SURVEY
OF
WORLD
CULTURES

SURVEY OF WORLD CULTURES

SOUTHEAST ASIA STUDIES, YALE UNIVERSITY
BY ARRANGEMENT WITH HRAF PRESS, NEW HAVEN

Indonesia

RUTH T. McVEY, EDITOR

HERBERT FEITH • HILDRED GEERTZ • EVERETT D. HAWKINS
MANTLE HOOD • ANTHONY H. JOHNS • DOUGLAS S. PAAUW
KARL J. PELZER • G. WILLIAM SKINNER • ROBERT VAN NIEL

Already Published in This Series

This study of Indonesia was developed pursuant to a contract between Yale University and the United States Office of Education, Department of Health, Education, and Welfare.

Jacket and title page designed by Sally P. Hargrove. Title page figure is Gatotkatja, a wajang character symbolizing Indonesian freedom. Jacket shows the mythological Garuda or eagle, traditional emblem of Indonesia.

ON THE ORIGINS OF THIS BOOK

In 1956, a research team at Yale University produced a three-volume monograph on Indonesia for the use of the Human Relations Area Files. The work, which was compiled by Stephen W. Reed (editor), Paul W. van der Veur, Richard J. Coughlin, Edward M. Bruner, Robert S. Bone Jr., Roswitha T. Djajadiningrat, Raden Mas Koentjaraningrat, Thomas W. Maretzki, Robert Van Niel, Jacob J. G. Syatauw, Isidore Dyen, Donald R. Fagg, Everett D. Hawkins, Douglas S. Paauw, Mohamed Sadli, John O. Sutter, and Karol van der Veur, was printed in a limited edition and had restricted circulation.

It was felt at the time that it would be most desirable to prepare a version of this report for general publication, since no comparably broad study of Indonesia existed in spite of the considerable need for one. At the same time, it was realized that this would entail an extensive revision of the monograph, since its original version had been tailored to the special needs of HRAF. Moreover, the rapid changes in Indonesian political and economic affairs which took place in the latter part of the decade soon outdated the 1956 report. In 1959, a research team at American University undertook a revision and updating of the work. This version was written by John Cookson (editor), Mildred Bigelow, George L. Harris, Howard J. John, Jean H. McEwen, and Florence K. Nierman.

When in 1961 the Yale Southeast Asia Studies Center found itself able to sponsor the preparation of a book for general publication, it was faced with the question whether to modify and build on these earlier versions or whether to undertake what would in effect be an entirely new effort. On the one hand, the previous monographs contained material of considerable and enduring importance. On the other, the events of the past several years had brought many qualitative changes to the Indonesian scene which could be dealt with only by a new approach. In addition, it was felt that the framework of the earlier versions, which provided brief surveys of a wide range of specific topics, was less useful for general publication purposes than a limited number of essays on broad aspects of Indonesian life. The changes imposed by time and purpose could not, it was decided, be accomplished by revision alone; and the present book has therefore been conceived and written as an entirely new work. Those associated with this volume are, however, keenly aware of their debt to the pioneering work done by their predecessors in preparing a scholarly introduction to Indonesia, and are grateful for their generosity in laying aside their claims for the publication of such a work in order to make this book possible.

PREFACE

Indonesia is the world's fifth most populous nation. It is also one of the largest, for its islands spread over an expanse of more than three thousand miles. Economically, it is one of the most important international suppliers of tropical agricultural products and a major source of the world's tin and petroleum. Although its sovereignty was recognized in 1949, the Indonesian people have ever since then been engaged in a revolutionary process more complex and taxing than the struggle for independence. This multifaceted revolution cannot be decided by arms or by political compromise, for it involves the transformation of an entire society into a mold as yet undefined, and within a time span made all too short by continuing economic and social crisis.

Because of Indonesia's importance as a nation, the seriousness of the problems that beset it, and the rapid rate of its economic, political, and cultural change, it is urgent that the country be well understood by the world outside. Unfortunately, however, Indonesia is one of the least known of the major states, for until the end of World War II virtually the only outsiders with an interest in the area were Netherlanders, and the double language barrier of Indonesian and Dutch inhibited the ready dissemination of expert knowledge to the rest of the world. It is only in the past decade that English-speaking countries—notably the United States and Australia—have acquired a number of specialists on Indonesia; very few of these scholars have yet attempted to deal with more than one facet of the country. The few general books on Indonesia that have thus far appeared in English have been largely journalistic and impressionistic in character. The reader who wishes to do more than scratch the surface must therefore piece together an image of Indonesia from an uneven mosaic of specialized books and articles—a weary and often unrewarding task. This book is an attempt to help bridge the gap between superficial impression and specialized knowledge concerning Indonesia. It is intended to provide an introduction to the major facets of the nation today; hopefully, it will be of use not only to Indonesia specialists who wish to acquaint themselves with aspects outside their field of competence, but also, and especially, to those who are strangers to the country.

Yet, while there is a pressing need for a study of this kind, it is also in another sense premature. Like most transitional societies, Indonesia is experiencing rapid and fundamental change; it is difficult to foresee the direction this transformation is likely to take, the more so since the academic tools for analyzing such change are themselves still largely in an experimental stage. As a result, no scholar dealing with the complexities of contemporary Indonesia can hope to avoid controversial and sometimes subjective judgments. It is not only a serious drawback that this book is written only by Western scholars and not by Indonesians; equally serious is the absence, by and large, of Indonesian scholarly analyses on which the Western student could usefully draw. It goes without saying that ultimately a definitive work on Indonesia can only be written—and no doubt will—by Indonesian scholars. In the meantime, we hope that this book, written by non-Indonesians who share profound interest in and broad sympathy for the young republic, will help to provide a basis for understanding the varied and changing nation that is Indonesia today.

The emphasis of this collaborative volume is on analysis rather than encyclopedic coverage, for it seemed to us that the reader would be better served by insight than by exhaustive but unsifted information. Although considerable exchange of ideas and criticisms took place in the preparation of the volume, the views presented in each chapter are its author's own; we did not consider it either possible or desirable to obtain consensus on so complex a nation. We have tried to treat the subjects under discussion in broad categories meaningful to the Indonesian context, and in doing so have subsumed certain important topics—such as religion, languages, health, and education—under other, more general headings. By no means all aspects of Indonesian life could be adequately dealt with, and not all of the topics discussed here have received equal attention. The greatest weight has been given to subjects of the widest concern: the society, government, human and material resources, and economics of modern Indonesia.

Since even the lengthier chapters can do no more than introduce the problems they consider, references for further study are provided in the footnotes and annotated bibliographies at the end of the book. For the use of those already engaged in Indonesian studies, works in Dutch and Indonesian have been listed in addition to those written in the major Western languages. The reader should bear in mind that the bibliographies are of necessity highly selective. In order to include as many works as possible in the available space, the bibliography of a chapter will not usually list studies referred to in the footnotes to it, nor will it duplicate works cited in one of the other bibliographies.

We have made grateful use of the advice and criticisms proffered by the following scholars, who served as consultants on the subjects indicated: Benedict R. O'G. Anderson, Cornell University (government and politics), Harry J. Benda, Yale University (history), Lance Castles, University of Indonesia (government and politics), W. M. Corden, Australian National University (government and politics), John M. Echols, Cornell University (literature), Clifford Geertz, University of Chicago (culture and society), Bruce Glassburner, University of California, Davis (economics), Susilo Hardjito, University of California, Los Angeles (music and theater), Benjamin Higgins, University of Texas (economics), Donald Hindley, Brandeis University (government and politics), Claire Holt, Cornell University (music and theater), George McT. Kahin, Cornell University (government and politics), J. D. Legge, Monash University, Melbourne (government and politics), Daniel S. Lev, Cornell University (government and politics), J. A. C. Mackie, University of Melbourne (government and politics), Achdiat K. Mihardja, Australian National University (literature), David Mozingo, University of California, Los Angeles (Chinese minority), Nugroho, Central Bureau of Statistics, Djakarta (agriculture), Francis Palmos, *Melbourne Herald* (government and politics), E. de Vries, Institute of Social Studies, The Hague (agriculture), Kampto Utomo, University of Indonesia (culture and society, agriculture), and Ann R. Willner, Harpur College (culture and society). Their comments on the early drafts of the manuscript contributed greatly to the scope and depth of the final versions presented in this volume.

We are deeply indebted to Harry J. Benda, who as acting director of Southeast Asia Studies initiated the project, shared in the planning of the book, and gave us the benefit of his valuable counsel on many occasions.

Our thanks are due to Robert L. Williams, Director of the Yale Map Laboratory, for preparing the black-and-white maps and charts for the book, and to the Ganaco Publishing Company of Bandung for graciously allowing us to use the color maps, which first appeared in the *Atlas Nasional*. We owe special thanks to Adrienne Suddard, of HRAF Press, who in many ways assisted us in the final stages of this volume.

Finally, we should like to express our gratitude for the financial assistance of the United States Office of Education, Department of Health, Education, and Welfare, which made the preparation of this work possible, and our appreciation of the unfailing courtesy and cooperation extended to us by its officers.

KARL J. PELZER
Director, Southeast Asia Studies

RUTH. T. MC VEY
Editor

Yale University
February 1963

CONTENTS

CONTRIBUTORS

HERBERT FEITH (Ph.D. Cornell University, 1961), Senior Lecturer in the Department of Politics, Monash University, Melbourne, Australia, became familiar with government practice and political life in Indonesia both as an employee of the Ministry of Information in Djakarta and on research visits under the auspices of Cornell University and the Australian National University. His publications include *The Indonesian Elections of 1955* (1957), *The Wilopo Cabinet, 1952-1953: A Turning Point in Post-Revolutionary Indonesia* (1958), and *The Decline of Constitutional Democracy in Indonesia* (1962), as well as several articles. A book of readings on Indonesian social and political thought is in preparation. His present research interest centers on consensus and legitimacy in Indonesia and on the country's administrative problems.

HILDRED GEERTZ (Ph.D. Radcliffe College, 1956) is a Research Associate in Anthropology at the University of Chicago. From her field research in Java and Bali, sponsored by the Center for International Studies, Massachusetts Institute of Technology, and her study in the Netherlands of Dutch sources on Indonesia have come numerous articles and a book, *The Javanese Family: A Study in Kinship and Socialization* (1961).

EVERETT D. HAWKINS (Ph.D. Princeton, 1934), Visiting Professor of Economics at the University of Wisconsin, has been for many years Chairman of the Department of Economics and Sociology at Mount Holyoke College. Other activities during this period included one and a half years as Visiting Professor of Economics at Gadjah Mada University in Indonesia, research trips to Indonesia and other countries of Southeast Asia in the summers of 1956 and 1962, and service as consultant to the United States government. He has written extensively on Indonesian labor affairs and is currently at work on a monograph, "Labor Relations à la Indonesia."

MANTLE HOOD (Ph.D. Amsterdam, 1954), Director of the Institute of Ethnomusicology at the University of California, Los Angeles, has studied the music and related traditional arts of Indonesia during stays in the Netherlands, Java, and Bali. His research has resulted in a number of articles for music journals as well as a book, *The Nuclear Theme as a Determinant of Patet in Javanese Music* (1954), and an essay, "Music, the Unknown," in *Musicology* (1963) by Frank Harrison, Claude Palisca, and Mantle Hood.

ANTHONY H. JOHNS (Ph.D. University of London, 1952) is at present Head, Department of Indonesian Languages and Literatures, Faculty of Oriental Studies, Australian National University, Canberra. His publications in the field of Indonesian history and literature have included *Rantjak DiLabueh: A Minangkabau Kaba* (1958) and a number of articles. Two monographs on Javanese religious history are in preparation, and he is planning a book on modern Indonesian literature in collaboration with the novelist Achdiat Karta Mihardja.

DOUGLAS S. PAAUW (Ph.D. Harvard, 1950) has taught at several American universities and recently spent two years as Visiting Professor of Economics and Chairman of the Ford Foundation Economics Project at Nommensen University, Medan, Indonesia. At present he is Director of the Development Planning Project, National Planning Association, Washington. His research has been primarily directed toward economic development problems of new nations, particularly in Asia. This interest is reflected in his numerous articles and reviews, a monograph, *The Economy of China and Manchuria* (1951), and a book, *Financing Economic Development: The Indonesian Case* (1960). Forthcoming is a comparative study of the economies of Southeast Asia.

KARL J. PELZER (Ph.D. Bonn, 1935), Chairman of the Department of Geography and Director of Southeast Asia Studies at Yale University, has long been recognized as an authority on the tropical agriculture of island Southeast Asia. His research in Indonesia and other parts of the area, which covered both the colonial and the postindependence periods, was reported in *Pioneer Settlement in the Asiatic Tropics: Studies in Land Utilization and Agricultural Colonization in Southeastern Asia* (1945), a study, "Land Utilization in the Humid Tropics: Agriculture," for the Ninth Pacific Science Congress (1958), and several articles. Nearing completion is a history of the development of plantation agriculture in Sumatra.

G. WILLIAM SKINNER (Ph.D. Cornell University, 1954), Professor of Anthropology and Associate Director of the China Program at

Cornell University, has done research on Chinese society in mainland China, Thailand, and Indonesia, specializing in the social structure and assimilation of the overseas Chinese in Southeast Asia. His major publications include *Chinese Society in Thailand: An Analytical History* (1957), *Leadership and Power in the Chinese Community of Thailand* (1958), and two works on Indonesia, *Local, Ethnic and National Loyalties in Village Indonesia: A Symposium* (1959), in which he participated as both editor and contributor, and *Communism and Chinese Culture in Indonesia: The Political Dynamics of Overseas Chinese Youth* (1963). In preparation is a book to be titled "Chinese Acculturation in Java."

ROBERT VAN NIEL (Ph.D. Cornell University, 1954), Associate Professor of History at Russell Sage College, has conducted historical research in both Indonesia and the Netherlands, his special interest being the development of Indonesia during the period of Dutch rule in the nineteenth and twentieth centuries. A translation of the Coolie Budget Commission report on *Living Conditions of Plantation Workers and Peasants on Java in 1939-1940* (1956) was followed by several articles and his study, *The Emergence of the Modern Indonesian Elite* (1960). He is now writing a history of the early years of the Cultivation System in Java, 1830-1850.

A NOTE ON NOMENCLATURE
AND SPELLING

Any standardization of Indonesian geographical and historical names is bound to be somewhat arbitrary and therefore unsatisfactory. If common modern Indonesian usage is followed consistently, we may satisfy the specialist but confuse the layman, who is familiar with Borneo but not with Kalimantan, and with Java but not Djawa. On the other hand, the use of English place names raises a number of objections. Not only is there sometimes more than one English equivalent, but many of the English versions are obscure and artificial; with increasing general reliance on modern Indonesian nomenclature they are moreover rapidly becoming anachronisms. Finally, the pronunciation of the Indonesian names is obvious from their spelling, which is more than can be said for some of the English equivalents.

The geographical nomenclature used in this book is the result of a compromise between Indonesian and English usage. Islands and island groups are referred to by their common and widely familiar English names; thus Sumatra (rather than Sumatera), Java (Djawa), Borneo (Kalimantan), Celebes (Sulawesi), the Moluccas (Maluku), the Lesser Sunda Islands (Nusa Tenggara), and West New Guinea (Irian Barat), to cite the major examples. All other place names follow the common modern Indonesian usage as given in the United States Board on Geographic Names, Gazetteer No. 13 (1955). In the case of historical names, modern Indonesian spelling has been used rather than English or Sanskrit derivatives; in some cases where more than one Indonesian version is current an arbitrary choice was made. For the sake of uniformity and ease in pronunciation, the Dutch *oe* has been replaced by the modern Indonesian *u* in spelling personal names, though a number of prominent Indonesians continue to use the older form. Indonesian pronunciation is generally similar to Latin; *dj* is equivalent to the *j* in just, *sj* to the *sh* in shoe, *tj* to the *ch* in chair, and *j* to the *y* of yellow. The accent is usually placed on the penultimate syllable.

Indonesia

CHAPTER I

Physical and Human Resource Patterns

KARL J. PELZER

THE INDONESIAN archipelago is the world's largest island complex. Stretching from mainland Southeast Asia eastward between Australia and the Philippines, it borders on three major bodies of water—the Indian and Pacific oceans and the South China Sea. The Republic of Indonesia embraces nearly all of this area, excluding only the eastern (Australian) half of New Guinea, Portuguese-ruled eastern Timor, and the British territories of North Borneo, Brunei, and Sarawak. The country has an east-west length of some 3,400 miles from 92° to 141° east longitude, and a breadth of about 1,000 miles from 6° north to 11° south latitude. For the greater part it lies south of the equator, which passes through the center of Sumatra and Borneo and through northern Celebes.

Indonesia's islands are commonly divided into three major groups. The Greater Sunda complex, which includes Sumatra (Sumatera), Java (Djawa), Borneo (Kalimantan), and Celebes (Sulawesi), is by far the most important part of the archipelago in terms of size, population, natural resources, and economic activity. The Lesser Sundas (Nusa Tenggara) form a chain of lesser islands stretching east of Java from Bali to Timor. The third group, the Moluccas (Maluku), lies north of the Lesser Sunda Islands and east of Celebes. The largest and most undeveloped land mass of the archipelago is its easternmost island, New Guinea, called Irian by the Indonesians. The western half of this territory remained under Dutch rule after the rest of the former Netherlands East Indies was transferred to Indonesian sovereignty, and it only came under the Republic's authority in 1963.

Viewed geologically the Indonesian archipelago is one of the world's most complicated structural regions. It consists of two relatively stable blocks of great age—the Sunda Shelf in the west and the Sahul Shelf in the east—between which lies a highly unstable area composed of deep-sea basins alternating with blocks that rise above sea level to form islands. The Sunda Shelf is an extension of the Asian mainland and forms a platform on which lie the Riouw Islands, Bangka, Billiton, and West Borneo. The Sahul Shelf links northern Australia with New Guinea and forms the bottom of the shallow Arafura Sea (see Figure 1).

During long geologic periods, sediments accumulated in the deep-sea area between the Sunda and Sahul shelves, building up to considerable thickness. Strong orogenic forces caused compressions and intensive folding during the Cretaceous and Tertiary eras, leading to the formation of what has been called the Sunda Mountain System.[1] This consists of two great parallel arcs, which are linked with the Himalayan Mountain System by the Arakan Yoma of Burma and the Andaman and Nicobar islands. The outer arc consists of a submarine ridge which in places rises above sea level to form islands. It includes the islands which lie parallel to the west coast of Sumatra, runs east beyond Java to form the Sumba, Timor, and Tanimbar islands, and then bends sharply to the north through the Kei Islands to Ceram and Buru. The inner arc is formed by Sumatra, Java, and the Lesser Sunda Islands from Bali to Wetar; similarly bending in a great hook to the north, it ends in the island of Banda in the Moluccas.

The crustal movements which led to the formation of this double-arc system have produced a striking dissimilarity between its two components. The islands of the outer arc are nonvolcanic; but those in the inner one are dominated by volcanism, which manifests itself in extinct and active volcanoes, solfatara, and fumarole fields. On the inner islands it is impossible to be out of sight of the volcanic cones, which continue to produce great lava flows and large quantities of ash. Since the Indonesian archipelago is for the most part a highly unstable section of the earth's crust, it experiences slight tectonic earthquakes every day; but destructive quakes are rare.[2]

Since each island tends to be a unit in itself, it is impossible to delineate major physiographic provinces for the country as a whole. In general, the islands each consist of highlands, plains of thin alluvium over the rock of the foothill regions, and low plains of deep alluvium, usually located along the coasts. The arrangement of these major components varies, however, from island to island. The highland core is usually substantial, since a large percentage of Indonesia's land area is mountainous, and some peaks (in western New Guinea) are eternally capped with snow. The development of coastal alluvial plains depends upon the geographic location of this core—whether it is centered or, as in Sumatra, located close to one coast. It is also affected by the shallowness of the fringing areas: alluvial plains build up easily along the east coast of Sumatra and north coast of Java, for example, as they

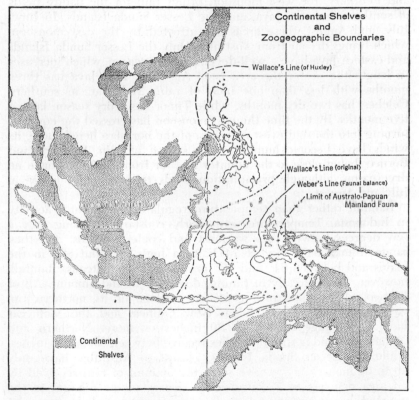

Fig. 1. Continental shelves of Southeast Asia and northwestern Australia and zoogeographic boundaries separating Asian from Australian fauna.

3

border on the shallow Sunda Shelf; but they do not develop readily along the opposite shores, which lie on the much deeper Indian Ocean.

As with all of Southeast Asia, Indonesia has a climate dominated by the monsoons, winds which blow from one direction in one season and from the opposite point in the other. The monsoon pattern of any given part of the archipelago depends on its location either north or south of the equator, its proximity to Australia or mainland Asia, and the position of the intertropical front—the area of convergence between the southern and northern tropical air masses. During the months of December, January, and February, the west monsoon brings rain for the paddy fields of southern Sumatra, Java, and the Lesser Sunda Islands. In June, July, and August, these areas are affected by the east monsoon, which brings dry air from Australia. Only the Lesser Sunda Islands and eastern Java have a well-developed dry season, which increases in length the nearer the area is to Australia. East Java has three months with less than one inch of rain; Makassar, in southern Celebes, has two dry months; while Timor has a dry season lasting five months. By the time the east monsoon has crossed the equator, turning into the southwest monsoon of the northern hemisphere, its winds have become humid and a source of rain. Sumatra and Borneo, being close to the equator and far from Australia, have no dry season, although precipitation tends to be slightly lower in July and August.

Rainfall rather than temperature regulates agricultural activity in Indonesia. Temperatures are nearly constant, differing only a few degrees between the warmest and coolest months, and they range from a daily low of 74°F. to a high of about 88° in the plains and between 64° and 80° on the interior plateaus. Rainfall, however, varies greatly in timing, distribution, and amount. All of Borneo, all of Sumatra except for portions of its northern tip, eastern and southern Celebes, New Guinea, and the Moluccas have an average rainfall of 80 inches or more. Northern and eastern Java and northern Celebes receive between 60 and 80 inches, while the Lesser Sunda Islands, closest to Australia, have only 40 to 60 inches. As we have seen, the amount of rain received by an area depends to a considerable degree on its relation to the moisture-bearing monsoon winds. It is also affected, however, by relief and altitude: mountain ranges and high volcanic cones

4

receive much more rain than do plains or foothill regions, while slopes on the windward side have higher rainfall than do those on the lee.

The fertility of Indonesia's soils is strongly affected by the climate. High temperatures lead to rapid chemical weathering of the parent rock,[3] while heavy rainfall in excess of evaporation causes a speedy leaching of the soil. As large parts of the country have a high level of precipitation, the leaching of the soil presents a serious problem to the cultivator. Those areas of the archipelago that have a well-developed dry season are less affected by the process, since during the dry months leaching is checked and the nutrient components are somewhat restored by the upward movement of water through the soil profile. On an island like Borneo, however, soils are subjected to constant leaching; and, since they are derived from sedimentary rock and have not been renewed by volcanic activity, they are mostly too poor to ever maintain a large population.[4] The fact that such an island supports a luxuriant tropical rain forest is no indication of the value of its soil, since these forests depend on decayed plant material for nourishment; they utilize this foodstuff almost completely, and hence no deep layer of humus is established.[5] Many unsuspecting investors and planters, misled by the luxuriousness of tropical growth in Borneo and similar areas, have undertaken expensive clearing operations for the planting of commercial crops only to discover that they were working with extremely impoverished soils. In general, soils of Indonesian regions having a population of less than thirty persons per square kilometer, whose inhabitants practice shifting rather than settled cultivation, should be examined very carefully before being considered for reclamation unless the land can be irrigated by tapping rivers which drain mineral-rich young volcanic highlands. The best permanent use to which poor soils can be put is to plant undemanding perennials. The crop best suited for this purpose appears to be the rubber tree, *Hevea brasiliensis*; it has been planted over wide areas of Sumatra and Borneo, having been introduced from the Amazon basin, where, too, the soils are infertile. The best Indonesian soils are those derived from young volcanic basic material; those which come from acid volcanic ejecta are less fertile. There is a very close positive correlation between the geographic distribution of young volcanic materials, soil fertility, and population density (compare the maps, Population Density of

Java and Geology of Java). Peasants, knowing that volcanic soils are rich, would rather risk the danger of eruption to cultivate the slopes of volcanoes than to move to less fertile regions where they may have to worry about food shortage. Poorer soils can be improved by irrigation with water containing volcanic silt, and dramatic rejuvenation can occur with the deposition of volcanic ash over an area of worn-out soil. Thus the 1883 reactivation of the Krakatau volcano markedly improved yields on the badly leached land of the Lampung area in southern Sumatra, which was covered with ash by the explosion.[6] Indeed, the best thing that could happen agriculturally to large parts of Sumatra and Borneo would be the occurrence there of severe volcanic eruptions.

Before prehistoric man began to clear land for his crops, all of Indonesia was covered by tropical rain forests. These forests were never uniform, however, but varied in accordance with altitude and rainfall and, to a lesser degree, with soils and drainage. The most remarkable feature of Indonesia's flora is its richness, which derives partly from the country's warm, moist climate and partly from its highly varied topography and vast sea-broken expanse.[7] Vegetation zones range according to altitude, from tropical beach formations and mangrove swamps through lowland evergreen rain forests to a series of more temperate zones:

ALTITUDINAL ZONES OF VEGETATION IN INDONESIA

Altitude		Vegetation
0–600	meters	Evergreen tropical rain forest of the lowlands
600–1000	”	Submontane evergreen tropical forest
1000–2400	”	Tropical montane rain forests, including mossy forests
2400–4000	”	Tropical subalpine forest
4000–4500	”	Tropical alpine scrub vegetation

Most of Indonesia is still forest-covered, although less than a fifth of the archipelago carries primeval forest. West New Guinea and southern and eastern Borneo lead the country with a forest ratio of over 80 per cent; in Java and Madura only 23 per cent is still forested, while in the Lesser Sunda Islands less than 20 per cent of the land is so covered (see the map, Vegetation of Indonesia, and Figure 2). Except in the high mountains, however, there is scarcely a region where man has not cut down at least

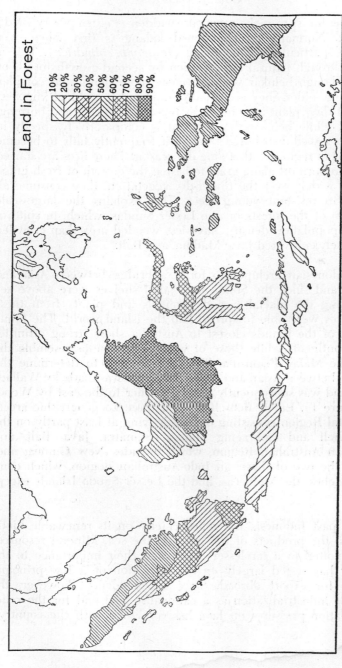

Fig. 2. Percentage of land covered by primary or secondary forests. Except for Java-Madura and the Lesser Sunda Islands, Indonesia is still heavily forested and allows extensive land use by swidden cultivators.

some of the forest to make room for swidden (i.e. temporary field) or *ladang*. Normally an abandoned ladang is first taken over by grasses, particularly *alang-alang* (*Imperata cylindrica*). This is replaced through natural reforestation by second-growth forest, or *belukar*. Though belukar woods become more dense and complex as they grow older, they are usually subjected to gradual impoverishment of their plant association by repeated clearing and burning. Moreover, while belukar development is comparatively speedy in areas with a well-distributed rainfall, it frequently fails to become established in regions with a long dry season. There fires are started annually to burn off alang grass to hasten the growth of fresh grass; spreading widely over the tinder-dry vegetation, they consume all but the fire-resistant young trees. This explains the large-scale destruction of the forests on the Lesser Sundas, which, in spite of their low population density, have less wooded area than crowded and intensely cultivated Java, Madura, and Bali.[8]

The Indonesian archipelago forms a bridge between Asia and Australia and since the Sunda and Sahul shelves were above sea level during the glacial periods, animals and plants from these land masses were able to spread into the island world. The fauna and flora of the islands closest to Australia show strong affinities to that continent, while those of western Indonesia resemble the life on the Malay Peninsula. The first attempt to determine the boundary between Asian and Australian types was made by Wallace in 1860 and was subsequently located farther to the east by Weber (see Figure 1). Later, Rensch defined three zoogeographic areas: an Oriental Region consisting of islands lying at least partly on the Sunda Shelf and embracing Malaya, Sumatra, Java, Bali, and Borneo; an Australian Region, which includes New Guinea; and, between the two of these, an Indo-Australian Region, which comprises Celebes, the Moluccas, and the Lesser Sunda Islands except Bali.[9]

In the past Indonesia has relied chiefly on its renewable biotic resources—the products of the soil and the sea. Mineral resources were exploited to a far lesser extent and their importance to the economy has rested largely on the extraction of a few principal products for export abroad. Since independence, however, the desire for industrialization as a nationalist goal and for the relief of population pressures on Java has combined with the country's pressing need for foreign exchange to give new importance to the exploitation of its mineral wealth. Indonesian planners tend to be more optimistic in their evaluation of the nation's mineral endowment than prewar geological investigations seem to warrant, but since these resources have not been fully surveyed no firm conclusions can yet be drawn as to the limit of available deposits. On the basis of what is known at present, it seems doubtful that Indonesia possesses the wide range of raw materials required for the development of a diversified heavy industry, though it could probably support limited industrial complexes utilizing the minerals that are available in sufficient quantity.

The map, Mineral Deposits of Indonesia, shows the geographic distribution of those mineral resources which were already being exploited prior to World War II. It will be noticed that this map does not show iron ore, a raw material vital for any heavy industrial development. Although Indonesia does possess extensive reserves of low-grade lateritic iron ore in Borneo and Celebes and small reserves of high-grade magnetite and hematite ore elsewhere, none of these were mined for export because of their inconvenient location, limited size, or low iron content; nor were they utilized domestically for lack of coking coal. Current Indonesian development plans, however, call for the creation of a small iron and steel industry, which presumably would make use of these deposits.

Crude oil, together with natural gas, was first extracted on Sumatra about 1890; today it constitutes Indonesia's most important mineral resource and prime earner of foreign exchange. The leading fields are located in tertiary geosynclines on the borders of the Sunda Shelf and extend along the east side of Sumatra, northern Java, and the east coast of Borneo. The leading production centers are in the Pakanbaru area of Central Sumatra, the hinterland of Palembang in South Sumatra, and the Balikpapan and Tarakan districts of East Borneo. Unlike all other mineral production, that of crude oil has risen since the colonial period from about 8 million tons in 1940 to 20.6 million tons in 1960, accompanied by an expansion of natural gas output from 1.3 million to 3.1 million tons.[10] Indonesia possesses extensive proven petroleum reserves exceeding nine billion barrels, and the prospects for expansion of the oil industry on both Sumatra and Borneo are good. There is a great need for new explorations, however, since the Indonesian government expects the oil industry to provide the country with development capital far above that received from its current level

9

of production. Moreover, the domestic demand for oil products is expanding steadily, cutting into the amount available to earn foreign exchange.

Tin deposits, located on the islands of Bangka, Billiton, and Singkep, are the country's second most important mineral resource. The mines on Bangka are Indonesia's oldest, having been opened at the beginning of the eighteenth century. On Billiton the first mine was started in 1851, and on Singkep in 1887. Most of the tin produced comes from alluvial deposits, but important primary reserves are known to exist on the three islands. Tin production has fallen in recent times, from a postwar peak of 36,400 tons in 1954 to 23,000 tons in 1960; the reserves are certainly large enough, however, to permit both rehabilitation and additional development of the industry.

Bauxite production started on the island of Bintam, off Singapore, in 1935 and rose rapidly thanks to the extremely favorable location of very large deposits on both sides of the Strait of Kidjang. So far the bauxite has been shipped abroad, but plans call for the development of an aluminum industry utilizing hydroelectric energy to be produced at the Asahan Falls in North Sumatra. As this industry will require only 120,000 tons of bauxite a year, exports could be continued, even at the present annual production rate of 400,000 tons.

Indonesia's leading coal fields are located in Sumatra; smaller ones are found in Borneo and Java, while the eastern portion of the country appears to be poor in this resource. Sub-bituminous and bituminous coal reserves have been estimated at 500 million tons, but reserves of lignite and brown coal, located principally in East Borneo, may amount to many billions of tons.[11] The first mines opened at Umbilin, in Central Sumatra, in 1892; the Bukit Asam mines, which today produce most of Indonesia's coal, were started in 1919. These two fields accounted for 1,400,000 of the 2,000,000 tons produced in 1940. Present-day production is down to 660,000 tons a year, or about one-third of the prewar output.

Other mineral resources which have been exploited on a small scale are nickel in Celebes; manganese, phosphate, sulfur, and iodine in Java; and gold and silver in Sumatra and West Java. Of these minerals, only manganese is now produced at a rate which comes close to prewar output, and its production has fallen considerably below the levels reached in 1956 and 1957. Current plans call for an increase in the exploitation of nickel, which is to be mined by a Japanese firm under contract to the Indonesian government.

Thus far we have discussed the land areas of Indonesia; but nearly as important are the seas which surround them, for they have deeply affected the country's economy, history, and culture. The seas both separate and link the islands of the archipelago, and in so doing present its government with administrative and logistic problems quite different from those of a country whose territory consists of one continuous area. Each island has tended to evolve its own social, cultural, and economic character; and the seas, by preventing mass migration, have aided minor groups to preserve their cultural and linguistic identity. Indonesia consists of a patchwork of diverse ethnic groups, whose differing economic interests and social attitudes seriously complicate the exercise of central political control.

At the same time that they have promoted a sense of separateness, the seas have linked the Indonesian islands. Prior to the development of an elaborate road system—which even today exists only on Java—travel took place by water along the coasts and between the islands rather than overland. Control of the coasts, particularly the shores flanking the Strait of Malacca, was far more valuable to a ruler than the deep administrative penetration of the hinterland, especially when the interior could be controlled economically by collecting tolls at the mouths of navigable rivers. Two kinds of civilization tended to arise on all but the narrowest islands—maritime-trading communities along the coast, and agrarian, noncommercial societies in the interior. On all the major islands but Java the major centers of population and power have been located in the coastal areas.

Just as the seas aid interisland communication but hinder central control, so they encourage outside penetration and handicap defense. Before the revolution in land transportation, island complexes such as Indonesia's were far easier to penetrate than were the continental land masses, and for centuries parcels of the archipelago have been held by foreign powers drawn by their economic or strategic importance.[12] Indonesia's lack of a common border with a powerful state has thus not meant its isolation, and the area as a whole has had a long history of economic, political, and cultural influence by foreign seafaring states. The importance of the seas for the control of the archipelago may be seen in the fact that for the greater part of the three and a half centuries the Dutch were active in the area they concerned themselves with domination of the coastal rather than the inland states, except when one of the latter was strong enough to challenge their position on the coast.

Control of the seas remains a central problem for the independent Republic, since the economic well-being of the archipelago is highly dependent on the maintenance of interisland shipping. Whenever the flow of shipping is interrupted—as it was during World War II and in 1958 when Dutch vessels were withdrawn from interisland trade—a serious crisis will arise, disrupting both the general economy and relations between the outlying regions and the center. The government must therefore assure the maintenance of adequate shipping facilities; moreover, it must see that they are not used for smuggling. Control of trade is relatively easy to achieve in countries which are landlocked or have only limited access to the sea, but it is extremely difficult in a vast archipelago with innumerable small and medium-sized harbors and nearby foreign ports which can serve as outlets for clandestine trade. Smuggling is as old in Indonesia as are the arts of shipping and state organization, but the conflict between central authority and particularistic trade has reached new importance in the years since independence, as economic difficulties and the weakness of the unitary state have combined to produce a situation extremely favorable to illegal commerce.

Although transportation by water does not require the energies and expense necessary to provide an adequate road system, it does demand adequate navigation and harbor facilities. An elaborate system of navigational aids must be maintained in Indonesian waters, especially in the Sunda Shelf area where the sea is shallow and coral reefs rise steeply to within a few feet of its surface. Moreover, an approach to the Indonesian islands by anything but shallow craft is rendered difficult by the hostile nature of their coastlines. The most inhospitable shores are those lined by mangrove swamps, as are long stretches of the Sumatra and Borneo coasts (see the map, Forests of Indonesia). In other areas, approaches are blocked by fringing or barrier reefs, while the outwardly inviting sight of sandy beaches lined by coconut palms indicates a landing endangered by strong wave action, tidal movements, and vigorous currents. With the growing size of ships

INDONESIAN POPULATION

Indonesian Population Density

persons per sq km

0-5

5-10

10-50

navigating in Indonesian waters, the number of suitable harbors has been decreasing; moreover, a large number of harbors which accommodated small coastal steamers as recently as 1942 can no longer be reached on account of heavy deposition of silt and the complete disruption of dredging operations.[13]

Indonesia is the fifth most populous nation of the world, exceeded in this respect only by China, India, the USSR, and the United States. The 1961 census showed a population of 97,085,000, and, since it is increasing at a rate of at least two per cent a year, the total number of Indonesia's inhabitants should pass the hundred million mark before the end of 1963.

The over-all average density of population in the archipelago is 51 persons per square kilometer. By this measurement Indonesia is not overcrowded, but the figure is highly deceptive. No less than 63 million Indonesians, or 65 per cent of the total population, live on the islands of Java and Madura, which contain only 7 per cent of the nation's territory. These islands have an average density of 477 persons per square kilometer, and some districts have densities of well over 1,000. The rest of Indonesia—the so-called Outer Islands—has an average density of just over 19 persons per square kilometer. Here, too, there is a wide range from area to area: less than two persons inhabit each square kilometer in western New Guinea, 7.6 in Borneo, 33 in Sumatra, and 321 in Bali (see Table 1). Indonesia suffers, therefore, not from absolute overcrowding but from an extreme maldistribution of its population.

The remarkable range of population density, which can be seen in the map, Indonesian Population Distribution, is closely related to mode of land use, percentage of land under cultivation, and soil fertility. High rural population densities are invariably associated with wet-rice cultivation, while sparse habitation is found where swidden, or shifting, agriculture prevails. A swidden cultivator requires as much as 10 to 15 hectares to support his family, while the Javanese peasant considers one hectare of paddy land (sawah) or two hectares of unirrigated land (tegalan) adequate for this purpose. Since wet-rice culture was introduced at a very early date in Java, the contrast between its population density and that of the other islands has built up over a long period of time to a point of great imbalance.

We lack the necessary statistical data for a precise historical

Table 1. AREA, POPULATION, AND DENSITY, BY PROVINCE, 1930 AND 1961

Province	Area		Population 1930			Population 1961		
	Square kilometers	Per cent of total area	Number (1,000)	Per cent of total population	Density per sq. km.	Number (1,000)	Per cent of total population	Density per sq. km.
Djakarta Raya	577	0.03	533	.88	923.7	2,973	3.06	5,152.0
West Java	46,300	2.43	10,864	17.89	234.6	17,615	18.14	380.0
Central Java	34,206	1.80	13,707	22.57	400.0	18,407	18.96	538.0
Jogjakarta	3,169	0.17	1,558	2.57	492.0	2,241	2.31	707.0
East Java and Madura	47,922	2.52	15,056	24.79	314.0	21,823	22.48	455.0
JAVA AND MADURA	132,174	6.94	41,718	68.70	316.0	63,059	64.95	477.0
Atjeh	55,392	2.91	1,003	1.65	18.1	1,629	1.68	29.0
North Sumatra	70,787	3.72	2,541	4.18	33.4	4,965	5.11	70.0
West Sumatra	49,778	2.61	1,910	3.15	38.4	2,319	2.39	47.0
Riouw	94,562	4.97	493	.81	6.7	1,235	1.27	13.0
Djambi	44,924	2.36	245	.40	5.4	744	.77	17.0
South Sumatra	158,163	8.30	2,062	3.40	13.0	4,847	4.99	31.0
SUMATRA	473,606	24.87	8,254	13.59	17.5	15,739	16.21	33.0
West Borneo	146,760	7.71	802	1.32	5.5	1,581	1.63	11.0
South Borneo	37,660	1.98	835	1.38	22.0	1,473	1.52	39.0
East Borneo	202,440	10.63	329	.54	1.6	551	.57	2.7
Central Borneo	152,600	8.01	203	.33	1.3	497	.51	3.3
BORNEO	539,460	28.33	2,169	3.57	4.0	4,102	4.23	7.6

Region								
North Celebes	88,578	4.65	1,139	1.87	12.8	2,003	2.06	23.0
South Celebes	100,457	5.28	3,093	5.10	30.7	5,076	5.23	51.0
CELEBES	189,035	9.93	4,232	6.97	22.4	7,079	7.29	37.0
Bali	5,561	0.29				1,783	1.84	321.0
Western Lesser Sunda Islands	20,177	1.06				1,808	1.86	90.0
Eastern Lesser Sunda Islands	47,876	2.51				1,967	2.03	41.0
BALI and LESSER SUNDA ISLANDS	73,614	3.86	3,460	5.70	47.0	5,558	5.73	76.0
Moluccas	74,505	3.91	560	.92	7.5	790	.81	11.0
West New Guinea	421,951	22.16	333	.55	0.8	758	.78	1.8
OUTER ISLANDS	1,772,171	93.06	19,009	31.30	10.7	34,026	35.05	19.2
INDONESIA	1,904,345	100.00	60,727	100.00	31.8	97,085	100.00	51.0

Source: 1930 figures from Departement van Economische Zaken, *Volkstelling 1930* (8 vols. Batavia, Landsdrukkerij, 1933-36); 1961 preliminary figures from Biro Pusat Statistik, *Sensus Penduduk 1961, Republik Indonesia* (Djakarta, 1962).

analysis of population growth prior to the present century. Earlier population estimates were made only for Java: in 1775 Radermacher reported that island to have two million inhabitants;[14] in 1795 Nederburgh found its population to be 3.5 million;[15] and in 1815 Raffles determined it at 4.6 million persons.[16] All through the nineteenth century population data were collected by district officers according to the number of households rather than the number of inhabitants; these surveys were first made at irregular intervals and then, from 1880 to 1905, at five-year intervals.

These early estimates have led to the wide assumption of a very rapid population growth on Java since the early part of the nineteenth century, an increase which has usually been attributed to the beneficial effects of colonial rule, particularly the introduction of such public health measures as smallpox vaccination.[17] There is, however, good reason to believe that these population figures are highly unreliable.[18] In the first place, the villagers quite rightly connected demographic inquiries with taxation and compulsory labor services and therefore deliberately underreported the number of households in their community, while at the same time the Dutch were not prepared to allocate the necessary funds to insure a reliable population survey. Very little was actually done in the field of public health during the last century, and it seems unlikely that hygienic measures could have caused the population to have risen as steeply as the early estimates would imply. Instead, it seems probable that Java's population must have been greater than reported at the beginning of the nineteenth century, and that the appearance of an extremely rapid increase was partly due to the gradual improvement of survey techniques.

Population growth was one reason for expansion of the cultivated area on Java, but another reason was that peasants migrated to escape the burdens imposed by the state. Even after the island was brought under a single power by the Dutch—in fact, until late in the nineteenth century—political control was far from uniform, and this encouraged considerable internal migration and clearing of forest land for new settlements. After 1870, however, the supply of new land was greatly reduced by the issuing of large blocks of the public domain to planters. Not long thereafter the younger sons of Javanese peasants found themselves compelled to work on plantations for lack of land on which to begin farms of their own,[19] but soon this source of employment was also filled. After about 1900, the rural population of Java grew faster than the area under cultivation, leading to a decline in the average farm size and the development of a landless rural class dependent on more fortunate villagers for employment as occasional farm laborers or as sharecroppers. By now the rural districts of Java—and also of Madura and Bali—are so overcrowded that a high percentage of their farms are less than half a hectare in size.

An example of the development of extreme rural overpopulation may be seen in the regency (*kabupaten*) of Malang in East Java, which was studied by Bennett in 1954-55.[20] In that area the population increased from 893,000 in 1920 to 1,110,000 in 1930 and an estimated 1,371,000 in 1953—a growth of 54 per cent in 33 years. In the same period the peasant-cultivated area was enlarged by only 11 per cent—from 175,700 hectares in 1920 to 194,400 in 1953. In other words, by 1920 practically all the cultivable land was already in use, and the population increase since then had to be absorbed by a decline in the amount of cultivated land per person, resulting in densities of up to 2,000 persons per square kilometer in the most fertile parts of the area.

In spite of such extreme pressures, the rural population of Java is not evenly distributed, as can be seen from the map, Population Density of Java. There are, in fact, sharp discontinuities: the region just south of the Malang plains, for example, has an average density of only 500 persons per square kilometer, one-fourth that of the overcrowded area to the north. This contrast results from the great difference in fertility between the young alluvial soils of the plains, which are irrigated by mineral-rich waters coming from regions of recent or continuing volcanic activity, and the thin soils overlaying tertiary limestone, which are highly pervious and thus unirrigable. A classical example of this relation between geology, soils, irrigation, and population density can be seen in the Jogjakarta region (see Figure 3). The district of Kotagedé, in a belt of young volcanic soils, is rich, lush, densely crowded, and devoted to intensive wet-rice cultivation. Separated from it by a sharp escarpment is the limestone plateau of the Gunung Sewu, on which lie the thinly settled, poverty-stricken, rather arid districts of Imogiri and Plajen. In this area the principal food crop is cassava, which is less desirable but can be produced on unirrigated fields.[21] An examination of the detailed census data of 1930—those of 1961 are not yet available—bears out this point for the island as a whole: in all districts of Java with a population density of less than 100 persons per square kilometer, under 30 per cent of the land was cultivable and less than 9 per cent of that portion was covered by sawah; in all districts with

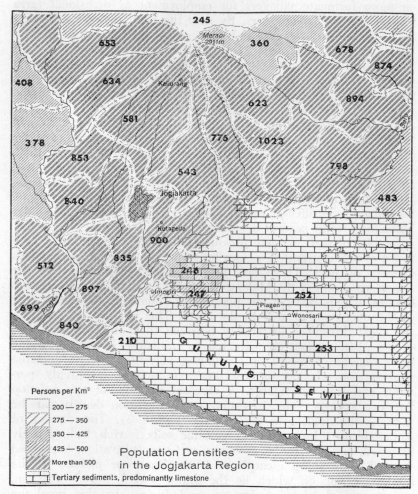

Fig. 3. Population densities by districts in the Jogjakarta region. There exists a close correlation between population density and geology, soils, and land use. The soils of the Gunung Sewu limestone region have a much lower carrying capacity than the rich soils derived from volcanic ejecta of Mt. Merapi.

18

more than 800 persons per square kilometer, over 50 per cent of the land was cultivable and more than 40 per cent of that was irrigated.

The present century, and particularly the period since independence, has seen significant migrations of population within the country, of which the movement of rural folk to the towns and cities has been the most important. In 1930 Indonesia had only seven cities with more than 100,000 inhabitants—six of them in Java —while by 1961 it possessed twenty-one in that category, eleven in Java, six in Sumatra, and two each in Borneo and Celebes (see Table 2). This growth is indeed alarming, for it does not

Table 2. CITIES OF INDONESIA WITH MORE THAN 100,000 INHABITANTS IN 1961[a]

Name	1930	1961	Per cent Increase[b]
Djakarta	533,015	2,973,052	558
Surabaja	341,675	1,007,945	295
Bandung	166,815	972,566	583
Semarang	217,796	503,153	231
Medan	76,584	479,098	626
Palembang	108,145	474,971	439
Makassar	84,855	384,159	453
Surakarta	165,484	367,626	222
Malang	86,646	341,452	394
Jogjakarta	136,649	312,698	229
Bandjermassin	65,699	214,096	326
Kediri	48,567	158,918	327
Tjirebon	54,079	158,299	293
Pontianak	45,196	150,220	332
Padang	52,054	143,699	276
Tanjong Karang/Telok Betung	25,170	133,901	532
Manado	27,544	129,912	472
Madiun	42,000	123,373	294
Pematang Siantar	15,328	114,870	749
Djambi	22,071	113,080	512
Pekalongan	65,982	102,380	155
Total	2,381,354	9,359,468	393

(a) In descending size, as of 1961.
(b) Calculated by the author.

Source: 1930 figures from Departement van Economische Zaken, *Volkstelling 1930* (8 vols. Batavia, Landsdrukkerij, 1933-36); 1961 preliminary figures from Biro Pusat Statistik, *Sensus Penduduk 1961, Republik Indonesia* (Djakarta, 1962).

reflect existing opportunities in the urban areas but rather the economically depressed and often politically insecure state of affairs in the rural districts. Growing urban congestion has led to death rates much higher than in rural areas, where the food is more varied and healthful and sanitary conditions are better. The sheer impossibility of providing employment, shelter, potable water, and other necessities to the newcomers has created social and economic stresses which have manifested themselves in high crime rates, prostitution, and juvenile delinquency.

Migration across Indonesia's national boundaries has not been of great importance in terms of numbers—although these are not small—but it has been of political and economic importance. Indonesians have a long tradition of emigration to Malaya, where they are readily absorbed since they do not face a linguistic or religious barrier to assimilation. Migrants come especially from Sumatra but also from Java, Borneo, and Celebes; there is little or no movement in the opposite direction. Chinese, Indian, and Arab immigration dates back to precolonial days; it was greatly stimulated by the economic expansion which began in the last quarter of the nineteenth century, but came to a near-standstill with the depression of the 1930s. Colonial rule brought the immigration of Netherlanders and the creation of an Indo-European population —on the eve of World War II there were about 60,000 Netherlands-born Dutch and approximately 200,000 Indo-Europeans in the country—but in recent years nearly all the Dutch, most of the Eurasians, and a goodly number of Chinese have left. Their departure has affected the economic and social structure of the country greatly, as will be explained in subsequent chapters, but because of the relatively small numbers involved it has had very little effect on Indonesia's basic demographic configuration.

The transferal of Java's excess population to the sparsely inhabited Outer Islands would seem an obvious answer to the country's major demographic problem but such a solution is not as simple as it appears on the surface: outside of the great demands it involves in financial outlay, organization, and cultural adjustment, the hard fact is that much of the outer territories is sparsely inhabited precisely because the land cannot support a larger population. Nonetheless, both the colonial and independent governments have carried on active transmigration programs as a principal way out of Java's demographic impasse. The first project was initiated rather hesitantly in 1905; subsequently the program

Table 3. PROJECTED POPULATION OF JAVA ACCORDING TO ALTERNATIVE COMBINATIONS OF FERTILITY AND MORTALITY, ASSUMING AN OUTMIGRATION OF ONE MILLION PEOPLE IN EACH FIVE-YEAR PERIOD, 1960-90

(*in thousands*)

State of nature	1960	1965	1970	1975	1980	1985	1990
(1) Constant fertility with slowly declining mortality	62,518	68,330	74,686	82,298	92,021	104,287	119,459
(2) Constant fertility with rapidly declining mortality	62,518	69,037	76,726	86,395	99,114	115,850	137,072
(3) Declining fertility with slowly declining mortality	62,518	68,330	74,326	80,999	88,893	98,002	108,595
(4) Declining fertility with rapidly declining mortality	62,518	69,037	76,348	84,992	95,653	108,644	123,565

SOURCE: Widjojo Nitisastro, "Migration, Population Growth, and Economic Development in Indonesia," adapted from Tables 51, 87, 88, and 89.

Table 4. PROJECTED POPULATION OF JAVA WITH CONSTANT FERTILITY AND RAPIDLY DECLINING MORTALITY, ACCORDING TO VARIOUS RATES OF OUTMIGRATION

(*in millions*)

Rates of outmigration	1960	1965	1970	1975	1980	1985	1990
(a) No outmigration	62.5	70.0	78.9	89.8	104.1	122.7	146.2
(b) Outmigration of one million persons in each five-year period	62.5	69.0	76.7	86.4	99.1	115.8	137.1
(c) Outmigration of one million *young* persons and their children in each five-year period	62.5	69.0	76.6	86.0	98.5	115.0	136.0
(d) Outmigration of five million persons in each five-year period	62.5	65.0	68.2	72.6	79.1	88.3	100.4
(e) Outmigration of five million *young* persons and their children in each five-year period	62.5	65.0	67.5	70.8	76.2	84.2	94.9

SOURCE: Widjojo Nitisastro, "Migration, Population Growth, and Economic Development in Indonesia," Table 75.

underwent various reorganizations and expansions, but government-sponsored migration in the colonial period never exceeded 60,000 persons a year. The postindependence record has been even less satisfactory: between 1951 and 1959 the project, now conducted by the Transmigration Service (*Djawatan Transmigrasi*), sponsored a total of 221,500 outmigrants, or an average of 24,600 persons a year. Various other official organizations have sponsored migration, particularly for veterans, and there are strong indications that spontaneous movement from Java, Madura, and Bali exceeds the number of those traveling with government assistance.[22]

To judge the effectiveness of transmigration as a solution to Java's overpopulation, we should observe Tables 3 and 4, which are based on calculations by Widjojo Nitisastro and represent population forecasts for that island according to a series of assumptions regarding fertility, mortality, and outmigration rates. The prospect they present is rather alarming. In the next thirty years—assuming constant fertility and rapidly declining mortality—the population of Java will more than double despite an annual outmigration of 200,000 persons. In the unlikely event that one million *young* people and their children leave Java each year, the island's population will increase by 32.4 million in the same period, for a total of nearly 100,000,000 persons in an area about the size of New York State. Transmigration will therefore not solve Java's demographic dilemma, though an active program can alleviate pressure and, by developing new land in the Outer Islands, help provide food for domestic consumption and crops for export. Indonesia's further hopes for the solution of its demographic dilemma rest on the improvement of present agricultural techniques, education, the lowering of the birth rate, and above all on the development of sources of livelihood outside the agrarian sector. All these measures, however, will take time to achieve; and it is an open question whether Indonesia will be able to realize them before the occurrence of a disastrous demographic crisis.

CHAPTER *2*

Indonesian Cultures and Communities

HILDRED GEERTZ

THERE ARE over three hundred different ethnic groups in Indonesia, each with its own cultural identity, and more than two hundred and fifty distinct languages are spoken in the archipelago.[1] Religious beliefs, too, are varied: nearly all the important world religions are represented, in addition to a wide range of indigenous ones. Economic adaptations include such differing modes as seminomadic shifting cultivation, sago gardening, smallholder rubber tapping, irrigated rice farming, highly capitalized plantations for export crops, small itinerant peddling, large-scale commerce, cottage industries, and modern manufacturing. Forms of community also vary, from small isolated villages to huge modern cities; the many different types of kinship systems include matrilineal, patrilineal, and bilateral patterns; while the traditional political structures range from tribes to kingdoms.

Nevertheless, not everything in Indonesia is diversity, and some generalizations can be made. Most of the languages belong to a single linguistic family, the Malayo-Polynesian, that is, they share many close cognate words and have highly similar grammatical structures. About ninety-five per cent of the Indonesians profess Islam alongside local indigenous religious beliefs, while an even earlier layer of Hindu-Buddhistic thought provides a further basis for cultural similarity over much of the area. The tenacious indigenous religions which merge with rather than merely surrender to Islam, Hinduism, or Christianity appear to be all of the same general species. Economic adaptations, though various, can be boiled down to a few representative types, and the same can be said of community forms.

24

Most Indonesians are peasants of one sort or another, that is, they are small-scale independent farmers who have some contact (however indirect) with the commerce in goods and in ideas from the cities. Few are so isolated as to be economically self-sufficient and unaware of cultural differences and of social change. At the same time, few are commercial farmers in the sense of systematic production for ever-increasing net profits. The highly capitalized plantations for export crops employ only a small portion of the total Indonesian population; most of the rest are subsistence farmers, cultivating their own land and selling part or all of its produce into urban market networks, but for personal livelihood alone.

They are peasants not only in an economic sense but also culturally, for they look away from their villages toward the towns for certain kinds of social and intellectual leadership. This is particularly true for Java, but urban centers today play significant cultural roles for much of the rest of Indonesia as well. In the past many towns had been the seat of royalty, who epitomized in their persons and way of life many important social and religious values of the villagers; today this function has been taken over to some extent by teachers, civil servants, professional men, soldiers, and political leaders—the new urban cynosures.

The basic spatial contours of Indonesia's social and cultural landscape have been influenced historically by the country's geographical setting of innumerable mountainous islands ringing the calm Java Sea. The coastal perimeters of the islands have culturally much in common because of the frequency and ease of contacts among them; but the inland peoples, cut off from one another by tropical forests and precipitous land masses, display widely diverging cultural forms. The interior regions are of two very general ecological types: first, those parts where extensive irrigated rice terraces can be maintained—primarily in the great river plains and volcanic slopes of central and eastern Java and Bali, and to a lesser extent in scattered pockets elsewhere in the other islands; and second, those areas where topography, soil, or rainfall patterns make wet-rice difficult and necessitate shifting farming or other economic adaptations.

These geographical distinctions are reflected in three broad types of Indonesian societies: the strongly Hinduized inland wet-rice areas; the trade-oriented, deeply Islamic coastal peoples;

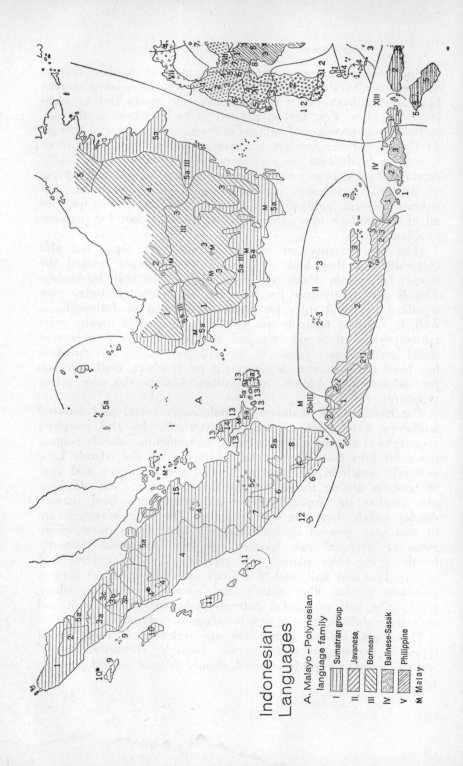

Indonesian
Languages

A. Malayo – Polynesian
language family

I.   Sumatran group
II.   Javanese
III. Bornean
IV.   Balinese-Sasak
V.   Philippine
M.   Malay

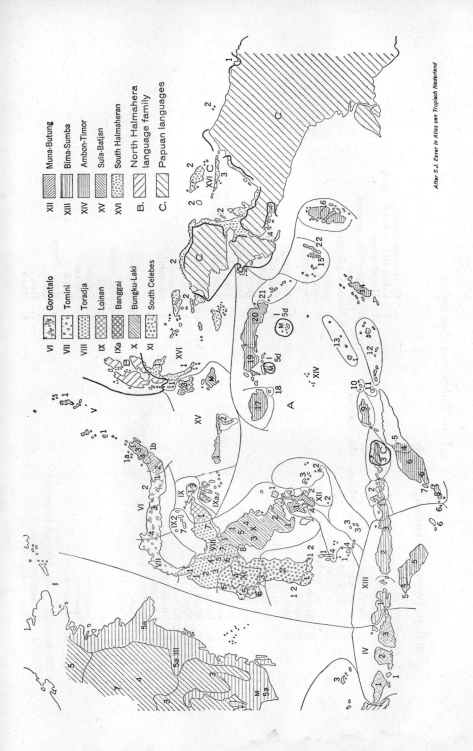

KEY TO *Indonesian Languages*

A. Malayo-Polynesian language family

I. Sumatran group
1. Atjehnese
2. Gajo
3. Batak dialects
   a. Northern group (Karo, Alas, Pakpak)
   b. Toba
   c. Simalungun
   d. Angkola-Mandailing
4. Minangkabau
4*. Lubu
5. Malay dialects
   a. Riouw Malay
   b. Djakarta Malay
   c. Kubu
   d. Moluccan Malay
6. Middle Malay
7. Redjang-Lebong
8. Lampung
9. Simalur
10. Nias
10*. Sichule
11. Mentawai
12. Enggano
13. Lontjong (along the coast of Bangka)
14. Lom
15. Orang Laut

II. Javanese group
1. Sundanese
2. Javanese
3. Madurese

III. Bornean group (Dayak languages)
1. Klemantan group
2. Iban group
3. Ot-Danum group
4. Kenja-Bahau-Kajan group
5. Murut group
B Badjau (sea nomads)

IV. Balinese-Sasak group
1. Balinese
2. Sasak
3. Sumbawan

V. Philippine group
1. Sangir-Talaud
1a. Bantik
1b. Bentenan
2. Mongondou
3. Tombulu-Tonsea-Tondano
4. Tontemboan-Tonsawang

VI. Gorontalo group
1. Bulanga
2. Kaidipan
3. Gorontalo
4. Buol

VII. Tomini group

VIII. Toradja group
1. Kaili
2. Kulawi
3. Pipikoro
4. Napu
5. Bada'-Besoa
6. Leboni
7. Bare'e
8. Wotu

IX. Loinang group
  1. Loinang
  2. Bobongko
  3. Balantak

IXa. Banggai

X. Bungku-Laki group
  1. Bungku-Mori
  2. Laki
  3. Laiwui
  4. Landawe
  5. Mapute

XI. South Celebes languages
  1. Makassarese
  2. Buginese
  3. Luwu
  4. Sa'dan
  5. Pitu-Uluna-Salu
  6. Mandar dialects
  7. Seko

XII. Muna-Butung group
  1. Muna-Butung
  2. South Butung
  3. Languages of the islands of Tukangbesi,
     Kalaotoa, Karompa, and Bonerate
  4. Wolio and Lajolo

XIII. Bima-Sumba group
  1. Bima
  2. Manggarai
  3. Ngad'a-Lio
  4. West Sumba
  5. East Sumba
  6. Hawu

XIV. Ambon-Timor group
  1. Kroe
  2. Solor
  3. Kedang, Alor, and Pantar group (on Alor
     some Papuan languages are also spoken)
  4. Belu (Tetum)
  5. Marae
  6. Timor (Dawah)
  7. Kupang
  8. Roti
  9. Wetar languages
  10. Roma
  11. Kisar
  12. Leti, etc.
  13. Damar languages
  14. Tanimbar languages
  15. Kai
  16. Aru
  17. Buru
  18. Ambelau
  19. West Ceram languages
  20. East Ceram languages
  21. Goram languages
  22. Banda

XV. Sula-Batjan group
  1. Taliabo dialects
  2. Sula dialects
  3. Batjan (nearly gone)

XVI. South Halmaheran–West New Guinea group
  1. South Halmaheran languages
  2. Nufor
  3. Windesi
  4. Kowiai, etc.

B. North Halmaheran language family (Ternate, Tidore, etc.)

C. Papuan languages

and the mainly pagan tribal groups of the mountainous interior regions. The three categories only crudely and tentatively summarize the basic forms underlying Indonesian diversity; nevertheless they provide a convenient framework for descriptive exposition.

The first category, the wet-rice growers of inland Java and Bali, comprises nearly half of the total population of Indonesia. The inland villages are sprawling and densely settled, and it is here that population pressures are rapidly becoming unmanageable. In the not-so-distant past there were fairly large kingdoms in Central Java and in South Bali. The culture of the inland peoples, although it is very distinctively their own, derives strongly from India of the first millennium, although Java acquired an important overlay from Islam after the fourteenth century. Both peoples stress formal etiquette and the proper recognition of status distinctions between aristocrat and commoner; spiritual and social refinement are highly admired. The arts—dance, music, drama, literature—are intensively cultivated. Of the two islands, Bali is the more traditional, for its indigenous social structure still functions today. The Javanese peasants are what might be called "posttraditional," for the combined impact of Islam and colonial commercial development broke the tight integration of its traditional social structure but did not produce a modern institutional system of the type found in Europe or contemporary Japan. The Javanese community, unlike most of those elsewhere in Indonesia, is almost "suburban" in its lack of distinct social boundaries and the near absence of institutionalized internal groupings. Moreover, the Javanese landscape is characterized by a thick scattering of large urban centers.

The second social type, the Islamic coastal peoples, includes such widely scattered groups as the Malays of Sumatra and Borneo and the Makassarese of South Celebes. The key to their similarities lies in their common history of participation in the international spice trade of the fourteenth to nineteenth centuries. At nearly every harbor in the archipelago there grew up a community of highly heterogeneous composition—Malays, Javanese, Makassarese, Moslem Indians, Arabs, Portuguese, English, Dutch, Chinese, and others—governed loosely by a local Moslem sultan. Ethnic heterogeneity and a commercial orientation remain significant characteristics of the coastal peoples. Islam—and a number of cultural patterns associated with it, such as respect for religious learning and law, and certain types of music, dance, and literature—is the most important unifying element. Many of the towns of twentieth-century Indonesia outside Java have crystallized around these former trading kingdoms, with the development of the modern governmental apparatus both increasing their ethnic heterogeneity and giving new civil-servant status to the local royalty.

The immediate rural hinterland of these Islamic coastal towns, outside of Java, is usually a sparsely populated region, with fishermen, craftsmen, coconut tenders, commercial gardeners, and wet-rice farmers living near the town, and shifting cultivators (still of the same coastal culture) located in the nearby hills. Beyond those hills, in the mountainous interiors, are the pagan tribal groups discussed below. While in the past the harbor sultans sometimes claimed these tribes as subjects and forcibly exacted tribute from them in the form of produce and slaves, the two worlds, coast and interior, had actually little to do with one another. This was in marked contrast to the Islamic market towns of Java, which were founded at an early date along that island's northern coast and which had strong and intricate relationships with the high civilization in the interior.

The tribal groups, classed together as the third category, display a very wide range of cultures. This grouping includes the Toradja of Celebes; the Dayak of interior Borneo; the people of Halmahera, of interior Ceram, of the interior of most of the Lesser Sunda Islands; and the Gayo, Redjang, and Lampong of Sumatra. Most of these mountain societies remained at least until the present century in virtual isolation from the outside world, each developing its own distinctive patterns of life. Many were, well into the last century, regularly engaged in war and head-hunting. Generally left untouched by either Hinduism or Islam, many of the tribal peoples have been the successful object of recent Christian missionary activity. Most are shifting cultivators of dry rice or gardeners of sago, maize, or root crops. When the opportunity presents itself they adopt wet-rice or commercial cultivation if they are genuinely profitable; however, many of these peoples inhabit marginal lands which are not capable of conversion to irrigated farming. Kinship ties are stressed by most of these groups instead of territorial or "feudal" political bonds, and they often have large corporate groups of kinsmen which own land, ritual objects, or status titles as a unit. Today, however, the process of administrative rationalization, which has brought the creation of regular territorial districts headed by civil servants, has gone quite far to alter the traditional community forms.

These three categories do not merely represent different kinds of economy, nor are they culture areas. They are better termed "sociocultural types,"[2] as they have been constructed on the basis of similarities in ecological adaptation, political structure, and stratification, and both social structure and culture pattern are taken into account. The three types are by no means exclusive; the categories are to be viewed not as sharply bounded pigeonholes, but rather as indistinct conceptual divisions into which many of Indonesia's three hundred ethnic groups can be crudely fitted. Aside from a number of small and peculiar groups which do not mesh with the scheme, there are several important ones which do not fit it at all. These latter, notably the Batak, Minangkabau, Minahassans, and Ambonese have undergone very rapid and extensive changes in the past century. A fully developed typology of Indonesian groups would have to include a dimension of change, and the distinction made here within the category of inland rice growers between traditional and posttraditional is a step in this direction.

Before starting on a more detailed examination of some sample communities, several remarks are necessary regarding the accuracy of these descriptions. Our sources of information on Indonesia are very uneven, some describing a prewar, pre-Republic situation and some very up to date. Most ethnological writings emphasize the traditional over the contemporary culture patterns, and it cannot be arbitrarily assumed this emphasis is erroneous. Much of Indonesian society retains its traditional forms today, although they may be somewhat altered to serve new uses; and with continued economic stagnation many of these traditional elements are likely to endure. On the other hand, the colonial experience and the events of the postwar period have set into motion exceedingly important changes, transformations which, however, are affecting different segments of the society at different speeds and which are difficult to estimate in the absence of specific recent research in each local situation. One of the most pervasive and potentially most powerful forces for change today is education in the Western form, which is rapidly being made available to every Indonesian child, rural as well as urban. Not only are local elementary schools multiplying, but their graduates are increasingly entering secondary schools and universities in the urban centers, with the result that peasant villagers may be becoming increasingly more receptive to novel ways. The general class structure of Indonesia appears to be changing, as the ranks of trained white-collar and professional workers grow. What the future social effects of this educational revolution will be remains to be seen; but they are certain to be important.

The Urban Network and the National Community

A network of national social institutions, notably of government administration, commerce, and education, threads over the entire archipelago, binding even the most remote village to Indonesian society as a whole. The nodal points of this institutional web are the numerous towns and cities of the country.[3] Speaking very roughly, this urban portion of Indonesia takes up between ten and fifteen per cent of the population. The 1930 census listed 171 towns and cities, with 102 on Java and Madura, 36 on Sumatra, and 33 elsewhere. Most of the largest are on Java, where they are disproportionately swollen by an overabundance of the poorest laboring groups; the towns of the Outer Islands, though similar in form, are considerably less filled out. Large or small, almost all have been growing at a constantly accelerating pace during the twentieth century, faster even than the "exploding" rural population. This steady flow to the cities has not, however, been accompanied by a comparable development of industry, with the result that many quarters of the cities (the *kampong*) have a strongly rural appearance, with simple sanitation facilities and housing suitable to the countryside but hopelessly inadequate for the crowded urban situation.

Dutch colonial civil servants and planters, and Chinese traders of the nineteenth century, provided the basic architecture and street plans for many of the larger urban centers (including a seventeenth-century system of unhealthy, useless canals in Djakarta). Some towns, such as Jogjakarta, have a formal basic layout reflecting the traditional social relationship between sultan, market place, and mosque. All, however, are marked by the fact that most municipal facilities—such as paving, sewage and water conduits, electricity, and telephone—were introduced during the first decades of this century and have not been improved since, nor in some cases adequately maintained. With the exception of certain modern business districts in the cities, the small Chinese retail store (the *toko*), a drab, windowless, tin-roofed warehouse with a removable wood wall facing the street, is the typical commercial building of urban Indonesia. While Djakarta has seen some new construction in the postwar period in the form of multistoried office buildings and an entirely new modern suburb, the housing shortage for both offices and residence at all income levels and in all towns and cities is acute.

Socially the cities and towns are sharply segmented according to ethnic identities, income class, and occupational groups, each entailing a distinctly different style of life; and this cultural segregation is partially reflected in spatial distribution into separate neighborhoods. With some exceptions, the members of the various cultural compartments hold themselves apart from the others, even though they may be in everyday contact in business and government, in shops and offices. The phrase "plural society" is nowhere so appropriate as when applied to Indonesian cities.

Apart from rapid nonindustrial growth and sociocultural compartmentalization, a third important characteristic of Indonesian cities is their social formlessness. Compared to Western cities, there is a serious inadequacy or even absence of community-wide institutions, such as public transportation, communication, recreation, and social welfare facilities. In part this is related to the cities' rapid growth and social pluralism, and to the general state of economic underdevelopment. It is largely, however, a heritage of the colonial situation, in which the interests of the urban administrations, where they existed as such, lay mainly with the colonial settlers rather than with the populace as a whole.

For the purposes of this survey, a structural distinction can be made between those large cities which are cosmopolitan in nature and the smaller urban centers which have primarily local orientations. The former I term "metropoles," the latter "provincial towns."

Djakarta, Surabaja, Bandung, Medan, Palembang, and Makassar are the most important of the metropoles. Their similarity lies not so much in their size as in the kind of structural relationship they have with the nation as a whole and with the external world. These cities serve both as connecting links to other nations and as integrating centers of economic, political, and intellectual life—either for all of Indonesia, as does Djakarta, or for extensive sections of it. In them are located the outposts of Western finance, the foreign diplomatic corps, the highest administrative and legislative organs of the national government, the central offices of Indonesia's many political and quasi-political organizations, most of its industrial and commercial establishments, and the main universities. Their newspapers are, or were, the most influential, and their inhabitants set the standards for urban living for the rest of the country.

The social composition of these cities can be only tentatively outlined, for no full study has been made of them. First, there are the foreign diplomatic and business communities, whose members, as temporary representatives of offices in their homelands, remain alien in style of life and attitudes, insulated to a large extent from the cultures around them. These groups mingle socially to varying degrees, are class-stratified within themselves, and form encapsulated subsocieties within the larger one. Formerly, of course, this group was almost wholly Dutch and many of its individual members had close ties with Indonesians. The other nationals in this segment have had, with a few notable exceptions, more fragile bonds to Indonesia, so that with the post-1957 expulsion of the Dutch these foreign communities have become even more alien to the general Indonesian scene.[4]

A second social segment of the cities is formed by the foreign merchant communities—notably the Chinese, but also numerous others such as the Indian and the Arab. The members of these communities are mainly engaged in retail trade, although in the great cities some have acquired considerable wealth as importers of luxury goods. In addition, there is a rather large professional class among the older, more established Chinese groups.[5] Another segment, formerly of importance but virtually extinct since 1958, is that of the Eurasians (usually referred to as "Indo-Europeans"). Part Dutch and part Indonesian in family background, but mainly Dutch in culture, this group was employed principally in government administration and in large Western commercial offices.

The urban Indonesians themselves have a highly complex class structure, one which is not yet very well understood. Two dimensions of variation, one based on social structure, the other cultural, provide a rough preliminary framework. The social structural dimension covers types of occupation and levels of income. The cultural dimension is defined at one pole by a single cultural pattern which might be termed the "Indonesian metropolitan superculture" and at the other by a large variety of traditional ethnic ways of life. The two dimensions crosscut each other in complex fashion to produce an extremely variegated urban population.

The Indonesian metropolitan superculture is still in the process of formation, and is at the most only two or three generations old.

Nevertheless for some Indonesians with the necessary education, occupation, income level, and individual family background it represents a coherent set of values and style of life. Since most city dwellers today are newcomers or second-generation migrants they are mainly "bicultural," that is, they retain certain features of their original regional culture for some areas of their life—family relationships and religion, for example—while participating in the metropolitan superculture for other concerns.[6]

It is in the areas of political ideology, artistic styles, and material culture that the content of the metropolitan superculture has been most elaborated. The foremost characteristic of the superculture is the colloquial everyday use of the Indonesian language, and directly associated with this language are the new Indonesian literature, popular music, films, and historical and political writings. Further, there are several fundamental social goals to which the bearers of the metropolitan superculture consider themselves committed—i.e. egalitarianism, socialism, economic development, and the advancement of the Indonesian nation.[7] The prime external symbols of adherence to the superculture are the acquisition of higher education, facility with foreign languages, travel experience abroad, and Western luxury goods such as automobiles. A nonindigenous social form closely linked to this national cultural complex is the voluntary association or committee, with its apparatus of officers, formal meetings, and so on. These organizations (political parties, labor unions, social welfare bodies, peasants' and women's groups, etc.) were found in profusion in every city and town during the 1950s; and as the metropolitan superculture extended its influence, they penetrated even into some villages. However, with the decline in independent political activity under Guided Democracy, there are indications that popularity of these voluntary associations may have diminished.

As with any cultural standard, only a privileged few have the ability or resources to model the whole of their lives according to its tenets; in this case it is the intellectual and political elite and the wealthy of the great cities who are bearers of the full metropolitan superculture. These are the top government officials, professional people, heads of political parties, high army officers, and successful businessmen, especially those of Djakarta. As social status goes down it is probable that in the case of most individuals the bicultural balance will shift toward the regional culture of his origin.

Below the urban elite groups comes a large and as yet unstudied urban middle class, made up primarily of middle-level civil servants and white-collar workers such as medical personnel, school teachers, and the middle ranks of the army and police. These elements are middle-class in terms of social status and general outlook but not in income, for many of their members are underemployed and poverty-stricken. Most of them identify themselves as *pegawai*, a term meaning specifically an employee of almost any rank in a large government or business office, but also connoting the more general outlook of the white-collar bureaucrat who aspires to attain the metropolitan superculture. Another segment of the urban middle class, somewhat overlapping with the pegawai group, is that of the skilled workers. Included under this heading might be the traditional urban occupations—the *tukang*, or craftsmen such as tailors, bricklayers, and blacksmiths, and the *pedagang*, the more successful market peddlers (peddling is a difficult skill practiced by a core-group of professionals) or small shopkeepers. Equally important are the newer skilled occupations such as those of electrician, railroad worker, truck driver, and automobile mechanic.

Some of the members of this urban middle class are new arrivals to the city, having come there from small towns or villages, while others descend from families with long urban residence. The latter segment consists principally of population groups which were given preference by the Dutch in education and employment—as for instance the Ambonese, Menadonese, and aristocratic Javanese —and of Moslem merchant families from the coastal towns of North Java, Sumatra, Celebes, and other areas of Pasisir culture. To what degree the members of the urban middle class are cut off from their traditional cultures, to what degree they maintain significant contacts with village kinsmen, to what degree the ethnic subgroups interact socially and intermarry are all as yet unstudied empirical problems.

Even less is known about the numerically much larger body of the urban proletariat—the laborers, servants, and small street peddlers, unskilled and illiterate for the most part, that increasingly swell the great cities. Socially and culturally, they appear to be in another world from the pegawai and skilled workers, and they participate minimally if at all in the metropolitan superculture. Their social allegiances and cultural identities lie in the villages from which they are for the most part recent migrants, though

37

some are old-time city residents whose forebears have followed minor city trades for generations. It can be reasonably supposed that the members of the lowest social stratum have generally migrated to the cities from the nearby countryside (in contrast to the white-collar workers, who may have been born some thousand miles away, generally in a small town), and that there is a constant revisiting of the home villages. Most of this group, at least in the first generation, live in neighborhoods made up mainly of the same ethnolinguistic group and continue to speak their original language at home and to maintain, with urban variations, the cultural patterns of their native villages. Whether or not, or to what degree, there is mobility up from the proletariat over the course of a generation or two, resulting in acculturation to the metropolitan superculture, remains a question.[8]

One of the more interesting characteristics of Indonesian urban development, in contrast to that in other Southeast Asian countries, is that it is not dominated by a "primate" city which funnels all national affairs. Although Djakarta is popularly termed the *pusat* ("center"), it is pre-eminent only in the fields of government, politics, finance, commerce, and to some degree education. Surabaja is the industrial city of Indonesia; Palembang is oriented around oil and smallholder rubber extraction and export; and Medan is marked by the plantation economy surrounding it, which provides the city with a multicultural quality even more pronounced than that of the average Indonesian great city.

The line between the metropoles and the provincial towns is arbitrary, and there are a good many cases which could fit either category. The main features which set the great cities apart are the dominance of ties to the international world and the extent and heterogeneity of the hinterland which they serve. The term "provincial" is used for the second group to indicate the outlying position of these towns, their relative lack of sophistication, and the corresponding closeness of their integration with the regions in which they are set. It is difficult, for instance, to state where Malang, Bandung, and Semarang fall; but for our present purposes such specific discussion is unnecessary. Because of their markedly regional character, the old Javanese court cities of Jogjakarta and Surakarta (Solo), while very large, can be seen as provincial towns in the present terms, and so can almost all the remaining cities of Java and most of those of the Outer Islands. Towns vary considerably in form and character according to the cultural orientations of their major population groups, or in response to the presence of special elements such as a busy harbor, a large university, an unusual number of secondary schools, or proximity to a Western-run oil camp. Nevertheless, since they all form a part of a larger interlocal system, they are more similar to than different from one another.

Compared to the metropoles, the towns are generally more stable in population; most are growing steadily but not spectacularly, and some are even unchanging or declining in size. Ethnic pluralism is just as significant in the towns as in the cities, but its intensity varies from one locality to another. Few if any Westerners live in provincial towns any longer. Javanese towns are mainly Javanese and Chinese in composition, with only a scattering of persons from other islands; towns elsewhere in Indonesia, in contrast, often have so many component groups that no one can overshadow the others numerically. For example, Kupang, on the island of Timor, consisted in 1950 of about 40 per cent native Timorese (speaking several different languages) and 60 per cent non-Timorese (including Rotinese, Savunese, Alorese, Waiwerangese, Florinese, Indo-Europeans, Chinese, Javanese, etc.).[9]

The life of the provincial town is typically focused on two main institutional complexes, government and trade, which generally coexist in complementary but distinctly separate social spheres, and frequently are found in separate locations in the town. Mills and factories are relatively few[10] and, in any case, are technologically very simple. Government offices, on the other hand, are numerous in every town, and well- (usually over-) staffed, since extensive rural areas are served from urban administrative posts and a wide range of functions are carried on by the government. Army installations and schools contribute further to the size and influence of the salaried, white-collar sector in these towns.

The pegawai groups of the small towns can be classed into two very general types: the "locals" and the "metropolitans."[11] The latter are those people who participate in the Indonesian metropolitan superculture to a greater extent than in the regional culture of their origin, their social orientation being mainly directed away from their immediate surroundings toward other towns and cities. The members of this "metropolitan" white-collar group are more geographically mobile than their "local" counterparts; many live in several different towns or even regions in the course of their lives, marry persons from distant localities, and subsequently visit frequently back and forth over wide areas. Even though they may be originally of the same culture, they have very little genuine social contact with the peasants around them. They are, in general, the top civil servants for the area, the professionals, and the representatives of Western or nationalized commercial enterprises. The "local" pegawai groups are those, correspondingly, whose main social weight lies within the town or region itself, and who identify predominantly with the culture of those surroundings. At its upper levels, this segment composes that portion of the political elite whose roots and strengths lie in the local society.[12] In many former areas of "indirect" colonial rule via the indigenous authorities—principally in the Outer Islands—government officials and political party heads are often descendants of the onetime local sultans and rajas. These traditional leaders are increasingly supplemented by a nonaristocratic elite emerging from the peasant and trading classes via the schools, the civil service, and the labor unions.

The commercial sector of the smaller urban centers has been dominated by Chinese, Arabs, and Indians; both wholesale export and petty retail trade has been in their hands. However, there are Indonesian trading groups of considerable antiquity, and with present governmental support they may, in some cases, be increasing in strength. In Java this group is large, mainly *santri* in religion, and its more successful members are quite "metropolitan" in orientation.[13] Little has been published on trading classes in the Outer Islands, although among various ethnic groups they play an important role: on Sumatra, for instance, the Minangkabau (traditionally peripatetic traders) and the Batak stand out as commercially oriented peoples; while on Bali, which is economically undeveloped, the new indigenous merchants come from the old nobility.[14]

As in the great cities, the mass of the population of the towns is illiterate and unskilled, only a step away in sophistication from the peasants of the surrounding countryside. In Java, in fact, there is little difference in outlook between the small-town proletariat and the peasantry, and there is a constant interchange of persons between countryside and town as economic conditions ebb and flow. In some towns, especially in the Outer Islands, there are neighborhood enclaves of poor laborers of an immigrant ethnic group whose point of origin may be a distant island; these groups are often Bugis, Makassarese, or Malays.

From the national point of view, the network of cities and towns forms an important integrating system, with the emerging metropolitan superculture serving as the connective tissue. From the point of view of the several regions, however, the urban centers play quite varied roles. In some areas, as in Java, the towns are deeply embedded in the local society; while in others—as apparently in some of the Lesser Sunda Islands—the town sits in the rural countryside like a foreign particle, essentially unrelated to and untouched by its surroundings. The range of this variation in types of urban-rural relationships in Indonesia still remains to be studied.

We shall now take up a discussion of the rural communities to which the great majority of Indonesia's people belong, centering it on selected groups whose sociocultural pattern can be considered broadly representative of the categories of rural society described earlier. These, we will remember, are the traditional and post-traditional wet-rice cultures, the Islamic coastal communities, the swidden agricultural societies of the interior, and, finally, groups which for various reasons fit into none of these major categories.

Posttraditional Wet-Rice Peasants: Java

The speakers of the Javanese language occupy about two-thirds of the island of Java, and totaled roughly forty million persons in 1961.[15] In the eastern portion, near the island of Madura, there are numerous enclaves of migrant Madurese inter-spersed with the Javanese population, while the mountainous areas of West Java are Sundanese. Both of these ethnolinguistic groups have rather different ecological adaptations and different cultures from the Javanese, and it is among the Javanese proper that the island's extremely dense population concentrations are found.[16]

The settlement pattern is one of broad stretches of rice paddy alternating with small tree-covered islands of dry land where the houses are clustered together, both crisscrossed by paved roads and unpaved paths which lead to the numerous urban centers. Few villages are more than fifteen miles from a town; most are much nearer. Townsmen, particularly the pegawai and merchants, rarely have houses in villages, and almost as rarely own agricultural land as absentee landlords; most villages are therefore fairly homogeneous both in economic condition and in general outlook. Yet urban standards are used in the villages—and have been for more than a thousand years—for estimating and displaying differences in social rank; and urban tastes in art, music, speech, clothes, and etiquette percolate out even to remote rural regions.

Traditional Javanese culture was from the earliest times given its fullest expression in the urban centers where the royal courts were located. The cities of Jogjakarta and Surakarta today are the capitals of the important remains of four classical kingdoms; and one of these, headed by the Sultan of Jogjakarta, who was a prominent nationalist leader during the revolution and has been Minister of Defense, continues to retain something of its political identity as a "special territory" (*daerah istimewa*) of the Republic. The central inland valleys which contain these royal remnants are still called "Mataram" by Javanese elsewhere, after the island's last great kingdom, which existed into the nineteenth century; and they are considered to be the source and repository of the finest and purest elements of Javanese civilization. The art forms—the stately, formally perfect dance, the intricate, subtle gamelan music, and the profound and engrossing shadow plays—all reach their highest development there, as do the myriad systems of Javanese philosophical mysticism (*ilmu Djawi*). Many of today's greatest Javanese artists and most renowned thinkers are aristocrats of "Mataram"; nobility of social status is thought nearly to coincide with nobility of soul, with wisdom, and with artistic proficiency. For the Javanese, external manifestation of inner character takes the form of an elaborate etiquette and an elegant verbal facility, both of which are found in their most finely modulated forms in the old royal heartland. The entire complex of strongly Hinduized aesthetic canons and theology forms what has been called the *prijaji* variant of Javanese religion, The term prijaji originally referred to the gentry way of life—that is, the courtiers and officials of the king—but now it implies the whole set of attitudes and moral commitments adhered to by nearly every white-collar Javanese, whatever his social origin.

A secondary stream of influence, representing another facet of Javanese culture, has its origins in the belt of commercial cities across the north coast from Tjirebon to Banjuwangi. To the outside observer just as "Javanese" as the inland regions—though perhaps not regarded as such by many of the Javanese themselves—this coastal territory was the area where Islam took root earliest and most firmly on the island in the sixteenth century. From the first, Islam was associated with an urban merchant and craftsman class, members of which traveled from the north coast over the entire region, spreading the Moslem faith as they went.

Islam is a strictly monotheistic religion; God, to its adherents, is omniscient and omnipotent, but distant. Mohammed is regarded not as a deity but as the human being who was chosen by God to be his spokesman, and through whom the words of God, the Koran, were transmitted. It is a highly moralistic religion; its followers are exhorted to lead wholly ethical lives. It is militantly universalistic—there are no social prerequisites to acceptance as a Moslem, such as membership in a particular cultural group. Only one action is required for a person to consider himself a Moslem: his making the statement that he believes in the one God and that he believes that Mohammed was the true spokesman of God.

For many Javanese the periodic confession of faith is the only outward sign of their Islamic persuasion, and most of their ritual and magical beliefs are Hindu-Buddhist or indigenously Javanese in origin. Nonetheless, they consider themselves Moslems. There are many—perhaps a third of the population—who follow orthodox practice more carefully, performing the five prayers daily, attending the services on Fridays in the mosque, keeping the month-long fast at Ramadan, learning to recite verses from the Koran, and if possible making the pilgrimage to the holy city of Mecca. These persons are referred to as santri and are found today in nearly every segment of rural and urban Javanese society, though their strongest representation has always been among the traders and craftsmen. Every town has a santri quarter (the *kauman*) usually near both the mosque and the market.

Santri and prijaji, cultural patterns bound up historically with the social roles of trader and gentry, represent two aspects of urban Java, two streams of sophisticate culture, both of which impinge upon and deeply affect the outlook of the mass of the peasants who form the base of the society. It would be wholly erroneous to think of the Javanese village as a closed community, self-sufficient and culturally insulated against the outer world; it is hard to imagine such a situation even at some earlier period of time. Nevertheless, there is a third Javanese religious tradition which has been especially associated with the peasantry; it is usually referred to as the *abangan,* in contrast to santri and prijaji. The three patterns, it should be noted, are fundamentally similar; they are not distinct entities, but rather variants of the more general Javanese values, behavior norms, and religious beliefs.

In the traditional social context of the village, the abangan religious system and its ethical correlates show themselves to be highly adaptive. The world of the Javanese peasant is one filled with myriad swarms of unseen local and ancestral spirits, hovering around all natural objects, human beings, and artifacts. The spirits are always ready, if angered or if they spot a weak point in one's defenses, to cause misfortune, particularly illness. They can also be influenced to attack an enemy by practitioners in black magic, who can be hired for the purpose. There are three defenses human beings can mobilize against them: the first is to feed the spirits regular offerings of rice and other food, flower petals, and incense; the second is to go to a curer (*dukun*) who by virtue of his superior psychic strength and magical potions can counteract and oust the spirits; and third, to maintain a strong, unperturbed heart, for psychological upset is thought to lower one's capacity to fend off the supernatural and is considered to be the underlying cause of nearly all illness. The principal reward for right thinking, right acting, and proper ritual observances is what the Javanese call *slamet*—well-being—usually described in negative terms as the absence of trouble, the holding off of misfortune. The principal way to maintain personal inner strength is to limit radically desires and impulses, so that one will be subject to no strong feelings of either pleasure or disappointment.

The central ritual set for every Javanese, but pre-eminently for the abangan, is a simple ceremonial meal called the *slametan*, at which various foods are presented to the spirits (a miscellaneous collection including indigenous Javanese ones, Hindu gods, Allah, and Moslem religious heroes). This meal must be attended and "witnessed" by all of one's immediate neighbors, a group of six or eight of those in direct proximity. Very brief and unpretentious, the slametan nevertheless symbolizes and gives periodic exercise to one of the most deeply felt values of the Javanese, that of mutual helpfulness and harmony among neighbors. Called *rukun* in Javanese, *gotong rojong* in Indonesian, the invocation of this ideal creates a pressure to be concerned with one another's well-being, and thus softens to some extent the tendencies to social atomism brought about by the absence of actual institutional requirements for cooperative endeavor.[17]

An allied Javanese value is the feeling that all villagers are equal, and that no member of the village has the right to hold himself aloof from his fellows unless he is in fact formally superior in status. However, toward persons who are actually socially superior—such as the village head, the town government officials, or older persons—an elaborate expression of deference is required; and they for their part are expected to respond with appropriate dignity. Celebration of status differences is a Javanese value as deeply held as that for egalitarianism among fellow villagers; and in fact it underlies the latter, for it is out of fear of belittling someone unjustly that the villagers attempt to be properly respectful and circumspect toward all. For townsmen of prijaji persuasion, the ideas associated with this etiquette of social inequality form a central part of their religious outlook and enter into all aspects of their life, including familial relations.

There are two levels of village governmental units, the lowest being the village itself, the *dukuhan,* which is headed by a *kamitua.* Above it is the *desa,* which is headed by a *lurah* and is actually a government-created grouping of several dukuhan for administrative efficiency. The lurah and kamitua were formerly appointed by the government officials above them, or elected by landowning villagers; today by and large they are elected by the entire adult citizenry. They have "permanent" tenure, but can be deposed at any time either by their superiors or by popular action. The lurah's main duties are record keeping, tax collection, the transmission of instructions from the central government, and the informal arbitration of local disputes. Both lurah and kamitua are local men, unlike the official who is their superior, the *tjamat,* who is in charge of a subdistrict (*ketjamatan*) made up of varying numbers of desas. The tjamat is a townsman—a prijaji in outlook usually— and his relationship with the peasants is generally some combination of traditional prijaji paternalism and bureaucratic formalism. The tjamat and the lurah together endeavor to bridge the gap between the central administration and the local peasantry, one reaching up from the desa and the other down from the subdistrict office.

The desa's territory includes the surrounding rice fields as well as the house land. The irrigation system, of crucial importance for wet-rice farming, is under the supervision of an official from the central government, which employs one or more village men to see that the works are properly maintained. In spite of the skill and in-

45

dustriousness of the Javanese farmers, there is not enough arable land for the rapidly rising population, and a steady lowering of living standards is the consequence. The land, however, has not gravitated into the hands of a wealthy few, but rather has remained in small peasant-held parcels.[18] Intricate arrangements of share-cropping and rental, through which the produce of each piece of land is spread among many persons, make it possible for the majority of the able-bodied men to have access to some land for cultivation. Many villages, acting as corporate units, hold residual ownership rights (*kongsèn*) to large sections of rice land which is often called somewhat misleadingly "communal land." Rights to use this kongsèn land are distributed to individual eligible villagers —sometimes annually, sometimes permanently to a man and his heirs—and the land is then worked by the user as if he owned it outright. Labor contracts are individual, whether they be in the form of wagework, sharecropping arrangement, or a mutual labor exchange. Few permanent groups of any sort exist for collective land ownership and cultivation, and a large portion of the land is owned privately in the Western sense.

Class stratification within the village is minimal, because there is little occupational differentiation and because economic differences fall within a very narrow range. In some villages land is fairly evenly divided, and mutual labor exchange (possible only where plots of land are approximately equal in size) is the rule rather than wage labor. In other villages, perhaps the majority, there is a fairly clear division between those farmers who own a little land and can act relatively independently and those who are landless and must depend on good personal, kinship, and neighbor relationships for sharecropping and wagework openings. Those in the upper group (the "landowners," who rarely own more than five acres) often have a patronlike relationship to those to whom they give employment, receiving deference and minor services in return for work opportunities and small gifts. The elite of the village are those members of the landed group who are culturally oriented in some degree toward the town. Some of them have sufficient cash resources to serve as wholesale middlemen, buying up village crops for resale in town. Others are members of the lurah's staff, and they and their families often form a local in-marrying upper stratum. In santri villages the wealthiest men make the expensive pilgrimage to Mecca, returning to receive the title of hadji and sometimes to open a village school for the teaching of the Koran. Most of the village elite place their children in modern Western-style primary schools, and increasingly nowadays send them into town to high school. There is no possibility for a lurah to be promoted up into the civil service bureaucracy, for the social chasm between the village and urban elite is too great; but there is some chance for his children to bridge the gap through acquiring a higher education.

The Javanese kinship system is bilateral and nucleating—that is, descent is considered the same through the mother and the father, inheritance is the same for daughters and for sons, the nuclear family of parents and young children stands essentially on its own and usually in a separate house, and obligations between kinsmen are minimal. There is a very high divorce rate (around 50 per cent of the marriages are subsequently severed), and children frequently live in a series of different family groups during the course of their childhood. There are no corporate kin groups. Few business partnerships are established between kinsmen, and inherited land is generally divided or given to one heir who then compensates the others for their shares with cash.[19]

Above the household there are no organized groupings for economic, ritual, or other purposes. Religion is a personal matter, involving, for abangan peasants, merely a few invited neighbors at an occasional slametan and, for santri, regular prayers and visits to a mosque. Mosques are usually self-maintaining and are not supported by any bounded social group. The village community, the dukuhan, does have some corporate features. It possesses a communal shrine (pundèn)—a small grave, cluster of trees, or spring which represents the burial place or first dwelling of the mythical original pioneers who cleared the primordial jungle and converted it to rice land (in Central Java this may have been a thousand years ago). From these settlers all current inhabitants are considered to have descended in spirit; and at their shrine small periodic ceremonies are held. There is also usually a communal graveyard just outside the settlement area, where the only village-wide religious ritual is held, an annual purification of the village of evil spirits (the ritual of bersih désa). The dukuhan (not the desa) has authority over the distribution of the village kongsèn land, which in some communities comprises virtually all, but in others only a small portion, of the cultivable land. Administratively, the dukuhan usually has several elective officials, who become part of the administrative staff of the desa head; they are usually compensated for their work by the granting of use rights on certain plots of rice land owned by the dukuhan as a whole.

In spite of these traditional communal bonds, the modern dukuhan is not often a strongly integrated group toward which its members have deep loyalty. In some areas where there has been a history of antagonism between the neighboring dukuhan (often based on religious differences between santri and abangan), the villagers feel considerable group identity; but in other localities the dukuhan merely represents a place to live. Marriages are contracted nearly as frequently outside the dukuhan as within it, and there is considerable internal migration as villagers move to town or to other rural areas in search of economic opportunity.

Javanese village social structure, in sum, is exceedingly simple and vague in form. Above the family there are few organizations—either territorial, economic, religious, governmental, or otherwise—in which the individual finds a prescribed or definite position. The strongest felt ties are toward the formless and temporary assemblages of immediate neighbors and the circle of closest kinsmen. There is a marked absence of concerted corporate enterprises, striking in comparison with the situation in most other parts of Indonesia, particularly Bali. Because Bali has close cultural and historical ties with Java, its present-day social structure may resemble in general outline the traditional one that Java left behind centuries ago under the combined impact of Islam and colonialism. Balinese society, which will be described in some detail below, is marked by strong, unambiguous social arrangements for living, for family relationships, labor, community cooperation, and social control, which are sanctioned by group religious ritual. It is the virtual absence of these sorts of institutions which makes the term "posttraditional" appropriate to Java: it is no longer traditional in form, but it is also not yet modern.

There are some indications that this structureless situation may now be changing with the introduction, since the revolution, of political parties and their affiliated groups into the rural countryside of Java. Even in the years before the war, urban Javanese society was alive with organizational activity. While outright political parties were restricted, numerous groupings flourished, all feeling themselves to some extent part of a nationalist movement; and by their side a wide assortment of nonpolitical associations arose, such as boy scouts, educational committees for the support of private schools, philosophical societies, and women's clubs. After independence these organizations attained even greater vitality, and became in fact the major channels for the townsmen's social interaction. Any coordinated town-wide action, such as the public observance of the national Independence Day, is directed by an *ad hoc* committee made up of the various chairmen from all the different important associations. The nonpolitical organizations are informally grouped into four or five clusters, called *aliran* in Indonesian from the word for "stream," each with a political party at its core. Thus there generally is in every town a complex of associations oriented about the Nationalist party, the formally disbanded Masjumi, Nahdatul Ulama, and the Communists.[20] The various groups within each aliran are headed by a small set of overworked leaders, and the consequence of this clustering is that all associational activity is politicized.

The town-based political parties moved into the rural sector with the holding of elections in 1955 and 1957, each bringing in tow many of the associations oriented about it. This new mode of social organization was received by the peasants with mixed feelings, some fearing its divisive effect on village harmony, others enthusiastically recognizing it as an encouraging sign of social progress and an alternate means to power and influence within the village. How extensively and permanently the formal organizational system will be adopted by the peasants remains to be seen; at present it is only a suggestion of one direction of structural development.

Traditional Wet-Rice Peasants: Bali

Bali, which possessed in 1961 a population of about 1,780,000, is located immediately east of Java, with only a narrow strait of water between them.[21] The kingdoms of medieval Bali were closely allied with those of Java, and many elements of their respective cultures are very similar. As we have noted, however, their systems of social organization are strikingly different. Bali is a much smaller island; its heartland, a limited region of fertile soils and heavy population, is located on its southern side, cut off by high mountains from the commerce of the Java Sea. As a result of this isolation, Islam and interisland trade completely bypassed Bali, while colonial government was not introduced until 1908. The Dutch at that time began a process of rationalizing the village and supravillage governmental structures, but this development has never gone so far as it has in Java. Commercial agriculture, too, has not yet reached Bali, with the minor exceptions of small coffee plantations in the mountains and a fairly lively cattle export trade.

Isolation has not meant cultural inertia; on the contrary, Bali is noted for the vigor, sophistication, and complexity of its arts—especially its music, dance, and drama, but also painting and sculpture.[22] In contrast to Java, where the practice of the arts, while more subtle and profound, is today largely confined to court circles and to a few professional dramatic and orchestral troupes, aesthetic expression in Bali is an activity pursued by large numbers of persons from all segments of the society. In Java, aside from rather crude popularized productions, new artistic creation has slowed down, and most effort is toward the preservation in detail of revered traditional masterpieces; in Bali, while earlier forms are still very much alive, there is also considerable improvisation and development. Art for both cultures has perhaps greater significance than elsewhere in the archipelago, possessing a central and dynamic religious meaningfulness. In Java this significance is philosophical and mystical, concerned with the achievement of psychological and moral inner stasis, while in Bali external ritual display and more direct aesthetic pleasure are involved.[23]

In Bali two sets of institutions provide frequent opportunities for aesthetic activity: the temples and the series of personal life cycle ceremonies. There are thousands of temples in Bali—each village has at least three or four—and they reflect many different functions and histories. Each one has a fairly fixed congregational group which maintains it physicially and performs the rituals required at it. These congregations overlap in membership; every Balinese belongs to a number of them, usually by reason of descent but sometimes by residence or magical command. He may belong to one representing his local patrilineal descent group, to one for a larger nonlocal descent group, to three village temples, to one or two temples for his rice fields, and to several others of no specific function. These are not sect temples, for the religious system is identical for all. Most of the Balinese temples are similar in form: two walled-in courtyards, connected by a narrow gate—the first a forecourt for the orchestra and for making preparations, the second the actual temple itself with altars and raised pavilions for offerings. The altars, walls, and gates are often elaborately and fairly carved, and during a ceremony they are decorated with many additional ornamentations of palm leaves, bamboo, colored cloth banners and

50

streamers, and so on. Every important temple ceremony takes the form of a gala party to which the distant gods are invited and requires an orchestra, processions and dances, and hundreds of deftly made offerings of food in intricate plaited baskets.[24] There may also be a cockfight and a dramatic performance in the evening outside the temple. The ceremony at many village death temples includes a special performance of the eerie dance-drama of the fight between Rangda the witch and Barong the bearlike dragon, during which some of the performers may spectacularly fall into trance and attempt to stab themselves with their own krisses.[25] Trance is a frequent, though not a necessary, element in Balinese rituals; it signifies the entry of the human body by one of the visiting gods, and does not take place outside of ritual contexts. The free release of emotions of aggression, sexuality, and disrespect that trance permits stands out in relief against the everyday behavior of the Balinese, which is quiet and controlled, unexpressive and decorous.[26]

The series of personal life cycle ceremonies are additional occasions for artistic performances and displays. The most important are teeth-filing, which ceremonially marks the entrance to adulthood (although in fact it may be postponed for economic reasons until middle age), and cremation. Other points in the life cycle, such as marriage or the achieving of the third month of life, may also be celebrated with more than simple ritual. Cremation is such a costly and elaborate festival that it is generally postponed for years after death, the body being buried at death in the village graveyard and disinterred at the time of cremation. Today mass cremations are most common in many parts of Bali; poorer commoners may share the ritual expense at a more wealthy Brahman priest's cremation, while poorer gentry may join the cremation of a better-off prince in their own descent group.

Gentry, priests, and commoners comprise only very general status categories in Bali; they are not distinctly separate groups, for they all share precisely the same culture, and their members are mutually and intricately related to one another. The main status distinction is that between gentry and commoner or, as the Balinese say, between the *djero* and the *djaba*, the "insiders" and the "outsiders," signifying those who live inside a "palace" and those who live outside. The latter represent at least 90 per cent of the population. With the exception of the supravillage political organization to be discussed below, aristocratic blood is not associated with superior position in, for example, economic power or artistic training. Aristocrats always command high deference in speech and posture from their inferiors, but little else. A "palace" is nearly indistinguishable in elegance and comfort from a commoner's home, and nearly everyone has about the same standard of living.

The traditional stratification system in Bali is neither a feudal system of landlords and serfs nor a Hindu caste system, although it has often been depicted as one or the other. While there were, prior to 1908, some service relationships between certain gentry and specific commoners which have been termed "feudal," these did not involve land or agricultural labor; aristocrats either did their own farming or employed sharecroppers. As for calling it a caste system, there is no society-wide layering into ascriptive corporate groups with distinct occupational functions, as is typical of the Indian caste system, nor are there any important ideas of ritual contamination by low groups of high ones. There are marriage restrictions between groups of differing rank, but these do not prohibit *any* marriage across status group lines, but rather prohibit women from marrying below their rank and men from marrying upwards.

What the Balinese system of ranking actually does consist of is difficult to explain in a short space. It is closely connected to the kinship system, which is also unusual in form and peculiar to Bali, being one of patrilineal descent groups which are largely endogamous, optional (i.e. a group of kinsmen may prefer *not* to organize themselves as a descent group, especially if they are not wealthy enough to support the activities entailed by it), and mainly localized. These kinship groups (called *dadia*) are corporate—that is, they are permanent organizations which endure even though their actual membership changes through birth, death, change of residence, etc. Each dadia owns a special temple and has several chosen leaders and a treasury. Gentry dadia are distinguished from commoner ones in that commoner dadia are confined in membership to kinsmen living within a single hamlet, while gentry dadia are nonlocalized and have members scattered over a wide region. The members of a dadia all have the same personal title. These titles are ranked, but their relative prestige is not entirely agreed upon by everyone, and as a result there is a constant undercover struggle for recognition of the superiority of one's own title. Even the border between gentry and commoner is sometimes indistinct and contested. Aristocratic titles are always explicitly employed in address, but commoner ones are merely understood, thereby creating even further grounds for competition. Such rivalry for prestige (in its purest sense, without economic perquisites) is an exceedingly important element in the Balinese social climate.

Before 1908, political life was based essentially on this system of competing titled descent groups, for the ruling kings were the heads of successful gentry kingroups who were able to achieve and maintain, however briefly, status ascendancy over an entire region. At the time the Dutch administration was instituted, there were six major kings and countless minor independent princes.[27] The six kingdoms were mapped, given territorial boundaries (which they had never had before) and transformed into the present-day governmental districts (*swapradja*). The smaller princedoms were incorporated into one or another district. Today the top government officials for all but two of these districts are the direct descendants of former kings, and much of the bureaucracy is manned by nobles.

As in the past, the real significance of the highest gentry lies not in its political position but in its function as organizing center for many aesthetico-religious activities. The ceremonies for the kingroup temples of the highest gentry families, for their personal life cycle festivities, and for certain regional temples for the general welfare, all involve the participation of thousands of commoners, both skilled and unskilled, as contributors and as spectators. Formerly the kings maintained communities of fine craftsmen—gold and silver workers, stone carvers, weavers, and the like; many of these crafts have declined and some are now supported by the tourist trade. Massive gentry cremations are still held from time to time, often with interesting modern overtones of national political meaning arousing reverberations in Djakarta.

One small segment of the aristocracy is the Brahmana priestly class, made up of a group of unlocalized dadia which are at the very top of the prestige ladder. Some Brahmana dadia were in the past closely associated with dominant princes by marriage and ritual ties, and today some top officials come from this rank; but more are, and were, merely farmers. Each Brahmana dadia usually has a priest (*pedanda*) who serves a varying number of clients, both aristocratic and commoner. A Brahmana priest is not connected to any temple (these have their own commoner ritual specialists) nor to any particular region, but is spiritual minister to individual families in various villages scattered over large distances. Every Balinese has such a tie to a specific pedanda; he goes to him, however, only on special occasions for the holy water which is needed for all ceremonies, most of his religious needs being met by the temples and their priests, and by folk curers and mediums.

Some writers have treated these two groups, the nobility and the Brahmana priesthood, as a superficial top layer which rests lightly over the "real" Balinese community, the village.[28] While in the legal sense—and Balinese make unusually precise legal distinctions —most institutions associated with the village are wholly independent of the supravillage political and religious systems, nevertheless these upper ranks form an integral part of Balinese society and give it much of its vitality.

It is hard, in fact, to separate out "the" village as a structural entity, for every actual community is made up of a variety of distinct associations, each with slightly different memberships and slightly differing territorial reference. Balinese social structure is in this quite unlike Java's, where the territorially bounded village, the dukuhan, performs nearly all social functions in a monolithic way. Balinese religious organization, as we have seen, is very intricately distributed among a number of different structures. Worship is never personal or familial as it tends to be in Java, but always takes place in an organized group. Each ritual association, centered on a specific temple, is usually also some sort of functional group. The dadia is one such group; another is the agricultural society.

There are hundreds of agricultural societies (subak) in Bali, each corresponding to a small section of wet-rice paddies. Each society represents not only a temple congregation but also an independent local irrigation system, for its members have constructed and maintain its dams and channels, with all members having equal responsibilities and equal rights. This fragmented organizational pattern is encouraged by the rough topography of Bali, where deep ravines, cut by rivers running rapidly and steeply from the central volcanic mountains to the sea, corrugate the land, leaving few extensive flat areas. Between the ravines rise long parallel ridges, with settlements strung along the top and paddies terraced down the ravine slopes on either side. Since the river lies below the fields, each society ingeniously taps it at a point some miles upstream, and leads the water down by aqueducts and tunnels. Down the course of a river there may be as many as fifty societies using its water, but each one is fully autonomous. Disputes between societies over water can only be arbitrated, for there is no superior authority. Formerly the princes used the agricultural societies as a means for taxing the peasants, and the royal tax official had some arbitration powers; today a government bureau performs the same functions. Actually there are few disputes, for, so far, there is plenty of water for everyone. At the outlets from the river and in the midst of each society's paddies are temples where the society holds its rituals and festivals. There are also certain religious rituals seasonally performed at the head of each river, which were formerly the duty of the local prince and today are performed by the staff of the irrigation office.

The agricultural societies are independent of any village organizations: unlike Java, where a village government has jurisdiction over both its house land and its surrounding rice fields, in Bali the two spheres are kept apart. Within any settlement cluster live members of many different agricultural societies, and a well-to-do farmer with several plots of land may belong to several different ones. All land is privately owned; it may be sold, pawned, or given to someone else at the will of the owner, but the ritual and irrigation work responsibilities are transferred with the title to the land.

Settlements—clusters of walled-in courtyards, with coconut and fruit trees, temples and other public buildings—range in size from small hamlets of twenty households to large communities of several hundred households. Large settlements are usually subdivided into smaller units, but in a variety of different ways. There are three types of social unit which correspond in a general sense to the usual notion of a "village." All three of these are present in every settlement, but they hardly ever have the same membership or territory. They are the Kahyangan-Tiga groups, the *bandjar,* and the governmental village administration, the desa.

The Kahyangan-Tiga is a set of three temples to which nearly every Balinese belongs; there are over a thousand of these sets on the island. One of the three components is the *pura pusèh,* or "origin temple," which represents the ancestral spirits of the present inhabitants of the area, going back to the first group who settled there. The second is the *pura balai agung,* the "great council temple," representing the host of deities and spirits which can bestow or withdraw the general well-being of the people and surrounding rice fields. The third is the *pura dalem,* the death temple, usually placed near the graveyard and at which the local dead and the gods of

55

death are placated. In some cases, and perhaps ideally, all three temples have the same congregation, but this is not always the case. Often part of the membership for one of the three comes from another settlement; sometimes the congregation is divided into three segments, each sharing the heaviest ritual obligations for one temple and making occasional token offerings to the others.

It sometimes happens that the membership of the Kahyangan-Tiga and the bandjar or "hamlet association" coincide; most often a bandjar community as a unit has ritual responsibility for only one of the three. The fundamental function of the bandjar is, however, not religious but governmental.[29] The bandjar is a council of heads of households, each with a required female co-member—usually his wife—to take care of ritual duties. It is witness to marriage, divorce, and inheritance transactions; it serves as prosecutor and judge of criminal offenses, and acts as local police. The bandjar sees to the building and maintenance of the public roads, bathing places, meeting house, market sheds, cockfighting pit, and the like. It generally is also a burial society, with every member required on penalty of fine to attend the funeral and participate in the cremation of every other member. It often owns a gamelan orchestra, and perhaps dancing costumes, which it can lend or rent out to private musical societies. It has powers of taxation, usually levied by means of bandjar-wide work parties which harvest land owned by members in return for a set fraction of the crop, which goes into the bandjar treasury. The council can also punish backsliders or criminals by means of fines, and in extreme cases by eviction from the village, for the bandjar usually owns all the house land and can decide who shall or shall not live there. Such evictions still occur from time to time, the ostracized one moving to another region or into the household of a wealthy prince as a dependent servant. Most decisions are made by the bandjar association unanimously in its monthly meetings, and there are elected chairmen who administer these decisions. In large settlements there are usually a number of bandjar, and often these are not territorial in jurisdiction but have their memberships interspersed through each other. Immediately proximate neighbors can and often do belong to different bandjar, different Kahyangan-Tiga temples, and different agricultural societies; can have different Brahmana priests; and, in the past, owed allegiance to different princes. Moreover, each neighbor may choose to join a variety of different special interest societies: orchestra clubs, dance clubs, or work associations for carpentry, brick making, roof building, mat weaving, and so on. In recent times there have been some attempts, mainly futile, to simplify the Balinese social organization; they were especially promoted by the Dutch, who found it unwieldy and confusing (although the Balinese consider it the reverse). One consequence has been the establishment of the government-defined village, the desa.

The Balinese desa is an affiliation of several nearby bandjar, under a single desa head, who is called a *perbekel* or *bendesa*. This man is generally a government appointee, a literate villager whose main functions are transmitting information from the government and keeping certain records of births, deaths, and the like. The bandjar which are joined together into a single desa often have little in common with one another, aside from proximity. Sometimes a desa represents a single Kahyangan-Tiga set, or the bailiwick of a former lesser lord, but these are the exceptions. The desa head is usually a man of considerable influence in his own bandjar, but he is only a peripheral outsider to the others in his desa.

The intricacy of Balinese social structure, with the remains of its "feudal" states, its many temple associations, ranked title groups, corporate kingroups, agricultural societies, hamlet associations, government villages and districts, and musical and dramatic groups, contrasts strongly with the simplicity of the Javanese. Plainly, social change due to contact with the Western world does not necessarily lead to increased complexity. However, the nub of the distinction between "traditional" and "posttraditional" societies is not the degree of complexity, but rather the firmness and distinctness of social institutions, the proportion of social statuses which are ascribed and permanent, and the predominance of primary, face-to-face social groupings. Even though Balinese society is densely populated, highly stratified, and complexly differentiated into diverse interpenetrating groupings, it is at the same time sharply localized. Nearly every relationship is both a personal one, in the sense that the actors have long been fully acquainted and know a good deal about one another, and also a clearly defined one, in the sense that the rights and responsibilities each has to the other are distinctly specified and enforced.

To be "traditional" does not mean to be inflexible in the face of new challenges; the innovations of the new Indonesia are being vigorously adopted, but within traditional channels. The upper levels of the government administration are, by and large, in the hands of the former aristocracy. Political parties, economic co-operatives and corporations, new art forms such as easel painting, all are channeled through one or more of the existing groupings—the bandjar, the titled kingroup, the petty kingdom, the agricultural society, etc. The existence of these older social forms seems in many cases to facilitate rather than impede the acceptance of the new and the reinterpretation of the old. This may also be true for many of those other peoples of Indonesia who were until this century still traditional in social structure.

Islamic Coastal Peoples: Makassarese and Sumbawans

The "coastal Malays" of the entire eastern half of Sumatra, of the Malayan peninsula itself,[30] of the islands between Sumatra and Borneo (e.g. Riouw, Lingga, Banka, Billiton), and of the coasts and river valleys of Borneo, including the highly mixed population of Bandjarmassin, are all very similar. These, together with the coastal peoples of Atjeh, South Celebes, Gorontolo in North Celebes, Ternate, Tidore, the Batjan Islands, the Goram Islands, West Java, Madura, Sumbawa, and small pockets on the other Lesser Sunda Islands, all have much in common culturally. Precisely how much, however, remains to be ascertained, for in spite of their evident cultural and social importance, the coastal peoples of the Indonesian islands have been slighted in research and reporting. Some very general features which appear to be present in all of them can be suggested.

These scattered peoples can be considered to have a single but rather heterogeneous culture, one which Pigeaud called the "Pasisir culture,"[31] from the Malay term meaning "coastal." The Pasisir culture grew up around the international spice trade of the fourteenth to eighteenth centuries, and was, from the first, closely associated with the spread of Islam. Elements from the original cultures of the participating groups—from the Malays, north Javanese, and Makassarese in particular—were joined by Arabic and south Indian traits in mixtures whose proportions varied with each location. The flow of traders and migrants among the islands during that period aided the process of cultural borrowing and exchange.

Thus Islamic beliefs and institutions and an orientation to market-ing activities are important distinctive features of the Pasisir culture. Another characteristic is a relative stress on literary forms of art—especially poetic epics, histories and moral tales—in contrast, for instance, to the Javanese high tradition emphasis on dance, drama, and music. Probably all of the Pasisir peoples have bilateral kinship systems; some, such as the Malays, have a system much like the Javanese, in which the elementary family stands quite independently of other kinsmen; while others, like the Makassarese, have strongly developed corporate kingroups which are formed on a bilateral basis. Lastly, most of these peoples have the same general, quite distinctive type of political and social system. In the past they were organized into numerous small independent kingdoms, each with a supralocal ruling class, a commoner class, and a dependent group of slaves. In these kingdoms—and to a large extent today—the level of status was tied to actual political power, so that the kings needed constantly to prove their charisma and wealth in order to maintain the personal loyalty of their followers, and there was and is sharp competition for positions of prestige at all levels.[32]

Ecologically, the Pasisir peoples have regimes which are quite unspecialized; that is to say, within a single narrow area many different environmental possibilities are exploited, from fishing and coconut-grove tending near the shore to wet-rice paddies, permanent gardens, and swidden farming in the near interior. This lack of ecological specialization contrasts considerably with that of most of the other social groups of Indonesia. In addition to their agricultural pursuits, large parts of the Pasisir populations were formerly engaged in interisland shipping and trade; how significant this seafaring element is today is unclear.

Adaptive variety in the Pasisir economy may take the form of village specialization, as we shall describe in Makassar and Sumbawa; or it may be more a matter of individual opportunism, as among the Malays of Borneo and Sumatra, who often have several different sources of income—combining, for example, wet-rice farming with fishing, rubber tapping, or peddling. Wet rice does not play such a dominant role in their economy, and their population densities never reach the levels of Java, Bali, and the Sumatran highlands. However, perhaps because the Pasisir peoples have such flexible modes of ecological adaptation, their districts are the densely settled parts of otherwise thinly populated regions. Bandjarmassin had a population density in 1930 of 47 persons per square kilometer compared to the general Borneo average of 4, while portions of Southwest Celebes reached over 100 as against most of the rest of the island, with less than 5 persons per square kilometer.[33]

One of the most dynamic of the Pasisir peoples, numbering about five million in 1961, occupies the southeastern arm of Celebes.[34] This population group was politically fragmented into many coastal kingdoms, of which the Makassarese and the Buginese are best known, all of them with essentially the same language and culture. During the period of international competition for the spice trade, and even as late as the nineteenth century, the people of this area were highly active as traders, navigators, pirates, and as colonizers of smaller principalities elsewhere in Indonesia. Sumbawa, for instance, was directly dominated and exploited by Makassar during the seventeenth century. The Buginese had colonies in the Riouw Islands, in Borneo, and in small enclaves elsewhere in Indonesia; and the principal Buginese kingdom, Bone, was long in commercial and frequently martial competition with the Makassarese kingdom of Goa.

The town of Makassar was, from the seventeenth through the nineteenth centuries, the harbor settlement for the king of Goa, who was called the Karaeng-Ri-Goa and whose actual capital was about ten kilometers inland. The king was really an energetic businessman with royal trappings, who derived a profit on all trade passing through his port, either by levying customs and tariffs or by commissioning and captaining the ships himself. A large segment of Makassar's population consisted of a colony of foreign merchants—Malays and Javanese forced out of their own area in the seventeenth century by Dutch activities, Moslems from India and the Near East, Chinese, Englishmen, and so on. The tie between the king and his Indonesian subjects was essentially a personal one, bolstered by magical and religious symbols and by strongly enforced sumptuary regulations. This political structure was similar in some respects to those of the Hinduized kingdoms of Java, but Makassar's commercial emphasis and multiple ethnic group composition made Goa very different from the central Javanese realms. The relative power of each Celeban king was by no means fixed, nor was the territory over which he ruled. New kings could (and often did) emerge from distant branches of the royal family to challenge the established ones and to attract some of their followers. The entry of Dutch power into this extremely unsteady political system stabilized it to some degree by strengthening the then existing royal houses. The Dutch conquered Makassar in 1675 in order to seize and enforce a trade monopoly on spices from the Moluccas; and thereafter they supported and controlled the kings of Goa. Actually, aside from the political effects of their presence, Dutch influence was very small in the region until 1905, when Netherlands forces conquered the remainder of the island, reorganized the local government, introduced their own men as "advisors" to the native regents, and began the process of transforming the royal families into civil servants.

About five kilometers south of the city of Makassar is the mouth of the Djene' river which before the construction of roads in this century formed the main transport link to the mountains and the central artery for the kingdom of Goa. The village of Balombaru at its mouth was visited by the anthropologist Raymond Kennedy in 1949. It had had, fifty years earlier, a flourishing market and harbor, which had provided the king of Goa with a lucrative income in custom duties and anchorage fees. By the time of Kennedy's visit, its people were no longer sailors and merchants but largely craftsmen and farmers. Kennedy met an aged sailor who recalled trips by native sailboat (*prau*) to Surabaja, Tjirebon, Semarang, Djakarta, Padang, Singapore, Bangkok, Penang, and even China. The village still had a small group of Javanese and Chinese residents, the former mainly skilled leather workers, the latter all storekeepers. There was a Western-style elementary school of six grades, several Islamic schools for reading the Koran, one mosque, and numerous neighborhood prayer houses (*surau*).

Kennedy reported that the Makassarese make sharp social distinctions between the aristocracy, who composed about a third of Balombaru's population, and commoners. Before 1905, there had been a large class of slaves; at the time of Kennedy's visit slave ancestry had not been forgotten, and the descendants of slaves were poverty-stricken and often dependent on wealthier villagers. The immediate family of the king of Goa formed another distinct social layer, not represented in the village. The village chief of Balombaru was a low aristocrat, while the district chief over him was a direct relative of the king; both proudly displayed the appropriate symbols of their ranks, such as the style of their residences, their clothes, and the kinds of deferential behavior they expected from their underlings. The head of the mosque, the *imam* (*imang* in Makassarese) had a position of prestige equal to that of the district head. The king of Goa was the governmental head of the

Makassar area, and Kennedy reported that he was held in greater awe by the peasants than any higher officials from other islands.

The division into royalty, aristocracy, and commoners, however, is not a simple threefold class system, although it has frequently been reported as such.[35] Another village study, this time one of a rice-growing community some fifteen kilometers inland, made by Chabot in 1940 and 1948, gives a much more sophisticated picture of the Makassarese stratification system. Chabot shows that, from the point of view of the Makassarese themselves, their society is not made up of three sharply bounded strata; rather, they see everyone from king to common man ranged on a continuous scale of prestige, with no one's position fixed permanently at one level. In many ways the Makassarese system appears to be like Bali's, but it is much more fluid. The great variety of economic opportunities—large areas of unopened land, chances to make money in trade or commercial crops—makes possible considerable mobility for a man with initiative and the backing of his kinsmen. Chabot demonstrates that there was a good deal of migration from territory to territory and considerable social climbing, both of which were generally engaged in by large kingroups moving as a unit. In fact, it is the peculiar structure of the Makassarese kinship system which provides the key to much of the population's social behavior.

Two main factors determine a man's rank: the status of his parents and other kinsmen, and his own present personal attainments in terms of wealth, office, or learning. The outward validation of his status is, however, the amount of the bride price of his sisters and daughters, which is publicly placed in the mosque records. While the amount of the bride price follows certain customary standards (so much for commoners, so much for gentry, etc.), there is considerable play in the price, and tense undercover bargaining enters every marital transaction. A woman may never marry for a bride price lower than her mother's, although she may for a higher one; and a man may never marry a woman above him. A high bride price is to the advantage of both parties, since it indicates that they are both high in prestige, and consequently there is a steady secular inflation in bride prices. The imang of each region sets the amount in each case, taking into account all the relevant aspects of the social situations of the bride and groom and their families. No one may receive a higher bride price than that of the sisters of the local ruler; however today, apparently as a consequence of changing bases for prestige and power, some individual families may actually command higher bride prices than the ruler, though the publicly announced price remains lower.

Marriage thus becomes an urgent political matter, one in which everyone's personal pride is deeply involved, for each marriage establishes the relative status of many different men. A deep but touchy pride, a determined insistence on full revenge for real or imagined slights, and a strong feeling of rivalry with all persons and groups are all said to be characteristic of the Makassarese.[36] Every Makassarese man strives to obtain high bride prices for his sisters, daughters, and female cousins, and at the same time to get as high status a wife for himself as he dares, even if he has to "steal" or elope with his bride. Elopements are very common, for then the affronted kinsmen on both sides are faced with a *fait accompli* which they are usually forced to accept against their will. However, elopement is often followed by vengeful cattle thefts or even murders.

Prestige and political maneuvering are consequently family matters; an entire body of relatives supports and is carried upward by a successful man, or conversely slows his progress. This body of relatives is a corporate kingroup, sharply localized, into which membership may be gained via either one's mother or father. Each person belongs by birth to several such kingroups, and he may choose which one to live and ally his efforts with. He can also remain independent, or even ally himself by marriage to an entirely unrelated group.[37] Each kinship grouping centers around one or two influential men—the more influential the larger the group, and vice versa. These kingroups are sometimes very large and cohesive, and, although land is individually owned, such kingroups tend to be wealthier than small ones, which do not have the resources for mutual aid. Marriages are usually endogamous to the local kingroup; these keep the property within the group and are less difficult to arrange. However, the leading families within a kingroup are pressed to arrange advantageous exogamous unions, for it is these which validate the family claim to rank, and it is through these that the group widens its political influence. Competition is quite intense among the men within the kingroup, even between brothers; and, possibly as a result of this friction, there is frequent splitting off of segments of the family, who move to other regions to open up new land. In Chabot's village, in spite of its almost total dependence on irrigated rice, nearly 20 per cent of the population changed residence during the course of a single year, many of them moving to or from quite distant villages. In addition, the village included a sizable colony of Buginese settlers, who had been attracted by available land. Such shifting about appears to be characteristic of both Buginese and Makassarese; and usually it is an entire kingroup, or a cluster of kingroups headed by a gentry one, which moves as a body to the new place.

The kingroup forms the nucleus for a localized community of worship. The spiritual entities worshiped are ancestors, but their material representatives are objects such as large stones or ancient pieces of regalia (flags, swords, umbrellas, plows, etc.). The sacred objects, called "ornaments" or "fetishes" in the Dutch literature, possess a powerful magical force which they confer on their owners. The more powerful and high-status a kingroup is, the more powerful its sacred ornaments are, in consequence, thought to be. Regular offerings of food and betel nut are made to them, while on important occasions animals may be sacrificed. Unattached families that live in the same settlement may participate in the rituals; the stronger the kingroup is, the more nonkinsmen it has as affiliated members.

The local king or prince was the head of such a kingroup—an especially high and powerful one—and the sacred ornaments of his kingroup were revered by the people of the entire region, rather than merely by the immediate locality, as is the case for ornaments of the present-day commoner groups. The same relationship held between the royal family and their subjects as does today between a leading family in a village and the rest of the community. When a king lost ground politically, the power of his ornaments was thought to wane, too; his kinsmen and followers diminished in numbers, and commoner villages could transfer their allegiance elsewhere. Similarly, when a king gained great power any other kingroups of which he was a member (for instance through his mother) could as a unit coalesce with his, and individual persons could affiliate with him either by marriage or as personal followers. In the opposite process, two brothers could set up rival kingdoms, each taking a segment of their kinsmen and followers with him.

Even the literature of the Makassarese seems to center on this tense complex of prestige and marriage. There are three main types of poetic works: first, a form of poem which is sung antiphonally between men and women and is employed in preliminary courting; in it all meanings are hidden under symbolic allusions, the "code" being so obscure that no one's feelings can be hurt by rejection of an offer. A second poetic form is the historical epic, reporting the battles and descent lines of the royal houses. The third is a mythic form, of which there are hundreds of examples, each of which gives the story of the origin of a sacred ornament and hence of its kingroup, and explains symbolically the status of the group relative to others. These myths appear to change over time in accordance with the changing rank order of the groups.

The bilateral and optional basis of the kingroup formation, the peculiar tie between kinship and status mobility, and the personalistic attachment of followers to leaders, explain in great part the high tendency to fractionating and lability of the traditional political structure in South Celebes. Some of these forces are still operating today, but in the absence of specific information it is difficult to evaluate their potency. In the Dutch reorganization of the government in 1905, distinct borders were drawn around villages and realms, whereas formerly such political domains had been defined by personal loyalties rather than territorial residence. At the same time, a new fixed hierarchical relationship between territorial units was set up, so that, for instance, small independent kingdoms were placed as "subdistricts" underneath larger regional districts headed by more powerful princes. However, political processes at the local level of village and subdistrict probably still follow the old patterns of competitive struggle between rival kinship groups, each one striving to bring about advantageous marriages, redress social slights, and gain general acceptance of the potency of their own sacred ornament and of their own male members.

Formerly, and to a large extent today, the corporate kingroup, focused on a sacred ornament, was the basic social unit of Makassarese-Buginese society. The village studied by Chabot had two such groups in it, plus a minority of unaffiliated families, and he suggests that in the not-too-distant past the village and the ornament worshiping kingroup were virtually identical. A Buginese mountain community, Ponre, studied by Friedericy around 1930 appears to bear out this theory. Here the ornament worshiping group and the village were the same; the head of the kingroup was the village head, and he had full authority over distribution of land and the timing of its cultivation. The village owned seven large plots of swidden land in the surrounding forest, each of which was farmed for two successive years, then left fallow for twelve. The entire community cleared the new field; rituals involving the sacred ornaments were performed, and then the village head distributed portions of the plot to individual households, who did the remainder of the work alone. A plot of this land was farmed by the entire village for the household of the headman, who did no agricultural work. He in turn paid tribute in the form of produce to higher gentry in the lowlands, but remained sovereign in his own group. Any political units larger than the village community had the form of temporary federations; this was the case even for the great kingdoms of Goa and Bone.

It is a common commitment to Islam that gives the Pasisir culture its main identity from region to region in Indonesia. Nowhere, however, does this commitment completely supplant the indigenous religion, and in each locality there is an interesting and usually complementary relationship between the two forms of worship, which are, in fact, not generally felt by the people to be separate traditions at all. Information on religious patterns in South Celebes is rather slight; but nevertheless some impressions emerge from Friedericy's description of the ritual specialists and their functions.

A considerable amount of "animistic" ritual is required for the sacred ornaments, and these ceremonies are carried out by non-Islamic priests, called *bissu* or *pinati*. The bissu are (or were) in charge of the highest, most powerful sacred ornaments—those of the great kingdoms of Goa and Bone—while the pinati perform ceremonies for sacred ornaments of lesser status, as well as agricultural, circumcision, funeral, and courting rites. Both the bissu and the pinati are generally from the commoner group. Village mosque and prayer house officials are commoners, but the imangs of mosques attached to the smaller kingdoms (the present-day districts) are apparently usually from aristocratic or very high commoner families. Before the advent of the Dutch, the highest princes of Goa and Bone, for instance, had a special royal Moslem official called a *kali*, who stood next to the king himself in rank—and probably wealth and power—and who came from a close branch of the royal family. Today this association between high status and Islam may be blurred. Also, the animistic side of Makassarese religion may be weakening, as it apparently has long ago for the Buginese, who have reportedly become stricter Moslems and done away with many of their indigenous practices. Throughout the area there are active chapters of Muhammadijah, a modernist Islamic social service and educational society which is dedicated to, among other things, the purification of Indonesian Islam and the elimination of animistic elements.

For a more circumstantial picture of the role of Islam in the local community we must turn to another Pasisir people, the western Sumbawans.[38] For most of the past four hundred years the cluster of little kingdoms lining the northern coast of the island of Sumbawa has been dominated one way or another by Makassar. At times the area was directly governed, at times merely exploited by piratic raiding, and even once, after a volcano nearly wiped out the entire population, it was resettled and redeveloped by Makassarese; so that over the years the influence from Celebes has been considerable. The political system, especially in its upper levels, is almost entirely adopted from Celebes; the royal family claims direct descent from the kings of Goa, and it was the Makassarese who brought Islam to Sumbawa. As in Celebes the densest portion of the population is in the wet-rice growing river valleys, where the court was also located, but a sizable number of people live in the surrounding foothill region and practice dry, shifting agriculture. It is one of these villages in the highlands of western Sumbawa which was studied by Goethals in 1954-56.

In the village of Rarak the mosque is the social center; its staff, headed by the *lebé,* includes most of the influential men of the village. The functions of the lebé extend considerably beyond his formal duties of conducting the Friday services and related religious activities. He organizes any community-wide religious rituals, advises in personal ceremonies such as those at birth and death, and is often also a shaman and practitioner of non-Islamic magical lore. It is he who announces when the seasonal agricultural round will begin and leads Moslem prayers over the newly opened swiddens. While land tenure and agricultural work are entirely individualistic, unlike the system reported for the mountain community of southern Celebes, a field owned by the lebé himself is usually the first one planted. Almost everyone in the community joins in working on it the first day, in return for which the lebé provides a festive dinner. In addition, the lebé, with the consultation of respected older men, settles most domestic legal disputes such as those connected with marriage, divorce, inheritance, adultery, and illegitimacy. The annual religious tithes required by Moslem law are of much more than incidental, personal significance, for their collection and redistribution serve to define the social structure of the village. Citizenship in the community requires contribution of the tithe, and the greater part of the fund goes to the support not only of the mosque personnel but also of the secular village government. Finally, Islamic schooling (learning to read Arabic script and to recite by rote portions of the Koran) is highly esteemed; most small boys are taught by one of the local mosque officials, while the more energetic and brighter adolescents travel some distance to board at a school for religious instruction. A man who has made the pilgrimage to Mecca, a hadji, has very high prestige in Rarak.

The village mosque personnel form one pyramid of leadership within the community; a second pyramid, which is locally almost as influential, is that of the secular village authority, consisting of the headman and his assistants. They are the lowest representatives of the civil government in Indonesia prior to 1908 they were the link between the village and the sultan of Sumbawa, serving simultaneously to protect the peasants from oppression by the court and to organize the periodic labor parties for work on the sultan's lands.

The headman serves also as arbitrator in local civil disputes, such as theft of livestock and land-claim quarrels. The forest land around the village may be used only by the members of the village itself; persons from the neighboring villages must ask permission to use a plot and then may farm it only temporarily. In Rarak, the act of clearing the land creates a permanent personal right to its use, a right which can be inherited; while in neighboring villages, use rights lapse each time the plot land is left fallow. Boundaries between plots of land and between village tracts are recorded only in the memories of the older, more experienced men of the village; it is these men together with the headman who adjudicate any cases of land disputes. In this area, the current population explosion is creating a considerable land shortage, even in the mountain districts, and such disputes are increasingly frequent.

Unlike the Makassarese, the western Sumbawans have no corporate kinship groups of any kind. The kinship system is bilateral, and the nuclear family is the main unit. The pattern of sacred ornament worship is present in Sumbawa only in aristocratic circles and is entirely territorial in reference. However, even in the very poor mountain village studied by Goethals, there were slight economic inequalities between families because of differences in soil fertility of the inherited plots of swidden land and individual variation in industriousness and farming skills. Marriage arrangements, as in Makassar but for different structural reasons, are closely associated with prestige, and negotiations can be long and tense. There is no bride price, but the cost of the wedding festival serves much the same function. The families of the bride and groom must each contribute an equal share in the cost, and each side tries covertly to force up the total expense of the feast in order to discredit the other's ability to pay. One result of this, as in Makassar, is a fairly high frequency of elopements.

This mountain community in western Sumbawa represents one extreme pole of the Pasisir culture, the other pole of which is perhaps to be found among certain Islamic sections of the modern business elite in Djakarta. Sharply limited by the marginal character of its land, Rarak is entirely agricultural and exclusively subsistence-oriented; none of its members are merchants, and there is little or no commercial activity. Yet it is not entirely turned in on itself; it is not self-sufficient culturally, but faces outward toward what it considers the civilized world—the Islamic world, represented politically in the past by the Sumbawan sultanate, in the present by Djakarta, and religiously by Mecca. Those few Rarak men who travel away from the mountains are the ones who go to religious schools in the lowlands, or, in a few highly influential cases, make the pilgrimage to Mecca. These trips to the outside world are a major prerequisite to prestige in the village.

In a muted, impoverished way, Rarak repeats the pattern of the other Pasisir peoples, a "centrifugal" motion which spins off its members away from their own valleys and islands, temporarily or permanently, into the outer world, where they restlessly strive after new wisdom or wealth. In this respect the Pasisir peoples contrast sharply with many other Indonesians, for instance the Balinese, or the Toradja discussed below, whose social structures could be termed "centripetal," for they hold their members tightly to them. The Balinese, in particular, are for all their sophistication and large numbers rarely found outside their own island, for the duties and satisfactions of their temples and villages constantly draw them back again. It may be Islam itself (and its catalytic impact on indigenous social structures) which is largely responsible for the centrifugal quality of the Pasisir societies; for Islam is tied to no locality, and asserts that any man may worship Allah in any mosque or prayer house. It is radically egalitarian and individualistic, upholding the value of personal effort toward salvation rather than communal responsibility. The Moslem stress on the study of religious law and learning, and on the holy pilgrimage to Mecca, further serve to persuade young men to look outside their local comunities to improve their status. It is unnecessary (and precarious) here to ascribe causal force to Islam; it is sufficient to suggest that Islam is eminently "suitable" to a trading economy, to a social situation which demands high individual initiative and the freedom of movement necessary to seize trade opportunities wherever they arise, both of which were characteristic of the Pasisir peoples at least during their great period before the present century.

Swidden Farmers of the Interior: The Eastern Toradja

To select one group as an example of the tribally organized shifting cultivators of the interior areas of Indonesia does much more violence to the actual complex situation than is the case for the previously discussed sociocultural types. A more refined typology is clearly necessary but is impossible without further field research. However, some of the dimensions of variation that may prove significant can be tentatively proposed.

The first of these is the permanency of settlement. In some areas there is only a limited supply of land in relation to the population, and each group stays within a specified locality, farming a fixed set of fields but allowing a fallow period of seven to twelve years for each plot. This was the case for the highland Buginese and the Sumbawan groups already discussed. Other parts of Indonesia have an ample supply of virgin forest, and the villages are considerably more mobile; this is especially true for interior Borneo. Most swidden groups combine permanent gardening with shifting cultivation in various proportions. In the permanent gardens they raise long-term tree crops such as sago, rubber, or coconuts, or short-term vegetables or spices. And, to varying degrees according to their location and the current state of the external market, many swidden peoples are today involved in cash-crop production. These factors of land supply and proximity to export outlets have had repercussions on the organization of the community—most directly on land tenure patterns, and indirectly on kinship organization, class differentiation, and political structure, all of which appear to be more highly developed in regions where land is in relatively short supply.[39]

A second dimension might be the presence or absence of the water buffalo as a traditional pivotal element in religious ceremonies and feasts. Not only does the presence of such cattle carry with it a cluster of related cultural and social traits, which cannot yet be adequately specified, but there are significant ecological ramifications as well. The grazing of the cattle on swidden land which should be permitted to lie fallow prevents full replacement of the tree cover and promotes the development of uncultivable grassy prairies, thus cutting down on the land supply. This appears to be especially the case in the drier portions of Indonesia, such as the eastern Lesser Sunda Islands and northern Sumatra.[40]

Two other possible dimensions which appear to be somewhat related are the type of kinship system (i.e. whether or not the community is segmented into exogamous unilineal groupings) and the degree to which Melanesian cultural patterns are present. Both conditions—unilineality and Melanesian influence—come together in the western Lesser Sunda Islands, the southern Moluccas, and the islands near New Guinea. A good example is the interior Alorese, whose social structure and ethos are more akin to the New Guinea coastal peoples than to the majority peoples of Indonesia.[41]

The Eastern, or Bare'e-speaking, Toradja represent only one possible combination of these variables.[42] Their region in the mountains of central Celebes is one of high rainfall, almost no dry season, and a very rugged terrain. Prior to their first extensive contacts with the West in 1892, they consisted of a very sparse population, spread thinly over a wide territory. The villages were very small, ranging from 40 to 200 inhabitants, and most were economically, religiously, and politically self-sufficient. Their villages were actually walled fortresses perched atop small hills, with water source, temple, and smithy below them and their fields generally within walking distance in the nearby valleys. Warfare— apparently mainly for heads, slaves, and revenge—was the normal social condition, and there was no political superstructure over the village.

Land tenure was not a problem; each village had sovereignty over the swidden fields around it where primary forest no longer grew, on the basis that village ancestors had been the first to clear them. Members of the other villages had to ask permission to use any of these fields—a request which rarely occurred, for there was more than enough land. Each year a new section of the secondary growth was cleared again, and each villager received as large a portion as he and his family could farm. Primary forest was free

71

to anyone willing to put in the labor of felling the trees and dense undergrowth. If a village grew too large for its territory, some of its members would leave and establish a new one in another region. Most marriages were endogamous to the village; if one was not, the couple could settle in either that of the husband or of the wife, depending on personal preference, local labor shortage, or housing. The spouse who left his natal community relinquished all rights in village land and in his family property; but his children could, if they chose, return to their parent's village at any time.

At the period of the Dutch take-over, each village was a localized corporate kinship group, containing no members who were not related to the others by blood or marriage. The village temple was dedicated to the actual ancestors of the group, forebears who would not be interested in protecting outsiders. The kinship system was cognatic and membership in a village was utrolateral, i.e. each person could choose to join either his father's, his mother's, or his spouse's village group. The same membership principle applied to what were apparently extended families, which owned as groups such property as sago or bamboo trees, water buffalo herds, and, probably, slaves where slaveholding existed. Each nuclear family household had its own rice storage barn, its own cooking hearth, and it could possess buffaloes or trees of its own. The property of the extended family was apparently used mainly for ceremonial feasts and bride prices.

The structural importance of the extended family is unclear, but the existence and size of the bride price suggests that it was a significant social unit. There was also a nonlocalized personal kindred which played a large part in these marriage payments. The bride price was paid by the father of the groom to the father of the bride, and until this had been paid no marriage was legitimate. It varied in size, sometimes including as much as three buffaloes, numerous sago trees, and many pieces of clothing. The members of the groom's family all contributed to the bride price, and he traditionally took a long journey to all the villages where he had kinsmen, asking for their shares. When his sister or daughter married in turn, these debts, apparently, were repaid. The amount of the bride price and the size of the wedding festivities could be neither more nor less than that of the bride's mother. While people were proud to pay and receive large bride prices, they apparently kept to this rule; and it thus was impossible to use them, as the Makassarese did, for social mobility, nor did the differences indicate important status distinctions.[43] The association of the bride prices of the mother and the daughter is interpreted by Kruyt as indicating that the bride price functions primarily to promote fertility, and he supports this further by citing the custom of paying the entire price a second time in cases of sterile unions.

It seems that the localized extended family and the nonlocalized personal kindred both took part in feuds and the paying of wergild, but this aspect is exceedingly unclear. Each localized extended family had a headman, who took care of the family property, and who, together with other family heads, governed the village. One among them was, by tacit agreement, the headman of the entire village. He had no power to make decisions on his own, but he could have great influence. It was he who represented the village to the outside, who served as host to travelers, and who probably did most of the village trading. The matters about which this group of family heads made decisions included the annual distribution of swidden land, the giving and attending of feasts and funerals, the building and repairing of the village temple, the witnessing of marriage contracts, and the sentencing of witches to death.

The Eastern Toradja were thus not a nation, nor a tribe, but merely a number of villages (with a total population of about 31,000 in 1930) with much the same culture and language. Kruyt's term for them, the "Bare'e-speaking Toradja," classified them together according to linguistic similarities. There was, however, considerable minor cultural variation among them, and certain important differences in social structure. Several sets of villages had long been in much closer contact with coastal peoples of Pasisir culture, notably the Buginese sultanates of Luwu and Mori. In these villages, but not in the others, there existed a hereditary slave class and also the rudiments of a supravillage chieftanship. The latter came into being through direct introduction by the coastal sultan who appointed certain village heads as his representatives to collect and deliver tribute. In these areas, the village headmen were more powerful and wealthier than their counterparts in the more remote regions. In addition to delivering tribute to the sultan, they apparently engaged in trade on their own, using their slaves to gather forest products such as rotan and rosin for sale in the market at the coast. Even in the 1890s economic differences were visible between the slaveholding groups and the non-slaveholding ones; the latter did their own farming and got a better yield from their land because they did more careful work; consequently, they enjoyed a better diet. The slaveholding villages used slave labor for much of the farming, which was much less efficient; the whole population of these villages had a poorer diet. On the other hand, because of their participation in trade, the slaveholding villages possessed a considerably larger amount of imported goods such as dishes, cloth, lamps, and even sewing machines.[44]

Slavery was an important institution in the localities where it existed, and in some villages at least half the population was slave. In the regions where there was no hereditary slave class, slaves were still found but in much smaller numbers. These were either captives in war or debt slaves who were permitted to buy back their freedom if able. The slaves were treated fairly well and allowed to set up households of their own; their bride price was paid for them, but their children remained the property of their master. Marriage between a slave man a free woman was punished by death, while that between a slave woman and a free man was strongly disapproved. War captives and debt slaves could be used as sacrifices, either within the village of their owner, or in an enemy village to which they had been delivered as compensation for a murder to end a blood feud, or in a village to which they had been sold. Some slaves were highly respected and even served as leaders in head-hunting expeditions. After Dutch administration was established, slavery was abolished; but the ex-slaves remained poor and disdained. They were considered by the free men as stupid, uncivilized, and lazy; and, as of 1932, none had ever been appointed village chief, nor had any entered the mission schools.

Aside from the distinction between slave and free, there was no class stratification. Chieftainship was not hereditary but based on personal characteristics. Individuals were respected for their courage in war, their leadership abilities, their ritual knowledge, or their possession of large numbers of water buffaloes. The buffaloes had little economic value; they did no farm labor nor load carrying, but served primarily as ritual sacrifices and food for feasts. Nevertheless they were highly valued, and each man attempted to build up a herd through bride price payments, trade, or the taming of wild ones. Children were often given a buffalo of their own, as a start for their own herd, and the small boys of the village were in charge of the buffaloes and took them daily to pasture. There was apparently no problem of overgrazing and erosion in this wet climate. A man with a large number of buffaloes had power and influence over others in his family, for he could lend the animals or give them away for ceremonial feasts, thus placing their recipients in his debt. Such differences in personal prestige and power were, however, comparatively negligible.

There were never any strong ties between villages, even in those regions where there were nominal supravillage chiefs. The fragile lines of the few intervillage marriages, and, occasionally, a tenuous tradition of an ancient common ancestor among a group of adjacent villages sometimes served to inhibit but not entirely eliminate bloodshed between them. A complex system of fines for insult or criminal offense was frequently substituted for warfare among very near villages, and where such friendly relationships obtained the members would attend each other's death feasts and occasionally serve as allies in war against a common enemy. With those exceptions, every village was perpetually hostile to all others.

Head-hunting was not the sole cause of warfare, but it was a significant aspect of it and a key element in the Toradja religion. The head of a dead man was considered to be a rich source of supernatural power; it represented not only an equivalent spiritual loss to the enemy, and a lure to bring about further enemy losses, but—much more importantly—it could be a highly potent offering to the ancestral spirits. No influential man could be buried, nor could a new temple be consecrated, without the offering of a human head. Regular head taking was necessary for the continued general well-being and fertility of both villagers and their crops. Every village had a temple, a wooden gabled building large enough to hold several hundred people, which was intricately carved with symbolic representations of water buffaloes, crocodiles and other reptiles, and human genitals. It was in this temple that the scalps were hung, while fragments of the skull were used as personal amulets or buried in the rice fields. The temple was primarily for the worship of village ancestors—those, that is, who had been given the proper second death ceremony.

The Toradja had two funerals, the first at death, the second some years later. Before the second funeral the ghost of the deceased was thought to be dangerous and capricious, and was kept through magical means as far away from the living as possible. The second ceremony, the death feast, transformed the spirit from an evil ghost into a guardian angel, who could then be worshiped and supplicated for aid and blessings. The death feast required the offering of a newly cut head, the sacrifice of water buffaloes and pigs, and the final cleansing of the putrescent bones of all the remains of mortal flesh. The central position of the death feast in Toradja religion became evident when the Dutch administration prohibited both head-hunting and the ceremony of cleansing of the bones, the first for the purpose of pacification, the second as a sanitary measure. With these two ritual supports gone, the entire religion was shaken; and while up to that time missionizing had been notably ineffective, the Toradja thereafter turned readily to Christianity.

It was not required that the head be one of an enemy slain in war, and a second equally acceptable source was purchase of a live human being from neighboring villages. Persons who were suspected of witchcraft or sorcery were tried by a magical ordeal, in which they dipped their finger in burning pitch; if the hand was not burnt they were innocent, but if, as in most cases, they were proved guilty, they were sentenced to death and sold to another village for execution. It appears that more people were killed in this fashion than in head-hunting raids, a fact which would indicate considerable internal conflict and suspiciousness within each small Toradja village.

Head-hunting itself was a very fearful undertaking, and it was preceded and accompanied by manifold ritual precautions. It was a test of manly courage, and to a large degree actually a religious act. Heads were generally taken only from enemies with whom one had a justifiable grievance. The success of a head-hunting expedition was proof of the moral righteousness of the victors; the corpse of a fellow villager whose head had been taken was not given a proper funeral, for he must have deserved his fate. The return from a fruitful raid was followed by several exciting days of ritual, feasting, singing, and dancing.

Sickness was thought to be caused by witchcraft or sorcery, or by the anger of the ancestral spirits or any of a myriad of other spirits, ghosts, and deities, who could entice one's life force or "soul" away from the body. Most treatment involved the services of a shaman—a woman who, with special training and daily observance of food taboos, had the power to call on her guardian spirit to travel with her to the underworld and retrieve the wandering soul of the patient. The main element in the curing ritual was the recitation by the shaman of a long litany in which the spirits were propitiated, and which described the trip of the shaman to the other world. The recitation took place inside a small, specially made, tentlike enclosure, and lasted an entire night. Men could not become shamans unless they were transvestites, but there were a number of male religious roles, notably those of agricultural ritual specialists, head-hunting leaders, bone handlers for death feasts, rain makers, and rain preventers.

Two main factors underlie the kind of social structure that was found among the eastern Toradja at the turn of the century. First, the form of religio-political system in which head-hunting and chronic but primitive warfare kept groups small and mutually aloof. Second, the system of shifting agriculture, which supports only a small, scattered population, and the need for some labor sharing, especially during the clearing of the land, required a community larger than the nuclear family, but the limits on land supply prevented very large groups from forming. Both of these factors have, to some extent, been altered since the coming of the Dutch. There has been nothing published on the social situation since the Indonesian revolution, but it can be assumed that the changes initiated by the Dutch have not been reversed.

Protestant missionaries arrived in 1892, but made no headway either in conversion or in attracting students to their schools until after 1905, when the foundations of Toradja belief were shaken by the above-described restrictions on religious practices: the prohibition of head-hunting and of ritual exhumation and cleansing of the bones of the dead. With several military expeditions, the Dutch put down all armed opposition and installed their own government. Most of the new laws operated to undermine the tightly integrated villages, replacing them with less strongly structured regional communities and a growing trend toward individualism. Warfare and head-hunting were abolished, and villages were forced to move from their hilltop fortresses down into the valleys, where roads were built connecting them. The purpose of relocation was to make a regional administration easier; and subsequently districts and subdistricts were created, with some village headmen promoted to lead them.

Wet-rice cultivation was introduced to promote more permanent settlements and provide a stronger subsistence base for the new, more densely settled communities. It failed in the first few years, ostensibly because of its unfamiliarity, possibly also because of its unsuitability to the land and climate; it is unclear from present

77

information what proportion of the farming is irrigated today. Coconut-tree cultivation for the production of copra was introduced in the coastal districts, coffee in the interior; the former is probably flourishing today, the latter because of changes in the world market probably not. The administration introduced monetary taxes, which had two consequences. First, it brought increased activity in the gathering of forest products such as rotan, copal, and ebony, which were traded to coastal foreigners (Buginese, Gorontolese, Minahassans, and, later, Chinese) for the needed cash. Second, a new responsibility was placed on individual initiative, for the taxes were not permitted to be paid by village chiefs in the name of all their dependents, but had to be provided by each man. A similar individualizing force was exerted by the considerable labor draft that the Dutch imposed in order to build roads and bridges over the whole territory. This demand, too, was placed on individuals; and although many villages attempted merely to send representatives, the Dutch insisted that every able-bodied man take part.

The common result of all these changes was the enervation of the kin-based village. Attacked on three sides—physically with the enforced resettlement into larger communities, politically with introduction of a superior authority and the promotion of individual responsibility, and religiously with the abolition of head-hunting, the bone cleansing ritual, and the execution of suspected witches—the old regime must have been completely undermined. Kruyt states that, with the exception of certain groups who became Islamic, the majority of the Eastern Toradja were converted to Christianity. In these new communities the church and the school must have become the new integrating centers for widespread areas, and kinship may have proportionately declined in importance as a structural feature.

Changing Highland Peasants: Minangkabau and Toba-Batak

Of the major Indonesian peoples who cannot be fitted into a primitive threefold typology of wet-rice, swidden, and Pasisir peoples, two are especially interesting and important. Both of them straddle several categories, and despite their rather striking contrasts to one another are fundamentally very similar in social structure and ecological adaptation. The Minangkabau and Toba-Batak are located in the high valleys of interior Sumatra; but both are highly centrifugal societies, with energetic representatives scattered over all the islands of the archipelago. They are both basically wet-rice cultivators, but they differ from the peoples of Bali and Java in that they are not exclusively committted to wet rice but employ swidden cultivation extensively on the encircling mountain slopes and swamplands, and in that they share very little of the Hinduized high culture of classical Java. They are, in fact, very like most of the swidden peoples in that their communities are internally segmented into corporate kingroups, which until very recently owned and controlled most of the agricultural land and composed the village political structure. From an historical viewpoint, the Minangkabau could also easily be treated as aberrant members of the Pasisir culture, for they have been Moslems for at least three centuries and played a significant role in the great pepper trade; however, they are an interior and not a coastal people, and their role in the pepper trade was primarily that of producers rather than merchants. Historically the Toba-Batak differ sharply from the Minangkabau, for they were virtually isolated from the world until the last century and have since become Christians.

Both societies are still largely traditional in structure, for at least until this century there were very few different social roles, and most of these were defined by narrowly ascriptive factors such as descent, age, and sex. Their villages were small, independent, self-sufficient, and tightly knit communities, within which the total life of their members was confined; there was little or no superordinant political authority as there was in Java, Bali, and the Pasisir kingdoms. The Toba-Batak and Minangkabau are further alike in that both have experienced extremely rapid social change in this century. With the advent of commercial agriculture and Western schools, their members suddenly confronted many different kinds of occupational opportunities and new paths to social prestige; and both societies have consequently experienced a thoroughgoing transformation which is by no means complete. The first stage of this change, for both Minangkabau and Toba-Batak, has been the sending out of large numbers of migrants—temporary and permanent, agricultural and urban; of these, the urban group swiftly came to form an outstanding and dynamic element in the national elite.

One of the features of Minangkabau society which has generated a good deal of interest is that its kinship system is matrilineal—that is, descent and inheritance are reckoned through the mother rather than the father, and it is a woman's brother rather than her husband who has authority over the family group. How such a system could work in conjunction with the patrilineal Islamic legal framework has excited a good deal of speculation; but no detailed village study has ever been made, and there is very little published material on postwar conditions.[45] It is difficult from the sources presently available to determine even the ideal structure of Minangkabau society, much less the actual present-day situation, in part because there is considerable variation from village to village in specific customs (for instance, in some communities the rule for succession to a titled status position is by primogeniture, in others it is rotation among the eligible sons or cousins, and in still others it is by selection of the most fit), and in part because there is considerable variation in village size and composition; and apparently a good many *ad hoc* social arrangements were and are permissible.

There were about five million persons of Minangkabau culture in 1961 (a reckoning which includes as Minangkabau all the inhabitants of the province of West Sumatra but excludes those Minangkabau residing elsewhere). Their language is closely related to Malay, being nearly comprehensible to Malay speakers, and on the eastern and southern borders of the area—in Siak and Djambi—Minangkabaus blend culturally and linguistically with Malays. The central area of Minangkabau culture is the group of valleys surrounding Mount Merapi, near the town of Bukit Tinggi. This is mainly wet-rice country, and population densities are high, averaging 117 per square kilometer in 1930.[46] It is also the area where traditional customs are held to most tenaciously. In a wide band around this core area is a less thickly populated region, also Minangkabau in culture, which includes the belt along the west coast near Padang and much of the vast swampy lowlands going down toward the east coast. These are the areas the Minangkabau call the *rantau,* a word originally meaning the lower reaches and bay of a river, but now connoting any area where one goes to seek his fortune. To *merantau* (literally "to go to the rantau") in Minangkabau means "to go abroad," an activity which, as will be seen, is highly characteristic of Minangkabau men but which must be understood against the background of the traditional village social structure.

Until this century at least, the Minangkabau village was essentially a federation of localized corporate kinship groups or lineages, each of which owned a section of the cultivable land near the village and had its own headman (usually called *pangulu*), who had authority over its land and over the actions of his kin. The village was governed by these lineage headmen as a group, sometimes with one among them acting as chief. Lineages varied in size, in generation depth, and in degree of internal segmentation; a prosperous and cohesive one might have had as many as 200 to 300 members. Individual newcomers to a village had to affiliate themselves with one of the existing lineages, and gradually, by various legal arrangements, to become full-fledged lineage members with full land rights. The lineages were sharply localized, that is, their membership did not extend beyond the borders of the village; for although each lineage had a proper name, and the same names were found in different villages, there was generally no functional connection between lineages with the same name in different communities, nor was it strongly forbidden to marry between them.

Landholding was the crucial function of the lineage; there was very little individually owned property, and each lineage distributed parcels of its land to its component families for their more or less permanent use. The offspring of each family had first rights to the land their parents had used, but should there be no offspring the land would revert to the lineage as a whole for redistribution. It could never be sold to someone outside the village, and even an intravillage sale was always revocable if the original lineage desired to buy it back. If a man through his own work acquired some property—for instance if he cleared a portion of the primeval jungle himself and converted it to farm land—he personally had authority over that piece of land and its produce, but at his death it became the property of his lineage unless he had already legally given it away to members of another lineage. In the latter case the recipient of the gift of land was not an individual but a lineage group. Thus there were two types of property: *harto pusako,* that owned by the lineage as a whole, and *harto pentjarian,* that which was owned by the individual who had obtained it himself—which could only be "private property" until its owner's death. There was a third form of property, called *harto ulajat,* which was under the authority of the village, the *nagari,* as a whole. This consisted mainly of forest tracts surrounding the village which had never been cultivated; and permission for their utilization had to be obtained from the village as a whole, with a tax being paid to the community on the harvest as well as on any other products of the forest. While the use of such terms varied considerably, the landholding lineage group was generally called the *parui'*, and its head the *mama'*. If there were several parui' within the village which considered themselves related, they were usually called a *kampueng*, and the head of the kampueng was termed the pangulu. The kampueng had residual rights to the land held by the parui'—the right, should one parui' die out, to redistribute its land among the surviving ones, and the right to be consulted on any pawning of the land. The kampueng lineage group was usually though not necessarily exogamous, but the parui' always was.

The village was governed in one of two ways, the so-called "democratic" or the "autocratic." In communities of the first type, village-wide decisions were made by a council of heads (pangulu) of all the established lineages; in the second the lineages were variously affiliated with one another so that there were four main sets (*suku*), each with a head (sometimes called *pangulu andiko*—"head pangulu"—or *pangulu kaempe' suku*—"pangulu of the four suku"); and among these four, one (the *pangulu putjak*, or "top pangulu") was the leader of the entire village. The terms "democratic" and "autocratic" are misleading; in both cases decisions in village affairs were arrived at through open discussion among the pangulu. "Democratic" villages are interspersed with "autocratic" ones over the entire Minangkabau territory; it is difficult to determine what economic or historical differences there were between the two types which might explain them. To be pangulu of a lineage was to hold a highly respected position; in most cases the incumbent was chosen from among a group of eligible men as the one most capable of leadership by ability, wealth, and moral stature. The position carried a title with it (e.g. Datuk, Radja, etc.), and an ambitious man strove to be chosen pangulu and to be given his lineage's title. The ambition of the lineage as a whole was to build up its prestige within the village as symbolized by its pangulu and to arrange marriages with equally respected lineages.

Settlements, of course, varied in size; only a large and long-established community would have a full complement of lineages, lineage sets, and their officials. Such a large village—a true nagari—usually also had a mosque, built and maintained by the village as a whole. Smaller settlements had prayer houses, where the men could gather for their regular prayers and for Koran reading but where no Friday services could be held. Very small, new hamlets often consisted only of a branch of one lineage which had moved out of an overcrowded village. In places at the confluence of transport routes there were, probably from very early times, busy market places where foodstuffs and textiles were bought and sold. The use of money, however, did not gain real headway until the twentieth century.

The degree to which there were class differences in traditional Minangkabau society, and how they have developed in postwar years, is unclear from the sources published thus far. Whether, for instance, sharp distinctions are emerging between wealthy commercial farmers and poor subsistence ones or between village and city people, or whether there was a very extensive noble class in the past which today is continuing to claim prestige, are all still unanswered questions. However, it seems clear that the Minangkabau never developed the finely graduated systems of rank nor the acute sensitivity to social distinctions that are found in Java and Bali. There had been, until the beginning of the nineteenth century, a "king" of all Minangkabau, *Jangdipatuan Basa* (literally, "he-who-is-named-ruler"); this line died out in 1844, seven years after the introduction of direct Dutch rule. There remained a small royal family and associated noble class, which had always formed a sharply isolated caste adhering to endogamous marriage and the custom of patrilineal descent. There has been considerable debate as to whether the ruler had much wealth or power, and there is good reason to suspect that he never had much authority over the people of Minangkabau. The royal family has little significance today. A group of considerably greater importance appears to be that of the pangulu and their immediate families—persons with authority over lineages or over villages, who were in a position to acquire property and, in the present period, to go into business and to educate their children.

It is at the domestic level that the fact of the matrilineal descent system has any real significance. Membership in a lineage, the right to use its land, and the right to be given the title held by the lineage are transmitted to a man from his mother's brother or his mother's mother's brother, not from his father or grandfather. It is his sisters and their children toward whom a man has the most responsibility and over whom he has the most authority. The stable domestic unit is the woman and her children, while the men shift around its periphery. In the old society each married woman had a room of her own in a long narrow lineage house, side by side with those of her sisters, her mother, and her mother's sisters. A man spent most of the daylight hours at his sisters' house, eating

83

there and working mainly on his sisters' land. He slept either in his wife's room or in the village prayer house, where all males above the age of seven could spend the night. The divorce rate was high, and men had little to do with their own children officially. The authority within the household was the *mama'*, who was not a husband but a brother of one of the older women. Women may have done much of the agricultural labor in nearby fields, leaving the men free to make long journeys to distant swiddens or for trade; during some seasons it is very likely that the villages were inhabited mainly by women, old men, and young children.

The Minangkabau are profoundly Islamic in religion, and some writers have assumed that Moslem doctrines, bound up as they have been with patrilineal Arabic civilization, were incompatible with matrilineal customs. Actually, there appears today to be little friction between the two points of view, although in the nineteenth century a long and disastrous civil war, the Padri War, was fought partially over religious issues. It seems rather that the Islamic institutions gave the traditional Minangkabau social structure a flexibility which it badly needed, especially at its weak point—the place of the young men in the society. For a young man in an old-style village is in a very uncomfortable position: he must wait passively to be asked in marriage by some girl's family, a bid which will come only after he has proved in some way his abilities and moral character; while at the same time in his own mother's group he has little status, for all the authority positions are taken up by older men. A chance to leave the village to go to an Islamic school and return a respected scholar, or to go abroad to earn money and return with splendid clothes and a worldly air, are both more exciting choices than merely to stay at home as an agricultural laborer more or less under the supervision of his mother and uncles. A man with property of his own, and the proved capacity to earn more, was more likely to be successful in customary ways, to make a better marriage, to maintain the esteem of his wife's family, and to gain the respect of his own lineage mates and ultimately the lineage's single honorific title. The trip abroad, merantau, became very nearly required for every young bachelor in traditional Minangkabau society.

There are strong indications that in the present century the lineage system is finally being undermined, as there have been radical changes in the agricultural base from a subsistence to a commercial orientation—changes which, supported by the ideas of individualism that are implicit both in Islamic theology and in modern secular thought, have been altering the system of group land tenure and thus attenuating the functions of the lineages. The distinction between harto pusako and harto pentjarian—lineage property and private property—has been further extended so as to permit private property to remain alienable even after its first owner's death. The size of lineage land itself is steadily diminishing, through the paring down of the branches of the lineage retaining authority over it, and through its outright sale. Schrieke, a sociologist who studied the problem in 1929, stressed the rapidity and astonishing extent to which commercial agriculture had been taken up by individual farmers, especially in the peripheral areas where wet rice was not feasible, and the concurrent extent to which land was leaving group control and becoming personal property. He stated that before 1910 Dutch colonial policy thoroughly inhibited any economic development in the Minangkabau region, for the government required the growing of coffee at fixed monopolistic prices, banned the export of rice, and blocked off trade routes to the eastern coast. With the removal of these barriers at the beginning of this century, there was an astonishing surge of individual cash-crop farming, transforming the economy within ten years into a fairly highly monetized one based on coffee, rubber, and coconut exports. The energy and shrewdness of the new Minangkabau businessmen, derived at least in part from their experience in traditional peddling trips abroad, has been demonstrated in their ability to exclude the Chinese merchants from the growing middleman trade in the Minangkabau towns, a feat that few other regions were able to accomplish. During the same period an educational revolution was underway, for the Dutch government introduced a number of elementary and secondary schools. By 1935, about five per cent of the total population was attending elementary schools, a low percentage by American standards but one equaled in Indonesia only in Minahassa, and in certain parts of Java.[47] A Minangkabau intellectual group grew up —novelists, poets, physicians, lawyers, political thinkers—most of whom, before the war at any rate, left their homeland for the greater opportunities of the cities.[48]

The Toba-Batak have been experiencing a similar social renascence, but not, apparently, at the expense of their traditional lineage structure.[49] As among the Minangkabau, the foundation of the Toba-Batak lineage's cohesion lies in its authority over cultivable land; but in the Toba-Batak region the modernization process has not yet apparently affected agricultural practices and land tenure. Rather than changing the modes of production themselves, the Toba-Batak response to contact with the modern world has been a flood of migration out from the heartland, leaving the traditional agricultural and land tenure forms basically unchanged. Where the Minangkabau have increasingly converted their shifting dry-rice fields, vegetable gardens, and even wet-rice lands to grow commercial crops such as coffee, rubber, and coconuts, the Toba-Batak are intensifying their wet-rice production, exporting rice to the growing market in East Sumatra, and abandoning their peripheral nonirrigable swiddens.[50]

There are nearly a million Toba-Batak[51] inhabiting the mountain valleys near Lake Toba and, increasingly, much of the lowland regions of eastern Sumatra. In the surrounding areas are a number of other Batak groups—the Karo, Pakpak, Simelungen, Angkola and Mandailing Batak—who speak various Batak dialects, some mutually unintelligible. These other groups have similar familial systems but differing ecological adaptations; of all of them, the Toba-Batak are the most heavily committed to wet rice. Some of the other Batak groups had broad territorial political organization and superordinant rajas in the past; but the Toba-Batak villages were always entirely independent of one another, and little more than a century ago they were engaged in constant warfare.

Toba-Batak settlements (*huta*) are very small clusters of houses standing like islands in the midst of rice fields. Formerly, the tiny huta was a complete village in itself; but today larger sets of scattered settlements, closely connected by kinship ties, form the basic community. In the village studied by Bruner near Balige, there were 38 huta, with an average of six households each. The members of this village belonged to a number of different but related patrilineal clans, which were in turn divided into a larger number of localized clan segments, which formed the corporate landholding lineages. Both the more inclusive clan, which is not necessarily confined to a single community, and the localized lineages are termed *marga*; but it is the smaller unit which is the significant Toba-Batak social group, for it alone is corporate and exogamous.

The traditional relationship between clan, lineage, and the organization of village and huta is understandable mainly under the conditions of an expanding population and an unlimited supply of new land, conditions which held until very recently. When an area became overpopulated, a group of relatives would move together to virgin territory, claim all the surrounding cultivable land for themselves and their descendants, clear some of it, and establish a new village. They usually kept the proper name of the lineage from which they stemmed, but lost their rights to the land they had left behind; and after several generations passed, they were often permitted to marry fellow clansmen of the former territory. The larger patrilineal group, the clan, which has branches in several villages, is of importance primarily at weddings and funerals, when as many as a thousand kinsmen including affinal relatives may gather.

As the new village prospered, other families from other clans would request or be invited to settle there, and would also open up land and found lineages. The patrilineal descendants of the pioneer lineage were termed the *marga radja,* the "ruling marga," for they were considered to have ultimate jurisdiction over all the village territory, and the headman or *radja* was traditionally chosen from among their ranks. If any member lineage were to die out, its land would revert to the marga radja, but otherwise it remained lineage property. Genealogical histories going back as far as twenty generations, and detailing the relationships between many scattered lineages and the lands associated with them, are kept carefully in unwritten form by men who specialize in such knowledge, and are recited especially at funerals.

For the Batak as for the Minangkabau, the affiliation between land and lineage is not that of ownership in the Western legal sense, but rather one of moral stewardship, what Van Vollenhoven called the "right of disposal." Individuals use particular plots as their own, and as long as they and their direct descendants continue to use the land they have full personal rights to it; but the lineage as a group maintains a residual authority over it and a responsibility to each individual in the group to see that he has some land to use. Among the Batak this is more than merely a legal arrangement: it is moral and ultimately religious, for the tie between the land and the lineage, as descendants of the original man who cut down the jungle, is sacred. It is for this reason that the lineage which first claimed all the land in a certain region for its own continues to receive the respect of the members of all groups arriving later, even though in actuality they have each cut out large tracts of the territory as their own lineage land.

87

Within a cluster of huta, then, there are usually a number of lineages, many of whom consider themselves patrilineally related at some distant generation. The male members of each lineage build houses next to one another, for residence at marriage is mainly patrilocal. Most of the marriages are within the community, and each marital tie links in very special ways all the members of both lineages, for the group which has received the wife into its membership is in a permanently subordinate position to those of her parental lineage, and is required constantly to demonstrate this inequality with services and ceremonies. It is only a relative condition of inequality, however; for every lineage has some to which it is superior and some to which it is inferior, and it is impossible for one to be superior or inferior to all others.

The whole complex of interpersonal relationships as defined by the kinship system—of solidarity among lineage mates, of subordinate service or superordinate authority statuses between affinal relatives, together with a rich assortment of ceremonies and feasts —is called by the Toba-Batak their *adat*. For them the adat is sacred; to forget or ignore its prescriptions is dangerous to both health and welfare, and to fulfill them is emotionally rewarding. Kinship is more than an economic relationship for the control of agricultural land; the fact that the term marga refers to the non-localized clan as well as the localized lineage indicates this. Ceremonies frequently bring together as many as a thousand people, all members of the clan immediately involved or related to it by blood or marriage. Weddings are especially large, for not only the lineages and clans of the bride and groom are concerned, but also all those to which they are related through the marriages of their lineage mates. One of the crucial ceremonies at a wedding is the distribution of specified parts of a sacrificed water buffalo or pig, each portion going to a lineage in special relation to the lineage of the bride or groom. This ceremonial recognition of wide-ranging links of blood and marriage reinforce the ties of everyday life. Mutual aid among kinsmen, even in the modern urban world of business and government offices, is exceedingly common among the Batak; and it is the tightness of the web of kinship surrounding them that gives the Batak people their outstanding resiliency in responding to twentieth-century challenges.

It was not until the middle of the nineteenth century that the isolation of the Toba-Batak villages was broken, with the almost simultaneous entry of three alien forces: Protestant missionaries, the Dutch government, and the plantations of the East Sumatran lowlands. The government brought local peace and limited opportunities for white-collar work; the missionaries brought schools and the skills necessary to hold salaried jobs; and the plantation economy introduced improved transportation facilities from the Toba-Batak highlands down to the coast, a market for surplus farm products, and, after 1950, large tracts of opened agricultural land into which Toba-Batak farmers, overflowing their small valleys, rapidly poured. Christianity has been adopted by about half of the Toba-Batak; a few have become Moslems, while the rest have remained what the Toba-Batak call *perbegu,* meaning "believers in spirits." The churches introduced a new regional form of social organization, gathering a number of nearby villages into one congregation and the children in a single church school. The consequence of this was that the small huta, once circumscribed worlds in themselves, have been supplanted by larger regional communities. This trend was reinforced by the Dutch introduction of government by larger territorial units, grouping huta and villages into administrative *"kampung"* and *"negeri,"* with elected headmen whose qualifications for office included sophistication in the ways of the outside world.

Thus, the traditional forms of political leadership have been giving way to new ones. Before 1940, the members of the marga radja, while by no means much more wealthy than commoners, occupied most positions of prestige. The children of these locally ruling lineages were given preference in the schools and in government positions, while most of the church elders and the first urban migrants entering the civil service and private business were from such groups. With the revolution in 1945-49, the Toba-Batak peasants repudiated to a large degree the legitimacy of such ascriptive social distinctions, and there was a general opening up of all avenues for upward mobility to everyone.

Aside from these changes in community structure, the most important recent social development has been the massive postwar migrations of Toba-Batak down from the highlands to become "squatter farmers," appropriating for their own use the land of the former tea, rubber, and tobacco plantations of East Sumatra. Agrarian migration is by no means new to the Toba-Batak; what has been new in the lowland movement is the inability of the pioneers to reproduce their former social system in the new location, as had been their former practice, and the substitution in the new settlements of a "posttraditional" form of community. The movements into the plantation areas have been voluntary and officially illegal; strictly prohibited before the war, the entry of individual farmers onto commercially planted ground was encouraged by the Japanese during the occupation in an effort to expand production of food crops. During the revolutionary period and the early years of the Republic, when Dutch colonial enterprise was being repudiated and the new government had not yet established a firm policy for the region, the squatters swarmed in rapidly and, once established, claimed on grounds of customary law the right to remain. Toba-Batak were not the only ethnic group to take land; there were already large numbers of Javanese, who had been brought to Sumatra before the war by the plantation companies as laborers, Batak from other regions, Coastal Malays, Minangkabau, and others.

The new villages were composed of representatives from all these ethnic groups, and there were no customary lines along which village organization could go. In one such community studied in 1955 by Clark Cunningham, 60 per cent were Javanese, 30 per cent were Batak, and 10 per cent were from other ethnic groups (Batu Bara, Asahan, Minangkabau, Bandjarese, and Chinese). The Batak came from widely scattered areas, and many of them spoke mutually unintelligible dialects. Because the migration had the form of the simultaneous entry of small families from many different lineages, there could be no marga radja with ultimate authority over the land, nor even large landholding lineages. Each nuclear family cleared its own plot and claimed ownership of it. The headman for the village was a government appointee, in this particular case a Javanese settler, and had no traditional buttress for his authority. The settlement pattern was determined by the already existing grid of roads through the former plantations, the result being a linear scattering of houses, rather than a cohesive clumping. In some cases the Batak villagers built their houses in a cluster, facing in on one another as in the mountain villages, and tended to keep their social life within the confines of this small neighborhood; but the community as a whole was splintered by ethnic differences. Even the different Batak dialect groups kept themselves suspiciously separate from one another. In such circumstances, the close connection between territorial political organization and the lineage system disappears, as the size, social heterogeneity, and amorphousness of the community grow and the functions performed by the lineages diminish. Nevertheless, the Batak nuclear family even in a posttraditional village is never as alone as Javanese families are; the marga and much of the ceremonialism associated with it remains exceedingly strong, and, in the city at any rate, fictional marga connections among the local group of displaced Batak develop.[52]

Other Forms of Community

Of the many other cultures and community forms in Indonesia we can only take a small sample. There are very small groups of agricultureless nomadic hunters and gatherers, the Kubu of East Sumatra and the Punan of Central Borneo. Until recently there had been considerable doubt as to whether these peoples actually existed, partly because of their elusiveness, and partly because both peoples merge culturally with their more sedentary swidden-farmer neighbors and probably represent only the poorest fragments of the latter groups, who are forced to inhabit uncultivable land. Needham has since done field work among the Punan (1951-52, 1958-59) and reports that the term covers a number of quite different tribes, some of whom are nomadic nonagriculturalists, and others more settled swidden peoples.[53] One of the largest of these is called the Penan, whose nomadic branch is socially fragmented into small cognatic kingroups, each almost completely isolated from the others, which eke out a precarious but self-sufficient existence on the products of the jungle. These minuscule communities are endogamous to varying degrees and are not subordinate to any larger sociopolitical unit. In a country of predatory head-hunters, the Penan are more often the victims than the aggressors, a fact further reinforcing their tendency to retreat into themselves.

Another unusual society is that of the Mentawai Islands off the west coast of Sumatra.[54] Long isolated from the rest of Indonesia, they lacked rice, pottery making, weaving, and even betel chewing until the beginning of this century. Their subsistence base was taro, a tuber which is grown in shifting gardens. Their religion was different not so much in its content (it appears to be the usual sort of Indonesian animism) but in its strong ritual emphasis on the taboo—the complete cessation of useful activity and of the eating of certain foods, for months at a time. During these taboo periods, the men of the village were almost completely immobilized; the women obtained all food, and the village was closed to outsiders. These periods of ritual abstention and inactivity were held on many different occasions: building a new house, clearing a new field, making a boat, felling a coconut tree, etc. Our picture of the social structure is obscure, for available data are incomplete and contradictory. The descent system has been variously classified by different anthropologists, one considering it patrilineal, another matrilineal, and a third bilateral. Apparently, the crucial concern of the Mentawaians was not descent but the ritual responsibility for the welfare of the group, which was mainly in the hands of most of the older men. These men, whose actions even in daily life were circumscribed by numerous taboos, were the heads of large houses in which lived an unknown number of their kinsmen. The house group was evidently patrilineal and exogamous, and there were usually several intermarrying houses within a village. The villages, however, were mainly endogamous; and when marriages were contracted outside a village, the husband moved to his wife's village and became a full-fledged member of her kingroup. The women did the agricultural labor on the outlying swiddens and had temporary houses there where they received lovers. Marriage was delayed, mainly because young men were unwilling to take on the ritual responsibilities of maturity, and one-third of the children were born outside wedlock. These children were not discriminated against; they merely became part of their mother's father's house group. After legal marriage the woman usually moved into the house, and subsequent children were usually members of their father's house group. Thus the kinship system was one in which membership in corporate groups was a function of several other factors beside descent. During this century missionaries have steadily but slowly made converts; today they claim nearly half of the 30,000 Mentawaians, and state that in Christian villages the ritual taboo periods and the house group as a significant social unit have simultaneously disappeared.

The Ambonese and Minahassans are also difficult to fit into any simple scheme, not because of their ethnographic peculiarities but because their social structures and cultures are a result of a transformation brought about by intense contact with the West. Originally both groups were primarily shifting cultivators, with small, dispersed populations, and were politically organized into small autonomous tribes with kingroups as their major social units. For both, contact with the West brought revolutionary changes, even to the extent, in Ambon, of the loss of the indigenous language, which was replaced by Malay and Dutch.

Ambonese relationships with the external world have been not only intensive but of long duration and with peoples of very diverse origins.[55] Starting at least as early as the fourteenth century, the Ambonese were participants in the commercial Pasisir society—as producers, however, rather than as merchants of the valuable spices. If there had been indigenous kingdoms in Ambon, which is unlikely, they were completely suppressed. The Ambonese were dominated first by the Islamic kingdom of Ternate, which forcibly eliminated head-hunting, introduced a regional rather than tribal form of social organization, and brought Islam to some villages. After that came the Catholic Portuguese, and then the Calvinist Dutch. Today, some villages are Christian and some Moslem; they often border on each other, and are virtually identical culturally except for religion. A highly composite culture grew up, with elements from sixteenth-century Portugal, Java, the Malays, and the seventeenth- and twentieth-century Dutch intermingling with the indigenous patterns. Essentially similar variants of this "creole Moluccan" culture are also found on the islands of Banda, Ternate, Tidore, and Batjan, which were all heavily involved in spice production.

It is no surprise then that Ambonese social structure is complex and difficult to unravel. Some of the most ancient-appearing features were demonstrably introduced quite recently, as for instance the landholding corporations of patrilineal kinsmen (the *dati*), which were brought about or at least given a permanent form by the Dutch. Most of the Ambonese population lives in small villages (*negeri*) which are made up of several localized exogamous patrilineal kingroups (*mata rumah*). These groups form the basis of the village political and class systems. Each lineage of importance owns a sacred spring, a sacred stone, an honorific title, and a number of cultivable plots of land outside the village—the dati lands—which are usually sago and pepper gardens. One (or perhaps several) of these lineages is considered to be the descendant of the man or men who first cleared the land. From these locally elite lineages are chosen both the village head (called by the elevated title of *radja*) and the village priest (*mauwang*), whose sphere is the placation of the founding ancestors and the gaining of their help in the agricultural cycle. This animistic priest amicably coexists with the Christian or Moslem religious leaders of the village. There are institutionalized links between the various lineages of a village concerning marriage choices: each lineage regards certain others as bride givers and yet others as bride receivers. There are complex exchanges of symbolic objects at the wedding, and each marriage is fraught with status significance for the group. This is apparently the underlying reason for the high incidence of mock wife-stealing which is engaged in with the girl's cooperation in order to present a *fait accompli* to the apparently outraged parents. Villages are primarily endogamous; each one has slightly different customs from the next, and formerly they made war on each other.

Because the Dutch made the town of Amboina their administrative center for the Moluccas, and because of the strenuous educational efforts of the missionaries, there is a large group of educated Ambonese, who are found throughout Indonesia in the civil service, the schools, and the hospitals. They formed an important part of the Netherlands Indies army, and after the revolution many chose Dutch citizenship and were "expatriated" to Holland; many others, however, actively supported the revolution and the Republic.

The Minahassans, similarly, have been much influenced by Dutch culture—in some ways even more than the Ambonese, for though their contact with the Dutch was much briefer it was more intense. Before the middle of the nineteenth century, the peoples of Minahassa were of little concern to the rest of the world; but with the advent of Dutch coffee planters and missionaries, the society was totally transformed within several decades from a head-hunting tribal group, probably much like the Eastern Toradja, to a settled peasant economy based primarily on cash crop cultivation, with a Christianized, highly Westernized culture. Apparently the indigenous social structure was based mainly on kinship organization, with cognatic kingroups much like those found elsewhere on Celebes. Unfortunately, there has been no modern study made in Minahassa. However, it would appear that these kingroups may still be important, especially among the Manado elite, though apparently they no longer form the basis for community organization. Today, because of the excellent missionary school system, the Minahassans form with the Ambonese an important segment of the civil service.

Finally, mention should be made of plantation communities, oil installations, and mines, especially those which exist completely independent of any indigenous local community, in which laborers as well as management live on the grounds and lead the whole of their lives within the company.[56] The membership of the upper levels in most of these organizations has, of course, changed totally in the last four years as the government has nationalized them; but the basic social structure is probably unchanged. There is a great need for studies of these plantation social forms and their place in the rest of Indonesian society.

Conclusion

> *Lain padang, lain belalang; lain lubuk, lain ikannja.*
> —INDONESIAN PROVERB

"Other fields, other locusts; other pools, other fish." The import of this folk saying, found in various forms throughout Indonesia, is that different places have differing customs. A less figurative version is *"Lain desa, lain adat"*—"other villages, other customary rules." The awareness of cultural variation is both profound and almost universal in Indonesia's peoples—they have lived with ethnic diversity for thousands of years. The consciousness of dissimilarity has two facets, one a sense of one's own specific cultural identity, and the other an attitude of tolerance for other mores. How specific the locus of identity is for an Indonesian, how extensive his cultural reference group is, varies considerably: for some isolated peoples it is the immediate small community, and all other villages are perceived as somewhat alien; for others, notably the Pasisir peoples, the differences perceived are more inclusive; for the most sophisticated metropolitans, the nation itself is the primary referent.

The proverb employs for its metaphor the biological process of speciation, the natural variation of living forms which grow up in differing environmental contexts. The same process can be seen at work at the cultural level in Indonesia, as each tiny community, set in its own small valley, keeping its marriages within its own group, develops over the generations its own peculiar customs and rules. Social and physical isolation breed cultural divergence. Every Balinese hamlet, Minangkabau village, or Toradja tribe has its own distinctive regulations which are slightly or markedly different from those of its nearest neighbors. *Lain desa, lain adat* in these situations has specific, concrete meaning, of which any new settler joining one of these villages is very much aware.

But cultural processes are not the same as biological ones, and Indonesia is again an excellent case in point. Physical isolation occurs only in the interior of the islands; for most of Indonesia the geography of island living does not entail seclusion, but rather the reverse. The seas among its islands are, in fact, great highways, and the traffic on them has been steady, at times heavy, and of international origin, for nearly two thousand years. Thus Indonesia's fundamental topography is that of a crossroads, a confluence of many ways. And the majority of its peoples have responded to the continuous onslaught of influences from alien cultures with receptivity, flexibility, and at the same time selectivity. The Javanese and the Pasisir cultures are both products of this process, both amalgams of elements from many sources. Much of Indonesia's diversity is explained not by the isolated development of its peoples, but by their differing histories of contact with and responses to the outside world.

It is this very diversity in values, outlooks, and capacities on the cultural level, together with the variety, openness, and adaptability of social forms, that are Indonesia's most basic structural features; and it is these which give the society as a whole its greatest strength and durability. If Indonesia is to survive as an autonomous and integral entity in the modern world, it must create for itself a new national organization and a coherent national identity, one which at the same time rests on a multiplicity of local community forms and identities.

CHAPTER *3*

The Chinese Minority[1]

G. WILLIAM SKINNER

VIRTUALLY all Chinese in Indonesia are either themselves China-born immigrants or descendants of earlier immigrants through the male line. Nonetheless, as a result of the considerable intermarriage and assimilation which have occurred in many parts of the country, one cannot determine who is and who is not a Chinese according to any simple racial criterion. There are, for instance, many persons in Java who are uniformly considered Chinese but are by ancestry less than one-quarter Chinese, while other persons who by ancestry are more than one-quarter Chinese consider themselves—and are considered by the local people—to be indigenous Indonesians. Among certain groups of Chinese, furthermore, change away from traditional Chinese patterns has been so marked that the obvious cultural indicators have become misleading or irrelevant. Many persons who are unambiguously Chinese neither speak nor read a word of any Chinese language, have forsaken Chinese deities and the ancestral cult, operate in a kinship system which is no longer male-centered, and have unequivocally rejected Chinese citizenship.

An adequate definition, then, relies in the first instance not on racial, legal, or cultural criteria, but rather on social identification. In Indonesia a person of Chinese ancestry *is* Chinese when he functions as a member of, and identifies with, Chinese society. The only reliable cultural sign of this self-identification as Chinese and of alignment with a Chinese social system is the use—at least in some form and some circumstances—of a Chinese surname. Available evidence indicates that the total number of Chinese so defined falls between 2.3 and 2.6 million.[2]

The migration which gave rise to Chinese settlement in Indonesia had its origin in the early junk trade of Chinese merchants from

97

southeastern China, and subsequent growth in the Chinese population has been closely tied to their economic role. Freed from the
stultifying effects of the imperial bureaucracy at home, the Chinese
overseas proved themselves eminently suited for economic development. The emphasis placed in their value system on industriousness, frugality, self-reliance, venturesomeness, and skill, together
with some extraordinarily adaptable and serviceable principles of
social organization, marked the immigrants out for economic success in a land of rich resources whose indigenous peoples were
quite differently oriented.[3] From the seventeenth century to the
twentieth, as the Dutch pressed ahead with their ever more systematic exploitation of the Indies economy, the Chinese were allotted
a growing number of roles which the Dutch could not themselves
fill. They were allowed to indulge their preference for entrepreneurial occupations and to build up a comprehensive commercial
and financial network extending from the major ports to rural
markets. The Dutch controlled the shipping and import-export trade
which fed and was fed by this network and took tax and revenue
cuts at several points in the system. In addition to being encouraged
to take up commercial positions intermediate between the Dutch
colonialists and the indigenous population, Chinese were directly
imported, from the 1860s to the 1930s, as laborers on the plantations and in the mines producing commodities for Western markets.
In the most recent stages of colonial development, overseas Chinese
were increasingly employed as foremen and white-collar workers in
Western enterprises themselves. Thus it is that the retrenchment of
Dutch business interests in the 1950s left the Chinese in a position to
dominate or control major segments of the nonagricultural economy
throughout Indonesia—a position which was both sanctioned by a
long history and tainted with colonialism, perpetuated by deep-
seated cultural differences and vulnerable to nationalistic attack.

The present distribution of the Chinese—I take 2.45 million as
a working total—among the major units of the archipelago is approximately shown in Table 1. At present, then, the Indonesian
Chinese are about evenly divided between Java and the Outer
Islands. It has by no means always been so, however. A century
ago the outer provinces were little developed and two-thirds of the
Indonesian Chinese lived in Java. From mid-century on into the
1920s, however, as tin mining on the islands of Bangka and Billiton
and plantation agriculture in the east coast residency of Sumatra

were systematically developed through the employment of imported Chinese labor, the Chinese population of Sumatra rapidly increased both relatively and absolutely (see Table 2). This trend, however, was reversed by the Great Depression, which severely restricted mining and plantation agriculture and led to a net loss of Chinese in many parts of Sumatra during the 1930s. The decline between 1956 and 1961 in the proportion of Indonesian Chinese residing in Java reflects primarily the fact that the Chinese repatriated in 1960 were very disproportionately from Java. Present indications are that within the Chinese population natural increase is somewhat lower in Java than in the outer provinces as a whole, but also that there is a small net migration of Chinese to Java from the rest of Indonesia.

Although at least half of the Indonesian Chinese live in Java, they form a mere two per cent of the total population of that crowded island. Java's major ports—for immigration as well as trade—are all located along the north coast of Java proper, facing the South China Sea, and in consequence the Chinese population is concentrated there. Chinese are least well represented in the relatively underdeveloped areas of eastern Java where Madurese is spoken. In the remainder of the island, the Chinese are more strongly represented in the Sundanese regions of West Java than in the Javanese areas further east, even though the Priangan, the Sundanese heartland, was opened by Indies authorities to Chinese settlement only in 1872.

The Chinese of Java are today overwhelmingly urban, a reflection not only of the mercantile origin of their settlements and of their continued preference for urban occupations, but also of the vagaries of government policy. During much of the nineteenth century the Chinese were required by the Dutch authorities to live in designated urban neighborhoods and could travel out of them only with permits issued by government bureaucrats.[4] The termina-

Table 1. DISTRIBUTION OF THE CHINESE POPULATION

	Chinese population	Total population	Per cent Chinese of total
Java and Madura	1,230,000	63,059,000	2.0
Sumatra	690,000	15,739,000	4.4
Borneo	370,000	4,102,000	9.0
East Indonesia	160,000	13,427,000	1.2
Totals	2,450,000	96,327,000	2.5

Table 2. GROWTH OF THE CHINESE POPULATION IN INDONESIA

(in thousands)

Year	Java Number	Java Per cent	Sumatra Number	Sumatra Per cent	West Borneo Number	West Borneo Per cent	Other Number	Other Per cent	Outer Islands Number	Outer Islands Per cent	Total
1860	150	67.6	....	....	....	....	....	....	72	32.4	222
1880	207	60.2	94	27.3	28	8.1	15	4.4	137	39.8	344
1895	256	54.6	159	33.9	38	8.1	17	3.6	213	45.4	469
1905	295	52.4	195	34.6	48	8.5	25	4.4	268	47.6	563
1920	384	47.5	304	37.6	68	8.4	54	6.7	425	52.5	809
1930	582	47.2	449	36.4	108	8.8	94	7.6	651	52.8	1,233
1956	1,145	52.0	605	27.5	271	12.3	179	8.1	1,055	48.0	2,200
1961	1,230	50.2	690	28.2	315	12.9	215	8.8	1,220	49.8	2,450

SOURCE: For 1860-1930, Departement van Economische Zaken, *Volkstelling 1930*, 7, 39-43; the estimate for 1956 is based on the registered population as published in *Penduduk Indonesia* (Djakarta, 1958); the 1961 figures are a projection made by the writer from the 1956 estimates.

tion of this quarter system in 1919 coincided with the onset of the great postwar wave of Chinese immigrants, and the result was a massive penetration during the 1920s of Java's rural interior by Chinese traders, for the most part China-born. Nonetheless, the Chinese population remained predominantly urban. In 1930, 58.4 per cent of the Java Chinese lived in cities and towns of 8,000 population or larger, and almost 10 per cent of the total urban population of the island was Chinese.[5] Chinese penetration of the countryside continued at slackened pace during the 1930s, but the war and revolution of the following decade brought a major reversal of the trend, as the Chinese sought security in the cities. Finally, in 1959-60, Indonesian authorities evacuated most of the Chinese alien population from the rural countryside in West Java. In consequence the Chinese of Java are more urban today than in 1930.[6]

When the Outer Islands as a whole are compared with Java, it is notable that Chinese form a higher proportion of the total population and are more rural in their distribution. The areas of heaviest concentration, i.e. where the Chinese form a fifth or more of the total population, are West Borneo (20.5), Billiton (25.2), the Riouw archipelago (27.9), and Bangka (32.0).[7] Chinese are also heavily concentrated along the east coast of Sumatra proper, from Deli and Medan on south through Bengkalis, but their proportion of the population in this coastal strip as a whole probably does not exceed 10 per cent. In all of these areas there are smaller districts in which the Chinese form an ethnic plurality—and in some even a majority—of the total population. Most of the immigrants to these areas were originally settled in rural districts to work in mines and on plantations; and as the mines played out, contracts expired, and plantations increasingly replaced Chinese with indigenous laborers from Java, many of the Chinese who elected to remain settled on the land as farmers and fishermen. In 1930 at least 70 per cent of the Chinese population in each of the areas mentioned was rural; though less marked today, the rural predominance clearly persists. It should also be noted that in the regions of great Chinese concentration, cities and towns are still more strongly Chinese than the districts in which they fall. In the case of Pontianak, the provincial capital of West Borneo, Chinese form nearly three-fifths of the total population.[8]

Chinese immigrants to Indonesia have come almost entirely from the two provinces of Fukien and Kwangtung, which are exceptional in China for their great regional diversity. Every immigrant to Indonesia has inevitably borne the stamp of the distinctive local culture peculiar to his native area. Linguistic distinctiveness underlies the cultural differentiation among these subethnic groups, and consequently they may be referred to generically as speech groups. The languages of the three major speech groups represented in Indonesia—Hokkien, Hakka, and Cantonese—are mutually unintelligible, differing one from the other as Italian differs from Spanish and Spanish from Portuguese.

Hokkiens were the first Chinese to settle in Indonesia in large numbers, and they formed the dominant group among immigrants until the middle of the nineteenth century. Their regional home is situated in southern Fukien, an area of outstanding importance in the annals of China's overseas trade. The strongly mercantilistic content which Hokkien culture consequently acquired in the course of centuries is still apparent in Indonesia. Not only are Hokkiens, by comparison with other speech groups, more often occupied in trade, but among traders Hokkiens are also more often successful. Hokkiens and their assimilated descendants are the dominant group in East Indonesia as a whole, in Central and East Java and on the west coast of Sumatra.

Moving from the Hokkien area south along the China coast, the next group encountered is the Teochius, who live in the hinterland of Swatow and along the coast southwest of that port. Although they speak a dialect which is mutually intelligible with Hokkien, they tend to accentuate their distinctiveness overseas. In Indonesia, Teochius are found largely outside Java, being concentrated along Sumatra's east coast (where they were preferred by plantation managers as estate laborers), in the Riouw archipelago, and in West Borneo, especially Pontianak and adjacent districts. Traditionally they have specialized in agriculture, and even today they are well represented in market gardening and other commercial agriculture. The past fifty years, however, have seen a steady advance of the Teochius in the whole range of commercial specializations, and in many areas where Hokkiens are poorly represented Teochius dominate trade.

Although Hakkas are among the major Chinese speech groups to have emigrated overseas, they are not a maritime people. Their heartland, which lies completely inland in Kwangtung province, consists primarily of mountainous, relatively unproductive terrain; and Hakkas more than any other speech group turned to emigration through economic necessity. Throughout the great migration waves from 1850 to 1930, Hakkas were the poorest of the Chinese immigrants from the mainland. They were first drawn to the Outer Islands of Indonesia to exploit mineral resources, and to this day Hakkas dominate Chinese society in the former gold-mining districts of West Borneo, while the contemporary dialect of the tin-mining island of Bangka is derived from the Hakka language. Beginning in the late nineteenth century, Hakkas began coming to West Java in numbers, attracted by the rapid growth of Batavia and by the opening of the Priangan to Chinese traders. Hakkas now predominate among the Chinese in Greater Djakarta and West Java.

The Hakkas' western and southern neighbors in China are the Cantonese, who are centered in the great delta of the Pearl or West River. Cantonese, like Hakkas, became well known in Southeast Asia as mineworkers, and their nineteenth-century migration to Indonesia was largely directed toward the tin mines of Bangka. Although they began to come in numbers to Java about the same time as the Hakkas, their circumstances were rather different. They normally came with more capital, and they brought with them an exceptional measure of mechanical and industrial skill. Cantonese were traditionally noted as skilled artisans, and they took advantage of their area's close contact with Europeans in Canton and later on in Hongkong to pick up some of the secrets of Western machinery and industrial success. Cantonese thus carved out a niche for themselves in Indonesia's cities—as skilled artisans, machine workers, and owners of hardware stores and small industries, in addition to their role in restaurant and hotel keeping, for which they are also known in the West. Far less numerous than either Hokkiens or Hakkas and more evenly dispersed than either throughout the archipelago, Cantonese are of only secondary importance in Chinese communities everywhere in Indonesia. They are disproportionately represented in Central and East Java, South and East Borneo, Bangka, and Central Sumatra.

It may be stated as a general rule that if a given area of Indonesia was settled by Chinese in appreciable numbers prior to this century, Chinese society there is in some degree dichotomous today. In one sector of the society, adults as well as children are Indonesia-born, the orientation toward China is attenuated, and the influence of indigenous culture is apparent. In the other sector of the society, the population consists of twentieth-century immigrants and their immediate descendants, who are less acculturated and more strongly oriented toward China. The significance and pervasiveness of the social line between the two sectors varies from one part of Indonesia to another. At one extreme is Java, where two essentially separate social systems exist within the Chinese population. At the other extreme are such areas as the district of Bagan Siapi-api on Sumatra's east coast, where the two sectors are unambiguously subsystems of a single society, the distinction between the locally rooted Chinese population (predominantly fishermen of Hokkien extraction) and the China-oriented population (mostly Hokkien traders) being merely one of cultural emphasis.

In every case, the formative period for the locally rooted society began when immigrants settled on the land, formed alliances with indigenous women—Chinese women almost never emigrated overseas prior to this century—and reared children who were taught to identify themselves as Chinese. Marriage among these mixed-blood descendants of immigrants led eventually to the development of a fairly stable society. This process began in the sixteenth century in Java, and the culture of the resultant society was stabilized by the eighteenth century. In West Borneo and Bangka the process began in the eighteenth century, and a culturally distinctive local society was formed only by the middle of the nineteenth century. In communities such as the cited case of Bagan Siapi-api, the process began as late as the last decade of the nineteenth century, and cultural stability is only now being achieved.

The locally rooted Chinese communities in Indonesia can be ranged along a gradient according to the degree of indigenous influence in their synthesized culture. In Bagan Siapi-api, the emerging culture is far more Hokkien than Malay, and the language of daily use is virtually unadulterated Hokkien. In West Borneo, rural settlement patterns are typical of certain areas in China which have been settled in recent centuries by Hakkas; and kinship and religion, for instance, are very close to the homeland prototypes. Nevertheless, the rhythm of life is Indonesian, and it is interesting to note that the Chinese in West Borneo eventually replaced the Hakka wet-rice cultivation complex, including the plow, sickle, and threshing box, with a locally evolved amalgam which includes the Dayak digging stick and the Malay harvesting blade. In northeastern Bangka, the indigenous content of local Chinese culture is still greater. The language used is an almost creolized Hakka dialect with heavy borrowings from Bangkanese

Malay, and the influence of Malay norms is evident in the material culture, settlement patterns, family structure, and religious behavior. We might next cite such cases as the established Chinese communities in the Minangkabau area of West Sumatra, Bali, Minahassa, and Ambon as examples of a still greater degree of indigenous influence in the syncretic culture of the locally rooted Chinese community. Finally, in the case of the old Chinese families of Java, virtually every aspect of the culture has been profoundly informed by influences from the local civilizations.

Position on this continuum is in part a function of the length of time which elapsed between the beginning of societal formation by the Chinese settlers and the arrival in significant numbers of immigrant China-born women. Among the many other relevant factors one must note the comparative cultural level of the indigenous population. The Chinese found much that was attractive and valuable in a highly differentiated, rich, complex, and literate culture such as that of the Javanese, considerably less in the simpler local culture of Bangka, where there were only a few representatives of a literate elite, and still less in the relatively impoverished, nonliterate cultures of the Borneo aborigines.

In Java the locally rooted Chinese community is known as *Peranakan Tionghoa* (Chinese children of the Indies).[9] From the eighteenth to the early twentieth century Peranakans dominated the local Chinese communities. Immigration from China was always moderate and assimilation to Peranakan society rapid, so that immigrant Chinese and their incompletely Peranakanized offspring formed but a small and transitory group. Beginning with the first decade of this century, however, several developments laid the basis for the rise of a stable, non-Peranakan Chinese society. First of all, the number of Chinese immigrants rapidly increased during the first three decades of the century.[10] Second, the proportion of non-Hokkiens among the immigrants steadily rose until Hakkas and Cantonese easily outnumbered Hokkiens. This development naturally retarded acculturation to the Hokkien-flavored Peranakan way of life. Third, the sex ratio of the immigrants became steadily more balanced, leading to a rapid increase in the number of families in which both parents were China-born. Fourth, the rise of Chinese nationalism gave the new generation of immigrants a strong national pride inimical to the de-sinification which accompanied assimilation to Peranakan society. And finally, in response to the new nationalism and the growing desire for modernization, a system of Chinese-language schools and a Chinese-language press were developed after 1900, thereby providing a potent means of preserving the Chineseness of the immigrants' children. Kuo-yü, the new national language of China promoted by the schools, emerged as a new Chinese *lingua franca* for non-Peranakan Chinese of different speech groups.

The society which took form in response to these changes is usually called *Totok*, an Indonesian term which, strictly speaking, refers to foreign-born immigrants but which is often extended to include the descendants of immigrants primarily oriented toward their country of origin, in this case China. In the outer provinces as a whole, Totoks easily outnumber the Indonesia-oriented Chinese in well-settled families. In Java, on the other hand, Totoks are outnumbered at least three to two by Peranakans.

It is proposed in the remainder of this section to limit discussion to that half of the Indonesian Chinese which lives in Java and to contrast Totoks with the Peranakans living there. The focus is narrowed in this fashion not because the Java Peranakans are in any sense typical of the locally rooted Chinese societies of Indonesia, but simply because they constitute the largest and by far the most important group of non-Totok Chinese about whom meaningful generalizations can be made.

In regard to livelihood, Totoks strongly prefer self-employment and are overwhelmingly found in entrepreneurial occupations. Peranakans, more diversified in their occupational distribution, show a preference for the professions and for clerical and staff positions in large enterprise. A 1957 study in a West Java town showed that among gainfully employed Chinese family heads, shopowners accounted for 80.5 per cent of the foreign-born Totoks, for 57.1 per cent of those Chinese citizens who were born in Indonesia, and for only 44.6 per cent of the Peranakans holding Indonesian citizenship. In the case of white-collar positions in large business enterprises, however, the corresponding proportions were 2.2, 6.1, and 15.4 per cent.[11] These occupational preferences reflect a marked difference in value orientation. Totoks more than Peranakans value wealth, frugality, work, self-reliance, and "nerve." Peranakans more than Totoks value the enjoyment of life, leisure, social standing, and security. A 1957 questionnaire study which I administered in Djakarta showed that in terms of career and success orientation Totoks were far ahead of indigenous Indonesians, and that in this regard Peranakans were considerably closer to the Indonesians than to the Totok Chinese.[12]

Within any city or town in Java, the Totoks are concentrated in the central business district, living typically in shop-house dwellings similar to those in the cities of southeastern China. Peranakans, on the other hand, are dispersed more widely through the town and are more eclectic in their housing, showing a distinct preference for modern Western architecture.

In many elements of kinship structure, the emphasis has shifted among Peranakans away from the patrilocal, patrilineal, and patriarchal bias which is basic to the traditional Hokkien system and which in general still characterizes contemporary Totok practice. Weddings may be held, and the bridal chamber prepared, in the parental home of the bride as well as of the groom. Daughters inherit along with sons, and in particular the inheritance of real property tends to follow marital residence; even the ancestral tablets and ashes are not infrequently inherited by daughters and their husbands in matrilocal cases. There is a distinct tendency in the ancestral cult to worship the lineal ascendants of the mother as well as of the father. Political, economic, and social authority, still concentrated within the family according to generation and relative age, is much more evenly distributed between the sexes among Peranakans than among Totoks. Social interaction with maternal kinsmen is normally as frequent and intimate as that with paternal kinsmen. Peranakan bilaterality is clearly reflected in kinship terminology: for instance, in the second and third ascending generations, kin terms do not distinguish maternal from paternal relatives. In accordance with the enhanced status of females, young Peranakans do not exhibit the pronounced preference for sons which Totoks still betray, and they show less sympathy for the persistence of polygyny than do Totoks.

The sex egalitarianism of Peranakans reflects not only their bilaterality but also the curiously selective Westernization of their kinship values. (In this regard, the adoption of a Dutch style of life by the Peranakan elite is critical; see below.) Western influence also appears in the Peranakan preference for fewer children, as contrasted with Totoks.[13] A 1957 survey in Djakarta[14] showed that among Peranakan couples the proportion of childless couples was significantly higher than among Totoks and that Peranakan couples with children had fewer of them on the average than Totok couples did.[15]

In a number of other respects, however, Peranakans are closer to traditional Chinese family values than are Totoks. It must be remembered in this connection that Peranakans had been shielded by barriers of both language and distance from the modernizing forces and social ferment which in the twentieth century so strongly affected social patterns and values in the coastal provinces of China. The above-mentioned household survey in Djakarta showed that among Peranakans both the proportion of structurally complex family types and the average number of extra relatives are higher than among Totoks, which suggests that it is the Peranakans who manage a closer approximation of the traditional Chinese ideal. Divorce is infrequent among both Peranakans and Totoks but, in their attitudes at least, Peranakans are stricter. Above all, Peranakans are more familistic: in choosing a spouse, considerations of family are more important to them than to Totoks, and arranged marriages, in fact if not in name, are more common among Peranakans. Peranakans also tend to be more nepotistic.

Ancestral rites are carried out by a higher proportion of families, and with greater regularity, among Peranakans—a fact which confirms both the reduced emphasis on traditional familism and the greater secularization of Totoks. In terms of activity and self-assessment, Peranakan youth are far more religious. While China-born immigrants tend to be strong temple worshipers, their children reject the deism of the Chinese religion far more thoroughly than Peranakan youth, among whom deity worship occurs more often at home than in the temple. Peranakans are also much more than Totoks likely to be Christians, the excellent schools operated by both Catholic and Protestant bodies providing the chief path to their conversion.[16] The Christianization of the Peranakan population must be interpreted in large part as a search for security and status in a rapidly changing society. During the colonial era, it meant identification with the power elite; in the period of independence it means identification with a segment of the native population which has been accepted within the national community.

Since the turn of the century, concerted efforts have been made to bridge the cultural gap between Totoks and Peranakans and to achieve first a unity of purpose and eventually a unified community. The endeavor has been made in the context of the Chinese nationalist movement, within Chinese voluntary associations, and above all in the Chinese-language schools. Early in the century, many Peranakans, embarrassed before nationalistic Totoks and

Western sinologues alike, took the initiative in an effort to purify (i.e. re-sinify) Peranakan culture. A single pan-Chinese movement eventually encompassed this effort and linked it with the struggle to unify Totoks of differing speech groups, and with the fight to achieve for all Chinese in the Indies a closer approximation of European status.[17] Success on a number of other fronts blinded the Peranakans to what was really happening within the movement: the Totoks had taken over full leadership by 1915, and by the 1920s it became apparent that unity of Peranakans and Totoks was to be had only on Totok terms, that is, through a thorough re-sinification of Peranakan culture. Twentieth-century changes, however, opened up more than one road to the modernization and social betterment which leading Peranakans had come to demand. The one route, which drew Peranakans to Chinese education and revolutionary Chinese nationalism, aroused Dutch fears and caused the Indies authorities to lay out another. Beginning in 1908, the earlier Dutch policy of cultural exclusivism was abandoned, and Dutch schools for Peranakan children were rapidly opened in the major cities and towns. Subsequent changes in the Indies legal system gave the Peranakan elite a status closer to that of the Dutch and Eurasians and more distant from that of the indigenous population, and held out the prospect of steady Chinese advancement in the context of, if not in league with, Dutch colonialism. The major Peranakan leaders chose the Dutch road and carried much of the community with them in the 1920s and '30s.

If the pan-Chinese Totoks lost the first round in the struggle for the Peranakan soul, they gained a second chance in the 1940s, when Totoks and Peranakans once again found common ground, this time in nationalistic opposition to the Japanese. During the occupation, the Japanese treated all Chinese subgroups with impartial disdain and forced all their organizations—Peranakan as well as Totok—into a single omnibus federation. During the revolution and after the transfer of sovereignty the Indonesian nationalists, too, seldom bothered with fine distinctions in dealing with the Chinese minority. As it happened, large numbers of Peranakans, unable to adjust to the revolution, came to believe that the consequences of Indonesian independence could be avoided through a retreat into Chinese nationalism. For fifteen years, from 1942 to 1957, the number of Peranakan children attending Totok-operated Chinese-language schools steadily increased, and a pan-Chinese community of interest appeared to be growing as the new Indonesian state treated its Peranakan citizens almost as poorly as it did the Chinese aliens. However, Indonesian policy began to change in 1957, and subsequent developments (see below) have tended to sharpen the line between the two Chinese communities. Today only Totok children attend Chinese-language schools, while Peranakan children are enrolled almost exclusively in Indonesian-language schools, sponsored in large part by Peranakan organizations. Almost none of the Chinese associations now include both Peranakans and Totoks; even the "pan-Chinese" organizations no longer pretend to a mixed membership or leadership. Although in the '20s and '30s Totoks not infrequently took Peranakan wives, they do so far less often today because of the ever more balanced sex ratio within the Totok community. In the 1950s, if not earlier, leaders acknowledged by both Totoks and Peranakans on Java disappeared from the scene; and today the chief links between the two communities are the now anomalous Chinese-educated Peranakans and the diminishing number of Peranakan women married to Totoks.[18]

Within the Totok sector of the society, the highest level of segmentation is the division into speech groups. These are less strikingly distinctive today than they were at the turn of the century, but speech-group membership remains crucial in structuring social relations. In the last analysis a Totok will relax fully among those with whom he can speak his natal tongue; he will more readily trust those of his own kind and will normally find his closest friends and opinion leaders among them. Speech-group membership provides the organizational principle of the most important voluntary associations in Totok society.

Among Peranakans, considerations of speech group are simply irrelevant. The highest level of segmentation in Peranakan society is that of social class, which is graded not primarily according to wealth, as among the Totoks, but rather, in the first instance, according to educational attainment and family standing.

Under the provisions of the Round Table Agreement of 1949, practically all Indonesia-born Chinese—being Dutch subjects of non-Dutch foreign origin—were given a choice of citizenship. They could obtain Indonesian citizenship by doing nothing or they could establish their status as citizens of China alone by formally rejecting Indonesian citizenship within a two-year period (1949-51).[19] With few exceptions China-born Totoks were not Dutch subjects and so had no choice.[20] The Indonesian Justice Department estimates that more than 390,000 Indonesia-born Chinese rejected Indonesian nationality at that time.[21] The majority of these were Totoks—for the most part children of China-born fathers—including many minors whose option was made for them by their parents.

The implementation of the Round Table provisions, however, hardly resolved the citizenship problems of the Chinese. Those born in Indonesia who did not reject Indonesian citizenship were legally citizens not only of Indonesia but also of China. In an attempt to remove this major source of contention between them, the governments of Indonesia and of the People's Republic of China signed a Dual Nationality Treaty in 1955. The instruments of ratification were exchanged only on January 20, 1960, when the two-year period of implementation began. According to the treaty and subsequent agreements, every dual national who wished to maintain his Indonesian citizenship had to appear prior to January 20, 1962 at a local Indonesian court and either (1) present a certificate from his local precinct registrar attesting that he had voted in the 1955 or 1957 elections, or (2) provide acceptable proof of having been born in Indonesia and (either in writing or orally) choose Indonesian and simultaneously reject Chinese nationality before the court. Dual nationals who failed to take these active steps have lost their Indonesian nationality. An additional agreement provided that children (born before the beginning, but not yet of age at the end of the earlier option period) of parents who rejected Indonesian nationality are not bound by their parents' decision and may choose Indonesian nationality within two years after attaining eighteen years of age.[22]

It is not possible at the time of writing to clarify the quantitative aspects of citizenship among the Indonesian Chinese. On the basis of available information it may be estimated that of the 2.45 million ethnic Chinese in Indonesia approximately one million are individuals born outside of Indonesia; about 200,000 are Indonesia-born individuals who as legal adults in 1949-51 rejected Indonesian citizenship; and perhaps 50,000 are children born of Chinese-citizen parents since 1949. These 1.25 million Chinese are unequivocally aliens in Indonesia, the great majority being citizens only of the People's Republic of China. The remainder of the Chinese population, it may be estimated, consists of about 200,000 teen-agers and young adults, born before the 1949-51 option period, whose parents then rejected Indonesian citizenship; and approximately one million dual nationals who have, as of January 1962, made their final choice.

The number who chose Indonesian citizenship was reduced by the requirement that all make an active option and by an impressive array of bureaucratic and legal obstacles.[23] In all probability, when the final count is made the number of Chinese holding valid Indonesian citizenship will fall between 600,000 and 800,000. It may be predicted that this number will include an easy majority of the Java Peranakans, but a smaller proportion of the less Indonesianized Chinese communities in the outer provinces.

The decade since the end of the first option period in 1951 has demonstrated that the Indonesian populace and government find it difficult to distinguish between foreign Chinese and Indonesian citizens of Chinese descent (hereafter called WNI Chinese).[24] Even in Java it is hard for the indigenous people to perceive the significance of the sharp cultural differences or to make allowance for the legal distinctions between the WNI Peranakan and the Totok citizen of China. In part this attitude has been inherited from the colonial period, when despite certain legal niceties all Chinese were lumped together as Foreign Orientals and controlled through a single structure of indirect rule. It is also not unrelated to the fact that WNI Chinese, for reasons beyond their control, were prior to 1960-62 not only citizens of Indonesia but also nationals of China, like all the other Chinese in Indonesia. It is significant, however, that the Indonesian view is based on the conviction, so often symptomatic of a prejudiced mind, that the minority in question is somehow immune to change: "Once a Jew (read Chinese), always a Jew." The form which this thinking takes is that Chinese of whatever stripe, being clannish and perduringly faithful to their native land, have remained unaffected by however many years or generations they have spent in Indonesia, and that they play every situation for what it is worth without regard to ultimate loyalties.[25] In the view of many Indonesians, the WNI Chinese differs from the foreign Chinese essentially only in that he found his self-interest best served by the opportunistic assumption of Indonesian citizenship. Indonesian business groups, in fierce competition with WNI Chinese as well as with aliens, are eager to perpetuate the view that all Chinese are the same and, in congruence with their typically Islamic orientation, to define that sameness in religious and moral terms.

Official discrimination against Chinese of whatever citizenship usually takes the form of preferential treatment for indigenous (*asli*) Indonesians. In the economic field, for instance, the national government has used its controls over credit facilities, import and manufacturing licenses, wholesale rights, and foreign exchange to favor not just Indonesian citizens but asli Indonesians.[26] In many governmental agencies even statistics are compiled in two categories —not citizens and aliens, but asli and non-asli (both citizen and alien). An Indies law of 1875 which prohibits the alienation of native-owned land to persons of foreign descent has not been altered since independence, so that WNI as well as foreign Chinese even today cannot buy farmland. In the field of education, quotas have been quietly introduced in most of the government-operated universities and professional schools to ensure that the great majority of entrants are asli Indonesians.

When the Indonesian government does distinguish between the WNI and the foreign Chinese in its policy, it is more often than not because the desired objective would be unworkable if applied to all Chinese, and half a loaf is better than none. For instance, in June 1954 a regulation was issued forbidding control of rice mills by "persons having citizenship other than Indonesian citizenship," a wording designed to encompass not only aliens but also WNI Chinese, who at the time were technically dual nationals. Only in September, after political opposition was mobilized and the infeasibility of the inclusive interpretation became apparent, did the Minister of Economic Affairs announce that the prohibition was intended to apply only to foreigners.[27] To cite an opposite illustration, in the summer of 1957 the military commanders in East Indonesia, eager to put an end to the propagation of foreign ideologies, closed all Chinese-language schools. It was soon borne in upon the military leaders that insofar as foreign nationals among the students were thereby deprived of an education in their native language, these closures contravened a number of international conventions and agreements and endangered relations with China. In consequence a limited number of the Chinese schools were allowed to reopen, but for alien students only. In this manner the adoption of a new national policy was precipitated, whereby WNI Chinese children are no longer permitted to attend Chinese-language schools.[28]

The prejudice and bitter resentment which is so often revealed in the formulation and execution of much of the government's Chinese policy flows in part from an Indonesian inferiority complex developed during centuries of underprivilege in their native land. During the colonial period the Chinese were markedly superior to the mass of Indonesians in both legal status and economic power, and almost all interethnic contact found the Chinese in a higher position than the Indonesians. In those relationships the Chinese' supercilious awareness of their favorable situation was only too often painfully evident. To the unfortunate legacy of superiority and inferiority feelings must be added another of suspicion and hostility, stemming in particular from the interethnic strife of the Japanese occupation and the revolutionary war. Indonesian nationalists will never forget the indifference or opposition with which many if not most Chinese regarded the revolutionary struggle.[29] It is the very class of Indonesians whose highborn families in prewar days had to endure Chinese swagger and who were in the vanguard of the revolutionary struggle who today man the civil bureaucracy and the army officer corps. It is therefore not to be wondered at if in government offices Chinese run up against discriminatory practices, an administrative dual standard, and occasional calculated disrespect.

The position of alien Chinese is not an enviable one. Throughout the past decade they have been restricted and harassed with increasing severity in almost every field of activity. A concerted effort was begun in 1954 during the first Ali Sastroamidjojo Cabinet to reduce the importance of foreign Chinese in the economy, and by 1957 the avowed policy of the ministries of Industry and Trade was to move gradually toward the exclusion of aliens from all lines of business. Aliens are forbidden to establish any new enterprises or to move or expand existing ones. In July 1957 the government decreed a head tax for foreigners, the amount of which could be paid without serious hardship by only a minority of Chinese aliens. Since 1957, when the elaborate private Chinese-language school system built up over half a century throughout Indonesia was decimated by government decree, many foreign Chinese children have had no school to attend in their own community. In April 1958 a military decree banned the publication of newspapers or periodicals in the Chinese language; the decree is no longer in effect, but less than half of the thirty-four Chinese newspapers published at the time of the initial ban have resumed publication.[30]

A crisis which very nearly jeopardized the entire position of the alien Chinese in Indonesia was precipitated by new regulations officially promulgated in November 1959. One, Regulation 10, prohibited aliens from engaging in retail trade in rural areas, and the other, an army ordinance applicable only to the province of

West Java, forced aliens in areas outside the towns to relocate. When formal protest from Communist China brought no satisfaction, Chinese diplomatic personnel in Indonesia encouraged the Chinese in West Java to evade the regulations and went so far as to interpose themselves between the Indonesian administrators and the affected Chinese. When Chinese aliens refused to obey orders to evacuate, army personnel became enraged and resorted to harsh physical measures to enforce compliance. Nearly eight months of diplomatic stalemate and interethnic abuse brought Sino-Indonesian relations to a nadir.[31] Repatriation of Chinese who wished to escape the deteriorating situation began in December 1959, and within a year some 96,000 had arrived in China.[32]

The prolonged incident made explicit just how weak and exposed the position of the foreign Chinese now is in Indonesia. In the first place, it demonstrated that the Chinese had few friends indeed in the recently altered Indonesian power structure. With the decline of the parties and the rise of army power, few checks on anti-sinitic politics remained. It appeared, in fact, that Sukarno alone had prevented army action which promised to turn tragedy into outright disaster for the alien Chinese. Secondly, the incident pointed up the limitations on the effectiveness of Peking's power in Indonesia. Concerned not to alienate the Indonesian Communist party or to forego Indonesia's diplomatic support, Peking could not afford to pull all the stops over its overseas citizens; and while it eventually forced concessions from the Indonesian authorities, these were kept to a minimum by the army and Foreign Ministry and never publicly acknowledged as such. Thirdly, the episode made apparent to the alien Chinese that mass repatriation *in extremis* was neither feasible nor particularly desirable. Chinese authorities found it so difficult and so expensive to resettle the first 40,000 refugees that they found it necessary to discourage further repatriation even before the crisis subsided. Most of the repatriates were settled in twenty-five Overseas Chinese State Farms, largely situated on Hainan Island, where they learned that "they must develop the spirit of labor and accept the idea that they are settled on the farm permanently."[33] When the word got back to Indonesia, further official discouragement through the Embassy was unnecessary to bring repatriation to a rapid halt.

To the Indonesian authorities, the political activity of foreign Chinese is a matter of great concern. During the decade from 1948 to 1958, the struggle between Communist and Kuomintang partisans permeated all levels of Totok society, and in consequence foreign Chinese in Indonesia are highly politicized. There is evidence to suggest that by 1957 a neutral or moderate position was fast becoming untenable. A study conducted in that year showed a sample of China-oriented Totok youth to be distributed as follows on the political scale: 43 per cent Communist or pro-Communist, 28 per cent mildly pro-Peking, 6 per cent neutral or equivocal, 5 per cent mildly pro-Taipei, and 19 per cent Kuomintang or pro-Kuomintang.[34] Speech-group membership is one of the most important correlates of political alignment among the Indonesian Chinese: Hakkas tend to be rightist, Cantonese intermediate, while Hokkiens are decidedly leftist.[35]

In 1958, following Taipei's aid to the rebellion which had recently broken out in Sumatra and Celebes, an officially sponsored campaign broke the Kuomintang as an effective force in Chinese politics. All Kuomintang organizations were banned, and eventually schools and businesses with Kuomintang connections were closed. Then, in late 1959, the army and to a lesser extent the civilian arm of the government took advantage of the campaign against foreign Chinese to weaken the Communist partisans within the Totok community. A number of Communists and pro-Peking leaders who had worked closely with the Embassy in an attempt to thwart the regulations of 1959 were imprisoned, deported, or otherwise harassed.[36] Pro-Communist fervor was undoubtedly cooled by the outcome of the 1959-60 crisis.

The present position of the WNI Chinese as a whole is only slightly less precarious than that of the foreign Chinese, but at least their commitment and the nature of the task before them have now been clarified. Those who persisted in opting for Indonesian citizenship in 1960-62 have pledged their allegiance to Indonesia and committed their children to ultimate integration within the larger society. The latter will come more smoothly now that WNI Chinese children are being educated only in schools where Indonesian is the language of instruction and where an Indonesia-oriented curriculum is enforced. Even today only a minority of WNI Chinese children attend Indonesian *public* schools, but the proportion attending schools where their classmates are almost all ethnic Chinese has steadily decreased since 1957. A large number of the formal voluntary associations with primarily Peranakan membership have in recent years substituted Indonesian for Chinese names and adopted an open membership policy.[37] Today one can find genuine cooperation between indigenous Indonesians and Peranakan Chinese in a small number of special-interest associations, business firms, professional offices, churches, and even government agencies. An increasing number of WNI Chinese are committed to broadening the scope of interethnic cooperation.

Encouraging signs can also be noted in the political sphere. The major vehicle for WNI Chinese political aspirations is BAPERKI, founded in 1954 and dedicated at the formal level to the achievement of full civil and human rights for all Indonesian citizens and at the operational level to protecting the special interests of WNI Chinese. BAPERKI quickly found the position which best served its objectives in a political arena dominated by anti-Chinese bureaucrats, army personnel, and Moslem business competitors—namely foursquare behind President Sukarno—and has adhered to it ever since with tenacity and to good effect. Meanwhile WNI Chinese have been able to participate effectively in predominantly asli political groups. In the 1955 and 1957 elections, WNI Chinese candidates were put up by a wide range of political parties. Especially in the two Christian parties and in the Indonesian Communist party, Chinese-asli cooperation has proved both genuine and effective.

Among the WNI Chinese who have some grasp of reality and the future, two groups predominate: on the one hand those who oppose assimilation at a forced pace and are determined to participate in Indonesian society and polity as a separate group, and on the other those who hold that voluntary and rapid assimilation is the only way to avoid discrimination or even persecution.[38] In recent years the second, more assimilationist point of view has been gaining, though it is not yet dominant. An anti-Chinese tract of 1958 held that WNI Chinese would have to substitute Indonesian for Chinese names if they were to convince Indonesians of their commitment to Indonesia: "As long as they are unwilling to do even this symbolic act it will be difficult to erase the prejudice of the autochthonous Indonesians against them."[39] In the years since, a growing number of educated WNI Chinese have been giving their newborn children Javanese or other Indonesian names. This indeed signals a trend which may prove inexorable: the further Indonesianization of Peranakan culture and the steady integration of the Peranakan social system with the larger society. One may now entertain the possibility that the WNI Chinese will eventually be accepted as true compatriots by their fellow citizens.

CHAPTER *4*

The Agricultural Foundation

KARL J. PELZER

DESPITE the Indonesian government's keen interest in industrialization, the economy of the archipelago is still basically agrarian. The primary production sector—which yields peasant food crops, smallholder and plantation export crops, livestock, fish, and forest products—provides well over half the national income and is a source of livelihood for more than sixty per cent of Indonesia's gainfully employed inhabitants. By far the most important of its divisions is that of peasant food crops, which alone accounts for more than one-third of the national income. It is, however, as a supplier of tropical export crops that Indonesia is best known, for it is one of the world's leading producers in this field.

The archipelago's wealth in tropical agricultural commodities has been proverbial for many centuries. Spices, grown mainly in the Moluccas, began to attract traders to the archipelago as early as the beginning of the Christian era—at first from China and India, later from the Middle East and the eastern Mediterranean, and since the end of the fifteenth century from the western Mediterranean and northwestern Europe. During the past three centuries the variety of Indonesia's agricultural export products has steadily broadened, in part as a result of an ever widening world demand for tropical commodities and in part because of the successful introduction of exotic plants from other tropical areas. The Portuguese and Spaniards were responsible for the introduction in the sixteenth and seventeenth centuries of such important crops as maize (corn), cassava, sweet potatoes, tobacco, red pepper, and a host of fruits and vegetables. The coffee bush, brought to West Java by the Dutch in the seventeenth century, spread from there to other parts of the archipelago. Tea, cinchona, rubber, oil palm,

118

sisal, abacca, and other less important economic plants reached the country in the nineteenth and twentieth centuries, during the heyday of Indonesian plantation agriculture.

The archipelago has owed its outstanding reputation as an exporter of tropical agricultural products in part to the fact that its topography provides enough diversity in altitude and therefore in climate to suit a wide range of economic plants. Moreover, parts of the country are endowed with highly fertile young volcanic soils and can thus support demanding crops. The majority of the Indonesian people are skilled and industrious cultivators who, though they possess a considerable degree of the conservatism characteristic of peasant societies, have successfully incorporated exotic crops into their agriculture. Finally, the agrarian, economic, and fiscal policies pursued by the Netherlands Indies government after 1870 encouraged the development of estate agriculture, attracting capital to this sector not only from the Netherlands but also from other European countries and the United States.[1]

The development of a plantation economy brought about the division of Indonesian agriculture into two major sectors: a highly scientific estate agriculture, extensive in its use of land and intensive in its use of labor[2] and capital; and a peasant agriculture, tradition-bound and—at least in Java—highly labor-intensive. The plantations, being capable of financing the construction and operation of factories, took over the cultivation of crops requiring complicated and costly processing, while the peasants concentrated on the production of domestic food crops and export crops which demanded little processing. In some cases peasants became satellite producers of such crops as tea and sugar, selling their output to nearby plantations for processing. Such products as palm oil, centrifugal sugar, and tea are typical plantation crops, while copra, spices, and kapok are produced by peasants; rubber and coffee take an intermediate position, being at home in both sectors. Between 1938 and 1958 some striking changes occurred, so that by now the peasant's share in the production of sugar cane, tea, and tobacco is markedly greater than it was in 1938 (see Table 1).

While this division is the most obvious one in Indonesian agriculture, the peasant sector shows regional, organizational, technological, and orientational variations which permit further divisions such as: permanent-field agriculture, carried on in the densely populated parts of the country, versus shifting-field, or swidden agriculture, which is characteristic of the thinly settled regions;

Table 1. PERCENTAGE OF INDONESIAN COMMERCIAL CROPS
RAISED BY PEASANTS AND PLANTERS, 1938 AND 1958

	Peasant		Planter	
Crop	1938	1958	1938	1958
Palm oil and palm kernel	0	0	100	100
Sugar[a]	1	33	99	67
Cacao	2	n.a.[b]	98	n.a.
Tea[c]	18	35	82	65
Rubber	48	63[d]	52	37[d]
Coffee	58	80	42	20
Nutmeg and mace	80	97	20	3
Tobacco	30	90	70	10
Kapok	83	93	17	7
Coconut products	95	99	5	1
Pepper	99	99.9	1	0.1

(a) In 1958 large quantities of sugar cane were raised by smallholders and
sold to sugar mills for conversion into centrifugal sugar.
(b) Not available.
(c) Both in 1938 and 1958 tea factories bought tea leaves produced by
smallholders.
(d) Exports rather than production.

SOURCE: 1938 figures from Department of Economic Affairs, *The Export
Crops of the Netherlands Indies in 1938*, Bulletin No. 175 (Batavia,
Landsdrukkerij, 1939), pp. 14-15; figures for 1958 calculated by
the author on basis of data taken from *Statistical Pocketbook of
Indonesia 1961*, pp. 56-59, 66.

subsistence versus market or export oriented agriculture; or irri-
gated-field versus dry-field cultivation.

Though the staple food of most Indonesians is rice, by no means
all peasants are rice growers, and in several regions of the archipelago rice is not the principal food. Maize is the staple in parts of
Celebes, Timor, Lombok, East Java, and Madura, while in recent
years cassava has become the main source of starch for villagers in
tertiary limestone regions of Java. Sago is the staple in parts of
eastern Indonesia; most of it is obtained from spontaneous stands
of the sago palm, although some ethnic groups such as the Toradja
of Celebes also plant it as a crop.

In Java, peasant-held land which is cropped continuously is
divided into three major categories: *sawah,* or irrigated land;
tegalan, or unirrigated land; and *pekarangan,* compound or mixed
garden land.[3] Intermittently cultivated land is known as *huma* in
Java and generally as *ladang*[4] in the Outer Islands. Of these types
of cropland, sawah is the most highly prized, followed by peka-

rangan; tegalan and ladang—unless planted with cash crops—are of lesser value. Of the more than thirteen million hectares of land in Java and Madura, about one quarter is occupied by sawah, suitable for the raising of wet rice, and somewhat over a third by tegalan, pekarangan, and fresh-water fish ponds (see Table 2). Agricultural land use in those islands has already passed its limits of safety. Java has been without arable forest land since before World War II, and inroads made since then in its forest reserves—which should cover 30 instead of the present 22.7 per cent of the area—have caused erosion and flood problems which can be checked only by reforestation of the most exposed land. Consequently any expansion of the sawah cultivation can take place only at the expense of the tegalan area, and settlements can expand only by encroaching upon either sawah or tegalan.

In contrast, the Outer Islands—except Bali—have plenty of room for extension of the cultivated area. There only one per cent of the land is devoted to sawah culture, which is important only in such small islands as Bali and Lombok and in relatively restricted areas of Sumatra, Borneo, and Celebes.[5] The size of the tegalan and pekarangan area of the Outer Islands is unknown; but in all prob-

Table 2.   LAND UTILIZATION IN JAVA AND MADURA, 1959

Classification	Hectares	Per cent of total area
Land used by smallholders		
Sawah area	3,484,000	26.4
Tegalan, pekarangan, fresh-water fish pond area	4,908,000	37.1
Tide-water fish pond area	107,000	0.8
Total	8,499,000	64.3
Land held by plantations		
Area planted	374,900	2.8
Area uncultivated	252,400	1.9
Total	627,300	4.7
Forest area	2,997,000	22.7
Other land occupied by settlements, roads, inland water, etc.	1,094,100	8.3
Grand total	13,217,400	100.0

SOURCE: Adapted from data given in *Statistical Pocketbook of Indonesia 1961.*

ability it is not much larger than that of sawah, the prevailing type of agriculture in these territories being swidden cultivation.

Swidden agriculture is characterized by slash-and-burn clearing, by a rotation of fields rather than of crops, and by short periods of cropping (one to three years) alternating with long fallow periods—up to twenty years or more, but often as short as five years. Swidden cultivators prefer to lay out their temporary fields in forest areas. By now, however, there is relatively little primeval forest left in Indonesia, so that the swidden farmer normally clears a parcel of second-growth forest (*belukar*) which may have been cleared innumerable times in the past. He may even have to turn to land covered with *alang* grass, which is far less fertile than that which has rested for several years under dense forest. The longer the fallow the larger the area needed to support a swidden cultivator, who on the average requires about ten times as much land as his sawah-cultivating counterpart in Java.

Swidden agriculture's requirement for extensive forest-fallow land renders somewhat deceptive the figure for land use in the Outer Islands given in Table 3, according to which less than ten million hectares, or 7.3 per cent of the land surface, are under dry-land cultivation. This represents only the land actually in production; to it should be added about 25 million hectares included under the headings "other forest areas" and "other land," for this inactive area is a necessary part of the swidden system.[6] This amount must be charged against the nonreserved forest areas, leaving 47.5 million hectares, or 35 per cent of the area, permanently covered by non-reserved forests. Since a reduction of the forest cover much below 40 per cent would involve serious risks to soil and water management, any large-scale expansion of cultivation in the Outer Islands requires the replacement of the present land-extensive swidden system by permanent-field agriculture. This has already become necessary in such densely settled sections of the Outer Islands as the coastal regions of East Sumatra and parts of South Sumatra.[7]

Swidden agriculture is one of the world's least understood land use systems and is often referred to in disparaging terms because of its "wastage" of cultivable land. As a matter of fact, in view of the low fertility of so many Indonesian soils, swidden cultivation is a rational system so long as the population density is low enough to permit fallow periods of sufficient duration to allow adequate recovery of soil fertility. Those who condemn the system also overlook the fact that it has played a very important role in the cultivation of smallholder rubber, which has spread with amazing rapidity in the Outer Islands since about 1910.[8] *Hevea brasiliensis*—a tree which grows best in the humid tropics up to an elevation of about 600 meters—fitted perfectly into the swidden system, despite the early predictions of government officials and planters that it would require the kind of care that only a well-run plantation could give. Swidden cultivators of Sumatra and Borneo planted rubber in ladang which they had previously used for one or two plantings of food crops, instead of letting a nondescript belukar cover it. At the end of a seven-year period the swidden cultivator—with a minimum of care by way of an occasional slashing of undergrowth —had a valuable garden, capable of producing latex for forty years or more if properly cared for. After three or four such plantings, the shifting cultivator turned into a rubber grower who—with a favorable price ratio between rubber and rice—could thenceforth afford to purchase his rice from the Chinese buyer of his rubber. Other

Table 3. LAND UTILIZATION IN THE OUTER ISLANDS, 1959[a]

Classification	Hectares	Per cent of total area
Forest reserves	14,789,100	10.9
Other forest areas	72,494,700	53.3
Total	87,283,800	64.2
Land used by smallholders		
Sawah area	1,500,000	1.1
Nonirrigated land	9,865,000[b]	7.3
Total	11,365,000	8.4
Land held by plantations	1,073,100	0.8
Other land including grass lands or *alang-alang*, swamps, inland waters, roads and settlements	36,217,100	26.6
Grand total	135,939,000	100.0

(a) Excluding West New Guinea.
(b) Estimated by allowing 0.3 hectare per person. A part of this area is planted with perennial crops such as rubber (±1,400,000 hectares) and coconut palms, pepper and coffee, a further part is occupied by pekarangan or compound gardens, but probably more than half consists of ladangs. Not included, however, are old ladangs under forest fallow.

SOURCE: Based in part on estimates and in part on data given in *Statistical Pocketbook of Indonesia 1961*.

crops which fit easily into the swidden system are coconuts, coffee, and pepper. However, the world requirement for these crops is not as great as for rubber, and both coffee and pepper are more demanding in regard to soils, climate, maintenance, and harvest labor. They therefore never gained so wide a distribution or so great an importance in the rural economy of the Outer Islands as has the smallholder cultivation of rubber.

A similar development of smallholder cultivation took place in West Java in the eighteenth and nineteenth centuries, when swidden cultivators planted coffee on a large scale in their old huma. By the end of the nineteenth century, however, virtually all shifting-field cultivation had disappeared from that island,[9] for population pressure had forced the conversion of the available land to permanent-field systems. Because of the lack of any land surplus, peasants in Java cannot afford to convert tegalan into rubber gardens, for even though such a shift might bring greater eventual profit, it would mean foregoing any yield for at least six years—until the rubber reaches its producing stage. As a result, peasant agriculture in Java is almost wholly devoted to raising food crops for subsistence, while a good part of that on the Outer Islands shows a marked commercial bent. The social and economic consequences of this orientational divergence have had considerable effect on recent political relations between Java and the outer regions, as will be described in subsequent chapters.

In Java the average peasant cultivates less than one-half hectare of land, which may consist of sawah, tegalan, and pekarangan, or a combination of pekarangan with one of the other two. Even so small a farm is thus divided into several tiny parcels. If the land consists mostly of sawah which is irrigated by a modern system supplying water during both the rainy and dry seasons, two rice crops can be planted during the year. A cultivator whose sawah is watered by a peasant-designed irrigation system, or who must depend on rainfall alone, has no possibility of raising a second rice crop. He may, however, plant a less moisture-demanding dry-season crop, such as soybeans, sweet potatoes, or maize. Tegalan, too, are often doublecropped—soil and moisture supply permitting—unless they are planted with a crop which requires more than four or five months to mature, such as cassava.

The practice of multiple cropping has spread in Java ever since the nineteenth century, as the per capita supply of land shrank and the average farm size declined. By now at least one-fourth of the plowed land in this island is producing more than one crop a year. The construction of numerous modern reservoirs has played an important role in this intensification of cultivation. The sugar industry as well as the government has engaged in the provision of modern irrigation systems and storage dams, for sugar cane requires twelve to fourteen months to mature and demands a considerable supply of water during the dry season. In consequence, peasants in the sugar-producing areas are in a generally favorable position regarding water supply, though the Irrigation Service gives their fields lower priority than the sugar lands in distributing the available water.

The principal crop raised by the Indonesian farmer is rice, the staple food for most Indonesians. We do not know the exact origin of domesticated rice, but all evidence points to the Southeast Asian mainland as its home. From there, long before the beginning of the Christian era, its cultivation spread into Indonesia. It did not, however, extend to the easternmost parts of the archipelago: rice is not grown in West New Guinea; even in the Moluccas it is unimportant, sago palm being the staple item of diet. In Indonesia, as in other parts of the Asian tropics, many different varieties of paddy are cultivated in accordance with a wide range of ecological conditions. The two major classes are upland or dry rice, which depends on rainfall alone for its moisture needs, and lowland or wet rice, which requires an inundated sawah for its cultivation. Dry rice is far less important than wet rice in Indonesian agriculture: in 1960, approximately 1.3 million hectares of upland paddy were harvested, as against close to 6 million hectares of irrigated rice.[10] One-third of the rice area harvested in the Outer Islands is devoted to dry-rice varieties, which are suitable to swidden agriculture and require relatively little manpower to cultivate. They often produce less per hectare than lowland paddy, however, and on Java and Madura, where land and not labor is in short supply, wet cultivation accounts for about 93 per cent of the rice area harvested.

Nonstaple food crops are referred to in Java as *polowidjo*, which indicates that they are subsidiary or secondary to rice. Over the last century secondary crops have come to play an important role in Java both as a part of the daily fare and as a source of cash. The major secondary crops are maize, cassava, sweet potatoes, taro, peanuts, soybeans, red (chili) pepper, and onions. Some of these are raised in tegalan the year round, others in sawah during the dry season. A failure of the secondary crops is fully as serious as is a poor rice crop, since they provide cash for the purchase of the daily food when the old rice crop has been consumed and the new one is still weeks away.

A further source of produce is the pekarangan which surrounds each house in the villages of Java and many homes in the towns. These gardens are carefully tended, well watered, and densely planted with a great variety of trees, bushes, and small plants. They are highly productive, and their leafy vegetables, pods, tubers, and fruits contribute greatly to the diet as sources of protein and vitamins A and C. Moreover, since there is always something to be harvested from the pekarangan, they provide a year-round source of cash.[11] Outside Java, pekarangan are best developed on Madura, Bali, and Lombok; they play a minor role elsewhere and are lacking completely in areas where swidden cultivation prevails.

According to surveys undertaken in 1957, 78 per cent of sawah owners in Java had less than 0.5 hectare and 90 per cent less than one hectare (see Table 4). Prewar village surveys have shown that many of the peasants who owned only tiny holdings were heavily indebted; they retained only a small share of the yield, the larger part going to moneylenders. At present the extent of rural indebtedness is unknown, since there are no official records; but it is clear that moneylenders exercise *de facto* control over a large share of the land by virtue of unrecorded agreements; thus peasants who appear to be independent and in control of their land are in reality sharecroppers. Peasants who depend upon the goodwill of their creditors are usually reluctant to volunteer information about their indebtedness for fear they will create difficulties for themselves if they speak frankly—especially if they have borrowed from one of the village officials. The moneylender-landlords, for their part, will not volunteer information, in order to avoid taxes. As a result, village records showing ownership of land do not reflect the true socioeconomic conditions in the rural areas.

According to investigations[12] conducted in a village of West Java by rural sociologists of the Agricultural College at Bogor, no less than 44 per cent of the heads of households engaged in agriculture had no land of their own; another 25 per cent owned only a piece of compound land in the village, and 23 per cent had less than one hectare of tegalan—not enough to provide a living. Thus no less than 92 per cent of the families in the village were compelled to work full or part time as tenant farmers or agricultural laborers. Of the 8 per cent that were independent, 6 owned from 1 to 5

Table 4. NUMBER OF SAWAH OWNERS IN JAVA, CLASSIFIED
ACCORDING TO AMOUNT OF SAWAH OWNED

Region	Less than 0.5 ha.	0.6 to 1.0 ha.	1.1 to 2 ha.	2.1 to 5 ha.	5.1 to 10 ha.	10.1 to 20 ha.	Over 20 ha.	Total
West Java	1,908,821	304,079	198,663	92,785	11,993	2,268	756	2,519,365
Central Java	2,956,974	376,875	187,844	70,227	6,373	754	137	3,599,184
East Java	2,278,143	393,332	237,814	111,394	13,968	1,748	421	3,036,820
Total	7,143,938	1,074,286	624,321	274,406	32,334	4,770	1,314	9,155,369
Per cent	78.03	11.74	6.82	3.00	0.35	0.05	0.01	100

SOURCE: Speech given by Deputy Minister for Agrarian Affairs before Supreme Consultative Council on January 13, 1960, U. S. Joint Publications Research Service, JPRS 5249, p. 7 (also available on Micro Card 17409, Nov. 1960).

hectares of land and 2 held more than 5 hectares. The leading families—i.e. those who owned more than five hectares—held about half the land in the village. For six months of the year they employed the landless to raise potatoes and cabbage on their tegalan; for the other half of the year these farmhands became sharecroppers, growing dry rice and maize on the same land. Similarly, a study of the *kabupaten* of Malang (East Java) showed that 16 per cent of all heads of households were completely landless, 64 per cent had insufficient land to support their families, and only 20 per cent had enough to be independent.[13]

Social stratification in Javanese villages shows a correlation with the amount and kind of land owned. Villagers who hold both sawah and pekarangan—with a house on the latter—have a higher standing than do those who lack sawah but own some tegalan land and a pekarangan with a house. Below this group come those who have only a house plot in the village, and they in turn rank higher than villagers whose houses stand on someone else's pekarangan. The lowest group of all consists of those who possess neither land nor house but live as boarders in another person's home. The numerical proportion of these groups in a given village is an excellent indicator of the local population pressure on the land.

The great shortage of land in Java has given rise to a considerable degree of rural underemployment; living standards in the crowded villages are very low, and radical peasant associations have won considerable support there. Similar characteristics can be observed in many of the sawah districts of the Outer Islands, particularly in North Tapanuli, South Sumatra, and Lombok. By contrast, the peasants of the swidden regions, especially those who own stands of commercial export crops, generally enjoy a higher income; what is most important, they still have room to expand the cultivated area in step with population growth.

Since sharecropping is so widespread a phenomenon on the Indonesian agrarian scene, the Sharecropping Law (No. 2/1960) promises to affect a very large percentage of the peasantry.[14] Its stated aims are to bring justice into the landlord-sharecropper relationship, to protect the weak sharecropper against the strong landowner, and to provide the sharecropper with adequate incentives for increasing production. The law authorizes the heads of the second-level autonomous regions to fix the ratio by which the yield is to be divided; a nationwide minimum portion for sharecroppers has been set, however, at one-half the yield on sawah and two-thirds on tegalan. All sharecropping agreements between land-owner and tenant must be registered; they may not involve more than three hectares per sharecropper and must be valid for at least three years for irrigated land or five years for unirrigated land. Agreements between moneylenders and peasant debtors must, according to the law, be concluded at the office of the village administration.

The Basic Agrarian Law (No. 5/1960) is also of great significance, for it replaces the previous colonial land laws and provides a keystone for future agrarian legislation. Whereas Netherlands Indies laws had considered final ownership of land to rest with the state, the new legislation is based on the concept of private property. Individual hereditary right of ownership (*hak milik*), the basic land right recognized by the law, may be held only by Indonesian citizens. It is not absolute, since the state may regulate the use of land under its authority to administrate the country's natural resources in the national interest. The new act also recognizes *hak ulajat*, or the right of adat communities to dispose of land and other resources not yet encumbered by hak milik; the state, however, reserves the power to override this right in carrying out development projects of national interest.

In order to assure hak milik to as many peasants as possible, the Basic Agrarian Law limits the amount of land which an individual may own under this right and forbids absentee ownership. The limits on such holdings have been determined according to population density, with a uniform minimum for subdivision of two hectares.[15] The stated purpose of this minimum limit is to ensure sufficient income to the Indonesian peasant and to prevent excessive fragmentation of holdings. Land in excess of the permissible maxima has been registered and is being taken over by the state for distribution among the landless rural population. Land reform committees have been established throughout Indonesia down to the third regional level (*kawedanaan*) to oversee this process; the fixing of the amount of indemnification to be paid the owners is left to the committees of the second (*kabupaten*) level. Whatever the specific amount, 10 per cent is to be paid into savings accounts in the local bank for cooperatives, farmers, and fishermen, while the remaining 90 per cent is to be issued in land reform bonds bearing a 3 per cent interest rate and redeemable in twelve years. Those who benefit from the program must pay for the land they receive within fifteen years, during which period they must be members of a peasant cooperative.

Since the land reform program is still in its early stages, it is not possible to evaluate its success. The Ministry of Agrarian Affairs estimated that as a result of the various land reform provisions about a million hectares would become available for redistribution.[16] While this would certainly give relief to many peasants, it cannot provide them all with the two hectares envisioned as the nationwide minimum holding; indeed, no land reform program could accomplish this, for in Java there is simply not enough land to go around. The fact of the matter is that the problem cannot be solved by a redistribution of the land, but only by a redistribution of the population or by the creation of employment outside the agrarian sector —either of which would have to be accomplished on a truly massive scale.

One of the consequences of the rural overcrowding caused by population growth is that food production has not kept pace with the steady increase in spite of very intensive land use. Because of the lack of statistical data on peasant food crops in the Outer Islands prior to World War II it is not possible to compare prewar with postindependence food production for the country as a whole; but it is safe to assume that output in the latter period, while higher than that of colonial times, has declined relative to the total population. In Java, the chief area of overcrowding, production in 1960 was only slightly above the level reached in 1940, and the per capita supply of major foodstuffs—production minus seed—declined markedly (see Tables 5 and 6). The low nutritional level resulting from the insufficiency of food production has concerned authorities ever since the beginning of the century. At present, the average Indonesian consumes only 2,125 calories a day (see Table 7), whereas the United Nations' Food and Agriculture Organization regards 2,300 calories as the desirable level.[17]

To help close the increasing gap between production and dietary need, Indonesia must import large quantities of rice and wheat flour, as well as protein foods and powdered and canned milk. In 1959 rice imports amounted to 603,000 metric tons, or 11.5 per cent of the value of all imports, as compared to an average of 240,000 tons (3.6 per cent of total import value) in 1938-40. Wheat flour imports averaged 132,000 metric tons in the 1955-59 period, compared with an average of 94,000 tons in 1938-40. Since Indonesia desperately needs its foreign earnings for capital goods and other non-agricultural essentials, it can ill afford its present purchases, much less an increase in the amount and range of its food imports. The government has therefore bent its efforts to raising domestic supplies, concentrating on the chief staple, rice. In 1958 it prepared a Three-Year Rice Production Plan, which aimed at achieving a production of 100 kilograms of rice per person a year—which, together with the equivalent of 60 kilograms of rice in the form of maize, cassava, sweet potatoes and other tubers, would bring Indonesia's per capita supply to a level deemed adequate by nutritionists.

The Three-Year Plan consisted of a short-range program for the intensification of production on land already under the plow in Java and the Outer Islands and a long-range program of extension

Table 5. PRODUCTION OF MAJOR PEASANT FOOD CROPS
IN INDONESIA, 1940, 1952-62

(1,000 metric tons)

Crop [a]	1940	1952	1954	1956	1958	1960	1961	1962 [b]
Rice (milled) [a]								
Java and Madura	4,664	4,160	4,817	4,756	4,963	5,022		
Outer Islands	n.a.	2,416	3,015	2,846	3,016	3,518		
Indonesia	n.a.	6,576	7,832	7,602	7,979	8,540	8,350	9,200
Maize (shelled)								
Java and Madura	1,900	1,204	2,153	1,431	2,012	1,779		
Outer Islands	n.a.	434	567	533	622	707		
Indonesia	n.a.	1,638	2,720	1,964	2,634	2,486	2,298	2,300
Cassava (fresh)								
Java and Madura	8,415	5,087	6,430	6,420	8,100	8,624		
Outer Islands	n.a.	2,448	3,139	2,710	3,178	2,518		
Indonesia	n.a.	7,535	9,569	9,130	11,278	11,142	12,106	12,000
Sweet potatoes (fresh)								
Java and Madura	1,418	1,260	1,063	1,502	1,750	1,394		
Outer Islands	n.a.	1,031	1,048	1,136	1,353	1,315		
Indonesia	n.a.	2,291	2,111	2,638	3,102	2,709	2,525	2,600
Peanuts (shelled)								
Java and Madura	196	127	204	178	191	211		
Outer Islands	n.a.	40	43	40	40	41		
Indonesia	n.a.	167	247	218	231	252	247	245
Soybeans (shelled)								
Java and Madura	294	266	362	310	380	388		
Outer Islands	n.a.	20	38	46	38	49		
Indonesia	n.a.	286	400	356	418	437	426	430

(a) Converted from dry stalk paddy to milled rice at ratio 100:52.
(b) Preliminary estimates.

SOURCE: For 1940 to 1960, *Statistical Pocketbook of Indonesia 1961*, pp. 52-53; for 1961 and 1962, *The 1963 Far East, Communist China, Oceania Agricultural Situation*, Economic Research Service, U. S. Department of Agriculture (Washington, March 1963), p. 43.

Table 6. PRINCIPAL FOODSTUFFS AVAILABLE PER CAPITA: PRODUCTION MINUS SEED

(*kilograms*)

Year	CEREALS			ROOT CROPS			Total Rice Equiv. of Cereals/Roots	PULSES		
	Rice	Maize	Total Cereals	Cassava	Sweet potatoes	Total Roots		Peanuts	Soybeans	Total Pulses
Java and Madura										
1936–40	89.0	42.2	131.2	171.3	27.4	198.7	209.1	3.6	5.6	9.2
1956	84.8	25.4	110.2	117.4	27.5	144.9	166.5	2.8	5.3	8.1
1957	83.0	22.9	105.9	128.9	28.7	157.6	167.1	3.0	5.0	8.0
1958	85.1	34.4	119.5	142.2	30.7	172.9	176.2	2.9	6.2	9.1
1959	84.3	24.5	108.8	155.0	25.4	180.4	178.9	2.9	6.0	8.9
1960	81.4	28.7	110.1	143.0	23.1	166.1	175.0	3.0	5.9	8.9
Indonesia										
1956	88.9	22.8	111.7	109.4	31.6	141.0	166.3	2.3	4.0	6.3
1957	87.1	21.2	108.3	118.5	31.1	149.6	166.1	2.4	3.7	6.1
1958	88.8	29.2	118.0	128.5	35.3	163.8	181.6	2.3	4.4	6.7
1959	89.7	22.5	112.2	140.6	31.9	172.5	179.0	2.5	4.4	6.9
1960	89.9	26.1	116.0	120.1	29.2	149.3	174.2	2.4	4.4	6.8

SOURCE: *Statistical Pocketbook of Indonesia 1961*, p. 215.

Supply — Utilization

Product	Production 1,000 m. tons	Imports 1,000 m. tons	Exports 1,000 m. tons	Changes in stocks 1,000 m. tons	Total supply 1,000 m. tons	Seed and waste 1,000 m. tons	Industrial 1,000 m. tons	Total (nonfood) 1,000 m. tons	Total gross 1,000 m. tons	Extraction rate per cent	Total (food) 1,000 m. tons	Net per capita — Per year kilograms	Net per capita — Per day calories
Rice	7,554	681	..	..	8,235	340	..	340	7,895	..	7,895	90.4	890
Wheat(b)	..	137	..	..	137	..	..	..	137	72	99	1.1	10
Corn	2,618	..	..	..	2,618	54	..	54	2,564	..	2,564	29.4	285
Total grain	10,172	818	..	..	10,990	394	..	394	10,596	..	10,558	120.9	1,185
Sugar:													
Centrifugal(e)	775	2	87	−21	711	..	..	..	711	..	711	8.1	85
Other(d)	289	..	..	..	289	..	..	..	289	..	289	3.3	30
Potatoes(e)	2,893	..	..	..	2,893	..	..	..	2,893	..	2,893	33.1	90
Cassava	10,972	..	21	..	10,951	550	660	1,210	9,741	18	1,753(a)	20.1	185
Soybeans	422	..	1	..	421	29	..	29	392	..	392	4.5	40
Peanuts(g)	229	..	3	..	226	27	..	27	199	..	199	2.3	35
Other pulses(h)	460	..	..	..	460	..	..	..	460	..	460	5.3	50
Other vegetables	11,540	1	18	..	11,523	1,154	..	1,154	10,369	..	10,369	118.8	70
Coconuts(i)	2,446	..	..	..	2,446	..	1,810(l)	1,810	636	..	636	7.3	70
Other fruits(j)	9,000	7	1	..	9,006	..	..	..	9,006	..	9,006	103.2	115
Meat(k)	205	..	4	..	201	..	..	..	201	..	201	2.3	15
Fish(l)	705	53	1	..	757	..	..	..	757	..	757	8.7	15
Coconut oil	474	..	1	..	474	..	..	..	474	..	474	5.4	130
Other veg. oils	164	..	148	−2	18	..	18	18	..	..	..	..	..
Total fats:													
As product	638	..	148	−2	492	..	18	18	474	..	474	5.4	..
Fat content	638	..	148	−2	492	..	18	18	474	..	474	5.4	130
Whole milk(m)	29	15	..	..	44	..	..	..	44	..	44	.5	(n)
Eggs	200	..	..	..	200	..	..	..	200	..	200	2.3	10
Total consumption													2,125

(a) Excludes alcoholic beverages.
(b) Wheat equivalent of wheat flour.
(c) Noncentrifugal.
(d) White and sweet.
(e) Raw.
(f) Dry weight.
(g) Shelled basis.
(h) Edible only.

(i) Coconuts used in making copra and coconut oil for domestic use or export. Includes tree nuts other than coconuts.
(j) In terms of fresh.
(k) Carcass weight. Production includes meat from animals slaughtered within the country, whether homebred or imported. Trade excludes meat from exported as well as imported animals.
(l) Landed weight.
(m) Trade and consumption includes the whole milk equivalent of canned and dried milk, if any.
(n) Less than 3 calories.

SOURCE: U. S. Department of Agriculture, *Food Balances in Foreign Countries: Part II. Estimates for 12 Countries in the Far East*, Foreign Agricultural Service, FAS-M-101 (Washington, 1960), p. 6.

of the area under cultivation in the less populous parts of the country. Implementation of the short-range program centered on the establishment of paddy centers, which were to aid the peasants by providing them with improved seeds, fertilizer, and cash credit (see Table 8). The peasants who received this aid were expected to repay the centers in cash or in kind from their increased yield.[18] It was calculated on the basis of a pilot project that by 1961-62 production would rise on the average by 8 quintals of paddy (4 quintals of milled rice), producing an additional 1,200,000 metric tons of milled rice. The plan foresaw Indonesian self-sufficiency in rice by the end of 1962,[19] but by the end of 1961 it was clear that this estimate had been unrealistic. Instead of the expected surplus of 390,000 tons of rice from the 1962 harvests, it is safe to assume a deficit of at least 1,000,000 tons for that year (see Table 8).

An important task assigned to the paddy centers was the collection of rice needed by the government for distribution to the armed forces, government employees, and estate laborers as well as for injection into the market in order to keep down its price to the consumer. As long as the difference between the government-controlled and free-market prices of rice was relatively small, the state was able to obtain a high percentage of its requirements (see Table 9). However, in 1960 prices began to soar on the free market, and the government was forced to offer the peasants one and a half meters of textiles at controlled prices in return for every half quintal of paddy in order to provide them with adequate incentive to deliver the rice quota. In 1961 free market prices of rice in Djakarta rose from Rp. 6.62 to Rp. 48.75; this increase, the product in part of serious drought, continued into 1962 and caused the government to fail in realizing its collection program.

It remains to be seen whether the paddy centers can play the role that is expected from them. On the one hand, average yields in Indonesia are very low, and it should be possible to increase them substantially by the use of better seeds, sufficient quantities of commercial fertilizers and pesticides, improvement of drainage and irrigation systems, and better preparation of the land. All of these remedies require sizable investments which the poverty-stricken peasants cannot afford. The aid provided by the paddy centers, if well administered and on a sufficiently large scale, should therefore do much to increase yields. So far, however, the centers have been handicapped by a lack of trained personnel, seed, and fertilizer. Moreover, the program requires the peasants to take the

TABLE 8. SUMMARY OF THREE-YEAR RICE PRODUCTION PLAN

Category	Unit	1959-60	1960-61	1961-62
Population[a]	1,000 persons	90,330	91,956	93,611
Rice requirements (at rate of 100 kg. per capita [year])	1,000 metric tons	9,033	9,195	9,361
Paddy Centers				
Number of centers		42	125	500
Area to be affected	1,000 ha.	100	500	3,000
Improved seed requirements	ton	5,000	25,000	150,000
Fertilizer requirement	ton	10,000	50,000	300,000
Paddy to be collected in settlement of credits: 6 quintals of stalk paddy/ha.	ton	60,000	300,000	1,800,000
Mass Intensification				
Area to be covered	1,000 ha.	303	1,240	2,000
Improved seed requirements	ton	3,200	60,000	100,000
Fertilizer requirement	ton	30,300	124,000	75,000
Insecticide requirements				
Phosphorus, sulphur, aldrin	ton	530	730	750
Endrin	liter	56,250	112,500	112,500
Agricultural tools required				
Mattocks	each	200,000	250,000	550,000
High pressure pumps	each	1,500	1,500	400
Water pumps	each	200	500	1,000
Rice Production Target	1,000 tons	8,780.4	9,061	10,050
Difference between rice requirement and production[b]	1,000 tons	−516	−406	+387

(a) Census of October 1961 showed that Indonesia's population came close to 97 million rather than the 92 million estimated by planners.

(b) Three per cent allowed for waste.

SOURCE: Planning Office, Department of Agriculture, *Three Year Rice Production Plan* (Djakarta, January 1, 1960).

risks without assuring them a price which is in line with the cost of living; they therefore have little incentive to increase rice production for sale on the government-controlled market. At best, it appears inevitable that rice imports will have to be continued for at least another two or three years; and it may require the completion of some of the long-range programs for irrigation, swamp drainage, and fertilizer plant construction before self-sufficiency can be achieved.

Agricultural exports play a critical role in the Indonesian economy, for they provide approximately two-thirds of all foreign exchange earned. Production is divided between large-scale plantation enterprises and small peasant holdings. The area controlled by plantations has always been small relative to the economic importance of the estate sector: approximately 4.7 per cent of Java and 1 per cent of the Outer Islands (excluding West New Guinea) are devoted to this form of agriculture. Not even all of this limited area is under production, however. In 1958 only 828,000 of the 1,800,000 estate-controlled hectares were actually planted with cash crops, the rest being either occupied by squatters, in fallow, or still under forest cover. Estates are highly concentrated in the residency of East Sumatra, which accounts at minimum for about 53 per cent

Table 9.   PADDY PURCHASED BY THE GOVERNMENT
IN JAVA, 1952-62

(metric tons of dry paddy in stalk)

Crop year	Quota	Purchased	Percentage collected
1952-53	800,000	495,724	62.0
1953-54	800,500	749,178	93.6
1954-55	994,000	791,743	79.6
1955-56	1,200,000	593,484	49.4
1956-57	800,000	514,006	64.2
1957-58	800,000	692,683	83.9
1958-59	900,000	324,687	36.0
1959-60	900,000	536,583	59.6
1960-61	1,000,000	544,804	54.4
1961-62	1,000,000	517,250	51.7
1962-63	1,400,000	....	......

SOURCE: 1952-53 to 1956-57, Leon A. Mears, *Rice Marketing*, p. 162; 1956-57, Mears, *Rice Marketing*, Supplement, Table A-13a; 1958-59 to 1961-62, data obtained by correspondence with Biro Pusat Statistik.

of the plantation area and 46 per cent of the land in production. This heavy concentration has given the region a vital importance in the Indonesian economy and at the same time has made it a center of conflict between peasant and planter interests.[20]

The oldest plantations in Indonesia, which were largely concentrated in the principalities of Central Java, date back to the early part of the nineteenth century. Between 1830 and 1870 estate agriculture received little or no encouragement from the colonial authorities, however. During this period the government relied on the compulsory production of export crops by the Javanese peasantry—the so-called Cultivation System, which is described further in the chapter on history. The Agrarian Law of 1870 provided for the gradual abolition of this system and opened the doors to plantation development in both Java and the Outer Islands. The planters were required, however, to lease the land on which they operated; unlike estate enterprises in most other parts of the world, those in Indonesia could not own land outright. Private ownership of land was restricted to ethnic Indonesians, and so no pattern of large land holdings by foreigners or Indonesians of foreign descent was established.

The only exception to this rule was a type of tenure, found mainly in West Java, which dated back to the period of the East India Company and the incumbencies of Governors-General Daendels and Raffles at the beginning of the nineteenth century. In order to raise ready cash the Company, and later the state, sold about 1.5 million hectares of land to private persons; and the owners of these "private estates" (*particuliere landerijen*) exercised seignoral rights over land normally held by the government.[21] Since the treatment of Indonesians living on these proprietary lands was all too often harsh and oppressive, the villagers in these areas frequently resorted to violence during the nineteenth century. In 1911 the Netherlands Indies government began the gradual repurchase of such lands,[22] but it was not until the passing of the Law on the Abolition of Private Estates in January 1958 that they completely disappeared.

With this exception, plantations have operated in Indonesia under one of two types of leasehold. In Java, sugar and tobacco planters rented land from Indonesian villagers, being permitted to use in any one period only one-third of a village's sawah area for the raising of estate crops. After the harvest the land had to be exchanged against another third, this system of rotation being designed above all to prevent planters from gaining a permanent hold on village lands. Contracts were usually closed with the village heads rather than with individual peasants, thus strengthening traditional tendencies toward communal landholding; in the periodic reapportionment of plots to individual cultivators, the village heads assigned each claimant a parcel in each of the three sections into which the village sawah area had been divided in order to make possible rotational leasing by an estate. This type of lease could be concluded, in the case of a sugar plantation, either for a single occupation of sixteen months or for several occupations extending over a maximum of twenty-one and a half years.

The interests of planters and peasants interlocked under leaseholds of this kind; but since the planters were much stronger financially and organizationally than their peasant partners, the authorities developed a complicated set of regulations designed to protect the latter against abuses. Even so, the equity of the peasant-planter relationship was a subject of considerable controversy; it continues to be one even today, although the sugar and tobacco estates have since been transferred to public control by the Indonesian government.

Since perennial tree crops do not permit an interlocking of peasant and plantation agriculture, all other estates—tea, coffee, cinchona, rubber, and oil and coconut palm—have leased land under the second system of tenure. By the Agrarian Law of 1870, all land to which no Indonesian could prove ownership or use was deemed to be public domain; it could therefore be applied for by non-Indonesians—in particular planters and plantation enterprises—for lease under a 75-year contract (*erfpacht*), which allowed for the mortgaging and inheriting of the land. This system was first applied especially to Java and Madura. In the indirectly governed parts of the outer territories, and especially in East Sumatra, plantation interests were able to obtain land from the local Indonesian rulers in the form of 75-year agricultural concessions; these were rather more favorable to the planters than the long leases of the directly governed regions in that they did not give clear precedence to peasant claims on the land.[23]

In 1957 only a small portion of estate lands belonged to government-owned and -operated plantations. The seizure of Dutch enterprises in Indonesia began at the end of that year, however, and in 1959 all Netherlands-owned concerns were nationalized, bringing some 542 plantations—held either as agricultural concessions or as long leases—under public administration.[24]

Table 10 classifies plantations according to the type of tenure rights they held just prior to 1960. In that year the Basic Agrarian Law abolished the regulations which had governed estate holdings since 1870. Agricultural concessions and long leases were replaced by *hak guna-usaha*—right of exploitation—which can be held by Indonesian citizens or by corporate bodies established according to Indonesian law, domiciled in the country, and having made application for the conversion of their previous rights to hak guna-usaha by September 24, 1961. Exploitation rights obtained by foreign companies as a result of the conversion of previous rights are valid only for the remaining time of the original tenure and in any case for not more than twenty years.[25] Land newly given out under hak guna-usaha may be held for twenty-five years, and this limit may be extended in cases where the crop planted requires several years before it begins to produce. Land held under hak guna-usaha may be inherited or otherwise transferred, and it may be mortgaged.

Since by the time the Basic Agrarian Law was passed all Dutch-owned plantations had been nationalized and were under PPN (Pusat Perkebunan Negara, or Government Estates Administration) management, the legislation mainly affected American, British, Belgian, and French concerns. Although most foreign companies applied for conversion of their agrarian rights to hak guna-usaha by September 1961, in late 1962 it is not yet known how much land has been returned to the government. The long-range future of foreign-owned plantations, however, is still uncertain, although the Indonesian government does not rule out further extension of the exploitation rights beyond the date of the current contracts. For years the authorities have insisted on the gradual replacement of foreign personnel by Indonesians and have accelerated this process by issuing entry and work permits to foreign employees sparingly. While this policy's aim of opening upper-level positions to Indonesian nationals is certainly justifiable, it has the unfortunate short-run effect of spreading still thinner the already scarce managerial, scientific, and technical skills available to the industry. The state-run enterprises are particularly ill-equipped in this respect, and unless they can be provided with competent staff, together with adequate funds, sufficient disciplined labor, and opportunities for expanding and replanting their crop areas, a further weakening of the plantation sector seems inevitable.[26]

Table 10. LAND HELD BY PLANTATIONS AND LAND IN USE CLASSIFIED ACCORDING TO TENURE, 1959, AND TOTALS FOR 1958 AND 1938

(1,000 hectares)

Territory	Agricultural concessions		Long leases		Private estates		State-owned		Leased from villages		Leased from principality		Total	
	Held	In use	Held	In use	Held	In use	Held	In use	Held	In use	Held	In use	Held	In use
West Java	..	..	248.7	142.8	67.9	26.2	18.1	11.9	5.5	5.1	..	..	340.2	186.0
Central Java	..	..	37.2	29.5	2.5	0.8	10.9	9.8	18.2	16.5	8.2	4.1	77.0	60.7
East Java	..	..	172.3	93.0	0.6	0.2	1.9	1.6	35.3	33.4	..	..	210.1	128.2
Java and Madura	..	..	458.2	265.3	71.0	27.2	30.9	23.3	59.0	55.0	8.2	4.1	627.3	374.9
North Sumatra	729.5	337.3	99.8	42.1	..	..	50.7	5.9	..	..	..	..	880.0	385.3
Central Sumatra	29.4	8.7	14.9	4.8	..	..	..	..	..	..	..	..	44.3	13.5
South Sumatra	..	..	90.1	32.0	..	..	..	..	..	..	..	..	90.1	32.0
Sumatra	758.9	346.0	204.8	78.9	..	..	50.7	5.9	..	..	..	..	1,014.4	430.8
Borneo	16.6	2.8	17.8	8.3	..	..	..	..	..	..	..	..	34.4	11.1
Celebes	2.2	1.2	4.1	3.2	..	..	..	..	..	..	..	..	6.3	4.4
Moluccas	..	..	6.8	5.1	..	..	..	..	..	..	..	..	6.8	5.1
Lesser Sunda	7.8	0.7	3.4	1.7	..	..	..	..	..	..	..	..	11.2	2.4
Indonesia 1959	785.5	350.7	695.1	362.5	71.0	27.2	81.6	29.2	59.0	55.0	8.2	4.1	1,700.4	827.7
Indonesia 1958	905.0	351.6	721.4	367.7	72.9	27.8	39.8	24.1	56.0	51.6	8.2	4.1	1,803.3	826.9
Indonesia 1938	941.3	410.1	1,011.0	543.6	340.2	45.8	31.2	25.8	101.8	100.4	59.6	45.2	2,485.1	1,170.9

SOURCE: Statistical Pocketbook of Indonesia 1961, p. 62-65.

Of the forty-odd commercial export crops grown in Indonesia, only eight—rubber, copra, sugar, palm oil, tobacco, hard fiber, coffee, and tea—are of major importance (see Table 11). In terms of quantity, agricultural exports reached their peak in 1928 with over five million metric tons but declined markedly after that year. Both the plantation and the smallholder sector share in this trend, with the important difference that by 1960 the volume of plantation exports had shrunk to a mere 17 per cent of that of 1928, while the volume of smallholder exports had only declined to 56 per cent of the 1928 level (see Table 12). Furthermore, while in 1928 the plantations accounted for 67 per cent and smallholders for 33 per cent of all agricultural exports, by 1960 the roles were almost reversed: smallholders furnished 62 per cent and plantations only 38 per cent. Except for rubber, all agricultural exports have fallen in volume (see Tables 11 and 13); none, however, has declined so heavily as has sugar.

Sugar was king among Indonesia's plantation crops during the first three decades of this century; and since the sugar plantations are located in Java, that island in 1928 contributed more than half the value of all agricultural exports. In 1928 the industry reached its apogee; since then, except for a brief recovery in the late 1930s, it has been on the downgrade. During the depression of the 1930s the number of sugar mills in Java declined from 180 to 94, only 84 of which were in operation in 1939. Sugar production was curtailed by more than 50 per cent during World War II, and the land no longer needed for sugar cane was used for the growing of rice and other food crops. During the struggle for independence about half the sugar mills were destroyed as part of the Indonesian scorched earth policy; some of them have since been repaired, and at present Java has 54 operating sugar mills. In the postrevolutionary period the sugar planters found themselves confronted both by a national government determined to wipe out the "colonial" aspects of the peasant-planter relationship[27] and by a peasant population well aware that the loss of two rainy-season crops and one dry-season crop was not adequately compensated for by the rental offered them. In 1958, following the seizure of all Dutch-owned enterprises in Indonesia, the administration of the sugar estates passed to PPN—the agency in charge of state-run plantations —and since then the sugar industry has been in public hands.

Despite the concentrated efforts of management in the postrevolutionary period, sugar production has not reached a level higher than

Table 11. PROPORTIONAL SHARES OF THE PRINCIPAL PRODUCTS IN THE VALUE OF EXPORTS

Year	Centrifugal sugar	Rubber	Copra	Palm oil	Leaf tobacco	Hard fiber	Coffee	Tea	Pepper	Cinchona	Tapioca	Total of these eleven products	Petroleum and petroleum products	Tin	All other
1928	23.8	17.6	6.8		6.1			6.2				60.5	9.1	5.6	24.8
1938	6.5	22.6	5.6	2.4	5.6	1.3	2.0	8.2	1.2	1.2	1.3	57.9	23.5	4.8	13.8
1940	5.5	39.2	1.3	1.0	4.1	1.1	0.8	5.2	0.4	0.9	1.4	60.9	18.1	8.7	12.3
1950	..	42.8	7.2	3.4	5.1	0.3	1.9	3.4	2.7	0.2	0.4	67.4	18.4	6.1	8.1
1952	..	45.4	5.5	2.8	2.4	1.1	1.9	2.5	2.0	0.2	..	63.8	20.5	9.2	6.5
1954	2.1	31.3	5.9	3.1	3.9	0.5	4.6	4.6	1.5	..	0.6	58.1	26.2	7.1	8.6
1956	1.9	39.0	4.2	3.0	3.1	0.7	3.2	3.2	1.0	..	0.1	59.4	27.6	6.9	6.1
1958	0.9	33.1	2.3	3.0	3.7	0.5	2.3	3.1	0.6	0.1	0.1	49.7	39.9	4.5	5.9
1959	0.3	45.0	3.0	2.1	2.6	0.3	2.0	2.2	1.4	0.1	0.4	59.4	30.7	4.0	5.9
1960	0.3	44.9	3.4	2.4	3.4	0.4	1.6	3.3	1.2	0.0	0.4	61.3	26.3	6.5	5.9

SOURCE: 1928, *Bank Indonesia Report for the Year 1953-54*, p. 84; 1938, 1940, 1950, 1952, 1954, *Statistical Pocketbook of Indonesia 1957*, p. 135; 1956, 1958, 1959, 1960, ibid, 1961, p. 144.

Table 12. GROSS WEIGHT OF PLANTATION AND SMALLHOLDER EXPORT PRODUCTS

(1,000 metric tons)

Year	Plantation products	Per cent of 1928 (1928=100)	Smallholder products	Per cent of 1928 (1928=100)	Total	Per cent of 1928 (1928=100)
1928	3,429.0	100.0	1,711.0	100.0	5,140.0	100.0
1938	2,157.3	62.9	1,290.0	75.4	3,447.3	67.1
1940	1,924.0	56.1	1,021.0	59.6	2,945.0	57.3
1955	828.9	24.2	1,192.2	69.6	2,021.1	39.3
1958	661.5	19.3	778.3	45.5	1,439.8	28.2
1959	645.3	18.8	1,058.0	61.8	1,703.3	33.1
1960	589.7	17.2	952.1	55.6	1,541.8	30.0

SOURCE: 1928, *The Export Crops of the Netherlands Indies in 1938*, p. 13; 1938-60, *Statistical Pocketbook of Indonesia 1961*, p. 115.

Table 13. VOLUME OF EXPORTS OF SELECTED AGRICULTURAL COMMODITIES

(1,000 metric tons)

Year	Centrifugal sugar	Rubber	Copra	Palm oil	Tobacco leaf	Hard fiber	Coffee	Tea	Pepper	Cinchona	All cassava products
1928	2,565	234	496	35	....	50	113	70	24	10	....
1936	880	315	508	172	48	77	95	70	78	9	285
1938	1,071	303	557	221	48	88	69	72	55	7	247
1940	804	545	256	178	27	93	40	72	32	7	226
1952	1	754	346	125	10	28	18	32	7	3	1
1954	212	723	298	147	18	24	37	40	13	1	143
1956	175	660	264	133	11	34	57	35	19	2	18
1958	88	577	126	131	21	28	28	35	12	4	21
1960	35	556	166	109	22	16	41	35	12	2	104

SOURCE: 1928, *The Export Crops of the Netherlands Indies in 1938*, pp. 23-24; 1936, 1952, *Statistical Pocketbook of Indonesia 1957*; 1938, 1940, 1956, 1958, 1960, ibid. 1961, pp. 127-39; 1954, ibid. 1958.

two-thirds that of 1938. The area under cane for milling in sugar factories climbed slowly to a peak of 55,000 hectares in 1960—as against 85,500 in 1938—but the yields of cane per hectare declined seriously, falling from 164 quintals of raw sugar per hectare to 104 quintals in the same period.[28] At the same time, relatively low sugar prices caused per capita annual sugar consumption to increase; and this, coupled with the absolute increase in population and continuing low production, brought about a drastic curtailment of exports in 1958-60. In 1961 shipments abroad were completely halted, although the International Sugar Agreement allowed for an export of 350,000 tons. In this manner Indonesia, thirty years ago one of the world's leading suppliers, has, at least temporarily, disappeared from the roster of sugar-exporting countries. As a matter of fact, the country at present has a shortage of sugar for domestic consumption, especially in the Outer Islands: in May 1962 the black market price of that commodity in Medan was reported to be Rp. 250 per kilogram. This circumstance has contributed to a rise in the production of types of sugar which are not processed by mills and therefore are not subject to government-set prices, such as non-centrifugal "cup" sugar and sugar made from the sap of the aren, lontar, and coconut palms.

The government has tried to increase sugar production in order to satisfy domestic needs and provide foreign exchange. Some of the factors contributing to the current depressed state of the industry are material or technical ones—poor seed cane, deteriorated irrigation systems, lack of fertilizer, poor cultivation and harvesting methods, and lack of labor, managerial, and scientific personnel. In addition, production is adversely affected by a conflict between peasant interests and government policy. The state wishes to keep sugar prices low as an anti-inflationary measure and in order to compete on the world market. To create adequate incentives by subsidy would be extremely expensive, particularly in view of the fact that recent rapid rises in food prices have made it increasingly profitable for the peasants to use their land for other crops. The government has therefore resorted to systems of "compulsory deliveries" and "compulsory surrender" of land for artificially low remuneration, which the student of Indonesian economic history will recognize as repetitions of eighteenth- and early nineteenth-century colonial policies. The land rentals paid by PPN are so low that the villagers have every incentive not to lease their land to the agency;

when pressed, they try to make available only poor land, and that as late as possible in the planting season.

The Land Use Law (No. 38/1960) enables the state to compel peasants to forego the better financial returns which would result from planting "nonvital" crops such as onions or tobacco in the interest of "nationally vital" produce such as sugar cane. In 1961 it was ruled that peasants living in sugar districts were obliged to sell cane, which they raised for their own account, to the local sugar mill for the most unprofitable price of Rp. 25 per quintal.[29] In January 1962 the government issued a decree specifying the hectarage of sawah that must be planted with cane for delivery to the mills.[30] Should this regulation be completely implemented, the sugar cane area of 1962-63 would exceed that of the immediate prewar period. At the same time, however, the government has shown a certain ambivalence in its policy of restoring the sugar production in its original area of concentration: in December 1961, for example, a high official of the Department of Agriculture declared that it would not be feasible to provide increasing amounts of land for sugar cane in Java, since the land was needed for other crops. In the future, he stated, it would be necessary to develop a modern sugar industry in the Outer Islands, where it would be possible to mechanize cultivation and to permit the cane to ratoon, thus following the example of modern sugar industries outside Indonesia.[31]

Whereas centrifugal sugar production has thus far been exclusively a Javanese industry and has depended on the existence of plantations and their processing facilities, rubber growing has developed in both Java and the Outer Islands and has been both a plantation and an independent smallholder activity. Rubber entered the Indonesian economy at a time when Java's arable land was almost all in use and when the areas which had been declared public domain were for the most part already in the hands of European planters. In consequence, although about 40 per cent of the estate rubber is located in Java only 1 per cent of the smallholder rubber is grown there. Peasant cultivation of rubber—which, as we have seen, fitted swidden agriculture admirably—is located for 75 per cent in Sumatra and 24 per cent in Borneo.

In 1928 rubber was second to sugar as the most important agricultural source of foreign exchange, but during the depression it took the lead and has held it ever since, producing almost half the value of all Indonesian exports in 1959 and 1960 (see Table 11). This expansion, coupled with the decay of the sugar industry, resulted in a reversal in regional contribution to the economy: Java, which at the beginning of the century produced about three-fourths the value of Indonesian agricultural exports—58 per cent in 1928— has become an absorber rather than an earner of foreign exchange. This period also marked a general shift from plantation to small-holder cultivation as the chief source of production for export. Ever since the late nineteenth century smallholders have contributed a steadily increasing share of Indonesia's agricultural exports, and their role could have been even greater during the colonial period had it not been for the government's policy of favoring planters over peasants.[32] Since the transfer of sovereignty, the peasant sector's share of the value of agricultural exports has consistently exceeded that of the estates. This has further strengthened the predominance of the Outer Islands over Java as an earner of foreign exchange since, as we have seen earlier, the shortage of land hampered the development of smallholder enterprises there.

Although smallholder rubber production expanded steadily during the prewar period, in 1940 plantation exports were still twice the value of smallholder shipments. This figure, however, is somewhat deceptive as a measure of the relative size of the two sectors at the time. It would appear that even before 1941 smallholders already had a substantially larger amount of land under rubber than did the planters, but they were not permitted by the government to utilize their productive capacity to the same degree in implementation of the International Rubber Restriction Agreement of 1934.[33] With the termination of the restrictions on tapping, the smallholder came into his own and, producing far more rubber than the planter, has become the chief earner of foreign exchange (see Table 14).

Rubber plantations tend to produce steadily to their capacity, showing little fluctuation in response to changes in price. Since Dutch-owned estates were replanted extensively in the early 1950s with trees of a high-yielding variety, the output of the plantation sector should increase in the near future, provided obstacles to greater production can be kept to a minimum. In recent years, however, plantation production has been plagued by widespread theft, labor problems, lack of spare parts and new equipment, loss of land due to squatting, and losses of both equipment and rubber as a result of the rebellion of 1958. Moreover, plantations located in the neighborhood of extensive peasant-rubber areas are beset by labor shortages when rubber prices are high, since laborers—especially the casual workers, but also some of the regular force living on the estates—will move into the smallholder sector of the industry, where they can earn considerably more money by tapping on a share basis. As plantation wages have tended to lag behind the rising cost of living, laborers who have turned squatters find it more rewarding to raise food crops, for which they can get a good price, than to seek employment on a plantation. As a result, the labor shortage has become acute in East Sumatra, an area which is planted with no less than 43 per cent of the country's estate rubber.[34]

Smallholders rarely tap all trees capable of producing latex; instead, their output fluctuates considerably. Variations in the course of a year of stable rubber prices are due to the fact that most smallholders do not devote all of their labor to rubber; they grow other crops, especially dry rice, and they may spend time fishing. There appears to be a connection between rubber output and rice prices: the rate of tapping falls off when rice prices are higher than those brought by rubber, and increases when the reverse is true. In the leading smallholder rubber districts of Sumatra and Borneo a shortage of tappers also handicaps production and is responsible for neglect of rubber gardens, poor tapping, and no tapping at all in inconveniently located gardens. Only when rubber prices are so high that additional tappers can be drawn from labor surplus areas and plantations by the offer of half and even two-thirds of the

Table 14. PRODUCTION OF PLANTATION AND
SMALLHOLDER RUBBER IN INDONESIA
(*1,000 metric tons*)

Year	Plantation	Percentage of total	Small-holder	Percentage of total	Total
1936	162	52.3	148	47.7	310
1940	283	51.6	266	48.4	549
1950	178	25.1	530	74.9	708
1952	299	37.6	497	62.4	796
1954	288	35.8	517	64.2	805
1956	266	36.8	456	63.2	722
1958	245	35.2	451	64.8	696
1960	217	35.0	403	65.0	620

SOURCE: Biro Pusat Statistik, *Rubber Statistics: Indonesia 1962* (Djakarta, B.P.U.-P.P.N., 1962), p. 17.

yield is full smallholder production realized. During the Korean war, which brought high world rubber prices, the smallholders produced record quantities, but since then their output has fallen off.

In recent years, with food prices greatly inflated and rubber prices kept low by means of foreign-exchange controls and over-evaluation of the rupiah, the incentives for the smallholders to maximize production have been notably lacking. On the other hand, the great difference between the official and illegal currency exchange rates and the considerable portion of export earnings retained by the central government have made it tempting for merchants to purchase rubber and other smallholder export crops at inflated prices and to smuggle them into Malaya or the Philippines, keeping the foreign exchange for themselves or converting it into merchandise for black market sale at home. This conflict between smallholder and commercial interests of the Outer Islands and the policies of the central government contributed greatly to the separatist tendencies which resulted in the rebellion of 1958. The restoration of central authority has not been accompanied by an improvement in the smallholders' position, and there is thus considerable danger that smuggling will continue or that the peasant will shift to the production of nonexport crops.

The position of peasant-grown rubber is further threatened by the fact that very few of the smallholdings are planted with high-yielding seed material—in contrast to the plantations, which by now have a considerable percentage of their land planted with selected and improved trees. Most smallholder gardens are thirty-five years old and over and are therefore in immediate need of replanting. But the peasants are reluctant to cut down trees as long as they are still producing latex, knowing that it takes at least six years for new trees to come into production. Replanting with high-yielding strains is imperative, however, because only such trees can produce efficiently enough to compete with synthetic rubbers, which have made great inroads into the natural rubber market in the postwar period.

If Indonesia is to maintain a market for its rubber, heroic measures for the planting of new lands and the complete replanting of the old stands should be undertaken over the next fifteen to twenty years. This is a huge task, considering the size of the area involved and the great organizational, financial, and labor investment which it will require. However, in view of the importance of rubber to the national economy, its capacity for yielding good returns even on relatively poor soils, and its perfect suitability to the ecology of Sumatra and Borneo, it would seem worthwhile for Indonesia to emulate Malaya in carrying out a large-scale program of extension and replanting of smallholder rubber.

The second most important smallholder crop is copra. This did not become an important export item until the last quarter of the nineteenth century, although the coconut palm is an ancient economic plant in the archipelago and is found wherever climate and soil permit. In the 1880s coconut palms were planted extensively on Sangihe Island by smallholders, and coconut plantations were begun on the islands of Talisse and Kinabohutan, north of Celebes.[35] The coconut palm, however, never became a significant plantation crop; about 95 per cent of the copra exports in 1939 were produced by Indonesian smallholders located above all in Sumatra and in Celebes or nearby small islands.

Commercial stands of coconut palm are planted in swidden areas, either in ladang under active use or in fields which have become overgrown with alang grass. For two to three years it is possible to plant upland rice, maize, pineapple, or robusta coffee between the young palms, and the return from these catch crops covers part or all of the cost of planting and maintenance until the trees begin to bear fruit. The palms usually number 100 to 120 trees per hectare; this area and density will produce on an average about 1,000 to 1,200 kilograms of copra a year. In view of the longevity of the palm it is extremely important that care be taken to select seed from high-yielding trees, since the difference in the number of nuts produced is very great between a poor and a good yielder. Since most of the palms now in existence were planted some sixty to eighty years ago there is a great need for rejuvenation of the coconut groves through replanting. Here, however, we meet a problem very similar to that besetting the smallholder rubber industry: the peasants are reluctant to cut down palms that are still yielding, even though production may have fallen off or the trees become so tall that harvesting is difficult.

Ever since the end of World War II Indonesia's copra exports have been considerably below prewar tonnage. To some extent this has been due to natural causes or neglect. For example, in the residency of East Sumatra extensive stands of palms died because the land flooded, owing to the heavy silting of rivers which in prewar days had been regularly dredged. The rhinoceros beetle and other pests have also lowered production. In part, however, the fall in recorded exports has not reflected an actual decrease in production but a conflict between the smallholders and the central government similar to that noted in the rubber industry. The coconut growers of Celebes and the islands to the north have smuggled sizable quantities of copra to Davao and other ports of the Philippines, where they can obtain a good price in foreign exchange, rather than sell it to government buying organizations, which pay them too little and too late. It has been estimated that in some postwar years up to 300,000 tons of copra were taken out of Indonesia illegally. The coconut growers' discontent over government purchase policies contributed to Celebes participation in the rebellion of 1958, during which time legal shipments came to a standstill. Since then, exports have been adversely affected by the shortage of shipping, which became acute following the withdrawal of the Dutch interisland fleet from Indonesian waters.

Livestock raising is important only in some of the Lesser Sunda islands. However, some 70 per cent of Indonesian cattle and buffalo are to be found in Java and Madura, where they are in the main kept as work animals on the farms. Since only about 5 per cent of Java's land area is under grass, the peasant who owns a draft or meat animal is confronted by the problem of obtaining adequate quantities of fodder. Furthermore, as is so often the case in the humid tropics, the native grasses are notoriously low in nutritional value and production. Livestock holding in Java could be raised by the use of fodder crops of a higher yield and nutritive content and by the substitution of the cut-and-carry system for grazing, which causes losses due to the trampling of valuable fodder plants. Proper grazing methods and improved grassland management could also contribute substantially to greater meat production in the Lesser Sunda Islands.

Because of the relative scarcity of livestock, meat is expensive and is consumed only in very small quantities by the average Indonesian. Protein intake is exceedingly low, having been estimated at 43 grams a day, as against a reference standard of 65 grams.[36] Even this figure, representing one of the lowest protein consumption rates in the world, may be too high, for Indonesia's usually optimistic Eight-Year Development Plan envisaged an increase to only 48 grams by 1968.[37] Of this, it was hoped to realize only 8 grams in the form of animal protein, the rest coming from such vegetable sources as soybeans, peanuts, and bean sprouts.

A small portion of the animal protein that is consumed comes in the form of poultry and eggs, since villagers frequently keep fowl, which are not fed but allowed to scavenge. In general, however, the peasants cannot afford to consume such meat and dairy products as they produce but must market them. Fish, rather than such items, is by far the greatest source of animal protein in the Indonesian diet, and both deep-sea and inshore fishing are important industries throughout the archipelago. Deep-sea fishermen usually devote full time to this trade, while those working inshore waters tend to use fishing as a supplement to farming or some other economic activity. The number of both sailing and motorized fishing vessels expanded greatly in the 1950s;[38] a further increase in the number of motorized deep-sea craft is greatly needed in order to reach fishing grounds too far from land for sailing vessels to exploit without the catch spoiling before it is landed.

In addition to its sea operations, Indonesia also has important inland fisheries utilizing fresh water ponds, or *siwakan,* and salt water ponds, or *tambak,* for fish farming. Fish-pond farming is especially well developed by the Sundanese of the Priangan region of West Java and by the Minangkabau in the highlands of West Sumatra. Lacking regular permanent fish ponds, Javanese peasants will also raise fish in their sawah if the water supply permits. In coastal regions of Java and Madura, mangrove swamps and young alluvial land not suited for crop production have been converted into salt and brackish water ponds on a large scale.

The total yield of Indonesian sea and inland fisheries in 1960 was about 760,000 metric tons[39]—410,000 from the seas and 350,000 from inland waters—compared to a total 1940 production of 460,000 tons. Despite this increase, the present annual catch is insufficient to meet the need for fresh and preserved fish products. However, the government is well aware that a fuller utilization of Indonesian fish resources would increase the protein supply without necessitating the allocation of precious agricultural land for the raising of livestock; and with the help of foreign aid it has been endeavoring to improve the exploitation of both sea and inland fisheries.

Indonesia is dependent on its exports of commercial crops to provide it with much of its essential imports and development capital; at the same time it needs a high level of food crop production to avoid the utilization of foreign exchange for agricultural imports. As we have seen, the production of both food and export crops is at present in a somewhat parlous state. Food production has lagged behind population growth, while the export of all commercial crops except rubber has declined since the prewar period. Though rubber production has remained high, its future is threatened by competition from synthetics, which the smallholders in particular are in a poor position to withstand.

A real improvement in both commercial and food crop production cannot be achieved without considerable government investment, not only in the form of money and materials but also in terms of organizational and scientific skills. There is a great need for the restaffing of the experiment centers which helped make Indonesian plantation agriculture famous before World War II, as well as for research in support of smallholder agriculture on a scale far larger than that undertaken in the colonial period. Technical and administrative skills are still very short in the state plantation sector and in the paddy centers; and the latter are further handicapped by their law-enforcing function, which makes it difficult for peasants to receive their advice and aid without suspicion. Above all, the peasants need education of the kind that will enable them to become better producers; there is a pressing need for an effective agricultural extension service which would establish a close link between the research and seed stations on the one hand and the smallholders engaged in cash and food crop production on the other. Granted that the Indonesian peasants are conservative, they are not so close-minded as to be unwilling to imitate convincing demonstrations which are in keeping with their economic resources and technical competence. Their conservatism is, in fact, largely a function of their economic position. Those who need help most badly are understandably the most reluctant to take risks and try out suggestions which have not been thoroughly tested in their locality, and it is therefore necessary that great care be taken in introducing innovations in such poverty-stricken areas as Java.

The Indonesian government is acutely aware of the need to raise agricultural production and has developed elaborate programs for this purpose. Thus far the plans have not generally been implemented in an effective manner. In part this failure has been caused by a lack of the funds, materials, and skills necessary to their execution. In part it results from the fact that programs developed in Djakarta often have proved unrealistic in terms of regional conditions or have been rendered ineffective by the many bureaucratic layers through which they must pass. We have noted, too, that in both food and export crop production there is a tendency toward conflict between the interests of the peasants and those of the central authority. The government, in sore need of revenue and foreign exchange, seeks to minimize the prices paid to the producers and to increase its control over crop production; the peasants seek to evade this by resorting to illegal marketing channels or by switching to the cultivation of noncontrolled crops. The political dangers of this situation have already been demonstrated by Sumatran and Celebes smallholder support of rebellion; but even from a purely agricultural point of view it has ominous implications. If the trend continues it may mean that peasants, though dependent on government assistance for the improvement of their crops, will become increasingly disinclined to accept state-sponsored aid and innovation. The already observable tendency to shift to the production of more profitable noncontrolled crops may lead to a neglect of those products most important to the economy and to a general disinclination to expand production beyond subsistence needs. The solution to the problem is not easy to foresee in view of the straitened circumstances of the government and its need for large quantities of foreign exchange and reasonably priced food for the burgeoning nonagrarian population. Nonetheless, if Indonesia's agricultural production is to expand in the future along rational lines, better regard for peasant interests would seem necessary.

CHAPTER 5

From Colonial to Guided Economy

DOUGLAS S. PAAUW

AMONG Southeast Asia's newly independent countries, Indonesia stands out for the rapidity with which it has destroyed Western social and economic institutions implanted by colonialism: Dutch enterprise there virtually ceased to exist less than ten years after sovereignty was transferred. The loss of Dutch economic enterprise and technical talent, the eradication of Dutch educational traditions—and even the Dutch language—as well as many other symptoms of the complete severance with the past have created a void which has greatly overburdened Indonesia's small elite and slowed constructive action in many areas of social and economic rehabilitation.

The chief architect of Indonesia's newly launched program of social and economic reform, President Sukarno, has defined the society's economic goals as Socialism à la Indonesia, Guided Economy, and Development. Socialism à la Indonesia has been enunciated as the concept of adapting the principles of socialism to Indonesia's cultural environment. Guided Economy (*Ekonomi Terpimpin*) has emerged in the Indonesian leadership's thinking as an attack on "economic liberalism" (relatively free enterprise); it represents the government's intention to intervene more directly in the economy to achieve its goals of Socialism à la Indonesia and Development. The present leadership's concept of Development is crystallized in its Eight-Year Plan, which was introduced in early 1961 and embodies President Sukarno's new concepts for general social progress. In the context of the plan, Development includes not only investment projects but also a program for the spiritual and social uplift of the Indonesian people. It is the view of the Indonesian elite now in power that Indonesia's experiment with

155

liberalism (this is the term employed) from the beginning of sovereignty in 1949 to roughly 1958 failed to promote the desired rate of social and economic progress.[1] It is their hope that Socialism à la Indonesia, Guided Economy, and Development will foster rapid progress toward a more prosperous society in which economic welfare will be more equally shared among Indonesian peoples.

In general, political stability and the relative degree of national unity have been important factors in the divergent rates of economic progress among Southeast Asian countries. Countries which have found it necessary to devote a preponderant part of national effort to political stability and establishing minimum conditions to assure central authority and administrative control have shown lagging rates of economic growth during the past decade. Indonesia has been the prime example of the relationship between political instability and economic stagnation.

Not all of Indonesia's diverse ethnic groups can be said to be solidly behind the leadership's policy of rapid eradication of Western colonial institutions. The tendencies to destroy the social and economic institutions associated with colonialism and to move with haste toward a centralized guided economy have emanated more from Java than the outlying islands. In part, the rebellion of 1958-61 reflected reluctance on the part of the outlying provinces to endorse the rate and direction of change precipitated by the national leadership. This central fact has impeded Indonesia's political unification as well as the integration of the scattered islands into a national economy.

Resistance among the peoples of the outlying islands to the President's new program for Indonesia's development reflects fear of centralization of authority as well as more moderate attitudes toward capitalism and foreign enterprise. Behind these attitudes we find both ethnic considerations and significant differences in historical experience. The contribution of foreign enterprise to local welfare was more real and obvious than on Java, the burden of colonial control less onerous, and the desire to maintain local autonomy more respected. Individualism in economic activity is more highly valued in many of the outlying islands than on Java, producing conflicts over the degree of economic centralization to be promoted by political decision.

The colonial administration did little to promote social and political integration among the many ethnic units that comprise Indonesia, and it is possible that the continuation of a strong foreign economic impact in Indonesia after independence hampered progress toward national unity. It is likely that fears of foreign exploitation of underlying differences among the peoples of the many Indonesian islands have prompted the tendency toward centralization of authority, as a means of welding Indonesian groups into a political entity. The costs of employing central power to quell local resistance and to achieve the degree of political centralization called for by the dominant strain of Indonesian nationalism, however, have severely limited the capacity to carry out programs of economic development.

The Structure of the Economy: Island Fragmentation

The geographical fragmentation of Indonesia into a large number of islands is basic to an understanding of the nation's economy. Integration of separate island economies into a national whole was not a major objective of colonial policy, and progress toward regional specialization and trade developed slowly. Nevertheless, such a pattern was beginning to emerge late in the colonial period, and belatedly Dutch officials foresaw that greater economic integration between Java and the outlying islands was essential to progress of the whole.[2] "In the decade preceding the Pacific war," writes one observer, "the Dutch were progressively welding Indonesia into a functional economic unit, with considerable interisland trade in foodstuffs and concentration of manufacturing in Java, which was becoming more and more the managerial nucleus for the whole system."[3]

During the nineteenth century, Dutch colonial investment had concentrated on developing export industries on Java, and that island was the main source of profits.[4] Western economic penetration promoted the growth of population by reducing mortality,[5] and it also led to the breakdown of the subsistence economy as Indonesians provided labor and land for export industries. The expansion of export crops, proceeding simultaneously with population growth, gradually reduced the supply of land available for traditional agricultural occupations. This produced underemployment of the growing labor supply, and the Javanese turned to additional occupations for the market, although Western enterprise absorbed only a small part of the surplus labor from the subsistence sector. Other opportunities for the Javanese were limited by the lack of available capital and by Western and minority group domination of the middleman roles in the growing export and domestic trades.

A shift in emphasis by foreign investment from Java to the outlying islands began to occur in the early part of the present century, coinciding with the final assertion of Dutch authority over most of the Outer Islands.[6] World demand for raw materials for industrial purposes was growing relative to demand for agricultural consumption goods, and these resources were primarily located outside Java. Wertheim attributes to this shift an important structural change in the Indonesian economy.[7] The Western impact on Java, reinforced by the growth of population relative to land resources, had gradually induced Indonesians to participate in Western economic activity and markets, but its main effect was to produce "an extension over an ever-widening area of the traditional pattern of rice cultivation on *sawah* land."[8] In this pattern of response, Wertheim characterizes the Javanese as passive:

> The ordinary peasant in Java continued to maintain a predominantly passive attitude toward the incursions of the money economy. He remained a farmer providing for his own needs, sought other income only when he was forced to, and tried to keep to a minimum the periods when he was no longer independent, but employed by a Western-owned undertaking. He preferred to leave profit seeking to the Chinese or the Arabs or even, in some cases, to the Indonesians who had outgrown the old traditional desa milieu—such a type, for instance, as the haji (the pilgrim returned from Mecca) or the immigrant from Sumatra.[9]

In the outlying islands, the impact of Western economic activity was quite different. The peoples of these regions were reluctant to accept employment in a subordinate capacity in Western enterprise, so that "these undertakings had to look abroad for their labor supply first in China, but later preponderantly in Java."[10] In general, the population's response was more dynamic:

> In the greater part of the Outer Territories the adaptation to modern economy was carried out by the Indonesians themselves. At a time when the Western rubber plantations were still in the experimental stage, Indonesians on Sumatra and Borneo—mostly Malays—were embarking on the cultivation of rubber on their own account on their *ladangs*. The cultivation of coconuts, too, formed an important source of income in large areas. The vast stretches of uncultivated ground provided a considerable proportion of the local population

with the opportunity to earn money for the purchase of imported goods, in addition to their usual occupation of subsistence farming. And even though there, too, nearly everywhere in the Outer Islands, the Indonesian became more or less dependent upon foreign middlemen or upon large Western businesses, the adaptation to Western economy was on the whole more dynamic in character than on Java or in Deli. By reason of the sparsity of the population, the *ladang* pattern of cultivation offered a better chance of dynamic expansion than did the *sawah* pattern on Java.[11]

Geertz offers an alternative explanation of the Javanese "passivity" in response to Western introduction of commercial crops and export processing facilities.[12] He believes that on Java government policy was effective in stifling indigenous cultivation of these crops; at one time Javanese producers had attempted to produce sugar cane on smallholdings, only to be thwarted by restrictions imposed by large Western producers supported by the colonial government. The greater responsiveness of peoples on the outlying islands in introducing peasant export crops, therefore, may have been largely a matter of the relative ineffectiveness of colonial government controls in repressing their initiative, while government power on Java was adequate to enforce its restrictive policies more completely. Expansion of smallholders' rubber exports during the government's restriction program in the 1930s suggests that the Outer Islands had some success in circumventing government regulations favoring European exporters.

Between 1900 and 1930, these divergent patterns of development led to a basic structural dichotomy between Java and the outlying islands. Densely populated Java began to show signs of economic stagnation; eventually food production failed to keep pace with population growth,[13] and after 1920 exports from Java expanded less rapidly than those from the outlying islands.[14] Rapid growth of several important export products (rubber, petroleum, tin, copra) on the outlying islands was causing important shifts in the colonial economy, shifts so significant that it was suggested in a major government report that the center of economic activity had moved, especially after 1928, from Java to Sumatra and Borneo.[15]

In concentrating on the development of the outlying islands after 1900, foreign investment not only created additional agricultural plantations but also promoted the rapid development of mining, raising the share of mineral products in Indonesia's exports from 16 per cent in 1910 to 30 per cent in 1939.[16] The same period saw

159

a growing response on the part of indigenous enterprise on the Outer Islands: smallholders' exports of agricultural products grew even more rapidly than plantation exports; by 1925 the value of smallholders' agricultural exports exceeded the value of estate exports on the outlying islands, and, by and large, this trend has continued. The important consequence of this was a shift in ownership and income in favor of indigenous enterprise; and since this did not occur on Java, Indonesian per capita income and the capacity to import grew more rapidly on the outlying islands than on Java. By the early 1930s, the value of exports originating from the Outer Islands exceeded that from Java,[17] and this relationship has been maintained.

During the first four decades of this century, therefore, the outlying islands were becoming increasingly integrated into the international economy, and, unlike on Java, this process was yielding substantial gains to the indigenous populace. As indigenous agriculture became increasingly specialized in production for export, expansion of food production was overlooked in favor of importing rice from export proceeds. Polak observed a close correlation between rice imports and export earnings, asserting that in the outer provinces "the fact is that net rice imports moved definitely with income earned by the Indonesian population from export crops and from wages earned in the estates."[18] His data for the period 1921 to 1939 show a rising trend of rice imports, correlating closely with export income changes and also reflecting clearly the income-reducing forces of the depression. All available evidence points to a widening disparity in per capita income between Java and the outlying islands.[19]

Prior to 1930, both Java and the Outer Islands were food-deficit areas, but for quite different reasons. The data referred to above suggest that outside of Java expansion of output by indigenous peoples took the form of producing for the world market, an opportunity provided by a favorable population-land ratio and the external economies made available by foreign enterprise. On Java, intensive cultivation of food crops failed to provide adequate supplies of food to match population growth, and Javanese peasants were unable to turn to cultivation of export crops. To a limited extent, Javanese were able to take advantage of land resources in the outlying islands by emigration for employment in the estate sector, but these emigrants generally tended eventually to return to Java. If the Javanese were not particularly successful in drawing

160

upon the land resources through factor movements—the transfer of labor, capital, or entrepreneurship—they also reaped little benefit of the more favorable population-land ratio on the outlying islands through trade. The importance of international trade completely overshadowed interisland commerce, and the failure of Java to industrialize left that island without goods to export in return for the land-abundant products of the outlying islands. Moreover, Java's capacity to trade its labor-abundant products for the land-abundant and capital-intensive ones of the Outer Islands indirectly, via trade, was limited by the colonial trading pattern, which produced large export surpluses to provide for transfer of profits and invisible payments associated with the regime.[20]

At the beginning of the Great Depression, therefore, there were growing discrepancies between Java and the outlying islands in economic structure as well as per capita income. The colonial pattern of development had promoted the evolution of these differences, but it failed to promote domestic integration and interisland trade which would further regional specialization and the equalization of factor returns and per capita incomes. Although in the colonial period the greatest disparities in incomes existed between ethnic groups—Europeans at the top, followed by Chinese and other minority groups, with the Indonesians at the bottom[21]—there were also disparities among Indonesians, the latter mainly reflecting the difference in economic conditions on Java and the outlying islands. Social and political obstacles prevented a tendency toward equalization of ethnic income disparities, while the lack of economic integration among the regions of the archipelago prevented equalization among indigenous groups. These disparities, continuing into the independence period, have had much to do with the stresses and strains among ethnic groups and among Indonesians from various islands.

During the 1930s, prodded into action by the drastic effects of the Great Depression on the Indonesian economy, the colonial government initiated a constellation of policies to expand production for local markets, to begin domestic industrialization, and to promote interregional trade.[22] Stress was laid on the achievement of self-sufficiency in rice production, the development of consumer goods manufacturing, and controls over domestic price and distribution procedures which would promote the more effective internal distribution of domestic output. Export controls were designed to limit production in order to exert a favorable effect on world prices, and numerous marketing boards were established.

Techniques to stimulate industrial production for domestic markets consisted mainly of protectionist devices, but government assistance in both financing and technical training was also attempted. Measures to promote self-sufficiency in rice were also basically protectionist: a variable import duty was imposed to yield domestic prices that would provide incentives to expand output. Interregional shipments to chronic deficit areas were subsidized in order to equalize supply. Some attention was also given to biotechnical improvements to increase yields, and new irrigation facilities were begun to extend rice cultivation in the outlying islands.

The experience during the 1930s is instructive, but the conditions were unusual. Despite the absence of a comprehensive plan and little coordination of the colonial government's efforts, considerable success was achieved in expanding output of rice and consumer goods manufactures. By 1940, Indonesia had become virtually self-sufficient in rice, following a long period of relatively large-scale imports.[23] Domestic output of a number of consumer manufactures, particularly textiles, cigarettes, and soap, expanded rapidly during the 1930s, replacing imports by substantial amounts.[24] Located mainly on Java, the growing manufacturing industry was primarily oriented toward the large Javanese market, but there was also some increase in exports to the outlying islands: about one-fourth of the output of Java's most important manufacture, batik sarongs, was consumed in the outlying islands in 1939.[25] Even more surprising was the fact that Java began to export relatively large volumes of rice to the outlying islands just prior to World War II—almost 200 thousand tons in 1940.

The slump in export markets for Indonesian products was a major factor promoting these developments.[26] On Java, the decline of the sugar industry provided the land for an expansion of rice production, while government policy provided the incentives. On the outlying islands, however, smallholders found it profitable to continue expansion of agricultural crops for the world markets, in spite of government restrictions and the fact that the agricultural estates were cutting back production as world prices fell below their production costs. In general, therefore, the shift from production for export markets to production for domestic markets was more pronounced on Java than on the outlying islands.[27] This may have been caused by the fact that the Javanese lived closer to the subsistence level and hence were more severely affected by price fluctuations. Moreover, the collapse of the sugar industry, Java's main agricultural export business, was more complete than that of the export industries in the outlying islands. Finally, the government rice and industrial development policies were principally designed to provide alternative economic opportunities on Java, where the impact of the depression combined with the population pressure on land to precipitate a serious crisis. In spite of the successes these programs achieved, objective Dutch scholars believe that the depression had disastrous welfare effects on much of Java's population.[28]

In spite of these qualifications, the responses generated by the depression promoted the first real tendency toward the economic integration of the Indonesian islands. Exports from Java to the outlying territories increased substantially. Apart from rice, these growing exports mainly took the form of consumer manufactures, the value of which more than doubled between 1935 and 1940.[29] The outlying islands themselves provided a substantial export surplus on world markets, which financed a persistent Javanese import surplus as well as the large invisible account deficit symptomatic of the colonial balance of payments. Interisland trade allowed partial compensation to the Outer Islands in the form of Java's export surplus, in addition to providing markets for Javanese rice surplus and manufactures; the Outer Islands provided primary products in return. Apart from the rice component, which was likely to be transitory because of Java's underlying population pressure on land, the beginnings of a viable pattern of trade and specialization was emerging. Nevertheless, as Table 1 indicates for 1938, the value of international trade was considerably greater than the value of interisland trade.

This emerging pattern was still embryonic at the time of the Japanese invasion of Indonesia; and wartime disruption reversed the process toward integration. Except for Japanese requisitions, foreign trade completely ceased during the occupation.[30] Interisland trade was halted by the loss of transport facilities and by Japanese policies preventing the movement of regional surpluses.[31] Agricultural plantations were turned over to food production, and facilities for processing export products were left idle or converted to other uses. Throughout Indonesia there was a shift of factors from market production to subsistence agriculture; transport and distributive assets were eroded, and the productive apparatus in the modern, capital-intensive sectors was severely crippled. Rehabilitation proceeded slowly during the immediate postwar years; it was not until the transfer of sovereignty in late 1949 that an independent national leadership could address itself to the major task of uniting the scattered islands into an integrated economy.

In the period since independence, many of the long-run trends resulting from the colonial impact on the economy have persisted. The shift toward the domination of export activities by the outlying islands has accelerated. Since 1956 even Borneo has passed Java in value of exports; the ratio of values of exports from the outlying islands to Java's export values has risen from 1.21 in 1940 to 6.70 in 1959.[32] Java has shown decreased export capacity, whether measured in volume or real value terms; this capacity has grown in the outlying islands, although primarily as a result of greatly expanded petroleum exports. Java's population pressure is reflected in its large rice deficits throughout the postwar period; the slack provided by converting land from export crops (mainly sugar cane) to food crops has been countered by rapid population growth. Improvements leading to yield increases have not been introduced on a scale adequate to meet increased demand for rice on Java, while extension of rice cultivation on the outlying islands, where practical, has been hampered by political difficulties and the shortage of capital to meet the high investment requirements of reclamation projects. Moreover, incentive factors have discouraged domestic supplies of rice from moving in interregional trade. Smallholders' agricultural exports have continued to grow relative to plantation exports; and despite foreign-exchange controls generally unfavorable to exports, agricultural producers in the outlying islands have

Table 1. INTERNATIONAL AND INTERISLAND TRADE, 1938

(*1,000 guilders*)

	Java	Outer Islands
Exports abroad	215,560	442,239
Imports from abroad	312,442	166,008
Balance[a]	−96,882	+276,231
Interisland exports	125,010	58,701
Interisland imports	58,701	125,010
Balance	+66,309	− 66,309

(a) Minus: import surplus; plus: export surplus

SOURCE: Centraal Kantoor voor de Statistiek, *Statistisch jaaroverzicht van Nederlandsch-Indië* [Statistical Annual of the Netherlands Indies] *1938,* Table 249, p. 336; Table 251, pp. 338-39.

been more inclined to produce for world than domestic markets. Smuggling of both exports and imports in the outlying islands appears to have been possible on a scale large enough to partially offset the discouraging effects of official controls; incentives for export production continue to be stronger than those for producing for domestic markets.

Local specialization of production within a national economy requires that the extent of local markets be widened. Village markets must be linked together by transport and larger distributive organizations. In independent Indonesia neither transport facilities nor distributive channels have expanded rapidly enough to promote the growth of national markets and to encourage regional specialization, despite the sound comparative advantage basis for inter-island specialization and trade based on Java's surplus of labor and the Outer Islands' surplus of land. Experience has shown that inter-island movement of labor is slow and expensive; in recognition of this fact the Indonesian government has recently de-emphasized its previously ambitious plans for large-scale resettlement of Java's rapidly growing population. Labor shortages have begun to appear in plantation and extractive industries on outlying islands, causing some absorption of local migrants from the agricultural sector. The process has been very slow, however, because "the Sumatran tends to regard plantation labour as inferior if not degrading."[33]

Since independence, the withdrawal of foreign commercial and managerial activities, the circumscription of the economic activities of the Chinese, and an increase in population pressure on already cultivated land have induced relatively large-scale population movements from agriculture and related activities on the outlying islands. The dramatic acceleration of this type of population shift in North Sumatra has been carefully documented.[34] The stigma against plantation employment has tended to persist, however, and the migrants have mainly moved into commercial, transport, and other service activities supporting capital-intensive production. Since 1958, however, the government has transferred increasing numbers of Javanese to the outlying islands to fill positions in the new but rapidly expanding government economic administration[35] and to staff military garrisons. This trend is beginning to force local migrants from the rural sector to accept labor employment in the capital-intensive sector.

The patterns of specialization and resource use that have emerged in Indonesia since independence hardly seem consistent with the country's underlying resource endowments. Java produces an increasingly large volume of manufactured consumer goods, distributed predominantly on that island; but the growth of Javanese manufacturing has been hampered by lack of market opportunities and supplies of raw materials—precisely what the outlying islands have to offer. Raw materials for Java's developing manufacturing industries are mainly supplied from abroad; and the other islands have looked overseas for markets for their primary products. They have tended to import consumer manufactures principally from abroad and only secondarily from Java; but supplies from both sources have dwindled as a result of shipping shortages, foreign exchange scarcities, and political vicissitudes. This difficulty has encouraged the Outer Islands to develop the local manufacture of consumer goods; in spite of Java's early start in manufacturing, competitive sources of supply grew rapidly in Sumatra and other islands during the 1950s.

Food supply, essentially defined in terms of rice, is basic in Indonesia's economy. As has been pointed out in the chapter on agriculture, virtually the entire country is now a food-deficit area, although the problem assumes its most serious proportions on Java. Consumer manufactures have not been made available in adequate supply, particularly on the outlying islands, to provide a basis for rice-manufactures exchange; and low purchasing prices have retarded the flow of rice to the government marketing agency designed to channel more rice to deficit areas. Shortages of rice have been frequent in urban centers in the outlying islands as supplies from abroad and from transshipment or export from Java have fallen. Since 1961 similar problems have plagued urban centers in Java.

In recent years, the transport problem has become particularly acute. Since Dutch shipping was barred from coastwise and interisland routes after 1957, shipping available for transport of domestic goods has fallen below the prewar and postindependence volumes.[36] Moreover, harbor facilities have deteriorated, and the small volume of interisland trade that moves is handled inefficiently, with delays, losses, and excessive risks. Distribution of consumer goods throughout the archipelago has been obstructed by the breakdown of the traditional middleman system in 1959-60 caused by the expulsion of Chinese merchants from rural areas. New government distributive channels, of uneven effectiveness, have been much less successful in replacing the disrupted traditional system on the outlying islands than on Java.

Markets in the outlying islands show the potential for absorbing growing quantities of manufactures. In some areas relatively large local markets surround capital-intensive industry, and these markets have shown strong demand for imported consumer goods, particularly manufactures. It is in these areas that local manufacturing has been stimulated by import stringency. Moreover, the outlying islands produce a disproportionately large share of Indonesian national income relative to their populations.[37]

The foregoing discussion has made no judgment concerning the optimum pattern of resource use in Indonesia. It does appear that there is a basis for considerable regional specialization, and it may even be true that a case could be made for concentration of manufacturing of consumer goods on Java, a position taken by Dutch experts during the 1930s and now endorsed by some of Indonesia's leading economists.[38] National markets have not developed since independence, however; the economy has not been integrated by an adequate transport and communications network and hence no viable pattern of regional specialization has emerged. Island fragmentation makes the problem of integration all the more difficult, for economic activity on each of the major islands continues to be more oriented inwards toward the economy of the island and outwards to foreign countries rather than toward national (interisland) markets.

Regional Trade Balances, Terms of Trade, and Specialization

The incentive problems that have impeded the growth of interregional trade and discouraged production for legal export can best be demonstrated by estimating present patterns of international and interregional trade and the trade balances that have accrued to each region. Serious hazards for such an estimate inhere, however, in the difficulty of rupiah valuation—given Indonesia's multiple exchange rates and its variable import duty structure—and in the fact that imported goods may be re-exported through Javanese ports. Official data, based on the legal exchange rate for exports and imports, give a distorted picture of the postindependence patterns of trade, the values of goods moving in trade, and regional balances. Exports are undervalued relative to import values; and products moving in interinsular trade which are agricultural or subject to price control (e.g. rice) are similarly undervalued. Prices of products with an import component—largely manufactured goods—reflect the effects of high import duties, while prices of agricultural commodities do not. Tariff and exchange rate policies, and to a certain extent price controls, have caused the terms of trade between primary products and industrial products to shift increasingly against primary products and in favor of industrial goods. It is this general issue that has been one of the most serious points of contention between the central government and dissident groups on the outlying islands, since the outlying islands tend to export primary products while Java's exports to other islands have been more industrial in nature.[39]

During the period 1952-59, the official exchange rate was held at rupiah 11.47 to U. S. $1.00 (although the official rate was devalued in August 1959, official trade statistics employ the old rate for the entire year). In fact, however, the official rates were not significant for determining the proceeds from exports, effective rates for import goods, or the terms of trade between exports and imports and among the islands. From June 1957 to August 1959 these relationships were primarily decided by the export certificate system, which was then operated in conjunction with import surcharges.[40] As that system worked out in practice, the exporter received varying fractions of the rupiah price of importing goods, depending on which of six categories were actually financed from export proceeds. During 1958 and 1959 (prior to the readjustment in August), exporters' proceeds worked out to rupiah 30.36 per U. S. dollar—the value of export certificates less a 20 per cent tax—while importers' payments for foreign exchange probably averaged about rupiah 68.3 per U. S. dollar, the figure resulting from the basic cost of foreign exchange certificates plus the average surcharge for the six categories of import goods. Revisions in 1959 and 1960 raised the effective export and import rates, but increased the already substantial discrepancy between the two.[41]

If these estimates are correct, they suggest that during the period 1957-59 export proceeds averaged about 44 per cent of the rupiah payments generated by foreign exchange earnings (and an even smaller percentage of the domestic retail prices of imported goods), although the system had been introduced as a concession to promote exports and to moderate dissatisfaction in the outlying islands. Moreover, with the value of export proceeds being frozen while domestic prices continued to rise, interisland trade was subject to progressively deteriorating terms from the Outer Islands' point of view.

This emphasis is essential to understand the extent to which foreign exchange policies tended to obstruct regional trade and specialization as well as to give more accurate measures of the relative values of international and interregional trade. Policies similar in effect to the system described have existed throughout the period since the transfer of sovereignty—although the particular devices have shown great variety.[42] Discrimination against producers of export goods discouraged exporting through legal channels; smuggling of both exports and imports has been a factor, but probably of decreasing importance, in reducing the central government's capacity to control foreign exchange. Since smuggled goods are presumably unreported in export and import statistics, official data underestimate the degree of export and import specialization in the outlying islands where illegal trade has been concentrated.

Foreign exchange policies have thus added to transport and market difficulties to prevent progress toward regional specialization, and exports of primary products from outlying islands to world markets and to Java have, therefore, failed to grow for incentive as well as organizational reasons. An estimate of the 1958 value of exports from the outlying islands and Java, and return imports, using both data as officially provided and as corrected by using the actual effective export and import rates is presented in Table 2. These figures show an export surplus for the outlying islands of considerable size, while the reverse was true for Java. In terms of the effective purchasing power of exports over imports, relative to world prices as a base, the outlying islands received only 13 per cent of their world export values in world import value—the disparity caused by the multiple rate system, the relatively heavier inflow of imports to Java, and the discrepancy between import and export values in the aggregate. Java fared considerably better: the adjusted value of its imports amounted to 148 per cent of exports. Perhaps this major discrepancy can be defended on grounds of equity, but it inevitably produced serious disincentive effects on exports from the Outer Islands, gave great impetus to smuggling attempts, and aggravated regional frictions.

Interisland trade figures, when stated in rupiah values, show Java as having a substantial export surplus to the outlying islands

Table 2. RUPIAH VALUES OF FOREIGN TRADE, JAVA,
OUTER ISLANDS, AND INDONESIA, 1958

(*million rupiah*)

	Official	*Adjusted*[a]
Exports		
Java and Madura	1,179	3,124
Outer Islands	7,835	20,763
Indonesia	9,014	23,887
Imports		
Java and Madura	3,945	4,616
Outer Islands	2,258	2,642
Indonesia	6,203	7,258

(a) Export values adjusted to actual effective export rate, i.e. 30.36; import values adjusted to average rupiah purchasing power of exports, i.e. 44 per cent of export rate.

SOURCE: *Statistical Pocketbook of Indonesia 1960*, pp. 109, 111. Both exports and imports at the official rate, i.e. 11.47.

(see Table 3). The problem in accepting these data at face value, however, is that they are not corrected for the fact that prices of Java's exports to the outlying islands were rising more rapidly than prices of the Outer Islands' exports to Java. If we were to assume that Java's exports reflected price trends of imported goods, while the other islands' export prices reflected price trends of Indonesia's exports, we would find the interisland balance substantially different.

It is impossible to correct for differences in domestic price trends which affect the terms of trade among the Indonesian islands. The data presented in Table 3, however, suggest that even using undeflated and uncorrected values for trade between Java and the outlying islands, the total discrepancies between export and import values is much greater for the outlying islands than for Java. They also suggest that the total value of Indonesian trade with the outside world exceeds the value of trade between Java and the outlying islands, even though rupiah values for the latter are inflated because of domestic price rises, a factor more or less eliminated from the international trade figures by using rupiah values at the more inflexible effective import and export rates. If corrections could be made for all of these factors, the impact of progressively deteriorating international and regional terms of trade for the outlying islands would presumably be seen much more clearly.

Technological Dualism

A second major structural characteristic of the Indonesian economy has come to be described as technological dualism. The dichotomous nature of Indonesian society had long been emphasized by Dutch writers.[43] It remained for contemporary economic analysis, however, to give us the tools to expose more clearly the fundamental economic dualism found in many underdeveloped countries. Indonesia exhibits an almost classic case of the type of technological dualism analyzed in recent literature;[44] Higgins believes that this model "fits the Indonesian case beautifully."[45]

Technological dualism refers to marked differences in productive techniques in two sectors of the economy, the one capital-intensive, with fixed proportions of capital to labor, and the other labor-intensive, with variable proportions. In an underdeveloped economy of the Indonesian type, these sectors encompass virtually all economic activity; there is little between them to bridge the qualitatively large gap in techniques.

In Indonesia, the economy inherited this feature from its colonial

Table 3. RUPIAH VALUES OF INTERNATIONAL AND INTER-REGIONAL TRADE, JAVA AND OUTER ISLANDS, 1958

(million rupiah)

Outer Islands:

Exports abroad	20,763
Exports to Java	5,685
Total	26,448
Imports from abroad	2,642
Imports from Java	12,802
Total	15,444

Java:

Exports abroad	3,124
Exports to Outer Islands	12,802
Total	15,926
Imports from abroad	4,616
Imports from Outer Islands	5,685
Total	10,301

SOURCE: Interisland trade computed from data in *Statistical Pocketbook of Indonesia 1960*, pp. 146, 147. Rupiah values of international trade were taken from adjusted figures in Table 2 (see above).

171

past. Dutch and other foreign investment poured into activities associated with producing primary products for export to the mother country and other foreign markets. A capital-intensive, modern sector focusing on plantation agriculture and mining became grafted to the traditional labor-intensive economy. Modern techniques of production introduced in the capital-intensive sector were not designed to absorb labor from the traditional economy, nor was the sector as a whole operated to raise Indonesian income. Spread effects in terms of introducing new methods beyond the sector and raising incomes of some Indonesians were incidental and more or less resisted by the colonial government. Proportions of capital and labor utilized in the productive process were determined by techniques available in metropolitan countries, by the constraints of colonial supervision of production and the exacting demands of the foreign market. These conditions not only produced a rather artificial, foreign-dominated sector alien to the traditional economy, but they also gave a distinct export orientation to the modern, developing sector of the economy. This latter aspect will be explored further in the section concerned with the dynamics of the Indonesian economy.

The traditional economy continued to devote its resources to small-scale agriculture and handicraft production of consumer manufactures; it is true, of course, that small-scale enterprise made some inroads in the production of export crops, but here too labor-intensive methods continued to dominate production. Potential linkage of the two basic sectors through markets was inhibited by foreign and minority group assumption of intersectoral distributive roles. This prevented the evolution of a demonstration effect toward modernization of techniques in the traditional sector; it tended to hamper the Westernization of the traditional sector by reducing possibilities for the transmission to it of attitudes which might have induced capital formation, a lowered birth rate, and other fundamental changes related to growth.

This basic dualism in the economy has had profound effects upon the pattern of development. Additions to capital formation were concentrated in the modern sector; consequently growth and technological change tended to be restricted to this sector. In the traditional sector, techniques of production did not change, and capital investment was scarcely adequate to keep existing productive facilities intact. An expanding modern sector, therefore, came to exist side by side with a more or less stagnating traditional sector. This general situation was true in spite of the provision of limited social overhead facilities on Java, of which irrigation was the most important. These facilities led to some improvement in the external factors affecting agricultural productivity, but by and large they failed to promote technical change within the productive unit. The scale of enterprise remained small, and techniques of production continued to be labor-intensive.

Population dynamics tended to perpetuate technological dualism and stagnation in the labor-intensive sector. Per capita income in the traditional sector on Java probably began to decline after the population explosion during the nineteenth century (described in Chapter 1). In this process the population-land ratio became increasingly adverse, and the presumption is that capital investment per worker began to decline as well. Polak's data on per capita food supplies on Java suggest a deterioration of consumption from 1920-35, with "a partial redress" in the period 1935-39.[46] These data are suggestive for two reasons. First, they suggest falling Indonesian food consumption during the 1920s—the heyday of the export-oriented capital-intensive sector. Second, they indicate that the labor-intensive sector was able to make gains at the expense of the capital-intensive sector during the depression in export markets through the transfer of land from plantation agriculture to food crops.[47]

The sharp cleavage between the traditional and modern sectors and the pattern of specialization in the modern sector prevented the growing population from finding employment outlets in the expanding sector of the economy; moreover, this cleavage was widened by the colonial policies which excluded Indonesians from many potential opportunities. Absorption of greater supplies of labor required heavy capital investment, since the capital-labor ratio was high in plantation agriculture, export processing, and mining. Opportunities for absorption in these primary activities as well as in commercial, government, and other service activities were further inhibited by political factors, since white-collar roles were mainly reserved for the non-Indonesian minorities. Although capital investment grew at a relatively rapid rate in the modern sector, its allocation to capital-intensive production failed to provide employment for the growing labor force generated within this sector itself. The traditional sector was forced to absorb its own population growth as well as the surplus from the modern sector. This situation produced ever-widening disparities between the per capita income in the two sectors. All of this applied to Java more than to the Outer Islands, since Java was the scene of rapid population growth and resultant pressure on land resources, which produced sharp discrepancies in per capita income between the two ethnically based sectors as well as smaller gaps between Java and the outer provinces.[48]

Independence did not automatically relieve this basic dualism, much to the consternation of many nationalist leaders. Prior to 1958, foreign interests continued to dominate the capital-intensive sector, and to the extent that private foreign capital has continued to flow in, it has also been devoted to its traditional outlets in plantation and mining (petroleum) enterprise. The government's capacity to provide capital for diversification of production has been severely limited by the necessity to finance all the paraphernalia associated with political independence. More recently, the government has devoted much of the resources at its disposal to Indonesianize the distributive, banking, and transport industries, all dominated by foreign finance and personnel at the time of independence. In this situation, the basically dichotomous structure of the economy has remained with little change, even though revolutionary changes have occurred in many areas of Indonesian society.

It is difficult to delineate the geographical confines of the Indonesian economy's two basic sectors. Some writers have drawn the distinction between Java as the traditional, labor-intensive sector and the outlying islands as the modern, capital-intensive sector. This simplified version of the dichotomy lacks realism. Only Sumatra possesses a greater share of estate agriculture and mining enterprise than any other island. Borneo has little estate agriculture and some mining installations. Celebes has little of either. On the other hand, Java is the site of relatively large areas devoted to estate agriculture, second only to Sumatra, and it also has a number of relatively large-scale processing and distributive installations for rubber and petroleum. As per cent of income produced from all sources, capital-intensive activities have undoubtedly been more important on most of the outlying islands than on Java, however.[49] Data showing the island distribution of some of the modern, capital-intensive activities are presented in Table 4.

Table 4. ISLAND LOCATION OF CAPITAL-INTENSIVE ENTERPRISE

	Java	Sumatra[a]	Borneo	Celebes	Other
Operating oil fields	1	9	3		
Oil fields not operating	2	3			1
Operating mines	2	6	2	1	
Mines not operating	6	2	9	14	
Planted area, agricultural estates (1,000 hectares)	374	432	10	15	8

(a) Including offshore islands.

SOURCE: U. S. Department of Commerce, *Investment in Indonesia* (Washington, 1956); *Statistical Pocketbook of Indonesia 1959*.

Composition of Output

Indonesia does not issue official annual data on its national income and product accounts, so that the composition of output is difficult to ascertain.[50] The first postwar estimate was made by a United Nations expert, S. Daniel Neumark, attached to Indonesia's former National Planning Bureau.[51] This estimate, completed in 1954 and covering the years 1951 and 1952, has served as the basis for revisions for those years and estimations of national income and product for subsequent years. Data on the national income and product variables have been submitted by the government to the Economic Commission for Asia and the Far East (ECAFE) and also to the Statistical Office of the United Nations; the estimates published by these sources are the only data now available that may be considered to be more or less official.[52] The Indonesian National Planning Bureau has also published estimates for the years 1953-58. It should be borne in mind, however, that all postwar estimates are based on limited data. The United Nations publishes Indonesian national account estimates with this warning: "The figures have been calculated by using rough estimates and extrapolations based on the national income estimates for the years 1951-52 prepared by Dr. D. S. Neumark."[53]

The advantage of Neumark's estimate is that his presentation shows considerable detail in the account "national income by industrial origin." Later revisions by Indonesian writers and the National Planning Bureau, as well as the estimates submitted to ECAFE and the UN Statistical Office, fail to provide enough detail to present a satisfactory picture of the composition of output.

175

Table 5 presents the National Planning Bureau's estimates for 1953 to 1958.

For the year 1952, an estimate of the contribution made by the labor-intensive and capital-intensive sectors to each component of the net domestic product, at factor cost, is presented in Table 6. This estimate gives a rough indication of the relative importance of the economy's two basic sectors in the economic activities listed in the Neumark breakdown by industrial origin.

All estimates reflect the overwhelming importance of agriculture (including forestry and fisheries) as a source of output. Neumark's figures show agriculture's contribution at about 56 per cent of total net output in 1951 and 1952; the National Planning Bureau's estimates show an average agricultural contribution of 55.6 per cent for the six years 1953-58; and the ECAFE tables show an average of 55.8 per cent for the nine years 1951-59. Smallholders' food crops and smallholders' export crops dominate agricultural output, contributing about 65 per cent and 13 per cent respectively to agriculture's total. Plantation crops represent about 6 per cent

Table 5. PERCENTAGE DISTRIBUTION OF NATIONAL INCOME BY SECTORS OF THE INDONESIAN ECONOMY

Sector	1953	1954	1955	1956	1957	1958
Agriculture						
Peasant food crops	36.2	36.9	36.2	36.6	35.5	40.4
Peasant export crops	7.9	7.9	8.0	7.1	6.7	3.6
Estate crops	4.5	3.8	3.8	3.5	3.4	3.2
Livestock	4.2	4.9	4.6	4.5	4.2	5.0
Fisheries	3.0	2.9	2.9	2.8	2.6	3.0
Forestry	2.3	2.2	1.4	1.4	1.3	1.6
Less export duties and statistical tax	1.1	.6	.9	.9	.9	.8
Total agriculture	57.0	58.0	56.0	55.0	52.6	56.0
Nonagriculture						
Industry	12.0	11.8	12.2	12.5	14.1	11.0
Services	23.1	22.5	23.2	23.4	23.1	19.3
Government	7.9	7.7	8.6	9.1	10.2	13.7
Total Nonagriculture	43.0	42.0	44.0	45.0	47.4	44.0
All sectors	100.0	100.0	100.0	100.0	100.0	100.0

SOURCE: Biro Perantjang Negara, *Report on the Execution of the Five-Year Development Plan 1956-1960: Covering the Years 1956, 1957, and 1958* (Djakarta, August 1960, mimeographed), p. 101.

of agricultural output, with a tendency toward decline over the years for which data exist.

The various estimates place the contribution of manufacturing at approximately 8 to 10 per cent of the value of total output for the years 1951-59. Undoubtedly this tends to underestimate the importance of manufacturing by omitting a substantial part of handicraft manufactures. It is likely that much of handicraft production is either excluded from the national product estimates or included in the contribution of small-scale agriculture. Even the recent extensive surveys of the manufacturing industries conducted by the Central Bureau of Statistics[54] failed to obtain data on the volume of handicraft manufactures during the years studied. Handicraft activity is almost inextricably associated with other

Table 6. NATIONAL INCOME OF INDONESIA BY
INDUSTRIAL ORIGIN, 1952

	Total (thousand Rp.)	Labor-intensive sector Per cent	Labor-intensive sector Thousand Rp.
Agriculture			
Peasant food crops	30,054,093	100.0	30,054,093
Peasant export crops	7,649,639	100.0	7,649,639
Estate crops	2,823,171	10.0	282,317
Livestock	3,132,190	100.0	3,132,190
Fisheries	2,687,666	100.0	2,687,666
Forestry	1,245,412	100.0	1,245,412
Total agriculture	47,592,171		45,051,317
Less indirect tax adjustment	−1,507,000	93.0	−1,401,510
Net agriculture	46,085,171		43,649,807
Mining	1,846,193	10.0	184,619
Industry	6,700,000	50.0	3,350,000
Transport and communications	2,491,801		
Trade, banking, and insurance	10,942,700	varies	6,586,043
Hotels, restaurants, and catering	224,000		
Entertainment industries	168,000		
Private building and construction	945,000	33.3	315,000
Rent	5,300,000	80.0	4,240,000
Free professions	500,000		
Domestic service	550,000	50.0	275,000
Central government, including defense	4,054,956	66.7	2,703,304
Local government	1,249,800	66.7	833,200
Government income from property, excluding estates	581,300		
NET DOMESTIC PRODUCT AT FACTOR COST	81,638,921		62,136,973

SOURCE: Paauw, *Financing Economic Development,* p. 208.

activities; much does not reach the market and is performed as a part-time occupation of labor that may not be involved in either the agricultural or industrial labor market. In this situation statistical coverage is virtually impossible; yet the omission tends to give a slight downward bias to the contribution of manufacturing to total product.

Manufacturing activities reported in the statistics cited are mainly indigenous enterprise concerned with the production of consumer goods. Table 7 presents data for 1958 showing the relative importance of the various types of manufactures in terms of percentage of total employees. These data were compiled by the Central Bureau of Statistics; coverage included 10,175 plants of medium and large size (i.e. with ten or more employees). The striking fact is concentration on manufacture of essential consumer goods. One-third of the employees were concerned with the manufacture of food and tobacco products, one-fourth with clothing. Eighty-eight per

Table 7. EMPLOYEES IN MAJOR INDUSTRIES IN INDONESIA, 1958

(*medium- and large-sized firms*)

Industry	Percentage of total employees
Food (including rice mills)	10.9
Beverages	1.5
Tobacco	20.6
Textile	16.3
Wearing apparel (including batik)	9.1
Furniture	1.5
Lumber	2.4
Paper	0.8
Printing	5.4
Leather	2.6
Rubber	5.0
Chemical (including soap, drugs)	6.7
Nonmetallic minerals	3.9
Metal products	3.7
Machinery, excluding electrical, manufacture and repair	1.7
Electrical machinery, manufacture and repair	0.6
Transport equipment	4.3
Miscellaneous	3.0
	100.0

SOURCE: Leon A. Mears, "Economic Development in Indonesia through 1958," *Ekonomi dan Keuangan Indonesia, 14* (1961), Table 6, 37. Computed from data in Biro Pusat Statistik, *Perusahaan-perusahaan Industri* [Manufacturing Industries] *1958* (Djakarta, 1960), Table 18, pp. 4-5.

cent of the 447,269 workers covered were reported to be employed in manufacturing plants on Java; another 7 per cent on Sumatra.[55] The significance of these figures should not be overemphasized, however. It is likely that statistical coverage is better for Java than for the outlying islands. Mears believes that manufacturing has become more concentrated on Java than prior to World War II,[56] but the statistical evidence behind this conclusion is dubious.

Table 8 presents data on the size (in terms of numbers of employees) of the manufacturing plants covered in the Central Bureau of Statistics survey; it shows that 56 per cent of the employees worked in plants with 100 or more employees, but only 11 per cent of the plants fell in this category. These data suggest that Indonesia has made some small progress in industrial development since independence, if not in raising the share of manufacturing in total output, at least in absolute measures of employment and firms. Just prior to World War II total industrial employment was estimated to be about 2,800,000, with 2,500,000 employed in small-scale industries and only 300,000 in factory industry.[57] In 1958, what may be termed factory employment totaled about 450,000 in manufactures for domestic consumption alone; employment in processing plants in the export industries would increase this total. The number of firms engaged in manufacture on a factory basis also apears to have grown substantially since the immediate prewar period.[58]

Table 8. MEDIUM- AND LARGE-SIZED INDONESIAN INDUSTRY
BY NUMBER OF EMPLOYEES, 1958

Number of employees per plant	Percentage of total plants	Percentage of total employees
10-24	50	13
25-49	26	15
50-99	13	16
100-249	7.5	20
250-499	2.1	13
500-999	0.9	10
1000-1999	0.4	9
2000 and over	0.1	4
	100.0	100.0

SOURCE: Mears, "Economic Development in Indonesia through 1958," Table 7, p. 38. Computed from data in *Perusahaan-perusahaan Industri 1958*, Table 18, pp. 4-5.

Until the 1930s industrial development consisted primarily of factory processing of agricultural and mineral goods for export and small-scale cottage industry for domestic needs. Significant growth of factories producing consumer goods for the domestic market did not begin until 1935, when the government began to promote this type of industry. Although these industries grew very rapidly between 1935 and the beginning of World War II, modern industry in Indonesia was still largely oriented toward the world market when the country gained its sovereignty in 1949. Small-scale handicraft industry was almost completely the domain of the Indonesian, while industrial processing for export was dominated by foreigners. Modern industries producing consumer goods such as textiles for the domestic market were owned by Europeans and the Chinese minority; and the Chinese also dominated the less capital-intensive consumer goods plants, such as rice mills and ice factories.

Under the impact of government policies to stimulate industrial development, Indonesian private entrepreneurship began to enter the (non-handicraft) manufacturing field on a significant scale during the first six or seven years after independence. Almost exclusively, emphasis was placed on the production of goods for local consumption. The government itself took the initiative for developing a number of large-scale manufacturing enterprises under its Industrial Urgency Program begun in 1951, but positive results were modest.[59] After 1958 the government's interest became more narrowly focused upon increasing manufactures of basic necessities to provide eventual self-sufficiency of these goods. This "sandan-pangan" program, begun in 1959, led to a close relationship between government and private entrepreneurs in the production of industrial necessities, with the government providing raw materials and controlling the distribution of output. This policy followed the political leadership's belief that government efforts to stimulate private enterprise of a more individualistic type through its earlier programs had failed. There is evidence that progress was made in expanding the volume of manufactures designed for home consumption since independence, particularly during the middle '50s.[60] Surveys conducted by the University of Indonesia have shown, however, that industrial development has continued to be plagued by insufficient supplies of raw materials, problems of importing and obtaining capital goods, problems of management and marketing and the lack of capital-goods producing facilities in Indonesia.[61]

The behavior of mining output in the national income accounting sense has been somewhat paradoxical. Neumark's estimate showed mining contributing just over 2 per cent of net national product in 1951 and 1952.[62] Later estimates indicate that mining's contribution jumped to 4-5 per cent of net domestic product in 1956 and 1957, but fell back to 3 per cent in 1958 and 2.5 per cent in 1959.[63] It is difficult to reconcile these results with data on output from mining enterprises. The output of petroleum, the major product, showed steady expansion, while tin output has fallen.[64] Outputs of minerals of lesser importance have also declined since 1957, with the exception of bauxite.[65] On the other hand, aggregate real domestic product also fell in 1958 and rose only slightly in 1959; and with the commanding importance of petroleum in mineral production, we would hardly expect significant decline in the share of mining in domestic product. It would appear, therefore, that petroleum has been undervalued relative to other mineral outputs.

Little is known about the details of the contribution made by the economy's other sectors to national product. The most important of these is the commercial sector, which includes in Neumark's estimate the components trade, banking, and insurance. In 1951 it contributed 15.2 per cent and in 1952, 13.4 per cent to net national income, while the related activities of transport and communications together provided about 3 per cent.[66] It is probable that these activities maintained about this level of contribution until 1957, when disruption of commerce and communications began to occur —first as a result of the rebellion and the eviction of the Dutch and later as a consequence of the government's efforts to reorganize distribution and other commercial activities. By 1959 distributive channels in the outlying islands had almost completely collapsed, and even on Java distribution of goods had slowed down. By 1961 the government had succeeded in partially restoring distributive channels on Java, and some improvement was apparent in other regions. In the intervening years the contribution of commercial and communications activities probably fell to less than 10 per cent of total product.

An important change over the years since independence has been the growth of the central government's contribution, including defense. Here again data are not available to show accurately the quantitative dimensions of the change. Neumark's estimates for 1951 and 1952 placed the government sector's contribution at just about 5 per cent. With the rapid growth of the administrative bureaucracy that occurred in the ensuing years and the even more pronounced expansion of defense facilities, the National Planning Bureau's estimates for the government sector—10.2 per cent of total national income for 1957, and 13.7 per cent for 1958—cannot be considered an exaggeration. It is reasonable to assume that this sector now (1962) comprises at least 15 per cent of national product.

Performance of the Economy

The dynamics of the Indonesian economy have undergone considerable change since Indonesia assumed sovereignty over the former Netherlands East Indies in 1949. In 1949, reflecting its colonial background, the modern sector was still closely tied up with the world market. Foreign trade had an important impact upon the economy, but this effect was transmitted through the modern producing and trading sectors, in which foreign ownership and enterprise were dominant. During the first few years of independence, the economy showed the same basic pattern of export orientation. By the end of the first decade of the new Republic, however, the export orientation of the economy had become less important. Exports had fallen significantly relative to national product, and the traditional sector had gained as an exporter relative to the modern sector.

These trends had begun to emerge during the 1930s, the last decade of firm Dutch control, although they became clearly apparent only after full independence was achieved.[67] During the mid-1920s, the value of exports relative to domestic product had been high as a result of expanding output for world markets and favorable market conditions. From 1925 to the onslaught of the depression in early 1930, the ratio of exports to domestic product was generally above 30 per cent, falling from 36 per cent in 1925 to about 30 per cent in 1929. During the 1930s the ratio continued to decline, leveling off at approximately 25 per cent by the end of the decade.

In calculating the ratio of export values to domestic product for the postwar years, we are confronted with the problem of rupiah valuation of exports. The estimates presented in Table 9 are based on rupiah values of export earnings at the rate of Rp. 11.40 to U. S. $1.00, the rate which was official from 1952 to 1959. This uniform rate is used to show rupiah values as determined by export volumes and world price levels. The declining ratio of export values to gross domestic product, therefore, partially reflects rapid Indonesian inflation relative to world price levels. Even with the domestic price factor eliminated from domestic product series, however, the ratio shows a significant decline over the decade of the 1950s (see Table 9).

This clear tendency is also reflected in the declining importance of production for export in the national income accounts. The change in the contribution of agricultural export production to national income from 1951 to 1958, is shown in Table 10. The share contributed by agricultural export activities fell from about 15 per cent of net domestic product in the early 1950s to about 10 per cent in 1956-57; the low contribution for 1958 (6.8 per cent) reflects the unusual circumstances of that year, particularly the impact of the rebellion.

The share of mining, the only other activity traditionally oriented toward export, rose slightly over the decade of the 1950s. Although an increasingly large part of mining output has been produced for

Table 9. RATIO OF EXPORT VALUES TO DOMESTIC PRODUCT

	Exports[a] (billion rupiah)	GDP[b] (billion rupiah)	Ratio (Exports to GDP, as percentage)	NDP[c] (billion rupiah, 1955 prices)	Ratio (Exports to NDP)
1951	14.8	66.0	22	104.4	13.2
1952	10.7	81.6	13	105.5	10.0
1953	9.6	86.6	11	112.5	8.5
1954	9.9	94.6	10	120.3	8.2
1955	10.8	125.1	9	122.6	8.8
1956	10.6	145.2	7	124.5	8.1
1957	11.0	171.0	6	134.5	8.2
1958	9.2	180.2	5	130.0	7.1
1959	9.9	210.1	5	132.0	7.5

(a) Valued at approximately Rp. 11.45 equals U. S. $1.00. The 1951 figure is raised from the value reflecting the official rate at that time (Rp. 3.81 = U. S. $1.00) to 11.45 = U. S. $1.00. Data are taken from *Statistical Pocketbook of Indonesia 1960*, p. 105, and rounded off to billions to make them consistent with the gross domestic product figures.

(b) Gross domestic product at current factor cost, as published by the United Nations *Yearbook of National Accounts Statistics, 1960*, p. 257.

(c) Net domestic product at constant factor cost of 1955. 1951-55 data from National Planning Bureau, "A Study of the Indonesian Economic Development Scheme," *Ekonomi dan Keuangan Indonesia*, 10 (1957), Table 1, p. 614; 1956-59 data from United Nations, *Yearbook of National Accounts Statistics, 1960*, p. 114.

183

domestic markets rather than export, the volume of petroleum exports has grown significantly over the decade; in this regard, petroleum has been unique. The volume of virtually all other categories of exports has shown a tendency to fall since 1951. Data on the behavior of export volumes by major commodity groups including petroleum are presented in Table 11.[68]

Petroleum production is the only field of enterprise in which foreign ownership and operation are still dominant. Despite the entrance of government firms into petroleum mining, foreign companies still accounted for about 90 per cent of crude petroleum production in 1959.[69] Several foreign-owned companies operate under special arrangements which allow them to use a part of their foreign exchange earnings for imports and reinvestment. At the time of this writing, negotiations are in progress that may provide new conditions under which these companies operate. Up to the present, however, the Indonesian government has not had complete access to the foreign exchange earned by foreign petroleum-exporting firms. This is significant because petroleum exports have been the only category of products showing appreciable growth since the prewar period and since independence.

The causes of the declining importance of exports are numerous and complex. Of primary significance is the dominant role of the

Table 10. AGRICULTURAL EXPORT SECTOR CONTRIBUTION TO NATIONAL INCOME, 1951-58

(*percentage of net domestic product at factor cost*)

Year	Smallholder export crops	Plantation export crops	Agricultural exports
1951	10.5	4.4	14.9
1952	10.1	4.9	15.0
1953	7.9	4.5	12.4
1954	7.9	3.8	11.7
1955	8.0	3.8	11.8
1956	7.1	3.5	10.6
1957	6.7	3.4	10.1
1958	3.6	3.2	6.8

SOURCE: 1951-52, Muljatno, "Perhitungan Pendapatan Nasional Indonesia untuk Tahun 1953/1954" [Estimate of Indonesian National Income for 1953/1954], *Ekonomi dan Keuangan Indonesia, 13* (1960), Table 3, pp. 192-93; 1953-58, National Planning Bureau, *Report on the Execution of the Five-Year Development Plan, 1956-1960,* English edition (Djakarta, 1960), Table 78, p. 101.

Table 11. EXPORTS BY COMMODITY GROUPS, 1939-60

(*gross weight: 1,000,000 kilograms*)

| Year | Animal products | Estate products | Vegetable products | | | | | Mineral products | Other products | Total[a] |
			Farm products	Forest products	Wood	Other	Subtotal[a]			
1939	33	2,669	1,287	131	417	74	4,577	7,468	24	12,103
1950	22	429	1,110	81	90	9	1,719	6,766	13	8,519
1951	39	547	1,403	100	92	20	2,162	7,507	27	9,735
1952	29	632	1,010	112	157	25	1,936	8,305	34	10,305
1953	23	752	987	118	155	20	2,033	10,309	47	12,412
1954	15	838	1,263	136	146	21	2,403	10,387	9	12,814
1955	25	829	1,192	91	167	20	2,299	10,134	18	12,476
1956	16	846	1,013	72	50	8	1,989	12,765	9	14,778
1957	14	785	1,060	77	148	21	2,091	14,758	10	16,872
1958	13	662	778	71	115	20	1,645	15,285	5	16,948
1959	18	645	1,058	92	57	12	1,863	12,779	8	14,669
1960	17	590	952	74	101	18	1,734	14,291	9	16,050

(a) Totals may reflect rounding of figures to nearest whole number.
SOURCE: *Statistical Pocketbook of Indonesia 1957*, p. 108; *1959*, p. 115; *1960*, p. 113; *1961*, p. 115.

government in expanding the money value of national product by continual deficit financing and by holding to an unrealistically low exchange rate which depresses export earnings. In addition, the government's efforts to revamp the structure of ownership and operation of the economy, and its success in wresting control of the capital-intensive sector of the economy from foreigners, have affected export production adversely.

One result has been to make the Indonesian economy less dependent upon fluctuations in the world market. There is little doubt that international market conditions have less influence on Indonesian employment and money income than during the colonial period. On the other hand, development and the standard of living have suffered severely, because export earnings and the capacity to finance imports have not kept pace with population growth and the growth of national product. The consumer goods component in the import account has been reduced as a result of balance of payments pressures and concentration on development objectives. At the same time, the falling capacity to import raw materials and capital goods for nascent industries has been a major obstacle to domestic industrialization, as Indonesian reports have emphasized.[70]

The Indonesian government has played a major role in changing the economy. Qualitative aspects are discussed elsewhere in this chapter; here we focus upon the government's quantitative impact in generating aggregate demand. During the last two decades of colonial rule, government expenditures varied between 10 and 15 per cent of gross domestic product. This ratio was maintained during the first six or seven years after the transfer of sovereignty,[71] although sizable budgetary deficits were required to achieve this level of government expenditures. However, after 1956, the gathering momentum of the trend toward Guided Economy increased the government's quantitative impact. Between 1957 and 1959 government expenditures averaged 19 per cent of gross domestic product,[72] and annual government deficits also reached new proportions. By 1959 expenditures had risen to 22 per cent, and the budget deficit to 7 per cent.

The government's greater role in generating expenditures has had two major consequences. First, as a growing source of personal income—reflected in the notable increase in the government payroll for military personnel, for the larger bureaucracy, and for the emerging corps of employees concerned with administration of the government's economic interests—the government has rendered

186

the nongovernment sectors of the economy less important in inducing changes in the society's income. Since government-generated income payments do not usually decrease, this change is likely to reduce fluctuations in personal income and provide stability of incomes and employment to an extent not found in the traditional or modern private sectors.

Second, the government's greater participation in the economy has aggravated the economy's inflationary bias. Growing government expenditures have not been matched by increased tax revenues; this has produced a volatile multiplier effect upon aggregate demand, a condition which is likely to continue at least until the readjustment in the society's organization has been more or less completed. Thus far, little thought has been given to devising a tax system to accord with the changing dynamics of the economy. The private enterprise-oriented tax structure inherited from Indonesia's colonial past will tend to become increasingly ineffective in financing government expenditures as progress toward the goals of socialism and Guided Economy continues.

As in any economy the more complex the patterns of specialization and division of labor, the greater is the need for a variety of incentives to assure that the essential economic functions will be performed. Mere subsistence economies—or subsistence sectors of an economy—may function well with passive incentives or relatively negative inducements. It is probable that one-fifth or more of total output in Indonesia is still produced for subsistence.[73] Even in this traditional sector, however, the expansion of output beyond minimum subsistence requirements, and the availability of its products for intersectoral transfers, are tied up with market incentives. The government has confronted this problem directly in its rice purchasing and distribution program, which is designed to insure adequate supplies of rice at relatively low and stable prices.[74] The government's domestic purchases have been insufficient to achieve its objectives, partly because its purchasing prices have been below prevailing free market prices[75] and partly because supplies of manufactured goods have been inadequate to prevent deteriorating terms of trade for products marketed by the traditional sector.[76] The government has raised its purchase prices, but continuing inflation has defeated the incentive effects of this policy, as the free market price of rice and prices of manufactures have risen more rapidly. In 1960, the government began experimenting with providing textiles at the official price in exchange for rice,[77] but distribution problems have prevented this effort from having widespread favorable effects; and efforts at stimulating rice production via the "Paddy Center" Plan, described in the preceding chapter, have not yet resulted in expanded output. Rice has become the largest single commodity import in value terms, accounting for almost 20 per cent of rupiah import values, a substantial rise from its share in the mid-1950s.

In sectors which produce exclusively for the market, the major problems of economic incentives have been associated with the government's expanded role in the economy. The adverse effects of foreign exchange control policies on private production for export have been discussed above. In addition to this continuing problem, output has stagnated in government enterprises and among private firms producing for the domestic market. Indonesian observers themselves recognize that old patterns of incentives to save, invest, and produce have been weakened by government policies vis-à-vis the private sector as well as within firms which operate as government enterprises, and that these changes lie at the heart of stagnation in the market sectors of the economy.[78] The current interpretation in Indonesia is that the private sector has a role in certain types of economic activity, but that private enterprise must be subjected to public and social control. "State enterprises must assume a 'leading and commanding role' vis-à-vis private enterprises in the same field of activity."[79] In practice this has meant official efforts to limit returns on investment in the private sector through the government's direct and indirect allocation of resources, often accompanied by fixing the prices of productive factors as well as prices of finished products. In the public sector, government policy has played down monetary incentives and material rewards by holding down wage and salary differentials.[80] The profit motive has been discredited throughout the system, and official controls have seriously weakened the relationship between the assumption of risk, the supply of effort, and legally obtained economic rewards. Although the political leadership has attempted to fill the void by appeals to patriotic and nationalistic motives, government policies have tended to replace incentives to positive economic performance in both the private and public sectors with incentives to obtain rewards through extralegal channels.[81] In general, therefore, the changing pattern of economic incentives has discouraged output and investment by deflecting a part of the economy's scarce supply of entrepreneurial and managerial resources to relatively unproductive activities.

In this situation, continual increases in aggregate demand, associated mainly with government deficit-financed expenditures, have not stimulated responses leading to rising output. Private enterprise is still significant in the Indonesian economy, but incentives are not strong enough to induce relatively full utilization of capacity in the private sector; and other factors have also been important in causing falling employment of existing capital resources. In the growing public sector, the government has failed to make investable resources available for expansion, and management has not yet shown the capacity or motivation to use existing resources efficiently.

What we are describing is the dynamics of an economy in transition, an economy whose leaders are searching for formulae to develop a growing socialist system. This search has involved discrediting and encumbering the incentive system which had evolved during the society's colonial history and continued well into independence. It is probably inevitable that drastic changes in Indonesia's economic system, growing out of the national leadership's antipathy to foreign economic control, should have eroded private enterprise incentives more rapidly than a workable new incentive system could be devised.

Output, Investment, and Consumption

Estimates of the behavior of Indonesia's aggregate output and related aggregates, as measured by national income accounting methods, should be viewed with great caution. Despite periodic interest in this field, Indonesia has lagged behind other leading Southeast Asian countries in improving the statistical services essential to national income and product estimation.[82] Estimates for the period since 1949 have not been issued regularly; no data are publicly available for the period after 1960. Moreover, the national income data available have originated from different sources, and the results are not consistent. In all estimates it has been necessary to fill statistical voids by extrapolation and guesses. These problems raise serious doubts about the usefulness of the results.[83]

The national account data, such as they are, point to the conclusion that Indonesia experienced a moderate growth of output between 1951 and 1957, but that stagnation or even retrogression of per capita income occurred after 1957, although this can be documented by national income data only for the period through 1960. Per capita income, moreover, appears to have been restored to the prewar level as late as 1955;[84] by 1959, therefore, per capita income probably still approximated the 1938 level.

The Economic Commission for Asia and the Far East (ECAFE) describes the performance of the Indonesian economy in rather similar terms:

> On the whole, although the economy made appreciable growth during the early independence period while it was rehabilitating prewar productive capacity, the expansion was not sustained. In recent years growth has slowed down to such an extent that the economy seems to be headed for stagnation.[85]

ECAFE'S evaluation of performance of the economy on the basis of national income data leads that agency to emphasize stagnation of real income (output) per capita in recent years:

> The most obvious symptom of Indonesia's economic weakness is the trend in its *per capita* income. Although the estimates are not altogether reliable, they suggest that national product increased at an average rate of 4 per cent during 1951-1957, declined by 3.2 per cent in 1958 and recovered in the following year by only 1.3 per cent. The relatively high average rate of growth, higher than in India or Pakistan, reflects little more than the restoration of pre-war production capacity, which makes relatively small investments appear to give significant increases in output. That process seems to have ended, because the high returns of the early 'fifties could not be sustained without stepping up the rate of investment. On the other hand, population has grown at an accelerated rate from an estimated average of 1.5 per cent during 1951-1955 to 2.5 per cent during 1955-1959, thus slowing down very substantially the rate of growth in *per capita* income. It is significant that during 1954-1959 *per capita* income remained virtually stagnant at approximately Rp. 1,500 per annum (except in 1957). In real terms, this level of *per capita* income is probably not far from the prewar level, as seems also to be the case in Burma. Growth during the postwar period thus represents largely a process of economic rehabilitation and an advance just sufficient to keep up with population.
>
> Recovery has not been accompanied by any significant change in the structure of production. Up to 1956-1957, as national product increased, the share of manufacturing rose and that of agriculture fell. However levels of national income during 1958-1959 were associated with a fall in the share of manufacturing and with a rise in the share of agriculture. In spite of significant mineral resources, mining plays only a small role in the economy, and accounts for only 3 to 4 per cent of national product.[86]

The basic series in the ECAFE evaluation, gross national product at factor cost at constant 1955 prices, should reflect the growth of output if based on adequate statistical information.[87] This series shows an average annual rate of growth of aggregate product in constant prices amounting to 5.2 per cent for the period 1951-57,[88] and 5.1 per cent for the period 1951-55. For the latter part of the decade, however, the average annual rate of growth of aggregate product falls to 2.1 per cent for the period 1955-59 and becomes negative for the years 1957-59.

The ECAFE estimates for changes in per capita real product show a rise averaging about 1.5 per cent per year for the eight-year period 1951-59. This result is based on the questionable assumption that the rate of population growth rose from 1.5 per cent during the years 1951-55 to 2.5 per cent in the period 1955-59. It is unlikely that the rate of population growth was lower during the more stable years of the first half of the 1950 decade, when aggregate output was expanding, than during the last half of the decade when political and economic instability were great and when aggregate output appears to have been relatively stagnant. The results of the recent population census in Indonesia suggest a rate of population growth of 2.5 per cent per annum for the period 1950-61,[89] which is difficult to reconcile with ECAFE's 1.5 per cent for the period 1951-55. This implies that the ECAFE estimates for per capita income and its growth show an upward bias for that period. On the other hand, the ECAFE population rate estimate for 1959 (2.8 per cent) appears to be too high. It would seem preferable to work instead with an average rate of population growth of 2.5 per cent for the entire period since 1950.

The various national income estimates that have been published by Indonesian sources do not differ significantly from the ECAFE estimates of the behavior of aggregate real product for the period prior to 1958. National Planning Bureau estimates published in 1957[90] show the average annual rate of growth for gross domestic product at factor cost from 1951-55 at 5.1 per cent, with this aggregate measured in constant 1952 prices, and 4.1 per cent measured in 1955 prices.[91] Muljatno's independent revision, published in 1960, shows net national product at factor cost, in constant 1952 prices, growing at an average annual rate of 5.5 per cent during this period.[92] These estimates do not diverge seriously from the average rate of growth (gross national product in 1955 prices) of 5.1 per cent suggested by ECAFE data. Finally, the National Planning

Bureau estimates for the period 1953-58, published in 1960, yield an average annual rate of growth in gross national product in 1955 prices of 4.7 per cent for the period 1953-57,[93] while the ECAFE data yield a rate of 5.3 per cent. There is agreement among the various sources, therefore, that aggregate real product grew at an average rate near 5 per cent from 1951 to 1957. Assuming the annual rate of population growth to have been 2.5 per cent, these estimates would indicate that per capita real product was growing at an average rate of about 2.5 per cent per year during this period. In the passage quoted above ECAFE attributes this achievement to the relatively easy task of rehabilitation of productive facilities from wartime and revolution damage. Data concerning capital goods imports presented below suggest, however, that the rate of investment may have been substantially higher in the first half of the decade than the second half.

Discrepancies in the national income and product estimates focus on the year 1958. At that time Indonesia suffered the brunt of the rebellion of dissident groups in the outlying islands, and this coincided with the first impact of widespread government assumption of control of Dutch economic interests and the ousting of Dutch managerial and technical personnel. The real questions concern the extent to which aggregate real product fell in 1958 and whether or not stagnation of output at a level substantially below the peak postindependence year of 1957 persisted in later years.

The ECAFE evaluation suggests that real gross national product fell by 3.2 per cent in 1958 and recovered slightly in 1959, by 1.3 per cent. These estimates are close to the results published by the United Nations in its 1960 *Yearbook of National Account Statistics*, which show a 1958 decline of 3.3 per cent in net domestic product in 1955 prices followed by a rise of 1.4 per cent in 1959.[94] These estimates, which rely on data submitted by the Indonesian government on questionnaire forms, differ significantly from those published by the National Planning Bureau, which prepared national product data for its report on the execution of the first Five-Year Plan and which utilized, according to that report, the work of Indonesian and foreign national income experts.[95] The Planning Bureau's estimate shows a major decline, amounting to 12.6 per cent for real gross national product and 12.9 per cent for real net national product. A comparison of the results for the years 1953-58 is presented in Table 12.

Table 12. ECAFE, UN, AND NATIONAL PLANNING BUREAU ESTIMATES OF ECONOMIC
AGGREGATES, 1953-58

| | Gross national product in 1955 prices | | | | Net domestic product at factor cost in 1955 prices | | | |
| | ECAFE | | National Planning Bureau | | UN | | National Planning Bureau | |
	Billion Rp.	Per cent change	Billion Rp.	Per cent change	Billion Rp.	Per cent change	Billion Rp.	Per cent change
1953	111.6		120.1		109.0		109.1	
1954	120.1	7.6	128.5	7.0	116.8	7.1	116.7	7.0
1955	123.9	3.2	127.9	— .5	121.5	4.0	118.9	1.9
1956	127.5	2.9	134.5	5.2	124.5	2.5	124.5	4.7
1957	137.5	7.8	144.7	7.6	134.5	8.0	134.5	8.0
1958	133.1	—3.2	126.8	—12.4	130.0	—3.3	117.1	—12.9

SOURCE: ECAFE data, ECAFE, Economic Survey of Asia and the Far East, 1961 (Bangkok, 1962), Tables 3-23, p. 109; National Planning Bureau data, National Planning Bureau, Report of the Execution of the Five-Year Development Plan, Tables 75 and 76, pp. 97-98; UN data, UN, Yearbook of National Accounts Statistics, 1960, p. 114.

There is some evidence that the UN and ECAFE series understate the decline in real product in 1958 by not taking the Indonesian inflation into sufficient account. In the UN net domestic product series, the implicit price deflator for 1958 is only 135 (1955 equals 100), yet available price indices for all major sectors show price increases between 1955 and 1958 substantially greater than 35 per cent.[96] For the agricultural sector, where prices during the late 1950s were rising less rapidly than in other major sectors, a National Planning Bureau study shows a general price rise of 42 per cent between 1957 and 1958 alone.[97]

There is agreement, however, on the fact of falling output in 1958 and continued stagnation in 1959. The various estimates also indicate similar conclusions about the sectors in which the decline was most serious. It is important to note, however, that important shifts took place within the agricultural sector. The share of food crops increased while export crops fell; the changes reported by the Planning Bureau between 1957 and 1958 show that peasant food crops rose from 35.5 to 40.4 per cent of national income, peasant export crops fell from 6.7 to 3.6 per cent and estate crops fell from 3.4 to 3.2 per cent (cf. Table 5).[98]

The decline in total output in 1958 and the continued stagnation in 1959—and presumably later years—represented a shift from production in export, industrial, and service sectors toward food crops production, particularly such supplementary crops as cassava and maize.[99] It is interesting to observe that this is much the same pattern of shifting economic activities that resulted from the impact of the Great Depression in the early 1930s, suggesting the hypothesis that such shifts are associated with retrogression in the market sector of the economy. The emphasis on supplementary crops clearly represents a shift toward the subsistence sector, while the same conclusion is suggested by the sharp decrease registered in government rice purchases for its distribution program in 1958. These purchases dropped from 639 thousand tons (79.9 per cent of planned purchases) in 1957 to 330 thousand tons in 1958 (35.5 per cent of planned purchases).[100] A general picture of falling output in the agricultural export sector, described in the preceding chapter, is presented in terms of index numbers in Table 13.

In addition to their effect on the export crops sector, the 1958 decline and subsequent stagnation spread through other sectors in the market economy. Manufacturing is reported to have suffered an especially severe loss in output.[101] Gains in petroleum and bauxite production were more than offset by losses in tin, coal, and other mineral products. The National Planning Bureau attributed the 1958 decline in aggregate output "to a considerable extent to the decline in production in the industry segment," arguing that "this was due in large measure to the shortages of industrial raw materials and spare parts for machinery and equipment."[102]

The alleged decline in manufacturing and related sectors cannot be fully documented by detailed data, yet there are many official complaints of inefficient use of existing industrial capacity.[103] The Central Bureau of Statistics data show a decline in the total number of manufacturing establishments (slightly over 6 per cent) and a decline in employment (4 per cent) between 1957 and 1958.[104] The same source reports substantial reductions in output

Table 13. INDICATORS OF PRODUCTION, 1951-52 AND 1956-59

	1951-52	1956-57	1958-59
	(per cent of gross national product)		
Sectoral share in gross domestic product:			
Agriculture	56	54	58
Manufacturing	9	11	8
Mining	2	4	3
Others	33	31	31
	(kilograms per capita per year)		
Cereal production:	96	107	112
	(index numbers: 1938 = 100)		
Production of agricultural export commodities:			
Smallholding agriculture			
including rubber	206	170	168
excluding rubber	59	53	34
rubber only	343	280	288
Plantation agriculture			
including rubber	67	74	70
excluding rubber	37	48	48
rubber only	150	150	134
Mineral production:			
Crude petroleum	111	190	232
Tin	121	106	82
Bauxite	201	111	149
Coal	63	53	42

SOURCE: ECAFE, *Economic Survey of Asia and the Far East, 1961,* Tables 3-24, p. 110.

of large weaving and knitting mills for both 1958 and 1959.[105] Moreover, low rates of utilization of existing capacity, caused by inadequate supplies of raw materials, were reported in the textile industry.[106]

Retrogression in other sectors cannot be supported by national income data; in recent years most estimates of domestic product by industrial origin have lumped together all of the service sectors and government. The National Planning Bureau report, however, showed the share of services in domestic product falling from 23.1 per cent in 1957 to 19.3 per cent in 1958, the latter well below this sector's share in the years 1953-57. The Bureau's data for shares by major sectors from 1953 to 1958 are presented in Table 5. The report indicates that the contraction of services in 1958 "was due primarily to the decline in the trade, banking and insurance segment which fell from a contribution of 12.6 per cent in 1953 to a low of 9.6 per cent in 1958."[107] The growth of the government sector is attributed to increased outlays for public administration and defense.[108]

There can be little doubt that value added in distributive trades, finance, and transport fell in 1958, reflecting the removal of the large Dutch component in these activities. It is likely that the contribution of these sectors to domestic product has continued to lag as a result of continuing pressures against other minority groups in these fields and the comprehensive reorganization of the distributive and financial apparatus. There is also a strong presumption that stagnation in these important sectors has retarded the revival of production in manufacturing and agricultural export activities. Stagnation in the trading sector is reflected in a marked decline in transport of all types. Freight movement by rail, shipping, and air are all reported to have fallen seriously in 1958 and, despite some recovery in 1959 and 1960, the volume of freight remained below that moved in the mid-1950s.[109] After the Dutch-owned KPM fleet was barred from Indonesian waters in 1957, interisland transport declined seriously,[110] and despite Indonesian emphasis on building a national fleet, shipping facilities are still below the volume available in 1957. Since 1958 a large part of available shipping has been diverted to military operations, first to quell the rebellion and more recently as a result of the West Irian problem. Air traffic in terms of distance flown and freight and passengers carried also fell drastically in 1958, and has failed to recover the previous high levels achieved in 1956 and 1957.[111]

All Indonesian estimates of investment are built from data on the rupiah value of imports of capital goods. An assumed local installation component—the cost of installing these goods locally—is added to the basic import item;[112] this component frequently varies from year to year. In some cases, an estimate of investment in the village sector is added to complete the rupiah value of gross investment.

The problem concerning the usefulness of the results is not so much a matter of the procedure employed—this method is commonly used in underdeveloped countries—but rather in the rupiah valuation of imported capital goods.[113] Throughout the period 1952-59, rupiah values for imported goods were derived from the official exchange rate, i.e. approximately Rp. 11.4 to U. S. $1.00. As domestic price levels have risen, this method of establishing rupiah values for imported capital goods yields a serious downward bias to the estimated value of domestic investment, affecting both the imported and local components No estimate has attempted to correct for domestic inflation.

This procedure produces estimates of Indonesian investment at rupiah values in terms of world price levels since the exchange rate is held constant. In deriving the ratio of Indonesian investment to domestic product, therefore, rising Indonesian price levels (relative to world prices) are reflected in domestic product values but not in the value of estimated investment. This has misled many observers to accept a ridiculously low investment rate for Indonesia, even during the years of relatively rapid growth of real product. Similarly, the procedure has produced erroneous conclusions about the incremental capital-output ratio since investment has been seriously underestimated relative to the value of product increments, suggesting an unrealistically low ratio. Since there is no satisfactory basis for determining the appropriate ratio of the value of imported goods to the total value of investment, there is merit in using only imports of capital goods to provide some indication of year to year changes in investment activity. This approach avoids giving the impression that the addition of arbitrary markups to unadjusted rupiah values of capital goods imports yields estimates of investment meaningful to a situation in which all other components of domestic product reflect rapidly rising domestic price levels.

Table 14 (column 1) presents the rupiah values of imported capital goods from 1951 to 1959, at the constant exchange rate of

Rp. 11.4 to U. S. $1.00. The unit value of imports has shown some degree of fluctuation over these years (see column 2); if the capital goods imports series is deflated by the index of unit value of imports, we obtain a rough measure of the real value of investment goods imported into Indonesia (see column 3).

Either series for the value of capital goods imports—rupiah values reflecting changes in world prices (column 1) or rupiah values with world price changes eliminated (column 3)—suggests that investment activity was relatively high in the period 1952-57, followed by a sharp drop in 1958 and 1959. The first series shows a decline in capital goods imports of 43 per cent in 1958; the second, in constant world prices, indicates a decline of 47 per cent. It appears clear that the sharp reduction in imported capital goods had much to do with the reductions in output.[114] In Indonesia, as in most underdeveloped countries, capital formation is still dependent on a high import component, since there is little domestic production of capital goods. This is less true for investment in the village sector, but even where investment activity is organized on a community development basis, capital goods are essential to the creation of productive capital.[115] There is every presumption that local

Table 14. IMPORTS OF CAPITAL GOODS, UNIT VALUES OF IMPORTS, AND DEFLATED VALUES OF CAPITAL GOODS IMPORTS

Year	Imports of capital goods[a] (million rupiah)	Unit value of imports[b] (1953 = 100)	Deflated value, imports of capital goods (million rupiah)
1951	2,460	116	2,121
1952	3,190	110	2,900
1953	2,604	100	2,604
1954	2,255	91	2,522
1955	2,219	91	2,438
1956	2,627	89	2,952
1957	2,924	88	3,323
1958	1,678	96	1,748
1959	1,620	83	1,952

(a) At the exchange rate of Rp. 11.4 = U. S. $1.00. Source: 1951-55, National Planning Bureau, "A Study of the Indonesian Economic Development Scheme," Table 2, p. 621 (omitting asbestos); 1956-59, calculated from data in Biro Pusat Statistik, Monthly Survey, January-February, 1961. Categories of items are consistent for all years.

(b) Source: ECAFE, Economic Survey of Asia and the Far East, 1959, p. 137; ibid., 1961, p. 198.

government investment, a major component of capital formation in the village sector, declined in the late 1950s after achieving fairly vigorous levels in the middle of the decade. The growing tension between central and regional governments, the rebellion of 1958, and the government's renewed efforts to centralize regional administration at the expense of local autonomy[116] have all discouraged local government investment and regional programs to mobilize and employ resources for local economic development.

It appears, therefore, that recent stagnation of per capita income is associated with a failure to maintain a satisfactory level of investment. In part this has resulted from government interference with incentives in the private sector, causing private investment to fall; and at the same time the government has failed to expand public investment. In fact, with the unusually severe security and budgetary problems of the post-1955 period, the government's capacity to allocate resources to capital formation has declined, and its real contribution to capital formation has also fallen.

The share of investment in government expenditures and the ratio of government investment to gross national product emphasize the deteriorating investment situation. The share of investment in total government expenditures reached a high mark of 20 per cent in 1954 but fell thereafter, amounting to only 11 per cent in 1957 and 9 per cent in 1958. The percentages shown for the latter years reveal an especially serious situation because government investment coincided with shrinking investment in the private sector.[117]

The statistical data cited suggest that the performance of the economy since independence, particularly since 1958, leaves much to be desired. Despite government development plans and political awareness of the problem, per capita income appears to have been relatively stagnant over the decade as a whole, beginning to decline in 1958. In fact, the years of seriously declining investment and output coincided with the first Five-Year Plan, 1956-61. In retrospect, it is apparent that the plan's effort was not large enough to overcome the forces of stagnation; it called for investment rates scarcely adequate to maintain per capita income.[118] During the first three years of its existence, when the plan was implemented under the general supervision of the National Planning Bureau, progress was made in initiating and extending a number of important projects. The output increases flowing from these projects, however, were inadequate to compensate for reductions in output resulting from political insecurity, the disruption caused by eviction of Dutch personnel in important sectors of production, and, finally, the negative response of the private sector to government attacks on the trading minorities as well as uncertainties about the future of private enterprise.

What has happened to consumption during the period since independence is by no means clear. It is probable that the gains in per capita output prior to 1957, and the decline after that date, were not closely correlated with per capita Indonesian consumption. For one thing, distribution of income has undergone considerable change as a result of independence and government policy. It is undoubtedly true that ethnic Indonesians receive a much greater share of domestic income today than at the time of independence. Inequality of distribution among the Indonesian, European, and "foreign Asiatic" (mostly Chinese) groups was a striking feature of colonialism: Polak's estimate of income distribution among them showed only 69 per cent of domestic income going to Indonesians in 1938, while 13 per cent went to Europeans, 10 per cent to foreign Asiatics, and 7 per cent to nonresidents.[119]

At the same time, there is little evidence that disparities in income distribution have been eliminated or even significantly reduced. It appears that upper-income foreign and minority groups have been replaced, at least to some extent, by upper-income Indonesians. Increasingly, positions of political influence have allowed Indonesians to receive disproportionately large incomes; frequently these positions are not associated with economic functions and thus are not part of a system of performance incentives. Moreover, there is evidence of growing concentration of land ownership in some areas, producing relatively high *rentier* income to wealthy Indonesians and "an ever growing class of landless peasants."[120]

An attempt to define more carefully the components of improved Indonesian per capita consumption further weakens the evidence for widespread improvement. The main items of Indonesian consumption—food and other essentials—appear to have shown no significant tendency toward a per capita increase in availability. Food production per capita has remained relatively stable over most of the years since the transfer of sovereignty, with a tendency toward increase in the mid-1950s followed by stagnation in the late 1950s.[121] Data released by the Central Bureau of Statistics on principal foodstuffs available per capita (with adjustments for seed, exports, and imports) suggest the same conclusion, even though the population deflator employed is shown by the 1961 census to have been too low.[122]

During the mid-1950s there had been a significant but temporary rise in imports destined for consumption, but this trend reversed itself late in the decade. The aggregate volume of imported consumer goods in the late 1950s was near the 1938 level; imported raw materials and auxiliary goods for domestic production were also near prewar volumes.[123] Higgins believes that domestic production of manufactures had expanded adequately during the period 1954-58 to raise per capita consumption of consumer manufactures, such as clothing and bicycles, despite falling imports.[124] Even during this period, however, imports of textile fabrics for use as producer goods, though they were high, did not reach prewar volumes (56 million tons in 1939; 44 million in 1957, the postwar peak; 23 million in 1958 and 27 million in 1959).[125] It is unlikely that increased domestic production of textiles, reflected in growing imports of raw cotton and yarns, has been adequate to compensate for reduced imports of textile fabrics, lower volumes of finished textile imports, and population growth. All import data for 1958 and 1959 suggest reduced consumption consistent with the sagging performance of the economy during that period. Volumes of imports of "essential goods" from 1952 through 1959 are presented in Table 15.

It is doubtful, therefore, that reducing the share of domestic

Table 15. IMPORT OF ESSENTIAL GOODS

(*1,000 kilograms*)

Year	All foodstuffs[a]	Rice	Textiles
1952	1,073,477	765,808	94,292
1953	610,236	371,500	156,192
1954	472,274	261,063	129,861
1955	337,006	127,784	146,834
1956	1,111,350	763,175	157,694
1957	827,314	563,438	134,030
1958	864,245	681,465	95,664
1959	745,340	604,154	97,849
1960	1,149,272	961,987	137,015

(a) Including tobacco and beverages.

SOURCE: Biro Pusat Statistik, *Monthly Survey*, January-February 1961, pp. 44, 56; ibid., March-April 1962, p. 54.

income received by foreigners and minority groups has led to improved per capita consumption of essential food and textile items; these are the most important items in the consumption pattern of peoples in low-income, underdeveloped countries. On the other hand, the real income increases accruing to Indonesians from redistribution have been taken out in the form of social services and the accouterments necessary for urban life, both important features of independent Indonesia. Per capita consumption of radios, automobiles, bicycles, trucks, and educational services have shown significant increases; presumably this is also true for housing and sanitation. Health facilities, however, have not been expanded rapidly enough to maintain the prewar number of hospital beds per capita, and the incidence of many serious diseases has increased. Relevant data are presented in Table 16.

Though the rapid urbanization that has occurred in postwar Indonesia has led to increased per capita supplies of urban services, there is legitimate question as to whether these increases should be considered tantamount to improved consumption. To an important extent, these changes have been associated with Indonesian assumption of new roles in the government bureaucracy, in com-

Table 16. SELECTED WELFARE STATISTICS, 1955-58

(*1940 = 100*)

	1955	1956	1957	1958
Licensed radios, per capita	410	430	475	488
Passenger automobiles, per capita	95	96	109	108
Trucks, per capita	370	370	415	347
Hospital beds, per capita	94	91	95	
School attendance, per capita	222	222	223	
School teachers, per capita	246	272	309	
Electricity consumed in homes and offices, per capita	246	258	267	263
Contagious diseases reported, per capita[a]				
Plague	76	24	3	
Typhus	121	119	131	
Paratyphus	129	117	123	
Diphtheria	85	83	101	
Bacillary dysentery	395	195	221	

(a) Java and Madura only.

Source: All entries except electricity, Mears, "Economic Development in Indonesia through 1958," Table 3, p. 30; electricity, basic data from *Statistical Pocketbook of Indonesia 1958* and *1960*.

202

merce, and in industry. From the viewpoint of the individual's welfare, the changed pattern of consumption should be considered partly as costs of performing economic functions in a new, urban setting requiring greater mobility and greater consumption of services indispensable to urban life. It is difficult to escape the conclusion that consumption by the average Indonesian, particularly of basic food and clothing, will not be substantially increased until the economy performs in such a way that real product per capita is raised over some considerable period of time. In other words, redistribution of income between non-Indonesians and Indonesians has had little effect in terms of providing continuing and real increases in welfare.

Inflation

This survey of Indonesia's economic performance would be incomplete without reference to inflation, perhaps the most revealing symptom of the economic forces that have prevailed since independence. The changing dynamics of the economy, described above, have had much to do with the persistence of rising prices. Inflationary trends have been reinforced by the national leadership's emphasis on rapid social and economic change to destroy those conditions which had promoted stability on a colonial basis. The economic impact of these policies has been to foster the rapid expansion of aggregate demand while deterring the growth of capital formation and output. Since 1958, moreover, security expenditures associated with the rebellion and the struggle for West Irian have been a major factor in increasingly large government deficits. These elements are reflected in the rapid rise in the money supply (see Table 18).

The history of recent inflation in Indonesia can be divided into three relatively distinct periods. The first phase of inflation was associated with the disruption caused by the Japanese occupation during World War II and the struggle for independence in the immediate postwar years. During these years, 1942-49, military occupation and civil strife severely reduced productive capacity; supply factors were the primary cause of inflationary price rises. The second period dates roughly from the transfer of sovereignty in 1949 to the outbreak of serious regional dissidence in 1957. This was a period of rehabilitation of productive facilities, during which the government leadership, in the first flush of independence, pursued aggressive policies to overcome foreign economic influence by strengthening Indonesian entrepreneurship. Output expanded rapidly, but the overly ambitious catalytic policies of the government led to relatively greater increases in aggregate demand. This was reinforced by the Korean war export boom in 1951, swelling rupiah proceeds to exporters and setting in force high import propensities which persisted in the following years of falling export proceeds. During this period price rises continued, but they were contained to a significant extent by the government's anti-inflationary policies, which had a deflationary impact when first instituted but which exerted little force after their initial impact. The final period, beginning about 1957, has been one of falling output and stagnation, coincident with rapidly rising aggregate demand generated by increasingly large government deficit-financed spending. Anti-inflationary policies have been continued, but their effect has been negligible. As a consequence, inflationary price rises have been particularly severe since 1957. Between 1951 and 1956, most price indices showed annual rises averaging between 8 and 12 per cent. Since

Table 17. FOODSTUFFS: WEIGHTED INDICES OF RETAIL PRICES, 1948-61

(average for year except where noted)

Year	Twelve foodstuffs Countryside of Java (1953 = 100)	Djakarta	Nineteen foodstuffs Makassar	Medan (Djakarta, 1953 = 100)	Pontianak
1948		47	44	57	
1949		45	39	49	
1950	49	54	53	72	
1951	88	89	86	103	
1952	117	94	87	96	117
1953	100	100	87	100	115
1954	97	106	94	110	120
1955	127	141	135	167	171
1956	153	161	161	168	186
1957	160	177	169	165	180[a]
1958	244	258	232	259	304
1959	271	311	272	338	425
1960	348	384	344	430	532
1961	565	524	424	530	644
1962	1,910[b]	1,248[c]	836[b]	968[b]	990[b]

(a) Average of three months.
(b) March 1962.
(c) April 1962.
SOURCE: *Statistical Pocketbook of Indonesia* and *Monthly Survey.*

204

20 and 40 per cent, with the first rapid rise occurring in 1957 followed by another spurt in 1958, the year of political and economic crises. During 1961 the available price indices showed rises between 50 and 100 per cent. Evidence on the behavior of various prices during these periods is presented in Table 17. Consistent and complete price series are not available; however, those presented, covering the period since 1952, give an indication of price trends in urban and rural areas.

Changes in the supply of money are presented in Table 18. Except during periods when the government was successful in repressing the effects of aggregate demand on prices through anti-

Table 18. CURRENCY, DEMAND DEPOSITS, TOTAL MONEY SUPPLY, AND RATE OF INCREASE IN MONEY SUPPLY, 1951-60

(*billion rupiah*)

End of	Currency[a]	Demand deposits[a]	Total money supply[a]	Rate of increase, money supply (in percentage)	Rate of increase, cost of living index[b] (in percentage)
1951	3.33	1.70	5.03		
1952	4.35	2.25	6.60	31	....
1953	5.22	2.27	7.49	14	....
1954	7.47	3.65	11.12	48	....
1955	8.65	3.59	12.24	10	8.0
1956	9.37	4.02	13.39	9	2.8
1957	14.09	4.82	18.91	41	25.2
1958	19.87	9.49	29.36	55	53.2
July 1959[c]	24.25	9.74	33.99	16[d]	32.9[d]
August 1959[c]	18.03	2.97	21.00	....	
December 1959	26.38	8.50	34.88	66[e]	5.7[f]
June 1960	32.26	10.30	42.56	22[f]	16.9[f]
December 1960	33.45	12.75	46.20	9[f]	n.a.
June 1961	35.08	13.78	48.86	6[f]	n.a.
December 1961	46.49	18.00	64.49	32[f]	n.a.

(a) Figures for 1951-59 are taken from annual editions of *Report of the Bank Indonesia;* for 1960-61, from American-Indonesian Chamber of Commerce, *Information Bulletin,* No. 688 (May 18, 1962), p. 3.
(b) Calculated from *Bank Indonesia Bulletin No. 19* (Third and Fourth Quarters, 1959), Table 54; ibid. *No. 20* (First and Second Quarters, 1960), Table 54.
(c) These figures reflect the effect of the monetary reform in August 1959.
(d) January-July 1959.
(e) August 26-December 31, 1959.
(f) Six-month period.

December 1956, however, annual increases have averaged between inflation policies, there is a rather striking correlation between the expansion of the money supply and the rate of price increases.[126] The major exceptions to this general relationship are the period 1952-56, when the government was able to exert strong anti-inflationary pressures, and the period just after the monetary reform of August 1959. This reform, which reduced the supply of money by almost 40 per cent, followed a period in which prices had risen with great rapidity: the Bank of Indonesia's cost of living index showed a rise of 53 per cent in 1958 followed by a rise of 33 per cent during the first seven months of 1959. Although the reform was followed by such rapid increases in the money supply that the previous level was reached within four months, the pace of inflation was significantly retarded through 1960 (see Table 18). The general correlation between the growth of money supply and the rate of price increases after 1956, as well as the more rapid rise in prices than money in the year prior to the monetary reform, suggest the dubiousness of the government's presumption of the existence of large idle balances (known in Indonesia as "monetary overhang" or "hot money").[127]

Socialization and Government Controls

A negative quality has characterized official economic policy since independence: the government has been more successful in destroying institutions and weakening the previous incentive systems than in replacing them. Indonesians view this process as an extension of the political revolution; state control is considered essential to building an economy consistent with Indonesia's social goals. "In order to reach this more just and prosperous society," writes Sadli, a leading Indonesian economist, "the revolution seeks to rebuild in a variety of ways the political, economic and social structure. The most important force in this revolution is the state and its government, which acting as the ' hammer ' must *guide* the changes and social structure. Guided Economy is thus but a part of the entire state policy which also includes Guided Democracy to organize the new structure of political life.[128]

Virtually all of Indonesia's political elite who have been concerned with economic policy agree that their economy should not be built along capitalistic lines. There is further agreement that the seeds of Western capitalism planted by colonialism should be eradicated. Beyond this, however, there is considerable basis for disagreement; and Indonesian political activity since 1949 has mainly revolved about the economic issues on which a consensus has not yet been reached.

The more clearly defined issues have concerned the rate at which the vestiges of capitalism should be uprooted and the means by which this should be done. A group of pragmatists have supported the view that the rate of eliminating capitalism, particularly foreign capitalism, should be gradual enough to prevent serious short-run disruption to the performance of the economy. This school of thought has espoused the promotion of development of Indonesian enterprise, whether public, cooperative, or private, as the means of achieving the agreed goal. The more radical political elements have supported a rapid rate of eradicating capitalism, particularly foreign capitalistic enterprise, regardless of the costs in terms of short-run economic dislocation. They maintain that this should be done by replacing capitalist by public or cooperative enterprise, and should be accomplished by nationalization rather than by gradual encroachment through strengthening Indonesian entrepreneurship. In the main, the radical group calls for immediate government action wherever private enterprise, foreign or domestic, controls economic activity construed to be important to Indonesian livelihood.[129]

Neither school of opinion has been completely ascendant since Indonesia's achievement of full sovereignty; but two fairly distinct periods can be identified. Prior to 1956 or 1957 more pragmatic, conservative policies were dominant, tempered by the inevitable compromise with the more radical groups essential to Indonesian politics. During this period, the intention to restrict capitalistic activity, particularly foreign and Chinese entrepreneurship, was clearly apparent; however, gradualism characterized the policies expressing this hostility. Government power and influence were exerted to effect the development of an indigenous group of entrepreneurs, who would be prepared to replace foreign and Chinese capitalists and would also be adequately oriented toward cooperative organization or sufficiently dependent on the government to be free from the capitalist taint. How this process would lead to the generally accepted goal of socialism was never fully clarified.[130]

Events in 1956 and 1957 led to the eclipse of the group espousing gradualism. By 1958, under the impetus of Sukarno's enunciation of Guided Democracy and Guided Economy, the balance of

207

power began to shift to the groups supporting rapid eradication of capitalism.[131] Cause and effect are not clear in the process of nationalization and the imposition of government controls that occurred after 1956. Nevertheless it is apparent that the government's share of enterprise was rapidly expanded, and that private enterprises of many types were replaced by public enterprise or subjected to government domination. The nation's political leadership, strongly supporting these developments, has continued to place emphasis on shifting the balance of power from private to public enterprise rather than on economic performance.

Sadli has described this pronounced shift in over-all economic policy as a return to the more radical goals of the revolution:

> The view of our revolutionary goals and methods is also very different if compared with the picture a short time ago. The political factor, i.e. the political consciousness in *the revolution's goals* has become more dominant. We have returned to a more revolutionary revolution, in which the political aims (of rebuilding the old structure) have become important again, frequently transcending the economic aims (to improve productivity). Thus, while before we sought to increase production with the existing variety of economic tools and institutions (private, foreign, and state), now the political character of the economic institutions must be screened and, where necessary, reorganized to be more in keeping with the revolutionary goal. In this way rebuilding the structure often becomes more important than increasing production.[132]

The economic impact of the government since 1958 reflects the success of the national leadership in translating the new ideology into action. While anti-Dutch and anti-Chinese attitudes supplied the immediate stimulus for the eradication of the country's major capitalist elements, the political impetus toward socialism is such that the weakening of private capitalism is likely to continue even though the Dutch economic foothold has been completely destroyed and the Chinese position seriously impaired.

In historical perspective, the Dutch colonial government itself had promoted the expansion of government intervention and controls, particularly after the depression of the 1930s had weakened the modern, export sector of the economy.[133] The Netherlands East Indies Government established the precedent of government interference both through public ownership and operation of certain important enterprises and through increasingly aggressive monetary, fiscal, and foreign exchange policies. Sovereignty itself conferred upon the state "extensive properties of the former colonial government"—in agricultural estates, mining, and public utilities.[134] Even the basic colonial law governing public enterprises (the Indische bedrijvenwet of 1927) was comprehensive enough to survive until 1961, when a new legal basis for government enterprises became essential as a result of the rapid growth of the public sector in production.

Extension of public enterprise since independence has been accomplished through two major processes. By far the most important has been the nationalization of enterprises previously owned by Dutch nationals, culminating in the virtually complete seizure of all remaining Dutch enterprise in late 1957 as a protest against Dutch refusal to yield on the West Irian issue. Shipping and other transport facilities—such as the major airline—had begun to be subjected to government control earlier, but the 1957 action laid the basis for complete state authority over the greater part of the modern sector of the economy. In this single wave of nationalization, more than four hundred agricultural estates were taken over, in addition to many commercial, industrial, and banking firms.

The second process leading to extension of public enterprise or direct public control has been more developmental in nature. The government itself has promoted the establishment of new enterprises through a number of public financial agencies. Most important of these is the State Industrial Bank (Bank Industri Negara), which began operations in 1951 with Rp. 500 million in funds made available by the government and Rp. 300 million in blocked foreign accounts (so-called Rurni accounts) converted to an involuntary bond loan to the Bank.[135] The Bank also has the authority to float its own bonds on the market, but its efforts at bond sales have been ineffective. Its developmental role has been somewhat different from the original intent, which was to finance large-scale industrial projects on a creditor basis; in most cases the Bank has emerged as the proprietor or parent company of the enterprises whose development it has financed. The firms now under its control add up to an impressive list,[136] and the Bank's flexibility in shifting from a purely financial to a managerial institution as well has appeared to enhance its effectiveness as an agency for promoting industrial development.

In addition to these major tendencies, which have been underway almost continuously since the transfer of sovereignty in 1949, the recent shift toward a more aggressive attack on capitalism has produced new avenues for extending government economic control. In early 1960 the government began a major effort to extend its control to traditional distributive channels, the impetus for this step arising from a directive issued in May 1959, which had provided that all alien traders should be removed from rural areas commencing January 1 of the next year.[137] It was the government's announced purpose that the resulting void in distributive channels should be filled by Indonesian cooperatives, which were to be aggressively fostered by the authorities.[138] In practice this meant that the Chinese and Indian traders who had traditionally handled the bulk of rural retail trade were to be removed, and that new distributive channels were to be organized at the initiative of the government on the basis of whatever was feasible and expedient.

Within a short period after the target date, the army supervised the removal of alien traders to cities or their home countries; the disposal of their assets was accomplished with equal alacrity. The expected collapse of rural distributive channels immediately ensued; even in larger cities supplies of consumer goods became scarce or unavailable as the government's stern measures created general apprehension among distributors. In most cases the anticipated appearance of retail cooperatives was not forthcoming, and the void in distributive facilities continued. Retail cooperatives have never been strong in Indonesia: they lack finance, administrative resources, and consumer support. The few experiments which had been made in this area were disappointing, for the cooperatives could not market goods at prices competitive with those of the old traders, and their lack of business experience led to large losses or such high prices that consumers avoided them.

As the distribution crisis worsened and popular resentment of the general shortages of consumer goods grew, the government was forced to enter the distribution field directly. The result was the establishment of government retail outlets known as *sandan-pangan* (literally clothing and food) stores.[139] These sprang up rapidly on Java during 1960 but did not begin to appear on the outlying islands until 1961. Demand for the goods distributed by these outlets was so great that rationing and long queues were necessary. Stocks were rapidly exhausted; and the government, in order to make good its continuing assurances of generous supplies, was forced to devise methods to otain increasingly large stocks of consumer goods for retail distribution.

To assure access to these supplies, particularly manufactures, the government undertook to involve itself more deeply in the intricacies of production, markets, and prices. Domestic producers of consumer manufactures were subjected to strict government controls, and the continued operation of private producers became dependent upon their compliance with the new regulations. Larger producers of consumer goods were obliged to make a part or all of their output available to the government; their profit margins became subject to official control, as the government specified legal prices of raw materials and finished goods. In the same vein, the government set prices at which private retailers could market their goods, and the military was called upon to assist justice department officials in enforcing these new controls. A network of economic police was organized to conduct investigations into the compliance of private retail traders and producers. Despite numerous arrests and occasionally severe punishments, the net result has been the continued disruption of the distributive system, widespread corruption, and exchange at black market prices in virtually all retail outlets except the state's own sandan-pangan establishments.[140]

Although the government thus made a determined effort to cope with the distributive collapse, it has not yet shown the administrative capacity to enforce the constellation of controls it erected to deal with the situation. There has been no tendency, however, for the government to falter in its determination to erect a new distributive system. Prospects are that controls will become more extensive and that their effectiveness in promoting state-controlled distribution will gradually increase as the government's administrative capacity grows.

During the period when controls over retail trade were being extended as a result of the campaign against rural alien traders, the government also attempted to strengthen control of output and distribution in the modern, industrial sector of the economy. Establishing its own outlets in both domestic and foreign markets, the government has attempted to induce foreign firms in some industries to sell directly to it at fixed prices rather than through marketing channels of the firms' choice. Estate producers of agricultural export products, as well as producers of industrial products for domestic consumption, have frequently complained that the government buying price has been set below their per unit cost of production. The government has countered by demanding detailed accountings of production costs; but these have rarely been submitted in sufficient detail to induce the authorities to consider seriously

211

the producers' growing complaints. Foreign companies which export primary products directly to a parent company at home have, however, apparently been exempted from marketing through the newly established official channels.

The government's aggressive entry into the marketing system, as an aspect of its new Guided Economy orientation, has resulted in the establishment of a vast new bureaucracy to supervise domestic and foreign trade. In conjunction with the reregistration of all private business firms in 1959, private firms were permitted to engage only in the importing of nonessential goods, and the number of private importers was restricted to 400.[141] The distribution of goods defined as essential by the authorities, whether of domestic or foreign origin, was placed under the control of the government.[142] A limited number of large state enterprises were entrusted with the importing of these goods; at present these companies "control the greater part of import trade."[143] In March 1961, a similar reorganization occurred in the export trade, concentrating exports in the hands of government trading enterprises and reducing the number of licensed private exporters. In the same month, the Central Management Board of the State Trading Corporations was established to "plan, coordinate and supervise" the activities of the government foreign trade apparatus.[144]

Although the extension of government ownership and control over economic activity has thus proceeded at an increasing rate, the scope of the state's direct influence is not as great as the above description of this process might lead one to think. The Indonesian economy continues to represent a mix between public and private enterprise. It is probable that the declining performance of private enterprise in nonagricultural sectors since 1957 has been more affected by the general change in Indonesia's political and economic climate than by the specific extension of public ownership and economic controls. Thus, recent attempts to express officially the basic Indonesian aversion to private enterprise have tended to impair private incentives to invest. Similarly, though the direct effectiveness of newly imposed government controls over private enterprise has been relatively weak, the long-run goal of subordinating private to public enterprise has been clear. Private entrepreneurs have therefore been inclined to adopt a short-run profit mentality emphasizing maximum returns from existing productive facilities with minimum replacement investment and virtually no expansion.

From the perspective of the economy as a whole, the extent of direct government control over production and exchange is still limited. Small-scale agriculture and cottage manufacturing—representing about 60 per cent of total output—continue to be operated on a private enterprise basis relatively free from government interference. Although the Government Rice Board purchases locally produced rice, and some smallholder export products are sold through government channels, private producers in the agricultural sector are, in principle at least, free to plan their own output patterns and they also have free choice in determining what share of their output to put on the market.[145] Some thought has been given to collectivization,[146] however; and the Paddy Center Plan, embraced in the current Eight-Year Plan, may be a first step in the direction of producer cooperatives.

In the plantation agriculture sector, the government now controls something over 50 per cent of total output, with the remainder in the hands of private entrepreneurs, mainly foreigners. The government's share of mineral production is probably less than one-third of the total (because of the predominance of petroleum, largely foreign-owned); its share of manufacturing, including handicrafts, is even smaller. In the domestic trade sector, the majority of goods are probably still distributed by private firms, although this is primarily because the government has failed to provide effective public channels to replace the disrupted traditional networks.[147] These firms have been subjected to an increasing number of restrictive regulations; but apart from the import and export trades, where state controls have been effective as well as comprehensive, the government's impact in the private trading sector has served mainly to promote corruption without achieving price and profit control objectives. Quantitatively, the government's direct control over investment, production, and distribution has not yet become dominant, though sooner or later it will become so if present trends continue.

It is hazardous to predict the long-run relationship between public and private enterprise, for Indonesian concepts of socialism, mixed economy, and control of private enterprise are vague enough to allow almost any specific interpretation the national leadership desires to employ. The concept of essential industries, which has been used in carrying out programs of government control in such areas as distribution, is equally flexible. Since 1959, Article 33 of the constitution of 1945 has provided the basis for the government's fundamental economic policy toward the organization of enterprise.

213

It calls for cooperative organization of the economy, government control of branches of production which are important to the state and the majority of the people, and the development of "natural riches" for the greatest popular welfare. From this article the spirit of Guided Economy has been distilled; but continuing controversy exists over the interpretations given to "state *control* of branches of production," with emphasis on the word "control," and "important to the state and which affect the life of the people."[148] Indeed, the dispute over the interpretation of "control" has existed since just prior to the transfer of sovereignty, when the term Guided Economy was being discussed among Indonesia's leadership as a possible basis for the Republic's economic policy.[149]

Writing in early 1962, Sadli suggests that the "guideposts" delineating the public, private, and cooperative sectors have not yet been set very clearly.[150] He believes that the leadership's current interpretation in Indonesia is that the private sector will be a permanent feature in the mixed economy, but that it cannot be allowed to grow freely lest it undermine the basis of socialism. Hence, "state enterprises must assume a 'leading and commanding' role vis-à-vis private enterprises in the same field of activity. All firms in such a branch are organized into so-called trade or industrial associations (Gabungan Perusahaan Sedjenis) which are to be presided over by state enterprises. State enterprises, as leaders of such groups, are expected to give guidance in matters of price policies, adherence to government regulations, and policies increasing production and efficiency, capital formation, etc."[151] The legal basis for subjecting private enterprise in the modern industrial sector to public control by these methods was provided in Government Ordinance Number 19, issued in August 1960.[152] In practice, the enforcement of this ordinance has led to the use of many noneconomic and nonperformance criteria in determining which private enterprises should receive the special favors and concessions needed to remain viable in the face of continuing shortages of raw materials, equipment, and foreign exchange.

National Development Plans

The extension of government ownership, operation, and regulation of economic enterprise has proceeded without the benefit of central planning devices to coordinate investment and production decisions. There is no body which directs the allocation of productive resources or investment among the various enterprises operated by the government, and there is little coordination between the numerous agencies empowered to influence the allocation of resources between the public and private sectors. Such efforts as have been made have impeded the flow of resources to both sectors, breeding corruption and endangering performance. Monetary policies, to be discussed presently, have been employed for this purpose, but, without the support of direct allocative controls, and in the context of inflation, they have had little effect in accomplishing the *real* shifts desired. In general, Guided Economy policies have weakened private enterprise, but the government has failed to mobilize for public endeavor the investment and entrepreneurial resources released by the faltering private sector.

In spite of this lack of over-all coordinating devices, the Indonesian government has consistently favored promoting economic development through state-sponsored development programs. It has announced many development plans, but none has been carried out with determination. More often than not, particular plans have been associated with specific political parties or leaders, and their fate has been tied to the political fortunes of their sponsors. This situation has reduced the effectiveness of the government's efforts at planned development; it has led to duplication of planning activities, abandonment of plans already underway, and waste of scarce administrative and economic resources.

In addition to periodic attempts to introduce plans of limited scope, three major development programs have been launched during the past decade. In 1951 the Ministry of Trade and Industry introduced the Urgency Economic Plan; in 1956 the First Five-Year Plan was launched; and in 1961 the Eight-Year Over-all Development Plan was begun, after being announced in 1960. This last program is currently receiving the focus of attention as the major vehicle of Indonesia's development, yet remnants of the two other plans are still being carried out.

The Urgency Economic Plan (Rentjana Urgensi Perekonomian) has been described as a "highly nationalistic attempt to diminish the nation's dependence on foreign trade by developing small, *nasional* (i.e. indigenous) industry to produce import substitutes by means of capital assistance and restriction of certain markets to indigenous sellers."[153] It is true that the plan was highly nationalistic. Its original objective was much more comprehensive, however, than the above quotation implies. In fact, the plan is instructive in its revelation of the early predisposition of Indonesia's political elite toward government initiative in all areas of economic development. Although its main focus was directed toward industrialization, this was but one of five parts of the Urgency Plan: cooperative development and direct efforts to promote popular welfare received considerable emphasis both in the plan itself and in the discussion it generated.

A Ministry of Economics commentary, issued just after the plan's announcement, reveals its ambition: "This urgency programme aims at promoting the development of Indonesian industry in all its layers, i.e., small, medium and large-scale industries. This is based on the consideration that, if the State wants to obtain in the shortest possible period the necessary productive apparatus to increase welfare, the government must give the lead in economic life."[154] One can detect here the consistent strain that eventually led to the Guided Economy shibboleth. Yet in retrospect Indonesians consider this to have been the period of their experiment with economic liberalism.

Government developmental initiative assumed a distinctive flavor from the Urgency Economic Plan, a flavor which dominated development policy until recently. The plan visualized Indonesia's national leadership as a group of men keenly attuned to the larger questions of Indonesia's economic growth; this group would be responsible for introducing critical innovations to trigger a process of spontaneous growth. The critical innovations in question came to be defined as credit and capital, and these were freely dispensed to selected Indonesian entrepreneurs under the "Benteng" assistance program. Behind this lay the further assumption that the supply of important complementary factors (e.g. technical and administrative skills) would be readily forthcoming from Indonesian society and culture once the necessary funds were available.

The field of small-scale industry became an interesting experiment to test these assumptions. Here, it was felt, it would be quite easy to capitalize on already established patterns of production and on proven entrepreneurial and technical skills. A program of direct assistance to such producers—the Loan and Mechanization Program —was established to supply these factors to no less than 72 kinds of industries on Java and Madura. It proved rather difficult to distribute this largesse, but eventually the Loan and Mechanization Program—which still exists—began to bear fruit in expanding output from Indonesian firms.[155]

The same delayed results were apparent in the government's efforts to expand and improve small-scale production through central processing establishments, the so-called Induks. This device was essentially an organizational innovation intended to promote the acquisition and thrifty use of capital goods which were beyond the reach of an individual entrepreneur, and at the same time to provide a means for gathering and disseminating useful technical know-how and marketing information. In essence a good idea, it was originally plagued by administrative inefficiency. Eventually the program was reduced to modest proportions, and considerable success was achieved. It is interesting to note that the Induk principle has been revived in the current Eight-Year Over-all Development Plan, which proposes that it be adapted to rice production under the Paddy Center program.

In the area of large-scale industry, too, it was the Urgency Plan's intent that the government's role should be essentially catalytic. Factories built with state-supplied capital and equipment were to be turned over to private, cooperative, or joint public-private management. Although the government's ambitious plans to build large-scale firms were carried out gradually—only a handful of firms were completed during the first several years—the anticipated surge of entrepreneurship to manage these new enterprises did not emerge. New factories lay idle or operated at less than capacity; in most instances the government itself was forced to assume direct or indirect managerial responsibility.

The failure of the government to realize its own objectives through the Urgency Economic Plan has had much to do with Indonesia's later planning efforts. Quick, spectacular results did not appear. Freely distributing economic resources—physical capital, credit, or special privileges of various sorts—had little immediate effect on output or the structure of the economy. Rapid ramification into wider circles of economic improvement was not perceptible enough to justify the large expenditures undertaken in behalf of the Urgency Plan. At the same time, these expenditures had begun to produce serious problems of economic stability by 1952, and their unstabilizing impact became even more serious when the "open perversion of the Benteng policy"[156] occurred during the tenure of the first Ali Sastroamidjojo cabinet (1953-55).

Among the important repercussions upon Indonesia's development policy produced by the failure of this experiment, perhaps the most significant was the sobering effect upon those planners who

217

had envisaged a dramatic response from an indigenous middle class, which they had viewed as ready to blossom if given capital and credit as well as political freedom from the Dutch. It led them to greater realism in establishing standards for assistance and in carrying out the Loan and Mechanization Program, a project which has now existed for a decade and has made an effective contribution to the development of small- and medium-scale industry.

The failure of the Urgency Economic Plan advanced the drift toward a more centralized economy. Its primary objective, the rapid development of a domestic industrial base, had had a strong emotional appeal. But when complementary social and economic elites did not come forth rapidly enough to implement the plan, this appeal waned; and at the same time the administrative inefficiency and corruption associated with the assistance program did irreparable damage to its whole approach. Though specific programs begun under the Urgency Plan were continued, a new general orientation was sought, resulting in a sharpening of the controversy between leaders seeking to accomplish the objective of economic independence by development activities and those favoring the more direct action of nationalization. The First Five-Year Plan, at least on paper, left the balance of power with the development-minded group; but it projected development with more direct central involvement than had been envisioned by its predecessor.

Indonesia's First Five-Year Plan was the product of extensive research. Minister of Finance Sumitro, earlier identified with the Urgency Plan, was primarily responsible for obtaining a team of foreign experts through the auspices of the United Nations to staff research positions in the National Planning Bureau. In addition this agency, which was designed to produce and assist in the execution of a national development plan, was granted ICA aid in the form of a team of American engineers.[157] When the First Five-Year Plan was published in 1956,[158] it reflected the years of professional research behind it, the experience gained from previous development attempts, and the political pressures to which economic policy was subject. When the Planning Bureau began its work, fundamental data and knowledge essential to sound planning were lacking. There was little organized information on Indonesia's natural endowments, or its labor and other human resources. There were no postwar estimates of national product and income or such component aggregates as investment, savings, and consumption.

Before the plan was released, the Planning Bureau had developed at least preliminary data in these important areas. The new program was drafted in terms of aggregate planning, showing projected increases in investment and national income beginning with estimates of these variables in a base year.[159] On the other hand, the plan's substance focused upon a large number of individual projects to be completed during the five planned years. A major technical deficiency in the plan was its failure to relate such project planning to aggregate planning, i.e. to the anticipated over-all changes in national income and investment. There was a sectoral breakdown of planned investment to be financed by the government, but inadequate consideration was given to alternative patterns of allocation of the plan's projected investment resources.

In its relative modesty, the five-year program reflected disappointment with the ambitious efforts of the Urgency Economic Plan. Its original version called for a total investment of 30 billion rupiah; this was raised to 35.2 billion in a 1957 revision of the plan. Of the total, only Rp. 12.5 billion was to be financed through the government, and of this only Rp. 9.5 billion from the national budget. The Rp. 9.5 billion to be financed through the government budget, considerably less than expended for development during the previous five years, apparently reflected a fear of generating further inflationary pressures, for by 1956 the indiscriminate use of government development funds had resulted in severe inflationary tendencies. It also reflected reluctance to tackle the problem of tax reform, a step that must be taken before Indonesia can undertake a large-scale development program without further aggravating the economy's instability.

The First Five-Year Plan, then, represented a reversal of the free-spending policies associated with the Urgency Economic Plan and the Benteng subsidy system which had developed from it. It also reflected some interest in utilization of more careful planning techniques and the establishment of a body of professional planners to draft economic plans and advise on their execution. There was significant progress in the coordination of development expenditures during the early period of the National Planning Bureau's existence (1952-56), and foreign observers believed that Indonesia was on the road to establishing successful institutions for development planning.[160] Later events suggest, however, that the experience gained by the Planning Bureau staff had little impact on long-run planning activity in Indonesia.

Most indicative of the political shift underway in Indonesia, the First Five-Year Plan reversed the policy of providing direct assistance to private Indonesian entrepreneurs. In some fields, such as agriculture, where private enterprise was not suspect, the plan included assistance of a technical rather than capital nature. In general, however, it concentrated on the development of public enterprise, leaving the private sector to fend for itself. This emphasis bcame even more apparent in the execution of the plan after 1957, when Dutch enterprise was taken over by the government. As a broad, costly national undertaking, the effort to create an Indonesian middle class of private industrialists was ended. Remnants of the Urgency program, in the form of personnel continuing to pursue the original objectives on a limited scale, remained in government departments concerned with industry; but the failure to incorporate into the Five-Year Plan the underlying philosophy of energizing private entrepreneurs by capital, credit, and political privilege meant its demise as a tool of social change endorsed by the leadership.

Political factors also began to affect the operation of the National Planning Bureau. Originally the Bureau reported to the National Planning Board, a body composed of top personnel in government agencies whose work was associated with economic development. In 1956, however, Bureau Director-General Djuanda was appointed to a newly established cabinet post as Minister of National Planning; this marked the beginning of a process which eventually led to the complete eclipse of the Bureau as a planning agency. With the withdrawal of the highly respected Djuanda from direct involvement with the Planning Bureau,[161] the way was opened for political attacks on the agency and its role in national planning. In August 1959 the National Planning Bureau was converted into the Bureau of Finance and Economics, an advisory body to the First Minister, and the task of drafting a new, eight-year plan was assigned to a politically oriented organization, the National Planning Council. The Bureau ended its work by issuing an objective report on the execution of the First Five-Year Plan during its first three years of operation.[162]

In 1957 a National Development Conference was convened in order to alleviate tensions in the disaffected areas by allowing regional representatives to express their views on economic development. The conference, whose decisions were incorporated into the five-year plan, recommended that major priority be given to three fields—food, clothing, and transport, particularly shipping[163]—and that the development effort be increased to the largest possible scale.[164] The government budget contribution to the plan was raised to Rp. 10.6 billion, with an additional Rp. 1.9 billion to be provided from foreign sources. The Planning Bureau's report compared expenditures during the three years 1956-58, with the revised total planned for the five-year period, 1956-60; these data are presented in Table 19.

The comparison indicates that government developmental investment totaled about three-fifths of the five-year investment target; i.e. superficially the rate of planned investment was being achieved. The Planning Bureau itself emphasized, however, that in real terms this was untrue.[165] Between 1956, when the plan was launched, and late 1958 the purchasing power of money had probably fallen by 40 or 50 per cent, based on the behavior of the various price indices available.

Shortly after the plan was launched, the security situation deteriorated, culminating in the rebellion of 1958. The ousting of virtually all Dutch enterprise in late 1957 caused serious disruption to production, investment, and distribution. The National Planning Bureau reported a decline of about 13 per cent in real national income for 1958. It is remarkable that the government was able to maintain any semblance of its investment program under these unfavorable conditions. As it was, the emergency forced major changes

Table 19. DEVELOPMENT INVESTMENT, 1956-58, AND PLANNED INVESTMENT, 1956-60

(*million rupiah*)

	Realized investment 1956-58		Planned investment 1956-60	
	Amount	Percentage of total	Amount	Percentage of total
Agriculture, fisheries, forestry	1,376.5	19	1,625	13
Power and irrigation	877.6	12	3,125	25
Industry and mining	1,364.2	19	3,125	25
Transport and communication	2,525.3	34	3,125	25
Education, social affairs, and information	1,188.0	16	1,500	12
Total	7,331.6	100	12,500	100

SOURCE: Biro Perantjang Negara, *Report on the Execution of the Five-Year Development Plan, 1956-1960*, p. 7.

in the plan's projected allocation of investment resources. Inter-island shipping reached a virtually complete standstill in 1958, and the government's efforts to obtain and put into operation a minimum interisland fleet necessitated a disproportionately large outlay for transport and communications—34 per cent of developmental capital expenditures for the period 1956-58. In this situation, the plan had little impact in terms of ordered economic development or even of accelerating the rate of capital formation.

It is possible that, even without the emergency conditions of the period, the five-year plan would not have altered the entrenched policy of uncoordinated investment expenditures. Capital expenditures continued to be undertaken at the initiative of separate ministries, either with or without direct cabinet concern with the details of their allocation. The National Planning Bureau deteriorated into an office concerned with collecting data, submitting reports and occasionally offering advice. During this period, there was no agency to coordinate or evaluate the investment activities of the various branches of the government, a task to which the Planning Bureau had hitherto made an impressive contribution. By early 1959, the First Five-Year Plan was virtually abandoned, although a number of already initiated projects were continued. Government interest began to focus instead on the appointment of a National Planning Council and the drafting of an alternative plan—the Eight-Year Over-all Development Plan.

In August 1959 President Sukarno named a seventy-member National Planning Council (Dewan Perantjang Nasional), urging it to produce as quickly as possible a plan for Indonesia's social, cultural, and economic development. This unwieldy body was chaired by Muhammad Yamin, a leftist leader and former Minister of Justice; its secretary-general was M. Hutasoit, an able and moderate administrator from the Ministry of Education. The new Planning Council was strikingly lacking in planning competence or experience. Its membership was selected on the basis of political considerations; it contained no professional economists or representatives from Indonesia's previous planning agencies. The council construed its task to be the completion of a comprehensive plan by Independence Day (August 17) 1960; and by that date the document that has come to be known as the Eight-Year Over-all Development Plan was essentially complete. In December it was approved by the first meeting of the Provisional People's Consultative Assembly, and it was officially inaugurated by the President on January 1, 1961.[166]

The Eight-Year Plan may have some value in mobilizing popular interest in national economic development. It has been widely publicized, after having been introduced with elaborate ceremony and symbolism; and the term "Pembangunan" (Development) is beginning to join other slogans (Manipol-USDEK, Socialisme à la Indonesia) as key symbols of the regime. It is conceivable that President Sukarno and his advisers had this in mind, selecting politicians rather than professional economists and planners to devise a politically attractive plan to replace those that failed to generate popular support in the past. If the new plan succeeds in exciting interest in general economic and social development at all levels of society, it will have accomplished a most important objective, one prerequisite to the success of any major development program.

It has been pointed out that the Eight-Year Plan possesses some strong points,[167] although they are obscured by the immensity of the document and the presentation of the essential lines of the plan's allocation of expenditures. A unique but confusing feature is its division of projects into two categories, A and B. The heart of the developmental focus of the plan, in the view of its designers, consists of the 335 projects in Category A. The total rupiah cost of these projects was estimated to be Rp. 240 billion, presumably at the 1960 value of the rupiah. At the official rate of 45 rupiah to U. S. $1.00, this would yield a cost in terms of U. S. dollars of five and one-third billion, spread over the eight-year period 1961-69.

One of the plan's many presentations of projected expenditures for A projects is given in Table 20. Since the categories in this table are not particularly useful for sectoral analysis of planned expenditures, two further presentations are given in Tables 21 and 22. Table 21 shows major categories of expenditure with elaboration by large projects, i.e. those involving planned expenditure exceeding Rp. 1 billion over the entire planning period. Table 22 presents a reclassification of the plan's allocation by major sectors, somewhat more useful for analyzing the plan's projected sectoral patterns of investment.

One of the important merits of the plan is its detailed listing of the A projects to be carried out in each category. It is apparent that preliminary work concentrated on project planning of this kind. All major projects are listed by planned location, and cost estimates in terms of rupiah and foreign exchange are given for most of them. Other details are also provided for the projects: the date of their introduction, the planned period of construction, and,

223

in some cases, the estimated effect of their completion on output. In addition to the 335 basic A projects, "reserve" projects are added —objectives somewhat lower in priority, to be introduced if financial resources prove to be more than adequate to finance the basic items. The one exception to detailed project planning is the category "Reserves for Special Projects," amounting to Rp. 30 billion—one-eighth of the total planned expenditure. Commentary in the plan documents suggests that this category of expenditures is to be reserved for military or security purposes, perhaps those of a construction nature. In one place, for example, the plan states that Rp. 210 billion will be made available to cover development projects in the "civil field," with the remainder reserved for "special develop-

Table 20. EIGHT-YEAR PLAN: "A" PROJECTS BY CATEGORY OF EXPENDITURE

Field	Number of projects	Rupiah cost (millions)
I. Mental and Spiritual		17,815
A. Education	43	16,261
B. Culture	9	1,554
II. Research	16	2,653
III. People's Welfare	11	6,188
IV. Government[a]	6	3,632
V. Special Development	1	30,000
VI. Production		108,062
A. Industry	81	52,022
B. Food	8	25,120
C. Clothing	7	28,945
D. Medicine	6	2,175
VII. Distribution (including transport and communications)	144	60,382
VIII. Finance[b] (including tourism)	3	11,288
Total	335	240,020

(a) Includes transmigration (1,000 M), buildings for National Planning Council and its Institutes (100 M), development of cooperatives for distributive production functions (500 M), seven modern prisons (26 M), improvement of and equipment for State Police (2,000 M), and National Law Institute (6 M).

(b) Includes expansion of tin mining (168 M), Village Development Bank to promote community development (10,000 M), and tourism (350 M).

SOURCE: *Warta CAFI*, Circular No. H 343 (February 21, 1961), p. 1.

Table 21.   EIGHT-YEAR PLAN: LARGE CATEGORIES AND ITEMS
RELATING TO "A" PROJECTS[a]

(million rupiah)

	National account	Foreign exchange	Total
Food production, of which:	13,992	11,128	25,120
Paddy centers	7,255	10,880	18,135
Irrigation	6,385		6,385
Clothing production, of which:	14,240	14,705	28,945
Spinning	3,910	3,910	7,820
Weaving	720	720	1,440
Raw cotton	900	1,500	2,400
Rayon	8,415	8,415	16,830
Industrial production, of which:	28,091.5	23,930.5	52,022
Chemical fertilizers	1,568	1,847	3,415
Electricity	7,075	7,075	14,150
Petroleum	2,050	1,800	3,850
Steel	3,050	1,881	4,931
Coal and coke	3,628	2,856	5,484
Aluminum	850	899	1,749
Other mining and quarrying	1,042	288	1,330
Cement	2,313	1,562	3,875
Paper mills	1,193.5	976.5	2,170
Sugar mills	2,500	2,500	5,000
Medicine: antibiotics	610	500	1,110
Highway repair, improvement, and extension (84 projects)			24,214
Bridges and ferries	600	400	1,000
Motorized transport equipment	60	4,364	4,424
Railways	3,000	4,000	7,000
Postal service	1,090	500	1,590
Telecommunications	2,942	3,232	6,174
Shipping and harbors	3,185	6,908	10,093
Air communications	2,180	2,305[b]	4,485[b]
Village Development Bank[c] (to finance community development and provide agricultural credit)	10,000		10,000
University development	9,232[d]		9,232[d]
Technical schools	1,848		1,848
Elementary schools	2,635		2,635
Hospitals and clinics	2,305		2,305
Housing bank	2,000		2,000
Transmigration	1,000		1,000
Police force improvement	2,000		2,000

(a) The largest of the 335 projects, Special Development (Rp. 30,000 million), is given no elaboration.
(b) Of which Rp. 900 million (U. S. $20 million) for purchase of aircraft and spare parts.
(c) To be financed as a branch of the Bank Pembangunan Indonesia in 1961.
(d) For development of public universities, except for subsidy of Rp. 250 million to private universities.

ment." In analyzing the plan's projected pattern of sectoral allocation, therefore, it is preferable to omit this category. Other components also appear to be less than strictly developmental investment, but their amounts are a much smaller percentage of the

Table 22. RECLASSIFICATION: EIGHT-YEAR PLAN, "A" PROJECTS

Category and major items		Amount (million rupiah)
Agriculture:		26,692
Food production	13,992	
Cotton production	2,400	
Community development and agricultural credit	10,000	
Forestry	300	
	26,692	
Industry		65,837
Textiles	26,090	
Chemical fertilizers	3,415	
Mining and quarrying	17,344	
Cement	3,875	
Sugar mills	5,000	
Paper mills	2,170	
Medicines	2,175	
Other	5,768	
	65,837	
Electric power		14,150
Transport and communications		58,980
Highways	25,214	
Motorized transport equipment	4,424	
Railways	7,000	
Air transport	4,485	
Communications	7,764	
Shipping and harbors	10,093	
	58,980	
Education and research		18,914
Health, housing, and special welfare projects		8,188
Law enforcement		2,032
Reserves for special projects (unspecified)[a]		30,000
Miscellaneous		15,207
Total		240,000

(a) Presumably, military and security installations.

SOURCE: Compiled from the project listing in National Planning Council,
Buku Ringkasan Pembangunan Semesta [Outline Book on Over-all
Development] (Djakarta, 1961).

total. Cultural expenditures (national shrines, museums, art galleries, etc.) represent a planned expenditure of only Rp. 1.5 billion, for example.

As a pattern of planned sectoral allocation of developmental investment, the distribution of categories of expenditure—with the omission of the Rp. 30 billion provided for special projects—appears to be relatively sound on the basis of Indonesia's prime development needs. The projects which make up the major categories also appear to have been rather well conceived and put together in a manner suggesting that the A projects deserve serious consideration as components of a feasible development effort. The allocation of 12 per cent of plan resources to social welfare and miscellaneous (culture, improvement of the police force, etc.) may be considered a minimum concession to the political pressure to which the planners were subject. The emphasis on industrial development is heavy (31 per cent of the total), but major expenditures in this category are realistic in terms of Indonesia's requirements and resources, with textile promotion and mining development receiving the lion's share of the industrial allocation (see Table 22). In the context of island fragmentation and market limitations, which we have stressed as major impediments to economic progress, the emphasis on transport and communications (28 per cent of the total) is consistent with sound development objectives. Electric power deserves emphasis, and its share (8 per cent) is justifiable on the basis of the universal shortage of industrial power in Indonesia. Expenditures for education and research (9 per cent) are weighted in favor of the dissemination of technical knowledge at all levels of learning. If carried out, this program of educational development will have an important impact on providing the human ingredient of development, recognized by all observers to be one of Indonesia's most serious deficiencies throughout the postindependence period. Agriculture's share (13 per cent) is somewhat low in view of Indonesia's serious food problem. On the other hand, output of chemical fertilizers is to be expanded under the industrial development program, and if this succeeds the greater supplies of fertilizers should have important effects on yields.

In striking contrast to these positive aspects of the plan, it virtually ignores the whole problem of estimating total resources available to prosecute the plan and allocating them to produce maximum developmental progress. The National Planning Council noted that plan investment expenditures would comprise 13 per cent of national income; in addition it expected investment expenditures to be undertaken by regional governments and private enterprise, so that investment might be expected to be 15 per cent of national income.[168] Yet the plan's discussion of financial resources is confusing. There is some recognition of the importance of stabilization to insure financial prosecution of the plan, but this cannot be considered as a serious part of the whole program.[169] Stabilization of the economy is, however, the foremost prerequisite for the success of any large-scale development effort in Indonesia. Without restoring relative price stability, aggressive project planning, even with relatively great foreign assistance, is almost certain to be self-defeating. Although government programs may develop additional productive facilities, inflationary finance and its consequences will continue to discourage production throughout the economy and reduce the efficient operation of new capacity. Indeed, the self-defeating nature of development without stabilization has been confirmed by experience in 1961 and 1962.

This question of finance was the thorniest raised in the National Planning Council and in the limited discussion permitted in the Provisional People's Consultative Assembly. The nub of the problem concerned the extent to which the Eight-Year Plan should call for popular sacrifice to provide resources for developmental capital formation. From the outset, the National Planning Council was in search of methods of finance which would not require large-scale sacrifice. During the summer of 1960, just before the plan was announced, the matter of finance had still not been settled, though various financial mechanisms smacking of gadgetry were mooted about. In the end, the plan emerged without a sound program to provide financing for its exhaustive lists of development projects, although many conflicting alternatives are proposed in its pages. The most that can be said is that the matter of finance was left to the hope that foreign assistance and investment would suddenly become of a much greater magnitude than Indonesia had experienced since independence—or had any reason to expect on the basis of its inducements to foreign investment.

It is on the matter of finance that the Category B projects fit into the plan. In brief, projects in this category are designed to provide the Rp. 240 billion needed to finance the Category A projects. The B projects are not necessarily developmental in nature; no domestic finance is provided for them. They represent, in fact, a financial panacea embodied in the opening of Indonesia's unused natural resources to foreign developmental capital. The National Planning Council mentioned oil, timber, and fisheries; cabinet discussion resulted in adding copra, rubber, tin, aluminum, and tourism to the list of natural resources to be used to attract foreign capital. Finance for development (Category A) projects is to be provided by sharing the profits from foreign development of these resources, with 50 per cent of the profits flowing to the foreign developer and 50 per cent of the Indonesian government. As late as March 1961, Chaerul Saleh, Minister for Basic Industries, maintained that 75 per cent of the financial requirements of the Eight-Year Plan would be yielded from developing the petroleum industry alone. This would work out to about U. S. $500 million per year (at the official exchange rate), roughly one and one-half times the total value of present annual petroleum production.

Almost as an afterthought the National Planning Council raised the subject of domestic finance, despite its disclaimers[170] about imposing a domestic burden on the Indonesian population to finance the plan.[171] In elaborating on the sources of domestic finance that might be employed without imposing serious sacrifice, the National Planning Council specified: funds frozen by the government during the 1959 monetary reform (Rp. 10 billion), profits of state enterprises, voluntary popular savings, sale of capital goods provided by the government to small-scale enterprise, and expanding production for export through appropriate measures. Few of these suggestions, if carried out, would in fact generate the *real* domestic savings required to offset government rupiah expenditures for development. In fact, therefore, the plan left the financing of domestic expenditures largely to inflationary devices. It is interesting to note that in 1961 a program of "guided savings" was introduced, again a departure from the no-domestic-sacrifice spirit that dominated the thinking of the National Planning Council. This new program provides that all government employees are required to deposit each month a minimum of 10 per cent of their salaries with designated banks.

No development plan can be prosecuted without supplies of local factors of production. If in fact relatively large amounts of foreign exchange are provided from Category B activities, and this foreign exchange is employed to purchase developmental *capital* goods—the intention of the National Planning Council—domestic savings will still be required to allow transfer of current resources such as labor, administration, and complementary building materials to developmental uses. The failure to provide domestic finance to meet these local development costs is an even more glaring deficiency of the Eight-Year Plan than are its unrealistic proposals for mobilizing great quantities of foreign exchange.

The whole matter of the Eight-Year Plan's execution is apparently still a controversial issue. Indonesia does not possess an agency with responsibility for administering its development plans. The National Planning Bureau, the Ministry of Planning, the Planning Board—all have been abandoned with the demise of the First Five-Year Plan. This has bred a situation in which conflicts among the various agencies concerned with economic policy are inevitable. The National Planning Council continues to exist, but without clearly defined responsibilities about execution of its plan. The cabinet, led by the President, may eventually assume responsibility for execution, but it is not an administrative body designed to carry out developmental projects. Separate ministries will apparently be given some responsibility for execution of projects within their competence. What is likely to emerge is a situation much like that surrounding past development efforts. "Project planning" of this kind is not synonymous with a national development effort, and it is doubtful that it will have significant results in raising real income per capita.

Experience in 1961 and 1962 bears out some of these conclusions. The Eight-Year Plan itself had provided that the majority of the 335 A projects be initiated in the early years of the plan, many in 1961. However, Presidential Decree No. 26, issued in late 1960, specified that first priority for actual implementation would be given to twelve Category A projects. This was followed by an announcement from the Ministry of Basic Industries and Mining, which was entrusted with the execution of the projects, specifying that ten projects would be initiated during 1961.[172]

It is an important commentary on the execution of the plan that foreign assistance had been obtained or was under negotiation for all the projects on this priority listing. Throughout 1961 projects were added to this list as tentative assurance of foreign participation become available. Among the major additions was the commencement of work on the long-planned tin smelter on Bangka with West German equipment and financial and technical assistance. Other projects have been activated as assistance became available from a wide variety of foreign sources: the United States, the Soviet Union and several Sino-Soviet bloc countries, Italy, the

United Kingdom, and Japan, to mention a few. Indonesian leaders have actively sought foreign assistance for these projects, and although no accurate estimate of the total volume or the actual conditions negotiated is available, the Eight-Year Plan has definitely accelerated the flow of intergovernmental loans and grants. Even private foreign investment has shown some inclination to participate; three new private foreign petroleum companies (Asmara of Canada, Union Pacific, and Pan American) have joined the three with longstanding operations, and there have been several other new applicants.

On the other hand, the government's 1961 budget was raised to RP. 83 billion from the previous year's Rp. 46 billion. Despite an optimistic estimate of tax and tax-like revenues, the new budget envisioned a deficit of Rp. 16.7 billion. The major factor in the great increase in projected expenditures was the allocation of Rp. 30 billion for economic development. Almost half of this was consigned to the food and clothing (sandan-pangan) program, plus relatively large amounts for construction and operation of the Asian Games facilities. In general, therefore, the procedure appears to be a matter of introducing spectacular, large-scale projects and those involving heavy foreign exchange costs as foreign financing becomes available, while attempting to finance smaller-scale domestic projects to which the leadership is committed from inflationary domestic sources. Even this compromise, however, is likely to accelerate instability and thwart the major short-run goal of increasing output of food and clothing.

Foreign Exchange, Monetary, and Fiscal Policies

In addition to its role in planning and controls, the government has had significant impact upon the economy through relatively aggressive monetary and balance of payments policies. The immediate direct effects of these policies have tended to fall on the modern, foreign-trade-oriented sectors of the economy, but secondary effects have been transmitted to other sectors. The dichotomy between the economy's two major sectors and the geographical fragmentation of the economy have, however, caused lags of varying length between the enforcement of policy changes and their final effects throughout the economy.

The apparent goals of economic policy during the ten years since sovereignty was achieved have been (1) establishing Indonesian control over economic activities carried on by foreigners and minorities, (2) encouraging distributional changes to yield a larger share of total product to Indonesian nationals, (3) promoting the development of the economy in terms of raising per capita income, and (4) maintaining economic stability. By the end of the first decade (1959), it appeared that priorities were assigned among these objectives in the order listed. Judging from policy decisions, the first two goals have consistently been more important to the government and the power elite than have economic development or stability. In the present context the goal of establishing Indonesian control over economic activities carried on by foreigners has been reformulated in terms of the Guided Economy provision of the 1945 constitution; that is, Indonesian economic control has become synonymous with government control.

The implications of these policy priorities for monetary and fiscal policy can be seen quite clearly in retrospect. Attempts to achieve the first three goals—Indonesian control, distributional changes, and economic development—have threatened the stability of the economy. Throughout the period since 1949, monetary and fiscal policies have been primarily employed to alleviate the unstabilizing effects of the pursuit of these objectives; it is only recently that they have been emphasized as major tools to pursue goals other than stability.

Throughout the decade of the 1950s the threat to economic stability implicit in the burdens of national unification and the establishment of a new nation was increased by the pursuit of the government's three prime economic goals. The government's capacity to collect tax revenues persistently lagged behind expenditures, leading to increasingly large budget deficits. Since 1958, the growth of the government's deficits has reached alarming proportions as a result of heavy military expenditures.

Increasing budget deficits and slowly rising—eventually stagnant —levels of output have produced widening disparities between the rates of growth of aggregate demand and output. Stabilization policies appear to have been relatively successful until 1954, but after that they were employed with diminishing effectiveness. This Indonesian experience suggests that an underdeveloped country may operate a disequilibrium economy with relative stability in the short run by employing policies attacking the symptoms of disequilibrium. In the longer run, however, the causes of disequilibrium must be attacked or the situation is likely to get out of control.

The Indonesian attempt to cope with disequilibrium through monetary-fiscal policy has consisted of a two-pronged attack. Balance of payments pressures were restrained by employing a variety of multiple exchange rate devices, supported where necessary by direct import controls.[173] Pressures on domestic aggregate demand were relieved by monetary policies designed to curb bank credit and excess public liquidity. Policies designed to alleviate balance of payments pressures, however, eventually produced serious effects on output, investment, and export incentives. Restrictive monetary policies tended to have a once-over and temporary anti-inflationary result, while also having disincentive effects on output and investment. It is probable that the recognition of these limitations on the persistent use of the stabilization gadgetry contributed to the decision to undertake more drastic action in August 1959, when the value of currency in circulation was reduced, bank deposits were frozen, and the international value of the rupiah was decreased.

The basic policies to restrain inflationary pressures have been operated with flexibility, applied with severity, and temporarily relaxed when their effects on the various symptoms of disequilibrium produced a crisis. Balance of payments controls exemplify the problem. The Indonesian Republic began with a fairly favorable balance of payments situation. Foreign stockpiling of raw materials prior to and during the Korean War raised prices of Indonesia's major export products. In both 1950 and 1951 this produced a positive balance in the merchandise account, allowing an accumulation of foreign exchange reserves simultaneously with increased volumes of imported goods. Although this generated rising prices in some sectors of the economy in 1950 and 1951, the inflationary impact of the export boom was not universal, and the government showed no great concern about the problem. The collapse of the boom in 1952, however, placed the economy in a precarious position. Inflationary pressures begun by the export boom were still being felt; but government revenues—largely foreign-trade oriented—suffered a severe decline, while public expenditures continued to grow. This produced a large budgetary deficit in 1952, and the budgetary stimulus to rising aggregate demand was much greater than the deflationary force of the balance of payments reversal.[174] These forces produced serious threats to the economic stability of the new Republic: domestic prices began to climb, and a sharp loss of

233

foreign exchange reserves occurred (from over Rp. 6 billion at the beginning of 1952 to Rp. 3.6 billion a year later).

During 1952 and 1953 several measures were introduced to halt the loss of reserves. In early 1952 the rupiah was officially devalued to one-third of its former value (from Rp. 3.80 to Rp. 11.40 per U. S. dollar), although the import rate was in fact unchanged and the de facto export rate devalued only from Rp. 7.60 to Rp. 11.40.[175] This was undertaken in conjunction with the imposition of varying rates of export duties—in effect a system of multiple export rates, but at slightly reduced levels from the export taxation implicit in the foreign exchange certificate system which had been in force from March 1950 to the time of the official devaluation in February 1952.

When this slight reduction proved ineffective, duties were revised downward later in 1952, again without significant result. Import licensing and foreign exchange allocation were tightened (essentially through a quota system), and multiple import rates were created under the import "inducement" system, which Benjamin Higgins aptly describes as "really a system to induce Indonesians not to import."[176] It required Indonesian importers to pay different surcharges, depending on the category in which the particular import goods were classified. Initially there was a free list, a prohibited list, a list requiring a 100 per cent "inducement" surcharge, and one requiring a 200 per cent surcharge. These measures, too, had little effect in relieving balance of payments pressures, since only a small percentage of goods were subject to the higher import rates and few were prohibited.

In late 1952 and during 1953 real teeth were put into import controls by the government's determination to restrict the loss of foreign exchange reserves during 1953 to a target figure of Rp. 1.3 billion (about one-third of the 1952 loss). Direct control through restriction of import licenses was employed if necessary; the first line of defense, however, was provided by tightening up the inducement system so that many more import goods became subject to rates above the basic official Rp. 11.40 per U. S. dollar, which remained applicable only to a narrowing list of exempted goods. In addition, an innovation with considerable monetary as well as balance-of-payments impact was introduced in late 1952: importers were required to prepay 40 per cent of anticipated import costs at the time of application for foreign exchange. In March 1953 the prepayment was raised to 75 per cent and extended to the surcharges to which the imported goods were to be liable.

By 1953 the government had thus established a system of balance of payments controls which were relatively effective in relieving pressures on foreign exchange reserves and which continued to provide a relatively large share of total national tax revenues. Moreover, certain devices—particularly the import prepayment plan— were effective in absorbing excessive domestic purchasing power. In 1953, the loss of foreign exchange reserves of Rp. 1.5 billion was near the target figure of Rp. 1.3 billion.

Essentially the same system of balance of payments controls, with minor variations, was maintained in the immediately succeeding years. In 1954, however, a serious balance of payments crisis arose, and was overcome only by drastic action during the second half of the year. The crisis followed a cabinet change in August 1953. The Ali Sastroamidjojo government, replacing the Wilopo cabinet, entered office determined to employ monetary and fiscal policy to replace colonial control of the economy by Indonesian enterprise, particularly in the foreign trade sector. During its first months in office, the new government freely dispensed import licenses and foreign exchange allocations to favored "Benteng" firms, and it encouraged the establishment of Indonesian firms in the import field. These policies resulted in a huge draft on foreign exchange reserves during the first half of 1954. Reserves fell by Rp. 1.2 billion during this period, though the targeted loss had been set at only one-half of this amount for the entire year. The liberal foreign exchange allocations produced an anti-inflationary impact, as greater supplies of imported goods flowed in against the increasing purchasing power emanating from the budget deficit. However, much of this anti-inflationary potential was dissipated through the corrupt practices that accompanied the ambitious attempt to create Indonesian firms.

In the second half of 1954, the threatening crisis evoked drastic government action. Reserve requirements were suspended as gold and foreign exchange holdings fell below the legal minimum cover of 20 per cent behind currency in circulation. The adverse publicity that accompanied this step forced the adoption of stringent measures to halt the further loss of reserves. Foreign exchange allocations and import licenses were drastically reduced, and "Benteng" subsidies in the import trades severely checked. These measures, together with adjustments in foreign debt and assistance, allowed

Indonesia to survive the crisis and to show a net loss of reserves for 1954 as a whole which was considerably smaller than that experienced during the first half of the year. The experience showed both the adaptability of the government's control system and its willingness to employ that system with flexibility.

Retrenchment continued during 1955, and a net foreign exchange reserve gain was shown for that year. Imports continued to fall in total value, and the volume and value of imported consumption goods fell more than proportionately. Consumer goods imports had totaled 763 million kilograms in 1954; in 1955 they fell to 444 million. In rupiah values, the reduction may be seen from the fall in imported consumer goods from Rp. 3.7 billion in 1953 to Rp. 2.7 billion in 1954 and to Rp. 2.1 billion in 1955.[177] This severe decline in imported supplies of consumer goods aggravated inflationary pressures on prices, since imported goods were an important component of Indonesian consumption.

The quickening of the pace of inflation, together with a cabinet fall in July 1955 involving a shift toward the more pragmatic Harahap government, brought an awareness that stabilization policies, while more or less protecting foreign exchange reserves, had lost considerable ground in the battle against domestic price inflation. Inflation had spread throughout the economy, finally reaching the relatively insulated rural sector and bringing increases in the prices of basic foodstuffs. There was also general dissatisfaction with the widespread corruption which by 1955 had permeated the administration of balance of payments controls. Foreign exchange allocation had become subject to political rather than market considerations; increasingly, reliance was placed upon direct controls rather than allocation by the market through the multiple import rate system.

The Harahap cabinet, in power from August 1955 to March 1956, became the vehicle for major reforms in the foreign exchange control system which had fallen into abuse and was apparently aggravating domestic price inflation. The new cabinet introduced measures to simplify and rationalize import controls, to eliminate corruption in their administration, and to shift the focus of monetary and fiscal policy from foreign exchange reserve protection to domestic price stability. Import surcharges were raised and exemptions reduced. A new Bureau for Trade and Foreign Exchange was set up to allocate foreign exchange on a completely impersonal basis. By avoiding the use of names on applications and their being processed through the applicant's bank, discrimination against Chinese traders was rendered impossible. Speed in processing applications was emphasized in an effort to increase quickly the flow of import goods, in order to counter the mounting inflationary pressures. All importers were required to deposit a minimum pre-payment of Rp. 5 million against future foreign exchange purchases and import surcharge payments. This drastic measure had an immediate effect in its significant reduction of money in circulation and hence of purchasing power.

These measures soon produced the anti-inflationary consequences they were designed to afford, but at the expense of sharply falling foreign exchange reserves. Within a few months the money supply was reduced by 5 per cent. Prices of import goods fell by almost 15 per cent during the second half of 1955, compared to a rise of 13 per cent during the first half of that year. The black market value of the rupiah, which had been rising at an alarming rate, began to fall.

The price and foreign exchange effects of these policies became fully apparent in 1956, however. During that year prices of imported goods, which had risen steadily since 1952, showed a significant decrease. The index price of 44 import commodities fell from 145 for 1955 to 136 for 1956 (1953 equals 100).[178] Foreign exchange reserves declined from Rp. 2.7 billion at the end of 1955 to Rp. 1.25 billion at the end of June, 1956, a year during which other Southeast Asian countries succeeded in making substantial increases in their reserves.

This brings us to the core of the problem faced by Indonesia during its first decade of stabilization efforts. The drastic measures enforced by the Harahap cabinet in 1955-56 exhausted the final potency of measures directed toward the symptoms rather than the causes of disequilibrium. Import prepayments, requiring advance payments of 40 per cent on their initiation in 1952, had been raised to 75 per cent in 1953 and to 100 per cent in 1954; and finally, in 1955, all import firms were required to deposit 5 million rupiah in advance of anticipated imports. Each of these steps had yielded perceptible reductions in the money supply and easing of inflationary pressures. By 1956, however, it was apparent that the use of this device had been pushed beyond the point of diminishing returns, and in that year the government was obliged to make net refunds to importers.

The multiple import rate policy had adverse effects upon exports and foreign exchange earnings. Exporters consistently received less than the rupiah proceeds of their foreign exchange earnings, yet their costs of production rose in response to the upward surge of domestic prices. In addition to this tax element in the differential export and import rate, a general export duty was in effect, and certain commodities bore additional duties. Finally, the severe cuts in imports reduced the access of export producers to raw materials and capital goods. Throughout the period after the collapse of the Korean boom, there was no significant rise in officially reported exports, and the presumption is that an ever larger volume was moving through illegal channels. Moreover, the burden of multiple exchange rate policies fell more heavily upon the more foreign-trade-oriented Outer Islands than on Java, and this aggravated growing political tensions between center and periphery. These factors produced a climate favorable to concessions to exporters; and several devices—most notably the export certificate system—were tried. None of these experiments succeeded in raising Indonesia's foreign exchange earnings, and they were rejected outside Java as inadequate to compensate for the heavy taxation and deprivation resulting from the multiple exchange rate system.

After 1956, therefore, the constellation of policies employed to protect foreign exchange reserves and to repress domestic inflation was not particularly effective in achieving either objective. Implementation alternated between stringent and liberal foreign exchange allocation, with prices responding slightly to these policy changes but, in general, maintaining a rapid rate of increase. Dissatisfaction with the impotence of policies mainly directed toward the balance of payments probably had much to do with the decision to employ the drastic measures included in the monetary reform of August 1959.

Just prior to the reform in 1959, a consumer price index based on 1953 as 100 showed a rise to 380, compared to 240 at the end of 1958 and 150 at the end of 1956.[179] On the other hand, wages of various groups stood at indices ranging between 135 and 210 in 1959 (1953 equals 100).[180] Ralph Anspach believes that this, along with serious output decreases, was the basic factor in precipitating the drastic 1959 measure. "The immediate impulse . . . is to be found in the steadily deteriorating economic situation reflected in a 17 per cent decline of total output in 1958 and in the rapidly advancing inflation that was causing great hardships among the common people."[181]

238

It must be emphasized that anti-inflationary policies and their impact should not be viewed only in terms of economic considerations. Hans Schmitt has argued that the variation in the use of fiscal, monetary, and foreign exchange policies during the period under review was an expression of a fundamental political struggle.[182] Schmitt's analysis suggests that political conditions in Indonesia were such that anti-inflationary policies of the type used between 1952 and 1957 had involved heavy political costs. In his view, foreign dominance in the economy continued until the final ousting of virtually all Dutch economic interests in late 1957. Inflationary policies were needed to strengthen Indonesian enterprise and to bolster the position of the bureaucracy in the conflict with foreign economic interests. Stabilization policies, with their orientation toward import controls, threatened the group of national importers "who had largely been recruited from the intelligentsia."[183] Efforts to encourage the Indonesianization of economic roles had focused on the import market, since this was the activity "easiest to enter."[184] On the other hand, inflation was more harmful to the economic interests of the Outer Islands than to important Javanese groups, giving a further political dimension to the conflict.[185] By 1957 economic considerations called for more drastic measures to cope with Indonesia's growing stability problems, and by 1959 the leadership appeared to be more receptive on political grounds as well. Later events suggest, however, that interest in stabilization waned after the 1959 measures.

The measures undertaken in August 1959 embraced both monetary and foreign exchange policies: (1) rupiah notes of 500 and 1000 denominations were reduced to 10 per cent of their face value; (2) 90 per cent of all bank deposits above Rp. 25,000 were subject to being "frozen" (this is the term used), the frozen deposits becoming a long-term loan to the government; (3) the exchange rate was devalued from the previous official rate of Rp. 11.40 to U. S. $1.00 to Rp. 45.00 to U. S. $1.00, with foreign purchases of rupiah subject to a 20 per cent exchange tax.[186]

The monetary measures had only a short-lived effect in reducing the money supply, but they did temporarily slow down the pace of inflation. Currency in circulation declined from Rp. 24.2 billion in July to Rp. 18 billion after the reform; demand deposits fell from Rp. 9.7 billion to Rp. 3 billion. In other words, the total money supply was reduced from about Rp. 33.9 billion to Rp. 21 billion by the "reform." That it was a temporary palliative in the face of a growing budgetary deficit is apparent from the rapid growth of the money supply after August. By the end of 1959, currency in circulation had risen to Rp. 26.4 billion and demand deposits to Rp. 8.5 billion, yielding a total money supply about Rp. 1 billion above the amount just prior to the monetary reform of a few months earlier. During 1960, the rate of growth in the money supply was about 33 per cent. The significant impact of the reform was its effect in causing the rate of price increases to advance more slowly than the rate of growth of money supply. The reverse had been true in the year prior to the measures (see Table 18). The lag effect in the reaction of prices to the growth of money supply had worn off by 1961, however, and once again the rate of price increases exceeded the rate of monetary expansion.

The conclusion that emerges from this account is that a drastic monetary action amounting to the confiscation of a large part of currency and deposits in circulation and the devaluation of the rupiah failed to halt the growing symptoms of the economy's disequilibrium, just as the previously employed constellation of stabilization policies eventually lost their force in repressing these symptoms. It should be added parenthetically that this may not have been the sole objective of the 1959 action, and that other goals of the reform may have been achieved. One observer viewed the monetary measures as part of a series of policies to strengthen the role of the state throughout the economy,[187] and another quotes President Sukarno on the deliberately anti-private-enterprise nature of the monetary reform.[188]

Little has been said in this discussion about fiscal policy proper— the use of government expenditures, revenues, and borrowing to affect the economy. The Indonesian government has, in fact, failed to emphasize fiscal policy for stabilization purposes. In 1952, the Wilopo cabinet recognized the importance of the budget deficit in generating inflationary pressures; it set up targets to keep the deficit within specified limits in 1953, mainly by attempting to reduce government expenditures. Some progress was made in this direction, but these efforts were soon abandoned after the Wilopo cabinet fell in June 1953.

In general, Indonesia has not employed tax and expenditure policies for stabilization. Expenditures have responded to the desires of particular ministries, the economic objectives espoused by the various cabinets, and the growing demands of the internal security situation. Tax and tax-like revenues have reflected changes in the aspects of government stabilization policy discussed above. Changes in revenues, therefore, have largely tended to follow changes in foreign exchange policies. In spite of some tax changes in 1960, there has been no determined effort to alter the structure of taxation to increase revenues, to restrain inflation, or to improve economic incentives. In short, the fiscal system has been residual to the other components of stabilization policy; no cabinet has attacked the problem of revising the tax system in order to adapt it to the purposes of a newly independent country confronting the related problems of economic stability and growth.

Throughout the period since independence, taxation has been primarily oriented toward the foreign-trade sector, as it had been during the last two decades of the colonial period. Until the collapse of the Korean boom, receipts from export taxes dominated government revenues, producing 54 per cent of total government tax income in 1951 and 43 per cent in 1952. Following the introduction of stabilization policies which emphasized balance of payments controls, import taxation became dominant, producing 39 per cent of total government revenues in 1953 and an average of 40 per cent since that year. No significant progress has been made since independence in increasing the share of revenues from income, consumption, or rural taxation. Except for revenue changes associated with foreign exchange policies, the tax structure has remained essentially the same as it had been in 1939, the last normal year of colonial control.

Much the same conclusion can be reached for the use of monetary policy. Apart from the foreign exchange aspects, particularly the import prepayment system, monetary policy has not been effectively employed for stabilization objectives. Credit has had an impact upon stability, but its impact has been one of aggravating inflationary pressures. Relatively large-scale credit expansion through the organized financial sector occurred throughout the period 1950-57.[189] During much of this time, expansion of credit reflected the use of government funds to strengthen Indonesian enterprise through institutional credit. The government undertook tentative steps toward credit regulation, but these had little impact on restraining bank credit.[190]

Beginning in 1959, the Monetary Board attempted to tighten controls over bank credit expansion, reinforcing special reserve provisions which had been on the books since 1957 by imposing credit ceilings. The special reserve provisions required private banks to: (a) invest specified fractions of their cash assets (cash on hand plus balances with the Bank Indonesia) in treasury notes and bills; (b) deposit specified fractions of their surplus cash (cash assets as defined in (a) less investments in treasury notes and bills) in a "Special Account" in the Bank Indonesia; and (c) maintain minimum specified ratios between cash assets and current liabilities. For banks with current liabilities exceeding Rp. 150 million, the fraction of cash assets to be invested in treasury notes and bills was raised from 10 to 20 per cent in October 1957, while the fraction of "surplus cash" to be deposited with the Bank Indonesia was raised from 50 to 75 per cent in April 1959. These measures failed to check the expansion of bank credit, since reserve-eligible securities were being continuously supplied by the growth of the government deficit.

The new credit ceilings introduced in April 1959 applied to all banks, private as well as governmental. The ceiling first imposed restricted credit from any bank to the volume outstanding at the end of August 1958. In August 1959 new ceilings were set for a number of larger banks; in some cases credit was restricted to the March 1959 volume, although in the case of four larger foreign banks the ceiling was lowered to that of November 1957.[191]

A number of exceptions were made to the enforcement of the credit ceilings, and these exceptions turned out to be of critical importance in determining their impact. The ceilings were not to apply in the case of credit extended to government enterprises engaged in the importation of essential commodities and the domestic purchase of rice. Just after the monetary reform, moreover, the Bank Indonesia was empowered to provide liquidity credits to enable banks to expand credit, and the Monetary Board made use of this power to waive the credit ceilings for banks at its discretion. The Board also permitted certain banks to default on the special reserve requirements "under certain special circumstances."[192]

Despite the new credit controls, therefore, the continued expansion of credit was possible. The Bank Indonesia reports that "the granting of credits by the 13 foreign exchange banks and the Bank Indonesia . . . showed a steadily rising tendency, so that at the end of March 1960 this total exceeded twice the total of the credits at the end of July 1959, i.e. before the government launched its measures in the monetary field on 25th August 1959."[193] At the end of December 1959 bank credits outstanding totaled Rp. 11,432 million, compared to Rp. 6,695 million called for by the existing ceiling.[194] The Bank Indonesia reported that "this addition in credit grants was principally due to the increase in credits given out to those sectors exempted from the credit ceiling regulations."[195]

It is apparent that the main impact of these monetary policies was in their effect on the allocation of credit rather than on the restriction of its volume. This conclusion is demonstrated in Table 23, which presents data on the volume of bank credit from major sources outstanding to public and private recipients, from December 1957 to March 1960.[196] In spite of the new quantitative credit controls, bank credit from the sources shown more than tripled in slightly over two years, accompanied by a dramatic shift in the relative shares absorbed by government enterprises and the private sector. During this period, the volume of bank credit outstanding to government enterprises (from the sources in Table 23) rose by Rp. 9 billion, compared to a rise of about Rp. 2.1 billion outstanding to the private sector. The share of government enterprises rose from 11.5 per cent in December 1959 to 61 per cent in March 1960. Since both Indonesian private banks and foreign banks rely predominantly on private enterprise for their lending business, this shift represented a weakening of their lending position relative to that of government financial institutions. Private Indonesian bankers complained that the credit controls were being enforced to discriminate against them; the basis of the selective enforcement of the controls, however, related to the maintenance of liquidity in enterprises which the government considered "vital," and these were largely public firms after December 1957.[197]

Newly independent Indonesia faces several major problems that must be solved before the performance of the economy is likely to improve. The foremost precondition to economic development is the establishment of relative stability. The government budget has been the primary cause of inflationary pressures, and the restoration of stability must focus upon the reduction or elimination of the budget deficit. Recent structural changes in the economy, and accompanying changes in distribution of income, have made the traditional tax system ineffective in maintaining the share of government income relative to national income. Tax reform is needed to allow the government to finance a larger part of its expenditures from current income. On the other hand, it is hardly likely that the government's inflationary impact can be adequately reduced without simultaneous reductions in government expendi-

Table 23. BANK CREDIT OUTSTANDING TO GOVERNMENT AND TO PRIVATE ENTERPRISES, DECEMBER 1957 TO MARCH 1960

(million rupiah)

	December 1957		December 1958		December 1959		March 1960	
	Govt.	Private	Govt.	Private	Govt.	Private	Govt.	Private
Bank Indonesia, Bank Negara Indonesia, and thirteen foreign exchange banks(a)	526	3007	1471	3654	5884	4456	9560	4578
Private Indonesian banks		950	......	1326	......	1507	......	1522
Total	526	3957	1471	4980	5884	5963	9560	6100

(a) Including foreign-owned.

SOURCE: *Report of the Bank Indonesia, 1959-1960*; and *Bank Indonesia Bulletin*, No. 20 (First and Second Quarter, 1960).

tures. Recent improvement in the internal security situation and the settlement of the West New Guinea problem may allow substantial reductions in military expenditures, the category that has dominated public spending in recent years.

Secondly, the government confronts the problem of establishing effective planning agencies and of improving public administration throughout the vast and growing economic bureaucracy. Coordination of planning efforts must be undertaken if government investment resources are to be effectively employed to raise per capita output. In the management of government enterprise, reform is needed to promote effective decision-making, to delineate lines of responsibility and to place emphasis upon performance rather than political criteria. Channels of administrative control between Djakarta and the far-flung economic interests of the government must be shortened, so that the central decisions can be readily made on the basis of accurate information. In the administrative reforms essential to prosecuting a development program, progress is partly dependent on abandoning the concept of complete control from the center. Delegation of decision-making authority to responsible individuals in the field would do much to enhance the performance of government enterprise. Improvement in communication facilities is also essential to better public administration: although decisions at all levels of operation are referred to Djakarta, communication between the capital and the outlying islands is often a matter of days or weeks. Improved communications are a basic prerequisite to uniting the scattered islands into an integrated economy followed closely by the necessity to develop transport facilities to levels which will encourage the growth of wider domestic markets, essential to the development of domestic industry.

Integration of the economy is related to the third major problem impeding short-run development of the economy, the question of national political unity. The settlement of political differences between Djakarta and the outlying provinces is essential to provide minimum security conditions for using present productive facilities to capacity; and this in turn is a first precondition for launching a program to enlarge productive capacity and improve technology through a vigorous and large-scale development program. The concept of a national program, and its acceptance by the Indonesian peoples, are scarcely realistic in the context of disaffected groups spread throughout the archipelago. The national leadership faces the problem of coping with this discontent either by genuine negotiation of differences that have existed since independence or by attempting tighter authoritarian controls than the central government seems ready or powerful enough to exert.

Economic progress requires that Indonesia's human and material resources be mobilized to solve these basic problems. Whatever the final interpretations on the issue of the public-private mix, incentives must be created to induce Indonesians at all social and economic levels to expand investment and output. Material and status rewards must be related to *economic* performance in both public and private enterprise, to encourage the allocation of resources to the many opportunities for constructive development, and to halt the diversion of resources to activities that hamper or retard economic progress.

The most critical unaccomplished preconditions to economic development in Indonesia, therefore, appear to lie in areas beyond the boundaries of economic analysis. Many of these are related to the presence or absence of the society's determination to organize itself for a massive assault upon economic stagnation. To borrow Hirschman's terminology, the government, and Indonesia's leadership generally, have failed to organize themselves into a "binding agent" for promoting economic development.[198] This critical factor is defined as "a 'growth perspective' which comprises not only the desire for economic growth but also the perception of the essential nature of the road leading toward it."[199] In most underdeveloped societies this perception would appear to include, first, essential reforms to enhance the feasibility of prosecuting a development program and, secondly, a realistic appraisal of the magnitude of the effort and sacrifice required to prod the economy from stagnation to the beginnings of growth. Neither has been apparent during the first decade of Indonesia's sovereignty.

Much of the Indonesian leadership's energy has been devoted to precipitating changes essential to assure Indonesian control over economic enterprise and the economy's resources. This concern does not of itself imply a disinterest in developmental goals and activities. However, having virtually completed its objective of wresting the control of important sectors of the economy from the Dutch, the leadership's developmental goals and visions have not crystallized into concepts likely to provide solutions to either the fundamental noneconomic problems obstructing economic growth or the economic problems inherent in self-sustained stagnation. For the leadership has viewed its task as one of attacking *symptoms* of underlying political and economic disequilibrium, and of achieving minimum conditions to trigger mechanisms leading to rapid and easy development, with little or no sacrifice on the part of Indonesian peoples. There is no evidence that it is prepared to attack the fundamental causes of social and economic instability; the Eight-Year Plan represents the culmination of this reluctance in its delineation of ambitious development objectives to be accomplished from resources external to the Indonesian economy. There are many competent Indonesian social scientists whose grasp of the realities of Indonesia's development task is profound and more relevant than the partial comprehension of foreign observers. The influence of this group of Indonesian experts has, however, been adumbrated by the transfer of planning authority to veteran politicians. This has resulted in the dissemination of unrealistic development goals and methods in the context of Guided Economy, Guided Democracy, and the "retooling" of social, cultural, and economic institutions. Perhaps these measures represent a circuitous route toward the integration of Indonesian society and the coalescence of its leadership into a "binding agent" that can promote development. If so, progress toward economic development will still require determined and realistic efforts to resolve the problems that have produced instability and retrogression in the economy and which represent continuing impediments to sound economic growth.

CHAPTER 6

Labor in Transition

EVERETT D. HAWKINS

LABOR ORGANIZATIONS are among the oldest mass groupings in Indonesia; they arose at the same time as the country's
first modern political associations, and they played a leading role
in the struggle of those movements to achieve national independence. Today, like the parties and other mass organizations, they find
themselves dependent upon and constrained by the patterns of
Guided Democracy, Guided Economy, and Socialism à la Indonesia which have been evolved by the nation's leaders to shape the
course of the Republic. It was easy for labor organizations to join
in the cry, "Down with Colonialism, Imperialism, and Capitalism";
it is much harder for them to help build a country with a strong
government, a viable economy, and a society based on Indonesian
traditions.

In comparison with the colonial period, all Indonesian cabinets
have been prolabor. However, although a certain amount of labor
legislation has been introduced, including reduction of the hours of
work, many of the older attitudes toward labor have not changed;
it is generally accepted, for example, that a manual worker is paid
little, produces little, and has little status. Moreover, the government, including its civil and military departments and corporations,
has become the major employer of labor in Indonesia; and the
public authorities, feeling that the country cannot afford work stoppages, have developed rules and administrative bodies to minimize
industrial disputes and to prevent strikes. Management in the
larger undertakings is no longer predominantly foreign, but the
exodus of alien personnel has made more severe the already serious
shortage of skilled, trained managers in both the public and private
sectors. In spite of all attempts to attain a single labor front, multiple
unionism persists, with most unions bearing close ideological ties to
certain political parties or groups.

248

Many of the patterns of industrial relations in Indonesia are not unlike those in other countries which have moved recently from control by a colonial elite to that of a new nationalist state.[1] Their development in the context of a competitive political system industrializing primarily according to market factors had not been completed, however, when the nation's leaders elected to shift to a semicompetitive political system, with industrialization regulated primarily according to a development program.[2] The changes arising from this decision have been so recent, so complex, and so affected by considerations governing the recently completed struggle for West New Guinea, that it is only safe to say that industrial relations, like other phases of Indonesian life, are still in a process of transition.

Because of the uneven distribution of Indonesia's population, the labor supply varies greatly from crowded Java, Madura, and Bali to less populated Sumatra, Borneo, Celebes, and most of the other islands. Programs to recruit labor from the densely to the thinly populated areas are still used to meet this situation, although less extensively than when the Dutch were extending their estates and other extractive industries to the Outer Islands. In addition, large-scale transmigration schemes have been evolved as a solution to overcrowding and underemployment on Java, but the numbers moving have never been but a small percentage of that island's annual increase in population. Most Javanese do not like to leave their homes even if whole villages are moved. Frontier regions offer less in the way of schools, hospitals, and other amenities, and the cost of living is higher. Furthermore, the cost of transmigration is high, transportation has recently been scarce, and the administration in new areas has often left much to be desired. These plans, therefore, have not solved the underemployment problem of Java, even if they may have helped the growth of certain parts of Sumatra and the other islands. This difference in the distribution of available manpower is still a fundamental factor in understanding differences in labor relations in various parts of Indonesia.[3]

Given the general oversupply of labor, most workers are anxious to hold on to their present source of employment. This reflects an overcommitment to a particular job; in fact, one might generalize that Indonesian workers are more job- than wage-conscious. This frequently results in more workers being on the payroll than necessary,[4] so that employers complain about high labor costs per unit of output, while at the same time workers talk about low subsistence wages. Indonesia, like India and many other economically developing areas, faces this major dilemma; an abundance of unskilled labor results not only in low wages and low productivity, but also in high costs.

Although the government has published 1961 census figures on total population by sex and province,[5] labor force data will be restricted to estimates until employment figures are released. The previous census, taken by the Dutch in 1930, showed about 21 million in the labor force out of a population of just over 60 million, while the National Planning Bureau estimated in 1953 that there were 30 million in the labor force out of a total population of approximately 80 million (see Table 1). The Manpower Directorate of the Ministry of Labor, with some technical assistance from the International Labor Office, has made a series of sample surveys, including one on the labor force in Java and Madura in 1958.[6] Although this study is much the most comprehensive survey now available, some of the rural and urban data are not strictly comparable since different time periods were used to survey the rural area (a year) and the urban area (only one week). This study indicates about 24 million in the working force out of a population of about 48 million in the rural areas (see Table 2). This would indicate a working force of almost half (49.93 per cent) of the population. In the urban areas of Java and Madura the working force in 1958 was 2.6 million out of a population of 8.2 million, or

Table 1. OCCUPATIONAL DISTRIBUTION OF THE INDONESIAN LABOR FORCE, CENSUS OF 1930 AND ESTIMATE OF 1953

(*millions*)

| | Totals | | Per cent | |
	1930	1953	1930	1953
Agriculture and raw materials	14.4	18.2	68.9	60.7
Industry	2.2	4.0	10.5	13.3
Transportation	0.3	0.8	1.5	2.7
Commerce	1.3	3.0	6.2	10.0
Professions	0.2	0.2	1.0	0.7
Government	0.5	1.8	2.4	6.0
Other	2.0	2.0	9.5	6.6
Totals	20.9	30.0	100.0	100.0

SOURCE: Biro Perantjang Negara, *Garis-garis Besar Rentjana Pembangunan Lima Tahun, 1956-1960*, p. 139.

Table 2. ESTIMATED POPULATION CLASSIFIED BY THOSE IN
THE WORKING FORCE (WORKING AND UNEMPLOYED),
THOSE NOT IN THE WORKING FORCE, AND THOSE OF
WORKING AGE, IN RURAL AND URBAN AREAS IN
JAVA AND MADURA, 1958

(*thousands*)

	Rural	Urban	Total[a]
Population	48,339	8,225	56,564
Working force[b]			
Working	23,945	2,621	26,566
Fully unemployed	192	201	393
Total	24,137	2,822	26,959
Not in working force	7,511	2,732	10,243
Total of working age	31,648	5,554	37,202

(a) The totals are not strictly comparable since different definitions were
used in the rural and urban areas.
(b) The working force in Java and Madura constitutes 47.77 per cent of the
population; the rural working force, 49.93 per cent; the urban working
force, 34.31 per cent.

SOURCE: Departemen Perburuhan R. I., *Report on Labour Force Sample
Survey in Java and Madura*, 1961.

only 34.31 per cent. If these totals are combined, the working
force in the rural and urban areas would be 26.6 million, or 47.7
per cent of the total population.

When this percentage figure is projected for a total 1961 population of 97 million in Indonesia, it indicates an estimated working
force of some 45 million; while if the 37.5 per cent figure used in the
1953 estimates were applied, the estimated labor force would be a
little over 36 million. The discrepancy of 9 million may be accounted
for in part by divergences in the definition of employment used
by the surveys. For example, over 7.5 million, or 31.61 per cent of
the 24 million in the working force in rural areas, were stated to be
members of the families who worked without wages (see Table 3),
while in urban areas less than 5 per cent were listed as unpaid
family workers by the 1958 study.[7]

One of the main reasons for the great difference between the
rural and urban working force in Java and Madura is the fact that
almost as many women work in the rural areas as men. This trend
toward higher rural than urban employment of women was also
found in a study made in the Special Region of Jogjakarta in

Table 3. ESTIMTED TOTAL NUMBER OF PEOPLE IN RURAL AREAS OF JAVA AND MADURA TWELVE YEARS OF AGE OR OVER WHO HAD JOBS, CLASSIFIED ACCORDING TO BRANCH OF ECONOMIC ACTIVITY AND STATUS, 1958

(thousands)

Branches of economic activity	Owners with workers	Owners without workers	Workers	Members of a family who work without wages	Total	Per cent of total
Agriculture	1,706	4,207	4,225	6,676	16,814	70.18
Mining	2	5	22	6	35	.17
Manufacturing	79	702	798	416	1,995	8.35
Construction	6	35	213	6	260	1.09
Public utilities	….	….	5	….	5	.04
Commerce	107	2,089	129	391	2,716	11.36
Transportation	7	142	105	3	257	1.04
Services including government	27	287	1,463	86	1,863	7.77
Total	1,935	7,467	6,960	7,583	23,945	100.00
Per cent of total	8.10	31.19	29.10	31.61	100.00	

SOURCE: Departemen Perburuhan R.I., *Report on Labour Force Sample Survey in Java and Madura, 1961.*

1959. In Gunung Kidul, the poorest agricultural area of Jogjakarta, every family surveyed counted the wife as a worker. Many women are part-timers, working in the busy agricultural season and engaging in trade on market days. In certain regions, too, women supplement their income by handicrafts such as weaving or batik waxing.[8]

Of the approximately 24 million in rural areas of Java and Madura classified by major branch of economic activity, over 70 per cent had agriculture as their main occupation; over 11 per cent were engaged in commerce; and the rest in manufacturing, construction, and so on (see Table 3). Because of the seasonal nature of agriculture and the generally low level of income, over one-quarter of the workers in rural areas had secondary occupations, principally in agriculture and commerce.[9]

In urban Java and Madura, out of a labor force of somewhat over two and a half million the leading sources of employment were services—including government, which engaged about a third of the workers—followed by commerce (see Table 4). In rural and urban areas together, the total number of employees, as opposed to owners or unpaid family workers, amounted to less than a third of the total labor force in the two islands. The 1958 study found less

Table 4. ESTIMATED TOTAL NUMBER OF PEOPLE IN URBAN AREAS OF JAVA AND MADURA TWELVE YEARS OF AGE OR OVER WHO WERE IN THE LABOR FORCE, CLASSIFIED BY BRANCH OF ECONOMIC ACTIVITY, 1958

(*millions*)

Branches of economic activity	Total	Per cent
Agriculture	0.12	4.58
Mining	....	....
Manufacturing	0.61	23.28
Construction	0.11	4.20
Public utilities	0.02	0.76
Commerce	0.73	27.86
Transportation	0.21	8.02
Services including government	0.82	31.30
Total	2.62	100.00

SOURCE: Departemen Perburuhan R. I., *Report on Labour Force Sample Survey in Java and Madura,* 1961, p. 37.

253

than a million people in both the rural and urban areas of Java who were included in the following occupational codes: professional, technical, and related workers; administrative, executive, and managerial workers; and clerical workers.[10] It is clear from the data provided in this study that white-collar workers made up a very small percentage of the labor force, that factory workers accounted for only about a tenth, that service and commercial employees made up almost a quarter, while agriculture and related occupations still were the predominant occupation for over 60 per cent of the labor force in Java and Madura.

Since Indonesia is passing through the demographic transition in which death rates are decreasing more rapidly than birth rates, a growing proportion of the population will live to be part of the working force. At present, a very high percentage of the population is below age fifteen and a very small percentage above fifty-five, the normal retirement age.[11] As the government comes closer and closer to its goal of compulsory education, and as the percentage of students going on to high school rises, the growth of the labor force will tend to slow down. Moreover, evidence indicates a slowing down of the rate of population increase during the 1940s because of war and revolution, and this means that in the 1960s relatively fewer newcomers may enter the labor force. These factors will not solve the unemployment or underemployment problem, but they may make it somewhat less serious for the immediate future than it might otherwise have been.

The Indonesian employment pattern shows clear variations according to national and ethnic groups. For all practical purposes the Dutch are no longer a factor in the labor market, but until 1957 they did fill a great many of the professional, managerial, commercial, and technical posts and even some of the more skilled trades. The Eurasians formed a second category, aspiring to the status of the Dutch but generally employed in somewhat junior positions. Many have already left Indonesia, and those who remain no longer enjoy privileged status; on the contrary, to gain acceptance they must try to be more Indonesian than the Indonesians. The Chinese were primarily the middlemen in internal trade. In rural areas they were often moneylenders operating under the *idjon* system of buying crops in advance of the harvest; and they also engaged in manufacturing and various crafts. Today the Chinese are still in these businesses, though in recent years their role has been considerably reduced by government measures.[12] There are still some foreign managers, traders, and businessmen in Indonesia. With the exception of the Chinese, however, the labor force is almost entirely Indonesian today, and the percentage will probably grow beyond the present 97.6 per cent[13] unless there is a change in political policy regarding Indonesianization of the economy.

Differences in population distribution, degree of commercialization, and traditional social and religious outlooks combine to produce important variations in labor relations among the Indonesian ethnic groups. The Javanese, for example, came into contact with commercialization and industrialization before most of the peoples on the other islands; they are therefore more used to the employment relation and more committed to earning a living through wage and salary payments.[14] The Bataks of northeast Sumatra tend, on the other hand, to dislike the employment relationship intensely, particularly as it applies to blue-collar jobs; plantation work on the area's numerous estates has had very little attraction for them. Consequently, the regional employment pattern shows recruits from Java filling the ranks of the estate laborers and Bataks holding white-collar and independent positions. This is only one of the ways in which ethnically related factors produce variations in regional labor patterns. Though it would not be proper to ascribe overriding importance in labor relations to these considerations, they should by no means be overlooked.[15]

Like all developing countries, Indonesia does not utilize its human resources nearly to the full. Unfortunately, over-all figures on employment are not available.[16] However, the Labor Force Sample Survey showed about 1.5 per cent unemployed in Java and Madura in 1958—less than 1 per cent in the rural areas but about 7 per cent in the cities.[17] As in many other countries, the percentage of unemployment is higher in the younger age brackets, i.e. among those who are just entering the labor force; approximately half the urban unemployed in this study were in the fifteen to twenty-four year age bracket.[18]

The low rural rate of unemployment is deceptive; the problem in the agrarian sector in Java is not an absolute shortage of jobs but the spreading of available work into too many hands.[19] The Labor Force Sample Survey estimated that there was an underemployment rate of one-third in the agricultural field in the rural areas in 1958.[20] Even if this figure is only approximate, it is clear from the supporting data that there is a great amount of agrarian underemployment in Java and Madura. Even in the peak season there were only

7.37 million workers who averaged eight hours a day, and over a million averaging only two hours; in the slack season the situation was reversed, with over 8 million averaging two hours a day and less than half a million working eight hours.[21]

With such a large amount of underemployment it seems safe to say that many local *gotong rojong* (mutual aid) projects, such as building schools, roads, and irrigation systems, could be carried on without even short-run reduction in crop yields and with increased returns in the future. Total human resources are great enough to support a substantial increase in industrialization. To recruit unskilled labor is not a difficult task in many parts of Indonesia, and certainly not in Java. There has already been a great movement to the cities, as is evidenced by the more rapid rise in city population than in the country as a whole.

In spite of its large labor supply, Indonesia still lacks enough trained and experienced manpower—managers and entrepreneurs, professional personnel, and skilled workers. This was in part due to the historical domination of the modern sector of the economy by Europeans and Chinese, and to the traditional preference of educated Indonesians for government service. Certain craft industries and petty commercial activities have customarily been Indonesian-run; but the number of Indonesians participating in the modern business sector, outside of those replacing Dutch personnel after the take-over of Netherlands businesses in 1957, has not increased rapidly.

The government's notably successful drive to reduce illiteracy—which declined from 93 per cent in 1941 to less than 50 per cent in 1958—has reflected a general desire by the population to acquire as much schooling as possible; education, in fact, is becoming a great source of labor mobility. Viewed from the standpoint of labor supply, however, the greatest needs are in intermediate and higher specialized (that is, non-liberal-arts) education. The government has made considerable efforts to expand facilities in this area, one of the most significant being the development of intermediate and high schools specialized in commercial, agricultural, teacher training, technical, and similar subjects. The number of students in these programs has been increasing and forms a larger percentage of students above the primary level than in many other Asian countries.[22] Because of this, and because of the generally acute shortage of educated personnel, Indonesia has not yet developed large pockets of white-collar unemployment as has India. Nonetheless, the problem does exist and much more needs to be done in relating the supply of the particular human resource to the demand for it, as well as in adapting the educational program to Indonesia's needs rather than to patterns followed in Holland or other more industrialized countries.

Indonesian labor unions have been politically oriented from the start, and most of them today are still concerned with political action, some of them actually functioning as the labor arm of a political party. The first Netherlands Indies union to include Indonesian workers was the Union of Rail and Tramway Personnel (VSTP); it was founded in 1908, though it was not until some five years later that Indonesians were represented in it in any numbers. In the colonial period Indonesian unions, which existed almost exclusively on Java, could be classified into three general categories: white-collar and professional workers and civil servants (for example, teachers, doctors, government pawnshop officials, customs officials); wage-earners and urban low-status salaried personnel (rail and tram workers, dockworkers, post-office employees, printers); and workers on sugar estates and other plantations.[23] As might be expected, the groups in the first category were usually more conservative in their political alignment, their members tending toward Budi Utomo, the moderate wing of the Sarekat Islam, and the less radical nationalist movements. The second category formed the mainstay of Communist support during the PKI's heyday in the 1920's. Though these unions were generally more radical than those in the first group, they were also much less stable—as early industrial labor organizations in most countries have tended to be. Except for the VSTP, they frequently resembled groups coming together temporarily to support a strike more than permanent labor organizations. With the third category, the lack of stability was even more pronounced. The sugar workers' PFB, organized by the Sarekat Islam leader Surjopranoto, was the only union of this type to achieve a degree of success. The union expanded rapidly during 1919 under the benevolent protection of the colonial government, which under its Ethical Policy sought improvements in the sugar workers' condition which the employers were not interested in granting voluntarily. At the height of its success the PFB boasted 31,000 members, the largest of any Indonesian union in the preindependence period. As soon as their wages had been improved, however, its members lost interest; and when the following year their leaders failed to win a strike which had been called to revive their enthusiasm, the organization melted away. It was followed by a series of leftwing unions which organized the estate workers with even more fleeting success. The PFB had been the principal component of the Sarekat Islam-sponsored Central Labor Federation (PPKB). Communist-controlled unions, of which the most important was the VSTP, participated briefly in this and other united groupings; but efforts at a common labor front usually dissolved quickly into a radical and a moderate concentration of unions.[24]

Part of the reason for the weakness of the prewar labor movement lay in the difficulty faced by union leaders in organizing and disciplining the largely illiterate workers; part of it lay in their own lack of experience and tendency to subordinate economic to political interests—in particular the drive for national independence and the ideological disputes which were then dividing the labor movement in Europe. Management was inclined to concede little or nothing, and on overcrowded Java strikebreaking was exceedingly easy. In addition, the government's attitude, especially after 1920, was openly on the side of management, it being argued that Indonesian welfare could only be served by the unhampered expansion of European-run enterprise. The colonial government gradually passed more stringent labor legislation, including antistrike measures. Since government workers, particularly salaried ones, were inclined to be more conservative, and since increasingly severe measures were taken against Communist and nationalist radical leaders, there was a general tendency for unions to become more moderate after 1929. Thus, whereas the Sarekat Islam's PFB and the Communists' VSTP had set the tone in the early stages of the labor movement, the principal association in the 1930s was the Federation of Public Servants' Unions (PVPN) organized by the gradualist Hadji Agus Salim.

The depression of the 1930s, which was severe in Indonesia and resulted in a substantial decline in wage rates and employment, put an effective check on union activity. Close on its heels came the Japanese occupation, which ended independent labor organization and subjected the Indonesian workers to great economic hardships. With independence, however, there was a rapid resurgence of union activity. Under the Republic, unions assumed an important role in economic, governmental, and political activity; they looked on themselves as arms of the revolution, and indeed not infrequently played a paramilitary role.[25]

Political affiliation continued to characterize the labor movement of the 1950s. The parties' efforts to develop mass organizations of their own—including, of course, unions—received additional impetus with the preparation for the 1955 general elections. By 1957 there were at least twelve labor federations, in addition to a number of regional and local groupings and a large quantity of unaffiliated independent unions (see Table 5). The principal federation was—and still is—the Communist-oriented SOBSI (Central Labor Organization of All Indonesia) which had been founded in 1946 and was the sole effective labor federation in the Republic. SOBSI is composed primarily of industrial unions but also includes some craft groups; it is generally conceded to be the largest, strongest, and most carefully organized federation, with the largest number of full-time union leaders. Three other federations of importance in the 1950s were the KBSI (All-Indonesian Congress of Workers) which claimed to be independent in spite of some PSI (Indonesian Socialist Party) officers; the SBII, which was started by the Masjumi party; and KBKI, which was organized by the Indonesian Nationalist party (PNI). The other federations were of less importance, some of them hardly being more than paper organizations.

In industries such as railroads, plantations, and oil, SOBSI unions appeal chiefly to rank-and-file workers, while the non-Communist unions tend to attract the white-collar *pegawai* employees. This, added to the relative organizational and financial weakness of the non-Communist unions, has made it difficult for SOBSI's rivals to compete for its membership. Attempts at creating a counterweight to SOBSI by combining the forces of the non-Communist federations resulted in the founding of the KBSI federation in 1953—an association which, however, suffered some serious disaffiliations the same year. In the late 1950s efforts were made toward a combination of the four Moslem federations, and in 1961 most of the members of the SBII and KBIM amalgamated into the Association of Indonesian Islamic Labor Unions (GASBIINDO). In a similar move toward consolidation, the KBKI has tried to absorb its fellow Nationalist federation, GSBI, as well as a number of local unions. The KBKI proved unable to maintain its own unity, however, and in January 1963 split into a faction dominated by Labor Minister Ahem Erningpradja and a group oriented about the PNI.

It is not easy to determine the exact membership of Indonesian trade unions. Multiple unionism makes it difficult for any one union to collect dues, and many members cannot afford to pay them

Table 5. ESTIMATED MEMBERSHIP AND POLITICAL ORIENTATION OF TRADE UNION FEDERATIONS, 1957-58

(*thousands*)

Federation	Political orientation	Registered June 30 1957[1]	Number of members reported by regional labor offices end 1957[2]	Trade union claims March 31, 1958[3]
SOBSI	PKI (Communist)	1,502	1,180	2,733
KBSI	PSI[a] (Socialist)	261	106	376
SBII[c]	Masjumi Party[a] (Moslem)	275	84	600
KBKI	PNI (Nationalist Party)	101	332	1,002
HISSBI	Partai Buruh (Labor Party)[b]	8	16	261
SOBRI	Partai Murba (National-Communist)	44	117	281
SARBUMUSI	Nahdatul Ulama (Moslem)	12	14	12
GOBSII	PSII (Moslem)	1	6	1
GSBI	PNI (Nationalist)	33	18	145
KBIM[c]	Masjumi Party[a] (Moslem)	42	10	42
O. B. PANTJASILA	Partai Katholik (Catholic)	....	....	61
SBKI	Parkindo (Protestant)	....	....	....
B. P. B. (Regional)		171	21	180
Nonfederated			378	
		2,450	2,282	5,694

(a) Disbanded in 1960.
(b) HISSBI is now associated with IPKI.
(c) Merged into the Moslem-oriented GASBIINDO.

Source: Ministry of Labor, (1) *Registered Trade Unions Period June 30, 1956 to June 30, 1957*, pp. 30-33; (2) *Report for Two Years April, 1957–April, 1959, p. 8*; (3) *Tindjauan Masa'alah Perburuhan, May, 1958*, p. 8.

in the first place. In only a few labor organizations such as the railway and communications workers' unions is the check-off system used, a system which gives an accurate count of membership and which also provides regular funds for union development. In some cases, workers may belong to more than one union, or move from union to union, depending upon whether or not a particular organization supports their grievance. They may also be willing to join in a strike or a demonstration by a particular union, though they otherwise have little real affiliation with it. The rank and file in Indonesia is relatively weak and depends to a great extent on leadership; but many of the labor leaders, particularly in non-SOBSI unions, have other full-time jobs and hence can devote only partial attention to their organizations.

Certainly the claims of trade union membership are highly exaggerated by all groups, and therefore the total of 5,693,898 union members claimed as of early 1958 is much too high (see Table 5). In some cases even the registered members or the membership reported by regional labor offices is probably too great. Prior to the rebellion in 1958 there were probably over 2 million members, most of whom did not pay dues regularly, and of this total approximately half were affiliated with SOBSI.

In the colonial period wage payments, even among the largest firms, tended to be made in goods and services as well as cash. During the 1950s some of the major companies tried with fair success to introduce modern industrial relations practices by going over to a so-called "clean" wage policy; but they were generally forced to relinquish this toward the end of the decade, since inflation and shortages of essential goods caused the workers to press demands for substantial payments in kind in addition to their money wage. Many employers, particularly on the estates and in the oil industry, where workers must live far from the cities, have come to provide such services as medical, educational, social, and recreational facilities, and housing for their workers and staff members.[26] Some foreign managers would have liked to get away from such activities, and have argued that they smacked of paternalism; but both labor and, in certain cases, the government insisted upon their continuance. At the end of 1961 the average married male worker with two children on the estates in East Sumatra received only a little over a fifth of his daily wage in cash, the rest comprising payments in kind, such as food and clothing allotments, housing, and medical and educational services (see Table 6).[27]

Table 6. MINIMUM DAILY WAGES IN SELECTED YEARS,
1951-60, IN CERTAIN INDUSTRIES IN INDONESIA

(*base year 1953 = 100*)

Industry and location	1951 Rp.	1953 Rp.	1955 Rp.	1958 Rp.	1960 Rp.	1961 Rp.
1. *Estates on Java, South and West Sumatra*						
Married with two children:						
In money	3.00	3.50	4.25	4.75	5.30	6.40
In kind	1.80	1.44	2.52	4.86	7.41	7.41
Total	4.80	4.94	6.77	9.61	12.71	13.81
Index number	97	100	137	195	257	279
2. *Estates in North Sumatra*						
Married with two children:						
In money	3.25	3.50	4.25	4.45	4.90	5.75
In kind	5.78	5.63	6.26	10.18	17.51	19.37
Total	9.03	9.13	10.51	14.63	22.41	25.32
Index number	99	100	115	160	246	277
3. *Sugar-cane estates*						
Married with two children:						
In money	4.00	4.00	4.50	4.75	5.25	6.00
In kind	1.65	1.65	3.20	5.95	9.32	11.44
Total	5.65	5.65	7.70	10.10	14.57	17.44
Index number	100	100	154	189	258	309
4. *Kretek* (*spiced cigarette*) *manufacturing industries*						
In money: males	....	....	4.00	5.50	6.00	7.50
females	....	....	3.50	4.50	6.00	7.50
5. *Tandjung Priok Harbor*						
Regular:						
In money	....	5.25	8.05	10.62	11.50	11.50
In kind	....	1.17	1.24	2.12	6.00	9.50
Total	....	6.42	9.29	12.74	17.50	21.00
Index number	....	100	145	199	272	327
6. *Building construction in Bandung*						
In money:						
Foremen	20.00	22.00	26.00	34.00		
Chief *tukang*	15.00	16.50	19.50	25.50		
Tukang (bricklayers, carpenters, etc.)	10.00	11.00	13.00	17.00		
Other (unskilled)	5.00	5.50	6.50	8.50		
Index number	91	100	118	155		

SOURCE: Ministry of Labor and *Statistical Pocketbook of Indonesia 1961*, pp.
248-49.

Wage payment systems in both private and public employment include as a rule extra payments according to the number of dependents in the family; and in addition awards are added for length of service. It is quite possible, therefore, for a young single person in a high rank to receive considerably less than an older person with a large family in a much lower rank. Because of the complexities of the wage system, including all of these payments in kind and bonuses, the incentive payments are apt to be so small that they have relatively little effect, although it has been demonstrated in Indonesia that payment by the piece does result in considerably greater output per person per hour.

Labor-management relations during the 1950s were made more difficult by the fact that the larger enterprises remained in foreign hands, and that nationalist feelings were thus deeply involved. The demanding standards of the colonial Dutch managers, lost during World War II and the revolution, were frequently not regained; why, the workers asked, should Indonesians labor long and hard for foreigners? It was a difficult transition from a period of autocratic, paternalistic rule to one where management was limited by trade union negotiation and government regulation—an adjustment which many foreign managers found hard to make.

Indonesian cabinets in this period understandably tended to take labor's side in demands on management, though at the same time concern for preserving production caused them to place limits on the extent to which disputes could be carried. The most important labor laws established in the 1950s were the Labor Code (Conditions of Employment), the Labor Disputes Acts of 1951 and 1957, the Workmen's Compensation Law, and the Collective Agreements Law. Although there are no official minimum wage laws in Indonesia, the minimum rates established by the government for its own workers in the various regions have tended to affect wages in the area; moreover, wage decisions established by government arbitration were binding on labor and management. The Labor Code, made applicable for all Indonesia in 1951, provided for a seven-hour day and forty-hour week, regulated employment of women and children, and established minimum hygienic standards in factories and workers' housing.[28] Although penalties are provided for violations and the Ministry of Labor (retitled Department of Labor Affairs in 1959) is charged with the code's enforcement, lack of staff has made it impossible to secure compliance, especially in the case of

263

smaller firms. The labor unions have insisted, however, that the larger companies at least meet the standards set by the code.

The Collective Agreements Law of 1954 is interesting not only for its establishment and guarantee of collective bargaining procedures but also because it protected plural unionism, the individual's right to work, and the employer's right to hire. All collective agreements, the law provided, were to be registered with the Ministry of Labor. Unions and employers were required to inform their members of the terms of the agreement and were subject to damages if they failed to comply with their provisions.

The general public and the governments of most countries are opposed to frequent strikes; in fact, many of the developing countries feel that they are less able to afford strikes than the more industrialized nations. Indonesia has been no exception to this trend. The most important labor regulation passed in 1951 was Emergency Act No. 16, which served as the basis for handling labor disputes in Indonesia until June 1958. This law did not prohibit strikes, but it carefully regulated the handling of disputes and in reality established a system of compulsory arbitration to determine wages, hours, and working conditions in place of a free system of collective bargaining.

Although the Act provided for the local and regional offices of the Ministry of Labor to try to settle disagreements through mediation, most of the cases went before regional disputes committees (Panitia Penjelesaian Perselisihan Perburuhan Daerah, or P4D). The decisions of these bodies were subject to appeal, and therefore many were referred—primarily by labor—to the Central Disputes Committee (PPPP Pusat, or P4P), which had the power to issue binding awards. From 1951 to 1958 the P4P handled 8,500 cases, or over a third of the more than 22,000 disputes referred to the Ministry of Labor. Although each case was handled on its own merits, decisions in one dispute tended to become precedents for others. Moreover, the P4P lumped together cases of a similar character—for example, all those of the estate unions on the east coast of Sumatra —and handed down one general ruling.

Over the years considerable criticism of this machinery developed, and a number of proposals were made for its change. Some of the unions criticized the legislation on the grounds that it interfered with their constitutionally guaranteed right to strike. A number of disputes suffered considerable delay in settlement because of the complexity of the issues involved or because so many minor cases had been referred to the Central Disputes Committee from the regions. It was occasionally pointed out that this system of compulsory arbitration made real collective bargaining impossible, since whichever side lost the argument at the bargaining table was bound to appeal to the government board.

In 1957 the Settlement of Labor Disputes Act introduced a number of changes in the arbitration arrangement, giving the regional disputes committees some power to issue binding decisions, and changing their composition from one comprising only government employees to one including five labor, five employer, and five government representatives. These functional groups seemed to work together harmoniously, since nine-tenths of the cases heard by the new P4P in its first year were decided unanimously. The number of disputes coming before the new central committee in that year was, however, very much less than before, not only because of changed legislation but also because of the anti-strike regulations taken in response to the developing national emergency and growing military control of the economy. By the first six months of 1962, the P4P reported, only 28 cases were decided and 102 appeals from the regional boards were rejected.

The record on disputes and strikes in this period can be seen in Table 7. Following the passing of the 1951 Act the number of hours lost during strikes declined sharply—from 54 million in 1950 to 7 million in 1956—although the number of disputes did not decrease until after 1957. With the introduction of the strike ban in 1957, the number of hours lost dropped radically again to less than one million in that year.[29] The hours lost through work stoppages continued to decrease the following year; but in 1959 they began a gradual rise to over 700,000 hours in 1961, largely because of illegal strikes which had political overtones and were centered on the estates of North Sumatra. This increase was not accompanied by a rise in the number of disputes or the number of workers involved, both of which, on the contrary, showed a tendency to decline.

As these figures suggest, the period since 1957 has brought profound changes to the position of labor and management in Indonesia. The seizure of Dutch enterprises at the end of 1957 took place with the participation and in many cases the leadership of the firms' Indonesian employees and their unions. Initially, a number of unions called for the businesses to be run by workers' councils; but the government did not accede to this, nor did it place the enterprises under private Indonesian management. Instead, they

Table 7. NUMBER OF DISPUTES, WORK STOPPAGES, AND WORKERS INVOLVED, 1950-61

Year	Disputes	Workers involved in dispute	Work stoppages	Workers involved in stoppages	Working hours lost by work stoppages
1950	180	....	184	490,539	54,489,897
1951	2,754	....	541	319,030	26,039,398
1952	4,003	....	349	132,963	6,152,377
1953	1,823	1,268,480	280	419,580	4,812,090
1954	2,963	2,304,747	347	157,582	2,385,730
1955	3,697	3,488,747	469	238,872	4,097,803
1956	3,896	3,111,957	505	340,203	6,968,931
1957	4,131	5,057,478	151	62,024[a]	863,257[a]
1958	3,350	2,975,922	55	13,578	98,060
1959	2,825	1,956,500	70	26,626	219,237
1960	1,096	833,235	64	14,577	306,462
1961	1,159	900,009	86	63,111	738,874

(a) In addition, 1,030,083 workers went out on strike and 7,218,706 hours were lost at the end of 1957 in the protest movement concerning West Irian.

SOURCE: Ministry of Labor, *Ekonomi dan Keuangan Indonesia*, 8 (1955), p. 458; *Tindjauan Masa'alah Perburuhan*, 10 (1959), pp. 44-49; *Statistical Pocketbook of Indonesia 1961*, pp. 243-45; and Departemen Perburuhan R.I. *Statistik Perburuhan*, Tahun 1961.

were put under government control—at first under the management of the army, which had already stepped in to take the initiative of the seizures from the unions. In this manner, three important developments of the Guided Democracy period were introduced: the replacement of foreign by Indonesian management, the substitution of state for private control, and the assumption by the military of a major role in all managerial affairs, including the field of labor relations.

To the extent that nationalist sentiment hindered labor-management agreement prior to the seizure of Dutch property, the take-over paved the way for more harmonious relations. New problems, however, arose to replace the old ones. In the first place, the exodus of Dutch personnel which followed the seizures made more acute the already great shortage of managerial talent. The breach has been filled by appointing army officers and politicians to management positions, by promoting foremen and other employees experienced in the business concerned, and by appointing Indonesians with some university training in management subjects, but no actual business experience. Obviously, such stopgap measures have their weaknesses, and these are felt in the field of labor relations.[30] The army managers, used to military discipline, are not accustomed to the give-and-take of a bargaining relationship; inexperienced civilian managers often hesitate to show a firm hand, preferring to yield the issue or pass the responsibility on to the higher bureaucracy. The workers themselves not infrequently have found it difficult to adjust to Indonesian managers, both because the latter often know little about the business and because the workers feel fellow Indonesians to be their equals, not their bosses.

It might be expected that, in view of the previously noted pro-labor attitude of the Indonesian government, the replacement of foreign management by Indonesian public control would strengthen the position of the labor organizations. This has not been the case: on the contrary, most of the older unions are today in a relatively weakened situation. One of the reasons for this is the decline of all politically oriented mass organizations, which has been effected under Guided Democracy. Of more immediate importance, however, is the fact that the government, as the principal managerial element in present-day Indonesia, naturally tends to view the position of management in a more sympathetic light than before. The new Indonesian managers do not talk about managerial prerogatives, but they do look upon certain union activities as interfering in their own field. Not only have a series of emergency measures aimed at maintaining production made almost all strikes illegal, but the government has felt it had to hold down costs, including wages, to try to reduce its deficits and to limit inflation. In 1961 it did, however, allow a 25 per cent increase in wages in the private sector to match increases to government employees.

The military has entered the field of labor relations not only through its assumption of a role in management but also by its establishment of supervision over labor unions. At the end of 1957 Nasution issued an order founding a Body for Cooperation between the Army and Labor, BKS-BUMIL, which was to advise the military on matters in the labor field and see that workers did their duty in firms taken over from the Dutch, that no sabotage took place, and that the plants were kept in good running condition. The fourteen labor groups participating in BUMIL were represented on its units on a basis of equality rather than in accordance with their strength.[31] BUMIL soon became involved in certain industrial disputes, though the jurisdiction of P4P and P4D was maintained over most cases. Whether the military officers in BUMIL learned more about the unions or the union leaders more about the military is a moot point; certainly the unions enjoyed anything but a dominant position in the relationship. Although BUMIL's importance had faded to the vanishing point by 1962, the army continues to play a major role in labor relations, principally by preventing nearly all strikes—political or economic—and by keeping under strict control the activities of labor unions, particularly those affiliated with SOBSI.

A move to unify all labor organizations into a single confederation was made early in 1960 by President Sukarno, who suggested it in the context of his drive for the creation of a monolithic National Front. In July 1960 Ahem Erningpradja, the Minister of Labor Affairs and president of the KBKI federation, held a conference of the leading trade union heads and certain government officials to discuss a draft regulation for the establishment of such a labor concentration, the Organization of Indonesian Workers Associations (OPPI).[32] SOBSI, not wishing to submerge itself in a body it was unlikely to control, refused to support the plan, while a number of modifications were proposed by other labor leaders. In the ensuing contest between SOBSI, its rivals, the army, and the President, various regional OPPI bodies were formed by non-Communist unions backed by the local military and without the participation of

SOBSI. Although the Minister of Labor Affairs found it necessary to abandon his original plan, there are indications that he is still working toward some form of united labor front. In the context of the West New Guinea drive, he organized a Joint Secretariat of Labor Federations composed of the six labor organizations represented in Parliament, SOBSI (Communist), KBKI (Nationalist), SARBU-MUSI (Moslem, Nahdatul Ulama), GASBIINDO (Moslem functional representative), GOBSII (Moslem, PSII), and SOBRI (Murba).[33] Even before the West New Guinea settlement in August 1962, however, this body had discussed other questions, including the extension of its membership to bring in a new series of Karyawan Organizations.

Army officers in important government managerial positions have taken the lead in forming these new groups; they were united as the Association of Employees of State Industries, which was to include all employees (karyawan, a term now commonly substituted for the more class-oriented (buruh, or worker) from the top management through the least skilled. The Association held its first national convention in August 1962 and claimed a membership of half a million in government trading companies, factories, and estates. SOBSI and others have called its components "company" unions. Certainly its leadership comes from management, and the first people to join in many government enterprises are the management and white-collar groups.[34] Although there was some indication that this was an attempt to supplant SOBSI unions with a new, less militant and more cooperative organization, it would seem that few, if any, inroads had been made into their membership by mid-1962, although some of the non-SOBSI unions were afraid of losses. In December 1962 the Karyawan Organizations held a convention in Djakarta; their representatives were addressed by Sukarno, to whom they pledged their loyalty. At the same meeting their Association changed its name to Central Organization of Indonesian Socialist Workers (SOKSI).

Related to this development has been the establishment of Enterprise Councils (Dewan Perusahaan), which the President urged in December 1961. These councils, made up of carefully screened government appointees from management, labor, the public, and—where appropriate—farm groups, are to advise the top managers in a given plant or industry. They are supposed to give labor a voice but to leave management in command, and it is hoped that their presence will enable all labor-management problems to be resolved without recourse to formal disputes. Since the workers' representatives are to be nominated by labor organizations having 30 per cent or more of the employees in the undertaking concerned, this should play into the hands of the larger unions and Karyawan-SOKSI. At the time of writing, these Enterprise Councils were still in the planning stage, one for the estates having been the first to be organized. It seems clear from the general statement of their purpose, however, that they are to constitute another "guiding" device which, if effectively implemented, would limit still further the traditional role of trade unions in Indonesia.

The Joint Secretariat of Labor Federations, the Enterprise Councils, and Karyawan-SOKSI are all manifestations of an increased tendency toward state guidance in labor relations, but all of them are so new that it is impossible at this time to predict their full import.[35] Furthermore, it is too soon after the agreement with the Dutch over West New Guinea to predict the possible roles of military and developmental factors in the future of Indonesian labor. It is clear, however, the labor organizations find themselves at the present in a generally most difficult position. Their principal weapon, the strike, has been taken from them, as was attested by the many arrests of union leaders following SOBSI-sponsored strikes on the North Sumatra estates in 1961. Conflict with management, which once earned approval as an attack on foreign imperialism, now earns opprobrium as an attack on the state. Some unions—principally the smaller ones—have attempted to advance their position by currying the favor of the military or governmental authorities, especially at the local level. Others have turned to the establishment of clinics and workers' cooperatives, but serious shortages of funds and supplies have hurt these projects. Given the severe inflation to which the country has been subjected, labor's principal demand is for substantial increases in money wages or payments in kind; government approval is necessary for the first, and the second depends on government distribution of cheap rice and textiles. The unions cannot force the issue; the efforts of SARBUPRI, the SOBSI-affiliated estate workers' union, to do so in 1962 through a strike on a privately owned North Sumatra estate under the slogan of "no rice, no work" met with quick suppression. It is difficult to measure the extent to which the workers have been disaffected by this situation. Almost all the unions are in straitened financial circumstances and must rely on sources other than dues-paying members. Although they have tended to deny decreases in their membership, few claim substantial increases, and it seems likely that total union membership has not grown since 1958.

On the other hand, though management is no longer seriously troubled by strikes or work stoppages, it nonetheless faces major problems in the labor field. Management—both public and private —must not only increase its own efficiency but also that of the workers, and there is at present very little incentive for the workers to raise their present low level of production. Unless the cooperation of labor is secured, and the workers given reasons—both economic and psychological—to increase their efficiency, Indonesia's path to the rehabilitation and industrialization of its economy will be a very difficult one.

CHAPTER 7

The Course of Indonesian History

ROBERT VAN NIEL

FRAGMENTARY stone and metal inscriptions dating back to the beginning of the fifth century A.D. provide our most ancient evidence of Indonesia's history. It is apparent from them that Indonesian civilization had already undergone influence from India, and we therefore have no real knowledge of the archipelago prior to its absorption of elements from abroad.[1] It would seem, however, that the earliest Indonesian political institutions above the village level were formed by local leaders who attempted to combine village and clan groups into larger, more stable communities under their rule.[2] As commercial contacts with India developed—the western Indonesian islands lay on the trade route from southern to eastern Asia and were sources of spices, gold, sandalwood, and other desired goods—local chieftains became acquainted with Indian social and political concepts. These, embodying a centralized, hierarchical state organization under a sacred king, aroused the interest of Indonesian leaders seeking a cultural vehicle for the legitimization and extension of their authority. Consequently, they made use of Brahmans from India to advise on the organization of government ritual.[3] The early Indonesian states thus assumed an Indianized form, though there is little evidence that the common people were affected by the adopted state culture.

Chinese chronicles, our second source of information on this early period, indicate that a number of Indianized states existed on Java, Borneo, and Sumatra during the sixth and seventh centuries and appear to have engaged in trade with India and China. These writings also make clear that Hinduism was not the only Indian religion introduced into the archipelago, for Buddhism was reported as being practiced in one of the Javanese kingdoms in the seventh century. It appears to have been of the Theravada school, which was widely popular in Southeast Asia; soon, however, that form was replaced by Mahayana Buddhism, which became temporarily dominant on Java and more permanently so on Sumatra.

The eighth century witnessed great changes in the political structures of the archipelago, changes which may have been stimulated by more active commercial and religious connections with Bengal. Among the many petty rulers of the country, strong kings arose who managed to extend their power over wider areas. Early in the century, Sandjaja, King of Mataram, achieved suzerainty over Central Java and may have extended his authority to Sunda (West Java), parts of Sumatra, and Bali.[4] The first of the great Central Javanese monuments, the Shaivite temple remains of the Dieng Plateau, dates from about the time of Sandjaja's reign. In Sumatra, the kingdom of Sriwidjaja, which was centered in the present area of Palembang, extended its influence to control the Straits of Malacca. Sriwidjaja adhered to Mahayana Buddhism, and the state became a stopping point for Chinese Buddhist pilgrims on their way to India. The power of this kingdom seems to have been based exclusively on its control of international trade; its heart lay upon the seas, not in the hinterlands of Sumatra. Sandjaja's Javanese state also engaged in commerce, but its control of the interior areas placed at its disposal a solid agrarian base and a much larger population.

In the latter half of the eighth century both the Sumatran and Javanese kingdoms appear to have come under the control of a single dynasty, that of the Sailendras (Lords of the Mountain).[5] Under their rule great Mahayana Buddhist monuments were built on Java. The most famous of these, the Borobudur, was built around 772 A.D. near the present city of Jogjakarta; it is an immense stupa, the terraces of which are decorated with sculptures illustrating Mahayana texts. The Javanese sculptors had already adapted Indian models to their own traditions, creating a structure associated with indigenous religious ideas and practices. The Dutch archaeologist Stutterheim, in his study of early Javanese civilization, concludes that during the ninth century both Hinduism and Buddhism were practiced on that island, Shiva and Buddha being regarded as manifestations of the same spiritual being.[6] Both were essentially court religions, not notably affecting the traditional religious practices of the villagers.

Late in the ninth century the Sailendra empire appears to have split into separate Sumatran and Javanese states. The Sailendras continued as rulers of Sriwidjaja, which remained loyal to Buddhism. The Javanese returned to Shaivite Hinduism, and its rulers declared themselves kings of Mataram. The monuments of Prambanan, built in this period on the Kedu plain near Jogjakarta, reflect their return to Shaivite worship. About the year 930, King Sindok moved the capital eastward from its original site in the Solo river area to the Brantas river valley, apparently in response to the extension of wet-rice agriculture and its accompanying irrigation systems into the latter region.[7] The rulers of this east Javanese kingdom, which was maintained until 1222, continued to use the title "King of Mataram."

On Sumatra, the Sailendra state of Sriwidjaja flourished as a religious and commercial center. It assumed close ties with India, where its kings established relations with Bengal and the Coromandel coast and founded Buddhist monasteries at Negepatem.[8] About the year 1000, Sriwidjaja seems to have reduced Java to submission, but its conquest was only a temporary one. A devastating raid by the Cholas of India in 1025 momentarily crippled the kingdom and gave Java the opportunity to recover. The Chola raids appear to have recurred sporadically, and gradually the power of Sriwidjaja waned. By the late thirteenth century the dominant position on Sumatra had passed to Melaju, a state which had its center near present-day Djambi and which was, by all indications, a vassal of Java.

Java's temporary conquest by Sriwidjaja delayed its development only slightly, for after the year 1000 the East Javanese state was reunited under the powerful king Airlangga. East Java, with its political center at Kediri, became more intensely cultivated and more densely populated, and commercially it rivaled and finally succeeded Sriwidjaja. Tuban and other ports on the Gulf of Surabaja became flourishing centers of trade which had contacts not only with Sumatra and the Malay peninsula, but also with Borneo and the Moluccas. Ternate was a Javanese vassal state at the time of the Kediri kingdom, and Bali seems to have been brought under control even earlier.

The East Javanese period appears to have seen the blending of Buddhism and Shivaism into a form of Tantric syncretism—the cult of Shiva-Budda—as the official religion, while the common people adhered to Shaivism blended with traditional practices.

This period also marked a flowering of Javanese literature, which, though it used Indian themes, was entirely Indonesian in rendition. Much of it was adapted to the popular *wajang* puppet dramas, and in this manner Indian cultural elements were communicated to the mass of the people.

An attempt by the last ruler of Kediri to bring the priesthood under more direct royal control seems to have provoked his overthrow and succession by a new East Javanese dynasty, which moved the capital to Singosari in 1222. The capital, the ruins of which are still visible today, was located not far from the present city of Malang. The most important ruler of Singosari was its last, Kertanegara, who reigned from 1268 to 1292. Concerned by expanding Mongol power in mainland East Asia, Kertanegara set out to strengthen his influence over neighboring areas. It is a matter of argument whether he pursued this aim by imperial conquest of the nearby islands and mainland or whether he sought a more symbolic mystical unity. Recent research tends to adhere to the latter interpretation.[9] In any event, Kertanegara felt strong enough to insult the envoys of Kublai Khan when they came to demand his submission. However, his forces did not succeed in preventing the ensuing Chinese expeditionary force from reaching Java, Kertanegara himself being slain by a rival ruler before it arrived.

Prince Widjaja, Kertanegara's son-in-law, managed to secure the backing of the Chinese force in his own bid for power, and in 1293 he founded a new dynasty, named Madjapahit after the settlement he founded on the Brantas river. Widjaja revived his father-in-law's program of expansion; and in spite of an initial series of revolts by its vassals, Madjapahit continued to extend its authority. Under the powerful leadership of Gadjah Mada, who was its chief minister from 1331 to 1364, the kingdom achieved what was probably the greatest power of any early Indonesian state. The extent of its rule is, like that of Kertanegara's kingdom, a matter of dispute. Contemporary chronicles, such as the *Negara-Kertagama,* speak of an empire controlling most of the islands and parts of mainland Southeast Asia, while the modern historian Berg suggests that possibly only East Java, Madura, and Bali were under Madjapahit's direct control.[10] Present-day Indonesian statesmen and historians tend to view the kingdom as a high point in the unification of Indonesia and hence as a major national historical symbol.

Under Madjapahit, government, culture, and society were controlled by an aristocratic elite, the *prijaji*. Both Buddhist and

Shaivite organizations flourished under the supervision of the state, which controlled religion through appointed officials. The servants of the king were granted control of one or more villages, which provided them with income by rendering as tribute a part of their produce. The administrative system and life at the courts do not seem to have differed markedly from that of nineteenth-century Java, with which we are more familiar. The world of the *kratons* (palaces) was not more sumptuous than in the latter-day principalities, but it did have a greater coherence and style which gave it a grandeur of its own.[11] Madjapahit's glory was short-lived, however; within a century of its founding the kingdom fell into decline. By 1389 its power was waning; by 1401 it had been torn asunder by civil war; and by about 1525 its last remnants had been destroyed in the rivalry of other Javanese states.

During the time of Madjapahit three exogenous elements which were to dominate Indonesian history from about 1400 to modern times—the Moslems, the Europeans, and the Chinese—made their appearance in the archipelago. European contacts at the time of Madjapahit were limited to the occasional traveler, one notable example being Marco Polo, whose account of his stay late in the thirteenth century was widely read in Europe. The Chinese had been in contact with Indonesia since earliest times, but the first large Chinese settlements seem to date from the period of Madjapahit. As a group the Chinese were to play a major role throughout the archipelago; their story is told in the chapter devoted to the Chinese minority, while the Moslem and European impact will be related here.

Historians generally agree that Islam came to Indonesia via the trade routes. The pattern of Asian commerce underwent changes starting in the late twelfth century which, especially after the fall of Bagdad in 1258, caused Moslem merchants to travel eastward in increasing numbers. Cambay in Gujerat became the great stapling port for the Moslem-controlled routes, and Moslem traders made their way as far as the spice islands of eastern Indonesia. We know that Madjapahit had Moslems as *shahbandars*, or chiefs, of some of their ports. It was only late in the thirteenth century, however, that there was significant conversion of Indonesians to Islam. By that time the expanding spice trade had resulted in the growth of powerful commercial towns along the northern Javanese (Pasisir) coast. The Pasisir city-states were governed by princelings who, in order to extend their authority against that of Madjapahit, sought the support of the Moslem merchants who controlled the trade routes; and in doing so they accepted Islam.[12]

If the adoption of Islam was initially a political convenience, it was far more than this in its ultimate effect. To the merchants of the archipelago's thriving ports, the new religion presented a life pattern that allowed them greater scope for individual development than did the rigid hierarchy of a Hinduized society. Moslem holy men, or *wali*, came to convert the people of the coastal cities and gained considerable fame as miracle workers.[13] Probably more influential in sustaining the religion was the nucleus of zealous believers who as teachers and scholars (*kijai* and *ulama*) formed the core of the Islamically oriented *santri* life pattern.[14]

The Islam that was brought to Indonesia had already been altered by mystical influences in India. During the course of its adoption in the archipelago it was fitted into existing social, cultural, and political concepts and thus acquired a distinct and heterodox form. Initially, the santri civilization appears to have been limited to the cities and larger towns; it seems to have penetrated into the interior regions of Java from the time of the decline of the coastal trading communities in the face of European competition.

In the non-Javanese parts of the archipelago, the influence of Islam appears to have been more direct. Minangkabau in western Sumatra and Atjeh in the north became Moslem strongholds, partly as a result of their commercial connections with Islamic centers. Traditional, or *adat*, authority remained strong in these areas, however, and not until the nineteenth century was Islam able to pose a serious threat to the old ruling class. In general, it was only in the nineteenth and twentieth centuries that Islam penetrated the rural interior of Indonesia so deeply as to disturb the traditional patterns of authority.

The early spread of Islam into the archipelago was closely tied to the rise of the city of Malacca, which was founded in the Malay peninsula about 1400 and which had won Chinese protection from incursions by Siam and Madjapahit. From its founding to its capture by the Portuguese, Malacca was a major center of Southeast Asian commercial activity, and it also became a focal point of the Islamic faith. It was Malacca which was responsible for the introduction of Islam into Java, whose Pasisir towns lay along the trade route to the Moluccas; and the Javanese in turn were instrumental in bringing Islam to the spice islands of eastern Indonesia.[15]

The capture of Malacca by the Portuguese in 1511 preluded the period of European influence in the archipelago. For more than half a century, Portuguese control of the city was contested by Indonesian rulers; often the Portuguese were hard pressed by these expeditions, but they managed to hold Malacca. Meanwhile they endeavored to expand their control of Malacca's trade routes to the east Indonesian islands in hope of securing a monopoly of their valuable spice trade. Shortly before the arrival of the Portuguese, the Moluccas (the so-called Spice Islands) had come under the control of Islamic merchant princes, the strongest of which were the sultans of Tidore and Ternate. For more than half a century, the Portuguese attempted to wrest from them control over the production and shipment of spices, but by 1570 Portuguese power in the Moluccas was so weakened that they lost all semblance of dominance in the archipelago.

With the Portuguese capture of Malacca, two Indonesian kingdoms arose to take over the commercial and political power once wielded by that city. On the island of Sumatra the sultanate of Atjeh became a competitor to the Portuguese and a successful monopolizer of the Sumatran pepper trade. Extending its control down the west coast of Sumatra, Atjeh converted the state of Minangkabau to Islam in the course of the sixteenth century. Atjeh continued to be an independent power of importance until the end of the nineteenth century, when it was finally subjected by the Dutch.

On the island of Java, the sultanate of Demak became the most powerful realm after the fall of Madjapahit. Under the patronage of Malacca, this Pasisir state developed important commercial connections with the Moluccas. When Malacca fell, Demak continued to expand independently, bringing about the establishment of a commercial settlement at Bantam on the western tip of Java. Bantam controlled commerce through the Sunda straits, which assumed new importance for Moslem merchants after the Portuguese became dominant in the Straits of Malacca. Throughout the greater part of the sixteenth century, Demak and its ally Bantam controlled the trade of Java.

Culturally Demak, though an Islamic state, continued many of the earlier Hindu traditions; one historian speaks of it as being a revival of Madjapahit's sea empire in Islamic dress.[16] Demak also controlled interior areas of Java, but its dominance there was contested by a new state which arose in Central Java late in the sixteenth century. This realm called itself Mataram, and, like the earlier kingdom of that name, it was centered near the present city of Jogjakarta. As the strength of the Pasisir city-states weakened under the Portuguese effort to eliminate transshipping points on the spice routes, Mataram was able to wrest control of the hinterlands from them. By 1600 its power extended throughout interior Java.

Mataram's greatest ruler was Sultan Agung, who reigned from 1613 to 1645 and who viewed his state as a continuation of Madjapahit. Since commercial and power relationships in the archipelago did not permit a revival of Madjapahit's imperial role, Agung was forced to base his authority in the interior and to concentrate on control of land and of rice production as the source of Mataram's strength. Although Agung utilized the older Hinduized state concepts in legitimizing his rule, he was careful for part of his reign at least to maintain the outward appearance of a Moslem prince, for by now Islam was a factor which no ruler could refuse to acknowledge.[17] He sought direct contacts with the heart of the Moslem world, and in 1641 he received the title of Sultan from Mecca. The reduction of the coastal city-states, which was accomplished under his rule, moved the center of Javanese cultural life to the interior,[18] where it experienced a last renaissance at the courts of Surakarta and Jogjakarta, whose political power gradually slipped to the Dutch.

In the late sixteenth century, various European powers had sought to poach upon the Portuguese monopoly of East Indian trade, the Spanish, English, and Dutch being among the most active of these. Before the seventeenth century had ended, the Dutch had won a position of commercial predominance over all their European rivals in the archipelago, and in increasing measure they were to affect Indonesian historical development.

The Dutch had come to Indonesia as traders, their principal aim being to obtain a monopoly over the spices of the Moluccas. Although it was not apparent at the time, this effort was actually a strategic error, for the importance of the spice trade in world commerce was on the decline.[19] In order to strengthen its hand in securing the spice monopoly, the Netherlands government had secured the combination of Dutch merchant interests into the United East India Company (Vereenigde Oost-Indische Compagnie), which was chartered in 1602 and existed for almost two centuries. The Company, although it began as a commercial venture, was to find itself increasingly involved in the politics of the archipelago.

When the Dutch first arrived in Indonesia in 1596, they put into the port of Bantam. At that time Bantam was, together with Atjeh, the most powerful state in the western part of the archipelago. Atjeh controlled the Sumatra pepper production, but Bantam was the commercial center through which much of this pepper entered world trade; moreover, with the decline of the Pasisir principalities, Bantam became the focal point for the Moluccan spice trade. The emergence of Bantam as the second great power on Java brought that state into frequent conflict with Mataram, a fact which was to be of no little significance in the establishment of Dutch power on the island.

At Bantam, Asian and European merchants traded on a basis of equality; their free competition drove prices upward, while the Bantamese rulers showed themselves adept at playing the rival merchants against each other. The Dutch, whose aim was to secure direct trade with the Moluccas and acquire a monopoly over its spice production, were not content to limit themselves to Bantam's free market; and as they proceeded to accomplish this aim their position in Bantam became increasingly untenable. Accordingly, they moved their base in 1619 to the town and factory of Jacatra, which was situated in a region contested by Mataram and Bantam.

The founding of Batavia, as the Dutch eventually named their settlement, was carried out under the leadership of Jan Pieterszoon Coen, a hardfisted man of action who twice served the East India Company as Governor General and was one of the major figures in Netherlands imperial history.[20] It was Coen who prosecuted most vigorously the Dutch aim of securing a monopoly over the Moluccan spice trade. The measures he employed to eliminate his competitors —including the English, who attempted to penetrate the Spice Islands about the same time as the Dutch—and to control the production of spices by the islands were so Draconian as to revolt even contemporaries, although their effectiveness was unquestionable. Whereas in other areas of Indonesia the Dutch continued for some time to trade as Asian merchants, without notably affecting the existing commercial and social patterns, the effect of their rigorous monopoly on spice production and sale in the Moluccas was to destroy all economic incentive among a formerly prosperous people. Temporarily their control was evaded through a clandestine spice trade which centered in Makassar in Celebes; but with the defeat of that state in 1668 the Dutch monopoly was absolute. The reduction of Makassar was only one of a series of maneuvers by which the Netherlands established control of the Indonesian seas between 1650 and 1680. During the same period the Dutch broke Atjehnese control over Sumatra and helped the Minangkabau kingdom re-establish its independence on the west coast of that island. Malacca had been captured from the Portuguese in 1641; the Dutch allowed it to fall into decay, for they wished to funnel the archipelago's international trade through Batavia, the center of Dutch power and the capital of the Company's far-flung operations in the East. Batavia now became the center of a vast Asian trade which for the Dutch Company was more profitable than the shipment of goods to Europe.

Batavia's future grandeur was not apparent at the start; indeed, it seemed as if the town would not survive the enmity of Bantam and Mataram. The rival realms were unable to combine their efforts to displace the Dutch, however, and singly they were unable to force the outpost to its knees. Bantam's power was not initially affected by the Dutch presence; indeed, that state reached its peak in the middle of the seventeenth century, establishing direct contacts with the Middle East and commencing the equipment of its own commercial fleet. When, however, the sultanate was weakened by a squabble over the succession, the Dutch saw their chance, and by maneuvering among the feuding family factions they achieved the destruction of Bantam's commercial position by 1684. In Mataram, the story was not dissimilar. In 1674 a revolt against Amangkurat I, successor to Sultan Agung, occurred as a result of his drastic efforts to reduce the independent strength of his vassals and of the Islamic teachers. The Dutch stepped in and restored him to the throne; thereafter, the Company used its military force as a decisive factor in settling revolts and internecine quarrels. In this process Mataram's rulers became more and more dependent on the Dutch. Gradually, their territory passed into Dutch hands, though the Company did not attempt direct rule, exerting control instead through the territory's existing Javanese administrators.[21]

In the late seventeenth century, the Company found its commercial policies in need of revision. Profits from its trade within Asia were declining, while prices for Asian products on the

European market had risen; it therefore seemed advisable to concentrate on the production of goods for the European market. Horticultural experiments on Java led, shortly after 1700, to the growing of coffee, which soon appeared to be a lucrative venture. In order to promote coffee production for the European market the Dutch began to assert their rights to collect tribute from those areas of Java which had come under their rule. Through a system of "contingents and forced delivery," first introduced in the Preanger area south of Batavia in 1723, they demanded coffee from the Javanese aristocrats as tribute payments. To oversee the production and delivery of this coffee, the Dutch appointed European supervisors—the first step in the creation of a European administration for the Indies.

In spite of the expanding use of the Preanger system of forced deliveries, the fortunes of the Company declined during the eighteenth century. In good part this was caused by developments outside Indonesia, but within the archipelago increasing speculation by the poorly paid Company servants began to have a telling effect. Practices such as the leasing of land and villages to Chinese for exploitation brought in some ready cash, but not enough, and the Company was forced to borrow funds to pay its dividends. It also showed a mounting inability to maintain order in the archipelago. Although Java was brought increasingly under its control, Borneo and Sumatra remained outside Dutch power. The Bugis, centered in Riouw, Kedah, and Johore, menaced shipping in the Straits of Malacca, while the seas of the archipelago were infested by pirates—often Indonesian seamen put out of legitimate business by Dutch shipping and production controls. By 1780 the East India Company was bankrupted; and in 1798 the Dutch government revoked its charter and assumed its assets and debts. The scene was thus set for a new era of Dutch rule in Indonesia.

With the placing of the Netherlands East Indies under direct Dutch government control, a policy dispute which was already emergent in Dutch colonial circles developed into a full-scale debate. Essentially, the argument concerned whether the Dutch should extend to the Indies the laissez-faire concepts then in vogue among liberal circles in Europe, or whether they should preserve the existing Indonesian social system to the greatest practical extent. This dispute was, in fact, to underlie Dutch policy decisions in Indonesia throughout the colonial period, and it was never satisfactorily resolved. Initially, the debate did not center about which policy would enhance the welfare of the Indonesians but rather which would bring greater profit to the motherland, this being the frankly stated purpose of colonialism at the time. It was only in the late nineteenth century that humanitarian considerations were introduced and the center of the dispute began to shift—at least for some of the participants—to the issue of promoting Indonesian prosperity.

The occupation of the Netherlands in 1795 brought into power the proponents of the liberal view. H. W. Daendels, a partisan of the French who became Governor General in 1808, introduced the new policy to Java, purging the existing Dutch administration and introducing numerous legal and administrative reforms. For the first time, the Europeans took the attitude that they had the right to press their ideas of government and administration upon the Indonesians, be it at first only in limited fashion. The concept of sovereignty was also extended to include ownership rights over all the lands of Java—though it is not certain that the princes who had ceded territorial rights to the Dutch had ever viewed their land titles in the Western sense of ownership.

Daendels' work of reorganizing the government on liberal lines was continued by T. S. Raffles, who assumed charge over Java in 1811 when the English occupied that island in order to secure their position in India during the Napoleonic wars. Of the many changes he introduced, the most significant was the land rent system. This concept, which Raffles developed from the land tax system of India, held that land was owned by the ruler of the country, who had the right to collect rent on it in accordance with its productive capacity.[22] The Dutch continued the policy after the island was returned to them in 1816, and they eventually managed to make it profitable; however, since such a taxation system requires careful land surveys and evaluations, and these were not prepared until the very end of the nineteenth century,[23] the application of land rent was for many years a rather haphazard and arbitrary process.

The confusion of Dutch policies regarding the positions of Europeans and Javanese led, in 1825, to the outbreak of the Java War, which was the last major outburst against Dutch rule on that island prior to the Indonesian revolution. The spark that touched off the conflict was the colonial government's abrogation of land rental contacts which had been closed between European entrepreneurs and princes of the Vorstenlanden—the Central

Javanese principalities of Surakarta and Jogjakarta which, after 1755, were all that remained of the kingdom of Mataram. The nullification of these contracts caused financial embarrassment to the Javanese lessors, who were already resentful of the various encroachments on the prerogatives of the nobility by Daendels and his successors. They turned for leadership to Diponegoro, a prince of the royal house of Jogjakarta who was an acknowledged opponent of European influence at the court and who had a great reputation as a mystical leader. Diponegoro raised the banner of revolt and proclaimed an Islamic "holy war" against the Dutch. The ensuing conflict was a guerrilla war which lasted until 1830 and was brought under control only with great difficulty.

The resulting devastation of large areas of Java considerably weakened the financial position of the colony. Its unprofitable condition had for some time been a matter of concern to the Netherlands and had caused the liberal *vs.* conservative policy debate to rage with increased vigor.[24] Finally, in 1830, the Dutch king appointed as Governor General J. van den Bosch, who proposed a system of colonial administration which promised rapid financial gain. Van den Bosch's plan, known as the Cultivation System (Cultuurstelsel) centered about the utilization of Java to grow products salable on the European market. These were to be raised by the Javanese on their own lands—or rather on the government's lands, which the Javanese were allowed to use and for which they had been paying land rent since the time of Raffles. The Javanese were to be compensated for growing these products—in part by having their land rent prorated against them—and were to receive additional compensation for the work involved in preparing the produce for market. Through the Netherlands Trading Society (Nederlandsche Handel-Maatschappij) which had been founded by the government in 1824 to stimulate economic endeavor, the Dutch were to ship the products to Europe and there bring them onto the world market.

Indigo, sugar, and coffee were the main products originally grown under the Cultivation System—although coffee should perhaps be excluded because its controlled production predated the system and it was grown on lands not normally used by the villagers for food production. But indigo and sugar were grown on part of the irrigated rice fields of the villages. In theory, their production was not to require more work than a similar area of rice and should have brought more revenue to the village as well as to the government. In practice, however, the forced cultivations did require more work, and the government also required corvée services (*heerendiensten*) for road work, dike building, etc. in increasing measure, so that the villagers found themselves burdened by the cultivation of the required crops. Compensation did not increase in accordance with the rising cost of living, and the safeguards written into the original concept were often ignored in practice. The Cultivation System did stimulate an increasing prosperity in many parts of Java and did provide entirely new economic possibilities for the island, but the Javanese population had all too little initiative and profit in the exploitation of these opportunities.

Under the Cultivation System, Java, as later India, came to supplant the West Indies as a producer of certain tropical products. Unlike the British in India, however, the Dutch did not have large quantities of manufactured goods to send from the motherland to the colony; the Cultivation System was therefore premised not on the laws of supply and demand but on the utilization of the traditional prerogatives of the rulers of Java. Reliance on the native Javanese patterns of authority meant reliance on the prijaji as the traditional governing class. The privileges of that group, which had been somewhat diminished under the liberal regimes of Daendels and Raffles, were accordingly restored in full by Van den Bosch, who also granted the prijaji hereditary rights; in return, they were expected to act as agents of the government for the forced production of the desired agricultural products. In order to supervise the system the European administration was also expanded, and Dutch officials came to stand next to the Javanese administrators as their mentors. It is now generally considered that this attachment of the prijaji to the Dutch administrative hierarchy led to their decline in the eyes of the Indonesians they ruled, detaching them from their traditional social base of support.[25] This lessening prestige was a long-term process, however, and not until the twentieth century was their position of leadership seriously threatened by other social groups.

In addition to its impact on the role of the prijaji, the Cultivation System altered the landholding pattern of Java. The government dealt with the village as a unit, both for the levying of taxes and for the recruitment of labor. Though individual landownership in the Western sense was not generally known in central and eastern Java, there had been a system of individual and familial dispositional rights over certain plots of ground. In many areas, the application of the Cultivation System rode roughshod over these rights and forced the population to accept a communalized system with periodic redivision of the land. In this process the role of the village headman was enhanced: he became the agent through which the colonial authorities dealt with the village and was given control over the village's most precious possession, its land. At the same time, the headman became more dependent upon the Dutch, for the authorities could reward him or punish him according to his performance in crop production. As a result the position of the village headman began to change in many parts of Java; in the eyes of the villagers he often became a source of governmental oppression rather than, as previously, the keystone of village solidarity and protection.

The village heads thus joined the prijaji as instruments of the Dutch colonial system. Their identification with an exacting governmental authority would seem to be one reason for the increasing popular influence of the religious teachers and scholars, who stood apart from and partially opposed to the governing groups. Gradually the santri groups spread out of the urban centers into the countryside; Islamic teachers became more frequent foci of anti-government unrest and came more and more to serve as symbols of Indonesian solidarity. Contacts with the Middle East, the heartland of Islam, became more frequent during the century, especially after the opening of the Suez Canal in 1869, and this resulted in a greater emphasis on religious orthodoxy.

The increasing penetration of the santri way of life was even more evident in Sumatra than in Java. As I have noted previously, the impact of Islam on that island, particularly in Atjeh and Minangkabau, had been markedly strong. In Minangkabau it led, even before the turn of the nineteenth century, to a struggle between the traditional adat chiefs and the Padris, religious reformers who sought to purify the Islam of the area by doing away with its pre-Moslem customs. The Dutch took the side of the adat chiefs, as they generally did against zealous Islamic groups; but not until 1837 did they succeed in subduing the Padris and bringing peace to the area. In Atjeh, a similar though less violent struggle for power between adat and Islamic groups began to develop. Here, however, the Dutch did not interfere, for their hands were tied by a treaty signed with England in 1824 by which Atjeh's independence was guaranteed as a buffer between Dutch power in the archipelago and British interests on the Malay peninsula. As a result, the power of the adat leaders in that area underwent considerable erosion in the course of the century.

In spite of the considerable profits which the Cultivation System brought the Netherlands, it was soon exposed to a heavy fire in the homeland, and this proved its eventual undoing. It was, first of all, against the mood of the times, which was increasingly influenced by the free enterprise leanings of the liberals. The Dutch constitutional changes of 1848, which gave parliament a voice in colonial affairs, enhanced the liberals' position, and after 1850 an avalanche of printed material appeared pointing up the advantages of a free enterprise system for Java. Since the system had rendered such profits it was not abandoned under these attacks but rather modified until, after the promulgation of a new constitutional regulation for the colony in 1854, it was reduced to a chaos of conflicting conceptions. "Free labor" *vs.* "forced labor" became the theme of the 1850s and '60s, though originally this argument had little to do with concern for the liberty of the Javanese peasant. It was rather the conservative, "forced labor" advocates who evinced a desire to protect the Indonesians against the destructive impact of unfettered Western exploitation, while the "free labor" liberals sought to open the country to private European enterprise. The free labor forces did, however, have the backing of some humanitarian-religious groups, and the strength of their moral argument was greatly increased with the publication in 1860 of the novel *Max Havelaar*. This book, written by the former colonial official E. Douwes Dekker under the pseudonym Multatuli ("Much have I suffered"), was an eloquent and scathing denunciation of the existing system of administration on Java; the furor that it created changed the debate over the colonial regime from a subject of purely parliamentary concern to a matter of general discussion. It may be doubted that Multatuli's intent was to see the Cultivation System supplanted by the liberals' program for the Indies, but in denouncing the existing state of affairs he did a good deal to achieve just that.

The formal demise of the Cultivation System and the beginning of the Liberal Period of colonial rule were marked by the adoption of the Agrarian and Sugar laws of 1870. The Sugar Law provided that government control over production of that commodity would gradually be diminished in favor of private enterprise. Sugar was at that time the most important product, together with coffee, to be grown under government control, all other crops having either been abandoned or placed earlier in private hands. Coffee was to remain under government control until 1917, but increasing quantities of this crop also came into private production. The Agrarian Law was designed to protect the Indonesian peasant against the envisioned penetration of free Western enterprise by limiting the landowning rights of non-Indonesians to urban plots. Henceforth, Indonesian agricultural lands could not be sold to private aliens. They could, however, be leased: if not under cultivation by a village they could be rented on a long-term arrangement, while if they were used by a village they could be leased through short-term contract. Where possible, these leases were to be closed with the individual landowner, otherwise with the village headman.

The Liberal Period in Dutch colonial policy, which lasted from 1870 to about 1900, was a time of great economic expansion. Until 1885 this took place on small private initiative, and after that under the guidance of large capitalist combinations. The production figures and the variety of new crops introduced in this era dwarfed the achievements of the Cultivation System; the plantation economy which was henceforth to characterize Indonesia now became firmly established. This burgeoning economic activity cannot be attributed solely to the efficacy of the liberals' free enterprise doctrines, for not only did private production of sugar, tea, and tobacco increase in this period but also the government-controlled production of coffee. One reason for the expanded activity was the opening of the Suez Canal, which stimulated trade between Europe and Asia. In the Netherlands itself, there was new national energy in all fields as that country emerged from its stagnation of the early nineteenth century. The Dutch themselves began to assume a new attitude toward a career in the Indies: no longer did they view the archipelago as a refuge for social outcasts and the surplus sons of well-established families, but rather as a place where new and rich opportunities awaited those who were willing to work for them.

The demands of the expanding Western sector of the economy and the increasing influx of European immigrants brought about a growing formalization of the European and Indonesian administrative corps during the Liberal Period. The European administration was expanded, and legal patterns of administration were introduced which were intended to protect the Indonesian against the arbitrary authority of his traditional leaders. The highest Indonesian governing officials, the regents, were treated more and more as civil servants; their hereditary prerogatives were gradually shorn away, and by the end of the century many had become little more than figureheads.[26] In this way, the authority of the prijaji, on which the Cultivation System had depended so greatly, was subjected to considerable stress. With the increasing number of Europeans in the archipelago, the officials of the European administrative corps became increasingly concerned with problems related to their own countrymen, thus accentuating the division between the European and Indonesian populations.

So far as the Javanese peasant was concerned, there is little indication that the introduction of the liberal system made much improvement in his life. Land rental arrangements were still often as not made with the village chief, and the peasant was pressured through the traditional system of authority to submit to the decisions made by his headman. In theory, the villages remained autonomous units, but in practice the administration interfered in village affairs whenever it deemed this necessary. With the growth of large-scale plantation enterprises after 1885 the Indonesian peasant was less able than ever to profit from the free competition proclaimed by liberal economic principles: indeed, investigations made after 1900 seemed to bear out the contention that the welfare of the Javanese peasant had actually diminished.[27]

Although the economic activity of the Liberal Period was concentrated, particularly in the beginning, in Java, the era was also marked by a Dutch forward movement on the Outer Islands. The Netherlands had evinced little interest in these areas earlier in the century. The Dutch had checked an attempt, promoted by Raffles, to consolidate British power in Sumatra through the establishment of a base at Benkulen, and, as we have seen, they played a role in settling the Padri War. Around the middle of the century, after James Brooke had established an independent state on Borneo's north shore, the Dutch made somewhat greater efforts to place the islands outside Java under their administration, but not until late in the century was this policy pursued with vigor. Bali, for instance, was conquered by the Dutch in 1849 as punishment for the looting of stranded ships; but no attempt was made to force Dutch policy on it thereafter. Economic relations in the archipelago were such, however, that its virtually independent areas did not prosper and could not compete with the Europeans commercially. The activities of these states were largely piratical in scope, and a good picture of their nature can be obtained from the novels of Joseph Conrad.

The initial stimulus to the Dutch expansion of the Liberal Period was the revived fear of further claims by other powers to the peripheral areas of the archipelago. Their major effort was directed toward Atjeh, whose continued independence had become a menace in European eyes because of its role in piracy along the Straits of Malacca. Accordingly, the Dutch obtained from the British a release from their obligation to respect Atjeh's independence, and in 1873 they engaged in war with the North Sumatran state. The conflict dragged on for three decades, and the Dutch only achieved the upper hand in the 1890s when they made an all-out effort to stamp out the zealous Moslem teachers who were largely responsible for the fierceness of the area's resistance. As earlier in Minangkabau, the Dutch befriended the local traditional chiefs against the power of the religious teachers; they established their control by partly restoring and partly creating an aristocracy whose interests were opposed to those of the Islamic elements.

The Atjeh War was the greatest of a number of conflicts which the Dutch fought throughout the archipelago in the late nineteenth and early twentieth centuries and which ended the independence of all the minor Indonesian states. The political unification and centralization which followed provided a stimulus for further economic expansion; and Sumatra now began to rival Java as an area of exploitation. On the east coast of that island tobacco plantations were established, and soon rubber and palm oil estates were opened there and on the west coast. Late in the nineteenth century oil exploitation began in South Sumatra, and petroleum was also discovered in Borneo. The days of Java-centered economic development had ended, and Indonesia as a whole was brought more directly into the modern economic world.

As Indonesia's export economy expanded, the costs of government also mounted. To the other problems raised by the Liberal Period was now added the fateful one of an unbalanced budget. Although the total nature of governmental receipts changed under the new economic policy, the taxation structure was never sufficiently revised to provide revenue for the increased demands for public expenditures.[28] The government had to borrow to meet mounting deficits, and before the end of the nineteenth century the East Indies were again a debit item in the Netherlands budget, as they had been at its beginning.

By the turn of the century, Dutch sentiment was ripe for a change in colonial policy. The feeling was widespread that free, unfettered liberalism had ceased to be a constructive force in Indonesia. This view was advanced strongly from the humanitarian side, which argued that the Netherlands owed Indonesia a "debt of honor" for the past profits it had drawn from the archipelago. Equally disturbed by the reports of a lessening Indonesian living standard were the manufacturing and commercial interests in the Netherlands, which had developed hopes of a market in the Indies. Both groups had increased their parliamentary influence in the late nineteenth century, and in 1901 they achieved the official inauguration of a new program of colonial administration.

The name of the new doctrine—the Ethical Policy—tells much of its philosophy and content. Essentially, it was a welfare program which, through devices not unfamiliar to modern aid and development projects, sought to stimulate and guide Indonesian economic, political, and social progress. It is possible here only to suggest the variety and scope of the measures introduced under this policy. The creation of new governmental departments in health, public works, and agriculture led to expanded activities in all these fields. New sanitation and hygienic measures, irrigation projects, agricultural extension services, and village banks and grain sheds altered the villagers' living conditions and brought them into more direct contact with governmental administration. They also contributed to a rapid rise in population, and emigration schemes were started in a vain effort at siphoning Java's surplus population to the less densely inhabited islands.

Considerable attention was also given to the extension of Western-style education, which before 1900 had been available only to a very few Indonesians. Although the number of Indonesians attending public schools expanded considerably during the remainder of the colonial period, the proportion remained small in comparison to the total population.[29] This limitation was particularly noticeable above the primary school level. For most Indonesians, Western-style education represented a means to entering government service, and during the first decades of the century the administration expanded rapidly enough to absorb virtually all those who qualified. Later, however, this was not the case and the government, fearful of the unsettling potentialities of an "intellectual proletariat," attempted not to educate more than it could employ.

In the field of government, Dutch policy moved toward reform in several not always compatible directions. One of these was toward greater decentralization of governmental authority, especially on Java. In one of its aspects this entailed the strengthening of the traditional Indonesian administrative corps: the regents, who had become so much the tools of their European advisors, were to be "detutelized." This intent, however, was quite canceled out by other developments of governmental policy. We have already noted the increasing interference in village affairs which took place in the Liberal era. This became much greater with the application of rural welfare projects during the Ethical Period, with the government exercising a policy of "gentle pressure" toward reform in the villages.[30] This governmental intervention was conducted through an expanding Western administrative and technical corps, into which increasing numbers of Indonesians were admitted. In this manner, the basic power patterns of Indonesian life were altered in the name of welfare and efficiency: Western administration and Western-trained Indonesians began to replace traditional sources of leadership and authority.

The role of the prijaji was diminished not only by these developments, but also by direct measures in the area of political affairs. In the interests of decentralization and the granting of a greater voice in government to the inhabitants of the Indies, authority was delegated to urban and district councils which, as they emerged in the course of the century, contained both Indonesian and European members. In 1916 the Volksraad (People's Council) was created from representatives of the major population groups to offer advice to the top echelons of the government.[31] The Volksraad soon grew into more than an advisory body, though it never was either truly representative or legislative. It served as a forum for airing political concepts and grievances, and it had the effect of further weakening the traditional role of the prijaji and increasing an awareness of the need for political groups organized on more modern lines.

The evolution of such new groupings had begun in 1908 with the establishment of Budi Utomo (High Endeavor) by a group of Javanese medical students in Batavia.[32] Budi Utomo's purpose was to promote Javanese cultural ideals; for almost a decade it remained nonpolitical, and it always restricted its appeal to a well-educated elite whose aim lay in strengthening the nation through reinforcing traditional culture patterns. Other regional associations followed the creation of Budi Utomo; they too represented small elites, and politically they were even more cautious than the Javanese organization.

If the first modern Indonesian movement was conservative and regionally based, the second was radical and scornful of ethnic boundaries. The Indische Partij (Indies party), founded in 1912 by E. F. E. Douwes Dekker, a grandnephew of the famous Multatuli, aimed at creating an Indies citizenship for all persons born in the country, and it spoke openly of independence for the colony. Its outspoken radicalism caused its leaders to be exiled to the Netherlands; their followers joined the association Insulinde and later formed the National Indische Partij (National Indies party). The nationalist slogans of the movement failed to catch popular fire, however, for in point of fact the Indische Partij and its successors, though they counted prominent Javanese political figures among their leaders, represented an effort of some Eurasians to identify with the educated Indonesians entering government service and thereby improve the economic status of both groups. With the awakening of Indonesian social and political consciousness, however, the majority of the Eurasians came to see their best chance in continued identification with the Dutch, and consequently they shifted their position from radical nationalism to staunch defense of colonial rule.

With the formation of the third major association, the Sarekat Islam, we come to the first party to achieve a mass following. Originally, it was formed as a merchants' protective association, the Sarekat Dagang Islam (Islamic Trading Union). Its sponsors were batik entrepreneurs of East and Central Java, who were, as most small Indonesian business groups, strongly santri in their orientation. The batik merchants' fears had been aroused by the activity of the Indies Chinese, who already composed the bulk of the urban independent middle class and who now began to appear in increasing numbers in the interior of Java, cutting into the Indonesian hold on the textile and batik business there. The merchants' association soon achieved a following that extended far beyond its original purpose, and in 1912 it acknowledged this by adopting the name Sarekat Islam (Islamic Union) and embarking on a more broadly religious and political venture.

A major reason for the remarkable popularity of the Sarekat Islam may be found in the new religious momentum gained since the late nineteenth century through the influence of Islamic reformism, which attempted to purify Moslem doctrine and to adapt it to the needs of the modern world as these had been advanced by the West. In some parts of Indonesia, especially the Minangkabau area of Sumatra's west coast, the reformist doctrines found rather widespread support against the traditional social order. In Java, reformism had an uphill struggle against the entrenched conservative religious groups; however, the new Islamic ideas did secure strong support from the urban commercial class which was beginning to develop around the turn of the century. More important than the actual number of their adherents, however, was the effect of these doctrines in bringing about a general revival of Islamic activity. Increasingly, Islam came to represent the Indonesians against their European rulers, against the Indies Chinese, and against the Christian missionaries, whose activities in the archipelago expanded rapidly after 1900. It was on this sense of solidarity through religion that the Sarekat Islam based its appeal.[33]

If Islam was the rallying point of the new movement, it was not its essence, nor was the Sarekat Islam principally a santri vehicle. Its chairman and driving spirit was O. S. Tjokroaminoto, a prijaji whose education was Western rather than Islamic. Tjokroaminoto was a charismatic leader of the first rank, and to many villagers he seemed the personification of the *ratu adil* (righteous prince), which legend had promised would liberate them from the many oppressions they suffered. If they differed regarding the exact nature of their grievances, they were united in attributing them to the colonial government, whose increasing activities in rural areas were the most obvious cause of the unsettling changes that were occurring in the traditional pattern of village life.

Riding the wave of Moslem religious revival and mounting social disorientation, the Sarekat Islam's membership grew rapidly. The organization was principally Java-centered, though it did have branches in other parts of the archipelago. Once its popularity had become apparent, other groups sought to gain control of the movement, among them the future Communist party. Marxist socialism had been introduced to the Indies by Dutchmen who founded the Indies Social Democratic Association (ISDV) in 1914; some of their Indonesian protégés made their way high into the central Sarekat Islam organization and propagated Marxist ideas there. At the same time, santri elements who disapproved of the mystical appeal which Tjokroaminoto made to the rural masses in the name of Islam also entered the competition for Sarekat Islam leadership. Chief among these was the Sumatra-born Hadji Agus Salim.

Competition between the socialist and Moslem groups for popular support drove the Sarekat Islam into ever more radical lines. By 1917 the organization was openly critical of the government, and within the next few years it had taken a hand in operating various labor and peasant organizations which fomented unrest in many parts of Java. The entrepreneurs and merchants who originally founded the association had soon lost their control, and as the Sarekat Islam proceeded on its radical course they dropped out of the organization. In 1920 the radical Marxists formed the Indonesian Communist party (PKI), which pushed labor and agrarian unrest with greater efficiency than the comparable Islamic organizations; and when the Communists were forced out of the Sarekat Islam in 1923 much of its remaining membership went with them.

The increasingly political role of the Sarekat Islam soon caused it to lose its claims of religious leadership to another organization, the Muhammadijah. That association, which had also been founded in 1912, was strongly impelled by reformist Islamic ideas; it was primarily nonpolitical, though some of its principal leaders were also for a time among the heads of the Sarekat Islam. Taking a leaf from the Christian missions' book, the Muhammadijah founded schools, clinics, and benevolent groups, while at the same time advancing its program of a purer and more progressive Islam. The movement grew in size and, spreading throughout the archipelago, won increasing support among the urban Moslem groups. During the 1920s, when reformist and pan-Islamic ideas seemed to be achieving dominance in religious thought, the more conservative Islamic groups formed their own association, Nahdatul Ulama (1926), which found its chief support among the rural Javanese santri.

Following its break with the Communists, the Sarekat Islam tried to re-establish its popularity on a more purely religious basis, but in this it failed; the active development of the Indonesian political movement was to occur after 1920 in secular, not religious, channels. For a time the PKI was the most active element in this movement, drawing the bulk of its membership from the growing urban proletariat and making intermittent efforts at gaining rural support. As increasing government restrictions placed its existence in jeopardy the party elected to stage an uprising, which took place in rural areas of West Java (November 1926) and West Sumatra (January 1927), where the Communists were able to take advantage of long-standing social discontent.[34] The failure of the revolt, which resulted in widespread arrests, marked the effective end of Communist activity in the colonial period.

With the fading of the Sarekat Islam and the destruction of the PKI, Indonesian political leadership came into more outrightly nationalist hands. The strongest leadership for the nationalist movement emerged from among the Indonesian students at Dutch and East Indies universities. In 1908 Indonesian students in the Netherlands formed an association which in time came to call itself the Perhimpunan Indonesia (Indonesian Society); during the 1920s it grew increasingly political in character and put itself forward as the advocate of national independence for Indonesia. The Perhimpunan Indonesia was strongly influenced by socialist ideas; the fact that the Dutch leftist parties were the most sympathetic to Indonesian aims, coupled with the rapid growth of European capitalist-dominated enterprise in the archipelago during the 1920s, helped to make socialist principles part of the program of every Indonesian nationalist group. The Perhimpunan Indonesia and its related associations were also deeply influenced by the principle of noncooperation with colonial government propounded by the Indian nationalists under Gandhi.

Returning Perhimpunan Indonesia members joined graduates from Indies institutions of higher learning in various Study Clubs which had been formed to provide a source of intellectual leadership for Indonesian economic and social development. In 1927 Sukarno, chairman of the Bandung Study Club, founded the Nationalist Party of Indonesia (PNI) in the hope of creating a united national movement. This political unity was not achieved, but Sukarno rapidly became the symbolic leader of the Indonesian independence movement. Sukarno's PNI was followed by other nationalist parties, most of them noncooperative. By and large, these groups were short-lived; government restrictions on them were severe, and their more outspoken leaders—including Sukarno, Hatta, and Sjahrir—were exiled to distant parts of the archipelago, not to return until the collapse of Dutch rule.[35]

Throughout most of this period, the government's policies had become increasingly uncongenial to the Indonesian political movements. Although the colonial authorities had welcomed the first Indonesian moves toward independent expression, their attitude became more guarded as the movements turned to open criticism and even urged the termination of the colonial relationship. The high-water mark of government concessions came in November 1918, when, responding to Indonesian attacks in the Volksraad and rumors of impending revolution in the Netherlands, the Governor General promised to consider broad political reforms. Soon thereafter, however, a reaction set in. The Dutch government came under the control of conservatives, while Netherlanders both at home and in the colony felt increasingly that in allowing scope for Indonesian political organization the government had opened Pandora's box. As a result, the Ethical Policy lost most of its proponents; after 1921 it lost ground rapidly to the conservative view that law and order rather than reform must be the overriding concern of the government. After the Communist uprisings of 1926-27 the authorities were careful to prevent any dissident movement from extending its strength to the general population. Instead of encouraging the evolution of Indonesian society, the government now sought to brake it by shoring up the prestige and power of the prijaji.[36]

An important factor in the more conservative attitude taken by the Indies Dutch after World War I was the changing nature of the European element in the archipelago. The twentieth century saw an unprecedented economic growth in Indonesia, much of it taking place on Sumatra, which came to outstrip Java in the value of its products. The benefits of this increased production went in large measure to the Europeans, whose numbers in Indonesia increased rapidly and who, unlike their predecessors in the colony, viewed themselves as temporary residents who were there to make their fortune and then return home. These Europeans sought a closer tie with the motherland than had their forerunners, and efforts at achieving an association between the European and Indonesian population groups gave way to an increasing exclusiveness of the two societies. East Indies society had always tended toward pluralism, but the separateness of the various social elements which now developed made this its central feature.[37]

The depression of the 1930s destroyed much of the prosperity founded on the export of agricultural commodities. With this reversal to the large capitalist-dominated economy, a trend that had long been underway came to the foreground: Indonesian entrepreneurs began to emerge as small producers, and Indonesian industries began to fill the need for low-priced products. It has been suggested that as trade and industry revived, a spirit of greater cooperation with the colonial government began to show itself on the part of the Indonesians.[38] Certainly the political movements, long dominated by the noncooperative wing, began to revise their stand. Noncooperation having led only to ineffective illegality, the Indonesian leaders now sought their strength in broader groups which could take advantage of Volksraad representation to express their ideas. In 1935, the more conservative parties united to form the Parindra (Greater Indonesia Party), while in 1937 the Gerindo (Indonesian People's Movement) was established by the moderate left. The Moslem organizations similarly united, chiefly to protest the government's limitations on the application of Islamic law: in 1937 the Muhammadijah and Nahdatul Ulama combined to form the MIAI (Great Islamic Council of Indonesia), and the following year a political organization, the Indonesian Islamic Party (PII), was established.

The cooperative efforts of the Indonesian political movements achieved little more success than their noncooperative ones, for the government displayed the utmost reluctance to make political concessions to even the moderate nationalists. In the face of this intransigence, the Indonesian groups consolidated their forces further, in 1939 forming the Indonesian Political Concentration (Gapi), in which conservative and radical nationalists united to press for an Indonesian parliament, and in 1941 creating the Council of the Indonesian People (Madjelis Rakjat Indonesia), which combined both secular and religious groups and called for a parliament and the adoption of the Indonesian national language, anthem, and flag.

These latter developments took place under the growing shadow of Japanese expansion toward Southeast Asia. Since the fall of the Netherlands to Germany in 1940, Japan had put great pressure on the Indies government to supply materials, especially oil, for the Japanese war machine. The Dutch adamantly refused, but they were in no position to defend the archipelago when, in March 1942, the Japanese pursued their objectives by invasion. The rapid defeat of the Dutch forces in the archipelago discredited the former colonial masters in the eyes of many Indonesians. The imprisonment of all Hollanders and most Eurasians by the Japanese not only added to the great humiliation of the former colonial regime, but also opened many administrative and technical positions to Indonesians. These factors, plus the initial expectation that the Japanese had come as liberators, served to create a certain but short-lived degree of enthusiasm for the Japanese.

The impact of the Japanese occupation was of the utmost significance in shaping Indonesia's future; without this experience it is inconceivable that the Indonesian state would have assumed its present form or would have had to meet some of its present problems. The removal of the Dutch dealt a profound blow to a social structure whose foundations had long been eroding. In spite of the increasing incursion of Western influence, traditional Indonesian social relations had remained remarkably stable up to the end of Dutch rule. The effect of Western encroachment had been muffled by the Dutch policy of supporting the traditional hierarchy and protecting the Indonesians as much as possible from the unsettling effects of outside influence. Now, however, the prop that had been shoring up the old social system was suddenly removed. In many areas the invasion produced a sense of disorientation which deepened profoundly with the further social and economic dislocations of the war.

The Japanese made little attempt to counter this process by bolstering the traditional hierarchy. Since the occupation of Indonesia was a military operation, the administration of the country was carried out, insofar as possible, by the military authorities and according to Japanese concepts. The Japanese were vitally interested in obtaining popular support for their war effort, however, and as Indonesian enthusiasm waned under the harshness of their rule, they sought to rally it by working through Indonesian leaders. In doing so, they turned not to the prijaji but to two groups whose interests were not identified with Dutch rule: the nationalists and the santri. Promising self-government to Indonesia in the near future, the Japanese sponsored the creation in March 1943 of the Putera (Center of People's Power), which was to include all former nationalist associations. Later the same year they sought to rally Islamic support by stimulating the organization of the Masjumi (Council of Indonesian Moslem Associations), which was to combine all Islamic religious groups.[39]

The nationalist leaders who headed the Putera had returned from imprisonment or banishment after the fall of the Dutch; chief among them were Sukarno and Hatta. They found themselves no longer leaders of small associations, subject to police surveillance and denied the opportunity to spread their views among the masses. Instead, they had at their disposal a massive, official organization which could reach the public through a radio and loudspeaker network extending to all the villages of Java. Moreover, they had access to the various youth, military, and paramilitary organizations sponsored by the Japanese, all of which provided fertile ground for indoctrination. The largest and most important of these was the Peta (Volunteer Army), which was trained by the Japanese but manned and officered by Indonesians; by mid-1945 the Peta numbered about 120,000 men, and it became the nucleus of the future Indonesian republican army.

The Japanese did not provide the nationalists with these opportunities unreservedly, however. Their sole purpose in allowing the organizations was to secure backing for their war effort, and when it seemed that the Putera was devoting more attention to Indonesian independence than Japanese victory, they replaced it in March 1944 with the more strictly controlled Djawa Hokokai. Nonetheless, the nationalists were able to make use of the organizations for their own ends, re-establishing a contact between the political elite and the populace which had not existed since the Communist uprisings of the 1920s. Perhaps more important, they were able to do so at a time when the Indonesian people, in a state of political, social, and economic upheaval, were seeking new leaders and new goals. At the same time, the fact of Japanese sponsorship was not without significance, for many members of the Putera and its associated groups became indoctrinated with the authoritarian concepts of their mentors, an influence which was to be felt to varying degrees throughout Indonesia's subsequent history.

As Indonesian disaffection increased with the changing tide of war and the extreme privations to which the populace was subjected, the Japanese made further concessions to nationalist demands, and finally established an Independence Preparatory Committee, headed by Sukarno, on August 7, 1945. By the time of Japan's surrender a week later, however, the promised grant of independence had not yet been received. The nationalist leaders were now faced with the problem of whether to proclaim independence on their own; Sukarno and Hatta preferred to wait for a go-ahead from the occupation authorities in order to avoid clashes with the Japanese troops, which, in the absence of an Allied force, were the strongest organized power in the country. Their view was not shared by the militant youth groups which had formed during the occupation on underground and semilegal bases in the major cities of Java. Leaders of these groups, demanding a declaration of independence completely free from Japanese sponsorship, kidnapped Sukarno and Hatta and persuaded them to make, on August 17, 1945, an unequivocal declaration of Indonesia's independence.

The fact that the Republic had declared its existence did not mean that it possessed the apparatus necessary for running a state. Far from it: a virtual vacuum of effective authority followed the Japanese surrender, increasing the already serious social disorientation and allowing it to find open expression. In Sumatra this reached the proportions of social revolution by the end of 1945. In Atjeh the aristocracy which had been placed in power with the Dutch conquest of that area was overthrown and decimated by resurgent religious elements. A few months later, local adat rulers in East Sumatra were similarly deposed by the populace, this time under radical secular leadership. In Java and elsewhere in Sumatra no one indigenous class bore the brunt of popular disaffection, and rejection of the traditional order was largely restricted to irregular extremist activities against Europeans and Chinese and to the removal of unpopular village heads and local administrative officials. Borneo, Celebes, and the islands of eastern Indonesia remained generally unaffected by such upheavals. Their social structure had not felt the corrosive effects of substantial Western penetration in the colonial period, and during the war they had been under the command of the Japanese navy, which, unlike the army on Java and Sumatra, had discouraged Indonesian mass activity of any kind. Finally, these islands were occupied rather rapidly by Allied troops, so that the Republic did not have a chance to extend its influence to more than a few small parts of the area prior to the end of the revolution.

Sukarno became president and Hatta vice-president of the newly founded Republic.[40] Within a week of the proclamation of independence a constitution was promulgated, based on a draft which had been prepared in the preceding months. It provided for a republican form of government, a "democracy led by the wise guidance of consultation-representation," and a cabinet which was to be responsible to the president. A representative council was to be elected by popular suffrage; until elections could be held Sukarno appointed a Central Indonesian National Committee (KNIP) which, representing the various Indonesian social groups, was to advise both the President and his cabinet. As it turned out, the KNIP, in an expanded form, was to serve the Republic for some years before elections could be held, and its role was to be considerably enlarged. Originally, the political forces of the nation were combined into a single front, the leadership of which rested in the hands of Subardjo and others who had been closely identified with the Japanese. Political leaders who had taken a strongly anti-Japanese stand during the war—the most prominent of these being Sjahrir and the former Gerindo leader Amir Sjarifuddin—protested what they felt to be collaborationist domination of the government and called for the replacement of the presidential system by a cabinet responsible to the KNIP. At the same time they and other political leaders who were not identified with the Subardjo group pressed for the replacement of the single front by a multiparty system. They were successful in both demands; in November the formation of political parties commenced, and in the same month Sjahrir became prime minister of Indonesia's first parliamentary government.

While it is difficult to assess the popular strength of the individual parties during the chaotic years of the revolution, we can make some generalizations on the basis of support of the more enduring major groupings. The Indonesian Nationalist party (PNI) gained the backing of the civil servants and administrators, who used their influence to broaden its base in the countryside; it was not the same party as Sukarno's PNI of the 1920s, though some of the old leaders carried over and the similarity of name may have accounted for some of its popularity. The Masjumi bore the same name as that of the Moslem grouping which the Japanese had encouraged, but it too was a new organization. Uniting both reformist and traditionalist Islamic groups, the Masjumi had wide rural and urban support and was believed to be the largest of the parties, though like the PNI it was not tightly organized. The Partai Sosialis (Socialist Party) combined the forces of Sjarifuddin and Sjahrir; its program was one of democracy and social revolution, and, though it did not boast a large mass membership, it had the best organization of the then existing political groups. The PKI also re-emerged in late 1945, but it remained a limited operation until mid-1948, many Communists joining other leftist parties and organizations instead of openly proclaiming their allegiance to it.

With the establishment of a multiparty system there arose a number of mass organizations which developed ties of varying intensity to the various political groups. Most important of these were the paramilitary organizations which evolved from armed youth groups established during the Japanese occupation and the early days of independence. Chief of these were the socialist Pesindo, the Moslem Hizbullah, and the radical nationalist Barisan Banteng. These groups, in addition to defending the Republic, played an important part in pressing the demands of their associated parties. They did not form the Republic's only military force, since within a few weeks of the proclamation of independence the government took steps which led to the creation of a national army, while in addition a sort of territorial home guard, the Laskjar Rakjat, came into existence. All of these forces, including the army, were made up of highly autonomous units whose operations were subject only to limited control by the KNIP or the National Committees of the areas in which they were active.

The Indonesian Republic had only a few weeks to organize itself before the landing of Allied troops. In September 1945 British forces arrived on Java to take the Japanese surrender and to evacuate prisoners of war. It seemed expedient for them to request the cooperation of the authority which had apparent control of the population, and accordingly they dealt with Sukarno's Republic. At the same time, however, it was necessary for them to think of the claims of their wartime ally, the Netherlands; and the British found themselves in the unhappy position of not fully satisfying either party to the evolving Dutch-Indonesian dispute and finally being accused of bad faith by both. Dutch troops and governmental officials began to arrive in limited but increasing numbers; at the same time, Indonesian militance began to mount. Striving to arrange a Dutch-Indonesian *modus vivendi* which would enable them to be quit of their task, the British succeeded by November 1945 in arranging talks between Netherlands and Indonesian authorities.

The parleys with the Dutch representatives in Indonesia which began on an informal basis in November 1945 were the first step in a long series of negotiations, agreements, misunderstandings, and conflicts which were to mark Dutch-Indonesian relations in the years to follow. The Dutch entered these talks quite unappreciative of the vast changes which had taken place in Indonesia during their absence. To them the Republic was the creation of Japanese puppets, and, still smarting from their own experience with fascist occupation, they refused to have anything to do with Sukarno. With growing evidence of the Republic's popular support

303

and the appointment of the anticollaborationist Sjahrir as prime minister, their attitude softened enough to make negotiations possible. Nonetheless, a profound disbelief in the validity of the Republic's claim to speak for the Indonesian people persisted, a feeling that was fed to no little extent by the belief that Holland must preserve its role in the archipelago if it was to recover the prosperity it had enjoyed before the war.

On the Indonesian side, negotiations were an equally controversial matter. Compromise was clearly necessary, for at best the Republic controlled only Java and Sumatra, and as Dutch troops continued to arrive the military position of the Republic became increasingly unfavorable. At the same time, however, revolutionary emotion in the Republic ran high, particularly on the part of the armed youth groups, from which the opponents of the government could secure powerful support at will by assuming an uncompromising revolutionary stand. Hence any government undertaking negotiations found itself in a very delicate position. The first major test of the government's ability to check such opposition came in 1946, when the nationalist-Communist leader Tan Malaka succeeded in forming the Persatuan Perdjuangan (Union for Struggle), which called for the abolition of political parties and a refusal to negotiate with the Dutch. Malaka's forces grew rapidly, backed by militant youth groups and political and military leaders opposed to Sjahrir. They succeeded in causing the cabinet's resignation but, being unable to unite on a government of their own, were forced to accede to a new cabinet under Sjahrir's direction.

The fortunes of Tan Malaka and his principal associates were temporarily eclipsed by their arrest in July 1946 after an attempted coup d'état, but the power of the opponents of compromise remained great. The subject of negotiations remained the principal axis around which the politics of the Republic revolved; by and large, the groups forming the government in power supported them as vital to the Republic's survival, while those out of power damned them as selling out the revolution. As the Republic's military and economic situation worsened, tempers frayed and views grew more vehement, until, as we shall see, they erupted into a major internal clash.

Whereas the Indonesian negotiators wanted recognition of the Republic as the sole authority in the archipelago, the Netherlands sought a federal, commonwealth arrangement. The Dutch had succeeded in re-establishing themselves in the islands outside Java and Sumatra, where they proceeded to set up states friendly to their position, putting them forward as potential partners for the Republic in the proposed federation. This federal scheme, which became increasingly explicit in the Dutch proposals, seems to have been little more than an attempt to counterbalance the power of a hostile Republic, and the Indonesians eventually accepted it only under pressure.[41] The collapse of the federation shortly after the transfer of sovereignty seems a natural consequence of the unhappy associations which the federal concept—in itself not without merit—had gained throughout the period of negotiations since 1945.

Dutch-Indonesian talks proceeded through the unsuccessful Hoge Veluwe conference of April 1946 to the eventual signing of an agreement at Linggadjati in March 1947. That pact was almost immediately subject to controversy regarding its interpretation; in July 1947 the Dutch, tiring of the debate, launched a "police action" to enforce their point of view. Militarily the move was quite successful, and the Republican-controlled area on Java was considerably diminished. Diplomatically, however, it had unfavorable consequences for the Dutch, for the Indonesian question, introduced into the United Nations by the Ukrainian S.S.R. in 1946, was now placed under the supervision of a Committee of Good Offices appointed by the Security Council. The committee succeeded in arranging a second agreement aboard the U.S.S. "Renville" in December 1947, but it was a patchwork affair which succeeded in only temporarily delaying the outbreak of a new clash.[42]

Within the Republic the concessions involved in the Linggadjati and Renville agreements resulted in major governmental shifts. Sjahrir, who signed the Linggadjati pact, was forced to resign in June 1947; he was replaced by his Socialist colleague Sjarifuddin, who in turn found it necessary to withdraw in the wake of opposition to the Renville concessions. With Sjarifuddin's fall an important change in political relationships took place. Hitherto, support for the government had come largely from the left-wing (Sajap Kiri) coalition, which included the Socialist, Labor, and Communist parties and the Pesindo. The Republican Fortress (Benteng Republik) group, which had strong support among PNI, Masjumi, and Tan Malaka adherents, formed the principal opposition. Now, however, the outsiders came into power; the new cabinet formed in January 1948 drew on Masjumi and PNI elements.

305

Moreover, to bypass parliamentary opposition to the Renville pact the cabinet was placed under Vice-President Hatta and made responsible to the President, not the KNIP. This reversal in governmental roles was succeeded by a change of party positions regarding the concessions to the Dutch: the Masjumi and PNI, having initially denounced the Renville agreement, now supported it; the left-wing groups, responsible for its signing, now denounced it. These changes brought to a head a long developing breach between Sjarifuddin and Sjahrir; the latter left the Socialist Party, taking a minority of its members with him, and formed the Indonesian Socialist Party (PSI), which supported the Hatta government. Sjarifuddin reformed the left-wing coalition into the oppositional People's Democratic Front (FDR). In addition to the support of the former left-wing parties, the front had the backing of Pesindo, the powerful labor federation SOBSI, and a good part of the armed forces, where Sjarifuddin, who had held the post of minister of defense since 1945, had built up a considerable personal following.

In succeeding months, tensions mounted within the Republic. The government, in order to cope with the socioeconomic situation in the territory left to it, instituted a program of rationalization which principally affected the army and labor forces, and persons displaced by these efforts swelled the ranks of the opposition. At the same time, the FDR became more clearly Communist, partly as a result of general disillusionment with America's position on the revolution, which was held to be pro-Dutch, and partly as a response by pro-Communists within the front to Soviet demands that Indonesia choose sides in the cold war. By mid-1948 tempers on all sides had worn thin, with clashes occurring between armed units of the FDR and its various opponents. Affairs came to a head in August 1948 with the return of the PKI leader Musso from lengthy exile in the USSR. Under his guidance, the FDR was reorganized to form an enlarged PKI which proposed to pursue more aggressively its claims to leadership of the national revolution. In mid-September the cleavage between the pro- and anti-government forces erupted into violence, as troops sympathetic to the PKI seized the city of Madiun. The brief but bloody insurrection which followed resulted in the death of Musso, Sjarifuddin, and other leftist leaders; the PKI went underground and did not emerge as an active political force until after 1950.

These events took place under the growing threat of a new

Dutch attack. Scarcely had the government completed its liquidation of the Communist forces when, in December 1948, the Netherlands launched its second police action. Dutch troops occupied Jogjakarta, the Republican capital, and interned the government leaders, including President Sukarno. An emergency government was formed on Sumatra, and the Republican forces adopted guerrilla tactics which made it impossible for the Dutch to consolidate their hold on Java. The Dutch action aroused considerable international opposition, and in January 1949 the Security Council called for the restoration of the Republican government and the completion of arrangements for the recognition of Indonesian independence; in addition it reconstituted its Good Offices Committee into the more authoritative United Nations Commission for Indonesia (UNCI). In the face of world opinion and economic pressure by the United States, the Netherlands accepted the Security Council resolution. Arrangements were made for the convening of a Round Table Conference in The Hague, which met from August to November under the UNCI's supervision and arranged for a transfer of Dutch sovereignty over all the Netherlands East Indies except western New Guinea, whose status was left for further negotiations. This last remnant of Dutch authority in the archipelago was a sop thrown to the Dutch conservatives to secure their parliamentary approval of the transfer. Some hopes were held that the territory might become a new tropical Holland, in which Eurasians and Indies Dutch might find a new home; but by and large the issue of its status, which was to cause the final wreckage of Dutch-Indonesian relations, was not then felt to be a major one. On December 27, 1949, the transfer of sovereignty took place, and the United States of Indonesia, a federation in which the Republic was one of sixteen component states, came into being.

The Indonesian federation did not last a year. It became all too evident that the political leaders of the non-Republican states had been held in their positions through Dutch power, and in many areas the movement toward the establishment of a unitary Republic became evident immediately after the transfer of sovereignty. Republican troops were dispatched to the various islands, where they released politicians kept in prison and thus spearheaded the abrogation of one state after another. In only one area was there substantial popular resistance to the movement for unification; this was in the South Moluccas, whose Christian population had supplied much of the manpower for the Netherlands Indies army and feared the consequences of undiluted rule by the Republic. The UNCI, which was observing the implementation of the Round Table Agreement, assumed a passive attitude toward the dismantling of the federation, and in August 1950 the creation of a unitary Republic of Indonesia was announced.

In 1950 Indonesia emerged as a fully independent state, but its problems of adjustment were just beginning. Both before and during the nationalist struggle, deep divisions among various groups within Indonesian society had manifested themselves. Now that the enthusiasm generated by the struggle against the Dutch no longer overshadowed other interests, these cleavages again rose to the surface. The multiparous political groupings which had existed within the revolutionary Republic were now compounded by the absorption into one state of leaders who had cooperated or compromised with the Dutch, as well as those who feared Javanese intrusion into the affairs of their regions. All this was added to the fact that the struggle for independence had been waged on a program of national liberation first, social change later. Thus, in spite of the profound dislocations which had taken place during the war and revolution, the basic social configurations of the new state were unresolved. The fact that the Dutch retained their economic position in the archipelago was not only a source of disillusionment to many, but also helped to enforce the status quo on what would otherwise have become a volatile economic situation. Indonesia emerged from its struggle an impoverished land, but revolution had raised the expectations of its people. Its leaders were trained in revolution, but not in the normal administration of a country. Under these circumstances, the vague ideals of revolutionary nationalism were insufficient to provide a cohesive guiding force for a society that needed complete re-evaluation of its aims, purposes, and ideals. Independence marked a milestone on the road to a new Indonesia; but it was only a milestone, not the end of the road.

CHAPTER 8

Dynamics of Guided Democracy

HERBERT FEITH

INDONESIAN GOVERNMENT and politics today is the government and politics of Guided Democracy, of a political order ushered in between 1956 and 1958 as a result of the disintegration, overthrow, and abandonment of the constitutional democracy of the earlier years of independence. To understand Guided Democracy, one must know something of the political order out of which it was born, and something of how and why this earlier order collapsed.[1]

Indonesian independence dates back, in many practical senses as well as the important symbolic one, to August 17, 1945, two days after the Japanese collapse, when Sukarno and Hatta proclaimed the Republic of Indonesia and thereby sparked four years of revolutionary warfare. In this discussion, however, we shall take our point of departure as December 27, 1949. It was on this day that the Netherlands finally relinquished its claim to sovereignty over Indonesia, and the Republic of the United States of Indonesia was born, a product of the Round Table Conference held at The Hague from August to November 1949.

The Republic of the United States of Indonesia (RUSI) was a federal state, incorporating the fifteen states and territories which the Dutch had built during the previous three years in areas they controlled, as part of their struggle against the revolutionary Republic of Indonesia (RI). But it was this revolutionary Republic, the sixteenth member of the federation, which dominated the federal structure. Those who came to power in December 1949 were predominantly leaders of the revolution; Sukarno became the new state's president and Hatta its prime minister.

Of the various groups of leaders of the revolutionary Republic, it was Hatta and the men of his general outlook who assumed

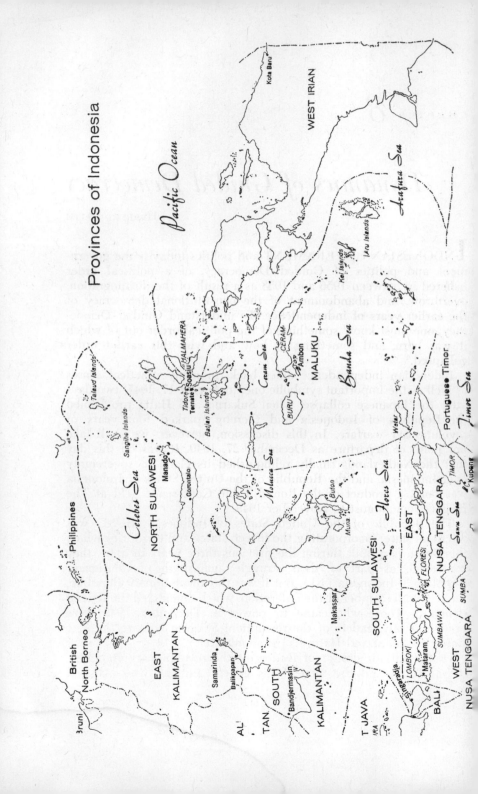

Provinces of Indonesia

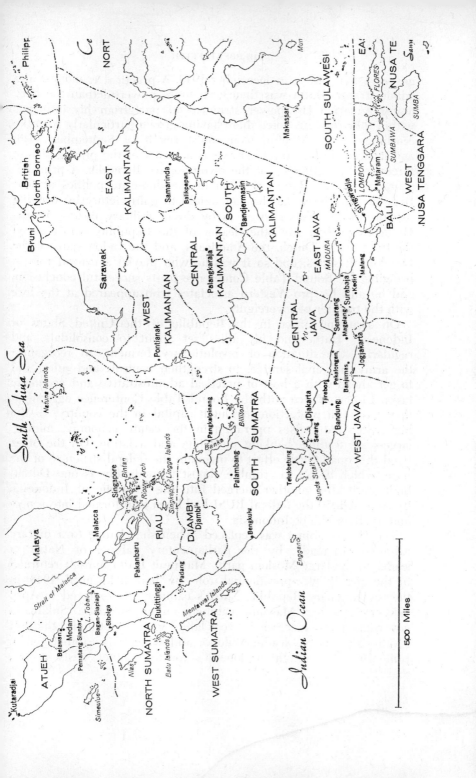

governmental power in December 1949. A practical economist and administrator, Hatta was then even more powerful than the fiery orator Sukarno. His power stemmed in part from his influence within the army, his voice there having grown particularly with the crushing of the Madiun Communist revolt of September 1948; and it also followed from his role as a leader of the pronegotiation forces in the leadership of the revolutionary Republic. A principal characteristic of Hatta's position in the domestic politics of that Republic had been that he had sought to gain victory by winning support in the West as well as by direct military means. It was Hatta, more than any other leader of the Republic, who enjoyed the trust of the Dutch, the Americans, and the Indonesians of the Dutch-built states; and so it was he who played a central role in bringing the Round Table Conference to its successful conclusion, and he and his pro-Western associates who appeared at the fore with the transfer of sovereignty.

On assuming office in the Republic of the United States of Indonesia, Hatta and his allies set about to consolidate and regularize the situation of revolutionary ferment, to reorganize the army and civil service, to strengthen controls and rules, and to get ahead with a host of practical administrative and economic tasks. In accordance with the Round Table Conference agreement they gave full protection to Dutch capital in the country, to the big Dutch enterprises operating in the estate economy, mining, large-scale trading, banking, shipping, and aviation. On the other hand they made little effort to maintain the federal structure of the state, which began to crumble almost immediately as one Dutch-built state after another merged into the Republic of Indonesia. By August 1950 the federal RUSI had been transformed into a new unitary Republic of Indonesia.

The Hatta cabinet was replaced, when the change to a unitary cabinet was made, by the parliamentary cabinet of Natsir, a leader of the large Moslem party, Masjumi; Hatta himself returned to the purely vice-presidential role he had held until 1948 in the revolutionary Republic. Natsir's cabinet was replaced in April 1951 by another Masjumi cabinet, under Sukiman. Sukiman's government was succeeded a year later by a cabinet under the PNI (Nationalist party) leader Wilopo; and when this cabinet fell in June 1953, it brought Indonesia's fourth cabinet crisis in less than three years.

In spite of the rapid succession and varying leadership of these cabinets, there was considerable continuity in their activities. The leaders of all of them were men whose outlook resembled Hatta's. They gave a high priority to establishing security, creating a more unified army, rehabilitating former fighters, and making the machinery of government more efficient. All of them devoted themselves to restoring and increasing production, stimulating development, and maintaining financial stability—and they offered no major challenge to the preponderant power of Westerners and Chinese in the economy.

All of these governments were, moreover, unspectacular in their foreign policies. And while they were active, through educational expansion and mass information campaigns, in spreading awareness of Indonesian nationality, they made few attempts to maintain nationalism as a source of intense personal commitment for those whose norms had been shaken by social uprooting. They were in fact humdrum governments, and as such incurred the hostility of many of the revolutionary generation, the young men uprooted from traditional society by the tumultous happenings of 1942-49, who had come to expect government and politics to provide their personal lives with meaning.

The attempt to operate a system of constitutional democracy was begun in this rational but uninspiring context. Support for the idea of democracy was almost universal in the Indonesian political leadership at the time. However, democracy was seen as a legitimating principle of government—*vox populi, vox Dei*—as a long-term goal, more or less synonymous with the "just and prosperous society" which Indonesian leaders of varied persuasions declared to be their aim. It was viewed as a matter of inducing popular participation, and by some as protection against tyranny. However, it was not seen as having representative functions, nor as necessarily linked with majority rule or with institutionalized opposition. There was, in fact, little support in the prevailing body of political ideas for the characteristic principles and mechanisms of constitutional democracy.

The fact that constitutional democracy was nevertheless adopted can be explained in part by the lack of other practical alternatives, in particular by the fact that no state party or cohesive army was there to take the reins. In part, too, it should be seen in connection with the attachment of a few individual leaders, like Hatta and Natsir, to the values of constitutional democracy *per se.* Finally, the sort of government it offered appealed to leaders who were concerned to consolidate a post-revolutionary situation, to establish order, rules, and controls at a time when political life was permeated by demands for symbolism and mystique. To these men, concerned with the dangers of anarchy and "demagocracy," constitutional democracy was attractive in that it combined the principle of popular sovereignty with a concentration on legality.

The operation of constitutional democracy in the period of these first four cabinets was reasonably effective. Cabinets were accountable to the parliament of the day for many of their actions, although this was not an elected body. The press was exceedingly free. Courts operated with considerable independence of the government. Demands for national loyalty were rarely used to silence the critics of cabinets. And nonpolitical administration characterized at least some major parts of the government apparatus.

The four cabinets had significant successes in the governmental tasks which they set themselves. They maintained controls fairly well, regularizing administration and restoring communications. They greatly reduced the volume of rebel and bandit activity, produced an increase in small and medium-scale industry, and restored rice production, up 23.2 per cent in three years.[2] Most export industries increased their output markedly, partly in response to the buoyancy of prices at the time of the Korean War. There was, moreover, a rapid expansion in educational facilities of every kind, and especially of secondary schools and universities.

The cabinets, however, met insuperable obstacles in trying to implement a number of their most important policies. They could not push through their efforts to have squatters cleared off the lands of foreign estates. They could not reduce the size of the civil service, and in fact allowed it to expand rapidly. They failed in their efforts to demobilize large numbers of soldiers. And after the middle of 1951 they made no further advance against the extremist Moslem rebel movement, Darul Islam, groups of whose guerrillas continued to hold important territory in West Java and South Celebes.

Most important, these cabinets failed to maintain their political support; opposition to them had become very powerful by 1952. Partly because Western-approved leaders were now no longer diplomatically necessary (as they had been in the period of revolution), partly because routinization and loss of *élan* was resented by many of the former revolutionaries, and partly too because of unpopular measures taken to deal with the post-Korean War slump in prices for Indonesia's exports, 1952-53 saw a general weakening of Hatta and others of his general orientation, and a corresponding rise in the power of President Sukarno and radically nationalist groups in the parties and the army. These latter groups won a major victory as a result of the "October 17 Affair" of 1952, when a group of army heads of broadly pro-Hatta orientation tried to force President Sukarno to have parliament dissolved but were foiled and subsequently removed from their offices. When the Wilopo cabinet fell eight months later, the pro-Hatta forces suffered a major defeat.

The next cabinet (July 1953-July 1955), led by the PNI's Ali Sastroamidjojo, broke the continuity of earlier policy orientation. Its leaders were closer to President Sukarno than to Vice-President Hatta in their view of what governments should do. Thus they paid less attention than their predecessors to the solution of practical administrative and economic problems and more to the pursuit of a vigorous and militantly neutralist foreign policy—the successful holding of the Bandung Asian-African Conference was one of their greatest achievements—and to efforts to realize the national claim to West Irian (West New Guinea).

Less afraid than the leaders of the earlier cabinets of the consequences of inflation or loss of production, they were correspondingly more active in supporting "Indonesianization" of the economy—assisting Indonesian firms to take over a bigger share of importing, banking, shipping, rice milling, and other areas where Dutch or Chinese business had until then remained dominant. Inflation was accelerated markedly in their period of office, making the prevailing exchange rate more unreal and so penalizing export producers.

Both the cabinet of Ali Sastroamidjojo and its successor, the short-lived government of the Masjumi's Burhanuddin Harahap (August 1955-March 1956), worked in a period of intense and bitter electioneering. For two and a half years before the double elections of September and December 1955 (for parliament and a constituent assembly respectively), campaigning exerted critical pressures on government. Ministers were obliged to make great efforts to advance the electoral interests of their parties—to collect money for them, to increase their power in crucial segments of the bureaucracy, and to make sure they stayed in office. Taken together

315

with the absence of major countervailing power from professionally oriented senior civil servants, this meant that technical considerations of administration and economic management were readily overridden.

In general these two cabinets were less effective than their predecessors in their efforts to solve the country's practical problems. Increases in export production were minor in these years, and the production of foodstuffs and industrial manufactures was also rising only very slowly. The cabinets did not prevent a further expansion of civil service numbers. They made little headway against the Darul Islam rebels in West Java and South Celebes, and Atjeh became a third area of sporadic battles against Darul Islam guerrillas in the course of their period in office. Matters of long-term policy were particularly neglected; they would receive attention "after the elections," it was said.

In addition to reducing the effectiveness of government in solving various economic and administrative problems, electioneering had important effects on the functioning of politics. Whereas alliances had been very fluid earlier, with the major cleavages often within parties rather than between them, the campaign situation produced a closing of ranks in most parties, and a more or less fixed clustering of all other parties around either the PNI or the Masjumi. The Communist party (PKI), growing rapidly in this period, was strongly behind the PNI. So were most minor nationalist parties and, usually, the conservative Moslem Nahdatul Ulama (NU). The small Socialist party (PSI) and the two small Christian parties (the Protestant Parkindo and the Partai Katholik) were aligned with the Masjumi. Between these two blocs of parties there was little acceptance of common fundamentals; each side, when in power, bent the rules of parliamentary democracy to suit its own purposes.

Moreover, the election campaign sharpened disagreement on the ends of the state and the nation. One central issue was whether the state should, as the Masjumi demanded, be based specifically on Islam; or whether, as the PNI argued, its religious foundations should be those of the Pantja Sila, which acknowledged merely "The One Deity."[3]

Ideological campaigning, brought to the village level, served to sharpen older communal divisions—divisions between Moslems and non-Moslems, and between communities where Islam is a major component of culture and others where Moslem profession goes along with a complex of pre-Islamic beliefs and practices.[4] And, with the elite divisions being projected into the body of society, it was not long before this process started working in the opposite direction, with newly sharpened communal divisions aggravating the cleavages in the elite. The Pantja Sila, previously accepted by Moslem political leaders as a symbol to which they could give at least tentative assent, now became anti-Moslem property; President Sukarno, as a vigorous defender of the Pantja Sila (and an active supporter of the Ali cabinet), came to be seen as a spokesman for one side in the struggle instead of a nonpartisan head of state.

The elections were held in an atmosphere of high expectations. Government and party leaders had promised repeatedly that elections would regenerate government and politics, that the tensions, divisions, and delays which resulted from campaigning would be redeemed by the over-all improvements which would follow from the polling. Election day itself, especially the day of the parliamentary election, was a momentous occasion—a ceremonial act of participation in the nation which was carried out with great dignity and seriousness. The balloting was orderly and free. Despite some pre-election intimidation by village officials and others in certain areas, these elections were generally fair. The choices made by village voters were meaningful—not as assessments of the performance of particular governments, but as quasi-ideological identifications by the villagers. The parties which emerged as successful—the PNI with 22.3 per cent of the vote, Masjumi with 20.9 per cent, Nahdatul Ulama with 18.4 per cent, and Communists with 16.4 per cent—were the ones which had succeeded in linking themselves with major social groups.[5]

However, those who had expected panacea effects from the holding of elections were quickly disappointed. Indeed, the year 1956 saw feelings of disillusionment expressed by a large number of groups and in a great variety of ways. The postelection cabinet, a PNI-Masjumi-NU coalition headed by Ali Sastroamidjojo, set about to bridge the earlier cleavage between the PNI and the Masjumi and to tackle the great number of governmental problems which had accumulated in the pre-election years. However, internal divisions made it hard for the cabinet to act with speed or determination, and it had been in office only a few months when its authority was subjected to a series of major challenges.

The first major opposition came from the leaders—and particularly the military commanders—of a number of regions outside Java.

317

Military commanders in the exporting areas of North Celebes and North Sumatra, seeing their areas' interests suffering as a result of exchange rate unreality, organized large-scale smuggling in the middle months of 1956.[6] Defending themselves publicly, they claimed that only by smuggling actions could they secure the funds needed for the welfare of their soldiers and their areas in general. The cabinet eventually succeeded in stopping these actions, but it did not punish the commanders or deprive them of the goods they had imported; and the government's authority fell sharply as a result. Noting Masjumi and Socialist sympathy for the regional commanders, politicians and political observers alike were confirmed in a conclusion they had first drawn from the elections: namely that the PNI, the NU, and the PKI were Java parties—each had obtained more than 85 per cent of its vote on the central island—and that the Masjumi and Socialists were predominantly parties of the Outer Islands.

In the second half of 1956 several abortive attempts were made by a former acting chief of staff of the army, Colonel Zulkifli Lubis, to organize a military coup in Djakarta. At the same time there were from many sides denunciations of the cabinet and the general state of the country, of various economic ills, of corruption, privilege, faction, and demoralization. These denunciations were combined in many cases with allegations that the parties and their leaders had failed the country. Lubis' supporters spoke openly of the need for military dictatorship; and in October President Sukarno urged that the parties should be "buried" and that "liberal democracy" be replaced by what he called "Guided Democracy," democracy with leadership.

To make the second Ali cabinet's plight even worse, the month of December 1956 saw a second wave of challenges from leaders of exporting regions outside Java. In Central Sumatra, two days later in North Sumatra, and after two more days in South Sumatra, bloodless coups were enacted in which the military commanders took power out of the hands of their more Djakarta-dependent civilian counterparts. In one case, that of North Sumatra, Djakarta was able to have the challenger overthrown from inside his command; but in the others it did virtually nothing, thus accepting a major loss of control. The challenging military commanders, who appeared to have considerable support in their own areas, declared that their seizure of regional power was temporary and its purpose corrective. They denounced Djakarta for overcentralization, corruption, and neglect of outer areas, for placing too many Javanese officials in these areas, and for leniency to Communism. They demanded that the Ali cabinet should resign and allow the Sumatran Hatta, who had resigned from the largely ceremonial vice-presidency earlier in December, to return to the government as head of a nonparty "business cabinet." Moreover, they threatened to sell their own export products directly, bypassing Djakarta and its exporter-penalizing exchange rate; and they made a beginning with carrying out the threat. The Masjumi, which sympathized with many of these demands, sought to have the cabinet resign, and, when this effort had failed, withdrew its own ministers.

What this complex series of postelection developments portended was clear to none of the observers of the scene and to few if any of the actors concerned; but it was obvious that the existing political order was under challenge. Moreover, it was showing remarkably little readiness to defend itself. Party leaders generally admitted that their parties were responsible for most of the evils for which they were blamed. There were only a few isolated defenses of the principles of parliamentary democracy. When the second Ali cabinet declared that the elected government's authority had to be maintained in the face of the regionalists' illegal actions to defy it, one widespread response was that the government was taking a formalistic and legalistic position. Those constitutionally in office were no longer seen as having the moral right to govern.

One proposal for a way out of the crisis was presented by the regionalists, who were in power in Central and South Sumatra—and in East Indonesia after March 1957—and who were linked in the military with the group of Colonel Lubis and in civilian politics with important parts of the Masjumi, the Socialist party, and the Protestant Christian party, Parkindo. Their solution, as indicated above, was "restoration of the Sukarno-Hatta duumvirate," by which they meant a return of Hatta to the prime ministership; in addition they stood for regional autonomy, greater power for the army, and anti-Communism.

The principal alternative was proffered by President Sukarno as he developed his ideas of Guided Democracy. When he spoke of Guided Democracy in October 1956, he said he had a formula or concept (*konsepsi*) of his own establishing it. Unveiling this concept in February 1957, he called for formation of a cabinet in which all major parties (including the Communists) would participate, and for the establishment of a National Council (Dewan Nasional), a high advisory body on which various functional groups—workers, peasants, national businessmen, and so on—would be represented and which would operate through consensus rather than by voting. Support for the President came from the PNI and various smaller nationalist groups, and most vociferously from the Communists.

There was also a third major group competing for power, the central leadership of the army under Chief of Staff Nasution. Major-General Nasution and his associates rarely spoke in public, and did not lay claim to an ideological position, but their demands were increasingly clear: more power for the army, to be obtained without directly challenging the President. In fact, for much of 1957 this central army group held a balance of power between the regionalists on the one hand and President Sukarno on the other. When Sukarno put his Guided Democracy proposals to the parties in February 1957 and several major parties (including the Nahdatul Ulama) rejected them, a compromise was reached largely on army-arranged terms. The second Ali cabinet resigned in mid-March; at this juncture the nation was placed under martial law, thus greatly increasing the power of the army commanders. The successor cabinet, formed in early April and headed by the nonparty man Djuanda, was based chiefly on the PNI and Nahdatul Ulama; though it was committed to the formation of a National Council such as the President had wanted, it did not include the Communists as his concept required.

For most of the rest of 1957 the position of the various contending groups remained deadlocked. For a time it would seem that Djakarta was moving toward a compromise with the regionalist leaders; but then relations would grow cooler again, with a military showdown appearing as the more likely solution to the regionalist challenge. Parliamentary institutions were more and more frequently side-stepped in this period; the parties were being edged off the center of the political stage, and many of their leaders were confused and demoralized. Only the Communist party, knowing what it wanted, remained vigorous and active: when provincial elections were held in Java in the middle of the year it emerged as the island's strongest party, with 27.4 per cent of the vote.[7]

Events came to a head in November and December 1957. In November the UN General Assembly considered a pro-Indonesian motion on the problem of West Irian. Similar motions had failed to obtain a two-thirds majority in earlier years, but this time President Sukarno threatened that Indonesia would act so as to "startle the world" in the event of the motion being lost. It was lost, nevertheless, on November 29. The accompanying sense of crisis was heightened a day later when an attempt was made (by Moslem youths, apparently acting at the behest of Zulkifli Lubis) to assassinate the President. On December 3, a group of workers took control of the Dutch shipping line KPM and a large Dutch trading company, and in the following days take-over actions of this kind snowballed. The cabinet, clearly divided on how to respond to these actions—which had the President's endorsement—did little to curb them. On December 13, by which time almost all Dutch firms had been seized, Chief of Staff Nasution decreed military control over them. The huge Dutch business establishments of estates, mines, banks, trading houses, and shipping thus passed into Indonesian hands, though a year was to go by before the take-overs were legalized by an act of nationalization. Most of the 46,000 or so Dutchmen still in Indonesia prepared to leave almost immediately.[8] Economically, the seizures resulted in chaos. Politically, however, they helped the Djakarta government, giving it an edge over the regionalists. This was both because radical nationalist actions of this kind were applauded by the political public at large, and because Djakarta acquired a large amount of patronage to distribute.

Three other events served to aggravate the regionalist contest. In December Natsir and two other leaders of the Masjumi, feeling themselves intimidated by government-protected youth groups, fled the capital for Padang in Central Sumatra. Chief of Staff Nasution sent an arms-buying mission to eastern Europe in the same month; and the navy was instructed to intensify its efforts to stop the rebellious regions from trading directly with the outside world. Finally, on February 10, 1958, Central Sumatran commander Lieutenant-Colonel Husein issued an ultimatum: unless a new cabinet was formed within five days, one led by Hatta and/or the Sultan of Jogjakarta, the regionalists and their associates in Sumatra would establish a government of their own. When February 15 came, and this demand had not been met, the Revolutionary Government of the Republic of Indonesia (PRRI) was proclaimed in Padang, with the Masjumi leader and former Bank Indonesia governor Sjafruddin Prawiranegara named as prime minister.

It was initially quite unclear who, in Indonesia and outside, would support this new government. The military commanders of Central Sumatra and North Celebes were clearly in support of the countergovernment, but commanders elsewhere, and notably in South Sumatra, remained uncommitted. Outside Indonesia, Secretary of State Dulles made statements which indicated sympathy with the Padang proclamation, and modern American arms arrived in Central Sumatra. No country, however, accorded the new government recognition or belligerent status. The United States refused to freeze Djakarta's overseas funds as requested by Padang; and the Caltex oil company, with its installations in Central Sumatra, continued to make foreign exchange payments to Djakarta.

The initial response of the central government was hesitant. Some bombs were dropped on towns in rebel areas, but Sukarno-Hatta talks went on at the same time, making it seem that a negotiated settlement was still possible. However, on March 7 a series of landings began in Sumatra, and as these met little or no resistance it became clear that Djakarta had no need to negotiate with its challengers. On April 17 Djakarta effected a landing at Padang, and took the city after virtually no fighting. By May 5, when Bukittinggi was recaptured, the Sumatran rebellion had been reduced to guerrilla proportions. The campaign waged in North Celebes in June and July was much tougher, but by its end the rebels had lost every major town. Guerrilla resistance continued for another three years, as did the rebels' overseas publicity activities, but the major victory had been won by mid-1958, in much less time than had been expected.

With this victory, the constellation of Indonesian politics changed markedly. Of the three earlier major contenders for power, one, the regionalist group, had been eliminated. The other two—President Sukarno and his followers, and the post-schism army, which accepted the President's claims to ideological hegemony—held power together. Thus the basis had been created for the relatively stable political balance of the subsequent years. Constitutional democracy was clearly a thing of the past. In addition, the turbulent postelection transition was now at an end.

Constitutional democracy was both overthrown by its opponents and abandoned by those who had earlier upheld it. Why did this happen? The explanation can be given largely in terms of the conjunction of two factors: the high level of political unrest, and the potentialities for dangerous division in the Indonesian polity.

Political unrest was particularly great after the 1955 election period; disappointment became acute as it became clear that no panacea-like over-all solution was emerging. Unrest had, however, been general throughout the period of constitutional democracy. The 1949-56 period had been one in which the promises of the revolution were expected to be redeemed; the earlier high hopes declined only slowly, while political freedom remained wide. It was a time of rapid urbanization, of quick expansion in numbers at school, of the doubling of press circulation and the tripling of the circulation of periodicals.[9] Parties had mobilized mass memberships, and various other kinds of modern organizations drew new adherents in large numbers. For all of these reasons, more and more persons wanted modern consumer goods and white-collar employment—the concrete manifestations of the promised better life.

But production and the openings for modern-type employment expanded only slowly; and therefore there were many whose aspirations to income and particularly status were not satisfied. Moreover, many of these were men who had been personally uprooted by social change, who had come to look to political authority as an appropriate source of norms for their own lives, and who had been bitterly disappointed by the selfishness, corruption, and factional bickering which they saw as characteristic of the governments of the day. Thus dissatisfaction was intense, particularly in the cities and towns, and with the open and pluralistic politics of Indonesian constitutional democracy, this dissatisfaction could find abundant political outlet.

Such expression, however, resulted in a dangerous aggravation of existing cleavages. History, as was noted in the preceding chapter, has left Indonesia with a complex legacy of social contrasts. Traditional economic and political organization was markedly different in different areas. Islam had a powerful impact on society in some areas and relatively little in others; Dutch rule was long and intensive in some parts of the archipelago and short and relatively unimportant elsewhere. Hence social and political values and orientations varied greatly in this postcolonial period, both between different ethnic groups and between different social segments within these groups. In particular one can discern a major contrast between a "Javanese-aristocratic" pole of political orientations and an "Islamic-entrepreneurial" pole. Thus a basis existed for the widespread acceptance of one of several mutually antagonistic ideologies, and as we have noted it required only the intensive pressing of interest demands, particularly in the electioneering situation, for those antagonisms to assume major proportions both in the political elite and in the body of society. As those enmities developed, consensus as to the ends of the state rapidly declined.

By 1956 consensus had been almost entirely destroyed. Conflict in the political elite had come to immobilize government,[10] growing to such importance in the civil bureaucracy and the army that the effectiveness of these bodies as instruments of control was seriously impaired. This incapacitation of government was particularly dangerous to the regime because the split which dominated all others—between the PNI-led coalition of forces and the Masjumi-led group—ran somewhat parallel to the division between Java and the Outer Islands and thus made secession and civil war real possibilities.

Under these circumstances the unrestricted propagation of sectional demands and symbols alarmed a large part of the political elite. Their perception of this threat to national existence and their role in it goes far to explain why there was little defense of constitutional democracy when it was challenged both by those who denounced "Djakarta" and those who condemned "liberal democracy." The same factor helps to account for the readiness of Djakarta in 1958 to use force against the PRRI: at that point most members of the political elite had already accepted the need for government to become tougher and more restrictive; the earlier effort to govern with a minimum of coercion had foundered for lack of adequate consensus, and one result was to endanger their positions.

At the same time, analysis in terms of the elite's responses to danger should not obscure the role of the broader political public in supporting the trend to a more authoritarian politics. As we have seen, the basic principles of constitutional democracy had never gained acceptance in Indonesia, except from a small group of leaders. The idea of institutionalized opposition, in particular, was regarded as foreign. The system was seen as bringing too many disruptive cabinet changes and as encouraging the organized sharpening of social tensions. The elections themselves discredited constitutional democracy in the eyes of some members of the political public: "Was it not money that brought the village voters behind that party?" and "How can my servants make sensible choices in these matters anyway?" were questions that were frequently asked. Finally, hostility to "liberal democracy" reflected resentment of the West, and of the pro-Western political leaders who had been its principal sponsors in Indonesia. With Western economic power still great in Indonesia, and with many Indonesians intensely ashamed of their country's continuing "backwardness," anti-Western sentiment was high. Fanning this sentiment was thus a ready way to political success.

By the middle of 1958, when the take-over of Dutch businesses had been accomplished and the PRRI rebellion had been reduced to guerrilla activities, the way was clear for a new political order to come into being. President Sukarno and the army had together amassed enough power to establish an alternative to constitutional democracy. That alternative—if the dominant governmental symbol of a period may thus be applied—was Guided Democracy.

It is a contention of this essay that Guided Democracy as a political system has been crucially affected by a particular relationship between President Sukarno and the army, a "stable conflict" relationship characterized by both common endeavor and continuing competition and tension between more or less equally matched partners.[11] I shall therefore begin this discussion by outlining the bases of Sukarno-army cooperation and dispute and examining several important facets of Indonesian political and governmental life in which their interaction has been of great importance—the civil administration, the Communist and pro-Western parties, the Indonesian Chinese, and, as a variant example, foreign affairs. In the following section I shall turn to the constitutional structure and ideology of Guided Democracy and to a discussion of how the system affects Indonesian society as a whole. A fourth and final section will be concerned with some aspects of the interaction of politics and economics in the period since 1958.

The Authoritarian Trend: Cooperation and Conflict

By mid-1958 political parties were no longer leading actors on the Indonesian stage. The Masjumi and the Socialist party had been discredited with a large part of the political public because several of their top leaders had been involved in the Padang rebellion. The PNI, Nahdatul Ulama, and a number of the smaller nationalist parties had saved more of their earlier prestige, but they too were seen as included under the President's continuing condemnations of "liberalism," the party system, and "Western-style democracy which has failed." They no longer had any significant degree of initiative in political developments. Only those parties which had never been in government in the previous eight years, the PKI and the much smaller nationalist-Communist Murba (Proletariat) party, had maintained their earlier prestige and *élan*, and the PKI was suffering from a growing number of army-imposed limitations on political activities.

By the middle of 1958 parliamentary institutions had in fact become fairly peripheral to politics—not only to the making of decisions but also to their legitimation. The elected parliament continued to function, as did the Djuanda cabinet, which saw itself as responsible to the legislature; but many of the most important issues were discussed at meetings of the presidentially appointed National Council and at *ad hoc* conferences of military commanders. A leading member of the army's general staff had voiced the opinion that there should be no election for another six years,[12] and in September 1958 Prime Minister Djuanda announced that the elections due a year later would not be held until some time in 1960. Moreover, an overt dismantling of existing parliamentary institutions had been at least threatened: among the matters discussed by the National Council from mid-1958 onward were various proposals for the incorporation of Guided Democracy in the country's constitutional structure—ranging from changes in the electoral law to such radical proposals as the banning of all parties and the replacement of the elected parliament by one consisting of representatives of functional groups.

In addition, there had been a marked diminution of civil liberties. Legal guarantees were more frequently brushed aside than before, particularly where men were arrested for allegedly abetting the rebellion. A number of newspaper editors were detained by authority of an army commander, and temporary bans were occasionally placed on papers. The army's power came to be felt in more and more areas of the economy. Various industries were named "vital," which meant that strikes were illegal there; numerous hoarders were punished severely; and in September 1958 the army took over the businesses of various Chinese persons declared to be sympathizers of the Taiwan government (which had aided the Sumatra-Celebes rebels).[13]

To many observers, the new political order looked like the emergence of dictatorship; but when they came to identifying the dictator, not one candidate was presented but two. Some, pointing to Sukarno's great influence over the cabinet, to the extraordinary prominence of the symbols of Guided Democracy in all public discussion, and to signs of the President's interest in ideas of a single state party, asserted that a Sukarno dictatorship was in the making. Others, noting the great number of actions taken by military decree on the basis of martial law regulations, averred that Indonesia was moving toward a military dictatorship. Indeed the possibility of military dictatorship was publicly discussed by a number of high government leaders, military as well as civil, following the series of military coups in Burma, Pakistan, and Sudan in October 1958.[14]

In fact, however, there were two distinct sources of initiative for the current set of moves away from constitutional democracy. *Both* President Sukarno and the army leaders inaugurated these moves, and they did so not as leader and follower or as part of a single power group, but as two partners between whom relations were competitive as well as cooperative. The emerging system of government was more authoritarian than the earlier one; government power was more concentrated, more widely pervasive in its impact, and more arbitrarily exercised; and open criticism of the government had become far more dangerous than before. But it was not a dictatorial system, because power was shared by two sharply distinct groups. Because there was competition between these forces, other groups were able to exercise influence by virtue of being able to support either of the "big two." This crucial aspect of politics has remained largely unchanged in the four years since mid-1958: despite the further increase in authoritarian controls and the corresponding decline of public liberties and rule of law, there has been no establishment of a monolithic regime.

The two partners in power do work closely together. They are bound to one another by various common attitudes and interests— notably hostility to parties, liberalism, and factional bickering. Moreover, they share an emphasis on the importance of the revolution as a source of legitimate authority; each of them has an interest in maintaining the argument that those who led the struggle for independence have a moral right to govern today. Their cooperation is possible because both of the parties accept a rough division of power, tacitly recognizing each other's rights over certain types of power and certain areas of its exercise. The articulation of values, the formulation and inculcation of state ideology, the fashioning of symbols, and the maintaining of a sense of momentum—these are almost exclusively Sukarno's field. He is in a dominant position with regard to foreign policy, and has the initiative in most public politics. On the other hand, the army is the predominant power in regional government, in the running of the former Dutch enterprises, to some extent in administration generally, and in the handling of rebellions. The division is by no means rigid, and when a particular area of government comes into the political spotlight the effect is usually to bring Sukarno-army conflicts to the fore there. But the tug-of-war relationship is not a continuous one in these areas, and moreover the division into two sets of areas has remained largely as it was when first established in 1958.

Why do the two parties accept this division? It is fairly clear why the President cannot deprive the army leaders of their share of power. He does not have a party of his own or any similar civilian organization; nor does he have a well-organized personal following within the army. But why does the army not secure itself a position of exclusive dominance over the government? The answer lies partly in the fact that the army is divided when it comes to playing political roles. It was originally formed in 1945 out of scattered local segments of various military, paramilitary, and youth organizations established under the Japanese occupation; its principal parent organization was the Peta, an Indonesian auxiliary army established by the Japanese in Java and Bali and composed of a number of battalions without a general staff. Disunity within the army was great in the period of armed struggle between 1945 and 1949, and the military was again sharply divided along regional and quasi-ideological lines for much of the period between 1949 and 1958. Its unity was strengthened by the defection and defeat of the regionalist rebels; moreover, the general staff's control over the regional commands has grown in the period since 1958. However, this latest period has also seen the emergence, re-emergence, or persistence of other divisions—between field officers on the one hand and holders of administrative and political positions on the other, between administrative rationalizers and wielders of solidarity symbols, between advocates and opponents of a purge of corrupt elements from the army, and between older officers and younger ones. Most important of all, it has seen the persistence of a pattern of cleavage between a more strongly Islamic group of officers, mainly non-Javanese, who are determined anti-Communists and suspicious of President Sukarno's relationship with the PKI, and a less strongly Moslem group, mainly Javanese, who have trust in the President and are willing to tolerate the Communists.

328

All of these divisions have come to the fore whenever the suggestion of a possible army seizure of power has come under discussion. It is not at all clear what political feeling exists in the soldiery or how it bears on the various divisions in the officer corps; but it is generally believed that Communist sympathies are widespread among soldiers in such areas as East and Central Java, where the Communists polled heavily in 1955 and 1957, and this almost certainly serves as a further brake on officer groups arguing for army action against President Sukarno.

Secondly, there is fairly widespread opposition among civilians generally to the idea of government by the army. This is partly a reflection of the army's unpopularity, which has grown markedly since the army began its large-scale movement into politics and administration in 1957-58. In addition, it reflects a common view that military rule is the very antithesis of democracy and popular sovereignty—very much more so than, for instance, rule by a single party or national movement. Thus the advocates of an army takeover are told that it would be hard to find acceptable justifications for this, that they would gain only grudging support from civil servants and the people generally, and so be forced to govern by something more like naked force. Neither General Nasution personally nor the army leaders as a group are seen as having an inborn or acquired right to rule Indonesia.

President Sukarno, on the other hand, is seen by many to have just this right. As an old-time nationalist leader, as the man who proclaimed independence, as an orator of great mass appeal, and as the first and only head of state, Sukarno is a cardinal symbol of both the nation and the state. Moreover his legal position is very strong. Being President, he has immense advantage over others when it comes to seeking validation of claims to power. One should not exaggerate the extent to which the President is actually legitimate in his present political role, the extent to which his authority is accepted voluntarily rather than because of the latent sanctions involved. The fact that he has given such greatly increased prominence to nationalist symbols and rituals, at the same time becoming more and more kinglike in his own actions, suggests strongly that legitimacy is an attribute he must constantly strive for rather than one he may take for granted. But because the Indonesian state of this period has few other major sources of legitimacy, consensus and legality each being weak, that attributed to Sukarno assumes great importance.

This means that other men in government need the President's endorsement. The army particularly needs this for its share of governmental power. Without it there would be less acceptance of its claim to civilian powers, both by the civilian bureaucracy and by the people at large—and thus presumably a need for the army either to yield these powers, which it would certainly be most reluctant to do, or to use them with greater and more overt reliance on force. The army thus needs the President. And the President needs the army—although this second statement has come to have somewhat less meaning in recent years as the army appears increasingly entrenched. However, this mutual dependence has not been enough to eliminate strain from the partnership, as we shall now see.

Conflict between the army and the President has important historical roots. There was hostility between the two in the later years of the revolution over the relative importance of diplomacy and armed struggle in defeating the Dutch, the President being then associated with the advocates of diplomacy. Later, in the period of constitutional democracy, they frequently stood at opposite sides of the parliamentary arena, giving indirect support to mutually antagonistic groups of parties; indeed, the antagonism between them as rival would-be heirs was one important factor sustaining the constitutional-democratic order. On at least two occasions—October 17, 1952 and June 27, 1955 (when the army boycotted the installation of the first Ali cabinet's candidate for the post of chief of staff, and so caused this government to fall)— there was an almost open clash between a group of army leaders and the President. In each case the army leadership was supporting positions adopted by Hatta, the Masjumi, and the Socialists, and Sukarno was associating himself with positions of the PNI (or the majority group of the PNI leadership) and the Communists.

The difference of ideological emphasis which this record suggests has continued to the present. It has clearly survived the rebellion, which placed some of the most strongly anti-Communist groups of officers outside the army. The army is certainly much more strongly anti-Communist than the President. It is also—though not uniformly —more strongly Islamic in orientation. In effect, then, the Sukarno-army relationship provides means whereby many of the most important conflicts between social and ideological groups can still be bargained out.

The two partners have markedly different orientations to government. Sukarno's view of Indonesia's problems centers on national unity and national spirit. He insists that nothing is more important than the maintenance of revolutionary *élan*, the creation and re-creation of a mystique and sense of momentum which will tie the people, or some important segments of them, to the government. A self-declared romantic, he is more concerned with formulating goals and articulating values than he is with specific economic or administrative problems, or with the political stability which might make it possible for these problems to be tackled most effectively.

The President's concern with ideology and enthusiasm finds more than an echo in the army. Many army leaders, particularly at levels below the very top, are men who have always thought fighting spirit a more important part of soldiering than the more technical and organizational aspects; this is one aspect of the legacy of the Japanese occupation.[15] Many of those who are not inclined by their personal skills and inclinations to a "fighting spirit" view have nevertheless been obliged, as spokesmen for the army, to place great stress on national spirit, revolutionary dynamism, and the army's calling to leadership. They have been obliged to do this because they have had to justify the army's wide powers over civil affairs—the fact that many army officers, and ex-officers supported by the army, are occupying high posts in administration and the running of state enterprises, posts for which they have much less technical competence than some of their civilian subordinates.

In spite of all this, however, it is a fact that the army leaders are generally more concerned than the President with routine efficiency in government. They are certainly more interested in stability of government than he; and although there are few among them who have a high degree of awe for the technical aspects of state management, the group as a whole seems to be more respectful of them than the President is.[16] While Sukarno declares admiration for Castro's Cuba, the army leaders see more to impress them in the Pakistan of Ayub Khan—although they think Ayub not revolutionary enough.

The Issue of the Army's Civilian Powers

A major area in which Sukarno-army tensions have been evident is the matter of the army's legal title to power in civilian affairs—in effect, its efforts to create a legitimacy independent of the President. With the proclamation of martial law in March 1957, Chief of Staff Nasution became Central War Administrator; his territorial commanders were made Regional War Administrators, and army commanders at the various lower levels acquired new rights within local government. Major-General Nasution and the territorial commanders used their powers increasingly with the outbreak of the rebellion in early 1958, issuing martial law decrees on a great variety of subjects, often in contravention of existing civilian legislation; and there was a parallel expansion in the power of regimental, battalion and company commanders *vis-à-vis* their civilian counterparts.

After the rebellion had been reduced to guerrilla proportions, President Sukarno made numerous efforts to lessen the army's civilian powers, and in this he had the support of a large part of the civil service. In December 1959 he succeeded in reorganizing the martial law system, establishing himself as head of a new Supreme War Authority (Peperti) and thus creating an institutional framework in which the regional military commanders were his direct subordinates. Soon thereafter, moreover, he was able to reduce the level of martial law powers in a number of areas.

Under the reorganized system, the military head of a particular region or locality has greater or less civilian powers according to whether the area is designated as being under a "state of war," a "state of military emergency," a "state of civil emergency," or free from emergency. Powers are divided in every case between a *kepala daerah*, or regional head responsible to the Minister of the Interior, and a military official responsible to the Minister of Defense and Supreme War Authority. But whereas final authority lies in the hands of the kepala daerah in "state of civil emergency" areas and districts where no emergency exists, it lies with the military commander in the case of regions under a "state of war" or a "state of military emergency" (see chart, A Simplified Picture of the Administrative Structure).

In practice, patterns of civilian-military relations differ from area to area. The impact of the army has been least in East and Central Java, where civilian administrative authority is strongly established and where there has been virtually no rebel or bandit activity. In these areas, most administration follows patterns set by the *pamong pradja* corps, a body of highly professional territorial administrators, with long traditions and very high status based on aristocratic origins.[17] Most regional heads are members of this corps—not only the subdistrict officers (*tjamat*) and district officers (*wedana*), but also most regents (*bupati*) and the two governors— and so are well equipped in terms of both training and ascribed authority for their twofold task of providing general authority and coordinating the work of the various departments which have branch offices in their areas. By and large, regional and local administration is efficient and authoritative in East and Central Java. Partly because of this, cooperation between army commanders and their pamong pradja counterparts is mostly close, with the army tending to stiffen pamong pradja authority rather than to undermine it. Martial law in East and Central Java is thus chiefly a matter of reserve powers, affording a basis for army action against strikers and Communist demonstrators, and for press control measures and the fixing of prices, but not for army inroads into local administration.

The opposite extreme can be found in some parts of West Java and in many Outer Island areas, especially where there has been fighting against rebel and bandit groups. In most of these districts, administration had been more indirect in the colonial period, and the process of converting traditional bearers of authority into members of a professionalized paternal administration had reached a far less advanced stage; in many of these regions, moreover, the traditional authorities had been repudiated for their part in the Dutch-built federal structure in the 1945-49 period. Thus the pamong pradja corps was relatively weakly established, having less internal cohesion than in East and Central Java, and less authority vis-à-vis other branches of the administration, political groups, and the population generally. Where areas of this kind were faced with major problems of civil insecurity, as in West Java, South Celebes, and Atjeh (regions of Moslem dissidence) or in Tapanuli, West Sumatra, South Sumatra, and North Celebes (the areas of PRRI fighting), the usual result was that the army made major incursions into government and administration at all levels. Thus not only staff officers and territorial commanders, but also sergeants and corporals at the level of the subdistrict gained power over civilian affairs. These incursions were difficult to reverse; the army's actual role did not diminish significantly when its formal powers were reduced by a change in the martial law level in a particular region. (Similarly, the practical effects were relatively small when the army in mid-1960 gave a type of nonactive status to officers who had been placed in charge of former Dutch enter-

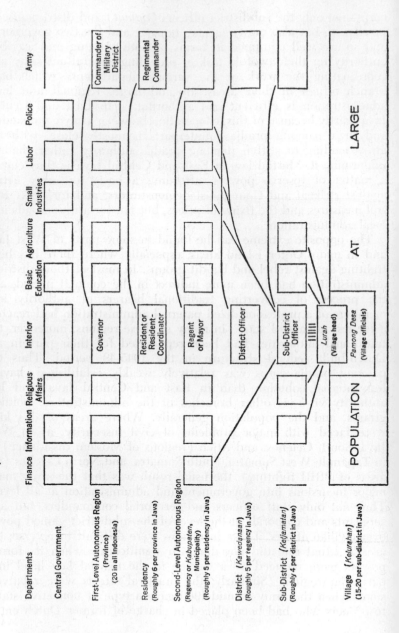

A Simplified Picture of the Administrative Structure

Departments	Finance	Information	Religious Affairs	Interior	Basic Education	Agriculture	Small Industries	Labor	Police	Army
Central Government										
First-Level Autonomous Region (Province) (20 in all Indonesia)				Governor						Commander of Military District
Residency (Roughly 6 per province in Java)				Resident or Resident-Coordinator						Regimental Commander
Second-Level Autonomous Region (Regency or Kabupaten, Municipality) (Roughly 5 per residency in Java)				Ragent or Mayor						
District (Kawedanan) (Roughly 5 per regency in Java)				District Officer						
Sub-District (Ketjamatan) (Roughly 4 per district in Java)				Sub-District Officer						
Village (Kelurahan) (15-20 per sub-district in Java)				Lurah (Village head) Pamong Desa (Village officials)						

POPULATION — AT — LARGE

prises. The many officers concerned continued to be addressed by their titles of rank and maintained close relationship with local army commanders, calling on support from them—and usually obtaining it—when they saw their positions challenged by civilian managers.)

Even though army power was not materially affected by reductions in the martial law level, army leaders did feel threatened by such changes, and particularly by the possibility that the President might succeed in eliminating martial law altogether once the PRRI rebellion had been ended. They saw it as most important for the army's morale, cohesion, and good name that some sort of legal or moral basis should seem to underlie its exercise of power in civilian affairs, and therefore they created a series of doctrines and organizational structures to provide such a basis.

In 1957, soon after President Sukarno had established the principle of functional representation, the army leaders took over this idea and set up a series of Cooperation Bodies—the Body for Cooperation between the Army and Youth, the Body for Cooperation between the Army and Labor, and so on.[18] Thus the mass organizations oriented about the major political parties were brought together under military auspices, with army officers given scope for both control over the separate organizations and the channeling of their joint activities. Subsequently, the various Cooperation Bodies were united in an army-led National Front for the Liberation of West Irian (FNPIB). This organization was later attacked by the President,[19] who supplanted it in mid-1960 with a National Front

NOTE ON A Simplified Picture of the Administrative Structure

The horizontal lines represent the effect on administrative authority of the introduction of martial law in March 1957 (as reorganized in December 1959). Broadly speaking, martial law makes it possible for the military commander in a particular area to exercise powers otherwise held by his counterpart in the hierarchy of the Department of the Interior. The extent to which he may exercise these civilian powers depends on the level of martial law existing in the area, being greatest in areas under a "state of war," less in areas under a "state of military emergency," and less again in areas under a "state of civil emergency."

This chart leaves out of account the special relationships created where autonomous powers are exercised by governmental organs at the province and regency or municipality level.

The parallels between army organization and civilian administrative organization are not as close as this chart suggests. Thus, there are only sixteen military districts, as compared with twenty first-level autonomous regions; similar discrepancies exist at lower levels.

of his own. The army, however, was not to be so easily foiled in its claim to leadership of the functional groups: in 1961 its leaders established a new Body to Develop the Potential of the Functional Groups (Badan Pembina Potensi Karja) to replace both the FNPIB and its constituent Cooperation Bodies. Nine months earlier they had strengthened their claim to a legitimate political role, as distinct from a governmental one, by securing army representation in parliament.

Similarly, army leaders have been active for a number of years in propounding a doctrine of territorial warfare—a form of defense in which military and political functions are merged, and the whole civilian population is involved under the leadership of the army. In March 1961 the army established a new Inspectorate for Territorial Operations and People's Defense, and this Inspectorate has provided numerous groups of pamong pradja officers, public prosecutors, students, and youth generally with short periods of military training and indoctrination. Training of this kind was intensified, particularly at the end of 1961, with the onset of a new phase of tension on the issue of West New Guinea and a subsequent series of moves in the direction of general mobilization. The army's claims to civilian powers have been buttressed in all of these ways, as they have been by repeated military emphasis on the army's dominant role in the revolution, and by the great attention given to celebrations of heroes' days, to graveyard ceremonies, and to the work of the army's Military History Service.

Most, if not all of these new doctrines and organizational arrangements have been initiated by army men in an effort to ward off presidential threats to the powers they hold over government and politics. In considering them, however, we should not fail to note that there have been important points in these activities where the interests of the President and the army have converged—notably in the stress on the revolution and the "spirit of 1945," and in the creation of a sense of crisis over West Irian.

Sukarno, the Army, and the Communists

It has been on the Communist issue that the army and the President have disagreed most frequently and persistently in the present period. This is partly a matter of differences of ideological orientation, divergencies which also reflect the ideological positions of the groups which have sought to have political representation through the army and the President respectively. Secondly, it results from a difference of time perspective between the two partners. The President is concerned primarily with the pattern of power in his lifetime—he was born in 1901—and probably believes that the Communists will not constitute a threat to the to the regime as long as he lives. The army leaders on the other hand, being mainly men in their forties, and pressed by their subordinates to consider the long-term interests of the army as an organization, tend to see the Communists as a major future challenge—to themselves, the army, and the regime.

Furthermore, Sukarno has needed the Communists' support to maintain his own power in the post-1958 situation. In all this period the President has had very little organized power at his disposal. He does have effective personal control over the organizational apparatus of a number of ministries, notably Information and Education. However, his power over armed units has always been small and has fallen in the course of these years: in 1958 there were a number of territorial commanders who sided with the President on some of the issues between him and the army leaders, but they had all been removed from their posts by 1961.[20] Sukarno had enjoyed his greatest military strength in the air force, but there has been a marked decline in his influence on its leadership, particularly since Air Vice-Marshal Omar Dhani replaced Air Marshal Suryadarma as its chief in January 1962.

Sukarno, having no party of his own, has little organized political support. Whatever hopes he has held for a monolithic state party have thus far remained unrealized. He did succeed in establishing a National Front in 1960; but, needing the existing parties as a political counterweight to the army, he was obliged to make so many concessions to them as constituent members of the Front that it emerged as little more than a loose confederation of government-supporting groups. Indeed, there is some doubt about whether the President ever wanted to establish a cohesive state party; the risk was always there that such an organization would be taken over by the army.

Lacking organized power, Sukarno is in permanent danger of becoming more dependent on the army than it is on him unless he can balance various other groups against it. Thus he has frequently sought the support of a whole range of political parties, notably the PNI, NU, and PKI. What is particularly important for the Sukarno-army relationship is that the President has persistently attempted to accord the Communists a status equal to that of the PNI and Nahdatul Ulama, and has restrained a number of army efforts to restrict the PKI's activities. The point here is not that Sukarno is pro-Communist; that would be a half-truth at best. It is rather that he depends on the PKI—as the largest party by electoral measurement, the only one with elaborate organizational machinery among villagers and the urban lower classes, and the one best capable of speedily providing him with a mass rally to address—to help him maintain his bargaining position vis-à-vis the army. This dependence is mutual. Experiencing repeated army efforts to restrict its freedom, and afraid of a major act of repression, the Communist party badly needs the President's shielding influence. Thus the PKI is not only a powerful ally of Sukarno, but it is also the most reliable, because of its great fear of the army.

It was in the middle of 1958 that the President made his first efforts to protect the Communists against too much army restriction on their activities. The contest became particularly intense in 1959, when army leaders tried to prevent the PKI from holding its sixth congress. They forced the party to postpone it several times, but eventually it was held, largely as a result of presidential pressure, and Sukarno himself addressed it with words of warm sympathy.

The Communist issue became particularly acute in the middle of 1960. On July 8, one year after a cabinet headed by the President had entered office, the PKI's Politburo issued a statement in which the government and a number of its leaders and policies were subjected to trenchant criticism. The President-Prime Minister received only praise, but the army was charged with making no serious attempt to crush the PRRI rebels; Foreign Minister Subandrio was condemned for exacerbating Indonesian-Chinese relations and for pursuing a policy of "needing imperialism rather than combating it"; Labor Minister Ahem Erningpradja was attacked for not defending the interest of the workers; and so on.

The army's response to this surprisingly forthright expression of opinion was vigorous. Reproduction of the statement was forbidden, all members of the Politburo were summoned to an interrogation; and in August the military commanders of the three strongly Moslem areas of South Borneo, South-Southeast Celebes, and South Sumatra-Djambi banned all Communist activity in their areas, and arrested a number of PKI party and mass organization leaders. This was followed by a protracted struggle between the army and the President, with the latter striving for a revocation of these bans. A temporary compromise arrangement made the activities of all parties temporarily illegal, and eventually in December 1960 and August 1961 the bans were lifted; but Communist activity continues to be heavily restricted in all the "Three Souths," as well as a number of other regions.

In late 1960, early and mid-1961, and early 1962 Sukarno repeated his previous efforts to have Communists brought into the cabinet, this time under the slogan NASAKOM (Unity of Nationalists, Religious People, and Communists). The President seemed interested particularly in having the Communists take the Finance portfolio, presumably in order to have them share blame for economic deterioration. These efforts were persistently opposed by the army; however, in March 1962 the party's Chairman, D. N. Aidit, and First Deputy Chairman M. H. Lukman were given quasi-cabinet status, being included in the newly formed State Leadership Consultative Body along with the President, First Minister Djuanda, eight deputy first ministers, and the heads and deputy heads of four high councils of state.[21] On all these matters there was marked conflict between the President on the one hand and the army leaders on the other. But when one looks at what has happened to the Communists as a result of Sukarno-army policies since 1958, one is forcibly reminded that this was a conflict between partners in power and not the rivalry of a group in control with one that was not.

A cursory glance at the position of the Communists in 1962 might suggest that they have fared very well. The party saw its old archenemies, Masjumi and the Socialist party, banned in 1960, and was itself spared. Claimed membership has risen markedly in both the PKI itself, which is now the largest Communist party outside the Sino-Soviet bloc, and in its labor, peasant, women's, and youth organization. At a time when other parties have done little more than keep a minimal organizational structure intact, the Communists have put hundreds of thousands of their members through training courses and have extended their indoctrination efforts to the general public. Close sympathizers of the party are now deputy governors of Central Java, West Java, and Djakarta; and party members are mayors of important cities and towns. Furthermore, the party is well represented on such high-status bodies as the Supreme Advisory Council, the National Planning Council, and since March 1962 on a new body, the State Leadership Consultative Body.

However, these gains—if they are indeed gains—have been heavily outweighed by the losses the party has sustained.[22] In order to remain a legal party, the PKI has had to write the Pantja Sila into its program, and to use such slogans as "National Interests above Class Interests." With the Damocles sword of banning hanging over their heads, the party's leaders have had to become active campaigners for the state ideology of President Sukarno, and their daily newspaper has been virtually forced to refrain from criticism of the government. The party itself has had to hand over a list of its members to the government. Its veterans' organization has been merged into an army-led Veterans' Legion, its boy scout organization into the government's Pramuka. Strikes are banned virtually everywhere, despite the serious decline in real wages in recent years. Much of the party's organization is under the indirect surveillance of the army; public meetings are rare and require army permission; and arrests of scores of Communists and Communist sympathizers are not uncommon in the provinces. As for the influence of Communist sympathizers in the officer corps, this has been reduced steadily since 1958 and is now believed to be slight. Almost all of the party's directly political periodicals have been banned since late in 1960, and its daily survives with a reduced newsprint allocation. Where its members and sympathizers sit in the appointed parliament and regional assemblies, or serve as mayors, deputy governors, or members of one or another high-level council, the PKI has usually gained responsibility without power; holding such posts has not helped the party to gain a significant foothold in the bureaucracy. On the other hand, there is evidence that some of the PKI persons concerned have had their revolutionary ardor cooled by occupying positions of high status.[23]

Thus the PKI is probably further from power in 1962 than it was in 1958—notwithstanding the rapid economic decline of the intervening years and the considerable volume of Soviet-bloc aid extended to the government. The party has indeed trained a large number of its two million claimed members, but its training has been for action within a moderate National United Front strategy, and it is doubtful whether the party now has any significant number of trained militants, even the few thousand who would be needed for a Bolshevik-type seizure of power. By its policy of support for President Sukarno, the party has saved itself from being banned, but it has paid for this freedom by accepting considerable emasculation.

Alternatively, it has been suggested that the PKI is "building up its prestige as the only solid, purposeful, disciplined, well-organized, capable political force in the country, a force to which Indonesia will turn in despair when all other possible solutions have failed"; and that it has a distinct chance of coming to power peacefully by appearing as "a tower of strength amid chaos."[24] However, despite the rhetoric of Guided Democracy (for instance NASAKOM—Unity of Nationalists, Religious People, and Communists), the Communists continue to be regarded as outsiders by almost all members of the political elite. It is true that the PKI's good organization, its freedom from evident clique conflict, its members' moral discipline and dedication to the task, and its popularity among peasants, workers, artisans, petty traders, and teachers are remarkable and widely admired. It seems highly improbable, however, that such admiration alone could bring the party to power; the latter could happen only if international or other developments induced a major loss of the will to power on the part of the ruling groups of the present period.

By 1960 there was evidently pressure from inside the party for abandonment of the pro-Sukarno strategy, for Sakirman, a member of the PKI Politburo of the party, found it necessary to reassure members who were asking whether Guided Democracy was not in fact "a semi-fascist political and economic system more criminal than liberal democracy."[25] By that time, however, a switch to a more militant strategy had been made immensely difficult by the growth of army power, and this was borne out by the vigorous response of the army to the criticisms which the PKI made of the Sukarno cabinet on July 8, 1960. Pointing to this response, Aidit and his intraparty supporters were able to argue that a more militant strategy would result in immediate repression of the party.

The pro-Sukarno strategy remains operative at the time of writing. It may well be true, as some observers have thought, that Aidit and his supporters are finding it increasingly difficult to defend it, and that a switch to something like a Yenan or "liberated area" strategy is in the offing. It is a plausible suggestion that Aidit's friendly gestures to Peking on Moscow-Peking issues—notably his sympathetic attitudes toward Stalin and Albania, expressed most articulately in late 1961[26]—may be concessions which he feels obliged to make to his left-wing intraparty critics, reportedly led by Lukman and Sudisman. One purpose of the continuing efforts of the President to bring the PKI into the cabinet may well be to deprive these critics of some of the force of their argument.

However this may be, it is clear that the PKI faces a devil-or-deep-sea choice as long as the over-all political situation remains as it is. It seems to be unprepared for a revolt, and thus is as unlikely to gain from a left-wing strategy (except perhaps in the long run) as from the current pro-Sukarno one. Moreover, its leaders fear the day when President Sukarno is no longer in the political arena. They might then be severely repressed or perhaps driven into rebellion at a moment of the army leaders' choosing. Alternatively, they might agree to enter some sort of association with the transformed regime; but they are unlikely to come to power early in either event, unless strongly aided by developments outside Indonesia's borders. Their principal source of hope would seem to be that "something might turn up" if they wait long enough and maintain their cohesion and *élan*.

It would appear that the army and Sukarno together have achieved a feat which neither of them could have wrought singly: they have lowered the boom on the PKI by degrees, with the President's partial protection serving at every point to weaken the influence of those elements in the party who advocate a break with the regime, and so making it unnecessary for the government to deal with a Communist revolt. The army's major demands have been met for the Communists are under close control. To the extent that the party has been weakened, the President has lost a part of his power leverage, but he is still able to use the PKI to gain concessions from the army.

The "Pro-Western Groups": The Anomalies of Pariahdom[27]

The position of the Masjumi and the Socialist party has been another source of conflict between the army and President Sukarno. The President has made repeated bitter attacks on these parties, linking them not only with "free fight liberalism," cosmopolitanism, intellectualism, and religious fanaticism, but also and more concretely with the PRRI rebellion, the Dutch, and the imperialists in general. The army heads, on the other hand, have been inclined to see the two parties as anti-Communist organizations which are best not destroyed unless and until the PKI—or better still all political parties—have been demolished. In fact, army disunity has been marked on this question: some officers, especially in certain of the regional commands, have sympathized actively with the Masjumi and the Socialists, and have employed individuals from these parties as their political assistants. Others have been strongly antagonistic to them because of their pro-Western orientation or their role in the rebellion, and have urged that the army dissociate itself from them completely. By and large, however, the Masjumi and PSI have usually been able to count on a degree of sympathy and protection from the military.

This source of conflict was clearly to the fore in 1960, when there developed strong resistance from parliament—the legislature elected in 1955—to the government's budget proposals. In March, therefore, the President suspended this parliament, and declared that he would replace it with a new, appointed *gotong rojong* (mutual aid) parliament. This body would not include Masjumi or PSI representatives or representatives of the small but army-connected IPKI (League of Upholders of Indonesian Independence); and half of its members would speak not for parties but for functional groups.

These intentions aroused widespread consternation among the parties, and shortly after they were announced some leaders of the Masjumi, the Socialists, IPKI, and the two Christian parties joined together to form the Democratic League (Liga Demokrasi), an organization which declared it would oppose the idea of the gotong rojong parliament and fight the influence of the Communists. During the President's absence on a foreign tour, the League grew rapidly, with branches springing up in a number of regions, and with various PNI and NU leaders becoming actively involved. Hatta, who had been almost silent on political issues for two years, now gave the movement indirect support with an article on "Our Democracy."[28]

The army was divided and uncertain in its response to the League. Several army leaders in Djakarta, and officers in a number of the provinces, gave it visible support despite its openly anti-Sukarno character. Similarly, it was army resistance which prevented the execution of an order sent by the President from overseas for the jailing of various League leaders. Indeed, it was chiefly army support which made the League into the important organization which it momentarily was.

Nonetheless, the army's heads remained cautious. Some of the League's leaders attempted to persuade them to take power out of the President's hands while he was overseas; but in this they were rebuffed. When the President returned home in June, army support for the League fell away fast. The gotong rojong parliament was sworn in in the same month, with only minor modifications of the plans Sukarno had announced for its composition (see Table 1). Thereafter, it seems, the army leaders made no major effort to protect the Masjumi and PSI. In August 1960 these two parties were banned on the grounds that they had failed to take a sufficiently strong stand against the rebellion; there were army attempts to have this matched by a similar ban on the PKI, but these were unavailing. In January 1962 most of the top leaders of the Masjumi and PSI were placed under arrest. Formally, at least, Sukarno was the winner in his tussles with the army on the role of these two groups.

Concerning the PRRI rebels, too, there has been intermittent tension between the President and the army. Most of the army leaders urged a negotiated settlement with the rebels soon after they had taken their towns and reduced the challenge to guerrilla proportions. This attitude reflected the officers' search for anti-Communist allies, and, more particularly perhaps, their concern to erase the "rebel sympathizer" stigma which attached to such anti-Communist groups as the Masjumi and PSI as long as the rebellion lasted. In addition, it reflected the friendly feeling which existed inside the officer corps toward many of the rebel camp's officers—old colleagues like Simbolon, Husein, and Kawilarang—who were seen as men of good will who had already paid heavily enough for their political errors. The civil war had, in fact, been characterized throughout by an extraordinary absence of ruthlessness on either side, resulting in part from feelings of affinity between the two officer groups involved.[29]

It is true that the army leaders were not of one mind on the matter of negotiation with the PRRI, and some saw a possible end to the rebellion as a threat to the army's title to civilian powers; however, there was a widespread inclination at least to see what the rebels would settle for. Thus, in the second half of 1958 and on several occasions in 1959, army envoys held secret discussions with rebel representatives in Singapore, Hong Kong, and Geneva. These negotiations were held in the face of presidential opposition, however, and this was one reason for their failure to arrive at a mutually acceptable formula of settlement. It was clearly of advantage to Sukarno that the PRRI men, as a group of his strongest opponents, should not be given an easy reprieve from rebel status; and that past association with these men should continue to discredit his other opponents, the Masjumi and the Socialists. Thus the President repeatedly insisted that the rebels could be rehabilitated only if they surrendered first.

Table 1. PARTIES AND PARLIAMENTARY REPRESENTATION: MARCH 1951, AUGUST 1956, JULY 1960

Parties, Associations, Functional Groups	March 1951[a]	August 1956[b]	July 1960[c]
Masjumi (Consultative Council of Indonesian Moslems)	49	57	....
PNI (Indonesian National Party)	36	57	44
PSI (Indonesian Socialist Party)	17	5	....
PIR (Greater Indonesia Association Party)	17	2	....
PKI (Indonesian Communist Party)	13	32	30
Fraksi Demokrat (Democratic Faction)	13	....	....
PRN (National People's Party)	10	2	....
Partai Katholik (Catholic Party)	9	7	5
Parindra (Greater Indonesia Party)	8	....	....
Partai Buruh (Labor Party)	7	2	....
PSII (Islamic Association Party of Indonesia)	5	8	5
Parkindo (Indonesian Christian Party)	5	8	6
Partai Murba (Proletariat Party)	4	2	1
Nahdatul Ulama (Association of Islamic Scholars)		45	36
Perti (Islamic Educational Movement Party)		4	2
IPKI (League of Upholders of Indonesian Independence)		4	....
Army (functional group)			15
Navy (functional group)			7
Air Force (functional group)			7
Police (functional group)			5
Workers (functional group)			26
Peasants (functional group)			25
Islamic authorities (functional group)			24
Youth (functional group)			9
Women (functional group)			8
Intellectuals and educators (functional group)			5
Not classified	26	....	....
Others	13	25	23
Total	232	260	283

(a) Adapted from Miriam S. Budiardjo, "Evolution toward Parliamentary Government in Indonesia: Parties and Parliament" (M.A. thesis, Georgetown University, 1955).

(b) Adapted from Parlaungan, *Hasil Rakjat Memilih Tokoh-Tokoh Parlemen* [Parliamentary Figures Elected by the People] (Djakarta, Gita, 1956), p. 34.

(c) Adapted from Biro Pusat Statistik, *Statistical Pocketbook of Indonesia 1960* (Djakarta, 1960), p. 38.

The army leaders, however, did not abandon their approach, and in early 1961 they entered a series of negotiations which finally led to the rebellion's ending. By that time the rebels were markedly weaker than before; their ammunition supplies were being exhausted rapidly, and they were finding it increasingly difficult both to obtain munitions overseas and to transport them to Sumatra or Celebes. Moreover, disunity in their ranks had reached serious proportions, contributing to demoralization. Thus, when one large group of PRRI rebels in North Celebes retired from the field between February and April 1961, a chain reaction was started, and one batch of rebels after another reported to government posts. By October of that year almost all of the PRRI's leaders and adherents had reported back, in addition to the men of two much older rebellions with which the PRRI had become allied— the Kahar Muzakar rebellion of South Celebes, dating back to 1950, and the Atjehnese Islamic rebellion which had broken out in 1953. Some 100,000 men, with approximately 20,000 weapons, accordingly abandoned the path of rebellion.

The rebels were not said to be "surrendering"; they were "returning to the fold of the Republic." In officially unadmitted fact, they returned on the basis of terms which each group of them had managed to obtain in negotiations with the army. Thus over 8,000 rebel soldiers, mainly from North Celebes, were sent to Java for retraining and reindoctrination, with the understanding that most of them would thereafter gain inclusion in the army. A number of former civil servants who had joined the rebel cause were reinstated, and rehabilitation payments were given to many of those not given government employment. Men who had been arrested and convicted in connection with the rebellion were released, and the returning rebel leaders did not have charges laid against them.

These terms appeared excessively lenient to President Sukarno, however. The President was particularly angered by several acts of settlement which the army leaders had negotiated while he was overseas, and there was a high degree of tension in Djakarta as a result. The President was able to insist that many of the returning rebel leaders should take a vow of loyalty to himself as Great Leader of the Revolution, as well as to the Republic, the Constitution, and the Political Manifesto he had proclaimed in 1959. In addition, he issued a set of secret regulations placing the rebels in "political quarantine" and barring them from employment in the army, civil service, and state enterprises. Early in 1962 most of the rebel leaders were brought to various parts of Java and the civilians among them were placed under *de facto* city arrest.

The army was certainly the principal victor from the ending of the rebellion. It gained prestige; and it gained the freedom to concentrate troops elsewhere—in the Darul Islam areas of West Java, in the islands facing West Irian, or the areas of Java where a Communist rebellion could break out. Moreover, its bargaining position vis-à-vis the President was enhanced. However, the rebels' return was less an army victory gained at the President's expense than a victory of the Sukarno-army regime as such—a triumph all the more significant for the fact that it occurred in a period of economic decline. With the elimination of the PRRI challenge and the Moslem rebel challenge in Atjeh and South Celebes, security was restored to virtually all parts of the country except the Darul Islam areas of western Java.[30] Moreover, with the dissolution of the countergovernment, a process of reorientation was begun on the part of those who had not previously accepted the Djakarta government as morally authoritative. Especially among members of the Minangkabau, Mandailing Batak, and Toba Batak ethnic groups of Sumatra, and among the Minahassans of North Celebes—the groups which had provided the rebellion with most of its leadership and support—there was a strengthening of loyalties to the current regime, or at least an increased determination to press demands within rather than outside its framework.

Thus, although there has been conflict between the President and the army on the role to be given to the Masjumi, PSI, and PRRI, this conflict has not weakened the Sukarno-army regime as such. On the contrary, it seems that in this, as in the matter of the Communists, the regime has been all the more effective in warding off challengers because of its coalition character. Just as Sukarno has provided the Communists with enough protection and status rewards to ward off the possibility of their going into rebellion rather than see their power greatly reduced, so the army leaders have succeeded, by a combination of military effectiveness and political generosity, in ending a rebellion of pro-Western elements. They have done this, moreover, at the same time the principal pro-Western political parties have been banned. Acting separately, but in the interests of their shared power position, Sukarno and the army have been all the better capable of dividing the actual and potential challengers to their regime into "moderates" to be absorbed and "extremists" to be isolated and neutralized.

Comparisons between the "pro-Western groups" position and that of the Communists are fraught with irony, however; for to assess the power of the pro-Western groups from their formal position, from the fact that the Masjumi and PSI have been banned and the PRRI dissolved, is to underrate them as much as one overrates the Communists from looking at their formal place of honor. To some extent, of course, loss of legal status has hurt the Masjumi and PSI. Many of their leaders are seen as political pariahs, and it is unlikely that they could again lead an open challenge to the government in the manner of the Democratic League. Many of their members in the civil service have been "retooled"— pensioned off, demoted, or taken from line posts to staff posts. A number of their activists, especially in Djakarta, have turned from politics embittered, often as much at the army as at the President, and now devote themselves to religious or mystical pursuits, to study or painting, chicken farming or fruit growing, stamp collecting, children, or gambling. The two groups' illegal publications are few and infrequent.

However, Masjumi and PSI men continue to have influential positions as army advisers and as political assistants in a number of regions; and former PRRI men play a similar role more informally. Masjumi influence continues to be great in the Islamic community; and PSI analysis of society and politics are accepted widely among intellectuals, both inside the government camp and out. Socially, there are numerous ties binding Masjumi and particularly PSI leaders to those in power. Largely because of these social ties, there is only a very blurred line between many of those in the regime and the Masjumi, PSI, and PRRI men outside it. The efforts of the President to sharpen this line have been distinctly less successful than the army leaders' efforts to draw one between the members of the regime and the Communists. Although the constitutional position of the PKI and pro-Western groups would suggest the very opposite, it is probable that the latter are considerably closer to future power—in the sense of participating in government decisions, though not of controlling them—than are the Communists, who lack their social ties to the ruling elite.

Political Aspects of Anti-Sinicism

The role of the Sukarno-army conflict in expressing conflict between social groups is exemplified particularly well in the development of anti-Chinese politics. Conflict over the position of the Indonesian Chinese came to a head in the second half of 1959 and early 1960 in connection with the implementation of Regulation 10 (1959), which banned aliens (noncitizen Chinese, Indians, Arabs, and so on) from owning retail businesses in rural areas. The effect of this and related regulations on the Chinese and the economy are discussed in chapters 3 and 5, but it is important to see them also from the point of view of political sponsorship.

While anti-Chinese feeling is widespread in Indonesian society, it is most marked among Indonesian business groups determined to expand at the expense of the Chinese, and in ethnic communities like the Minangkabau and Sundanese where business elements play a major role. Many of these entrepreneurial groups and communities adhere strongly to Islam, which provides a business ethic and often also a rationale for hostility to the Chinese, who are seen as heathens, pork eaters, and tools of the Communists. It is not surprising therefore that Regulation 10 was the work of a minister of the Nahdatul Ulama, or that it was in West Java, the area of the Sundanese, that the regulation was carried into effect most thoroughly and unmercifully.

It is by no means easy to trace the course of intragovernmental controversy on the matter of implementing Regulation 10; however, it is clear that tension was considerable between groups demanding a tough anti-Chinese position and others arguing for restraint. The hard 'approach was advanced most actively by the army leaders in West Java, and it seems that they had considerable support from within the general staff, as well as the enthusiastic backing of Masjumi, NU, and some PSI newspapers. What exactly the men of the tough school wanted to achieve is unclear—although one gets hints of it from a West Java army regulation barring aliens from residence (as well as trade) in rural areas, and from a proposal presented to the Indonesian Youth Front congress of February 1960 that the principles of Regulation 10 should be extended to towns and cities. There was strong opposition to these more far-reaching proposals; and it came not only from the Communists and a part of the PNI, but also and most decisively from President Sukarno. Assessments differ as to whether he acted primarily in response to the very heavy diplomatic pressure exerted from Peking, for fear of the economic consequences of wholesale expulsions, or to put an end to a situation in which his domestic rivals had the initiative on a popular antiforeign issue; however, it is evident that his intervention was of major importance in preventing the anti-Chinese campaign from assuming much larger proportions than it did.

Foreign Policy: An Area of Tacit Agreement

It is difficult to speak of the period since 1958 as an entity in Indonesian foreign affairs, for much of the country's recent posture in foreign relations dates back well beyond that year. The idea of an independent foreign policy was evolved gradually in the years of revolutionary warfare, when the leaders of the Republic, seeing the world being divided into two mutually hostile groups of nations, responded with repeated declarations that Indonesia would remain outside each of these blocs. By 1950 the symbol of an independent foreign policy was an integral part of Indonesian nationalism; but in the early years of the decade this independence was mildly expressed, involving no assumption of militantly anti-American or anti-Dutch positions and no attempt to act out hero roles on the international stage.[31] Indonesia repeatedly rebuffed United States efforts to align it militarily against the Communist states, and in 1952 the Sukiman cabinet was brought down largely because it had agreed to accept American military aid on ideologically unpalatable conditions. In most of its external relations, however, Indonesia acted as a state in the American sphere of influence. Having obtained full independence on the basis of the largely American-steered Round Table Conference, the new state sent an ambassador to Washington in 1950; it was to appoint them to Peking and Moscow only in 1953 and 1954.

After 1953, relations with countries of the Communist bloc became much closer. Trade with these countries, until then virtually nonexistent, grew rapidly, and there were numerous indications of a new political cordiality, particularly with China. After 1953, moreover, Indonesian cabinets were more active and militant in pursuing foreign policy objectives; their vigorous efforts to establish Indonesia as a leader of the world's anticolonialist forces came to a head in 1955 with the holding of the Bandung Asian-African Conference. Indonesia's claim to West Irian was asserted more and more vociferously in these years, and governments tended to associate themselves with radical nationalist feeling rather than to restrain it, as had their predecessors of 1949-53. Western businessmen operating in Indonesia found the political climate increasingly unsympathetic. In 1956 Indonesia abrogated agreements it had made with the Netherlands at the time of the Round Table Conference, and subsequently repudiated the Netherlands Indies government debts it had assumed with the transfer of sovereignty. The next and biggest step came in December 1957 when Dutch enterprises were seized and the last large group of Dutch citizens left Indonesia.

Between 1958 and 1961 a principal purpose of Indonesian diplomacy was to counter the overseas activities of the PRRI rebels. Efforts were made to persuade neighboring Southeast Asian governments to expel PRRI agents from their countries and to prevent them from shipping supplies to rebel-held areas of Indonesia. However, probably the biggest single focus of diplomatic activity in the post-1958 period, and particularly since early 1960, has been the struggle for West Irian.[32]

With the seizure of the remaining Dutch businesses in December 1957, Indonesia had played one of its strongest cards in the Irian game; there would be no point thereafter in threatening action against Dutch business. However, the quick successes of the Indonesian army in its actions against the PRRI rebels suggested that military action might provide all or part of an alternative course of action. By early 1960 the Indonesian navy and air force had been greatly strengthened, and the possibility of an invasion of the disputed territory became more real. The Netherlands responded by sending its aircraft carrier Karel Doorman into New Guinea waters, and Indonesian spokesmen declared repeatedly that if a clash occurred the blame would lie with the Dutch. In August 1960 President Sukarno abrogated diplomatic relations with Holland. In late 1960 and early 1961, small armed groups of Indonesians landed in the disputed territory, where they were arrested by the Dutch.

Since about 1958, Netherlands policy within West New Guinea had been increasingly favorable to the growth of representative institutions, and in early 1960 it was announced that elections would be held for a New Guinea Council, which would have a Papuan majority and power to make recommendations on the territory's political future. In early 1961, when the voting took place and Holland made statements suggesting that an independent state might be established about 1970, it became apparent that a markedly anti-Indonesian Papuan nationalism was arising. With Indonesia purchasing a growing quantity of arms from the Soviet

Union—and designating them specifically as means of liberating West Irian[33]—the situation came to look increasingly explosive. It was at this point that the United States took its first major step to intervene in the conflict: it decided to reject a Dutch invitation to attend the ceremonial opening of the New Guinea Council on April 5, 1961.

Both Indonesia and the Netherlands sought support for their positions on the West New Guinea issue at the UN General Assembly of late 1961; but each side failed to gain a two-thirds majority for the resolution submitted on its behalf. Thereafter, the quarrel entered a critical stage. On November 10 President Sukarno openly threatened a military attack on the disputed area; and in early December it seemed that the threat might be carried out, for the President had promised to give his "final command" on December 19. When the December 19 speech was delivered, tension declined: the President's instructions were merely to "defeat the formation of a Dutch-colonial-made Papuan puppet state," to raise the Indonesian flag in West Irian, and to prepare for general mobilization. However, Indonesian political and military spokesmen continued to speak in threatening tones, and more and more civilians, particularly students, were called up for military training. The sense of crisis ran particularly high after January 15, 1962, when Indonesian and Dutch naval vessels fought an engagement off the West New Guinea coast, in which an Indonesian motor torpedo boat was sunk, with a loss of over fifty lives. After a few days it became clear, however, that Indonesia would not take any immediate retaliatory action.

By early 1962 there were signs that the Netherlands might be willing to meet the bulk of Indonesia's demands. The Dutch prime minister declared in early January that his government was willing to negotiate with Indonesia on the West New Guinea issue without stipulating, as it had previously done, that the discussions should be on the basis of self-determination for the people of the area. Shortly thereafter, the Australian government changed its position on the issue, edging away from the word self-determination and declaring that the all-important point was to see that a peaceful solution was found. When Robert Kennedy visited Indonesia and the Netherlands in the following month it became clear that the United States was actively engaged in finding a solution on broadly pro-Indonesian terms. Its efforts seemed close to success in late March, when Indonesian and Dutch negotiators met near Washington in the presence of ex-United States Ambassador Ellsworth Bunker; but Indonesia withdrew from these negotiations after only two days, and landed a new batch of armed infiltrators on the contested island at the same time.

In the months following these negotiations Indonesia seemed to hover uneasily between military and diplomatic courses of action. On the one hand more soldiers were landed in West Irian in a slow-motion invasion by parachute and by sea; in Indonesia itself, the domestic atmosphere was kept tense by repeated declarations of martial intent, air raid training, and the drilling of students and other youths. On the other hand diplomatic channels were used to press for a settlement of the West Irian issue on terms more favorable than those proposed by Ellsworth Bunker. In the end, victory was achieved largely via the diplomatic front: a final series of negotiations, undertaken in the United States with the mediation of Bunker, brought an agreement signed on August 15, 1962 which represented a virtual capitulation by the Dutch. West New Guinea's administration was to be under a United Nations Temporary Executive Authority between October 1, 1962 and May 1, 1963, during which time its functions would be transferred from Dutch to Indonesian officials. Thereafter the territory would be administered by Indonesia, but with the proviso that a plebiscite should be held with UN advice and assistance by 1969 to determine whether or not the inhabitants wished to remain with Indonesia. With the signing of the agreement, Dutch citizens rapidly began to leave West New Guinea, and Indonesia commenced efforts to win the cooperation of the new Papuan elite.

The West Irian campaign was one to which both President Sukarno and the army contributed actively. It helped the President to maintain his image as the leader of the continuing Indonesian revolution. It was also in line with army interests in some important respects, for it provided a rationale for major new purchases of arms (for the army as well as the other services) and for extending the influence of the army among students, youth organizations, and the civilian population in general. To the extent that it channeled dissatisfactions produced by the very high food prices from October 1961 onward, it served the interests of both governmental partners; but this was probably of particular value to the President, as the party more seriously threatened by such dissatisfactions.

Moreover, full as agreement was on the importance of the West Irian campaign, there were major divisions of opinion on what was desirable strategy. In general the army appeared to favor a "clear-cut" solution, either diplomatic or military. For much of 1961 its leaders seemed to stake their hopes on a diplomatic victory gained as a result of United States and other Western pressure on Holland. In the second quarter of 1962 the emphasis changed, with a highly influential group of officers arguing, "Now that our preparations are as far advanced as this, let us fight with all we have and win decisively." President Sukarno on the other hand argued for a "rallying the people" approach. Rather than seek a victory which would seem to be a gift from the imperialists, and rather than run the risks of all-out warfare, he advocated mass rallies, the enlistment of volunteers, and the sending of small numbers of soldiers and volunteers to West Irian—but without the abandonment of diplomatic avenues. As this was the way in which victory finally came, it served to increase his prestige more than the army's.

The dual sponsorship of the West Irian policy, reflected in the combination of diplomatic, agitational, and military efforts toward achieving Indonesia's goal, has not been so apparent in other aspects of foreign affairs. Here one voice has dominated, that of the President; for this is one of those areas which, by the earlier-described silent concordat between Sukarno and the army, has been allotted to one of the partners as his special sphere.

Having close control over much of Indonesia's foreign relations, the President has handled them in a flamboyant and intensely personal way. In the four years since mid-1958 he has made six overseas trips of between two and ten weeks' duration, usually to a large number of countries and almost invariably with a large entourage—including many of the top government leaders, on whom important decisions must wait. One of these trips, to the Summit Conference of Non-Aligned Countries held at Belgrade in September 1961, saw Sukarno emerge as a principal spokesman of the uncommitted world. In the same period seven heads of state and five heads of government have visited Indonesia, as well as vice-presidents, crown princes, numerous foreign ministers and ministers of defense, generals, and admirals. Each of these visitors has received bountiful hospitality, the attentions of a large number of government leaders, and usually cheering crowds—workers being given paid days off by government order.

From many of the President's declarations on cold war issues and many of the positions taken by Foreign Minister Subandrio, it would seem that the country's stance is one of neutralism with a markedly pro-Communist tinge. Indonesia refrained from criticizing China for its Tibetan actions of March-April 1959; it likewise abstained from criticism of the Soviet resumption of nuclear testing in 1961. It has cordial relations with Ho Chi Minh's Vietnam and cool ones with Ngo Dinh Diem's. President Sukarno has been feted lavishly on each of his visits to Moscow and Peking, and in July 1960 he was awarded the Lenin Peace Prize; the following April was officially declared a Peace Month in Indonesia, the celebration of which was in the joint hands of an army officer and the head of Indonesia's PKI-inspired World Peace Committee. Relations with China were seriously disturbed by the 1959-60 crisis over Indonesia's alien Chinese residents, but by 1961 cordiality had been re-established. Throughout these years the Indonesian press has been full of attacks on (Western) imperialism; attacks on Moscow or Peking have been made far more rarely. Its position is summed up in President Sukarno's formulation that the world struggle is one between the "old dying forces" (capitalism and imperialism) and the "new emerging forces" (nationalism and Communism).

The Soviet Union for its part has given Indonesia great quantities of aid, both economic and military, particularly since 1960, and it has supplied the Indonesian forces with up-to-date equipment such as TU-16 long-range bombers, which it has provided to no country in the Soviet-Chinese bloc. Clearly Indonesia plays an important part in Soviet strategy in the Asia-Africa-Latin America area. On the face of it, it would seem that this large and important country, with its unique combination of a large Communist party and a friendly non-Communist government, provides Moscow with an unusually good chance of pulling off a major cold war break-through.

On the other hand Indonesia's trade is still mainly with the West and Japan, from which it continues to receive more economic aid than from the Communist bloc. Its army and navy, and probably also its air force, are controlled by men of anti-Communist orientation, and its military planning is reportedly concerned chiefly with possible threats from China. Furthermore there is no indication that the receipt of large military supplies from the Soviet Union and its European allies has made the Indonesian armed services politically dependent on Moscow or increased the influence of Communists or Communist sympathizers among the officers. The armed forces continue to be a formidable barrier to a PKI assumption of power, and anti-Communist sentiment is strong in the Indonesian political public. As for a drift to Cuba-like dependence on Moscow, this also seems unlikely. A non-PKI government would have little reason or necessity to forfeit the position from which it can obtain aid from Washington as well as Moscow. Unless confronted by a major change in the situation of its neighbors, the present Indonesian regime is, in its cold war posture, likely to remain like Ghana, Guinea, the United Arab Republic, and Iraq, rather than assume the position of Cuba.

Why then has Indonesia taken pro-Communist positions on so many cold war issues? The answer lies partly in the fact that, as a Jacobin, the President is attracted by much of Communist ideology. A man actively concerned about his place in history, he wants to be a Sun Yat-sen, not a Chiang Kai-shek. Moreover, he derives great prestige from tributes paid to him by the leaders of Russia and China—tributes which the West has never matched. Most important of all, his pro-Communist international posture is part and parcel of his domestic political position, and particularly of his mutually protective relationship with the Indonesian Communist party. But whatever the President's beliefs and ideological positions, he represents only one half of the Indonesian government. By virtue of the informal agreement with the army, he has day-to-day control over foreign policy—and particularly over its ideological formulation. However, this control does not extend to decisions which his military partners see as of major importance for Indonesia's future.

As for the Soviet Union, its aims in Indonesia are probably more modest than is sometimes thought. Moscow may indeed have hoped to contribute to the likelihood of an Indonesian-Dutch war. However, its principal goal for the foreseeable future is likely to be to maintain the advantages it now enjoys in Indonesia, rather than to seek new gains. Large-scale Russian military and other aid could thus be interpreted as an attempt to keep President Sukarno in power, and so make sure of a continued flow of friendly words from him, to forestall a major repressive action against the PKI, and to maintain influence vis-à-vis Peking within both the Indonesian government and the Indonesian Communist party.

Looking at the changes which have resulted from almost four years of this tug-of-war relationship between President Sukarno and the army, one finds that they are surprisingly few. The changes wrought in the relationship of these two to the other political forces have been immense, but between the two a balance has been maintained on terms much the same as those struck in mid-1958. Indeed, there has been a tendency for changes in the position of each of the partners to cancel each other out.

On the whole the army appears to have increased its effective unity; it has secured budget allocations, grown in size,[34] and become better equipped and better trained. The general staff's control has been enhanced, with the neutralization of most pockets of Communist influence in the officer corps, and particularly with its increased capacity to replace regional commanders when it wants to. However, four years of sharing hegemony have tended to blunt the army's sense of a separate political purpose. Much of the army's drive to power has become spent as officers have become involved in a host of relatively small political, administrative, and managerial tasks. Material comfort has frequently mellowed these officers' reforming zeal, and the experience of responsibility has tended to lessen their confidence in the army's capacity to solve the country's problems. Finally, the 1958-62 period has seen the growth of an increasingly vigorous popular dislike of the army, thus making it more and more difficult for the army to bid for top power on the moral claim of championing reform.

Similarly, the President's position has both advanced and regressed. Between 1958 and 1960, in the period when he was building the institutions of Guided Democracy, he evinced a great ability to provide men with something to believe in and hope for; but by the end of 1960 these institutions had all been brought into existence, and from that time on the President's symbols of reassurance grew less and less compelling. In addition, the dissatisfactions resulting from aggravated economic hardship appear to threaten the President's position in that, the army being virtually immovable, demands for immediate and radical change are usually addressed to him and not to the military. On the other hand, it seems that the President is far less widely blamed for the government's economic and administrative shortcomings than is the army: in East and Central Java, at least, it appears to be common for villagers to see Sukarno as a great and good leader whose ill fortune it is to be surrounded by venal and predatory advisers. Moreover, increased importance has come to be attached to President Sukarno's legitimizing capacity as other sources of legitimacy have lost their significance, and particularly as routine has been disorganized and laws and rules have become more and more unreal.

However, despite this tendency for the balance-destroying factors to be counteracted, the Sukarno-army equilibrium remains a tenuous one, marked by unremitting probing. Conflict between the two reached a high point in August 1961, at the time of the PRRI "returns," when the President criticized the army in his Independence Day address,[35] which he interrupted to shout "Sit down, green shirt!" (a term of abuse for the army) at a soldier in the audience. A sense of the instability of the Sukarno-army relationship has been generally shared by Indonesia's political participants and observers. Rumors of impending drastic change have had frequent currency, at least within the small and diminishing group of the politically informed. There have been numerous stories asserting that President Sukarno was mortally ill, that the army would take power and exile or imprison the President, and occasionally that the PKI or some part of it was about to switch or be provoked to rebellion. In March 1960 an air force pilot strafed two of the President's palaces, and a West Java cavalry unit attempted a simultaneous move on Djakarta, apparently aiming to effect some sort of a coup there; in January and May 1962 the President came close to being a victim of assassins. The Sukarno-army balance is not expected to outlive the President; indeed, few men doubt that Sukarno's disappearance would set tremendous changes in motion, and thus assassination attempts, like rumors of illness and impending coups, focus attention on the instability which underlies the balance.

We have observed in our discussion of the Sukarno-army relationship, that a major trend of politics since 1958 has been toward an increase in the power of these two forces vis-à-vis that of Indonesia's other political components. A closely related tendency has been toward strengthening of the scope and intensity of government power exercised over the society as a whole; and it is the evolution and effects of this governmental dominance which we shall examine next.

Toward a New Constitutional Framework

We have seen how government and politics had begun to have a distinctly authoritarian cast by the middle of 1958. By that time parties and parliament had lost most of their earlier authority, civil liberties had come into increasing disrespect, and power seemed to be less in the hands of the Djuanda cabinet than in those of President Sukarno and the army. This whole situation was often described by reference to President Sukarno's symbols of Guided Democracy; but the President himself insisted that Guided Democracy had yet to be achieved, and a great deal of public attention was devoted to the matter of how this should be done.

By that time there was overwhelming support from the political public for the symbol of Guided Democracy; the only group opposing it outright was the Masjumi. The symbol, however, had no exact referent, and every group supporting it tried to endow it with its own ideas of political reform. When Murba party men argued for Guided Democracy, they frequently advocated the establishment of a single state party or national movement. When Communists used the symbol with approval, it was usually with reference to the President's Konsepsi of February 1957 which called for the PKI's inclusion in the cabinet. Army men supporting Guided Democracy coupled this with insistence that the army should do much of the guiding. As for the PNI, the NU, and the Christian parties, their whole emphasis was on minimizing the leadership: "We are for democracy with leadership," they would say, "but not for leadership without democracy."

All of these points of view were presented in the Constituent Assembly, which was to formulate a permanent constitution to replace the provisional one which had governed the Republic since 1950. This body, elected in December 1955 and sitting since November 1956, was regarded by many, however, as politically outdated, a relic of the old "liberal" days. Its numerous sessions had produced agreement on only minor features of a new constitution, and its composition suggested that it would probably be deadlocked on the issue of Islam and the Pantja Sila. Moreover President Sukarno, who had pioneered the whole idea of Guided Democracy and kept the initiative on the matter of giving it clearer shape, was not a member of the Constituent Assembly. All this meant that relatively little attention was granted this body's debates.

The various possible ways of giving form to Guided Democracy were discussed most thoroughly in the closed sessions of the National Council. There the President himself took an active part in debate, and a variety of his ideas were tested and modified by Roeslan Abdulgani, his chief assistant in matters of ideology and political remodeling. The Council's discussions initially ranged widely—over such matters as Indonesian socialism, "over-all national planning," simplification of the party system, and the role to be played by functional groups. In late 1958, however, their focus was gradually narrowed to the matter of an electoral law. Here disagreement centered on the relationship to be established between the parties and the functional groups—workers, peasants, youth, national entrepreneurs, artists, and so on—which the President urged should receive corporate representation in Indonesia's future legislatures. Sukarno, supported by the Murba party, by various radical nationalists of no party affiliation, and by most of the army leaders, argued for the functional groups to have half of the total representation in a new parliament; and the President insisted on a dominant role for the government in drawing up lists of the functional group candidates. The parties on the other hand, and especially the Nahdatul Ulama, wanted to keep functional group representation down to one-third and sought to have a role in selecting the groups' candidates.

The situation was close to deadlock at the beginning of 1959, but on February 20 the government regained the initiative by an entirely new proposal—submitted to it earlier by a conference of military commanders—which urged that Guided Democracy should be implemented by a return to the constitution adopted by the Republic at the time of the outbreak of revolution in 1945.[36] The chief structural feature of this constitution was the provision for a strong executive president who is responsible not to parliament but to a larger and less frequently assembling People's Consultative Assembly. A return to it in 1959 would thus formalize the weakened position of parliament and the increased power of President Sukarno, and at the same time take the President out of his figurehead position and give him direct formal responsibility. In addition the symbolism of the year 1945 was important in connection with the repeated calls then being made by the President for a "return to the spirit of the revolution."

Announcing its proposal for a return to the earlier constitution, the cabinet declared that it would ask the Constituent Assembly to vote for it without amendment. Since this meant asking the Assembly to accept a non-Islamic constitution, it was coupled with a proposal that its adoption should be "with acknowledgment of the Djakarta Charter of June 22, 1945, as an historic document"—a reference to an earlier compromise formula providing for the "sovereignty of the people, with an obligation on adherents of

Islam to follow Islamic law." In addition, the February 20 announcement contained a declaration of intent on the controversial matter of the election law: a National Front representing all political groupings would be established; it would aid the government in endorsing a list of candidates for parliament, half of whom would represent parties and the other half functional groups. Parties would have the right to put up candidates of their own, subject to the provisions of a party simplification law—aimed at reducing the large number of minor parties—which would be passed before the elections. Members of the armed forces would be disenfranchised and their chiefs given the right to name thirty-five members of the legislature.[37]

The months after this announcement were ones of mounting tension. In order to secure passage of the package formula, the government needed a two-thirds majority in the Constituent Assembly. The PKI and PNI campaigned for its adoption, and the Masjumi was clearly opposed; but the position of the Nahdatul Ulama, whose vote was crucial, remained entirely unclear. The President, and to a large extent the army, committed their prestige to the formula; but several of the parties showed a somewhat unanticipated readiness to defend their own power and the NU finally adopted the position that it would oppose the proposal unless the government agreed to have the Djakarta Charter incorporated into the 1945 constitution and not merely acknowledged along with it. The government refused, and when the constitution was voted on in late May and early June, it failed three times, with NU opposition, to gain the necessary majority.

The government's immediate response to this impasse was a decision by Chief of Staff Nasution to ban all political activities for the time being. This was an unexpectedly tough action, and showed the parties how weak their power position actually was. Stronger measures followed: on June 29 President Sukarno returned from a two-month trip abroad, and a week later he dissolved the Constituent Assembly and declared the 1945 constitution operative by decree.

Three days after he had proclaimed the new constitution, the President, in an extraordinary display of speed and determination, announced the creation of a new ten-man Inner Cabinet, headed by himself as Prime Minister and Djuanda as "First Minister," with Nasution assuming the post of Minister for Security and Defense Affairs alongside his position as Army Chief of Staff. At

361

the same time the President named the three service chiefs and several other high functionaries as ministers ex officio, and several days later he named twenty-three junior ministers. In most aspects of political composition this cabinet resembled its predecessor; but the armed services' representation rose from two ministers to eleven, and all ministers were obliged to resign their party affiliations. The cabinet's program was given in the form of three terse and modest points: Food and Clothing for the People, the Restoration of Security, and Continuation of the Struggle against Imperialism.[38]

Before the month was out the President had introduced a whole range of further innovations. High civil servants and senior men in government enterprises were instructed to divest themselves of political party membership. Members of the elected parliament were obliged to take an oath of loyalty to the new constitution if they wanted to keep their seats, and parliament itself was deprived of its rights of inquiry and interpellation. At the same time two new high councils were established, the forty-five-member Supreme Advisory Council (Dewan Pertimbangan Agung, in effect a revamped National Council), headed by Roeslan Abdulgani, and the long-promised National Planning Council (Dewan Perantjang Nasional), with seventy-seven members under the chairmanship of the Murba-sympathizing ideologue Muhammad Yamin. PNI, PKI, and NU were well represented on both of these councils, as were the Murba party and several smaller groups—but not the Masjumi or PSI. The army's earlier ban on political activities was lifted, but mass rallies and demonstrations remained forbidden. The death penalty was decreed for economic sabotage—hoarding, black-marketeering, and corruption.

Carried out to the accompaniment of a whole series of new slogans like "retooling for the future," and symbolic actions like street-cleaning campaigns, these various changes of political structure had something of the character of an ideological *tour de force*. To a large number of civil servants and soldiers at least, it seemed that a new era of governmental vigor and determination had dawned. Some of this new sense of hope was sustained in the weeks after July, as the government continued to act rapidly not only in establishing new symbols and rites, but also in such changes as the complete overhaul of organization and personnel in regional government.

While this new spirit lasted, the parties felt obliged to accept their humiliation in silence. All of them except the Masjumi agreed to support the new constitution, and only a few members of that party resigned their seats in parliament rather than take the new vow. Furthermore, when the overhaul of regional government was announced in early September, it was only the Communists who protested strongly, although all of the parties were seriously hurt. All heads of regions were freed from their earlier responsibility to elected regional councils, and from the need to work with executive assistants elected by and from these councils. Governors, as heads of first-level autonomous regions (roughly equivalent to provinces) were made subject to appointment and removal by the President; second-level regional heads (regents and mayors of large cities) were placed directly under the Minister of the Interior. The parties' influence was further reduced by numerous changes of personnel; many of these new appointees were officials of the pamong pradja corps, and among the others were a number of army officers.[39]

The new atmosphere favorable to the President and the army did not last, however. One development which helped to dissipate it was the action of the army in arresting the Acting Chief Public Prosecutor, Gatot Tarunamihardja, after he had found evidence of high army officers being involved in smuggling and corruption. The President succeeded in freeing Gatot soon thereafter, and in transferring some of the officers involved in the malpractices; but the army heads insisted on the chief prosecutor's dismissal which when obtained resulted in general cynicism about the regeneration of government the 1945 constitution had supposedly brought.

Even more important in shattering the wave of hope and pro-government feeling was the monetary purge of August 25, 1959 (see Chapter 5). When it became clear at the end of the year that even this radical act of surgery had done little to curb the rapid inflation, the government's political prestige fell very low. At that point the parties recovered their resolution, and together began to use the parliamentary forum to attack the cabinet on a number of its economic policies, particularly several aspects of the very large budget it had submitted for 1960.

In response to this counterstroke, the President acted with a decisiveness that left his critics again floundering and acutely aware of their weakness. In March 1960 he dissolved the parliament which had threatened to throw out the budget, endorsed the same budget by decree, and announced that he would establish an appointed gotong rojong (mutual aid) parliament. On June 25 he installed the new legislature, which consisted of 283 members representing political parties (chiefly the PNI, NU, and PKI, and without the Masjumi or PSI), as well as functional groups and the armed forces (see Table 1).

In the following month, President Sukarno issued a decree on party simplification. This set out various ideological tenets to which parties were obliged to assent; it also required all parties to submit membership lists to the government, with 150,000 members in at least 65 regencies being the minimum for continued existence.[40] In August the President named a 58-man Central Board of the new National Front, the composition of which was somewhat similar to that of the gotong rojong parliament, although further on the Sukarno end of the Sukarno-army scale. At the same time, the Masjumi and PSI were declared illegal.

By August 1960 the major battles in this series were over. Thereafter there were no more serious attempts by the President to weaken the parties as such, and no major acts of open resistance by the parties—at least not until March 1962, when electoral legislation was discussed again. This halt in the contest occurred partly because there were no more liberal pieces of constitutional machinery for the President to destroy or the parties to defend. And indeed the formal institutions of Guided Democracy had virtually all come into existence by that time[41] (see chart, The Political Institutions of Guided Democracy). There remained only the establishment of the 616-member People's Consultative Assembly (Madjelis Permusjawaratan Rakjat), formally the highest organ of state under the 1945 constitution, whose appointed interim equivalent was to meet in November 1960.

More important, the President had evidently concluded that he would derive no advantage from a further lessening of the parties' power. Until 1960 he had worked fairly closely with the army in weakening the parties; and it had seemed in the first half of the year that this would lead to the establishment of a strong state party or front with which the existing parties would actually be merged. But some time in the second quarter of 1960 the President decided in favor of a weak National Front, which left the parties organizationally intact; and this was reflected in the composition of the gotong rojong parliament. Sukarno's retreat may have been caused by fear that a strong National Front might come under army control, or simply that it would leave him without the organizationally distinct allies he needed when it came to measuring strength against the army. In any event, after mid-1960, the PNI,

The Political Institutions of Guided Democracy

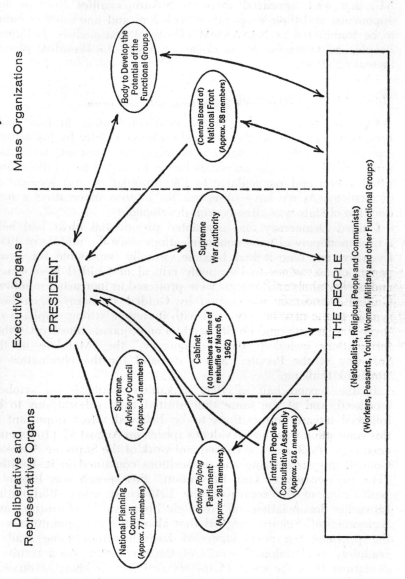

| Deliberative and Representative Organs | Executive Organs | Mass Organizations |

Body to Develop the Potential of the Functional Groups

(Central Board of) National Front (Approx. 58 members)

PRESIDENT

Supreme War Authority

Cabinet (40 members at time of reshuffle of March 6, 1962)

Supreme Advisory Council (Approx. 45 members)

National Planning Council (Approx. 77 members)

Gotong Rojong Parliament (Approx. 281 members)

Interim Peoples Consultative Assembly (Approx. 616 members)

THE PEOPLE
(Nationalists, Religious People and Communists)
(Workers, Peasants, Youth, Women, Military and other Functional Groups)

NU, and PKI appeared more as Sukarno's allies than as his opponents; and their cooperation with him and one another came to be formulated as NASAKOM (Unity of Nationalists, Religious People, and Communists), a slogan on which the President placed increasing stress.

Manipol-USDEK: The Advent of an Ideology

Until the reintroduction of the 1945 constitution in July 1959, President Sukarno kept the political initiative chiefly by his actions and promises directed toward remodeling the constitutional structure; but thereafter the emphasis began to switch to symbolic and ritual action and particularly to the formulation and inculcation of ideology. As we have observed, his interest in creating a new doctrine of state was already well developed.

Guided Democracy and associated presidential ideas had held a near-monopoly of mass communications since the middle of 1958. Even by that time it had become virtually impossible for newspapers or magazines to be openly critical of Guided Democracy, and new symbols and slogans were proffered in increasing numbers. Guided Democracy was joined by Guided Economy—a cardinal symbol in the new battery—and with it came a strong emphasis on "over-all planning" and on the need for an economic blueprint. Other formulations included "work democracy," the "Mandate of the Suffering of the People," and a demand for the elimination of "textbook thinking."

In the second half of 1959, Sukarno's emphasis on symbols increased, and at the same time shifted from exhortations to be followed toward propositions to be believed. Most important in this connection was the President's speech on August 17 (Independence Day) 1959, and the subsequent work of the Supreme Advisory Council in systematizing the propositions contained in it. Entitled "The Rediscovery of Our Revolution," this speech was largely a justification of the return to the 1945 constitution. Elaborating his earlier denunciations of "free-fight liberalism," "reformism," and "compromise," Sukarno argued that all of the disappointments of the previous ten years stemmed basically from some leaders' readiness to abandon the rails of the revolution. As a result of deviations from the spirit of the revolution, four kinds of dualism had arisen to make men hesitant and weak: dualism between leadership of the government and leadership of the revolution, dualism between the just and prosperous society and the society of capitalism, dualism on the question of whether or not the revolution had been completed, and dualism on whether democracy was to serve the people or the people, democracy. But now, with the return to the rails of the revolution, these ambiguities had been decisively set aside, and the crucial step had been taken toward realization of the "just and prosperous society" for which the revolution had been fought. Thenceforth there would be radical renewal in all fields. There would still be difficulties aplenty, but there was now the "mental momentum" by which those could be overcome.[42]

There were in fact few new themes in this speech, but it was important for its connection with the reintroduction of the revolutionary constitution. Three months after he had given it, the President declared its text to be the "Political Manifesto of the Republic," and at the same time he endorsed a set of expository notes on it composed by the Supreme Advisory Council.[43] There thus came into existence a catechism on the basis, aims, and duties of the Indonesian revolution; the social forces of the Indonesian revolution, its nature, future and enemies; and its general program, covering the political, economic, social, mental cultural, and security fields. Early in 1960 the central message of the celebrated speech was stated as consisting of five ideas—the 1945 constitution, Socialism à la Indonesia, Guided Democracy, Guided Economy, and Indonesian Personality—and the first letters of these five phrases were put together to make the acronym USDEK. With "Political Manifesto" shortened to "Manipol," the new creed became known as "Manipol-USDEK."

Manipol-USDEK had genuine appeal to many in the political public.[44] There had long been considerable support in this civil-servant-dominated public for the President's emphasis on all pulling together, on national interests being put above the interests of one's group, and on the possibility of coming to unanimous agreement through patient consultation.[45] This was partly because harmony and solidarity are strongly held values in most Indonesian societies, and partly because Indonesians had become acutely aware of the disruptive effect of the divisions between them in the preceding years. In addition many were attracted by the idea that what Indonesia needed above all was men with the right state of mind, the right spirit, the true patriotic dedication. "Returning to our own national personality" was attractive to many who wanted to withdraw from the challenges of modernity, and also to those who wanted to believe in the current political leadership but were aware of its failures to modernize as fast as such countries as India and Malaya. And for members of some Indonesian communities, notably for many Javanese, there was real meaning in the various complex schemes which the President presented in elaboration of Manipol-USDEK, explaining the peculiar significance and tasks of the current stage of history.

Perhaps the most important appeal of Manipol-USDEK, however, lay in the simple fact that it promised to give men a *pegangan*—something to which to hold fast. They were attracted not so much by the content of this pegangan as by the fact that the President had offered one at a time when the lack of a sense of purpose was sorely felt. Values and cognitive patterns being in flux and in conflict, men looked eagerly for dogmatic and schematic formulations of the political good. One common response to Manipol-USDEK was "it may not be a very good or complete ideology, but an ideology is certainly what we need."

Indoctrination: The Press, Education, and the Civil Service

It was only in some sections of the political public, however, that Manipol-USDEK was sympathetically received; in others there was marked suspicion. Vague as it is, Manipol-USDEK is not an attempt to synthesize all of the main patterns of political orientation in Indonesia, for it contains virtually no element of the political outlook characteristic of organized Islam. It is doubtful whether any state ideology could bridge the gap between the Javanese-aristocratic pole of political orientations and the Islamic-entrepreneurial pole, but certainly Manipol-USDEK does not. Thus many strong Moslems, particularly non-Javanese, saw the new formulation as something foreign to their own ideas.

Manipol-USDEK was therefore imposed, and with a generally increasing measure of constraint. Indeed, it has been the principal justification for efforts at thought control: a large part of the process of such control has come through regulation of the press, under the banner of the Manipol-USDEK formulation that the press must serve as an instrument of the struggle to complete the revolution.

The bridling of newspapers and periodicals has been common practice since the middle of 1958, but press control was markedly intensified in 1960 and 1961. In 1960 newspaper editors were obliged to take vows of acceptance of the state ideology, and several Masjumi- and PSI-sympathizing periodicals had their licenses permanently revoked for refusal to comply. In 1961 the government began a program of coaching journalists in the thought of Manipol-USDEK. Total press circulation had been reduced by that year to an average of 710,000 copies (for 65 dailies) from a 1959 level of 1,039,000 (for 90 dailies).[46]

The character of the Indonesian press was thus radically altered by early 1962. A great number of papers remain, representing many parties and political creeds, but each one is obliged to devote a large part of its four pages to unabridged government declarations, most of them heavily repetitious and dealing with ideology rather than policy. Only very small amounts of space are devoted to news of the world outside Indonesia, and there is little or no printing of news from a journal's own reporters. The rigidity of press censorship varies widely between different cities and towns, depending largely on the attitude of the military authorities in the area concerned, and a greater degree of freedom is allowed in most other cities than in Djakarta. It is relatively easy to break through the censorship barrier by subtle insinuations—in fact efforts to do this, though risky, have become a popular pastime of many intellectuals. Outright criticism of the government is rarely permitted anywhere, however, and there is no direct criticism of its ideological formulations at all. More important still, a great deal of news of importance is simply never found in the press.

Similarly, there has been an intensification of controls over various other sources of information. Late in 1961 all owners of printing presses and duplicating machines were obliged to register them with the government. Bans have been placed on more and more books, both of Indonesian authors and foreign ones, and efforts have been made to restrict the reporting of foreign journalists. However, in most of these fields the difficulties of implementing controls are greater than in the case of the press and periodicals, and in practice many of the regulations have been executed with remarkable patchiness. Thus most owners of banned material make very little effort to hide it, whether it be an economics textbook by the outlawed Professor Sumitro Djojohadikusumo or an issue of *Time* magazine.

It has apparently been fairly easy to introduce Manipol-USDEK into the curricula of primary and junior secondary schools, as it has been to include it in various information and propaganda campaigns designed for the population at large. However, a number of difficulties have been encountered in senior secondary and university education. Senior secondary school students appear to have responded readily to many of the ideology's demands, and most are said to be unresponsive to antigovernment political appeals. But, in the cities at least, very few have enthusiasm for the government's cause, and their political conformism is often combined with an irreverent cultural escapism. Thus they continue to be strongly drawn to rock-and-roll, jitterbugging, and various other banned Hollywood cultural exports which the President has repeatedly denounced as against the Indonesian national personality.

Within the universities Manipol-USDEK has been met by hostility, cynicism, and a great deal of indifference. The ideology appeals to some idealistic students because it has brought a new emphasis on universities involving themselves with the problems of their society, on shorter and more practice-oriented courses, and on students interrupting their education for government work in remote areas. Moreover, a large number of university persons, both faculty members and students, are in general accord with the values to which Manipol-USDEK gives expression. Many others, however, are alienated by these values and resent the President's attacks on "intellectualism," "Dutch thinking," and "textbook thinking" as attacks on their freedom. Moreover, most members of the university community judge the ideology as an intellectual system, and a large number of them hold it in contempt on this count.

In March 1961 the President appointed Iwa Kusumasumantri, a radical nationalist with some Murba and PKI associations, as Minister of Higher Education and Sciences, evidently in an attempt at intensifying his drive to establish Manipol-USDEK in the universities. Acting with speed and determination, Iwa established a series of new controls over students going overseas for study. Each of these would now need to have the minister's personal approval, to swear that he believed in Manipol-USDEK, and promise not to marry overseas. In addition, Iwa made numerous changes in curricula and textbooks, especially in the social sciences. He urged students to report signs of lingering liberalism in their professors, and established new government controls over private and semipublic universities and academies. Most important, he rapidly and unceremoniously dismissed and demoted a number of university presidents, deans, professors, and other teachers largely on the basis of political considerations.

Many of these measures were highly unpopular, and intra-university conflicts were fanned very high. Partly because of this, Iwa incurred the great hostility of the army leaders and so was replaced by a nonpolitical man, an established academic, in the cabinet reshuffle of March 1962. The new minister quickly undid a number of his predecessor's measures, and the drive to impose the state ideology on the universities has thus met with an important defeat. There continues to be a large number of university teachers who are widely known to be tongue-in-cheek in their acceptance of Manipol-USDEK, or to be accepting the ideology with the attachment of private interpretations which are radically different from the government's.

A third major group on which Manipol-USDEK indoctrination has been focused is that of civil servants and employees of state enterprises. In the Political Manifesto speech itself, great stress was placed on "retooling"—the renovation of the leadership of the revolution, all the state agencies, all instruments of production and distribution, and all parties and social and economic organizations. Since then, a large number of high and middle-level civil servants have been "retooled," more or less arbitrarily demoted or pensioned off, in what is in effect a mild but continuing purge. The survivors and new appointees are made acutely aware that their positions depend on active loyalty to the current political leadership and its symbols.

It is against this background that indoctrination programs have been pressed among government employees. Since late in 1960 indoctrination committees have been established in the various departments of the central government and in the capitals of provinces and second-level regions. As a result of the work of these committees, groups of civil servants have been given short-term courses in Manipol-USDEK, in effect being made to study a number of the President's speeches together with reformulations of them by the Supreme Advisory Council and its deputy-chairman (until March 1962), Roeslan Abdulgani. The government servants thus trained have then served as instructors in their own departments, usually giving weekly lectures to their fellow employees. In addition, new vows of a narrowly defined patriotism have been made obligatory for public officials.

In the civil service arena the government's indoctrination program has been fairly successful, meeting with considerably less open opposition than in the universities. At the same time, as in so much of the symbol-imposing process, there has been a tendency for programs to fizzle out imperceptibly when they are no longer new, dramatic, or spectacular and come to be seen as burdensome to administer. Furthermore, in this as in several other areas where indoctrination programs have been established by the President, rival campaigns have been instigated by the army. The military leaders have consistently supported the phrase Manipol-USDEK and many of its ideas; indeed, some of these, and especially the concept of a national pegangan, have come to be held with considerable tenacity by officers and men. (Manipol-USDEK ideology often helps army men to justify their new power and privilege, before themselves as well as others—which does not of course mean that their belief is insincere.) But in speaking to the members of their own force, the army leaders have usually reinterpreted Manipol-USDEK to make it an anti-Communist creed as well as an antiliberal one. Since 1961 they have established indoctrination programs of their own as part of schemes for military training, and thus many students, university graduates, and civil servants of various kinds have been instructed in the army leaders' version of the ideology. In one sense, then, pluralism has crept into the effort to inculcate a single doctrine.

Authoritarian Control: Its Rigors and Laxities

Since 1958 Indonesian government has become increasingly authoritarian and restrictive, and its controls have come to bear heavily on more and more fields of activity. It is extremely difficult, however, to make generalizations about the kind of political system which has evolved as a result. One set of distinctions may be made between the scope of power wielded by the government (how many aspects of the people's activity are affected by its decisions), the weight of its power (how intensely its decisions affect these aspects), and the concentration of its power (how widely the making and implementing of decisions is shared).[47]

It is the scope of power which has grown most spectacularly in the years since 1958. We have seen how government controls have been extended to the press, the publishing and importing of books, and the life of the schools and universities. A similar process has gone on in the area of voluntary organizations. Some of these have been banned—various small religious and mystical sects established in village areas,[48] such urban and internationally linked bodies of small membership as the Rotarians, Freemasons, and Rosicrucians, and the directly political organizations such as Masjumi, PSI, the Democratic League, and a host of smaller parties. Others, like the various veterans' leagues and scouting bodies, have been merged into government-run organizations; and most of the rest—the ten remaining political parties, their affiliated mass organizations, and business, professional, religious, and cultural associations—have been obliged to make declarations of support for the government and its ideology and often to work with the government on particular projects.[49]

Similarly, legal institutions have been deprived of their autonomy. In February 1960 the Chairman of the Supreme Court was made a member of the cabinet, and six months later the President denounced the principle of the separation of powers. In actual practice the administration of justice has come to be an ancillary aspect of the maintenance of government power. Particularly at the national level, but also at others, the decisions of the Prosecutor's Department on whether or not to bring men to trial are heavily influenced by the government's political calculations.

Thus law has become of little importance as a restraint on government action. Legality continues to play an important role in conflicts within the government and its bureaucracy, but the man who is outside them must find political rather than legal means for the redress of his grievances. If he has access to the politico-bureaucratic world he can usually obtain some satisfaction by taking his case up with one of a number of competitive cliques within it. But if he has no such access and is too poor to buy it, he may be helpless before arbitrary official action—whether he is an urban civilian whose house is seized by the army, a Chinese storekeeper whose stocks are stolen by a police-protected gang, a poorly connected professional man framed on a charge of speculation, or a villager in a revolt-torn area who must give his daughter over to a sergeant.

Probably the biggest expansion in the scope of government activity has come in the field of economics. The new economic functions of the state are discussed fully in Chapter 5 and so we shall merely list some of the most important of them here. The biggest single step toward expansion of the government's economic role was taken in December 1957 with the seizure of all remaining Dutch business establishments—the many estates, banks, trading firms, manufacturing establishments, and the interinsular KPM shipping line. Subsequently the government reorganized foreign trade, assuring considerable advantage in both importing and exporting to the state trading firms (most of which had been seized from the Dutch) and radically reducing the role of private traders, both Indonesian and foreign. Indonesian private business was dealt another severe blow by the monetary purge of August 1959, when all bank deposits of over Rp. 25,000 lost 90 per cent of their value.

With the implementation of the ban on aliens in rural retailing, and the consequent exodus of large numbers of Chinese from this and other sectors of the economy, the "national" private business-men recovered somewhat. However, when it became clear that the Chinese exodus was producing widespread dislocation in the distributive trade, the government stepped in again, licensing fixed-price shops for essential commodities, and decreeing controls on prices charged in various other types of transactions—sugar, rubber, and rice sales, hotel, restaurant, and bus services, and so on. Thus there has been a large increase in the scale of the government's own participation in economic life, and an even larger increase in its controlling and regulating activity. Attacks have been made on Western, Chinese, and Indonesian private business, with the result that each of these sectors has been weakened and made more dependent on political and bureaucratic connections.

Government intervention and control are in some measure felt in every field of Indonesian activity. Nonofficial groups continue to exist, but all of them depend on the government in a variety of ways, and the government persists in efforts to absorb and in-corporate them, at least partially. Thus they are repeatedly pre-sented with demands that they acknowledge the government's ideological claims and declare their own activities part of the national cause. They are asked, in effect, to agree that the political values established by the government should override the specific norms of their own areas of activity; and efforts are made to change the distribution of prestige to make it accord more fully with this primacy of political goals.[50] Thus the government condemns and belittles economic activity carried out for its own sake, just as it condemns "art for art's sake," "science for science's sake," and "sport for sport's sake." In its eyes the efficiency of a manufacturer or trader is not proper grounds in itself for social prestige, nor is the professional achievement of the lawyer, the doctor, the scholar, or the painter. Each of these men becomes worthy of respect to the extent that he demonstratively accepts the government's leadership and promises to participate resolutely in "over-all development." The government is by no means entirely successful in this effort to make all prestige a derivative of political power, but it actively maintains the attempt.

When we turn from the scope of power to its weight or intensity of impact, the picture is rather more complex. The government's power is fairly heavy where it is exercised on workers and peasants, groups whose capacity for political defense is usually slight. Strikes have been banned in all "vital enterprises" since August 1957, and this category has grown to the point where strikes are illegal virtually everywhere. With the army inclined to act promptly to jail union leaders violating the strike ban, strikes have in fact been extremely rare since 1958—this despite a trend for real wages to decline.[51]

The degree to which government power impinges on the peasantry is more difficult to establish, and the situation varies greatly between regions. However, it is clear that the government has been taking more from villagers in the present period than it did between 1949 and 1958. Rural taxation may not have risen above its very low pre-1958 levels. But there has been a marked increase in unpaid labor services demanded by local authorities under the slogan of gotong rojong (mutual aid). The government has acted with greater toughness than before 1958 in evicting squatters from estate and forest land, as well as from many urban areas, with a death toll of at least six persons resulting from one clash near Kediri in November 1961. Growers of rice, sugar, tobacco, and other commodities have been made subject to new restrictions or obliged to sell their produce at artificially low prices to government purchasing organizations. In addition efforts are made by subdistrict officers, locally stationed soldiers, information officers, and members of National Front teams to inculcate the government's ideology. However, this indoctrination activity is apparently superficial in most areas. Its effects on village society would seem to be much smaller than the impact of party competition in the years before 1958. On the other hand, the government's impact has grown as a result of schemes, introduced in the post-1958 period,

375

whereby villagers are taken from their agricultural work for a short period of military training.

The weight of these various measures has been relatively light in East and Central Java, where the pamong pradja has generally remained in control of local affairs, and where the army's role is peripheral. Their impact has been notably heavier in West Java and the Outer Islands, and especially in areas afflicted by rebellion. The element of arbitrariness has also tended to be greater in these areas, the villagers having few means of redress against capricious actions by lower-rank military officials. In West Java the army involved villagers heavily in various efforts to destroy the Darul Islam rebel-bandits, and in 1961 it introduced the highly unpopular policy whereby thousands of villagers, armed mostly with no more than bamboo spears, were obliged to form a "fence of legs" around rebel-held mountains. It was in West Java, too, that twenty-six persons died in 1960 as a result of a clash between the army and village members of a new and aggressive religious cult.

The weight of government power has grown and been particularly heavy on traders in the 1958-62 period. Chinese merchants have been hit hardest, but Indonesian businessmen too, all except the best-connected, have had to do business in an atmosphere of extreme uncertainty, have been forced to violate numerous regulations to survive, and are always afraid that their turn might come to fall victim to the Draconic measures periodically taken against hoarders, speculators, black marketeers, and corruptors.

Among civil servants and the employees of government firms the weight of government power is markedly less, but its deprivational consequences are still considerable. The monetary purge of August 1959 brought ruin to many in this community. Inflation has been a major cause of suffering among various groups of salary earners, especially civil servants and employees of state firms. Very many government employees have found compensation for the falling real value of their salaries through corrupt or more or less corrupt dealings—some indeed have found much more than compensation—but numerous others have been unable or unwilling to take part in such practices and have suffered materially as a result.

In addition, civil servants and others in the urban white-collar community have been hit by various more directly political measures. "Retooling" and threats of "retooling" have taken a heavy toll of civil servants' peace of mind, though very few have been deprived of their salaries. Fear has grown as men have denounced their rivals for being "absent during the revolution," "liberal" or "a-national" in their thinking, or "colonial" (routine-bound) in their methods of work. There has been a parallel growth of mistrust, with no member of the civil servant community knowing quite how much sincerity or hypocrisy to attribute to his fellow members' avowed enthusiasm for Manipol-USDEK. Similarly, the decline of public liberties has penalized numerous journalists, writers, and university teachers, who have been unable to write or say what they believe, and in some cases have been forced to perjure themselves to the point of losing self-respect in order to keep their positions.

Nonetheless, the machinery of political control falls far short of totalitarian proportions. Political arrests have been relatively rare and usually for short periods, and until the big arrests of Masjumi and PSI leaders in January 1962 it could be said that only a handful of prominent persons were involved. Several intelligence organizations are active, mails are intermittently and selectively censored, and telephones are occasionally tapped. Many persons outside the government find it difficult to gain permission to travel overseas. But there continues to be a group of city dwellers who discuss political issues in cafés and restaurants. Torture, concentration camps, and "brainwashing" techniques are certainly no part of the government's armory; and whereas Manipol-USDEK is avowedly a creed of enthusiasm, its inculcators are usually content in practice with lip service frequently paid. In the words of the Dutch proverb which is frequently cited in comments on totalitarian-sounding government declarations, "The soup is not eaten as hot as it is cooked."

In programs of political control, as in most other fields of government action, immense discrepancies exist between policy statements, laws, and decrees on the one hand and the government's actual behavior on the other. Such discrepancies have been designated as "formalism,"[52] and the social theorist Fred W. Riggs has argued that they are characteristic of a great range of activity in transitional (posttraditional, preindustrial) societies.[53] In the field of political controls "formalism" often results from the fact that policy declarations are made for the sake of the symbolism concerned, or as a part of a legitimizing ritual, and are not intended to be implemented. In these instances, the government is concerning itself with the responses of persons who judge it for its moral vitality and good intentions rather than on the basis of its

377

performance of policy tasks. The Indonesian government's actions were "formalistic" in this way when it brought in legislation (under the land reform program) providing for a minimum plot size of two hectares in Java—average plot size in Java being well under half that.[54] The same characterization can be made of the government's March 1959 announcement of compulsory military service for all males between eighteen and twenty-three, and of the declaration of Foreign Minister Subandrio in May 1962 that foreign as well as local journalists would thenceforth have to work within the framework of the Political Manifesto.

In other cases the hope may indeed have existed that a particular program could be implemented as announced, but in actual fact it called for degrees of power and administrative efficiency which the government lacked. Taxation policy affords a number of instances of this. Another is the 1960 regulation to reduce the number of *betjaks* or trishaws in Djakarta from approximately 60,000 to 15,000, to limit the betjak drivers to particular parts of the city, and to set prices for particular routes. Efforts to implement this regulation were abandoned soon after they were begun. Thirdly, discrepancies between declared policy and actual implementation may be a product of political antagonisms inside the government and bureaucracy. Here one might cite the example of the President's efforts to bring the universities under the sway of Manipol-USDEK; these efforts were frustrated largely because of army resentment of Minister Iwa's actions. Granted the fact that political antagonisms are so important inside the government, groups seeking to resist particular policies can usually find support and protection from some part of the flaccid colossus.

This brings us, finally, to the matter of the concentration of power. In describing the scope and weight of government power as horizontal and vertical dimensions of its exercise, we have been discussing the output of government decisions. We must, however, also look at these decisions and their implementation from the point of view of input, asking how widely power is shared.

An examination of the legal situation would suggest that power is concentrated to a phenomenally high degree. Under the 1945 constitution President Sukarno is accountable only to the People's Consultative Assembly, a body which need not be elected, and need not meet more than once in five years. To date only an appointed Interim People's Consultative Assembly has ever met. The present parliament is also appointed, and in any event the

President is not accountable to it; moreover, its rules provide that it should legislate by unanimity or, if this proves impossible, refer the particular matter back to the President for a "Regulation to Take the Place of a Law." The government continues to promise general elections at which some proportion of the members of parliament would be chosen by the people, but there are no indications at the time of writing that elections are actually being prepared.

Public liberties receive relatively few references in the constitution. Furthermore, as we have noted, governors and other regional heads are representatives of the President, with responsibility solely to him and none to any regional assembly. Appointed regional assemblies replaced elected ones in 1960 and 1961. Finally, there is even doubt about whether the President is legally required to remain within the framework of the 1945 constitution—which he, after all, reintroduced by decree. Constitutionally Indonesia is now as close to being a perfect autocracy as it was to being a perfect decentralized parliamentary democracy under the constitution of 1950, the electoral legislation of 1953, and the regional autonomy legislation of 1957.

It would, however, be more than folly to draw conclusions about the actual distribution of power from an examination of these legal and constitutional provisions; the situation is clearly "formalistic" in the extreme. As we have seen, President Sukarno has vastly more power over the formulation of government declarations than over the implementation of programs. With regard to the latter he is merely one of two major partners. Indeed, the notion of a Sukarno-army partnership conceals a much more complex pattern of power sharing, for as we have pointed out earlier, the two governmental giants reflect and depend on a broad range of social and political interests. For all the advantages that their organization and near-monopoly of violence gives them in political combat, the army leaders cannot make decisions in a vacuum. They must negotiate continuously to maintain the cohesion of their force, and, as each of the officers and officer groups they deal with has relationships of mutual dependence with civilians, they must speak for a host of civilian interests. In point of fact, the army's general staff fulfills many of the same functions as the executive of a large party which is a member of a coalition cabinet.

Moreover the same is to some extent true of the President. He occasionally makes a major decision on the basis of very little

379

consultation with others; the monetary purge and the dissolution of the elected parliament appear to be examples of this. These, however, were decisions of the once-over type; much more usually Sukarno has needed support from a number of cliques and powerful individuals if his decision is to be implemented, particularly if the action he proposes finds opposition within the military. Thus most of the President's decisions on controversial issues result from a long and complex process of bargaining, usually involving several key civilian ministers and often leaders of the major parties.

Not only the army leaders but each of these civilians has the power to harm Sukarno politically by not cooperating with him. First Minister Djuanda can threaten to resign, as he has on a number of occasions; the threat is a powerful one because Djuanda is one of the very few top government men who understands the language of the economists and has high prestige among those members of the political public who are concerned with the solving of economic problems. The heads of the Nahdatul Ulama can threaten to criticize the government as insufficiently concerned with Islam. Even such relatively impotent bodies as the gotong rojong parliament, the Supreme Advisory Council, the Working Committee of the National Planning Council, the Continuing Committee of the Interim People's Consultative Assembly, and the Central Board of the National Front can exercise significant influence, because it is an important blow to the President's prestige when one of these Guided Democracy agencies offers him open criticism. Some of the leaders of these councils are courtiers, vying with one another for a favored position in the President's entourage and greatly fearing dismissal from their official posts; but others, like Chaerul Saleh, Chairman of the Interim People's Consultative Assembly, have made themselves into heads of cliques, and so have power resources which would not fall away if they fell from grace. Such men are in a position to make Sukarno bargain with them.

Thus a good deal remains of the diffuseness which characterized intraelite relations in the years before 1958. The parties are much weaker, the President and the army very much stronger. But the political elite, including to some extent its military component, continues to be made up of loosely interdependent cliques, and this reduces both the weight of power and its concentration.

An even more extreme contrast between formal rules and practice emerges as one looks at power concentration geographically, examining relations between Djakarta and the regional governments.

Relations on this axis are crucially affected by the position of the regional military commanders, a group of sixteen immensely powerful men, whose will is usually more important for developments in their area than that of their civilian counterparts, the governors. These men are by no means warlords. It is necessary for them to heed most demands made on them by the army's general staff, and to desist from overt criticism of government ideology. Failure to meet these two requirements could cause them to be removed; it is apparently easier now for the general staff to replace a regional commander than at any time since 1952. However, within these broad limits the regional commanders are able to respond to political pressures in their areas of command, which are in most cases their own areas of origin.

The result is that numerous laws and regulations made for the whole country are applied or ignored in a particular area on the basis of decisions taken by its military commander, or by a triumvirate of the commander, the governor, and the police chief. Thus at least one regional commander refused to implement a decision of late 1958 to raise the price of government rice injected onto the market. Several commanders refused to implement fully the monetary purge of August 1959, or immediately made compensatory disbursements. Some have effectively resisted Djakarta's pressure on them to create a Manipol-USDEK ideological climate in their regions.

Conversely, military commanders often initiate action of their own. If Djakarta is slow in responding to a regional government's request for it to authorize money for particular projects—and Djakarta is usually slow in these situations—a particular regional commander may take the issue up with the general staff in Djakarta. Where it is a matter of political importance this may well produce results. If it does not, the commander may take action himself, imposing taxes on local export products or tolls on the movement of goods between regions, in order to build a bridge or a barracks, a monument or a university hostel.

How much army-protected smuggling goes on at the present time is not clear but it is probably less than in the mid-1950s. However, "legal barter" continues to be permitted to some areas; this means that a proportion of the foreign currency earned by certain products exported by these areas can be used directly by the exporters concerned without having to be converted into rupiahs at the official exchange rate. Wherever there is army-protected

381

smuggling or "legal barter" military authorities are usually well-provided with foreign exchange, which serves to increase their effective autonomy.

In the matter of handling rebellions, the regional commanders also enjoy a wide independence of action. This was particularly clear in the way in which the Atjehnese and South Celebes revolts were brought to an end in 1961; both Atjeh and South Celebes have "native son" military commanders, who acted as intermediaries between Djakarta and the rebel leaders. Finally, a number of regional military commanders have shown themselves willing to take repressive measures against the Communists in the face of strong opposition from President Sukarno. The best publicized instance of this was the earlier described ban imposed on Communist activity in 1960 by the commanders of South Borneo, South-Southeast Celebes, and South Sumatra-Djambi. However, Communist activities have been severely restricted in many other areas, including Java.

There certainly continues to be active resentment of Djakarta in a number of regions, especially outside Java, and overcentralization remains one of the charges leveled at the national government. In actual fact, however, power is not particularly highly centralized. If one may use the term federal for a situation in which legality is so easily sidestepped, the present governmental system is one of *de facto* federalism.

Perhaps the biggest changes in power concentration have developed where the government impinges on workers and peasants. Party organization projected into these social groups before the elections of 1955 and 1957-58 gave their members improved facilities for making demands felt by their employer, by the village head, or by the tjamat (subdistrict officer). In many places this organization had not taken firm root before the chilling winds of Guided Democracy began to blow, and it consequently withered on the vine. Parties continue to exist as units of informal social action in many villages, especially in the more detraditionalized areas of Java[55] and in the urban kampongs; and political demands are often pressed through them in nonpublic ways. There is, however, very little public political action by party branches. This is partly because army permission is required for political meetings in almost all areas, but more particularly because, in the absence of elections, the central leaders of most parties see little point in spending their energies on political organization at this level.

Communist organizations continue to protect workers and peasants effectively in many areas, but most of the non-Communist parties now have no need for lower-class support. These parties are therefore not only much weaker and less active than before; they have also come to speak more exclusively for the urban white-collar groups. The effects of these changes on the workers' and peasants' position have been all the greater because of the increased impact of army power on these groups (especially outside East and Central Java), and the diminished importance of law and rules as restraints on government action.

Indonesian authoritarianism clearly does not lend itself to easy generalization. The veil of constitution and official ideology is one-colored; but when one looks beneath it the power-exerting process seems a mass of dapples and speckles. But two conclusions may be drawn from the argument here. First, neither the weight of government power nor its concentration is as great as its scope. The government pervades almost all types of activity in Indonesian society and incorporates or partially absorbs many of them, but it has no comparably complete position of domination or mastery over society, nor is it itself a rigidly exclusive or impermeable organization. Second, there is a contrast between the urban white-collar community, which is most strongly affected by the increased *scope* of government power—through press control, indoctrination programs, "retooling," and so on—and the lower class groups which are hit (perhaps as hard, or harder, but less visibly) by the increased *weight* of power—through the strike ban, requirements for gotong rojong labor, and the holding down of prices for agricultural produce.

In most discussions of contemporary Indonesian affairs two major questions are raised: "Why is it that politics is so frequently an obstacle to the solving of economic problems?" and "Why, if the economy has been running so badly, are the powers-that-be still accepted?" The following section is an attempt to discuss these questions in relation to one another, to analyze the politics of economic decline.

Symbols, Politics, and Economics

One important point at which Indonesian politics and economics are intermeshed is in their imagery. The Indonesian government devotes great attention to symbols, ceremonial, and exhortation; it concentrates on the formulation and proclamation of goals, and on ritual demonstrations of its power to achieve them. These activities serve functions of the utmost importance in maintaining the regime in its present form; on the other hand, they frequently detract from the government's capacity to achieve the very goals it has set. Building the image of the "just and prosperous society" becomes a substitute for the prosaic administrative and economic tasks necessary for realizing that society.

Concern with symbols is important in the first place in that it has meant that attention is detracted from economic tasks to tasks of other kinds. Thus the government has devoted a great part of its resources to fashioning the insignia of national power and prestige. The Indonesia of 1963 has cruisers and destroyers, long-range bombers and missiles. A militarily insignificant state in 1957, it can now claim to be a second-class military power. In the same period, giant stadia have been built to enable Indonesia to play host to the 1962 Asian games, and work has begun on two other projects dear to the heart of the President—the building of a Freedom Mosque, to be the largest mosque in the world, and the construction of a National Monument, which is to be higher than the Eiffel Tower, larger than the Borobudur monument of eighth-century Java, and to last a thousand years. At the same time, as we have seen, great attention and resources are devoted to the President's travels overseas and the visits of foreign dignitaries to Indonesia.

This passion for symbols does not merely channel resources to noneconomic activities; it is also carried right into economic and administrative tasks. This is partly a matter of building prestige projects into the economy: thus Indonesia has recently acquired an atomic reactor, and work has begun on the building of a steel mill in West Java. It is also a matter of infusing ceremonial and ritual into predominantly technical work—the Eight-Year Over-all Development Plan was drawn up by an unwieldy committee of non-economists headed by a prominent ideologue; it presented the plan in the form of 17 volumes, 8 parts, and 1945 clauses, these numerals spelling out the date of Indonesia's proclamation of independence.

Recent years have in fact seen an immense increase in the prominence of ceremony and ritual in all aspects of public life. Special days abound, from National Awakening Day to Electricity and Gas Day, and on such days and numerous other occasions speeches are given at all levels of government. In these the meaning and purpose of particular activities are expounded in terms of Manipol-USDEK and various more short-lived clusterings of symbols—the Seven Duties, the Five Evils, the Three-Fold Command of the People, and so on—and men are exhorted to work with confidence, imagination, and enthusiasm, to avoid hesitancy and the mere following of routine. Similar themes are stressed on the increasingly frequent occasions when badges and medals are conferred on Heroes of the Revolution. Furthermore there is great concern with nomenclature: streets, movie theaters, and state enterprises are given new and more national names. Dramatic phrases are used to describe what might otherwise seem prosaic activities: the army establishes a Prosperity Command to increase rice production, and students are "mobilized" to cope with teacher shortages in outlying areas.

Some observers dismiss these various activities as frills, and others explain them in terms of the importance of ceremony in traditional Indonesian cultures. Each of these interpretations, however, overlooks their political functions. The fact is that all these symbolic actions, whose prevalence has increased so greatly in the present period, serve to make political authority a little more readily and voluntarily accepted by some parts of the population. Thus they help both to maintain the existing regime and to maintain it without further use of coercion; and they are particularly important in buttressing the positions of one group of men powerful within this regime.

Some of these actions, like the President's hoe-swinging ceremony which inaugurated the Eight-Year Plan in January 1961, are in effect promises of future achievement. Others are achievements in themselves, accomplishments which are secured at relatively low cost and are readily visible. They frequently succeed in eliciting a response like, "The economy is in a mess, and there is a terrible lot of corruption, but at least Indonesia counts for something these days. If you look at our air force, or at the role we are playing in Asia, you can't say the government isn't doing anything."

Not all of the symbolism focuses attention on what the government is doing, however, or even what it plans to do. A great deal is an effort to create an image of what the government *is*. Thus the President's trips, and especially the return visits of powerful overseas leaders, serve to picture him as a world leader. By speaking frequently of the suffering of the people, he establishes an image of the government as deeply concerned with the lot of the poor; and by formulating the tasks and duties of the times he meets the traditional expectation that kings should link the present with the past and future and give human life its appropriate place in the cosmic order of things.

Most important, symbols and ritual make it possible to act out the central doctrine of the regime, the doctrine that the revolution is still being fought. The President was ritually underscoring this doctrine when he abrogated diplomatic relations with Holland in August 1960 and seven months later denied Great Britain the right to be Holland's diplomatic representative in Indonesia. He did much the same with every fiery assertion that the West Irian issue would finally be resolved by the power of the Indonesian masses; and the same point comes through whenever the President or anyone else denounces routine in the name of dynamism and renewal.

The importance of this particular doctrine can scarcely be exaggerated. It is partly that a sense of crisis serves to make material deprivation more acceptable: if the struggle against imperalism is still all-important, guns must come before butter. There is, however, more to the doctrine of the unfinished revolution than that. For if indeed this is a period of revolution, if its tasks are essentially the same ones which were faced in the days of the guerrilla struggle against the Dutch, then it follows that the national leaders needed today are men who can rally and inspire the people to fight against the enemy and men who can organize the actual shooting; Indonesia therefore needs the leadership of specialists in symbols and military activity, not of specialists in economics or administration. Thus the doctrine serves to justify the great power now wielded by President Sukarno and the army; and it helps to explain why little influence lies in the hands of men like Hatta, whose claim to power lies in their skills in running a modern state.

Nor is this a matter of the power of the top leadership only. For there are men in every part of government service and public enterprise who are holding positions for which they lack the prescribed technical skills, and who feel themselves threatened by the availability of others who have them. Many of these incumbents are civilian politicians, men who owe their position to the power of their party or group, or to the favor of the President. Others are army officers or ex-officers, men who have come to have power over civilian affairs since martial law was proclaimed in

March 1957, or since the Dutch enterprises were taken over at the end of that year. If the government were to speak less and less of the need to complete the revolution and instead to declare economic development as the principal challenge of the present period, describing this as a slow and difficult task, then men in both of these categories—whether they are section chiefs, estate managers, or regents—would soon have their postions contested in the name of the government's ideology by others who could claim greater technical competence. And such others exist. They include not only many who had influential administrative posts before 1958 and have now lost them, but also a relatively large group of young men of formal training, who actively resent the obstacles placed in their career paths by what they frequently call the "older generation."

Thus a conflict exists throughout the administration and the state-controlled economy between men who justify their positions on political or military grounds and others who lay claim to these same positions on grounds of superior technical skill. The men of the first group may look to the President or the army leaders for protection; those of the second group look to leaders like First Minister Djuanda for protection, and often to men like Hatta and the PSI's Sjahrir for political guidance. The situation may be seen in terms of a figure T, whose horizontal line is the Sukarno-army axis, and whose vertical line runs between both of these on the one hand and on the other the more amorphous group of Djuanda and the open or unavowed supporters of Hatta or Sjahrir.

The issues on this vertical axis are less easily visible, partly because the advocates of efficient administration and economic management rarely speak in public. Moreover, these issues are sometimes regarded as of little intrinsic importance because they seem to have no concomitant in economic ideology. Since Sukarno, Nasution, Djuanda, Hatta, and Sjahrir all describe themselves as socialists and as men who seek an adaptation of socialist methods to the particular conditions of Indonesia, many observers see the differences between them as no more than disagreements on methods of implementation. The fact is, however, that sharply contrasting policy alternatives are presented by men at the opposing extremes of our vertical axis—those who would gear society primarily to maximizing production, and those who would place most emphasis on sustaining the mood of revolutionary struggle. At the top political level this conflict is raised whenever the

387

government's relations with the foreign oil companies are under discussion, or whenever Asian Games expenditures or outlays for arms purchases are brought up. At lower levels it arises again and again over appointments or budget allocations; and whenever it is raised the men of the Djuanda type labor under disabilities because of the doctrine of the unfinished revolution. That they frequently do win their point occurs partly because of Sukarno-army rivalry; thus the army tends to support their demands for conciliatory policies toward the foreign oil companies, while Sukarno supports their efforts to limit expenditures on arms. Ideologically, however, they are weak, because they have few officially acclaimed symbols to which to appeal. If they argue too strongly for sticking to precedent they will be charged with being colonial; if they advocate material incentives they may well be called liberal. Hence they usually argue in a somewhat defensive vein: "Of course this is still a revolutionary situation, of course we must struggle for West Irian; but we must also make our economy more efficient, for how else shall we build the just and prosperous society?"

The doctrine of the unfinished revolution thus protects a wide range of interests at all levels of government and administration. It is not that all who appeal to it are inefficient or lacking in achievement orientation. There are many Sukarno men and many army officers whose interest and ability in economic and administrative work are unquestioned; one thinks of such prominent figures as Chaerul Saleh, the Minister of Basic Industries and Mining, of Major General Djatikusumo, the Minister of Land Communications, and of numerous others like them at lower levels. The point is that there are also men of these two groups whose high positions in administrative and economic agencies cannot be justified on administrative or economic grounds; and because such men are important to the Sukarno group and the army group as power entities, the leaders of these groups must find other ways of justifying their incumbency. Both therefore have an interest in the doctrine of the unfinished revolution, and in a general stress on symbols and exhortation, on enthusiasm rather than technical ability.

It is clear that the passion for symbols is fraught with high economic and administrative costs. To assess these one cannot merely count the time which civil servants spend at ceremonies or which workers devote to cheering state guests. One must look at the whole wastage of skills which occurs because men of the

Djuanda and Hatta kind are in a permanent position of political inferiority. More broadly still, one must consider the effects on administrative and economic operations of a persistent effort to make criteria of loyalty prevail over criteria of technical competence. This effort has undoubtedly been an important cause of the pronounced tendency of recent years for rules to be bent to the will of the individual official and for legal controls to lose much of their force. Rules and controls, routine, precedent, and the specific definition of tasks—all these have been worn down, and one reason for this is that they are walls protecting the technician against the leader, the competent man against the man with the right spirit, the man who can do a particular job well against the man who can give meaning and purpose to the totality of jobs.

Inflation, Corruption, Overregulation, Controls

To explain the preponderant importance of loyalty criteria in administration and economic management, we must look also at several further aspects of the functioning of government machinery, particularly the problems of inflation and corruption, and the closely related phenomena of overregulation and the ineffectiveness of legal controls. The extraordinarily rapid development of inflation since 1957 is described in Chapter 5. It is related there to deficit budgeting and low production, and to the rapid destruction of Western economic institutions implanted under colonial rule. Here we shall describe its administrative effects, and then discuss its political dynamics.

While the urban cost of living index has risen steeply, civil servant salaries have been raised by only small ratios, and most government employees now have salaries whose real value is markedly smaller than it was in 1958, when it was already extremely low. The drop has been considerably greater for a large group of salaried employees of the former Dutch enterprises, for these men had their salaries lowered by government decision (from their earlier levels, which were far above those of civil servants) as well as by inflation.

Some of the persons in these two categories have responded to the situation by taking on out-of-office work, or by engaging in more of this work than they previously did. This is made easier in the case of civil servants by the fact that working hours are between 7:30 A.M. and 2:00 P.M.; it is in fact usual for civil servants to have second jobs as teachers, clerks in private employment, translators, journalists, cloth traders, poultry breeders, and so on. Other salaried persons have been able to supplement their earnings by rents from private land or by subsidies from rich members of their families. However, undoubtedly the biggest source of salary supplements is corruption.

There was a good deal of corruption before 1958, much of it widely publicized; but evidence from a wide range of observers suggests that it has grown greatly since that year. At the highest level, there are the stories of prominent men having large bank accounts overseas. Cabinet ministers, top civil servants, and army officers are often alleged to have received private commissions paid by foreign suppliers; and evidence is cited of conspicuous wealth among members of their families. Moreover, rumors recur that particular men were "retooled" because they knew too much of the doings of their superiors.

At a somewhat lower level one hears stories of young lawyers who enter the prosecutor's service and buy large houses and cars within a short time of graduating. Numerous tales are current of contract splitting and the doctoring of books in the case of particular government firms, and of the illegal sale of products by officials of government estates. Civilians speak of army men in charge of stores of scarce supplies who hoard these in order to raise their backdoor price. Figures are occasionally quoted for what it costs a student to enter a particular university division, what it costs a Chinese to enter such a division (under the unofficial quota system), what it costs for a government-endorsed scholarship to a particular country overseas, and so on.

At still lower levels there are many stories of backdoor sales by owners of sandang pangan stores, the frequently empty fixed-price shops for rationed and other essential commodities. There are the accounts of policemen being unwilling to come to the scene of an accident without payment, and of the officials of personnel and finance sections offering to "rush through" payments and promotions for a small consideration. And, finally, the scattered evidence suggests that payment for services is a regular feature of much of government at the regency, district, and subdistrict levels. In many of these instances, corruption is partly institutionalized. A more or less fixed tariff exists for particular licenses and permits, varying according to the purchaser's status, income, and ethnic classification, but not subject to arbitrary change by the official concerned.

In these lower-level cases, increased corruption is often a result of growing overregulation. It has been pointed out in the chapter on the economy that the volume of government regulation has grown rapidly since 1958. There are now many more areas in which government controls operate—over prices, wages, rents, fares, crop shares, and so on. In addition, the army plays a much increased regulatory role, so that there are a large number of official transactions for which permits are necessary from military as well as civilian agencies. Finally, there has also been a growth in the number of civilian agencies and offices from which approvals are required for particular transactions. An extreme instance is the one of the tennis players who had to fill in a form in nine copies and take it to each of twelve government agencies whenever they wanted the use of a municipal court for a day. But cases not quite as extreme can be cited by almost any person who has had to deal with rationing, health, police, or immigration authorities in recent years without the benefit of privileged status.

The connection between overregulation and corruption is particularly clear where a ruling is unrealistic—where farmers, traders, or consumers are instructed to accept a particular deprivation, which they consider quite unfair, without being given any material incentive to do so. One thinks of the decree of March 1959, when inflation was running high, to have all prices put back to their December 1958 level; traders felt no obligation to obey this decree, which would mean selling their stock at prices much lower than those for which they had bought it, and so they violated the decree and bribed the officials charged with enforcing it. The results are similar from regulations requiring certain groups of villagers to sell a large part of their rice crop at depressed prices; these requirements are widely disobeyed, as are the restrictions on the movement of rice between regions. In every case, however, something must be paid to a particular official. Hence the not uncommon observation that "under Guided Economy the price of an article is determined not by supply and demand but by the number of officials through whose hands it must pass."

Overregulation is closely related in turn to the need to absorb more and more secondary school graduates in the government service. For some years now junior and senior secondary schools have produced sizable numbers of graduates for whom no acceptable employment existed except in the government service and state enterprises. Because of the political dangers of leaving these persons either unemployed or obliged to take employment of a kind seen as incongruous with their training, the government has put most of them on its salary roll; and this has been justified by the fact that the volume of regulatory work to be done has increased. The effort made at the time of the 1959 money purge to ban all further admissions to the civil service proved as impossible to implement consistently as measures of this kind taken in earlier years, and the ban was formally lifted in 1961. Thus overregulation serves as a further instance of economic costs being sustained for political gains: an increased level of corruption forms part of an arrangement whereby education is prevented from producing political challenges to established authority.

The more spectacular forms of corruption—the private commissions, kickbacks, and rackets which are found at higher levels of the administration—call for a different type of explanation. They are far less fully institutionalized, and they certainly continue to arouse active resentment. Low salaries are an important factor here, too—and indeed in higher measure than at lower levels, for the egalitarian pattern of salary differentiation means that higher civil servants are more seriously underpaid by market measurement than are lower civil servants. But it is not so much overregulation which makes it possible for corruption to provide salary supplements at this level; more important is the ineffectiveness of legal controls.

In the period since 1958 the effectiveness of legal and other institutionalized controls has greatly lessened. This is particularly clear in the case of budgetary control. Budgets have come to contain more unfilled columns in these years, denoting the fact that the government has denied information to parliament and the public on a number of defense and other allocations and on deficit spending generally. The power of the Department of Finance to coordinate and supervise the expenditure of other departments and agencies of the government has fallen markedly in the same period. The central bank has lost much of the control it previously had regarding overseas purchasing by particular departments; the Committee for the Coordination of Overseas Credits was replaced in 1961 by a more directly political body, the Economic and Upbuilding Council, which seems to be less inclined to impose a rule-based coordination on the several departments using overseas credits.

The institution of the secretary-general, or permanent head of a government department, has been largely destroyed; most ministries now have not one secretary-general but a number of *pembantu utama* (principal assistants of the minister). In departments where the secretary-generalship survives, the incumbent is seen in much the same light as a pembantu utama—not as a senior professional administrator but as an able man willing to carry out the *politik menteri* (minister's policy) in full loyalty. Indeed, dependence on the politik menteri has become a central feature of much of administration. Routine contact within departments has declined, and there has been further heightening of the long prevalent tendency for even the most minor decisions to wait for the minister personally. Whereas these trends have been notably observable in what may be called the "idea departments"—Foreign Affairs, Education, Higher Education, Information, Religion, Justice, and Labor—they are found to a lesser but still significant extent in the technical departments as well. All ministers are subject to a variety of effective political controls, but the legal checks on them are in most cases extremely weak. The same freedom from institutionalized controls extends to a large number of other officeholders—military commanders, heads of state enterprises, regents, prosecutors, and so on. Each of these men has very wide freedom of action within his own sphere as long as he is assured of protection from others who are more powerful.

This decline in the effectiveness of legal controls is by no means simply a result of the existence of corrupters eager to protect their positions. It must be explained in far broader terms as the result of an increase in the importance of intrabureaucratic conflict, which in turn follows from a blurring of the line between politics and administration. When the role of the parties began to decline, many hoped that this would lead to a corresponding decrease in the importance of politics within the administration, and that the government would thenceforth be able to "get on with the job." Party-based conflict within the bureaucracy was indeed greatly diminished; but there continued to be major clashes of both opinion and interest about what "the job" was, and so politics, while changing its cast, lost none of its importance. In fact it gained in importance, as far as administration was concerned, for as the powers of parties and parliament declined there ceased to be a clearly delineated political sphere in which conflicts could be resolved. Thus a pattern emerged in which no barriers exist between politics—defined as the sphere where goals and policies are chosen and bargained out—and administration—defined as the sphere where goals and policies, once chosen, are implemented. Top-level decisions and pronouncements are either made in very vague terms, or, if they are detailed prescriptions, are treated as if they were merely broad lines of guidance. Policies actually implemented are most frequently the result of battles between politician-bureaucrats: ministers, top civil servants, general staff officers, regional military commanders, and the cliques and alliances formed among all these.

As the job of the bureaucrats has become more and more one of choosing between policies as well as implementing policies chosen, so battles between rival cliques and "empires" within the bureaucracy have grown in importance.[56] It is not that senior civil servants are any less interested in getting administrative work done. On the contrary, they are drawn into political conflict by their very determination to move ahead with their programs, for they find that they cannot obtain the resources which these programs require without support in key places. It is this which forces them to concentrate on building and maintaining their political positions and those of their agencies, and to make their appointments and promotions with a view to this rather than to rewarding efficient performance of tasks. It is this which forces them to be tolerant of corruption when they find it among their associates and subordinates. And it is this which produces the situation in which every agency set up to enforce controls is either ineffectual or allied with a bureaucratic "empire" and so incapable of enforcing controls against it.

The fact that inflation, overregulation, and corruption have all grown more serious in the period since 1958, and that legal controls have become less effective, does not constitute the whole picture of Indonesian administration. A number of factors are working in the opposite direction. First, the increased dominance of government has enhanced administrative effectiveness in a number of situations. This is the case in many parts of East and Central Java, where the pamong pradja's position has been strengthened as a result of the decline of the parties and where the army adheres to its motto of "We support (the civilian government), we do not disturb it." Similarly, most government heads now have a greater capacity to enforce certain types of measures against their employees—in the matter of transfer orders for instance. Second, there are some agencies which are better administered now than four years ago because of the entry of young, well-trained, and achievement-oriented persons into positions of responsibility. Finally, it has been argued that administration has been improved in certain regions as a result of increasing effective autonomy there. Nonetheless, the outstanding features of the recent period, and the features which call for explanation, are inflation, corruption, overregulation, and the decay of legal controls.

To the extent that it has its roots in high deficit financing, one may regard inflation as a response to demands made on the government. Seeing the current political situation as threatening, government leaders have tended to respond readily to the demands of various groups for subsidies, protection, bonuses, and projects, accepting inflation as the economic price to be paid for political survival. Inflation has resulted also from declining output, however; indeed, this is the more basic aspect of the matter, for deficit financing would be relatively minor in its adverse effects on economic functioning if it helped to expand output.

Why then has the government taken the apparently big political risks which are involved in allowing production to decline? One part of the answer to this question is contained in the earlier discussion of the doctrine of the unfinished revolution. Falling production is a consequence of a consistent tendency for both major and minor decisions of government to be more heavily influenced by specialists in symbols and military affairs than by specialists in administration and economics. There is, however, a further major factor involved. This is the fact that falling production forms part of the cost of a general political transformation which has benefited a social group to which the government is closely tied, and this in turn brings us to the next aspect of our discussion.

The Increased Power of the Bureaucracy

When one looks at the distribution of political and economic power in 1962 and compares it with that prevailing before the middle of 1956, it is clear that a major transformation has taken place. It has involved the destruction of Dutch economic power in the country. It has involved a major reduction in the power and wealth of the Chinese minority. Most important of all, it has involved the political incapacitation of the Masjumi and to a large extent of the entrepreneurial groups associated with it. These groups still exist, but they are far weaker and far more heavily dependent on government connections and favors than before. All of these changes have contributed to the lowering of production; and all of them have increased the power of the politico-bureaucratic elite and the social groups linked with it—notably politicians "on the inside," military officers and civil servants, and the businessmen who are connected with them.

It is not difficult to explain the connection between falling production and the blows which have been dealt to the Dutch and Chinese business communities. Falling production followed fairly directly from the losses of skilled personnel—Dutch business executives, accountants, and estate research men; Chinese storekeepers, processors, and graders of raw materials. Partly, too, production has fallen because of the intensified capital flight which has accompanied the departures of personnel. But why should production have fallen as a result of the political incapacitation of the Masjumi and the entrepreneurial groups linked with it? In this case there was no emigration of skilled personnel and probably no great amount of capital flight. Nonetheless, the change contributed greatly to the diminished effectiveness of the government as a promoter of high production, for it helped bring about the maladies of economic administration we have described above by removing the one major extrabureaucratic group which had hitherto exercised countervailing power against the bureaucracy.[57]

Before 1956, if one may oversimplify for the purposes of the argument, politics was a struggle between a Masjumi-led group of forces linked with independent business and a PNI-led group with ties to the bureaucracy and bureaucratically dependent business. By 1958 the group linked with independent business had sustained a major political defeat, and so politics became principally a matter of conflict between different segments and "empires" of the civilian and military bureaucracy and their offshoots. Thus the Masjumi's demise was of major importance in creating a situation in which most decisions about what the bureaucracy should do are made in a bureaucracy-dominated political arena or within the bureaucracy itself—the condition of merged political and administrative functions we have described earlier.

It is not only through the increased importance of intra-bureaucratic politics that government has become less effective in the promotion of production. This same result seems to have been achieved by the very fact that the bureaucracy is not compelled by forces outside itself to perform its tasks vigorously and efficiently. It is not only that there are no strong outside groups which can tell the bureaucracy what to do; in addition, there are no outside groups which can insist that the bureaucracy does well what it does do. To a large extent the bureaucracy has lost its instrumental character and become a law unto itself.

The individual civil servant or army officer is subject to numerous checks and controls: his own position depends on the continued support of the heads of an intrabureaucratic or largely intrabureaucratic "empire," and he must avoid acting in ways which are politically embarrassing to them. But the embarrassment to the heads of these "empires" is evidently not very great if their supporters and subordinates are lazy, inefficient, corrupt, or excessively inclined to restrain the flow of trade; the bureaucratic chiefs appear to be under markedly less pressure to punish their subordinates for shortcomings of this kind than were their predecessors, the party-politician ministers of the period up to 1956. The principal reason for this, I would suggest, is that the powerful politician-administrators of today have less need than their predecessors to maintain support from groups outside the bureaucracy. With the political incapacitation of the Masjumi and the independent business groups linked with it, the way was cleared for society to come under the near-exclusive dominance of the bureaucracy as a social group.

The political incapacitation of a country's business groups need not necessarily mean that the bureaucracy becomes more powerful and less instrumental in character. This consequence is avoided where power passes into the hands of a small, tightly knit, privileged, and rigidly exclusive state party of the type of the Communist party of the Soviet Union, a party which is in the bureaucracy but not of it, and so is in a position to dictate to it. But this is not what has happened in Indonesia: there the intermeshing and interdependence of political elite and bureaucracy is so great that the elite can rarely force the bureaucracy to do things that it does not like doing. One might say that those who have deprived the independent business groups of Indonesia of their earlier ability to exert a measure of control over the machinery of state are not rival would-be masters of the bureaucracy, but rather the bureaucrats themselves and politicians who are so close to them in social position, orientation, and interests as to be virtually indistinguishable on these counts. Now subject to no controls from any group outside itself, the bureaucracy has no need to accept the restrictions and discipline which administrative efficiency demands of it.

Those who have gained from this whole pattern of change are not merely a handful of men, a few thousand of the ninety-seven million Indonesians. On the contrary, the group of beneficiaries includes a large segment of the swollen civil and military bureaucracy, the personnel of government firms, various categories of private businessmen to whom the politician-bureaucrats are indulgent, and certain religious, cultural, and professional groups with access to the powerful. This is certainly a significant proportion of the country's effective political public, the two million or so—mainly city dwellers of relatively high social status—who read newspapers and have opinions on national politics. It is true that not all members of the bureaucracy have benefited from the changes; many of its most competent and scrupulous members have suffered considerable deprivation because they have lost power within the administrative structure. These same men and many others have suffered as a result of the new sense of insecurity which has followed from programs of indoctrination and "retooling." But for those who have remained or grown powerful within the structure the increased might of the bureaucracy vis-à-vis other social groups has brought a number of advantages.

These advantages are particularly great in the case of the bureaucracy's military arm. It is frequently pointed out that an overwhelming majority of army members, from generals to privates, are richer, more powerful, and higher in social position than they were before 1956. Benefits have also accrued to a large number of civilian officials, high and low, who have succeeded in swimming with the political stream. These men have gained greater power as individuals—for instance, power to waive regulations in the case of friends, power to accept relatives as new employees of their offices, or power to be selective in compensating businessmen from losses they sustained as a result of inflation or of the 1959 monetary purge. Many of the same officials have also gained in prestige, as honor based on political and bureaucratic attainments has increased at the expense of that deriving from noble birth or achievement in non-political spheres of activity. Many of them have further gained in real income—not only through corruption, but also by acquiring the use of previously Dutch- and Chinese-owned houses and cars.

Income gains of this kind only rarely accrue to a single individual or family, for favorably placed bureaucrats are subject to strong moral pressure to share their gains with others less fortunate. Within the Indonesian bureaucracy, as within the Javanese village and small firm, wealth brings obligations with it.[58] Thus the section chief or estate manager who acquires a large sum of money, honestly or corruptly, must usually share a part of this with many of his white-collar subordinates. Similarly, overseas trips are dealt out by turn: the moral sanctions are heavy against an official of a particular department who tries to get himself a second or third trip when another man of comparable rank has not had one. Thus it seems probable that a sizable proportion of the wealth redistributed as a result of the political changes we have described has trickled down to the middle and lower reaches of the bureaucracy.[59]

It would certainly be misleading, therefore, to speak of the post-1958 political transformation as simply a leveling down. Many people have seen their material position improved, despite the fall in Indonesia's aggregate income; and as far as prestige and power are concerned, quite as many have been raised as have been pulled down.

The whole change of the period since 1957-58 is well described in President Sukarno's metaphor, "return to the rails of the revolution." Between 1949 and 1956 an attempt had been made by one part of the political elite to "dam up" the revolution,[60] to stabilize the power situation on a pluralistic basis, leaving Dutch capital powerful and allowing considerable autonomy to Indonesian businessmen and religious, cultural, and professional groups; developments since then reflect the victory of those who wanted a more fundamental restructuring of society on "national" and "revolutionary" lines, involving the destruction of virtually all centers of power outside the government itself. The Indonesian political leadership of the period since 1957-58 has been following a pattern established in the Russian revolution—and there are parallels with the French revolution too—in depriving business and other nongovernmental groups of what autonomy they had and forcing them to come into direct dependence on itself.

But in the Indonesian case, unlike the Russian, this restructuring of society has not resulted in a really powerful political elite, one which is cohesive and capable of inducing planned economic and social change on a far-reaching scale. What has emerged is a divided elite, one whose members must continue to concern themselves primarily with the struggle for power among themselves. It is an elite whose weight of power is relatively low, in the sense that its impact on society is broad and all-encompassing rather than intense. And it is a conservative elite, in that it is unwilling or unable to make a determined effort at modernization. The roots of these three characteristics must be sought in a variety of factors; one of them is the dominant position of military officers and symbol-wielders within the elite, but perhaps the most important is the fact that the political elite is itself deeply imbedded in the bureaucracy, that it acts more as a servant of the bureaucracy as a social group than as its master for the changing of society.

This dependence of the political elite on the bureaucracy is important in sustaining the elite's divisions, because the bureaucracy is itself a representative instrument, channeling the demands of influential groups in society. It is also important in limiting the weight of the political elite's power, because the elite cannot use the bureaucracy to implement policies which harm either the bureaucracy's own interests or those which part of it represents. Finally, the bureaucratic matrix is important in making the political elite conservative, in the sense that it is unwilling to initiate resolute efforts to modernize the society. Any such effort would require major changes in the personnel of the political and bureaucratic leadership—in effect much increased power for the Djuanda and Hatta-Sjahrir types—and it would also involve diminished power and prestige for the bureaucracy as a social group.

Maintaining Power in a Period of Economic Decline

The preceding discussion has described the processes which have contributed to economic decline, but at the same time helped the government in one way or other to maintain its power position. This can be said of most of the ritual activity in which the government is so heavily involved; it can be said of expansion in the size of the bureaucracy; and it can probably be said of the whole process of change whereby the bureaucracy has grown in power, prestige, and presumably also income. It remains for us, however, to attempt a systematic answer to the very broad question introduced earlier: "If the economy is running so badly, why are the-powers-that-be still accepted?"

This question is one which has arisen repeatedly in the minds of Indonesian intellectuals. Noting the downward curve of so many of the principal economic indicators, experiencing the growth of corruption and administrative chaos, and seeing the failure of Draconian measures to rectify economic or administrative short-comings, many of these intellectuals have wondered why the Indonesian people submit quietly to this deterioration. Politically well-informed Indonesians have said repeatedly throughout this period—and indeed for many years before 1958—that "this situation just cannot go on; something radical must happen soon" or that "if this goes on much longer we must hit rock bottom soon, and then things will certainly change." Events so far have proved these men wrong, however, at least for the period since 1958. Continuing economic decline has led to no radical political action other than the three attempts on the President's life, the irresolute challenge of the Democratic League in 1960, and a few isolated acts of resistance to the army and police in rural areas. How is this tolerance of material deprivation to be explained?

First of all it should be said that the extent of material deprivation suffered is much smaller than some of the indicators suggest, particularly the indicators of falling production and falling over-seas earnings, because of the inflow of foreign aid. For various reasons—principally ones connected with cold war bidding, but also others having to do with intensified competition for a share of the Indonesian market—Indonesia has been receiving aid on a very large scale since the beginning of 1956. The total value of this aid is extremely difficult to calculate, partly because the term "aid" includes such a wide range of relationships, but estimates of an annual inflow of $150-200 million since 1959 are common and a useful rough indication. The importance of such a sum is clear if one compares it with the 1960 export figure of $840 million.

Most of the aid has come in the form of cheap long-term loans, particularly from the Soviet Union, but also from the United States through its Export-Import Bank, from Japan, from several East European countries, and from China. West Germany, Japan, France, Italy, and Great Britain have extended trade credits—in effect loans on terms less favorable to Indonesia. American agricultural products sold at low prices form a third major component of aid. Smaller sums have been contributed in the form of capital gifts (including Japanese reparations) and technical assistance (including that provided multilaterally under United Nations and Colombo Plan auspices).

The actual uses of these funds are many. Large sums have been provided in the form of military supplies, especially by the USSR, which extended a loan of $450 million for arms in January 1961. Foreign aid is being used in virtually all major construction projects of the Eight Year Over-all Development Plan—for steel, chemical and fertilizer plants, cement, paper and tire factories, the building of hotels and roads, and the opening of land—as well as to buy food. Moreover, it has enabled several thousand Indonesians to travel and obtain training overseas. All of these are uses to which the Indonesian government attaches importance, and all of them have relieved pressure on the government's meager resources of foreign exchange. However, the value of this large-scale aid was diminishing rapidly in 1961 and 1962, as ever larger sums had to be set aside annually for interest and amortization payments on the loans.[61]

Foreign aid notwithstanding, per capita income has shown a net decline in the 1958-62 period; and we must therefore seek further reasons for the lack of radical action against the regime. One explanation is that income has been redistributed to favor the politically important. Thus civil servants, officers, and well-connected businessmen drew benefits from the take-overs of Dutch enterprises in 1957 and from the seizures and cheap purchases of property connected with the subsequent anti-Chinese campaigns. Members of these groups gain at the expense of workers and peasants through strike prohibition and the various regulations holding down the prices which peasant growers receive for their rubber, rice, or copra; and it is they who profit from overregulation. Similarly, government funds are made available for large numbers of leading Moslems to make the Mecca pilgrimage every year, with the result that some of the edge has been taken off Islamic hostility to the government. This does not cover all the groups whose alienation could endanger the regime, but it mollifies an important section of them.

Second, prestige is made to accrue to many who are not adequately rewarded in terms of income. One way in which this is done is by the distribution of badges and medals for heroism in the revolution; another is through the establishment of the many governmental and advisory councils of large membership and diffuse powers. And civil service expansion has a similar effect: while the new civil servant may have a very low salary, and low total income, he is often heavily rewarded by the mere fact of admission to the group of guardians of the state—and so perhaps deprived of his willingness to oppose the regime. The same can be said about "retooling" in government departments and firms, for this seems to have enabled a number of competent men in their twenties and thirties to rise fast.

A third and most important factor which helps to explain why Indonesians accept the current power arrangement is that they have very few alternatives. As we saw in discussing the Sukarno-army relationship, the government of the post-1958 period has been strikingly successful in dealing with its domestic enemies. Using a judicious combination of repression and incorporation, the government has crippled or neutralized most of the groups which might want to challenge its position. This has been achieved partly by a strengthening of the armed forces and especially by its increased cohesion and identification with the government. It is also a result of the regime's great "absorptive capacity," of the fact that power is shared between a number of groups which are sharply distinct, but which at the same time have a common interest in preserving the power situation of the present. Furthermore, it is related to the government's centrist position in the cold war, which enables it to keep its would-be challengers in two mutually antagonistic camps; and it has much to do with the fact that since mid-1958 neither China, Russia, nor the United States has been actively concerned to change the Indonesian power situation. For all of these reasons great obstacles now stand in the way of any group of leaders, Communist, regionalist, or Islamic, who might attempt to gather support for an act of open revolt. The situation does indeed contain a great number of possibilities for a coup of some sort, for a major or minor shift within the group of those in control of government. But no outside group is now in a position to bid for power.

The present power constellation is buttressed further by the various control mechanisms discussed earlier. The sustained threat of "retooling" serves to keep many government employees from participating in *sub rosa* politics. Political arrests have a similar effect which extends to much of the urban white-collar group; among them the feeling is widespread that "one has to be careful about whom one is seen with." Moreover, various government practices impede the flow of political information. This is the case not only with press control, the censorship of mails, and the various restrictions on group association, but also with the government's demand for repeated affirmations of support for its ideological formulations, for this requirement forces men to withhold or disguise the expression of their political feelings. The inaccessibility of detailed poltical information is particularly important in stabilizing the current political balance, for it is obviously dangerous to attempt any sort of coup unless one can make accurate assessments of political feeling over a range of different groups.

Moreover, the government appears to have had considerable success in its efforts to focus attention on issues on which its own position has overwhelming support. It does this by the doctrine of the unfinished revolution, by repeated emphasis on the primacy of the fight against imperialism. It has done so by keeping the struggle for West Irian in the forefront of political attention, by encouraging anti-Chinese sentiment, by ceremonies recalling the heroism of the nationalist movement and the revolution, and by foreign policy actions which give rise to a feeling of national pride. In all of these ways the government highlights conflict between Indonesians and outsiders, and by the same token it distracts attention from conflict between rulers and ruled inside the country. The government's involvement in these kinds of activities is largely continuous, but they often receive particular emphasis when disaffection becomes immediately threatening to some of the key groups in power; for in these crisis situations channeling is a principal means of inducing catharsis.[62]

However, channeling would not be the effective technique it is if it were not possible to base it on a considerable amount of more or less voluntary acceptance of the powers-that-be, and we must therefore consider consent as a factor supporting the present distribution of power. It is immensely difficult to write accurately about real political attitudes in a period when these rarely find public expression. I shall, however, hazard some generalizations about these attitudes in the centrally important urban white-collar community. My basis is a series of discussions held with a sample of members of this community in Djakarta, Bandung, Jogjakarta, and Medan between August and December 1961.[63]

The first thing to be said is that to many or most of the members of this community Indonesia seems to be in a bad way. The optimism of Manipol-USDEK is shared by very few, these being mainly the more buoyantly extroverted among high school and university students. Most other white-collar urbanites see the country's condition in a far more gloomy light—as characterized by corruption or hypocrisy, confusion, material suffering, or the government's inability to get things done.[64] To most of them these seem more important features of the situation than Indonesia's increased military strength and international importance or the hope expressed in the Eight-Year Plan.

However, only a small proportion of the urban white-collar persons who see their society as sick are bitterly resentful of the government. Cynicism is widespread among them, but most of it is mild and good-humored, as the political jokes and parodies suggest. A characteristic saying is "Things are pretty bad, but they could be an awful lot worse." This may then be followed by: "One can still live reasonably well if one uses one's wits"; "It is still possible to have influence if you are careful"; or "There is really still quite a lot of freedom left to us." Similar remarks are "There are still a lot of good men in the government" and "The situation in some of the regions is pretty hopeful." Those who make comments of this kind are clearly not taking the government's assertions at face value, but they are also not rejecting them outright. They may offer one of the following explanations: "It is not the government itself which is bad, just certain people in it"; "It is the older generation which causes the trouble"; "This is a period of transition"; or "All Asian countries are having difficulties like this."

Dissatisfaction is thus frequently coupled with acceptance in the urban white-collar community. Some observers have attempted to explain this in terms of a supposed Indonesian disposition toward patience and docility, but one can account for a great deal of it without resorting to psychocultural interpretations. Comparing current urban white-collar attitudes to politics with attitudes before 1957, one notes a marked fall in the level of expectations. It is as if men felt that the riotous feasting had now inevitably come to its end. This fall in expectations is partly due to the fact that 1945-49, the period of utopian hopes and vast opportunities for social mobility, has receded further into the past. More particularly, however, it is a result of the decline of the parties and the broadening of political restrictions. With the virtual disappearance of open politics, large numbers of white-collar Indonesians have become politically incapacitated; unwilling to participate in the riskier practices of *sub rosa* politics, they respond to their inability to change the country's situation by making a virtue of necessity. So from "Things are lousy, but what can we do?" they have gone on to believe that "Actually the situation is not nearly as bad as it might be."[65]

Moreover, many of the white-collar group are thoroughly baffled by the country's situation. They cannot wholly accept the government's interpretation that the country is moving with all determination along the path of progress, restrained only by the continuing need to do battle with imperialism, liberalism, and individualism. On the other hand most of them cannot reject this entirely, for to do so would mean breaking with the nationalism of 1945, whose symbols continue to have strong appeal for them. Outright rejection of the government's interpretation is possible for a small group of fully trained Communists and members of the Masjumi—men who have clear and firmly held alternative systems of belief and interpretation—and it is possible for a small group of sophisticated intellectuals, particularly for persons who have lived overseas long enough to observe nationalism from the outside. But white-collar urbanites who are not schooled in any such alternative way of looking at the world are almost obliged to take the view that "there is something in what the government says" or that "Manipol-USDEK is basically the right idea; it is only its execution which is bad." Some are pushed to this position because it follows from their values and patterns of perception as nationalists. Others, hearing the government speak in terms of their own beliefs and hopes, find that they have no grounds of principle on which to base their opposition, and are therefore influenced by persistent government propaganda.[66] Both groups are uncertain and confused in their political views: they see the country's situation as disappointing and shameful, but they have no coherent set of ideas about why this is so, who is to blame, and how improvements might be brought about. Hence they are content to be inactive; they can see no cause worth fighting for.

Having set forth these various aspects of how the government's authority has continued to be accepted in a period of economic deterioration, I now hasten to point to some of the factors endangering such acceptance in the future. There is no doubt that deep dissatisfactions have developed which could quickly find political expression once a movement had started for a disruption of the present political balance. Some of these are dissatisfactions which have resulted directly from the economic change of recent years; and most of them are ones with which the government could more easily cope if the economy were not in a period of decline, if the regime had a greater volume of material rewards for distribution.

Dissatisfaction is found among numerous non-Javanese of various social groups, who see the government as one of Javanese, founded on a Javanese military victory over other ethnic groups. Because the Javanese have provided a disproportionately large number of government officials, the power shift favoring the bureaucracy at the expense of other groups has tended to benefit ethnic Javanese to the detriment of others. Moreover, within the group of government employees there are many non-Javanese persons who believe they cannot rise higher because they are not Javanese or culturally Javanized.

Similarly there are many committed Moslems, both in and outside the white-collar group, who are basically unreconciled to the present regime. Although the government has ceded a number of practical concessions to the Islamic community in the 1958-62 period—positions for Nahdatul Ulama leaders, an expansion of the activities of the Department of Religious Affairs, repressive controls over new religious sects, and so on—it has persistently stood on the non-Islamic side whenever Moslem and Pantja Sila symbols have been presented as alternatives to one another. It is to the pre-Islamic or non-Islamic strands of traditional culture that the President has gone in his efforts to propagate a "Return to Our National Identity," and so he has antagonized the Moslems, especially those of the modernist, antisyncretistic Masjumi. Masjumi Moslems are politically incapacitated now, or almost so, but they are actively resentful of the present state of political affairs and have an ideological basis for opposition to it, and their incapacitation could thus well be short-lived.

The various groups outside the white-collar community should each be discussed in terms of their grievances and orientations to them, but here information is extremely scarce. Among the wage workers of the cities and towns dissatisfaction seems to be acute, but it is apparently combined with a strong feeling that they themselves cannot initiate protest. Hence perhaps the readiness of labor unions to obey the strike ban—although this can also be traced in large part to the pro-Sukarno strategy of the PKI, the party of the most strongly class-conscious workers. Urban worker dissatisfaction is perhaps reflected in increased thieving, but it has not found expression in rice riots or other illegal demonstrations, and there is little evidence of a strongly organized urban underworld.

It is even harder to make generalizations about the peasantry. The occasional bloodshed arising from the government's clashes with squatters or members of mystical sects is certainly no adequate basis for a conclusion that peasant unrest has assumed threatening proportions. It may well be that the attitude in the peasantry as a whole remains, or has become, one of acceptance.[67] Moreover, there are groups of peasants whose economic position has improved steadily and who are well satisfied with the government. However, there is dissatisfaction among the wealthier peasants or farmers who grow rubber, copra, and other smallholder products for the world market; many of these men are actively resentful of the artificial exchange rate, the government-arranged marketing schemes, the bad condition of roads, and other restrictions on trade.

Furthermore, there seems to be both dissatisfaction and the will to act on it in the group which stands between the white-collar urbanites on the one hand and the workers and most peasants on the other. These are the men of modern skills who are denied the privileges of white-collar status—such as electricians, mechanics, truck drivers, and the urban small traders. Some of them are Communists and others are modernist Moslems. But the ideology of the present government has little appeal to them, being regarded as a collection of *prijaji* (Javanese aristocratic) and *pegawai* (civil servant) platitudes. Their sense of being outsiders in relation to the government is a product in part of their bitter resentment of government officials for corruption and the trading of favors within their group, and in part of their dislike for a white-collar community which asserts its social superiority over them and allows only a few of their members to enter its ranks.

In addition there are many in almost all social groups who see the 1945 constitution and Manipol-USDEK as nostrums which have failed and gone stale. This together with the droughts, floods, earthquakes, and volcanic eruptions of 1961 and 1962, all traditional evil omens, has brought many to believe that the present *djaman* (era) may be approaching its end.

For all of these reasons the government's position is shaky, and probably becoming shakier with every further development of economic deterioration. In one sense the government is continually fighting for its life. For President Sukarno and his associates the threat is more or less immediate: it is the threat of an army-made coup or an assassination. For the military leaders as a group the problem is more long-term: can the army (and the civilians with whom it is associated, now or in a post-Sukarno period) prevent another Kuomintang-type debacle? Can it strengthen its position sufficiently to forestall possible regionalist and PKI revolts, particularly in the face of hypothetical Communist advances in mainland Southeast Asia?

It is in looking at the shakiness of the government's position that one sees what is perhaps the most important aspect of interaction between economics and politics. With threats to its very existence looming large, the government is pushed to concern itself first and foremost with problems of political control. So it concentrates on strengthening the army, building up the machinery of political indoctrination, and structuring political situations in such a way that attention is focused on the common values and interests of rulers and ruled. But by doing this it further strengthens the military men and wielders of symbols, not least vis-à-vis the specialists in economics and administration. In effect, it turns the priorities still further away from the administrative and economic problems which must necessarily be tackled with determination if the trend toward deterioration is to be reversed. Here then is the tragic vicious circle: many of the problems of political authority would begin to solve themselves if the economy could be made to expand; but since the nation is in a period of economic decline the government must put political control first, even at the expense of further damage to the economy.

CHAPTER 9

Genesis of a Modern Literature

ANTHONY H. JOHNS

T HE TRADITIONAL literature of Indonesia is both ancient in origin and widespread in extent, for it includes almost everything written before the beginning of the twentieth century and is still preserved in a variety of forms in many of the regional languages of the archipelago. Of the regional languages Javanese has the richest extant literature, the oldest work of which dates back to the tenth century A.D. This, a version of the Ramayana, reflects such an accomplishment of style and mastery of form that it must be the product of a far older literary tradition, nothing of which, unfortunately, has survived. The loss of Malay literature has been just as great. There are no literary works surviving in that language which can be dated earlier than the fifteenth century; and there is no surviving Malay work in which Arabic loan words are absent and which is not written in the Arabic script. Yet it is unthinkable that a Malay Buddhist empire of the magnitude of Sriwidjaya should have been deficient in the arts of literature. Numerous inscriptions in Malay of Sriwidjayan origin which have been discovered in South Sumatra, and likewise ninth- and tenth-century Malay inscriptions from central and western Java, bear adequate testimony to the role of Malay even during this early period. Further, certain peculiar features of the oldest examples of the use of the Arabic script for writing Malay (i.e. the doubling of consonants) can only be explained by an older tradition of writing in a syllabic script of Indian derivation, similar to that still used in Java. Everything has been lost, however, apart from a few inscriptions and four lines of a poem written in Indian-type characters carved on a stone found at Minye Tudjuh in Atjeh.[1]

The only extant regional literature able to compare in age with that of the Javanese is that of Bali. Many other regions, however, have literary works of at least two or three hundred years' vintage, the products in turn of more ancient traditions. One can instance the histories of Makassar,[2] works in Madurese and Sundanese (written, like Javanese, in a script of Indian derivation) and works in Atjehnese and Minangkabau written in the Arabic script. Some of these have been published, but a far greater quantity exists only in manuscript.[3]

The types of literature subsumed under this general heading "traditional" are manifold and disparate. In Malay, they include romances (*hikajat*), chronicles (*sedjarah*), works on Islamic theology, mysticism, and law, and various types of verse: the *pantun*, in its basic form a quatrain with alternate rhymes, the *sja'ir*, a narrative poem consisting of quatrains, and the *gurindam*, a rhapsodical type of "free verse."

All these forms are clearly distinguished from "modern" literature by certain common characteristics. Few of the traditional works had as their purpose entertainment as an end in itself. A large proportion was devoted to the welfare of the state, to the practice of right religion and right morals. Sophisticated literature being centered on the court, it had necessarily to be dedicated to the king. The myths and legends of Indian origin, which were adapted in various ways to the Indonesian context, provided entertainment, it is true; but they also had a strong ethical content and presented in figure various aspects of the profoundest and most esoteric doctrines of the nature of God, man, and the universe. Much of the regional "folk" literature likewise had the end of establishing the mythical genealogy and mores of the group from which it originated.[4] In none of these works, in fact, do we find the author expressing a standpoint of his own, giving an individual critique and analysis of life around him. He is, in a sense, presenting a view of his culture as it sees itself, and as it would like itself to be. There cannot be for him any of that agonizing sense of doubt, that questioning and criticism of the bases of social life, and the analysis and presentation of the predicaments of individuals out of which Western literature is made.

The type of literature to which we attach the unsatisfactory term "modern" makes only a fleeting appearance in the Indonesian area in the nineteenth century, in the works of Abdullah bin Abdul Kadir' Munsji (1797-1854). Abdullah was a Malay of Tamil descent who spent much of his life at Malacca and there became a close friend of Thomas Stamford Raffles, who inspired him with his liberal ideas and passion for knowledge. It was from Raffles and his associates that Abdullah gained sufficient insight into an alien civilization to look critically upon his own society and to condemn its shortcomings. His autobiography, the *Hikajat Abdullah* (The Story of Abdullah),[5] is a landmark in many ways. It is quite clearly the work of an individual presenting a personal point of view; it is one of the earliest expressions in the Indonesian world of the encounter between East and West; and it is written in a style that could be called at least semicolloquial, quite unlike the monotonous semirhythmic prose of the so-called classical tradition. Abdullah, though he was not a great writer, is thus of major importance, foreshadowing and illustrating a development of literary and social consciousness which was only to become manifest in Indonesia some fifty years later.

In traditional Indonesian society, reading did not form part of a pattern of private leisure. Leisure tended, in fact, to be not private but public, consisting largely of listening to the recitation of traditional stories on specific social occasions, and of participating in dance or drama—activities which combined both recreational and religious functions. A modern literature, on the other hand, is written to be read in private, so that the author, as an individual, meets the reader as an individual, in the privacy of his own home. Without the habit of private reading, individual authorship is virtually impossible, and thus the development of a modern literature required a change in the social pattern of the audience as well as a new attitude toward life on the part of the writer.

Both of these prerequisites were met as a result of the Dutch impact on traditional Indonesian society. This encounter not only brought about structural changes in the Indonesian community, but it also introduced Western education and with it a corresponding increase in literacy and the development of the reading habit. The most important single contribution of the Dutch to the development of Indonesian literature was the founding of the organization which made this extension of the reading habit possible. In 1908 the colonial government appointed a commission to advise on the provision of reading matter for "natives and native schools." The commission submitted its report in 1911, and the first publications under its auspices included versions of local stories and legends, and translations from European literature of such classics as *The Three Musketeers* and *The Count of Monte*

Cristo. In 1917 the Commission was given the title of Balai Pustaka (The Hall of Good Reading). Balai Pustaka's libraries and agencies expanded rapidly throughout the archipelago, developing a considerable reading public. Further, the foundation gave new life in varying degrees to the traditional literatures of the regional languages, including Malay versions of Hindu legends. More important, it presented real opportunities to new Indonesian writers: any author could submit his work for consideration to Balai Pustaka, and if it were accepted and published it was guaranteed a wide circulation.

The publications of Balai Pustaka would not, by themselves, have been sufficient to transform Malay into Bahasa Indonesia, the language of the modern Indonesian nation. It was rather an emotional, nationalist impulse which achieved this—the determination of the Indonesian elite to develop a language able to cope with the experiences implicit in the expression "modern world," and thus to assert an Indonesian cultural and national identity over and against that of the Dutch. It is because it lacked this impetus that neither Malay, as a regional language, nor any other of the regional tongues—not even Javanese, with its radiant literary tradition—has yet been able to establish itself as a language of the modern world.

The formal adoption of Bahasa Indonesia as the language of Indonesian nationalism took place at the All-Indonesia Youth Congress of 1928, when leaders of the country's future elite pledged themselves to one fatherland, one people, and one Indonesian language. The Malay which they chose as the basis for the new tongue was far from being a national language ready made. Only a minority of the peoples of the Indonesian archipelago speak Malay as their mother tongue. However, the historical circumstances which led to the development of Malay both as the *lingua franca* of commerce and the cultural language of Islam throughout the archipelago had given it a remarkably wide distribution; and this in turn meant that it was not regarded as the prerogative of any particular area.

A second problem in the utilization of Malay was that traditional Malay was not in any sense a modern language. European pedants who had arbitrarily settled on the seventeenth century as the Golden Age of Malay were contemptuously critical of this attempt to develop Malay as a language of the modern world. Anything not classical had, by definition, to be bizarre; and Bousquet, writing in 1939, could speak of "that preposterous language Malay."[6] It was to the formidable task of creating for Bahasa Indonesia a sophisticated, modern literary content that the pioneers of Indonesian literature addressed themselves.

To achieve this aim, three young writers—Takdir Alisjahbana (b. 1908 in Tapanuli), Armijn Pané (b. 1908 in Tapanuli), and Amir Hamzah (b. 1911 in Bindjai)—founded, in 1933, a literary and cultural periodical which they called *Pudjangga Baru* (The New Poet). At birth, it was a monthly periodical devoted to language, literature, culture, and the arts. In its third year it declared itself the bearer of a new spirit into literature, the arts, and society; one year later, it set itself the task of fostering that spirit of dynamism which would create a new Indonesian culture. Far-reaching aims indeed! *Pudjangga Baru* continued publication until the Japanese occupation in 1942, and during the nine years of its prewar life it regularly included essays on art and culture, poetry, short stories, and on one occasion a complete novel.

The works in Malay and Bahasa Indonesia published by Balai Pustaka and those appearing in *Pudjangga Baru* are the most accessible and probably the most important examples of prewar Indonesian literature. They are not the only ones. There was a mass of reading material in Bahasa Indonesia published in the prewar years: newspapers, magazines, almanacs, novelettes, and works on religion were put out both in Batavia and the provinces. On the whole, however, the works coming from these two main streams—the sophisticated *Pudjangga Baru* and the more popular Balai Pustaka—are sufficiently representative for us to form a picture of the early development of Indonesian poetry and prose.

Formal realism, an acute and critical analysis of society, interpreted and presented in prose according to the individual *Weltanschauung* of the author—these are for us the distinguishing features of a novel; and at the same time, as we have seen, they distinguish a modern from a traditional literature. The first efforts on the part of Indonesians to write in this genre were naturally halting and sometimes confused. They were further handicapped by the absence in Bahasa Indonesia of an accepted naturalistic prose style. It will be remembered that the English novel is a comparatively recent development in literary history, and that it did not and could not develop until writers such as Swift and Dryden had established a naturalistic prose style: then, and then only, do Richardson and Fielding appear on the scene.

The first Indonesian work which can properly be described as a novel is *Sitti Nurbaja* (the title is a girl's name) by Marah Rusli (b. 1898 in Minangkabau), which appeared in 1922. It was followed by several others, among the most important of which are *Salah Asuhan* (A Wrong Upbringing) by Abdul Muis (b. 1890 in Minangkabau), which was published in 1928; *Karena Mentua* (Because of the Mother-in-Law), written by Nur Sutan Iskandar (b. 1893 in Minangkabau) and published in 1932; and *Kalau tak Untung* (If Fortune Does Not Favor) by Selasih (b. 1909 in Minangkabau), which appeared in 1933.[7]

These novels, and the group they represent, are similar in theme and treatment, dealing with the predicaments of young people caught between the old world and the new. At home these youngsters are expected to live according to the traditional pattern of life and are at the mercy of all its sanctions if they disobey. At school, and through their contacts with Europeans and Eurasians, they have learned of the existence of a different world, where the individual can aspire to be economically independent, personally responsible for his actions, and unhampered by the claims of the extended family and clan. The conflict between the two ways of life is brought most sharply into focus when the question of marriage arises: is the choice of a spouse to be a personal or parental responsibility?

Virtually all the novels of this period are characterized by an atmosphere of despair. Death, in fact, is the most favored plot solution. In *Sitti Nurbaja*, the heroine is murdered and the hero killed in a clash with the Dutch. In *Karena Mentua*, the hero stabs his wife by accident while attacking his mother-in-law, and in despair kills himself. *Salah Asuhan* is similarly a tragedy, written with the didactic purpose of illustrating the disruptive effects of a Western education and the perils of a mixed marriage.

Salah Asuhan has obvious shortcomings: the style is dull and ponderous, the relationship between certain episodes is forced, and the eventual suicide of the hero, Hanafi, may have symbolic value but lacks dramatic effect. Nevertheless its merits are considerable, and it is probably the best prose work to appear in Bahasa Indonesia until 1939.[8] Abdul Muis possesses to a large degree that breadth of vision which is essential to the novelist. His characterizations, particularly that of the spoiled and impetuous heroine, Corrie, are consistent and credible. Nowhere does he indulge in moral judgments on his characters or preach against a mixed marriage as such; it is fate in the form of the total colonial situation that is responsible for the tragedy.

Some of the author's attitudes to his characters and their predicaments are of special interest. Abdul Muis, it is clear, appreciates the value of a Western education and is obviously influenced by European ideas. Yet why did this Western education have such an appalling effect on Hanafi, who is completely alienated from his own people, and how could this have been avoided? Abdul Muis' only suggestion is that Hanafi's Western education should have been tempered by Islamic religious training. This is all very well, but there is not the least trace of an Islamic ethos in the book. The conduct of the couple is nowhere measured against the moral imperatives of Islam; the author makes no comment on the non-Islamic character of their wedding, and even on his deathbed Hanafi only thinks of the life to come as an opportunity to meet again his beloved Corrie. Marah Rusli, in *Sitti Nurbaja,* similarly leaves his characters quite unmoved by any element of Islamic teaching. The hero on his deathbed does, it is true, exclaim *Allahu akbar;* but his expectations are of meeting again his beloved and mother, not of appearing before the throne of God. The absence of Islam as an effective mediator or alternative between Westernism and traditionalism is a striking and general feature in the novels of this group.

Kalau tak Untung belongs to the same same class of problem novel and has the added distinction that it is the first important contribution to Indonesian literature by a woman. Although it lacks the scope of *Salah Asuhan,* in some respects it marks important advances. One of the most striking features of the book is its excellent construction and the polished and easy style of narrative. Some of the incidental vignettes of the scenes of traditional village life are strikingly vivid, and the presentation of the traditional ethos and its atmosphere highly successful.

As in the previously discussed novels, the theme of *Kalau tak Untung* is one of star-crossed lovers, Masrul and Rasmani. However, while the characters of the other novels tended to lay the responsibility for their troubles on fate, *Kalau tak Untung* makes it clear that it is Masrul's consistently weak and selfish character that is to blame. On the other hand, the heroine, Rasmani, is almost too good to be true; but at times she expresses herself with quite remarkable passion, considering the period when the book was written.

416

The book is further notable for its effective use of letters in the development of the plot and its skillful symbolic use of dreams to create atmosphere and to express dread and uncertainty on the part of Rasmani. In one such dream, just after Masrul has left home, she see him dressed in bridal attire, but blindfolded, led by a man with a limp. In another, having walked a long distance and being overcome by thirst, she picks a coconut from a palm with low-hanging fruit but finds it dry; she picks another, likewise dry; eventually she finds one with milk, but on drinking it becomes dizzy and collapses in a faint.

Another novel, quite different in style, is *I Swasta Setahun di Bedahulu* (I Swasta's Year at Bedahulu) by I Gusti Njoman P. Tisna (b. 1908, Bali), which appeared in 1938. It is important for several reasons, not least because it provides an instance of a Balinese, thoroughly versed in his own regional culture, making an original contribution to the development of the Indonesian national language. The majority of the earlier authors—and all those we have described—had been Sumatran. The atmosphere of their works is somewhat gloomy; that of the Balinese is radiant with sunlight, even though the book could hardly be called happy. Further, it is a historical novel, set in tenth-century Bali. Faults the work certainly has: characterization is not very convincing; the style is simple, even monotonous; and little is made of the historical background, though the book is full of incident. However, the reader is able to savor from its pages something of the richness, the texture and fragrance of Balinese life, as well as its underlying philosophy.

Thus far we have discussed the works of writers publishing through Balai Pustaka. On the whole, the authors associated with the periodical *Pudjangga Baru* were more sophisticated, although it would be misleading to suggest that there was always a clear-cut distinction between the two. For example, one of the three founders of *Pudjangga Baru*, Sutan Takdir Alisjahbana, wrote several novels which were printed by Balai Pustaka in addition to his numerous essays and poems published in *Pudjangga Baru*.

Alisjahbana is one of the most exciting personalities in this early period of the development of Indonesian literature. Although trained in law, he was self-educated in many other fields. Like Abdullah, he was a Europophile, and in many other respects he is reminiscent of his fellow writer of a hundred years earlier. Again and again he urged a thorough modernization of Indonesian life through Western education and an inculcation of the dynamism and acceptance of material values that had made Western superiority possible. In his endeavor to promote Indonesia's modernization, he wrote on politics, social questions, linguistics (including a grammar of Bahasa Indonesia), culture, and education, in addition to his novels and poetry.

Today, little of Alisjahbana's writing has much value in its own right. This is not meant to denigrate his remarkably penetrating intellect; but he spread himself over so many fields and led a life of such incessant activity that it was impossible for his work to have real depth. Moreover, his uncritical enthusiasm for Western education made his treatment of linguistics and culture correspondingly superficial. At one point he suggested that it would be advisable to kill off some of the lesser regional languages and dialects, including his native Minangkabau. Alisjahbana's poems are mostly sentimental and his novels of very minor literary value, being little more than vehicles for his ideas. When all this has been said, however, there remains the remarkable virility and even brilliance of his prose style, his wit, breadth of vision, incisiveness and integrity in debate, and his absolute devotion to his cause. Moreover, Alisjahbana gave generous encouragement to new writers: it was he who, when Balai Pustaka's editors were too shocked to admit Armijn Pané's *Belenggu* (Bondage) for publication, accepted it at once and issued it in two numbers of *Pudjangga Baru*.

Armijn Pané, who like Alisjahbana was one of the three founding members of *Pudjangga Baru*, is the finest prose writer of the colonial period. His single full-length novel, *Belenggu*,[9] is the only book written in the Dutch colonial era which can be judged as a fully mature novel, without any qualifications as to the time when it was written or the inexperience of its author. The theme is simple: the eternal triangle—a husband, Sukartono, and his wife Tini, who are unable to understand each other, and the other woman who is able and willing to give Sukartono the love and tenderness he does not find at home. Because Armijn dealt with his theme seriously and frankly, the book was attacked from many quarters as immoral and obscene; and an animated correspondence, praising and condemning the work, appeared in the succeeding numbers of *Pudjangga Baru*.

The events the novel presents are tragic, but the tragic predicament develops not from the pressure of exterior circumstances but through defects in the characters of the protagonists, and thus the book is in the same line of development as *Kalau tak Untung*. But whereas the action of the earlier novel took place against a rural setting, *Belenggu* is set in Batavia, the metropolis. The characters are representatives of a new type of Indonesian—the successful urban couple who possess a car, use a telephone, and who both have professional interests. The novel has remarkable merits: the dialogue is alive, the style lucid, and the plot construction symmetrical. Further, Armijn has succeeded in presenting with remarkable vividness the streams of consciousness of two individuals, each misunderstanding and at odds with the other. His picture of an emancipated couple, who outwardly appear sure of themselves but whose inner life is still hollow and confused, has quite broad implications for the historian of Indonesian society.

Some of Armijn's short stories in the collection *Kisah antara Manusia* (Stories of People)[10] are striking from the standpoint of psychological analysis, compactness of construction, and range of social observation and criticism. Where else in Indonesian fiction in 1935 can one find a description of men dressed as women, waiting in dark corners to sell themselves to wealthy perverts, or any allusion to the unemployment that forced them into such degeneracy?

We have already noted that very many of the early writers originated from Sumatra, and in particular from the Minangkabau region. This, in the first instance, is probably due to the relative ease with which writing in Bahasa Indonesia came to them.[11] Writers of Javanese origin wrote in either Dutch or their own regional language (Sundanese or Javanese as the case might be).[12] Attempts were certainly made to introduce modern literary forms into Javanese: Purwadaminta, for example, wrote Javanese sonnets. On the whole, however, the regional languages reflected little of the renewal of literary vigor that was manifest in the development of Bahasa Indonesia, and since independence they have been left even further behind.

The evolution of a modern poetry during the colonial period was as striking as the development of prose. The first author of note to attempt to write Indonesian-language verse which made use of Western poetic forms and concepts was Muhammad Yamin (b. 1903, Minangkabau). One of his earlier and more famous poems is *Tanah Air* (My Fatherland),[13] which appeared in 1920. In it Yamin, standing on the hills of his native Minangkabau, sings

419

lyrically of the beauty of its forests and gorges, rice terraces and lakes. None of his poetry can be called deathless, but his efforts opened new roads and revealed boundless possibilities for the development of a new poetry. Another pioneer of a new era in poetry was Rustam Effendi (b. 1903, Minangkabau), who declared in one of his poems: "I repudiate all the old forms and rules, because I write according to the promptings of my spirit."[14] The thought is clear enough, even though the verse in which it is expressed can hardly be called elegant.

The writers associated with *Pudjangga Baru* quite early developed a theory of art which had a profound influence on the poetry of this period. It was by no means original, for it reflected the ideas of the Dutch literary revival of the 1880s, an extreme romanticism whose worship of beauty at times approached the blasphemous. The clearest expression of this concept of poetry occurs in an essay by Armijn Pané in the first issue of the periodical *Pudjangga Baru*. Summarized, its theme is broadly this: an artist is the servant of his spirit (*suksma*) and must follow faithfully the promptings of his psyche in whatever he has to express. He is a child of his time and of his society, more sensitive than others to the nature of his surroundings and accordingly more conscious of the enduring sorrow of the world.[15] J. E. Tatengkeng (b. 1907, Celebes) expressed the same idea more vehemently:

> Art is inspiration!
> Art is feeling!
> Art is the inspiration of the imagination!
> Art is the most beautiful possible feeling expressed
>   in the most beautiful possible form![16]

Perhaps more important, the pervading melancholy of these Dutch poets found an echo in the rootlessness of the pioneers of *Pudjangga Baru,* who, as Armijn Pané pointed out, were separated from their traditions by the intrusion of a new type of world. Thus their somewhat lugubrious romanticism was partially to be attributed to their own disillusionment with the colonial society in which they were living.[17]

It is perhaps surprising that it should be the poetic ideas of the 1880s rather than of a later Dutch period that had such an influence on Indonesian poetry. The probable answer is that the works of the "Eightiers," finding their way into high-school textbooks during the 1920s, were the only specimens of recent European verse with which the new generation of Indonesian writers were at all familiar. In any case, the romantic poetry of this Dutch generation was exactly the sort of verse that would influence comparatively young writers without a training in literary criticism.

Not all the early Indonesian poets shared the enthusiastic pro-Westernism of Takdir Alisjahbana, and throughout the issues of *Pudjangga Baru* there ran a debate between those who found their inspiration in the achievements of the West and those who looked to the traditional values of Indonesian and Asian civilization.[18] Sanusi Pané (the older brother of Armijn, born in 1905 in Tapanuli) typifies the latter group. True, he used Western verse forms; but the themes and ideas of his work were basically Asian. Indian religious ideas dominated his mental make-up, and the titles of his poems—"The Taj Mahal," "To Kresna," and "Arjuna"—give a fair idea of his interests.

The most outstanding of the colonial poets was Amir Hamzah. He left two small volumes of original verse: *Njanji Sunji* (Songs of Solitude), published in 1937, and *Buah Rindu* (The Fruit of Love), which, though it was published later, in 1941, comprises poems written at an earlier period than those of the other book. Amir Hamzah was brought up in the literary traditions of a Malay court and thus, more than any other of the new generation of writers, was steeped in the Malay literary tradition. He did not begin to write, however, until he went to Java to further his studies at the age of fourteen or fifteen. Although it is frequently noted as his principal distinction that he gave new life to a moribund tradition of Malay poetry, by far the most important influences on his poetry came from Java, both from his years at a Dutch Protestant school in Batavia and as a student of Oriental literature in Solo. There is a significant proportion of Javanese words in his verse, and his complex patterns of alliteration and assonance clearly owe much to Javanese verse forms.

Amir's earliest poems give the impression of melancholy and depression; they have an obvious relation to the various types of traditional Malay verse, notably the quatrain. These early verses are characterized by the tone, imagery, and even some of the basic emotions of the pantun—though little of its wit. Yet there is a difference: even the earliest poems bear the stamp of a personality, and from the very beginning there is a conscious if imperfect adaptation of the form to suit his needs.

The poems of *Njanji Sunji* belong to a different world. Here

421

Amir has passed beyond the stage of conventional adolescent emotions and no longer has any need to rely on the quatrain or the traditional verse forms. In the best of these poems, the intensity of his theme creates its own form, and his mastery of word choice and construction of phrase is magnificent. These poems are a starkly honest communication of his spiritual life: of his trust in God, of his rebellion against Him, of God's hiddenness and mysterious silence, and eventually of Amir's acceptance of that silence. Some of the poems are too one-sided for greatness, but a few have that perfect balance and flawless restraint of expression that is the hallmark of true poetry.

It is sometimes suggested that Amir Hamzah belonged to the "Indo-centric" group of writers associated with Sanusi Pané. It is true that he translated Asian and not Western verse into Bahasa Indonesia; but unlike his "Indo-centric" colleagues, he neither used the sonnet form nor showed any other influence of the Dutch generation of the 1880s. Strikingly enough, certain of his finest poems reflect a study of the Old Testament, and in fact he translated part of the Song of Solomon into Bahasa Indonesia.[19] It is clear that as a poet Amir Hamzah must be considered not as the representative of a school or tendency but as a distinctive and uncompromising individual.

The Japanese occupation marked a new stage both in the consolidation of Bahasa Indonesia as a national language and in the development of Indonesian literature. It destroyed the presuppositions and complacencies of an entire generation and stimulated a surging feeling of national liberation. The Dutch language was suppressed and Bahasa Indonesia given legal status in its place. The Japanese encouraged literature, the visual arts, singing, drama, and the film, in every case making use of Bahasa Indonesia; but they also introduced a rigid system of censorship and attempted to ensure that every cultural expression served directly the ends of the Greater East Asia Co-prosperity Sphere. For many of the writers, the extreme misery of the Japanese period made it seem that man had been stripped of all pretense and artificiality, left naked in his essential humanity.

Some writers identified themselves with the cause of their Japanese masters and wrote poetry that was in every sense committed. The majority of the sophisticated and intelligent writers, however, resented the oppressive censorship of the Japanese

Kulturkammer and attempted to find some way around it; or else they wrote as their minds and hearts dictated, keeping the result until publication was possible. One means of evading the Japanese censor was by the use of symbols. The technique was not always successful, but some writers did succeed in introducing such a degree of ambiguity into their work that it meant one thing to the Japanese and another to the Indonesian readers. Some of the most successful and effective poems which passed the censor were those clearly written with the author's tongue in his cheek. One by Rosihan Anwar (b. 1922, Minangkabau) described in vibrant language the author's feelings as he wakes early in the morning and hears the tramp of youth on the march. Various exalted thoughts pass through his mind, after which he strides whistling cheerfully to the bathroom.[20]

Two really major literary figures emerged during the Japanese occupation: Chairil Anwar (b. 1922, Medan), who initiated a remarkable efflorescence in Indonesian poetry, and Idrus (b. 1921, Minangkabau), who created a new Indonesian prose style. Together, they established the viability of Bahasa Indonesia as a language of the modern world.

Idrus has not produced any large-scale work; his most important writings (none of them published until after the Japanese surrender) are short stories and vignettes. As a stylist he is famous as a pioneer of the new simplicity. We have already indicated that one of the problems facing Indonesian prose writers was to develop a prose style emancipated from the cumbersome and involved style of the past, one which could express everyday experience vividly and incisively. It is Idrus' success in this that is his great achievement: his sentences are short and compact, his style pithy, and, even more important, his descriptions of scenes and individuals are utterly convincing. In *Kota-Harmoni* (From Kota to Harmoni)—a bitter commentary on life during the Japanese occupation, embodied in a tram ride through Djakarta—the sharp querulous dialogue, the heat, the smell, the dust are all presented so vividly that to read the story is to experience them.

The same is true of *Och, och, och* (Oh! Oh! Oh!). This time the theme of the story is a train journey from Sukabumi to Djakarta; once again we are struck by the vivid realism, the unconventional and striking metaphor. The story exposes mercilessly the general corruption and loss of morale: the ticket inspector who allows the ticketless onto the train for a consideration of 25 cents; the con-

423

ductor who allows them to remain for an additional bribe; the callousness of the Japanese at the check point who confiscate all the rice on board; the organized smuggling of cloth, and even drugs—for all the youth of Djakarta have syphilis! These, like the majority of Idrus' sketches, are savage and biting, but the underlying irony leaves the reader with a feeling of pity and disquiet rather than disgust.[21]

What Idrus did for prose, Chairil Anwar did for poetry. Of Minangkabau descent, he was born near Medan but went to Djakarta shortly before the Japanese occupation and achieved a certain importance shortly after with the founding of the Japanese's Central Cultural Office. As a personality he contrasts strikingly with Amir Hamzah. Whereas Amir Hamzah had been prepared to accept in an agonized submission the burdens that fate imposed upon him, Chairil Anwar fought with a demonic vitality to impose his own standards. This is the significance of his poem *Aku* (My Self), in which he describes himself as a wild beast, rejected by his peers. He refuses to accept the pattern of life around him, where the bourgeois screen of the neatly arranged house, the dignified dress, and formal handshake hides a fundamental, ineradicable selfishness. He wishes to live for a thousand years, but in his own way and on his own terms, never surrendering to the dumb crowd.

During the Japanese occupation Chairil Anwar disregarded both censorship and the interests of the Pacific war. Consequently, few of his poems were published until the Japanese surrender. One important exception, however, was *Diponegoro*, which appeared in the Japanese-sponsored newspaper *Asia Raja* and was one of the few poems to pass the censor without sacrificing its integrity as art. Chairil probably knew little about the messianic leader of the Java War; but he called on the name Diponegoro to express his own devotion to liberty and readiness to sacrifice himself for a great cause, his flaming vitality and confidence in the inevitable victory of truth. Every word, every syllable is vibrant with life, expressed with a compression that reaches its climax in the leaping, muscular vigor of the last four lines, each consisting of a single disyllabic word.

Chairil's work reflected the many sides of his personality. He possessed a dedication to art, a relentless passion for artistic truth which was doomed never to reach fulfillment. His works, to use Eliot's words, are a series of raids on the inexpressible; every attempt is a different kind of failure. This is expressed in various of his poems, particularly in *Tjintaku Djauh Dipulau* (My Beloved Is Afar Off, on an Island). The beloved is a symbol for his ideal of perfection; he is never to reach her, for death calls him: "Direct your barque to my embrace." Another strand in Chairil's work is his revulsion from life, evident in an early poem headed *1943*, written at the sight of an infant in perfect health but infected beyond redemption by its first sip of life, life which is a deadly poison. There is his patriotism, expressed in *Tjerita buat Dien Tamaela* (A Story for a Girl, Dien Tamaela), and in *Krawang Bekasi* (two Javanese place names), a free rendering of Archibald MacLeish's *The Young Dead Soldiers*. There is likewise his religious intuition, which is extraordinary although hardly orthodox Moslem; even though this is rarely expressed, let alone elaborated upon, it reveals itself in such poems as *Doa* (Prayer) and *Isa* (Jesus).

Chairil Anwar died of typhus in 1949 at the age of twenty-seven. In spite of this brief career, it is impossible to overestimate his contribution to modern Indonesian literature. He made Bahasa Indonesia do things it had never done before, and gave it a heightened capacity for poetic and cultural expression it would never lose.

The new generation of poets which came to prominence with Chairil Anwar in 1945 looked back with something akin to contempt on the literary work of the writers associated with the prewar *Pudjangga Baru*. Chairil rejected their preoccupation with a poetic language and their tendency to wait for inspiration instead of draining life to the dregs in search of it. He exclaimed: "If we look back, we find that *Pudjangga Baru*, born in the year that Hitler seized power in Germany, printed only one shallow article on fascism throughout the course of its history. Its founders were dedicated to 'renewal,' but their use of the word was meaningless because they lacked any foundation of literary knowledge in the broadest sense."[22]

Asrul Sani (b. 1926, Minangkabau) complained of the older generation's attempts to create beauty by the use of a conventional "poetic" language; Rivai Apin (b. 1927, Minangkabau) considered much of their emotional expression to be empty posturing, indicating such rhetorical expressions in Alisjahbana's poetry as: "O poinciana!" "O banyan tree!" "O hevea fruit!" In the same vein Sitor Situmorang (b. 1924, North Sumatra) asserted, perhaps not quite fairly, that the poets of *Pudjangga Baru* may have known what literature was but that they lacked the conviction and élan of the new generation. Sitor added that Takdir Alisjahbana and his contemporaries were rooted in the colonial situation, and that Takdir was virtually obsessed with his comparison of Western progress and Indonesian backwardness.[23]

On the side of the older generation, Armijn Pané denied that there had been any cleavage in the development of Indonesian literature resulting from the Japanese occupation, while Takdir Alisjahbana declared that the realism of *Belenggu* was in advance of much of the realist writing produced after the war and that Rustam Effendi was as much an innovator as the postwar writers. He, too, denied any gulf between the two generations and—moving over to the attack—claimed that many of the new writers were more influenced by the books they had read than by life.[24]

If the younger generation was united in criticizing the old, it was divided as to its own orientation. Two main attitudes emerged, one of them coalescing into Gelanggang (Forum), a cultural organization which had been founded by Chairil Anwar in 1946. Among its members were the writers Asrul Sani, Rivai Apin, and M. Akbar Djuhana (b. 1925, East Sumatra), and the painters Muchtar Apin, Baharadin, and Henk Ngantung. Its mouthpiece was a supplement to the political and cultural weekly *Siasat* (Scrutiny) likewise called *Gelanggang*. From 1950 onward this supplement was under the direction of Asrul Sani and Rivai Apin, and in it the group published their declaration of faith: "We are the legitimate heirs to the culture of the whole world, a culture ours to extend and develop in our own way." Their whole emphasis was thus on the international, intercultural human encounter with reality, echoing the universal humanism proclaimed by Chairil Anwar.

The confession of faith issued by *Gelanggang* was answered a few months later by the prolegomenon of the Lembaga Kebudajaan Rakjat (People's Cultural Institute, popularly referred to as Lekra), which began: "In cognizance of the fact that the people are the one and only source for the creation of a culture, and that a new Indonesian culture can only be created by the people, the Lembaga Kebudajaan Rakjat has been founded on the 17th day of August 1950." It described Lekra's principal cultural aim as "art for the people," which it explained as a combination of "critical realism" and "romantic revolutionism." Among the founders of Lekra were the writers A. S. Dharta (its secretary-general, b. 1922, Bandung) and Sobron Aidit (b. 1934, Bangka, the younger brother of the Communist party leader D. N. Aidit).

Although these formal declarations of purpose were made after the ending of the revolution, the origin of the differences they expressed can be traced in part to the circumstances of the struggle against the Dutch. Bujung Saleh (b. 1926, Djakarta) noted that the division of Indonesia into the Republic and a series of Dutch-sponsored federal states between 1946 and 1950 was reflected in the divergent attitudes of writers in the two areas. If in a Dutch-occupied city such as Djakarta slogans like "universal humanism" were in vogue with the concomitant notion of *l'art pour l'art*, in the area of the Republic, art was as much a weapon as was a rifle, and the dominant literary concept was *l'art engagé*. This cleavage was expressed slightly differently by Sitor Situmorang in his analysis of the difference in meaning between "human dignity" as understood by Chairil Anwar and "humanity" as understood by the painter Affandi. For Chairil, human dignity was contained and expressed in the individual; for Affandi, humanity is achieved by man as of a social creature acting in harmony with his environment.[25]

The enduring conflict between these two groups has evidenced itself in complex ways. At one point it is expressed in the debate outlined above; at another it becomes a revival of the prewar dichotomy between the Europophilism of Takdir Alisjahbana and the "nativism" of Sanusi Pané. At still another point it assumes a partisan political form, for Lekra has become the cultural spokesman of the Communist party, while the loyalties of the Gelanggang writers have tended toward the now-banned Socialist party (PSI). Neither the Islamic parties nor the nationalist PNI have attracted writers of purely literary ability; and Lekra has managed to gather unto itself virtually all those artists who do not fall consciously into the universal humanist, individualist group associated with Gelanggang. It is one of the truly remarkable achievements of the Indonesian Communist party that it has largely succeeded—at least among the Javanese—in making itself the exponent of the interests and values of the common man by identifying itself with his culture.

This cleavage of sociopolitical orientation naturally has colored the critical assessment of the literary merits of one group by the other. A principal bone of contention between them is the use of the term "Generation of '45," which has been popularly employed to designate those writers who came to prominence with the proclamation of Indonesian independence. The phrase sounds so compelling and inevitable that one tends instinctively to accept it as having arisen concomitantly with a clearly defined group of writers, headed by Chairil Anwar. It was not coined, however, until 1949, when it was employed by Rosihan Anwar; and even at that time there was much acrimonious discussion as to whether it was a meaningful expression or not.[26]

The term "Generation of '45" lends itself, in fact, to as much ambiguity as does "Pudjangga Baru," with which it is frequently contrasted. Landmarks of this kind in literary history are labels more of convenience than of fact; in adopting them uncritically one runs the danger of mistaking an undefined part for a complex whole. Clearly the year 1945 did not inaugurate a completely new era in Indonesian literature, although for a small, highly gifted group it did symbolize a major breakthrough. Not all of this limited coterie, however, accepted the phrase as meaningful for themselves: Idrus, for example, rejected any association with it. In addition, Lekra critics, claiming a sociopolitical content for the term, denied it to Chairil Anwar and the Gelanggang group (who were after all the outstanding writers of the immediate post-1945 years) on the grounds that they were interested in the problems of the individual rather than the promotion of the social good.[27]

Although Chairil Anwar has remained perhaps the outstanding poet up to the present, several other fine poets have appeared. At the same time, so much has been written, scattered throughout so many periodicals, that it is difficult to form any reliable judgment of the merits and directions of modern Indonesian poetry.[28] However, one important collection, appearing in 1950, was *Tiga Menguak Takdir* (Three Penetrate Fate),[29] a selection of their own poems by Chairil Anwar, Asrul Sani, and Rivai Apin, the three founders of Gelanggang.

It may be debated whether the three writers collaborating in this book selected their best or most representative work to be included in it; but it remains undeniable that each spoke with his own highly individual and distinctive voice. We have already discussed Chairil. Of the remaining two, Asrul Sani is, in my view, the more outstanding. There is a certain calmness, steadiness, and even ethereal quality of vision apparent in several of his poems that is highly personal. Although his best poetry does not lack emotional impact, its force is quite different from that of the restless urgency and frustration of Chairil Anwar. Teeuw finds the key to Asrul Sani's approach in a sentence from one of his essays: "This [i.e. individuality in literature] is the one means of salvation in a type of democratic society that is bent on stifling all aristocracy of spirit." Thus, Teeuw declares, Asrul Sani is haunted by the fear of losing his individuality in the mob, and one of his favorite symbols is the solitude of the sea, far from the pressures of everyday life.[30] Among the most moving of his poems are *Anak Laut* (A Child of the Sea), *Pengungsi* (Refugees), and *Sebagai Kenangan kepada Amir Hamzah, Penjair jang Terbunuh* (In Memory of Amir Hamzah, the Slain Poet).

One of the most important poets subsequent to Chairil Anwar is Sitor Situmorang, who was born in 1923 of Christian Batak descent. In a special way he is a spokesman for the plight of many Indonesian intellectuals of today; and from this standpoint he is perhaps even more important than Chairil Anwar. Much of his inspiration and many of his attitudes derive from a sojourn in France and Italy made during 1950. On his homecoming he discovered that the place he returned to was no longer home; and the dominant theme of several of his poems is his bewilderment and sense of loss at this realization. Frequently we find a fugal counterplay of ideas in the development of this theme: how he appears to others and how he knows himself to be. Thus in the poem *Si-anak Hilang* (The Lost Son) he describes in simple quatrains the reactions of his parents and the people of his village on his homecoming from Europe—the traditional idyllic return of the wanderer, as it appears to them. The grievous revelation, however, comes in the last couplet of the poem. When all the family are asleep, the waves murmuring against the shore of Samosir tell the awful truth: the son has not returned home; what was home is home no longer.

Many of Sitor's poems are deeply personal and can only be understood through knowledge of his life. J. U. Nasution, in two most interesting essays,[31] shows how Sitor's Christian faith has gradually been eroded by Sartrean existentialism. One might add by sensuality, for certain of the poems of *Wadjah tak Bernama* (A Nameless Face) are oppressively, even crudely sexual. Yet with or without an explicit faith, Sitor is still profoundly religious in temperament. These tensions between faith and doubt, between Europe and Indonesia, between homelessness and a longing to

429

find a home, are the raw materials of which great poetry can be made.

Another important collection of poems, *Ketemu di Djalan* (A Chance Meeting), appeared in 1956. Like *Tiga Menguak Takdir*, it consists of a selection of the work of three young poets—in this case A. Rossidhy (b. 1938, West Java), Sobron Aidit, and S. M. Ardan (b. 1932, Medan). It is eminently useful as a documentation of the development of Indonesian poetry but is difficult to evaluate. All three authors were at the time of publication very young, either in their late teens or early twenties, and each is likewise still finding his way. My own feeling is that Rossidhy is more successful as a short-story writer than as a poet, and several of his poems in this volume are marked by irritating mannerisms. The writer Toto Sudarto Bachtiar (b. 1929, Djakarta), reviewing the volume, commented that of the three it is Sobron Aidit who is the most successful in achieving a valid poetic expression. He added, however, that the fifteen poems which represent each author cannot serve as a basis for any final judgment of the talent of these writers, particularly in view of their youth.[32]

Two further poets deserve individual mention, the first of them being the just-cited Toto Sudarto Bachtiar. H. B. Jassin has called him "the poet of Djakarta at eventide,"[33] for his verse reflects his knowledge and love of the metropolis. Some of his poems, such as *Gadis Peminta-minta* (A Beggar Girl) are simple and moving. Others, however, such as *Lagu Orang-orang Malang* (A Song for the Luckless Ones) are difficult to understand because of their compression, symbolism, and ambiguous syntax.

Another younger poet who speaks with a distinctive voice is W. S. Rendra (b. 1935, Solo). His volume *Ballada Orang-orang Tertjinta* (Songs of Lovers), published in 1957, is impressive in its capacity for emotional intensity, fine sense of language and atmosphere, and its promise for the future; but the book is still clearly the work of an adolescent. The dominant themes are almost exclusively sex and death, and he overworks puns such as *dara* (hymen, virginity) and *darah* (blood).

Prose development during the postwar period has been equally striking, although full-length novels have been few. Perhaps the most important single novel is *Atheis* (An Atheist) by Achdiat Karta Mihardja (b. 1911, West Java), which was first published in 1949. In it Achdiat delineates with great power one aspect of the confrontation of the Indonesian villager with the modern world.

Hassan, the hero of the story, is a pious youth from the village who, on his first arrival in the city, indulges in heroic asceticism. On meeting an old school friend, Rusli, however, he is confronted first by dialectical materialism, second by the beauty of Rusli's friend Kartini, and thirdly by the aggressive and vituperative independence of the anarchist Anwar, who believes in no God and respects no man. This combined assault is too much for Hassan's faith. He attempts to discard it, but finds his attempt to live as an atheist agonizingly unsuccessful. In the end, dying, he utters the Moslem confession of faith. Of course, the situation presented to us is not wholly representative. Not every village youth is as pious or ascetic as Hassan; neither is the city a hotbed of anarchism and dialectical materialism. Achdiat has in fact focused on certain elements in a general situation and, developing them with such power as almost to transcend realism, wrings from us pity and horror at the sufferings of simple folk involved in a world they cannot understand.

Another important book, first published in 1950, is *Djalan tak ada Udjung* (A Road with No End) by Mochtar Lubis (b. 1919, Minangkabau). The hero of the story, Guru Isa, is a coward. When fighting against the Dutch breaks out, he commits himself to the Indonesian side, not because he is a patriot but because he is afraid to do anything else. His comrades, who see only his actions and are unaware of his motives, regard him as a hero; but he does not deceive himself. Yet when arrested he withstands torture where his flamboyantly courageous colleagues are forced into betrayal of their friends. He has become the man his friends thought him to be. He has, in fact, solved the problem that we referred to earlier as central to much of Sitor Situmorang's poetry.

Pramudya Ananta Tur is by far the most prolific of the serious writers in Indonesia. He was born at Blora in 1925; during the revolutionary struggle he served as a war correspondent, was captured by the Dutch, and spent two years in prison. During this period of internment he wrote extensively and gathered an immense amount of material for future work. One of Pramudya's most important novels is *Keluarga Gerilja*, which was first published in 1950. The title literally means A Guerrilla Family, but a rendering such as A Family in Hell would better convey the content of the book. The story focuses on the agony of a family split by the conflict of loyalties—the father to the Dutch-sponsored Federalist state, the sons to the Republic. The sons in a guerrilla

431

plot kill their father; and the action of the novel takes place in the three days between the sentencing of one son and the time he is shot. In this book, Pramudya goes beyond realism in much the same way as Achdiat does in *Atheis*, creating ideal characters to communicate his own vision of human life and values. At the same time, although Pramudya as a man is passionately committed both politically and as a nationalist, he is not writing propaganda. The kernel of his feeling is revealed in the prayer of the second son: "Perhaps these my sins You do not account for sins, because it is You who have brought to birth this new people. Also because we—because I—am on the weaker side, and am defending myself. Indeed, we are on the weaker side. But all the sins I have committed are for me *still* sins. I have sinned against myself; I have sinned against humanity; I have sinned against the families [of others]—the families of those soldiers that I have killed. I have sinned against their love, which has been in vain."[34] The scene is reminiscent of Arjuna sorrowing over his duty to do battle against his kinsfolk, the Kurawas. Nor is this an accident: Pramudya is an ethnic Javanese and was brought up amid the symbolism, imagery, and motifs of the Mahabharata.

Perburuan (Pursuit), which also appeared in 1950, reveals the same qualities and interests as *Keluarga Gerilja*. The central figure in this novel is an Indonesian officer, Dèn Hardo, who took part in an unsuccessful rising against the Japanese, was pursued, and lived the life of a beggar. This work, too, has specifically Javanese overtones. Like many of Pramudya's heroes, Dèn Hardo is larger than life, and is reminiscent of Arjuna: his long sojourn in the cave echoes Arjuna's asceticism in the grotto on Mount Indrakila, and his disregard for material comforts, broad humanitarianism, and capacity for miraculous escape from the Japanese strengthen this impression.

In addition to his novels Pramudya has written many, very many, short stories. He likewise shows considerable skill as an essayist and critic. In one article appearing in *Kisah*,[35] he gives a fascinating account of literary creation as he understands it. Pramudya's art is one of immense power and consummate skill; and perhaps the most striking feature of his style is its immediacy. He has the ability to create overtones and a sense of dimension, combined with remarkable economy. Everything he writes (in his best work) is a living, functioning part of an organic whole; and his studies of

432

the encounters and sufferings of his heroes can only be compared in their intensity to those of Dostoevski.

Sitor Situmorang has likewise written many short stories. One significant collection is *Pertempuran dan Saldju di Parijs* (A Conflict and Snow in Paris), which appeared in 1956. One of the stories in this group, *Ibu Pergi ke Sorga* (Mother Goes to Heaven),[36] illustrates a theme we referred to earlier, the loss of the sense of home. The hero of the story returns from Djakarta to his village in north Sumatra. It is Christmas, and his mother is in the last stages of tuberculosis. Everything seems smaller than it once appeared to him, and the intimate cycle of village life no longer has any meaning. The parson's invitation to him to read the lesson strikes him with a dumb and embarrassed dismay. His mother's death gives him no sense of loss, and the parson's assurance that she is in Paradise carries no conviction.

Achdiat Karta Mihardja has published two collections of short stories: *Keretakan dan Ketegangan* (Fissures and Tensions) in 1956, two of which have subsequently appeared in English;[37] and *Kesan dan Kenangan* (Impressions and Memories) in 1961, the reminiscences of a round-the-world trip the author made in 1957. At first there appears to be no unity of theme underlying the stories, apart from the fact that almost all Achdiat's characters are unfortunate. However, closer examination reveals a connecting theme in the author's philosophy of life: fate is cruel, providence enigmatic; only love can give life any value or meaning.

The short story, it should now become clear, is the most popular and accomplished prose form in modern Indonesian writing, and at the same time a comparatively new arrival on the Indonesian literary scene.[38] It has the merit of permitting the author to deal discreetly with the manifold aspects of the fantastically rich canvas of contemporary Indonesia; the tensions, jealousies, and adventures of rural life; contrasts and conflicts between the city and the village, the new world and the old; reminiscences of adolescence, of the colonial past; satiric evocations of the present situation, of its absurdities and pathos.

The comparative absence of large-scale works, however, aroused disquiet among certain Indonesian intellectuals, and as early as 1949 some of them detected a crisis in Indonesian literature. This was one of the discussion themes at a meeting of the Dutch-sponsored foundation for cultural interchange, Sticusa, held at Amsterdam in 1953, in which several Indonesians participated,

433

including Asrul Sani and Takdir Alisjahbana. The concept of a crisis, particularly as it was developed at this meeting, was peculiar to the Gelanggang group of writers and was accordingly labeled by Lekra's adherents as the complaint of salon critics who had written themselves out.[39]

In this controversy, the questions raised by Sudjatmoko in the first issue of *Konfrontasi* (Encounter)[40] in 1954 are important and well put:

> We are bound to the short story, and apparently cannot progress beyond it. There are many works in this form that have merit, and the fluency of their language is evident, but we are still waiting for literary works of major calibre. . . . It is clear that almost all our short stories develop exclusively within the minor framework of the psychology of the individual; so that the question arises as to whether our incapacity[in this field] is merely a matter of shortness of breath, and a lack of mastery of the major forms of literature, or is caused by our inability to use weightier literary materials that are more difficult to handle.

> If this is the case, then we have to admit that our claim to the rank of human beings who have broken loose from the values of their old life, which formed an important element in our revolutionary literary "renaissance," has foundered in this psychologism [sic?], in minor experiences and slight reverberations of the spirit which are only sufficient to produce our short stories and poems. If this is the case, then we must ask ourselves whether the dramatic element implicit in our revolution, and the questions of humanity and society associated with it have not been plumbed and experienced by our writers.[41]

On the other hand, to say that Sudjatmoko's questions are well put is not to suggest that one can accept without reservation his answers. It may well be that he and those he represents are looking for the wrong things in the Indonesian situation, and thus misrepresent the contemporary literary scene. This is perhaps the reason why Takdir Alisjahbana and Asrul Sani were so concerned with the idea of decline in Indonesian literature at Amsterdam in 1953. They looked at the finest contemporary Western writers and wondered why Indonesian literature did not seem to reach an equivalent standard, without considering the view that Indonesian writing would develop in relationship to a society whose concerns are vastly different from those of the individual-oriented West.

434

The critic H. B. Jassin, in fact, dismisses Sudjatmoko's views quite brusquely:

> There is nothing we can say . . . particularly if a person has already defined his standards in a slighting manner, [declaring] that what he calls the psychology of the individual and "the minor experiences and reverberations of the spirit which are only sufficient to produce our short stories and poems" are of no significance to him. Because *a priori* he turns up his nose at the sight of these shorter works, he is not going to reach the essential life they embody, which may not perhaps fall short of what is portentously called: "the dramatic element implicit in our revolution, and the questions of humanity and society associated with it."[42]

In an interesting and realistic article, Nugroho Notosusanto summarizes the opinions of those who claim that Indonesian literature is in a state of crisis: the majority of new writers are young, many of them still at school; they are perhaps productive, but do not produce work of real competence or value. To this he adds the pertinent question: is there anything abnormal or regrettable in this; is not this youthful enthusiasm for writing rather a cause for encouragement?[43] One might even go further and say that a really effective short story requires as much art as a full-length novel, and that the best short stories of authors as young as Rendra and Rossidhy have a maturity of expression, poise, and balance that belies their youthfulness. At the same time, we might also note that in the most recent period there are signs that some of the longer forms of narrative are returning to popularity.[44]

In his Independence Day speech of August 1959, President Sukarno laid down "National Personality"[45] as the official Indonesian cultural motif. The implication of the slogan is that writers must have a social function, must be aware of their role as spokesmen of a national identity.[46] Clearly, part of Sukarno's aim in promulgating this state ideology was to dissolve the internationalist-"nativist" dichotomy by imposing a version of the socially oriented "nativist" view which would be meaningful for the entire community. It is still too early, however, to determine whether the official philosophy is going to result in a major change of direction in Indonesian writing; and it is difficult to assess whether, by using the concept "National Personality" as a criterion, it is possible to distinguish between the short stories written in *Kisah* up to 1957, and those which have appeared in *Sastra* since May 1961.[47]

On the other hand, it is certainly meaningful to ask whether a modern literature is still an exotic growth in Indonesia; whether the modern Indonesian writer is writing as an Indonesian, with his background and traditions forming an organic and distinctive part of his work, or whether he is using a European-acquired skill in a European way, with his own background appearing only as local color. If the first of these two alternatives is the more accurate description of the contemporary Indonesian scene—as I believe it is—then the best Indonesian writers are, and in fact have long been, expressing and developing a national personality.

Not everything that has been produced is of high excellence, and not many works have the major and compelling stature of Achdiat's *Atheis;* but the cumulative effect of the shorter pieces of good writing in poetry as well as prose is impressive. It is not only the amount of creative writing that is important, but the amount of criticism, discussion, and evaluation going on, particularly among younger writers and students. These critical works, appearing in periodicals and newspapers, must be read to gain any full understanding of Indonesian creative writing.

Indonesian authors still face many difficulties, but so do creative writers anywhere. Their greatest problem even if not all of them have been explicitly aware of it—has been to create a common literary tradition in a new language, appealing to the public of a new nation. Serious literature is unlikely to have a mass market, but with the continued spread of education in Indonesia one has a right to expect a far larger proportion of educated readers than exists at present.[48] With a larger reading public, writing will certainly become a better economic proposition than it is at present. The vitality of literary enthusiasm is indicated by the number of literary clubs scattered throughout the country,[49] while an increased emphasis on modern Indonesian writing has resulted from the revision of educational curricula, especially in the literature departments of the universities in Djakarta and Bandung.

The new writers have a complex technique to master. As Edwin Muir remarks: "To the novelist of fifty or a hundred years ago, life obediently fell into the mould of a story; to the novelist of today, it refuses to do so."[50] In another essay Muir adds: "The writers of this century have certainly been troubled by the problem of an era of transition; but it is clear that they have also been troubled by the desire to convey a new sense of experience."[51] These are precisely the problems faced by the Indonesian writer, and in particular the novelist. He is confronted with the immense tasks facing the mid-twentieth-century novelist who seeks a new means of individual expression—but without a tradition of two hundred years behind him on which the European novelist can call.

At the same time, the new writers no longer have to face one of the major obstacles to the first Indonesian literary generation— the need to create a language suitable to a modern nation. The area of thought, experience, and expression that present-day Bahasa Indonesia can serve to communicate with subtlety, grace, and exactness—not to mention pungency if required—is remarkable. It is adequate for the expression of Christian, Moslem, and Hindu belief, and all the needs of administration, scholarship, law, and commerce. Nothing could be more misleading than to imagine contemporary Bahasa Indonesia as a kind of superimposed *lingua franca,* without an organic vitality of its own.

CHAPTER *10*

The Enduring Tradition: Music and Theater in Java and Bali

MANTLE HOOD

AMONG THE three thousand inhabited islands of the Republic of Indonesia, a rich diversity of ethnic and religious backgrounds has produced a bewildering array of art forms. The Indonesian motto "Bhinneka Tunggal Ika" (Unity in Diversity) may apply to the arts only in the most general tems. Countless regional and local variants in techniques, designs, and subject matter have developed as a result of contact with or insularity from outside influences from China, Indochina, India, the Middle East, and the other islands of the archipelago itself.[1] Thus Indonesian art has produced such extremes as the elaborate Hindu-inspired sculpture of Bali, the result of Indian influences conveyed from ancient Java, and the severe ancestor figures of Nias, produced in isolation from the outside world. Throughout the archipelago artistic development has been generally rich, whether it has functioned as an expression of religious conviction or as the servant of utilitarian necessity. It has reached its highest development in the inseparably entwined arts of music, dance, and poetry, and in the creation of handicraft and art objects from natural materials. Some local artistic traditions, generally the less sophisticated ones, have succumbed or are fading under the pressure of outside influences[2]—a case in point being the Nias sculptures, which failed to survive the misdirected efforts of a Protestant mission. What might be termed the grand tradition of Indonesian art has shown an amazing viability, however, and it is this—the performing arts of Java and Bali—which we shall discuss here.[3]

The greatest stimulus to Javanese and Balinese art forms and the inspiration for their continuance and development is the Hindu

438

literature of the Mahabarata and Ramayana. These epics of immense length and bewilderingly complex episodic structure recount the miraculous deeds of the Hindu gods and heroes, a mélange of mysticism and magic in Indonesia which has been enriched by the autochthonous beliefs of the Javanese, Sundanese, and Balinese peoples, who continue to regard this classical literature as the story of their own ancestry. Indeed, *wajang purwa* or the "old stories" based on this Hindu literature provide an essential key to understanding contemporary societies on Java and Bali.

The principal form of presentation is the puppet play. In Central Java the appropriate vehicle is known as *wajang kulit* (kulit, leather). In the palace of President Sukarno, in the various Javanese royal courts, in countless villages the revered characters of wajang kulit are brought to life by the skilled hands of the *dalang* or puppeteer as materialized silhouettes of the spirits of the ancestor figures. The performances are presented in celebration of the crisis events of life such as birth, marriage, circumcision, and for the alleviation of epidemics and similar calamities; they enact any one of hundreds of stories which collectively represent every conceivable moral and ethical situation. The intimate world of the individual, "the thousand natural shocks that flesh is heir to," as well as the cosmos within which he dwells, are encompassed by a single story. The allusion to *Hamlet* is not inappropriate, since European scholars have compared the quality of some of the literature of wajang kulit with the finest works of Shakespeare.

These flat leather puppets are intricately carved from buffalo hide and painted on both sides, in conformity with strict rules of craftsmanship, to portray character type and dress.[4] The placement and shape of nose, eye, mouth, moustache, the presence or absence of body hairs or chin whiskers, the inclination of the head, the hair arrangement, the headgear, clothing and jewelry, and other details rendered by the carving and coloring determine rank, character, and ultimately the specific identity of the puppet. Facial and body colors depict temperament and mood: e.g. a black face with gold body indicates a refined warrior in a state of firm resolve or anger; a green face is appropriate for the cowardly warrior.

The refined character has an almond-shaped eye, a long pointed nose running in a straight line from forehead to tip, a slightly bowed head to indicate modesty, an absence of chin whiskers, and a minimum of jewelry and finery. These attributes are perhaps

439

best typified by the character Ardjuna. The coarse character has a round eye, a bulbous nose, a defiant angle of head, body and chin hairs, and an ostentatious display of finery. These qualities are typified by a character like Burisrawa. Subtle variations of any of these basic features provide an immediate index to character. A complete cast, allowing for several duplications of a single character in order to depict different ages or emotions, may number as many as three hundred and fifty puppets.

The dalang sits cross-legged before the *kelir,* a white screen bordered by red, holding the puppet with one hand by a central supporting rod made of buffalo horn and with the other manipulating two slender rods which articulate the arms at the shoulder and elbow. Above his head an oil lamp, the *blĕntjong,* or in modern times the less effective glare of an electric light, casts a shadow of the puppet, which from the other side of the screen takes on a lifelike quality as the flickering lamp creates the illusion of a breathing figure. By moving the puppet toward and away from the screen the dalang can exaggerate its size and enhance the supernatural impression of the performance.

This arresting aspect of wajang kulit has falsely suggested the translation "shadow play." According to Mellema and others the puppet itself and *not* the shadow is the important consideration.[5] Traditionally, wajang kulit was performed in the *pringgitan* of the Javanese house, a space leading from the formal front pavilion or *pendapa*—the male part of the house—to the intimate living quarters of the house proper—the female part of the house. Thus, the screen closed off the inner rooms in which sat the women and children, who were allowed to see only the shadowy aspect of the performance. On the dalang's side of the screen sat the men, who could see all of the puppets stuck into a lower or upper base made of the trunks of banana trees laid end to end—the five Pandawas and their followers, representing the good party, at the dalang's right and the hundred Kurawas and their followers, the bad party, at his left. It is believed that originally this type of performance was a male initiation rite in which the dalang functioned as a kind of priest. Poerbatjaraka, on the other hand, offers convincing evidence that traditionally the shadow-side of the screen was the most important and suggests that the segregation of the sexes at a wajang performance is a fairly recent development.[6] As documentation he cites literary sources and the Balinese practice of mixed sexes watching wajang. Today, at any rate, anyone may sit on either side of the screen.

The deepest respect persists for the dalang, who in the many functions of his art is justly regarded as a versatile and highly educated scholar. The dalang has a sacred responsibility, for through his religious convictions he is given the spiritual strength required to bring to life the figures of wajang. He must know all the levels of the Javanese language: the ancient poetic tongue Kawi, classical Javanese, two levels of low Javanese, three levels of high Javanese, and special vocabularies reserved for the royal courts and for the gods. He must develop a wide range of voice changes in order to accommodate the appropriate personification of the different characters. He must possess a great memory in order to retain the formalities and intricacies of many plots. He must be skilled in weaving topical humor—sometimes light, sometimes ribald, but always funny—into his stories, for it is the touches of contemporary invention that make wajang kulit the most popular and liveliest of arts. It requires great manual dexterity to manipulate two or three puppets simultaneously in a fierce battle scene. At his left against the side of the wooden chest used for storing the puppets, he underscores the dramatic action with sharp raps of the wooden *tjempala* held in the toes of his right foot and beaten against a set of metal plates, or with his left hand raps out signals to the large gamelan orchestra sitting behind him. He must sing all the songs and, by poetic imagery and indirect reference, indicate to the leader of the gamelan what piece is to be played next. And all of this must be accomplished in one continuous performance lasting through the night without intermission from about eight o'clock in the evening until six o'clock the next morning.

The wajang night begins with an overture by the gamelan, and then with proper ceremony the dalang removes from the middle of the screen a large leafshaped leather *gunungan* or *kayon*. This beautifully carved piece, simulating a mountain or tree, symbolizes the entire ritual of wajang. A gunungan is painted on both sides in an elaborate coloration of the symbols carved in silhouette. Another leather piece in the same form but painted red replaces it to depict fire and other natural elements. Sometimes the back of the gunungan is painted red, eliminating the need for a substitute piece. The gunungan is used to open and close the performance, to indicate changes of scene, and to represent a forest, a valley, a mountain, a fire, the gateway to a palace or temple, a river or ocean, wind, the raging of the elements. In the center of the gunungan is the entrance to a temple guarded on either side by a large *buta* or giant. On both sides of the temple roof is a *bledĕgan,* the representation of thunder and lightning, and at the vortex of the gable is a *kala* head, guardian against evil spirits. Up the center of the gunungan is the tree of life around which is wound the holy naga or serpent. On either side of the base of the tree is a tiger and a buffalo, and birds and monkeys are sometimes included in the elaborate details.[7]

The first period of the wajang night lasts until midnight. During this time the dalang introduces the principal characters and deliberately suggests the beginning of the plot, a fight between the forces of good and evil. The leading character of the drama, however, usually does not appear until shortly before midnight; it is only then that the audience may be sure which story is being presented. The first time period of the wajang night is compared by some to the youthful period of life, to childhood and adolescence. It is here that young children learn to value the Javanese ideal of refinement in manners and are given instruction by the dalang in the form of moral and ethical advice. At midnight the *gara-gara* or raging of the elements occurs, leading into the second period of the wajang night, which lasts until three in the morning. During this period the *panakawan* or clowns play an important role, to counterbalance fierce fighting and further involvements of plot. Symbolically it is regarded as reflecting the young adult's struggles in society. During the third period of the night the complications of plot intensify until finally at the eleventh hour good triumphs over evil and a philosophical dénouement symbolizes the maturity and wisdom of old age. The final battle ends with a victory dance, the *tajungan,* performed by Bima, one of the most beloved heroes of the Pandawas, or someone related to him—e.g. Baju, his father, the god of wind. If these characters are absent from a particular story, then the tajungan is performed by one of the leading heroes. A final meeting in the palace of the good party follows, and sometimes, as an entertainment for the festivities, a dancing girl in the form of a round wooden puppet (*golĕk*) dances for the pleasure of the assembled victors. And finally at dawn the dalang respectfully places the gunungan back in the center of the screen.

The role of the panakawan, mentioned as figuring prominently in the second period of the wajang night, has a peculiar significance throughout the Javanese versions of the Indian stories. These clowns function as servants in the palace of the five Pandawas, the good party, under the names of Semar and his three sons Pétruk, Garèng, and Bagong. Togog and Bilung are attendants for the bad party, the hundred Kurawas, cousins of the Pandawas. These servants translate the high and poetic language of their lords into the common vernacular, each expressing his own characteristic type of humor and mimicry. Their deformed shapes and feigned stupidity, their awkward and clumsy deportment, their topical witticisms and deceptive wisdom make them favorite characters with Javanese audiences. Their grotesque forms and purely Javanese names set them apart from other wajang figures, evidence to some scholars that these characters originated in pre-Hindu times and are, therefore, additions to the Indian stories. It may be significant, in this connection, that although the panakawan masquerade in their ridiculous roles as court fools, they sometimes rescue a desperate situation for their mighty masters by rendering good advice.

The particular background of Semar illustrates his vital role in the literature and justifies the great depth of feeling which the Javanese have for him. According to legend, the principal servants of both the good and the bad parties, Semar and Togog, were originally gods themselves, brothers of Batara Guru (Shiva). Semar's name was Sang Hjang Ismaja, and Togog was called Sang Hjang Punggung. In their godly forms these two were as handsome as the other gods. One day, the story goes, Sang Hjang Punggung (Togog) picked a quarrel with Sang Hjang Ismaja (Semar), and they began fighting. Batara Guru ordered them to stop but they did not heed his command. Then Sang Hjang Tunggal (the One God), father of all three, banished the two fighting gods from the heavenly kingdom and as punishment forced them to live among mortals, Semar as servant to the Pandawas and Togog as servant to the Kurawas.

In the course of the wajang story all the servants address their masters in high Javanese and are answered in low Javanese. When one of the gods visits the palace of the Pandawas, all of the princely heroes assume positions of respect, so that their heads are lower than his, and address him in the highest level of language and are answered by him in low Javanese. The only exception is Semar, who remains standing and speaks to the god in Ngoko (low Javanese) and is answered in high Javanese. This respect

443

and veneration shown for Semar—god that he was, but servant that he is—makes a profound impression on the Javanese people.

Of the hundreds of stories drawn from the Mahabarata a sequence of particular significance is the Bharata Juda. This series of twelve related stories depicts the final destruction of the gods and heroes of the Mahabarata. The first two evenings form a prelude and the last two a postlude to the main body of episodes. Although one or another of the eight central stories may be presented in connection with some special event or crisis, to the best of present knowledge it was not until as late as 1957 that the complete Bharata Juda was presented in a performance of wajang kulit. During the former reign of Sultan Hamengku Buwana VIII of Jogjakarta the present head of the court musicians, Kangdjeng Rija Madakusuma, sang the long epic poem, on successive days, in its entirety as a private performance. This great tragic drama is considered such a powerful and sacred text, according to informants, that a public wajang performance of the complete story was considered dangerous to the very survival of man. Grave economic and political conditions in 1957, however, were cited as justification for risking the complete presentation in the belief that "things could not get much worse and they might get better."

It was decided not to present the two evenings making up the prelude, and the rest of the episodes were scheduled to be given one night every two weeks until the entire series was complete. An overwhelming response brought people from all over Java to the city of Jogjakarta for this special series. After the second presentation the demand of spectators so far exceeded the number that could be accommodated that each story was repeated a week after its initial offering. In the third story of the central group, one of the tragic scenes depicts the death of a favorite hero, Abimanju. The large building in which the performance was being presented, Sasana Hinggil, was filled to capacity and overflowing. Outside loudspeakers carried the sound of the dalang's voice, the sound of the tjempala indicating appropriate action, and the accompanying music to thousands of people jamming the large *alun-alun* or public square immediately south of the palace. During the course of the performance, precisely at the moment of Abimanju's death, Central Java was violently shaken by an earthquake—an uncommon occurrence in this land of volcanoes. True to his sacred trust, the dalang continued his performance without the slightest hesitation. This evidence of great spiritual strength

444

calmed the audience and the series proceeded without further threat of calamity.

At the conclusion of the final episode of the Bharata Juda, shortly after six o'clock in the morning, a very special form of wajang—a short presentation lasting about one hour—was given by another dalang honoring the performance of the Bharata Juda and the puppeteer. During this performance the dalang being honored replaced the leader of the gamelan as the *rebab* player, a clear indication of the important relationship between drama and music.

In 1958 the Bharata Juda was given again, this time including all twelve evenings, one a month. The deep emotional effect of this series of stories on the Javanese people is indicative of the vital significance of this literature in their lives. Among the many refinements of Javanese society is the ideal of concealing the emotions—it is sometimes said that there is a Javanese smile for every emotion, and it is considered bad manners to speak or laugh too loudly. The deep impact of the tragedies of the Bharata Juda, therefore, is apparent when during the course of these performances unabashed tears streak the faces of the audience.

There are many symbolic interpretations of wajang. "Mysticism recognizes the wajang purwa performance as the symbol of the cosmos. The banana trunks are the symbol of the surface of the earth where all the creatures carry out their functions in the way fixed by and through the power of the dalang. The puppets come to life under the influence of the dalang and therefore are dependent on him. But on the other hand, the dalang is dependent upon the puppets because he would not be able to realize his power without them. In the same way man is dependent on God and God on man. Both complement each other and form a two-part unity. The one cannot exist without the other."[8] It is also believed that the performance itself has a powerful protective effect on the audience. Whether the listener is attentive or asleep he is guarded against evil influences the whole night through.[9]

Another type of puppet which uses flat leather figures is *wajang gedog*. This form of wajang relates the stories of the autochthonous Pandji cycle. Pandji is a culture hero who in some of his romantic adventures and heroic deeds is reminiscent of the Hindu hero Ardjuna. He numbers among his virtues excellence as a gamelan player and gongsmith. The large gongs of Central Java are famous throughout the Western world of music for their deep and sonorous tone quality, and the sacred art of fabricating these gongs

445

is only entrusted to a man of great spiritual strength. During working hours, traditionally, he takes the name of Pandji Sepuh, Pandji the Old One, and his co-workers and assistants bear the names of Pandji's half brothers, his servants, a younger sister, and others in the Pandji retinue.[10] It is believed that the assumption of these professional names will assure necessary protection from evil forces to which the artisans in such a responsible task are subject.

In Java and Bali, there are two principal gamelan tuning systems: the five-tone system known as *sléndro* and a seven-tone system called *pélog*. For the accompaniment of wajang kulit gamelan sléndro is appropriate; for wajang gedog a gamelan tuned to the seven-tone pélog is used. In Central Java, though wajang gedog is now seldom performed there, this tradition is still maintained.[11] Musicians in Central Java consider the musical compositions which accompany wajang gedog and therefore performed on gamelan pélog, more complex, more difficult and more beautiful than those used by gamelan sléndro for wajang kulit.

In Bali the stories of the Mahabarata are also presented with flat leather puppets under the general name wajang purwa or *wajang palwa*, or specifically wajang kulit. These performances are not accompanied by a large gamelan but by a pair or quartet of instruments tuned to sléndro and known as *gendèr wajang*. In addition to the various calendrical rites and transitional rites (except circumcision) observed in Java by a presentation of wajang performances, the Balinese perform wajang kulit at the time of cremations. For the stories of the Ramayana, drums and a few gongs are added to the quartet.

The Balinese puppets are less refined in their carving and coloring than those of Java and their relative size is somewhat smaller. The equivalent of the Javanese gunungan or kayon, the opening symbolic piece which establishes change of scene, etc., is rounded at the top instead of pointed and depicts the tree (*kayu*) of heaven, rather than a temple gate. According to the Balinese this tree grows from the top of Mahaméra, the mountain (*gunung*) on which the gods dwell.[12] The figures of the puppets are more naturalistic than those of Java, a factor which has occasioned considerable speculation as to the relative age of the two traditions.[13] The realistic head and body conformations have been taken by some as evidence that the Balinese tradition is of greater age than that of its Javanese counterpart. During the Singasari

446

dynasty, beginning in 1222, and continuing through the period of the Madjapahit empire in East Java a number of monuments depict in bas-reliefs wajang figures closely resembling those used in Bali today. Tjandi Djago, built in 1268, has bas-reliefs, inspired by a mixture of Buddhism and Shivaism, which represent the panakawan or clowns of wajang. In the main court of Tjandi Panataran, the largest and most important monument of East Java (begun during the Singasari dynasty and completed in the time of the Madjapahit empire) the story of Rama is represented in the style of the wajang figure. The bas-reliefs which conform most precisely to the wajang style of Balinese puppets are found on Tjandi Surawana, built in the fourteenth century near Kediri.[14]

The strong influence of the kingdoms of East Java on Balinese culture during this period accounts for the similarity between the figures depicted on bas-reliefs and the present-day puppets of Bali. It is well known, however, that wajang kulit was already very popular and widespread in Java as early as 1000 A.D. The naturalistic wajang figures of Bali, therefore, do not represent an older tradition than those of Java, although their lifelike stylization would seem to have remained virtually unchanged for the past seven or eight centuries. According to some, it is possible that the original Javanese puppets resembled closely the naturalistic style of contemporary Bali. It may be that with the collapse of the Madjapahit kingdom and the advent of Islam the Moslem prohibition of making images of the human figure resulted in wajang puppets with highly stylized facial and body contours to achieve a symbolic rather than a naturalistic representation.

Although the origin of wajang kulit may never be determined with certainty, there are several factors which suggest that it might be indigenous to Indonesia. The technical designations of the wajang apparatus are all pure Javanese;[15] the borrowed Hindu repertoire is limited to the broad outlines of the Indian epics, the construction and details of the stories following their own pattern; the shapes of the panakawan are remarkably different from those of the other puppets and their names are old Javanese, pointing to the possibility of a survival from an ancient ancestor cult. The Hindu stories were strongly influenced by the oldest Javanese literature, and the wajang figures in turn influenced the style of bas-reliefs. This chain of influences is not surprising, since the literature, the Hindu stories, and the bas-reliefs all portray the same persons and events.[16]

Among the Sundanese in West Java, the most popular form of presentation for the stories of the Hindu classics is *wajang golĕk*. These are round or three-dimensional wooden puppets dressed in traditional batik and other appropriate types of material. The puppet has greater mobility than the leather figures used in wajang kulit. The wooden arms articulate at the elbow and shoulder, and the head is fixed to the end of the central supporting rod, which runs through an internal channel the length of the body. This construction enables the skillful dalang to cause a puppet to dance, turn its head, and "breathe" most naturalistically as he manipulates the body and arms in relation to the head, which can also be turned from side to side by a movement of the central rod. The puppets are mounted in a base composed of banana tree trunks in an arrangement similar to that used in the Javanese wajang kulit, although the central "screen" has no cloth but only a frame. This suggests that wajang golĕk is a younger tradition that has retained the symbol of the kelir of wajang kulit. The accompanying Sundanese gamelan orchestra, which will be discussed presently, is smaller in size than the Javanese gamelan.

Wajang golĕk is also performed in Central and East Java to portray the stories of the advent of Islam. This literature is based on the conquests of Prince Menak, who prepared the way for the teachings of Mohammed. The golĕk puppets of Central and East Java are distinct from one another and from those of Sunda (West Java) in their stylization.

The histories of the empires of East Java form the repertoire of *wajang klitik*, which is acted out with flat wooden puppets finely carved and painted and having movable leather arms. Like wajang golĕk, the "stage" is framed without a screen, and gamelan sléndro is used for accompaniment.

Wajang bĕbĕr, a form practically extinct, employs a dalang who recites a narrative as pictures painted on cloth or paper are rolled from one supporting pole to another. The literature is related to that of wajang gedog.

A discussion of the major forms of puppet theater is incomplete without an introduction to the inseparable accompaniment of the gamelan orchestra in Java and the quartet of instruments known as gendèr wajang in Bali. The full gamut of emotions running throughout the long course of the wajang night is reflected and deepened by the expressive power of the musical accompaniment. There is appropriate music for each principal type of character when he first makes his appearance, music which accompanies battle scenes, love scenes, the clowns, tender and tragic music performed at the death of a favorite hero, meditative music, dance music, heroic music—every dramatic emotion and situation has its appropriate musical counterpart.

"[Gamelan] is comparable only to two things: moonlight and flowing water. It is pure and mysterious like moonlight, it is always the same and always changing like flowing water. It forms for our ears no song, this music, it is a state of being, such as moonlight itself which lies poured out over the land. It flows murmuring, tinkling, and gurgling like water in a mountain stream. Yet it is never monotonous. Sometimes the sounds flow faster and louder, just as water also sometimes speaks more loudly in the night only to sink back again quietly."[17]

Just as a still photograph is unable to capture the spirit of dance—which is movement itself—so verbal descriptions of musical sounds have little meaning for those who have never heard the music that is being described. The motion picture is a far better medium for dance than the still photograph, but even in this presentation, "presence" created by natural setting, audience rapport, etc., is lacking. For most types of musical reproduction the phonograph record is reasonably satisfactory; but for the rich sounds of struck bronze which typify Javanese, Sundanese, and Balinese gamelan even this medium is inadequate In most musical cultures of the Orient, there is a far greater sensitivity to sound itself than seems to be true of Western societies today—although in former times such a consideration seems to have been important also in the West. An accurate application of the term "gamelan" must take into account this particular sensitivity to sound.

"Gamelan" is usually translated by the word "orchestra." A Western orchestra is known, first of all, by its location—Boston, New York, Los Angeles—then by its conductor, and perhaps, to local residents, by the concertmaster and one or two of the soloists in the orchestra. No one would think of identifying a major Western orchestra by the particular instruments used. A gamelan, on the other hand, acquires its reputation and fame, and often a proper name, through the especial beauty of sound created by the specific instruments making up the ensemble. Gamelan may be defined, then, as a particular set of instruments usually maintained through a greater or lesser period of time. Its physical location may be some indication of the musical style associated with it, and its conductor will probably be known to local residents. But its unique reputation rests on the actual sound of the ensemble itself.

Prototypes of the modern gamelan can be found depicted in the bas-reliefs of monuments such as the Borobudur, Tjandi Prambanan, and Tjandi Panataran, along with the prototypes of musical instruments known in India today. The fact that the Indian instruments no longer exist on Java attests to the strength of the indigenous musical tradition. The oldest surviving actual instruments, probably more than a thousand years old, are sets known as *gamelan munggang*. These instruments have only three tones and are used for very special occasions in Central Java. Equally venerated are the sacred *gamelan sekati*, used during the Moslem holy week. These gamelan date from the sixteenth century and are tuned to the seven-tone pélog system. In former times they were used for the accompaniment of a fight between a tiger and a buffalo, for special occasions of state, and other "masculine" or outdoor events.

During the Hindu-Javanese period and up to the advent of Islam in Java, two types of gamelan could be distinguished: the strong or loud-playing ensemble used for outdoor occasions and the soft-sounding group of instruments used for indoor events. No later than the sixteenth century, these two groups had been combined into one gamelan. Even today all gamelan distinguish between loud and soft styles of playing. During loud playing the soft-sounding instruments are silent; in soft playing all of the instruments are used, but the loud type is played softly.

Except for some ancient ensembles, gamelan are tuned in either of two major tuning systems—in fact, a complete gamelan will be made up of a double set, one tuned to five-tone sléndro and one to seven-tone pélog. No two gamelan, however, are tuned in precisely the same way. There is also considerable flexibility in the "completeness" of the ensemble, so that a village may possess a gamelan consisting of about twenty or twenty-five instruments which is regarded as complete, while one of a number of gamelan belonging to a nearby palace may consist of as many as seventy-five instruments.

The most magnificent gamelan, of course, are found in the *kraton* (royal courts) of Central Java. Today gamelan outside the palace proper are in some instances made available in the pendapa of princely residences to gamelan clubs composed of young people, which meet for rehearsals with unfailing regularity. Sometimes these groups show a real break with tradition by includ-

ing girls among the instrumentalists. Although there were special
female instrumental performers in the past, regular gamelan players
were always men except for female singers and the fairly common
practice of the dalang, who for wajang kulit performances has his
wife play the gendèr. In Jogjakarta these young gamelan players
hold annual competitions which are judged by leading professional
musicians from the radio station, the palace, and the conservatory
of gamelan studies in Solo.

The Chinese have long been lovers of gamelan and frequently
own very fine sets which are also available to clubs. Well-to-do
Javanese often count among their possessions a complete gamelan,
and they encourage the practice of both music and dance, which
together with wajang kulit performances are indispensable to
various calendrical and crisis events of life. Sometimes two or more
sons inherit a gamelan from their parents, and as they go their
separate ways may divide the instruments between them or sell
their estate—practices which tend to break up excellent gamelan.

Very fine gamelan handed down through successive generations
often carry a proper name: for example, the one now housed at the
University of California at Los Angeles is called Khjai Mendung,
Venerable Dark Cloud. Some large gongs also acquire proper
names, and these and other types of instruments may be considered
as *pusaka,* i.e. heirlooms which have acquired magical powers.

There is a firm tradition which prohibits anyone from stepping
over an instrument. This veneration and respect for gamelan is
also seen in the practice of burning incense every Thursday night
before the big gong. In the poorer villages the gamelan are smaller
and of lesser quality; but the importance of their function in society
makes them no less respected than the more impressive sets.

On his first exposure to Javanese gamelan the Western observer
is inclined to hear a complex and undifferentiated sound, undeni-
ably beautiful but enigmatic. As he listens, he may begin to
distinguish first the sounds of the rapid figuration played by the
soft-sounding instruments, the deep, sonorous tones of the large
gongs, and perhaps the subtle rhythms of the drum. The lack of
sharp dynamic contrasts or sudden changes in tempo gives the
superficial impression of timelessness and amorphous form. In
actuality there is an endless amount of variety and change based
on a principle which was also tried briefly in Western Europe
during the early Middle Ages. Once this principle of organization
begins to become apparent, the listener realizes an inexhaustible

wealth of musical variety. A simplified explanation of "stratification," therefore, is essential to understanding gamelan practices in Java and Bali.

A large Javanese gamelan may have as many as thirty or thirty-five instrumentalists, a male chorus of fifteen singers, and three female soloists. Unlike the primary tradition of the Western orchestra, founded on a large harmonic complex which moves in vertical structures, the gamelan moves in as many as twenty-five different horizontal strata. For a time in the Middle Ages Western church music was also composed on this principle of stratification: three different voices performed in such a way that the lowest voice had note values of long duration, the middle voice a melody that was more active, and the highest voice the most active line. When, as in gamelan, these strata are increased up to twenty-five different lines, the resulting complexity is one which requires a considerable exposure to appreciate. Precise modal, structural, and rhythmic rules govern the behavior of each melodic stratum, and provide the basis for group improvisation. The principal melody of the *gending* or orchestral composition is played by the *saron* family. This basic melody is divided into its longest phrases by strokes on the large gong, subdivided into shorter phrases by *kenong, kempul, ketuk, kempjang,* or *engkuk-kemong.* In a complete gamelan there is a kenong or a kempul tuned to each pitch of each tuning system, and the long melodic line thus made possible is a kind of abstraction of the main melody. The other gongs mentioned are, of course, also tuned to specific pitches of the two tuning systems, but are represented by fewer instruments and provide, therefore, more rhythmic than melodic variety. Sets of horizontal gongs which look like inverted kettles, called *bonang,* occur in three sizes and perform abstractions or elaborations of the main melody, depending on their range. Several types of drums are used by a single player, sometimes in combination, sometimes singly, to direct changes in tempo and dynamics. All of these instruments belong to the loud-sounding part of the ensemble.

The most important instrument of the soft-sounding group and the nominal leader of the entire gamelan is a two-stringed bowed instrument known as the rebab. This is an Arabic term which does not appear in the literature until the sixteenth century. There is recent evidence, however, which suggests that only the name is Arabic and that it was applied to a bowed lute known as early as the eighth century under the name gending[18]—a term now used to indicate an orchestral piece of music. The rebab guides the flow of improvisation, paraphrases and anticipates the vocal lines, indicates to the drum (which passes it along through various rhythmic signals) changes in tempo and dynamics, and weaves these responsibilities into an improvised melodic line. In strong playing the rebab player delegates his authority to the drum. The family known as gendèr consists of instruments with thin bronze keys suspended over bamboo resonators played by padded, disk-shaped *tabuh* or beaters. The instruments occur in three different ranges, and the middle-sized instrument, *gendèr barung,* is considered one of the most important instruments in the soft-playing ensemble. This is especially true in the course of the wajang kulit performances, where the gendèr has a responsibility to the dalang or puppeteer. It supplies reciting tones, accompanies his songs, participates in modal preludes, and consequently is seldom silent throughout the long night. The *gambang* is a kind of xylophone, and the *tjelempung* is a type of zither plucked with the thumbnails of each hand. The *suling* is an end-blown flute which makes intermittent melodic commentary in the course of the long phrases. The male chorus and the female soloists each have independent melodic contributions, guided by the rebab and "decorated" by the activities of the flute.

The metal keys of the gamelan may be made of any one of three different grades of bronze or brass or iron, or may even be imitated in bamboo, an ensemble known as *gamelan bumbung.* A three-quarter length hood made of woven bamboo leaves mounted over a frame is worn when a tropical rain descends without warning on the workers in the rice field. Sometimes one finds a *kawongan,* as they are called, which has fastened inside its frame six or seven fibers tuned to either sléndro or pélog, two others which represent the deep and high sounds of the drum, and two representing gongs. Two or three owners of this type of musical kawongan will sit back to back in the shelter of their hoods, plucking out the principal melodies of the large gamelan and singing to this accompaniment until the downpour ceases.

The songs sung, whether by the chorus and soloists in the large gamelan or by the peasant in the rice field, are the highest type of poetry, with very strict meter. The caesura and the final vowel of each line are the determinants of the poetic form. One of the finest bodies of vocal literature, one that is extremely popular throughout Java, is known as *matjapat.* These solo songs are often heard on the radio as two-hour performances, with intermittent relief for the soloist provided by regular gending played by the full gamelan. Matjapat includes a number of different meters distinguished according to the number of syllables to the line, the number of lines to the stanza, and the final vowel of each line. The subject matter treats chronicles of great length representing epics, ethical and mystical expositions, riddles, etc. Matjapat songs of an educational nature are said to be "sung for children."

There is an inseparable relationship between gamelan and dance theater. General characterization, specific characters, and particular moods and types of action in the dance drama have their appropriate musical accompaniment. Audiences are so familiar with this close interrelationship between gamelan and dance that it is possible to broadcast over the radio a performance of "dance," the audience being able to follow the movements of the dancers through the sounds of the gamelan and the keprak or woodblock.

It was mentioned earlier that the five-tone gamelan sléndro is used to accompany wajang kulit. Each of the three time periods of the wajang night has a corresponding musical mode. The emotional impact of the musical accompaniment for puppet or dance theater is considerably heightened by the employment of "vocal tones." These are pitches used in addition to the five or seven tones to which the bronze keyed instruments are tuned. The rebab, the suling, and the voice can perform as many as ten tones in the so-called five-tone sléndro system and nine tones in seven-tone pélog. Occasionally a vocal tone or "bronze-key" tone may be borrowed by one system from the other. This greatly enriches the melodic resources of the gamelan.

In West Java the Sundanese have carried the principle of added vocal tones to a highly complex development. Through a system of submodes known as *surupan* as many as seventeen vocal tones, for example, are available in sléndro. This great sensitivity to pitch discrimination has resulted in the development of an esthetic based on the mild clash of dissonances resulting from the simultaneous occurrence of vocal tone and bronze key. The gamelan of Sunda are tuned to the same basic systems as those of Central Java, but the ensembles are inclined to be smaller and their style of playing quite different. In Central Java the entire gamelan complex, including chorus and female soloists, forms a homogeneous sound in which no one role is featured; in West Java the solo voice, the rebab, and the drums have played, especially since World War II, an increasingly important soloistic role. Through the availability of many vocal tones the rebab and the voice have developed a style of virtuoso performance which requires great control of pitch and articulation. The drummer performs on four instruments simultaneously and has developed an exciting and dramatic idiom. When the Sundanese gamelan accompanies dance, the drums are especially prominent.

An important instrument in West Java which may be used as part of the gamelan or as a principal instrument in a small chamber group is the *ketjapi*. It is a boat-shaped plucked zither, occurring in two sizes, which is often combined with flute and voice. The unaccompanied vocal literature mentioned above as matjapat is also very popular in Sunda. As in Central Java, various size gongs determine the structure of the gamelan piece, different musical forms being determined by the particular periodicity of these instruments. Stratification in the Sundanese gamelan is not so complex as in the Javanese, but the rich tradition of vocal tones introduces a different order of complexity.

With little difficulty the untrained ear can perceive marked stylistic differences between Sundanese and Javanese gamelan. Consistent with the dance style, the gamelan music of Central Java might be considered more highly stylized and perhaps "abstract," while Sundanese gamelan is quite lively, animated, and fluent. In East Java gamelan is closely related to that of Central Java, but it also bears an unmistakable resemblance to certain rhythmic and dynamic features of Balinese music.

For most Western ears Balinese gamelan is immediately attractive —for the simple reason that it corresponds more closely to the Western ideal of dynamic contrasts, of sudden shifts from fast to slow and loud to soft. The most brilliant orchestral ensemble in the Orient, Balinese gamelan achieves its singular appeal not through the principle of stratification nor the complexities of vocal submodes but through an extraordinary precision in ensemble performance. Thirty to fifty players perform in the large traditional *gamelan gong* or the modern *gamelan gong kebyar* in a standard of perfection expected in the West only from the string quartet. Balinese musicians seem to operate on the principle that if two players play interlocking parts as fast as possible—that is to say, each player plays every other note but at his full capacity for speed—the result will be a performance twice as fast as either of them can play. These shared or interlocking parts require the most precise rhythmic

455

timing. And because Balinese Hinduism, with its constant demand for music and dance, is genuinely accepted as a way of life, a good gamelan club in Bali will rehearse every night of the week. It is little wonder that an incredible standard of performance is achieved.

One of the most important distinguishing features of the two types of gamelan mentioned is a curious tuning principle. The instruments are built in pairs, and one is pitched slightly higher than its mate. As the corresponding keys of the two instruments are struck simultaneously, musical beats result which give to the entire gamelan its famous "shimmering" quality of sound.

The traditional gamelan gong and gong kebyar are both tuned to a five-tone scale of the seven-tone pélog system. In Javanese gamelan, although all seven tones are available, three different sets of five tones are selected from the seven to form three different modes. By comparison, therefore, Balinese gamelan gong may be said to possess the principal scale material of one mode in pélog. It is believed that the various pélog tunings found on different Balinese gamelan derive in the first place from the ancient ensemble known as *gamelan gambuh,* a much smaller group of instruments which utilizes all seven tones of pélog.

The traditional style of gamelan gong in Bali has a number of general features in common with Javanese gamelan. Form and structure are regulated through the periodicity of various size gongs, and to some degree melodic elaboration is achieved by stratification. One instrument which assumes considerable importance in the evolution from traditional gamelan gong to gong kebyar is known as the *réjong.* Originally this instrument consisted of a pair of wooden rods shaped like dumbbells with a small kettle mounted on each end of the wooden support. It was played by two players, so that each player could produce two different pitches. The four tones played on this pair of instruments were used to produce a great variety of rhythmic and melodic permutations, performed as interlocking patterns by the two players. This interlocking part or *kotèkan* provided a kind of "rhythmic spice" to the otherwise fairly simple orchestral piece. As the new dance style kebyar developed, the instruments of the gamelan were gradually modified, until today the réjong consists of twelve kettles arranged in one long frame played by four musicians. Although the idiomatic patterns have remained about the same, the range and volume of the instrument have tripled and taken on the added function of supplying rhythmic-harmonic "shock waves." The rapid figuration and interlocking parts characteristic of the réjong in the modern gong kebyar are also performed by a large family of *gangsa,* a generic term used in Bali to refer to various sizes of bronze (gangsa) instruments which in basic construction resemble the gendèr family mentioned in connection with Java. The Balinese gangsa, however, is played with a single hardwood mallet, so that twelve or fourteen of these instruments are capable of producing an extremely brilliant and dynamic style. There are two drummers required in both traditional and modern types of gamelan, and they also play interlocking rhythms, often at a great rate of speed. Pairs of small hand cymbals known as *tjĕng-tjĕng* underscore the dramatic action of the dancer and reinforce the most rapid, rhythmic pulsations of the gamelan. The potential of musical interpretation available to the kebyar dancer, therefore, is virtually unlimited.

Gamelan légong, a somewhat smaller and more delicate ensemble, accompanies the dance of the same name. The drums used for légong are smaller than those in gamelan gong or gong kebyar. Traditionally the réjong is not used at all, but in recent times some gamelan also have included this instrument. A pair or sometimes a quartet of gendèr, each instrument played with two hardwood disk-shaped *panggul,* are characteristically lead instruments. In contemporary times, however, légong may also be accompanied by the usual gong kebyar, in which case the gendèr is played with a single panggul. The suling or end-blown flute is used with traditional gamelan gong, gamelan légong, and sometimes with gong kebyar. A small rebab, formerly present in traditional types of gamelan, is less often used today.

Gamelan gambuh consists of several gambuh—very large end-blown flutes—a rebab and several types of gongs and drums. Unlike other types of Balinese gamelan, it is probable that the style of gamelan gambuh has changed very little during recent years; this type of ensemble and the dance theater associated with it are not very popular today. Another kind of ensemble, which utilizes a five-tone pélog scale, is known as *gamelan djogét.* This gamelan, whose instruments are made of bamboo, accompanies a flirtation dance performed by an attractive young lady who invites first one and then another male spectator to dance with her.

The sléndro tuning system is used in Bali only by the gendèr wajang quartet that accompanies the all-night wajang kulit performances. This type of instrument is similar to the Javanese gendèr except that it has only ten instead of thirteen to fifteen keys. It is played with hard wooden panggul. The quartet creates a variety of moods in response to the theatrical demands of the stories; for example, a piece such as "Rébong" is appropriate for love scenes, while "Lagu Délem" identifies the specific character Délem, the principal attendant of the bad party. One of the most moving and deeply tragic pieces of the repertoire is "Tlutur," played at the death of one of the heroes.

An important ensemble known as *gamelan angklung* performs, among other occasions, at cremations. The instrument after which this type of gamelan is named is made of bamboo. Two or three pieces of bamboo, tuned in octaves and therefore representing one pitch at two or three octaves distance, are suspended freely in a frame, and the tone is produced by shaking the instrument. These bamboo angklung are combined with a number of instruments of the gangsa type made of bronze, as well as by gongs and drums. Frequently such an ensemble, which has only a four-tone scale, does not include the bamboo instruments, although it still bears the name gamelan angklung.

The angklung as an instrument is best known in West Java, where the Sundanese combine several sizes in large ensembles and use them to accompany folk dance (*djogét*). They also serve an important function in the public schools, where sets of angklung tuned to five-tone sléndro and seven-tone pélog are used for teaching Sundanese music, and special sets tuned to the Western twelve-tone system for teaching Western music.

One of the most important functions of gamelan in Java and Bali is the accompaniment of dance. The close relationship between music and the puppet theater in establishing characterization, emotional mood, and dramatic situation also applies to the relationship between music and dance. Indeed, dance and puppet theater are in many aspects two sides of the same dramatic coin.

The literature of the puppet plays forms the foundation of the dance drama. When the role of the puppet is enacted by living dancers, the form is known as *wajang wong* or *wajang orang* (wong is the Javanese and orang the Indonesian word for human being). As in the puppet performances, the most highly stylized form of dance is found in Central Java. Great muscular control and coordination produces a deliberate but dynamic movement of torso, limbs, and head. Imitating the gestures of a flat leather puppet, the dancer appears to move in a two-dimensional plane. This is especially apparent in the male dancer, whose arms operate in an angular movement, hands forming various of the Hindu mudras, his feet, knees, and thighs spread out at an extreme angle so that his body appears to be nearly flat. In the female dance, the legs are held close together, the knees always slightly bent, and the movements are extremely small and refined. The most severe examples of this type of stylization are found in the city of Jogjakarta; movements in Solo (Surakarta), the other major variant of Central Javanese dance, are more fluid. In West Java, the Sundanese style of dance is closely related to the Central Javanese but tends to be more active and somewhat less angular. Balinese dance is the most dynamic of the three types. All of these different styles resemble closely the various dance positions depicted on the bas-reliefs of early monuments.

In Java, the classical dance was fostered by the royal courts and emulated by the villagers. It was not until 1918 that a dance school in the classical tradition, Krida Beksa Wirama, was founded outside the palace in Jogjakarta. Its establishment made it possible for any young person to study the dance tradition of the courts; this was a great stimulus to dance in Central Java and encouraged the formation of similar clubs. In Bali, although the courts were formerly the primary centers of dance, with the lessening of princely wealth and the importance of communal life under Balinese Hinduism the centers of activity became the village clubs that specialize in particular types of dance and music appropriate to various religious functions.

In the classical dance, the physical attitude of the dancer at any given moment requires a complementary mental and spiritual attitude. Whether the literature be religious, historical, or animistic (this last the basis of some types of folk dance), it is intimately identified with the life of the individual as a member of his society. The unmistakable rapport between audience and a performance of wajang kulit becomes much more intensified for the individual dancer when he accepts the responsibility of representing one of the gods or heroes of this literature in the context of the story fragment. At every rehearsal of a dance club there may be anywhere from forty or fifty to several hundred children watching open-eyed, fascinated by the serious determination with which the teen-agers and young adults refine the movements of their repertoire and add to it an increasing number of new roles. This

459

children's gallery of observers is made up of infants from two years old to boys and girls around eight or ten. At the latter age they have already witnessed six or eight years of rehearsal, not to mention the highly impressive spectacles of the formal performances themselves. By this time they are eager to begin their own lessons, and through close observation and their own childish efforts at imitation they have acquired the underlying spirit with which the serious dancer must approach his subject. Traditionally the dance is taught by imitation and rote learning, verbal instructions from the teacher being restricted to minimal explanation. Very slowly the student learns his first dance—rather than a basic set of dance principles—and accumulates within the limits of this one role specific names for specific movements. He also learns the important structural elements of the accompanying gamelan orchestra, so that he understands the various signals from the keprak, the wood-block that directs and underscores the dancer's movements, in relation to the *gongan, kenongan,* and *kendangan,* a variety of gongs and the dance drum that mark the temporal divisions of the musical sentence. The gestures of arms, hands, and fingers, based on the mudras of India, must be very precisely executed for the critical eye of the sophisticated audience, because very slight changes in the details of movements indicate a different charac-terization. Head, torso, and leg movements are also an index to characterization; but perhaps because they are relatively less flexible than the arms, hands, and fingers, they represent the more general aspects of characterization.

The formal dance area is the pendapa, the large pavilion men-tioned earlier. This approach to the Javanese princely residence has a polished tile floor on which no one dare set foot before removing his shoes, a gesture of respect for the head of the household. It has a sloping tiled roof which rises on four sides to a central vortex, the last two-thirds of the span being hipped at a sharp angle. The interior of the roof is usually teak, and the large wooden columns which support it are sometimes richly carved at the base.

As the dancer appears at the far edge of this impressive pavilion and moves unobtrusively along one side until he has come abreast of the dance area proper, he is already in character, even though his dance role has not yet begun. On this entrance, his walk is not the easy, relaxed movement of a dancer awaiting his cue, but rather a tense, somewhat angular stride which manages to simulate a personified puppet. As he kneels to execute the *sembah*—the

460

formal supplication to the gods—before entering into the living role which is his responsibility, his own personality as an individual is set aside and he enters into the spirit of his characterization fully. The serene detachment of classical dance in both Java and Bali, the highly impersonal execution of flawless details, and the highly complex vocabulary of dance movement relating the fabulous stories of great literature; the stylized delivery of the dalang as he recites a narrative link between episodes in the ancient poetic language of Kawi (even on the island of Bali); the enhancement of changing mood and dramatic action by the large gamelan and chorus—these elements in combination create a unique and unforgettable theatrical experience.

In Central Java the classical dance may be divided into five broad categories distinguished according to the literature from which they are derived and the individual dance style associated with each. Wajang purwa, the literature of wajang kulit, traditionally features a large cast of characters enacting stories based on the Hindu Mahabarata and Ramayana. The dance style is in the very finest tradition of the kraton. *Langen mandra wanara* is a kind of opera performed in Jogjakarta, in which the principal characters dance on their knees and also must be accomplished singers. The stories are taken primarily from the Ramayana, but sometimes episodes from the Mahabarata are also used. *Langendrija* is the Solonese version of opera, in which the leading characters dance in a standing position and are also required to sing. The stories are taken from the tales of the legendary, villainous Red Knight Menak Djinggo, whose exploits occurred in East Java. *Wajang topĕng* is a masked dance drama based on stories from the Pandji cycle. Occasionally stories in wajang topĕng are derived from historical sources. Wajang golĕk is the danced version of the Arabic stories of the Menak literature, in which the stiff movements of the round wooden puppets are imitated by the dancers.

Characterization in the classical dance drama may be divided into three large categories: *halus*, the refined male dance; *gagah*, the strong or coarse male dance; and *puteri*, the female dance. The halus classification is subdivided into *kalang kinantang* and *impur;* both of these subdivisions are in turn subdivided into *déwa* and *lugu*. Each subclassification denotes a subtle distinction in the vocabulary of arm, hand, and finger movements which might easily escape the notice of the untrained observer. Gagah characters are designated as *kalang kinantang, impur, kambeng, bapang, panakawan,* and *buron wana.* Most of these divisions are also subdivided into subtly distinct types. Kalang kinantang, for example, has four divisions: *déwa, lugu, radja,* and *keték.*[19] The panakawan characterizations are named after general types as well as specific characters: *tjantrik,* disciples or servants, *sétanan,* ghosts, and *emban,* a female attendant usually danced by a man; specific characters are Semar, Pétruk, Garèng, Bagong, Togog, and Bilung. In these groupings the broad features of characterization between refined and strong types are established by head, torso, leg movements and hand positions as well as casting according to physical type; the principal divisions within each main category, and especially the subdivisions within each of these, require a mastery of subtle movements to define the appropriate type and specific character. Bapang, for example, in the gagah category, includes five varieties of giant parts. One of these, buta Tjakil, designates a specific character—a "small" giant who is extremely popular in the dance theater and in wajang kulit.

Although attempts have been made to add as great a variety of subdivisions in the puteri or female dance as are known in gagah, classifications in this category tend to be much more restricted. Formerly all women's roles were danced by men. Gradually, women began to take these roles and finally, in the Solonese tradition, it became common for women to dance the roles of some of the refined male characters such as Ardjuna.

The most famous types of classical female dance are known through specific compositions, e.g. *bedaja* and *serimpi.* These two compositions utilize a common dance vocabulary and are the most popular in the tradition of the kraton. Bedaja is usually performed by nine dancers, but sometimes as few as five or seven, and depicts a story from the Mahabarata or occasionally from other sources. These are highly stylized, lyrical dances. The serimpi are performed by four principal dancers, sometimes assisted by four attendants, and enact an episode involving a fight. The basic pair of this quartet represents two jealous princesses who do battle; the second pair simply adds a symmetrical duplication. Rarely serimpi may be performed by only two dancers. A special composition performed by two dancers in this style is called "Sari Kembar" (Twin Flowers) or, by one dancer, "Sari Tunggal" (One Flower), and there is no fighting included. The dance vocabulary of bedaja and serimpi represents the apex of stylization.

Outside the kraton walls a type of professional solo dance has developed known as *talĕdĕk*. Although a good many movements used by talĕdĕk are similar to those of bedaja and serimpi, the dancer is not bound by the traditional transitional movements between dance positions but is free to move more casually. This type of female solo dance is used for pure entertainment, is often of a flirtatious nature, and is especially appropriate for male stag parties.

The solo female dance known as *golĕk* (as distinct from the wajang golĕk mentioned earlier) represents a combination of the bedaja and serimpi techniques with those of talĕdĕk. A well-known Solonese dance which is a fusion of talĕdĕk and classical styles is "Bondan"—a simple story portraying a young mother taking care of her baby.

In Central Java two famous professional theaters based on classical dance have been established. Sriwedari, located in Solo, has a very large following and represents a somewhat popularized style of the dance drama which at times approaches musical comedy. In Semarang the famous Ngesti Pandawa is a highly successful theater based on the Solonese style. Ngesti Pandawa has established a fine reputation for its excellent dancers, imaginative staging, lighting, and supernatural effects. In recent times, this theater has also instituted entr'actes in the form of a chorus of female dancers and singers performing in a "folk" or "popular" style in modern costuming and portraying topical themes. Ngesti Pandawa also embarks on tours, setting up almost overnight a large bamboo theater in another city and performing to packed houses for a two- or three-month engagement.

There are two principal types of folk dance drama in Central Java: *srandul*, dances based on legendary tales and current events, and *pradjuritan* or *djaran képang*, derived from the Menak or Arabic stories. These are often performed by an itinerate troupe. In pradjuritan there are eight principal dancers riding bamboo horses, as well as clowns and attendants. Frequently minor characters enter into a state of trance. In an unrefined version, known as *djatilan*, the story seems to be unimportant and the riders of bamboo horses, aided by the monotonous repetition of a few gongs and the drum, become entranced and imitate faithfully the antics of a horse: pawing the ground, eating grass, etc.

Mention should also be made of three types of folk drama which include incidental dance. One of the most popular forms in Central Java is *ketoprak*. The stories cover in melodramatic fashion a wide

463

range of subjects, including legends, myths, the Menak Djinggo, and Pandji stories, as well as historical accounts of former kingdoms and of the miracles wrought by the Walis who spread Islam throughout Java in the sixteenth century. Another popular type of Central Javanese folk drama, in which dance plays a very minor role, is *dagelan*. These comic dramas are based on topical stories and current events and inevitably have a happy ending. The most famous folk drama of East Java is *lodruk*, a type of melodrama based on a wide variety of stories, including modern situations, and in which dance is incidental. All lodruk roles are taken by men, who often acquire great fame for their flawless ability in imitating women. Although formerly these types of folk drama were sometimes performed by itinerant groups, today they are usually located in a professional "home theater."

A variety of dance excerpts taken from the different types of classical dance drama as well as the solo talĕdĕk or golĕk may be combined to form a single dance program. Sometimes the excerpts will be nothing more than a solo dance such as the masked Kelana, depicting a warrior preparing himself for battle; or they may involve several characters, with the choreography climaxed by a fight. In most recent times some interesting dance experiments have taken place, including a few tentative experiments in introducing movements borrowed from the modern dance schools of America in combination with the classical tradition.

The cities and villages of West Java, like those of Central Java, have developed and acquired a reputation for individual styles of dance. Such places as Bandung, Garut, Sumedang, Kuningan, Tjiamis, and Sukabumi have become known for their particular dance specialties. The Sundanese divide dance (*igel*) into two basic types: *ébéng*, or classical dance, and *djogét* or folk dance. Each of these in turn are subdivided into specific dance styles, though in recent times there has been considerable borrowing and combining of the different types.[20]

Ébéng is closely related to the classical dance of Central Java and may be divided into three principal types: *ébéng najup*, *ébéng topèng*, and *ébéng mamarung*. The literature which forms its basis is drawn from the Mahabarata, the Ramayana, and the Pandji cycle. Characterization in the classical dance is divided into two groups, *ngalamba* and *lejepan* designating the introductory and main sections of the refined type of dance, and *monggawa* indicating the strong or powerful dance style. The refinements of characterization differ in detail from those in Central Java, but in principle are similar. As indicated earlier, the Sundanese dance is less severe in its stylization than the Javanese, body and limb positions being less "two-dimensional" and all movements correspondingly marked by a greater fluidity. There is considerably more movement of the upper torso, especially emphasized by a supple rocking of the shoulders. Basic leg positions of the male dancers are not so elevated as those in Central Java, and the movements of the female dancer are less restricted than those of the Javanese.

Djogét designates a variety of folk dances, some of which have also influenced the classical dance. Some types of djogét may be accompanied by an ensemble of angklung, others require a full Sundanese gamelan, and some are accompanied principally by an Arabic drum (the *rebana*). One popular type of djogét is known as *pentjak*, a kind of fighting dance known rather generally throughout Indonesia.

Like similar presentations in Central Java a complete *lakon* or story may be presented by a large cast of characters, or a smaller group may perform a fragment of a lakon. Sometimes, especially since World War II, programs are made up of several solo or duo dances portraying characters from the wajang together with modern creations based on various animal figures or on different kinds of social themes such as planting rice or the fight for independence. *Topěng*, or mask dances, are especially popular in West Java. A great stimulus to the art of dance in West Java is provided by local and regional competitions among various dance clubs.

To enter into the fabulous world of Balinese dance and drama, the reader must seek further than the few pages available here.[21] In a society where the cultivation of performing arts and plastic and graphic arts is as important as the cultivation of rice, even the average person becomes to some extent a talented artist. This strong creative impulse has produced a wealth of artistic forms, fashioned and refashioned continually within a flexible tradition founded on a blending of religious faith, magic and superstition, and the supernatural reality of good and evil forces. The duality of a belief founded on the coexistence of both gods and demons may take the healthy form of a ferocious monster carved in stone and placed before the entrance of a temple gate to frighten away evil spirits. This counterbalance between the forces of light and dark is similarly represented in dance and drama, in the conviction

465

that it is better to recognize evil and deal with it than to ignore it and be conquered by it.

There is such a profusion of music and dance performances in Bali that almost any night of the week within the radius of a few kilometers one has a choice of a variety of presentations. In celebration of a wedding, a tooth-filing ceremony, a cremation, the honoring of local temple gods, the dance dramas unfold wherever space for a performance is to be found. This may be in an open courtyard with the barren dust as a stage, before a temple gate, at a crossroad, or in a graveyard with the open sky as a roof and towering palm trees forming a proscenium arch. Perhaps a temple wall and ascending stairs leading to the gateway may provide a bejeweled backdrop, as countless little oil lamps flicker in the small niches up the face of the wall. The dance area is encircled by hundreds of human beings of all ages and rank sitting, squatting, and standing in a tightly packed mass around the "central stage." In the immediate vicinity are a number of low tables or stalls where many kinds of food and drink, cigarettes, and betel are sold. Each stall or table lighted by a little lamp is served by a *dagang*, a young girl who may be skilled at flirtatious and seductive glances, wit, and repartee. Through such early training these little girls may later become excellent dancers, for this order of expressivity is a hallmark of Balinese dance.

Characterization in Balinese drama and dance may be classified as *halus* or *manis*, indicating the refined type of character, or *keras*, denoting the strong or coarse character. Principal female characters regardless of rank are always refined. Whether theirs is the role of a queen, a demon, a princess, the part requires a very sweet (manis) voice and refined movements. Originally these roles were enacted only by men, as is still the custom in such forms of dance drama as topèng, the masked play, and wajang wong. Some eccentric female roles are almost always performed by men. Two leading roles typical of this type are found in *ardja*, a kind of opera which is both spoken and sung. The principal role of Tjalonarang is that of a witch Rangda; and because the part is considered a particularly dangerous responsibility it is usually performed by an older male priest.

In most forms of the Balinese dance drama, minor female roles are quite important. The *tjondong* is the female attendant of the leading lady and has the specific function of introducing her before her formal appearance, waiting on her in various ways, and sometimes performing an extremely important part in the course of the drama. In most forms of the dance drama the tjondong will resemble as closely as possible the physical type of the mistress she is serving and performs in a dance style that is very similar. The tjondong role is known by different names in different types of dance drama; in Tjalonarang four such attendants are known as *sisia,* and the most important tjondong role is that of the daughter of the witch or a female disciple studying magic.

Although the eccentric female characters and their respective attendants are inclined to be somewhat mannish in their movements, it is in the male roles that a clear distinction between alus and kras characterization emerges. Certain specific characters such as Ardjuna and Rama will always appear as refined types, marked by delicate movements and a soft and winsome voice delivery. The principal king in wajang wong, topèng, gambuh, and ardja is always an alus role, and his enemies, human or demon, are kras. Apparently the requirements of alus and kras are not so rigidly enforced in Bali as in Java, because occasionally when a suitable mask is not available a substitute may be used which reverses the style of characterization. Therefore, an alus king may don a kras mask and perform accordingly, with complete understanding on the part of the audience that this is only an expedient. In male warrior roles like *baris* and *djauk,* even such refined characters as Ardjuna and Rama will move with great dynamic and sometimes violent tension. Of the two types, baris is more elegant, being performed without a mask, while djauk requires a fierce-looking mask with bulging eyes and all of the kras features.

There are two important male attendants for the principal characters, the *penasar* and the *kartala.* It is the penasar's responsibility to keep the action moving, to interpret the high language of the principal character into the vernacular, and often to display his basic stupidity by serving as butt for the pranks of the kartala, who is the principal clown. The pranks and improvisation of the penasar and the kartala make them the most popular figures in the drama. Frequently it is they who hold the stage and keep the audience entertained for a greater or lesser period of time while the principals are deciding among themselves offstage precisely which episode they wish to present. Sometimes this byplay between the attendants will stretch to several hours' duration before the drama at last begins. The kartala might be compared to the Shakespearean fool, often feigning foolishness in his mockery of

467

of the pompous penasar, but also revealing that he is a rather clever fellow.

In large productions penasar and kartala are sometimes doubled or tripled. In gambuh the roles of the penasar and kartala are replaced by those of panakawan: Semar, Turas, Tak, and Gogo. In ardja the attendants are known as Punta and Widjil. In wajang wong they are known as Tualèn and Merdah, serving the good party, and Délem and Sangut, attending the bad party.

Although it may be said that all forms of the dance in Bali are connected with some form of religious expression and in a sense are offerings, certain ones can be clearly defined as ceremonial dances. Among these types of ritualistic offerings is a slow dance known as *mabuang,* performed by men and connected with the pouring out of wine or milk. Another type of offering, for men or women, is known as *mĕndet* and may include old and young women, priests and boys, and a group of tiny shy girls. Two especially beautiful forms of the ritualistic dance are *redjang* and *gabor,* the latter having a greater variety of movements. These two forms of dance are usually performed by women but occasionally also by men. All of the ritualistic dances at times tend to merge into combinations, so that it becomes difficult to differentiate one type from another.

One of the most brilliant and dramatic dances among the ceremonial forms is known as baris. Originally the name "baris" referred to a line or file of soldiers, and many forms of baris consist of little more than gesturing and posing with lances, bows, or shields by groups of men and boys numbering anywhere from four to as many as sixty. The most impressive types of baris, however, are known as solo or dramatic baris. Characterization is achieved through statuesque posing, tentative advances, and cautious withdrawals, all extremely deliberate movements which will suddenly give way to a violent outbreak of dynamic tension expressed by a quivering and trembling in all parts of the body. Perhaps no figure in the Balinese dance world is so impressive as a fine dramatic baris.

There are a number of types of trance dance[22] and dances of magic involving different kinds of *barong,* the most exciting of which is Tjalonarang. The barong, which may take the form of various animals or giants, is a distant relative of the witch Rangda and stands as a buffer between the village and this personification of evil. He is assisted by young men possessed by the spirits of *buta-kala* or demons, who fall into trance and attack the witch. Rangda, however, places a spell on them, as a result of which they perform an agonizing kris-dance with the pointed ends of the weapons against their chests. As they fall prostrate, one by one, jerking and trembling in paroxysms of the trance state, the barong nuzzles them with his beard and the priest sprinkles them with holy water. Suddenly the action ceases, the Rangda mask is carried away, and slowly the dancers, and sometimes even the barong, must be revived from their trance.

Gambuh deserves special mention. Considered by some the forerunner of all forms of dance drama and music in Bali[23] gambuh is considered old-fashioned by most Balinese and enjoys very little popularity. It is concerned with the splendid pomp and circumstance of the powerful kraton of East Java in the fourteenth century, and, except for a few short passages spoken by the king's personal servants, the language is fourteenth-century Javanese. No sentimentality or comic relief is a part of gambuh; the servants and clowns are confined more closely to interpretive roles, which may account for this form's diminishing popularity. The themes are taken from the Balinese version of the adventures of the Javanese culture hero Pandji, from a Javanese historical romance known as Rangga Lawé, and the Javanese-Islamic cycle Amad Mohammed. But in this form of dance drama the story is really not so important as the large cast of characters, their flamboyant dancing, and the unusual musical accompaniment, gamelan gambuh, which we have earlier discussed.

Wajang wong is, in Bali, a rather old-fashioned form of dance drama not seen in too many villages today: it is related to wajang kulit and based on the story of Rama. Although it affords considerable spectacle, wajang wong is most admired for the beauty of its poetry, which is recited in ancient Kawi. Some festivals may include a week-long presentation of wajang wong, with different episodes being performed each day but not in any logical order of succession. *Parwa* is a dance drama based on the other major cycle used for wajang kulit, namely the Mahabarata. A wajang wong festival usually includes a parwa festival, the two forms alternating on the same day. In wajang wong all but the alus characters wear masks; in parwa only Tualèn, servant of the good party, and Délem, attendant of the bad party, are masked. The style of parwa bears a closer resemblance to that of gambuh than does wajang wong.

The stories of the masked play topèng are historical, like those of gambuh; but their manner of presentation is entirely different. They are very direct in nature and form a kind of chronicle of historical-mythical events. Whereas in gambuh the story is overpowered by dance ritual, in topèng a dramatic episode is featured, and in ardja, mentioned earlier as a kind of opera or musical comedy, the story continuity is usually given from beginning to end and the emphasis is on both singing and the plot. In this last form, the gamelan is limited to percussion instruments and flutes, which serve as an occasional accompaniment with long periods of rest to accommodate the extended comic dialogue. Ardja's themes include stories found in gambuh, Kawi versions from the Mahabarata as found in parwa, and also modern Chinese stories of passion. The beautiful girls who play the romantic leads of ardja are especially popular.

Probably the best known dance of Bali is légong. Here a rather involved plot with a great many different versions is often entrusted to three little girls, though it may include additional characters. In this most abstract dance form of Bali the girls, without change of costume, dance style, or other visible indications, represent the King of Lasem, his two wives, the tjondong, the penasar, and a bird of ill omen. This extreme distillation of dance story does not interfere with the exquisite beauty of the performance—indeed, the "story" does not really seem to matter.

A new style of dance which developed in the 1920s and was made popular by the famous teacher and dancer Mario is known as kebyar. This form of dance enjoys great popularity. In it, for the first time, the dancer is allowed to express himself in relation to the sounds of the gamelan. Whether performed in a squatting or standing position, by man or woman, kebyar is an exciting exchange between the dramatic musical effects of the large orchestra and rapid and sensitive interpretations in dance movement. The style has had a profound influence on the gamelan itself, leading to the formation of a new type of musical ensemble, the gamelan gong kebyar which we have described earlier.

The deep-rooted significance of music and dance in the lives of the Javanese, Sundanese, and Balinese peoples represents a priceless cultural treasure within the vast storehouse of Indonesian arts. Every performance of wajang kulit, wajang golèk, wajang wong, and other forms mentioned in the foregoing pages attests to the powerful viability of this heritage. Here, individuals of noble birth

from the palaces and unschooled peasants from the rice fields—
from babes in arms to the most aged—sit side by side the whole
night through, enraptured as the ancient dramas unfold in their
panoply of costume, music, movement, and poetry. This is a
heritage of religion and morality, ethics and sanctions, superstitions
and beliefs, histories and myths—hoary with age, but constantly
new as it passes through the tempering fires of contemporary times.

Notes and Bibliographies

Notes and Bibliographies

NOTES AND BIBLIOGRAPHY FOR *Physical and Human Resource Patterns*

1. R. W. van Bemmelen, *The Geology of Indonesia, 1A* (The Hague, Nijhoff, 1949), p. 3.

2. Ibid., pp. 188-224, 257-68.

3. The lower temperatures of highland regions tend to retard leaching, unless this is offset by higher rainfall. See E. C. J. Mohr, *The Soils of Equatorial Regions with Special Reference to the Netherlands East Indies* (Ann Arbor, Edwards, 1944), pp. 146-51.

4. E. C. J. Mohr, "Climate and Soil in the Netherlands Indies," *Science and Scientists in the Netherlands Indies,* eds., Pieter Honig and Frans Verdoorn (New York, Board for the Netherlands Indies, Surinam, and Curaçao, 1945), p. 253.

5. Karl J. Pelzer, "Land Utilization in the Humid Tropics: Agriculture," in *Proceedings of the Ninth Pacific Science Congress, 1957, 20, Climate, Vegetation, and Rational Land Utilization in the Humid Tropics* (Bangkok, 1958), 125.

6. Mohr, *The Soils of Equatorial Regions,* pp. 528-33.

7. Van Steenis has estimated the total number of flowering plants at 20,000 species, while Richards holds that the Indo-Malayan region is richer in plant species than are either the American or the African tropics. P. W. Richards, *The Tropical Rain Forest* (Cambridge, University Press, 1952), pp. 229-30.

8. F. J. Ormeling, *The Timor Problem: A Geographical Interpretation of an Underdeveloped Island* (Djakarta, Wolters, 1955), pp. 171-97.

9. Ernst Mayr, "Wallace's Line in the Light of Recent Zoogeographic Studies," *Quarterly Review of Biology, 19* (1944), 1-14; Bernhard Rensch, *Die Geschichte des Sundabogens: Eine Tiergeographische Untersuchung* (Berlin, Bornträger, 1936), p. 251; and the symposium on "Biogeographic Division of the Indo-Australian Archipelago, with Criticism of the Wallace and Weber Lines and of Any Other Dividing Lines and with an Attempt to Obtain Uniformity in the Names Used for the Divisions," *Proceedings of the Linnean Society of London, 154th Session* (London, 1942), pp. 120-65.

10. Biro Pusat Statistik, *Statistical Pocketbook of Indonesia 1961* (Djakarta, 1961), p. 86.

11. Van Bemmelen, *The Geology of Indonesia, 2,* 47.

12. For a discussion of this principle, see Derwent Whittlesey, *The*

Earth and the State: A Study of Political Geography (New York, Holt, 1944), p. 60.

13. Bagan-Siapiapi, one of the world's leading fishing harbors, was formerly accessible to coastal steamers. Today the town is separated from the Rokan River by a wide belt of mangrove-covered mudflats, so that even small motor boats must anchor a considerable distance from the former landing places. Goods and passengers have to be transported in small dugouts—which at low tide are dragged through the mud. Similar changes have interrupted coastwise shipping in other parts of East Sumatra.

14. J. C. M. Radermacher and W. van Hogendorp, "Bijvoegsels tot de beschrijving der Sundasche eilanden" [Additions to the Description of the Sunda Islands], *Verhandelingen van het Bataviaasch Genootschap van Kunsten en Wetenschappen, 3* (Batavia, 1781), 2d printing (1824), 272-96.

15. Cited in "Bevolking van Java en Madoera," *Tijdschrift voor Nederlandsch Indië, 2* (1839), 160.

16. Thomas Stamford Raffles, *The History of Java, 1* (London, Black, Parbury, and Allen, 1817), 63. Despite Raffles' use of the term "census" in his report, his figures were not based on an actual count but on oral reports made by villagers, who were called together at "the chief station of each division" to report the size of the population of their respective villages to investigating British officials. The village heads reported the number of *tjatjah*, or households, and were expected to separate peasant cultivators from other inhabitants. Ibid, *2* (1818), Appendix L, No. II, paragraphs 31-40, pp. CCXLVIII-CCXLIX.

17. Vaccinators were employed in Java as early as the British Interregnum (1812-16), being paid at that time by land allotments. After the restoration of Dutch rule vaccinators continued to be used, but their number was very small, and only a small percentage of Java's population was immunized against smallpox during the nineteenth century. See Widjojo Nitisastro, "Migration, Population Growth, and Economic Development in Indonesia" (Ph.D. thesis, Berkeley, University of California, 1961), p. 55.

18. For a most valuable critical examination of Indonesian population data, see the thesis by Widjojo Nitisastro cited in the previous note.

19. This development was foreseen much earlier in the century by Commissioner General du Bus, who in 1827 recommended a policy of encouraging Europeans to develop plantation agriculture rather than to rely on the readiness of the Javanese peasants to produce cash crops in response to adequate incentives. Du Bus predicted that very quickly a landless class would come into being which could be expected to work for European planters. See Daniel W. van Welderen Rengers, *The Failure of a Liberal Colonial Policy: Netherlands East Indies, 1816-1830* (The Hague, Nijhoff, 1947).

20. Don C. Bennett, "Three Measurements of Population Pressure in Eastern Java," *Ekonomi dan Keuangan Indonesia, 14,* 97-106.
21. Mohr, *The Soils of Equatorial Regions,* pp. 650-52.
22. For a study of the prewar government-sponsored emigration of land-seeking Javanese, see Karl J. Pelzer, *Pioneer Settlement in the Asiatic Tropics: Studies in Land Utilization and Agricultural Colonization in Southeastern Asia,* American Geographical Society, Special Publication No. 29 (New York, 1945); on postwar spontaneous emigration of land-seeking Javanese, see Kampto Utomo, *Masjarakat Transmigran Spontan Didaerah W. Sekampung (Lampung)* [Settlements of Spontaneous Migrants in the Wei Sekampung (Lampung) Area], (Djakarta, P. T. Penerbitan Universitas, 1957); and on recent migrations of a non-Javanese people, see Clark E. Cunningham, *The Postwar Migration of the Toba-Bataks to East Sumatra,* Yale University, Southeast Asia Studies, Cultural Report Series No. 5 (New Haven, 1958).

BIBLIOGRAPHY

Atlas Nasional Seluruh Dunia untuk Sekolah Landjutan, Djakarta, Bandung, Ganaco, 1960. This modern atlas was prepared especially for use in Indonesian schools. Three pages containing six maps are reproduced in this volume.

Atlas van tropisch Nederland [Atlas of the Tropical Netherlands], Batavia, Topographical Service of the Netherlands Indies, 1938. This prewar atlas—although highly dated in so far as it depicts social, economic, and political conditions—continues to render good service as a general reference work.

BEMMELEN, R. W. VAN, *The Geology of Indonesia,* 2 vols. in 3 pts. The Hague, Nijhoff, 1949. Vol. 1 of this valuable handbook deals with the general geology and Vol. 2 with the economic geology of Indonesia.

BRAAK, C., *Het klimaat van Nederlandsch-Indië* [The Climate of the Netherlands Indies], Verhandelingen No. 8, Koninklijk magnetisch en meteorologisch observatorium te Batavia, vol. 1, Batavia, Javasche boekhandel en drukkerij, vol. 2, Weltevreden, Kolff, 1921-29. Vol. 1 of this monumental handbook treats general aspects of Indonesia's climate, and Vol. 2 presents the regional climatology.

BRAAKE, ALEX L. TER, *Mining in the Netherlands Indies,* New York, Netherlands and Netherlands Indies Council of the Institute of Pacific Relations, 1944. Mining policy and the mining industry of Indonesia prior to World War II are briefly surveyed.

LEEDEN, C. B. VAN DER, *Het aspect van landbouwkolonisatie in het bevolkingsprobleem van Java* [The Agricultural Resettlement Aspect in Java's Population Problem], The Hague, Excelsior, 1952.

477

This Ph.D. dissertation, presented at the University of Leiden, examines Java's population and concludes that mass migration cannot solve it.

MOHR, E. C. J., "The Relation between Soil and Population Density in the Netherlands East Indies," *Comptes rendus du Congrès Internationale de Géographie Amsterdam 1938*, 2 sect. IIIc (Leiden, Brill, 1938), 478-93. This paper is important for understanding the problem of uneven population distribution in Indonesia, showing that in Indonesia population density is a function of the nature of the soil and this, in turn, of the presence of active volcanoes.

————, *The Soils of Equatorial Regions with Special Reference to the Netherlands East Indies*, trans., Robert L. Pendleton, Ann Arbor, J. W. Edwards, 1944. Part I deals with the genesis and morphology of tropical soils, while Part II presents a detailed regional treatment of the soils of Indonesia and their utilization.

NITISASTRO, WIDJOJO, "Migration, Population Growth, and Economic Development in Indonesia: A Study of the Economic Consequences of Alternative Patterns of Interisland Migration," Ph.D. thesis, Berkeley, University of California, 1961. The author examines the population growth of Java during the nineteenth and twentieth centuries, calculates Java's population for 1960 on the basis of the 1930 census data, and analyzes the effect that various rates of emigration from Java will have on that island's population growth between 1960 and 1990.

PELZER, KARL J., *Pioneer Settlement in the Asiatic Tropics: Studies in Land Utilization and Agricultural Colonization in Southeastern Asia*, New York, Institute of Pacific Relations in cooperation with the American Geographical Society, 1945. This study, based on prewar field work, treats of agricultural land use as well as problems of population distribution and interisland migration.

RICHARDS, P. W., *The Tropical Rain Forest*, Cambridge, University Press, 1952. Although this is a general treatment of the ecology of the tropical rain forest, the volume is important for the understanding of the Indonesian forests and contains numerous references to Indonesia.

STEENIS, C. G. G. J. VAN, "Maleische vegetatieschetsen" [Malaysian Vegetation Sketches], *Tijdschrift van het Koninklijk Nederlandsch Aardrijkskundig Genootschap*, 52, Ser. 2 (1935), 25-67, 171-203 363-98. This is a comprehensive account of the vegetation of Indonesia; the map accompanying this article is also published in *Atlas van tropisch Nederland*.

WERTHEIM, W. F., "Sociological Aspects of Inter-Island Migration in Indonesia," *Population Studies*, 12 (1959), 184-201; re-issued as Publikatie No. 3, Sociologisch-historisch seminarium voor Zuidoost Azië, Universiteit van Amsterdam. This valuable article utilizes observations made during a 1956 visit to the pioneer settlement districts of South Sumatra as starting point for a general discussion of the problems of interisland migration.

NOTES AND BIBLIOGRAPHY FOR *Indonesian Cultures and Communities*

1. The number of ethnic groups depends on how they are classified. M. A. Jaspan distinguishes over 360 groups in his *Daftar Sementara dari Sukubangsa-bangsa di Indonesia* [A Provisional List of the Ethnic Groups in Indonesia] (Jogjakarta, Panitya Social Research, Gadjah Mada University, 1958). Raymond Kennedy's classification, which is given in an appendix to this chapter, gives 54 groups, but many of these should be further broken down into 10 or more distinct peoples.

2. The theoretical development of the approach employed in this chapter has been carried out by Julian H. Steward in *Theory of Culture Change* (Urbana, University of Illinois Press, 1955), especially Chapter 5, in which the earlier concept of culture area is criticized. See also Julian H. Steward and Louis C. Faron, *Native Peoples of South America* (New York, McGraw-Hill, 1959); and the issue of the *American Anthropologist*, 57 (1955), devoted to "New Views on the Anthropology of Latin America," particularly the articles by Wagley and Harris, Oberg, and Wolf.

3. This section is based on field research in the small Javanese town of Modjokuto, which has been described by Clifford Geertz, "Religious Belief and Economic Behavior in a Central Javanese Town," *Economic Development and Cultural Change*, 4 (1956); and by Hildred Geertz, *The Javanese Family* (New York, Free Press, 1961), Chapter 1. It is also based on personal, unsystematic observations of Djakarta, Surabaja, Malang, Jogjakarta, Den Pasar, Singaradja, Tabanan, Padang, and Pakan Baru. Another important source has been W. F. Wertheim, *Indonesian Society in Transition* (The Hague, W. van Hoeve, 1959), Chapter 7. Others were: *The Indonesian Town*, eds. W. F. Wertheim et al. (The Hague, van Hoeve, 1958); The Siauw Giap, "Urbanisatieproblemen in Indonesië" [Urbanization Problems in Indonesia], *Bijdragen tot de Taal-, Land- en Volkenkunde, 115* (1959).

4. Leslie H. Palmier, "Western Communities in Southeast Asia," *Yale Review*, 1958.

5. For a discussion of the Chinese minority, see Chapter 3.

6. Edward Bruner, in his "Urbanization and Ethnic Identity in North Sumatra," *American Anthropologist, 63* (1961), explicitly denies that an Indonesian superculture exists. This disagreement is most likely based on semantic differences in interpreting the term "superculture." See also Edward Bruner, "Kinship Organization among the Urban Batak

of Sumatra," *Transactions of the New York Academy of Sciences, 22,* Series II (1959).

7. For a discussion of the methods and effect of government efforts in securing this commitment, see Chapter 8.

8. H. J. Heeren, ed., "The Urbanization of Djakarta," *Ekonomi dan keuangan Indonesia, 8* (1955).

9. F. J. Ormeling, *The Timor Problem* (Groningen and Djakarta, J. B. Wolters, 1956), p. 118.

10. For a study of a weaving mill in a small Javanese town, see Ann Willner, "From Rice-Field to Factory: The Industrialization of a Rural Labor Force in Java" (unpublished Ph.D. dissertation, University of Chicago, 1961).

11. Robert Merton developed this distinction, terming them "locals" and "cosmopolitans" in studies of American communities. See his "Patterns of Influence," in Robert Merton, *Social Theory and Structure* (rev. ed. Glencoe, Free Press, 1957).

12. See Leslie H. Palmier, *Social Status and Power in Java* (London, Athlone Press, 1960), for a study of a small-town elite group.

13. Clifford Geertz, "Religious Belief and Economic Behavior in a Central Javanese Town," *Economic Development and Cultural Change, 4* (1956).

14. Clifford Geertz, "Social Change and Economic Modernization in Two Indonesian Towns: A Case in Point," in Everett E. Hagen, *On the Theory of Social Change* (Homewood, Ill., Dorsey, 1962), Chapter 16.

15. This is an extremely rough computation, derived by combining the population totals for the provinces of Central Java and East Java, plus Jogjakarta, and minus the regencies on the island of Madura. The East Java figure still includes an indeterminate number of Madurese speakers living on Java. On the other hand, there are numerous Javanese speakers in West Java and Djakarta who are excluded from this estimate. The 1961 census figures, here and below, are from *Sensus Penduduk 1961 [Population Census 1961] Republik Indonesia* (Djakarta, Biro Pusat Statistik, 1962).

16. This section is based primarily on the fieldwork of the Harvard team that studied the town and villages of Modjokuto in 1952-54, some of which is still unpublished. Published materials include: Hildred Geertz, *The Javanese Family* (New York, Free Press of Glencoe, 1961); Hildred Geertz, "The Vocabulary of Emotion: A Study of Javanese Socialization Processes," *Psychiatry, 33* (1959); Clifford Geertz, *The Religion of Java* (Glencoe, Free Press, 1960); Clifford Geertz, "The Javanese Village," *Local, Ethnic and National Loyalties in Village Indonesia,* ed. G. W. Skinner (New Haven, Yale University, Southeast Asia Studies, 1959); Clifford Geertz, "Ritual and Social Change: A Javanese Example," *American Anthropologist, 59* (1957); Robert R. Jay, "Local Government in Rural Central Java," *Far Eastern Quarterly,*

15 (1956); and Alice Dewey, *Peasant Marketing in Java* (New York, Free Press of Glencoe, 1962). Other sources are listed in the bibliography.

17. The term *gotong rojong* has two meanings which are often confused. The first meaning is the norm for cooperation and mutual aid. The second and more fundamental meaning is the actual customary practices of labor and produce exchange as they exist in the Javanese peasant village. Koentjaraningrat, in *Some Social-Anthropological Observations on Gotong Rojong Practices in Two Villages of Central Java* (Ithaca, Cornell University Southeast Asia Program, 1961), has ably shown that the motivation of these practices is not idealistic but is based on hardheaded calculation of expected reciprocity, and that the practices are dependent on an agricultural economy and a fairly even distribution of land.

18. For a further discussion of Javanese agriculture and land tenure, see Chapter 4.

19. Koentjaraningrat, pp. 11, 20-21, shows that this is more true of urbanized villages. In remote villages, inherited land is held as a single estate for several generations, with no legal change in its status, but it is divided de facto, and worked individually by each heir.

20. This was the case in 1954; the reader will note that in Chapter 8 an argument is presented for significant changes in this pattern in the most recent years.

21. This discussion is based mainly on personal fieldwork (1957-58), the results of which are largely unpublished. Preliminary papers are: Hildred Geertz, "The Balinese Village," in *Local, Ethnic and National Loyalties in Village Indonesia;* Clifford Geertz, "Form and Variation in Balinese Village Structure," *American Anthropologist, 61* (1959); Clifford Geertz, "Social Change and Economic Modernization in Two Indonesian Towns: A Case in Point," in Everett E. Hagen, *On the Theory of Social Change* (Homewood, Ill., Dorsey, 1962); and Clifford Geertz, "'Internal Conversion' in Balinese Religion," in Bastin and Roolvink, eds., *Essays in Honour of Sir Richard Winstedt* (Oxford, Oxford University Press, in press). Other references are noted in the bibliography.

22. See Chapter 10; also Miguel Covarrubias, *Island of Bali* (New York, Alfred A. Knopf, 1956), and Beryl de Zoete and Walter Spies, *Dance and Drama in Bali* (London, Faber and Faber, 1938).

23. This description focuses on the social structure of Bali; for a perceptive analysis of the island's cultural patterns, ethos, and basic personality structure see Gregory Bateson and Margaret Mead, *Balinese Character* (New York, New York Academy of Sciences, 1942).

24. Jane Belo, *Bali: Temple Festival,* Monographs of the American Ethnological Society, 23 (New York, 1953); and the articles by Goris, Grader, and Swellengrebel in *Bali: Studies in Life, Thought and Ritual,*

eds. W. F. Wertheim et al. (The Hague and Bandung, van Hoeve, 1960).

25. Jane Belo, *Bali: Rangda and Barong*, Monographs of the American Ethnological Society, 16 (New York, 1949), and Bateson and Mead, *Balinese Character*. For a description of the dance in this volume, see Chapter 10.

26. Jane Belo, *Trance in Bali* (New York, Columbia University Press, 1960).

27. There are no adequate English terms for the different levels of Balinese royalty and nobility, for nearly every kingdom had different terms and titles, and in any case the political system was very different from that of European monarchies and feudal states. The same terminological difficulties appear in regard to the Javanese classical kingdoms and to the kingdoms of the Pasisir societies discussed below. In all cases, I arbitrarily use the words "king" and "prince" for positions of political authority in the traditional states. A case could be made for the use of the word "sultan," but it is often just as misleading and foreign as the word "king."

28. Covarrubias, *Island of Bali*, Chapter 3.

29. R. Goris reverses this stress, stating that the community is above all religious in function. He feels that the Kahyangan-Tiga temple set marks the boundaries of the essential Balinese village, and that any variations from this correlation are modern developments (R. Goris, "The Religious Character of the Village Community" in *Bali: Studies in Life, Thought and Ritual*). The approach I am following here asserts that, although worship provides the foundation of almost every kind of Balinese organization, the regular absence of a single multifunctional village community, in which religious, legal, social, and other activities are all performed by a single social structural group, is basically characteristic of Balinese social structure. See Clifford Geertz, "Form and Variation in Balinese Village Structure," *American Anthropologist*, *61* (1959).

30. Important studies on Malaya include: Raymond Firth, *Malay Fishermen: Their Peasant Economy* (London, Kegan Paul, Trench, Trubner, 1946); Rosemary Firth, *Housekeeping Among Malay Peasants*, London School of Economics Monographs on Social Anthropology, 7 (London, 1943); Judith Djamour, *Malay Kinship and Marriage in Singapore* (London, Athlone Press, 1959), and J. M. Gullick, *Indigenous Political Systems of Western Malaya* (London, Athlone Press, 1958).

31. Th. Pigeaud, *Javaanse volksvertoningen* [Javanese Folk Drama and Dance] (Batavia, Volkslectuur, 1938) pp. 347-49, 477-78.

32. Lack of data prevents me from making this list more precise, but there are no doubt a good many specific customs which are also characteristic of the Pasisir culture, such as the ritualistic regard for weapons and the use of Arabic musical instruments. A distinction should

be made between the Pasisir culture and the Pasisir peoples, the latter being those subsocieties of Indonesia which most completely adopted the Pasisir culture. At its peak the Pasisir culture was very dynamic, and it strongly influenced many of Indonesia's other cultures: central Javanese santri are full-fledged carriers of it, and even the high culture of the gentry prijaji is shot through with Islamic elements. The Minangkabau are a marginal case, and could easily be considered as one of the Pasisir peoples. Even the Balinese kris dance has been attributed to Pasisir influence (Pigeaud, p. 478).

33. E. C. J. Mohr, "The Relation between Soil and Population Density in the Netherlands Indies," *Science and Scientists in the Netherlands Indies*, eds. P. Honig and F. Verdoorn (New York, Board for the Netherlands Indies, Surinam, and Curaçao, 1945), pp. 260-61.

34. This section on Makassarese-Buginese social structure is based mainly on the following: H. Th. Chabot, *Verwantschap, stand en sexe in Zuid-Celebes* [Kinship, Class and Sex in South Celebes] (Groningen and Djakarta, J. B. Wolters, 1950); H. J. Friedericy, "Ponre: Bijdrage tot de kennis van adat en adatrecht van Zuid-Celebes" [Ponre: A Contribution to the Understanding of Custom and Customary Law of South Celebes] *Bijdragen tot de Taal-, Land- en Volkenkunde van Nederlandsch-Indië*, 89 (1932); H. J. Friedericy, "De standen bij de Boegineezen en Makassaren" [Classes of the Buginese and Makassarese] *Bijdragen tot de Taal-, Land- en Volkenkunde van Nederlandsch-Indië*, 90 (1933); and Raymond Kennedy, *Field Notes on Indonesia: South Celebes, 1949-1950* (New Haven, Human Relations Area Files, 1953).

35. Kennedy, *Field Notes;* and Friedericy, "De standen."

36. Chabot, *Verwantschap*, pp. 120-32, 211-26; and also H. D. Mangemba, *Kenallah Sulawesi-Selatan* [Introduction to South Celebes] (Djakarta, Timun Mas, 1956), pp. 9-15, 117-23.

37. Chabot gives no native term for these kin groups; and it appears from other sources that the terms vary considerably from locality to locality, and that an identical term may be used for groups of differing organization and scope. Technically, the type of corporate kinship grouping described by Chabot is called a "non-unilineal descent group" (Ward Goodenough, "A Problem in Malayo-Polynesian Social Organization," *American Anthropologist*, 58 (1955).

38. This section on Sumbawa is based on Peter Goethals' reports: "The Sumbawan Village," *Local, Ethnic and National Loyalties in Village Indonesia;* "Task Groups and Marriage in Western Sumbawa," *Intermediate Societies, Social Mobility and Communication*, ed. Verne F. Ray (Seattle, American Ethnological Society, 1959); and *Aspects of Local Government in a Sumbawan Village (Eastern Indonesia)* (Ithaca, Cornell University Southeast Asia Program, 1961).

39. For a further discussion of swidden and smallholder cash crop agriculture, see Chapter 4.

40. A pioneering attempt to classify the ecological adaptation systems of Indonesia is G. J. A. Terra's "Farm Systems in Southeast Asia," *Netherlands Journal of Agricultural Science, 6* (1958). In this article Terra divides Indonesia's swidden peoples into those with and those without cattle. A fine study of the interaction of cattle-tending and swidden cultivation in a climate with a marked dry season and modern postwar economic and social problems connected with these is: F. J. Ormeling, *The Timor Problem: A Geographical Interpretation of an Underdeveloped Island* (Groningen and Djakarta, J. B. Wolters, 1956). See further, in this volume, Chapter 4.

41. Cora Du Bois, *The People of Alor* (Minneapolis, University of Minnesota Press, 1944). See also F. A. E. van Wouden, *Sociale structuurtypen in de Groote Oost* [Types of Social Structure in East Indonesia] (Leiden, J. Ginsberg, 1953).

42. This description is based entirely on the excellent work of the missionary-ethnologist Albert C. Kruyt and his associates. Kruyt lived with the Bare'e-speaking Toradja from 1892 until 1932. N. Adriani and A. C. Kruyt, *De Bare'e-sprekende Toradjas van Midden-Celebes* [The Bare'e-speaking Toradjas of Central Celebes] (2d rev. ed. Amsterdam, Noord-Hollandsche Uitgevers Maatschappij, 1950); Albert C. Kruyt, "The Influence of Western Civilization on the Inhabitants of Poso (Central Celebes)," in *The Effect of Western Influence on Native Civilisations in the Malay Archipelago,* ed. B. Schrieke (Batavia, G. Kolff, 1929); R. E. Downs, "Headhunting in Indonesia," *Bijdragen tot de taal-, land-en volkenkunde, 111* (1955); R. E. Downs, *The Religion of the Bare'e-speaking Toradja of Central Celebes* (The Hague, Excelsior, 1956).

43. It is not clear from the published reports why there was no steady inflation in bride price and continuous shifts in status reflecting social mobility, as was the case in Makassar; but it is quite clear that both inflation and mobility were absent.

44. It is unclear from Kruyt's descriptions to what extent these Western trade goods were present in Toradja regions before the twentieth century.

45. The description of Minangkabau society supplied here is largely drawn from the following sources: B. Schrieke, "The Causes and Effects of Communism on the West Coast of Sumatra," *Indonesian Sociological Studies* (The Hague and Bandung, van Hoeve, 1955); Ahmad Dt. Batuah and A. Dt. Madjoindo, *Tambo Minangkabau* [Minangkabau Traditions] (Djakarta, Balai Pustaka, 1956); Anthony H. Johns, *Rantjak Dilabueh: A Minangkabau Kaba,* Cornell University Southeast Asia Program, Data Paper No. 32 (Ithaca, 1958); P. E. de Josselin de Jong, *Minangkabau and Negri Sembilan: Socio-Political Structure in Indonesia* (Leiden, Eduard Ijdo, 1951); M. Radjab, *Semasa Ketjil Dikampung* [Childhood in the Village] (Djakarta, Balai Pustaka, 1950).

46. Nathan Keyfitz and Widjojo Nitisastro, *Soal Penduduk dan*

Pembangunan Indonesia [The Problem of Population and Indonesian Development] (Djakarta, Pembangunan, 1955), p. 39.

47. *Atlas van tropisch Nederland* [Atlas of the Tropical Netherlands] (Batavia, Koninklijk Nederlandsch Aardrijkskundig Genootschap, 1938), Map 9a.

48. For a discussion of Minangkabau writers, see Chapter 9.

49. The main materials for this part were: Edward M. Bruner, "The Toba Batak Village," in *Local, Ethnic and National Loyalties in Village Indonesia;* Edward M. Bruner, "Kinship Organization among the Urban Batak of Sumatra," *Transactions of the New York Academy of Sciences,* 22, Series II (1959); Edward M. Bruner, "Urbanization and Ethnic Identity in North Sumatra," *American Anthropologist,* 63 (1961); Clark E. Cunningham, *The Postwar Migration of the Toba-Bataks to East Sumatra* (New Haven, Yale University, Southeast Asia Studies, 1958).

50. According to Cunningham, *The Postwar Migration,* pp. 67, 73.

51. See Bruner, "The Toba Batak Village," p. 118.

52. For a discussion of estate vs. squatter agriculture in the area of Batak migration, see Chapter 4, and for a description of the economic aspects of the relations of the Bataks to immigrant groups, see chapters 5 and 6.

53. Rodney Needham, "The System of Teknonyms and Death-Names of the Penan," *Southwestern Journal of Anthropology,* 10 (1954); Rodney Needham, "Mourning Terms," *Bijdragen tot de taal-, land- en volkenkunde,* 115 (1959).

54. See Edwin M. Loeb, "Mentawei Social Organizations," *American Anthropologist,* 30 (1928); Edwin M. Loeb, "Mentawei Religious Cult," *University of California Publication in American Archaeology and Ethnology,* 25 (1929); Edwin M. Loeb, "Sumatra: Its History and People," *Wiener Beiträge zur Kulturgeschichte und Linguistik,* 3 (1935); Warner Muensterberger, "Oral Trauma and Taboo: A Psychoanalytic Study of an Indonesian Tribe," in *Psychoanalysis and the Social Sciences,* 2, ed. Geza Roheim (New York, International Universities Press, 1950); P. Suzuki, *Critical Survey of Studies on the Anthropology of Nias, Mentawei and Enggano* (The Hague, Martinus Nijhoff, 1958); Anthony F. C. Wallace, "Mentaweian Social Organization," *American Anthropologist,* 53 (1951).

55. Frank L. Cooley, "Ambonese Kin Groups," *Ethnology, 1* (1962); F. D. Holleman, *Het adat-grondenrecht van Ambon en de Oeliassers* [Customary Land-tenure Laws of Ambon and the Uliasse Islands] (Delft, W. D. Meinema, 1923); Raymond Kennedy, *Islands and Peoples of the Indies* (Washington, Smithsonian Institution, 1943); Charles Robequain, *Malaya, Indonesia, Borneo and the Philippines* (London, Longmans, Green, 1954).

56. See Chapter 6 for a discussion of some aspects of labor and management in these enterprises.

BIBLIOGRAPHY

ADRIANI, N. and A. C. KRUYT, *De Bare'e sprekende Toradja's van Midden-Celebes (de Oost-Toradja's)* [The Bare'e-speaking Toradjas of Central Celebes (The Eastern Toradjas)] 2d rev. ed. 3 vols. Amsterdam, Noord-Hollandsche Uitgevers Maatschappij, 1950. A full, detailed, and reliable ethnography, covering demography, history, social structure, religion, marriage, family, agriculture, trade, crafts, dance, games, and modern developments as of 1935.

BATESON, GREGORY and MARGARET MEAD, *Balinese Character: A Photographic Analysis*, New York, New York Academy of Sciences, 1942. An incisive analysis of the Balinese ethos, accompanied by photographs which support and supplement the verbal analysis.

BELO, JANE, *Trance in Bali*, New York, Columbia University Press, 1960. A detailed, evocative, complete study of all the manifestations of trance and their social and cultural contexts in Bali.

BRUNER, EDWARD M., "Kinship Organization among the Urban Batak of Sumatra," *Transactions of the New York Academy of Sciences,* 22, Series II, 1959. A comparison of social structure between village Batak, and Batak in Medan in 1957-58.

——, "Urbanization and Ethnic Identity in North Sumatra," *American Anthropologist, 63,* 1961. A consideration of the problem of the effects of urbanization on Toba-Batak attitudes toward their traditional institutions.

CHABOT, H. TH., *Verwantschap, stand en sexe in Zuid-Celebes* [Kinship, Class, and Sex in South Celebes], Groningen and Djakarta, J. B. Wolters, 1950. A modern anthropological study of a Makassarese village in 1940 and 1948, with particular attention to kinship, social stratification, and psychological patterns.

COOLEY, FRANK L., "Ambonese Kin Groups," *Ethnology, 1,* (1962). Brief but informative description of Ambonese kinship system.

COVARRUBIAS, MIGUEL, *Island of Bali*, New York, Alfred A. Knopf, 1956. Competent ethnographic description of Balinese culture by the well-known artist, with drawings by himself and photographs by his wife.

CUNNINGHAM, CLARK E., *The Postwar Migration of the Toba-Bataks to East Sumatra,* New Haven, Yale University, Southeast Asia Studies, 1958. A good analytic study of the agrarian migration of the Batak, both prewar and postwar, with a comparison of two communities—one a highland village, the other a new multiethnic-group village on a former plantation—based on field research in 1955-56.

DEWEY, ALICE, *Peasant Marketing in Java*, New York, Free Press of Glencoe, 1962. One of the "Modjokuto" studies of a small town in East Central Java, focused on small-scale marketing operations.

DOBBY, E. H. G., *Southeast Asia*, London, University of London Press, 1950. A comprehensive study of environmental conditions and human adaptations of mainland and island Southeast Asia.

DOWNS, R. E., *The Religion of the Bare'e-speaking Toradja of Central Celebes*, The Hague, Excelsior, 1956. Summary description of religious beliefs and practices based on publications by Adriani and Kruyt, with an interpretation according to the theories of social and ideational dualism of Levi-Strauss.

DU BOIS, CORA, *The People of Alor*, Minneapolis, University of Minnesota Press, 1944. A brief description of the culture and social structure of the people of interior Alor, followed by extensive consideration of the development of individual personality in the society, supplemented by verbatim reports of interviews with a number of Alorese and reports on psychological testing.

——, *Social Forces in Southeast Asia*, Cambridge, Harvard University Press, 1959. A synthesizing overview of the major structural tensions and directions of social change in the area.

FREEMAN, J. D., "The Iban of Western Borneo," in *Social Structure in Southeast Asia*, ed. G. P. Murdock, Viking Fund Publications in Anthropology, 29, New York, Wenner-Gren Foundation for Anthropological Research, 1960. Kinship and community structure of the Iban-Dayak, who are located partly in Indonesian Borneo, partly in Sarawak.

FRIEDERICY, H. J., "Ponre: Bijdrage tot de kennis van adat en adatrecht van Zuid-Celebes" [Ponre: A Contribution to the Understanding of Custom and Customary Law of South Celebes], *Bijdragen tot de Taal-, Land- en Volkenkunde van Nederlandsch-Indië*, 89, The Hague, Martinus Nijhoff, 1932. Brief study of political and economic systems of a mountain community, Ponre, in the Buginese area.

——, "De standen bij de Boegineezen en Makassaren" [Class-Structure of the Buginese and Makassarese], *Bijdragen tot de Taal-, Land- en Volkenkunde van Nederlandsch-Indië*, 90, The Hague, Martinus Nijhoff, 1933. A full description of the class-structure of the nineteenth-century Buginese and Makassarese kingdoms, primarily from the point of view of the elite.

GEDDES, W. R., *Nine Dayak Nights*, Melbourne, Oxford University Press, 1957. An informative and readable popular account of Dayak society, together with a long folk tale.

GEERTZ, CLIFFORD, "Ethos, World-View and the Analysis of Sacred Symbols," *Antioch Review*, 17, 1957. The relationship between Javanese values and Javanese metaphysical ideas as summed up in the shadow-puppet play, the *wajang*.

——, "Form and Variation in Balinese Village Structure," *Ameri-*

can Anthropologist, 61, 1959. Main principles of Balinese social structure and three sample communities.

——, *The Religion of Java,* Glencoe, Free Press, 1960. The main variants of Javanese religious beliefs and rituals, and their social and cultural contexts.

——, "Religious Belief and Economic Behavior in a Central Javanese Town: Some Preliminary Considerations," *Economic Development and Cultural Change, 4,* 1956. Examination of the effect of differing Javanese religious patterns on economic endeavor.

——, "Ritual and Social Change: A Javanese Example," *American Anthropologist, 59,* 1957. A funeral in a Javanese lower-class neighborhood and its social implications.

GEERTZ, HILDRED, *The Javanese Family: A Study of Kinship and Socialization,* New York, Free Press, 1961. Anthropological field study in a small Javanese town.

GOETHALS, PETER R., *Aspects of Local Government in a Sumbawan Village (Eastern Indonesia),* Ithaca, Cornell University Southeast Asia Program, 1961. Leadership and decision making at the village level in a Sumbawan swidden-cultivating group.

GULLICK, J. M., *Indigenous Political Systems of Western Malaya,* London, Athlone Press, University of London, 1958. While outside the actual borders of Indonesia, and representing the late nineteenth-century political systems, the Malay kingdoms described here are similar in many respects with the kingdoms of Atjeh, East Sumatra, Makassar, etc., before the twentieth century.

HAAR, B. TER, *Adat Law in Indonesia,* trans. E. A. Hoebel and A. A. Schiller, New York, Institute of Pacific Relations, 1948. Highly useful compendium of social organization of Indonesia, based almost entirely on Van Vollenhoven's conceptual schemes.

HOLLEMAN, F. D., *Het adat-grondenrecht van Ambon en de Oeliassers* [Customary Land-tenure Laws of Ambon and the Uliase Islands], Delft, W. D. Meinema, 1923. A historical and sociological study of land-tenure customs in Ambon.

JAY, ROBERT R., "Local Government in Rural Central Java," *Far Eastern Quarterly, 15,* 1956. Concise and sophisticated description of contemporary Javanese village social structure.

JOHNS, ANTHONY H., *Rantjak Dilabueh: A Minangkabau Kaba,* Ithaca, Cornell University Southeast Asia Program, 1958. A specimen of a traditional narrative poem which gives considerable insight into the ethics and value system of the Minangkabau, together with a useful introduction by Johns.

JOSSELIN DE JONG, P. E. DE, *Minangkabau and Negri Sembilan: Socio-Political Structure in Indonesia,* Leiden, Eduard Ijdo, 1951. A reconstruction and interpretation of the "ideal" social structure of the Minangkabau, in the tradition of the elder De Jong, Rassers, and Levi-Strauss.

KAMPTO UTOMO, *Masjarakat Transmigran Spontan Didaerah W. Sekampung (Lampung)* [The Society of the Spontaneous Transmigrants in the Area of Sekampung in Lampung], Djakarta, Penerbitan Universitas, 1957. A careful, modern anthropological field study of Javanese pioneer communities which came on their own initiative to open up new land for wet rice in South Sumatra.

KOENTJARANINGRAT, *Beberapa Metode Anthropologi dalam Penjelidikan, Masjarakat dan Kebudajaan di Indonesia* [Several Anthropological Methods in Investigations of the Society and Culture of Indonesia], Djakarta, Penerbitan Universitas, 1958. Survey of methods and theories which have been applied in cultural anthropological research in Indonesia, with special attention to ethnography, social organization, religion, native law, cultural diffusion, culture dynamics, and culture change. Includes a very full bibliography.

————, "The Javanese of South Central Java," in *Social Structure in Southeast Asia*, ed. G. P. Murdock, New York, Viking Fund Publications in Anthropology, 1960. A sophisticated, brief analysis of the kinship system of the Javanese.

————, *Some Social-Anthropological Observations on Gotong Rojong Practices in Two Villages of Central Java*, Ithaca, Cornell University Southeast Asia Program, 1961. A careful and reliable field study of the various forms of mutual aid that come under the general term of *gotong rojong*, and their concrete significance in differing village situations.

KUPERUS, GERRIT, *Het cultuurlandschap van West-Soembawa* [The Cultural Landscape of West Sumbawa], Groningen and Batavia, J. B. Wolters, 1936. Social-economic history and geography of West Sumbawa, with particular attention to the nineteenth and twentieth centuries, based on research in 1931-32.

NEEDHAM, RODNEY, "The System of Teknonyms and Deathnames of the Penan," *Southwestern Journal of Anthropology, 10,* 1954.

NOOTEBOOM, C., "Economisch onderzoek van de inheemsche samenleving in Zuidwest-Celebes" [Economic Investigations of the Native Society of South West Celebes], *Koloniale Studiën, 6,* 1938. A brief comparison of social patterns of economic exchange in East Sumba and Southwest Celebes.

ORMELING, F. J., *The Timor Problem: A Geographical Interpretation of an Underdeveloped Island,* Groningen and Djakarta, J. B. Wolters, 1956. Detailed social-geographical study of Timor, based on field research in 1953.

PALMIER, LESLIE H., *Social Status and Power in Java,* London, Athlone Press, 1960. A social-anthropological field study of two Javanese towns and their elites, both Javanese and Chinese.

————, "Western Communities in Southeast Asia," *Yale Review*, 48, 1958. Suggestive sketch of the culture and social structure of the western enclaves, especially those in Indonesia.

PELZER, KARL J., *Pioneer Settlement in the Asiatic Tropics: Studies in Land Utilization and Agricultural Colonization in Southeast Asia*, New York, American Geographical Society, 1945. An important social geographic study of attempts to open new land to wet-rice cultivation in the Philippines and in South Sumatra.

PIGEAUD, TH., *Javanese volksvertoningen: Bijdrage tot de beschrijving van land en volk* [Javanese Dramatic and Dance Performances: Contribution to the Description of Land and People], Batavia, Volkslectuur, 1938. A complete, authoritative description of the form and distribution of Javanese dramatic and dance styles.

PIJPER, G. F., *Fragmenta Islamica* [Islamic Fragments], Leiden, E. J. Brill, 1938. Important essays on Islam in Indonesia.

RADJAB, M., *Semasa Ketjil Dikampung* [Childhood in the Village], Djakarta, Balai Pustaka, 1950. A richly detailed autobiography of a village-bred Minangkabau, covering the years 1913-28.

RAKA, I GUSTI GDE, *Monographi Pulau Bali* [Monograph on Bali], Djakarta, Indonesian Republic, Ministry of Agriculture, 1955. A reliable survey of agricultural and social conditions in 1954.

ROBEQUAIN, CHARLES, *Malaya, Indonesia, Borneo and the Philippines*, trans. E. D. Laborde, London, Longmans, Green, 1954. The geography, economy, and political structure of the region, with special attention paid to the impact of colonialism.

SKINNER, G. WILLIAM, ed., *Local, Ethnic and National Loyalties in Village Indonesia: A Symposium*, New Haven, Yale University, Southeast Asia Studies, 1959. Articles on Sumbawa (Goethals) Bali (H. Geertz), Java (C. Geertz), Sunda (Palmer), and Toba Batak (Bruner), with an introduction by Skinner.

SNOUCK HURGRONJE, C., *The Achehnese*, 2 vols. Leiden, E. J. Brill, 1906. Thorough and reliable study of the culture and social structure of Atjeh in 1891, including political structure, ritual and belief, domestic life and law, literature and games.

————, *Het Gajoland en zijne bewoners* [Gajoland and Its Inhabitants], Batavia, Landsdrukkerij, 1903. Ethnographic description of the Gayo.

SUZUKI, P., *Critical Survey of Studies of the Anthropology of Nias, Mentawei and Enggano*, The Hague, Martinus Nijhoff, 1958. Full, annotated bibliography of all relevant materials, plus a brief sketch of each of the cultures and the major sources on them.

TERRA, G. J. A., "Farm Systems in South-east Asia," *Netherlands Journal of Agricultural Science*, 6, 1958. A pioneering attempt to classify the types of ecological adaptation to be found in Indonesia.

VOLLENHOVEN, C. VAN, *Het adatrecht van Nederlandsch-Indië* [Customary Laws of the Netherlands Indies], 3 vols. Leiden, E. J. Brill, 1906-33. The first, and still the most important, attempt to classify and characterize the social structures and culture areas of Indonesia.

WALLACE, ALFRED RUSSEL, *The Malay Archipelago*, New York, Dover Publications, 1962. First published in 1869, this detailed and objective account of Wallace's seven years of travel and zoological research throughout the islands gives many acute observations of their society and culture more than one hundred years ago.

WERTHEIM, W. F., *Indonesian Society in Transition*, 2d rev. ed. The Hague and Bandung, W. van Hoeve, 1959. A stimulating analytic study of the social history of Indonesia as a whole, with particular attention to modern developments. Covers political structure, economic system, stratification system, urbanization, religion, labor movements, nationalism.

WERTHEIM, W. F. et al. eds., *Bali: Studies in Life, Thought, and Ritual*, 5, The Hague and Bandung, van Hoeve, 1960. A selection and translation of some of the most important prewar studies of Balinese culture and religion by Goris, Korn, and Grader, plus a new introduction summarizing Balinese religious concepts by Swellengrebel, and an interesting description of a modern "revitalization" movement in 1949 by Franken.

——, *The Indonesian Town: Studies in Urban Sociology*, 4, The Hague and Bandung, van Hoeve, 1958. More precisely: the Javanese town. Includes a general discussion of urban development up to 1938, a study of living conditions in Batavia of the laboring class in 1937, a study of differential mortality rates by ethnic group in Bandung, and a description of the unusual appanage town of Kuta Gede near Jogjakarta.

WOUDEN, F. A. E. VAN, *Sociale structuurtypen in de Groote Oost* [Types of Social Structure in East Indonesia], Leiden, J. Ginsberg, 1935. A comparison of kinship systems in Tanimbar, Kei, Timor, Roti, Savu, Sumba, Flores, Seran, Buru, and Celebes, based on sketchy and vague published materials.

NOTES AND BIBLIOGRAPHY FOR *The Chinese Minority*

1. The writer conducted field research in Indonesia for two years (1956-58) under the auspices of the Cornell Modern Indonesia Project. Unpublished field data collected at that time provide support for many of the statements not otherwise documented in this chapter.

2. The most nearly complete of the recent tabulations of the registered population which supply figures for the Chinese separately is that for 1956, which is set forth in *Penduduk Indonesia* (Djakarta,

Biro Pusat Statistik, Seksi Demografi, 1958). An estimate based on these statistics for 1956 indicates a total Chinese population in Indonesia of 2.2 million. Assuming that the rate of natural increase in the Indonesian Chinese population is 3.0 per annum—approximately that of the Chinese in Singapore and Malaya—we arrive at an estimated 2.55 million for 1960. During 1959-60, however, approximately 100,000 Indonesian Chinese were repatriated to China, leaving us with a corrected estimate for 1961 of 2.45 million.

3. Edward J. Ryan, "The Value System of a Chinese Community in Java" (unpublished doctoral dissertation in anthropology, Harvard University, 1961).

4. Wouter Brokx, *Het recht tot wonen en reizen in Nederlandsch-Indië* [The Right to Reside and Travel in the Netherlands Indies] ('s Hertogenbosch, C. V. Teulings, 1925).

5. Computed from the results of the 1930 census (*Volkstelling 1930*), which showed a total population of 3,523,550 living in urban centers of 8,000 population and larger, of whom 340,025 were Chinese.

6. According to the registration figures for 1956, Chinese constituted between 10 and 11 per cent of the total population of all the officially designated municipalities in Java. The range is delimited by Jogjakarta, in which Chinese formed only 4.5 per cent, and Tjirebon, in which they formed 20.8 per cent of the total population in 1956.

7. The percentage for West Borneo is based on the registered population as compiled by the provincial government in January 1956 and obtained in Pontianak. The other percentages are based on the registered population for 1956 as given in *Penduduk Indonesia* (Djakarta, 1958).

8. Elsewhere in the outer provinces the Chinese population is thinly dispersed apart from the commercial urban centers, in which the Chinese proportion of the total population falls within the range already established for Java.

9. The development of Peranakan society is briefly outlined in G. William Skinner, "The Chinese of Java," in *Colloquium on Overseas Chinese*, ed. Morton H. Fried (New York, Institute of Pacific Relations 1958), p. 2 ff.

10. The annual recorded average of Chinese immigrants to Java and Madura, 3,464 during 1900-03, had risen to 12,172 during 1927-30. *Volkstelling 1930, 7, 49.*

11. Giok-lan Tan, "The Chinese Community in a Sundanese Town" (unpublished master's thesis in sociology, Cornell University, 1961), p. 53.

12. The questionnaire, a multipurpose paper-and-pencil schedule, was administered in Chinese and Indonesian to 1,725 high-school seniors.

13. In the questionnaire study of high-school seniors, the number of

children desired by Totok respondents was significantly higher than the number desired by Peranakans.

14. A sample of households in Djakarta was surveyed in January 1957 by the Ministry of Health. The Ministry kindly made the raw data available to the writer, who made an analysis of family composition.

15. For instance, of all households consisting solely of husband, wife, and children, 51 per cent of the Totok but only 41 per cent of the Peranakan cases included four or more children.

16. For example, in one Sundanese town no less than one-sixth of the total Peranakan population were formal members of Christian churches. Giok-lan Tan, "The Chinese Community," p. 473.

17. Lea E. Williams, *Overseas Chinese Nationalism: The Genesis of the Pan-Chinese Movement in Indonesia, 1900-1916* (Glencoe, Free Press, 1960).

18. It should not be supposed that either side wholly welcomes the widening split between Totoks and Peranakans. In the Totok mind, the Peranakan who deliberately strengthens his ties with Indonesian society and gives his allegiance to the Indonesian state has betrayed his heritage and deserted his true compatriots in the hour of their adversity. And even as the Peranakan moves toward Indonesian society and de facto citizenship, he cannot wholly suppress a sense of guilt at his own apostasy. Neither Totok nor *asli* Indonesian permits him to overlook any opportunistic elements in his motivations.

19. For an analysis of the tortuous history of Chinese citizenship in Indonesia see Donald E. Willmott, *The National Status of the Chinese in Indonesia, 1900-1958* (Ithaca, Cornell University, Modern Indonesia Project, 1961).

20. Since Indonesia took official cognizance of Chinese citizenship only as it related to the People's Republic on the mainland, as opposed to the Taiwan-based Republic of China, certain anti-Communists among the Indonesia-born Chinese did not reject Indonesian citizenship in 1949-51 even though they had no particular desire to retain it. Pro-Nationalists among the China-born who could not bring themselves to assume citizenship in the People's Republic were, after 1950, "stateless" in the eyes of the Indonesian authorities.

21. David Mozingo, "The Sino-Indonesian Dual Nationality Treaty," *Asian Survey, 1* (1961), No. 10, 30.

22. Ibid., p. 26.

23. These are detailed in Mozingo, pp. 26-28.

24. WNI stands for *warganegara Indonesia* (Indonesian citizen). As a rule the initials are applied only to citizens of foreign extraction.

25. See, for example, A. J. Muaja, *The Chinese Problem in Indonesia* (Djakarta, New Nusantara, 1958), pp. 9-10.

26. For details see Willmott, *The National Status*, pp. 74-76, 87-90.

27. Ibid., p. 89.

28. Ibid., pp. 86-87.

29. Muaja, pp. 7-8.

30. For details see Willmott, pp. 70-76.

31. For details see David Mozingo, "New Developments in China's Relations with Indonesia," *Current Scene, 1* (1962), No. 24, 1-3.

32. *Jen-min jih-pao,* February 15, 1961. Cited in "Overseas Chinese Resettled," *China News Analysis* (No. 362), March 3, 1961, p. 7.

33. Ibid.

34. The study in question is described in footnote 12.

35. This differentiation appears to have its origins in the sociopolitical position of the speech groups early in the century. Hakkas were prominent among supporters of Sun Yat-sen's revolutionary movement, as one might expect from their poverty and marginality early in the century. Using the nationalist movement to advance themselves within the Chinese community, they became so intimately involved with the Kuomintang that they were left little scope for maneuver when the KMT met with disaster. By contrast, the relatively wealthy and well-established Hokkiens eschewed revolution and were thereby diverted from commitment to the KMT. In consequence they found themselves more flexible in the postwar world, better able to make a realistic adjustment to political change. Moreover, as the dominant overseas merchants among the Indonesian Chinese, Hokkiens were inclined to back the political force destined to control the mainland Chinese ports with which they customarily traded.

36. In this connection, see Arslan Humbaraci, "Anti-Chinese Feelings in Indonesia," *Far Eastern Economic Review, 27* (1959), 389-90.

37. Willmott, pp. 104-05.

38. See the more comprehensive analysis in Willmott, pp. 100-03.

39. Muaja, p. 36.

BIBLIOGRAPHY

CATOR, W. J., *The Economic Position of the Chinese in the Netherlands Indies,* Oxford, Basil Blackwell and Mott, 1936. One of the most valuable studies of the Indonesian Chinese available in English, drawing on the extensive Dutch literature to provide demographic, legal, educational, and political information as well as a comprehensive survey of the economic position of the Chinese in the Indies. Detailed treatment is given to the Chinese in Java (30 pp.), West Borneo (43 pp.), Bangka and Billiton (32 pp.), and Sumatra (43 pp.); East Indonesia receives little attention.

CH'EN I-LING, *Yin-ni hsien-chuang yü hua-ch'iao* [The Present Situation in Indonesia and the Overseas Chinese], Taipei, Chung-yang wen-wu kung-ying she, 1954. Of value for its description of Chinese communities in Java, Celebes, West Borneo, and South

Sumatra. A final chapter gives hurried treatment to four overseas Chinese problems—citizenship, education, indigenous economic nationalism, and Communism.

CH'IU SHOU-YÜ, *Tung Yin-tu yü hua-ch'iao ching-chi fa-chan shih* [The East Indies and the Historical Development of the Overseas Chinese Economy], Shanghai, Cheng-chung shu-chü, 1947. A representative Chinese view of the role of overseas Chinese in the development of Indonesia. It surveys the economic geography of Indonesia, mentioning the Chinese where relevant. A lengthy final chapter provides an historical sketch of Chinese migration and settlement, a general treatment of the economic position of the Chinese, and an account of immediate postwar developments of interest to Chinese businessmen.

FROMBERG, P. H., *Verspreide geschriften* [Collected Writings], Leiden, Leidsche Uitgevers-maatschappij, 1926. Fromberg (1857-1924), for many years a judicial official in the Indies administration, was the best friend the Indonesian Chinese ever had, and it was with loving gratitude that the Chung Hwa Hui, the Chinese association in the Netherlands, published this collection of his works. The bulk of these writings concerns the Indonesian Chinese, including his 1911 classic, *De Chineesche beweging op Java* [The Chinese Movement on Java], a sympathetic account of the origins, objectives, and development of the pan-Chinese movement, then in full swing. This volume is still the best available source on the customary law of Peranakan society, and provides essential data for the social scientist who would attempt an analysis of traditional Peranakan culture and society as well as for the historian of the pan-Chinese movement itself.

GROOT, J. J. M. DE, *Het kongsiwezen van Borneo, eene verhandeling over den grondslag en den aard der chineesche politieke vereeninging in de koloniën* [The Kongsi System of Borneo: A Treatment of the Basis and Nature of Chinese Political Association in the Colonies], The Hague, Martinus Nijhoff, 1885. The classic history of the unique saga of the Chinese kongsis in Borneo, by an academically trained sinologist who served for some time as a civil servant in West Borneo. The sinological learning and the sociological insight evidenced in the work are both remarkable for the time.

LIEM TWAN DJIE, *De Distribueerende tusschenhandel der Chineezen op Java* [The Distributive Commerce of the Chinese on Java], The Hague, Martinus Nijhoff, 1947. A solid if unimaginative economic history, interesting for its description of the development of the Chinese role in Java's internal trade from early times to the 1920s and its treatment of factors in Java and abroad which led to the decline of the Chinese distributive trade during the 1930s and early 1940s.

MOERMAN, J., *In en om de Chineesche kamp* [In and around the Chinese Camp], Batavia, Landsdrukkerij, 1929. One of the richest sources available on traditional Peranakan culture. Moerman clearly immersed himself in Chinese lore while in Java, and his book is a valuable if somewhat naive account of what he had come to admire. Most of the material appears to relate to the educated Peranakans of West Java.

MUAJA, A. J., *The Chinese Problem in Indonesia*, Djakarta, New Nusantara, 1958. This pamphlet is a sophisticated piece of anti-sinicism published in English most probably for the benefit of the Western economic advisors to the Indonesian government. Almost all of the relevant arguments, modes of thinking, prejudiced beliefs, and myths which typical Indonesians collectively manifest are conveniently brought together here in small compass.

Nederlandsch Indië, Departement van economische zaken, *Volkstelling 1930, Deel VII, Chineezen en andere Vreemde Oosterlingen in Nederlandsch-Indië* [Census of 1930, Volume VII, Chinese and Other Foreign Orientals in the Netherlands Indies], Batavia, Landsdrukkerij, 1935. Since the 1961 census utilized a short questionnaire it is unlikely to replace this volume of the 1930 census, which provides a mine of information on Chinese life in Indonesia which no student of the social or economic position of the Chinese in twentieth-century Indonesia can afford to ignore. Its detailed tables are supplemented by extensive interpretive discussion in Dutch, with English summaries.

NIO JOE LAN, *Riwajat 40 Taon dari Tiong Hoa Hwe Koan—Batavia 1900-1939*) [Forty Years of the Batavia Tiong Hoa Hwe Koan (1900-1939)], Batavia, Tiong Hoa Hwe Koan, 1940. The Tiong Hoa Hwe Koan, which began as the organizational vanguard of the pan-Chinese movement and later became essentially an educational foundation, was a potent force among Indonesian Chinese during the period covered by the volume. The author, a Peranakan scholar, captures the flavor and feel of the era with unerring skill. The language of this edition—the now dying dialect of Chinese Malay—contributes to the effect, as do over 120 pages of photographs and some 30 pages of reproduced documents.

ONG ENG DIE, *Chineezen in Nederlandsch-Indië: Sociografie van een indonesische bevolkingsgroep* [The Chinese in the Netherlands Indies: Sociography of an Indonesian Population Group], Assen, van Gorcum, 1943. A wide-ranging study by a Peranakan Chinese born and reared in Java. It contains a demographic analysis and brief outline of Chinese economic history in the Indies, together with good summary treatments of the Chinese as workers, traders, industrial entrepreneurs, agriculturalists, and artisans, and useful descriptions of family life, education, and the juridical position of

496

the Peranakans on Java. Unfortunately, such important sociological matters as social stratification and Peranakan-Indonesian relations are given only the briefest notice.

SANDICK, L. H. W. VAN, *Chineezen buiten China: Hunne beteekenis voor de ontwikkeling van Zuid-Oost Azie, speciaal van Nederlandsch-Indië* [The Overseas Chinese: Their Significance for the Development of Southeast Asia, and Especially of the Netherlands Indies], The Hague, M. van der Beek, 1909. Its inclusion of the texts of relevant regulations, reports, and other primary documents make this volume invaluable to the historian of the Chinese in Java on this count alone. Of special usefulness are the sections treating immigration, the development of the quarter and pass systems restricting Chinese residence and travel, and the legal position of the Chinese. Java is given fullest treatment, followed by West Borneo and the East Coast of Sumatra.

SKINNER, G. WILLIAM, "Change and Persistence in Chinese Culture Overseas: A Comparison of Thailand and Java," *Journal of the South Seas Society*, 16, 1960. Attempts to explain why it was that prior to this century descendants of Chinese immigrants in Java normally maintained their Chinese social identity generation after generation, whereas in Thailand they normally assimilated to indigenous society with some rapidity. The implications of this analysis for the present and immediate future of the Chinese in Java are also explored.

TOER, PRAMUDYA ANANTA, *Hoa Kiau di Indonesia* [The Chinese in Indonesia], Djakarta, Bintang Press, 1960. A defense of the Indonesian Chinese written at a time when they were under strong Indonesian nationalist attack. The book, banned shortly after publication, is an effective piece of argumentative journalism which illustrates the enlightened view of a small group of sophisticated intellectuals.

VLEMING, J. L., JR., ed., *Het chineesche zakenleven in Nederlandsch-Indië* [Chinese Business Life in the Netherlands Indies], Batavia, Uitgave Volkslectuur, Landsdrukkerij, 1926. The collective effort of some twenty-five sinologists, accountants, and auditors in the employ of the Indies Revenue Auditing Service, this volume is valuable for its remarkably comprehensive treatment of the business culture of the Chinese, a topic little studied even in China proper, and for its descriptive survey of Chinese economic activities in the various regions of the archipelago as of the early 1920s.

WILLIAMS, LEA E., *Overseas Chinese Nationalism: The Genesis of the Pan-Chinese Movement in Indonesia, 1900-1916*, Glencoe, Free Press, 1960. The first monographic treatment in English of any period in the history of the Indonesian Chinese, based for the most part on the Dutch literature and on archival materials available in the Netherlands. The documentation is exceptionally thorough and the facts well presented, though the author's conventionally historical

497

approach causes him to slight certain facets of the pan-Chinese movement which the social scientist would be eager to plumb.

WILLMOTT, DONALD E., *The Chinese of Semarang: A Changing Minority Community in Indonesia,* Ithaca, Cornell, 1960. The first study conducted according to the premises of modern social science which has been published about any Chinese community in Indonesia, this work presents a reasoned and comprehensive overview of the large and predominantly Peranakan Chinese population of a major Javanese harbor city. Somewhat deficient in ethnographic detail, it is exceptional in that it eschews the synchronic treatment which so often impairs community studies; its focus is sociocultural change, and the treatment of this aspect is well grounded in theory.

————, *The National Status of the Chinese in Indonesia, 1900-1958,* Cornell University, Modern Indonesia Project, Ithaca, 1961. This extremely useful monograph is a competent treatment of an important study providing, in addition to historical background, a thorough discussion of the Sino-Indonesian Treaty on Dual Nationality which was finally ratified in 1960 and a wide-ranging analysis of the position in 1958 of alien Chinese and of Indonesian citizens of Chinese descent. The author's treatment of intergroup relations, based more on attitudinal than on structural analysis, is easily the best available in English.

NOTES AND BIBLIOGRAPHY FOR *The Agricultural Foundation*

1. During and shortly after World War I American firms—such as the United States Rubber Company and Goodyear Rubber Company—had a far more encouraging reception in Indonesia, where they were able to lease all the land suitable for rubber cultivation that they wanted, than they did in the Philippines.

2. Tea, sugar, and tobacco estates, in particular, are both labor and capital intensive.

3. While the term *sawah* is used throughout Indonesia, the terms *tegalan and pekarangan* are readily understood and generally used only in Java and Madura, since they refer to a type of land use best developed only by the Javanese and Madurese. Javanese settlers have carried tegalan and pekarangan cultivation into the Outer Islands, especially into South Sumatra.

4. In parts of the Outer Islands the term *ladang* no longer refers exclusively to temporary fields, or swidden, carved out of the forest but also to dry land which is in continuous use, either for the raising of annuals—land which the Javanese would call tegalan—or dry land which has been planted with tree crops, such as rubber or coffee.

498

5. Even though sawah culture is practiced in parts of Atjeh, Tapanuli, East Sumatra, the Minangkabau region of West Sumatra, and in the Javanese settlement districts of South Sumatra, sawah occupies only 1.8 per cent of the total Sumatran area.

6. This estimate is based on the assumption that five million hectares form the active ladang area, which is used for two years and then lies fallow for ten years. Therefore 25 million hectares under forest and grass fallow are the counterpart of 5 million hectares of currently cultivated ladang.

7. For a further discussion of factors affecting the Indonesian cultivation pattern, see Chapter 1.

8. Jacob Ozinga, *De economische ontwikkeling der Westerafdeeling van Borneo en de bevolkingsrubbercultuur* [The Economic Development of West Borneo and Smallholder Rubber Cultivation] (Wageningen, Zomer en Keuning, 1940), pp. 237 and 262-65.

9. Swidden cultivation in Java is still found only in relatively thinly settled portions of Bantam, in the western part of the island.

10. Biro Pusat Statistik, *Statistical Pocketbook of Indonesia 1961* (Djakarta, 1961), p. 51.

11. For a further description of the uses of pekarangan, see G. J. A. Terra, "Tuinbouw" [Gardening], in C. J. J. van Hall and C. van de Koppel, *De landbouw in de Indische archipel* [Agriculture in the Indies Archipelago] 2A (The Hague, van Hoeve, 1948), 630-31.

12. H. ten Dam, "Cooperation and Social Structure in the Village of Chibodas," in *Indonesian Economics: The Concept of Dualism in Theory and Policy* (The Hague, van Hoeve, 1961), pp. 347-82. A Dutch version was published in *Indonesië*, 9 (1956), 89-116.

13. Don C. Bennet, "Population Pressure in East Java" (unpublished doctoral dissertation, Syracuse University, 1957), p. 138.

14. Sharecropping is known under various local names: *maro* or *mertelu* in Central and East Java, *nengah* or *djedjuron* in the Priangan district of West Java, *memperduai* in the Minangkabau area of West Sumatra, *tojo* in the Minahasa region of Celebes, and *njakap* in Lombok. In 1960 the Ministry of Agrarian Affairs estimated 60 per cent of all peasants to be sharecroppers.

15. The following maxima of sawah and dry land (*tanah kering*), based on population density by regencies, or kabupaten, are allowed:

Density per sq. km.	Sawah		Dry land	
Less than 50 persons	15	hectares	20	hectares
51-250 "	10	"	12	"
251-400 "	7.5	"	9	"
Over 400 "	5	"	6	"

16. Decree of the Minister of Agrarian Affairs No. SK/509/Ka, August 22, 1961. This land is to be derived from the following sources: (1) lands in excess of the permissible maxima set by Act No. 56/Prp/1960;

(2) lands of absentee owners; (3) former private estates and proprietary lands (*particuliere landerijen*); (4) former principality lands; (5) former plantation lands returned to the state; and (6) other lands directly administered by the state (speech delivered by the Minister of Agrarian Affairs at the Conference on Village Community Development, August 10, 1961.

17. *The World Food Deficit: A First Approximation* (Washington, Foreign Agricultural Service, U.S. Department of Agriculture, March 1961), p. 22.

18. The original plan called for repayment to be made by delivery of from 5.5 to 6.5 quintals of paddy per hectare. However, some Central Java chapters of the Barisan Tani Indonesia (Indonesian Peasant Front, an association closely allied to the Communist party) objected to this on the grounds that it resembled the *idjon* system—i.e. moneylending in return for payment in kind at harvest time, a form of indebtedness with which the Javanese peasant was all too familiar. In late 1961 the government therefore began to allow repayment in cash, which the peasants preferred.

19. This calculation was based on population estimates which were proved by the 1961 census to be in error by about 4 million. Rice needs were thus 400,000 tons more than initially calculated, and increased thereafter at the rate of 200,000 tons a year.

20. Karl J. Pelzer, "The Agrarian Conflict in East Sumatra," *Pacific Affairs, 30* (1957), 151-59; and Clark E. Cunningham, *The Postwar Migration of the Toba-Bataks to East Sumatra* (New Haven, Yale University, Southeast Asia Studies, 1958).

21. Among the perquisites held by owners of private estates were the rights to collect one-fifth of crop yields, a fee on fruit trees and other profit-yielding trees and shrubs, a tax on land occupied by buildings, and a fee on land covered by fish ponds. They could also appoint village chiefs, approve elected village officials, and dismiss them from office.

22. The Dutch parliament had authorized the first repurchase of a private estate in 1910.

23. For a detailed discussion of land laws established in the period of colonial rule, see J. G. W. Lekkerkerker, *Concessies en erfpachten voor landbouwondernemingen in de Buitengewesten* [Concessions and Long Leases for Agricultural Enterprises in the Outer Islands] (Groningen, Wolters, 1928); and G. J. Nolst Trenité, "Agrarische regelingen" [Agrarian Regulations], in *De landbouw in de Indische archipel, 1,* 286-309.

24. Prior to 1959 there were thirty-five government-owned estates, operated by PPN (Pusat Perkebunan Negara, or Government Estates Administration), a part of the Ministry of Agriculture. In 1959 the PPN-Baru (new PPN) was created to administer the plantations acquired in

that year by nationalization; and in 1960 the two bodies were merged under the title PPN.

25. The United States Rubber Company received exploitation rights for a period of twelve years with the understanding that further extension will be considered provided that the company in the meantime undertakes research and development work. However, the Indonesian government insisted upon cession of no less than 30 per cent of the planted area.

26. J. A. C. Mackie, "Indonesia's Government Estates and Their Masters," *Pacific Affairs, 34* (1961), pp. 337-60, gives an excellent account of PPN operations and a most informative summary of the many problems besetting the plantation sector. See also Douglas S. Paauw, ed., *Prospects for East Sumatran Plantation Industries: A Symposium* (New Haven, Yale University, Southeast Asia Studies, 1962). This symposium deals with the tobacco, palm oil, and rubber industries of East Sumatra. For a further discussion of labor and management problems confronting the estates, see Chapter 6 of this volume.

27. Among the measures taken by the Indonesian government to eliminate injustices in the sugar districts was the repeal of such regulations as a 1923 law forbidding the purchase of peasant-produced cane by the sugar mills, and a ruling of the prewar Irrigation Service discriminating against Indonesian cane-growers by allotting them less irrigation water during the dry season than was granted to European planters.

28. *Report of the Bank Indonesia, 1958-1959* (Djakarta, Kolff, 1960), p. 197.

29. Supreme War Administration Decree No. 4/1961.

30. Decree No. SK/XIV/1/KA, Djakarta, January 31, 1962. The regulation which was based on the powers granted by the Land Use Law, identified each mill and stated the amount of land to be planted with sugar, but left it up to the local and regional heads to establish the quotas for individual villages. The decree called for a total of 95,680 hectares to be planted in sugar, of which 77,340 were to be planted by the sugar plantations and 18,340 by peasants for delivery to the mills.

31. Speech by Amin Tjokrosuseno of the Department of Agriculture, delivered at the Conference on Sugar Production at Tjipajung in December 1961.

32. This was particularly evident in the sugar and rubber industries. For the latter, see P. T. Bauer, *The Rubber Industry: A Study in Competition and Monopoly* (Cambridge, Harvard University Press, 1948), pp. 208-15. Cases of favoritism were defended by Netherlands Indies officials with the argument that the interests of the state were best served by a strong plantation industry capable of competing on the world market.

33. Whereas the plantation rubber area is exactly known, the smallholder acreage has only been estimated on the basis of a census count of

trees, undertaken in the late 1930s. A preliminary figure, based on the assumption that smallholders had planted 850 trees per hectare on the average, gave a total of about 700,000 hectares under peasant rubber; a second estimate, assuming a lower density of trees, indicated an area of 1,300,000 hectares. Whichever figure one accepts, it is apparent that the smallholder area was considerably larger than that of the estates. In allotting production quotas under the rubber restriction agreement, the Netherlands Indies government favored the plantation by a ratio of 100:71.5.

34. The virtual collapse of the old labor-recruiting organization which for many years imported laborers from Java also contributed to the development of a labor shortage.

35. S. J. Hickson, *A Naturalist in North Celebes* (London, J. Murray, 1889), pp. 72-73.

36. *The World Food Deficit*, p. 22; and Erich W. Zimmerman, *World Resources and Industries* (New York, Harper, 1951), pp. 190-91.

37. *Rantjangan Dasar Undang-undang Pembangunan Nasional-Semesta-Berentjana Delapan Tahun: 1961-69, Disusun oleh Dewan Perantjang Nasional Republik Indonesia* [Draft of a Basic Bill for an Eight-Year National Over-all Development Plan: 1961-69, prepared by the National Planning Council of the Republic of Indonesia] (Djakarta, no publisher, no year), vol. 5, part 13, p. 2742.

38. In 1951 Indonesia had only about 100 motorized fishing vessels; these increased to 1,462 by 1959. Between 1954 and 1959 the number of sailing vessels rose from 97,000 to 176,000. See Biro Pusat Statistik, *Statistical Pocketbook of Indonesia 1960* (Djakarta, 1960), p. 84; and also *Indonesian-U.S. Cooperation: A Report (October 1950—June 1955)* (Djakarta, United States Operations Missions in Indonesia with the cooperation of the Indonesian State Planning Bureau, 1955).

39. Of this, Java and Madura produced 100,600 tons from sea and 113,000 from inland fisheries. Sumatran sea fisheries contributed 145,000 and inland fisheries 54,000 tons; Borneo 65,000 and 156,000; Celebes 36,000 and 22,000; the Lesser Sunda Islands 21,000 and 2,000; and the Moluccas 42,000 tons from sea fisheries and none from inland ponds (*Statistical Pocketbook of Indonesia 1961*, p. 83).

BIBLIOGRAPHY

ALLEN, G. C. and AUDREY G. DONNITHORNE, *Western Enterprise in Indonesia and Malaya*, New York, Macmillan, 1957. Several chapters trace the historical development of plantation agriculture in Indonesia from the nineteenth century to about 1955 and describe the impact of World War II and early postwar changes.

BAUER, P. T., *The Rubber Industry: A Study in Competition and Monop-*

oly, Cambridge, Harvard University Press, 1948. In this authoritative study of the structure, history, and economics of the rubber industry during the nineteen thirties and forties in both Indonesia and Malaya the author is highly critical of such prewar and immediate postwar policies as the ban on new planting of rubber and the policy of favoring the plantation industry at the expense of the smallholder.

BEERY, LAWRENCE A., JR., *Smallholder Rubber in Indonesia*, Djakarta, International Cooperation Administration, 1956. Mimeographed. This valuable summary of the smallholder rubber industry, prepared by an American technician, stresses the need for large-scale planting of high-yielding rubber in order to preserve Indonesia's position in the world market.

BOEKE, J. H., *Ontwikkelingsgang en toekomst van bevolkings- en ondernemingslandbouw in Nederlands-Indië* [Development and Future of Smallholder and Plantation Agriculture in the Netherlands Indies], Leiden, E. J. Brill, 1948. This historical survey of smallholder and Western plantation agriculture ranges from the seventeenth to the present century with special emphasis on government policy during the nineteenth century. To whom does the future belong? Not to the smallholder, is Boeke's answer.

Department of Economic Affairs, *The Exportcrops of the Netherlands Indies in 1938*, Bulletin of the Central Bureau of Statistics, No. 175, Batavia, Landsdrukkerij, 1939. The Department of Economic Affairs published annually a detailed statistical analysis of the export sector of Indonesian agriculture, covering acreage, production and quantity, and value of exports for smallholders as well as planters.

GRETZER, W. K., *Grundlagen und Entwicklungsrichtung der landwirtschaftlichen Erzeugung in Niederländisch-Indien*, Berichte über Landwirtschaft, Neue Folge, No. 146, Berlin, Paul Parey, 1939. This is a detailed survey of prewar Indonesian agriculture, its physical base, its human element, agrarian structure, and the major crops—both annual and perennial—produced either by plantations or by small Indonesian farms. Separate chapters deal with animal husbandry and forestry, agricultural export, and the impact of the Depression on Indonesian agriculture.

GRIST, D. H., *Rice*, London, Longmans, Green, 1953 (2d ed. 1955). The best comprehensive treatment of rice, the staple food of Indonesia.

HALL, C. J. J. VAN and C. VAN DE KOPPEL, eds., *De landbouw in de Indische archipel* [Agriculture in the Indonesian Archipelago], 3 vols. in 4 pts. The Hague, van Hoeve, 1946-50. This is the most comprehensive treatment of Indonesian agriculture by outstanding agronomists and other specialists. Vol. 1 deals with general aspects; Vol. 2A with food and medicinal crops; Vol. 2B with crops having stimulating properties and with spices; Vol. 3 treats of industrial crops. Each article is followed by a bibliography.

KOLFF, G. H. VAN DER, "An Economic Case Study: Sugar and Welfare in Java," in *Approaches to Community Development*, ed. Phillips Ruopp (The Hague, van Hoeve, 1953), pp. 188-206. The author, well-known for his studies of Javanese agriculture, examines the prewar adverse influences exerted by the sugar industry on peasant agriculture in Java and discusses possibilities of improving the relationship between industry and peasant by means of developing peasant cooperatives.

LEKKERKERKER, J. G. W., *Concessies en erfpachten voor landbouwonder-nemingen in de Buitengewesten.* [Concessions and Long Leases for Agricultural Enterprises in the Outer Islands], Groningen, Wolters, 1928. This is an invaluable study of the agrarian legislation affecting plantation agriculture prior to the Basic Agrarian Law of 1960.

MEARS, LEON A., *Rice Marketing in the Republic of Indonesia*, Djakarta, P. T. Pembangunan, 1961. Sponsored by the Institute for Economic and Social Research, Faculty of Economics, University of Djakarta, this detailed survey of the rice marketing system and related aspects was prepared to provide a basis for planning and policy.

METCALF, JOHN E., *The Agricultural Economy of Indonesia*, Agriculture Monograph No. 15, Washington, U.S. Department of Agriculture, Office of Foreign Agricultural Relations, 1952. This very useful survey of Indonesian agriculture compares the immediate prewar with the postwar situation and brings out the problems which beset the Indonesian agricultural economy as a result of Japanese military occupation and the Indonesian revolution. The survey makes extensive use of the dispatches sent by the U.S. Agricultural Attaché from Djakarta during 1950 and 1951.

PELZER, KARL J., "Land Utilization in the Humid Tropics: Agriculture," in *Proceedings of the Ninth Science Congress of the Pacific Science Association 1957, 20*, Special Symposium on *Climate, Vegetation, and Rational Land Utilization in the Humid Tropics* (Bangkok, Secretariat Ninth Pacific Science Congress, 1958), 124-43. Although this paper deals with agricultural land use in the tropics around the globe, it refers frequently to Indonesia.

TEMPANY, SIR HAROLD and D. H. GRIST, *An Introduction to Tropical Agriculture*, London, Longmans, Green, 1958. Despite its non-regional treatment of tropical agriculture, this book is invaluable for the understanding of Indonesian agriculture.

United States Economic Survey Team, *Indonesian Perspectives and Proposals for United States Economic Aid: Report to the President of the United States*, New Haven, Yale University, Southeast Asia Studies, 1963. This report, based on a survey conducted in 1961, contains valuable sections dealing with agriculture.

NOTES AND BIBLIOGRAPHY FOR *From Colonial to Guided Economy*

1. This is clearly stated, for example, by the Governor of the Bank Indonesia in a recent annual report: "As was the case in the field of politics where experiments in liberal democracy appear to have failed, in the economic field also experiments in liberal economy have led only to a dead end, because the spiritual and material identity of Indonesia were ignored." *Report of the Bank Indonesia, 1959-1960*, p. 2.

2. The case for economic integration of Indonesia is argued forcefully in the "Visman Report," published in 1941. In the economics chapter of that publication, Dr. Egbert de Vries wrote, "It is already apparent that Java, Sumatra, Borneo, and Celebes form an economic whole since these regions complement each other; it is a matter of vital importance for the peoples of these regions that the leading central apparatus intervene to promote further integration." "Het economisch leven," *Verslag van de commissie tot bestudeering van staatsrechtlijke hervormingen* ["Economic Life," *Report of the Commission for the Study of Constitutional Reforms*], *1* (Batavia, 1941), 31.

3. Charles A. Fisher in W. Gordon East and O. H. K. Spate, *The Changing Map of Asia: A Political Geography* (London, Methuen, 1950), p. 211.

4. W. F. Wertheim, *Indonesian Society in Transition: A Study of Social Change* (The Hague, W. van Hoeve, 1959), pp. 63-67.

5. Ibid., p. 93. This conclusion is disputed by Widjojo Nitisastro, largely on the basis of doubts about the quality of statistical data. See Widjojo Nitisastro, "Migration, Population Growth and Economic Development in Indonesia" (unpublished dissertation, University of California, Berkeley, 1961), pp. 222-24.

6. Wertheim, *Indonesian Society*, p. 97.

7. Ibid., pp. 97-99.

8. Ibid., p. 96.

9. Ibid., p. 95.

10. Ibid., p. 97.

11. Ibid., pp. 97-98.

12. Clifford Geertz, *The Social Context of Economic Change: An Indonesian Case Study* (Cambridge, Center for International Studies, M.I.T., 1956), pp. 47-49.

13. Evidence for this assertion can be found in J. J. Polak's study, *The National Income of the Netherlands Indies, 1921-1939* (New York, Institute of Pacific Relations, 1942), pp. 71 and 74. Polak's indices of production of main foods on Java and Madura, which he considers to be based on very good data, show stagnation of output during the 1920s and expansion during the 1930s, the latter—as suggested below—resulting from the conversion of export crop lands to food crops production following the slump in world markets. Even this expansion failed to

restore caloric values of Javanese consumption per capita (of seven main food crops) to the 1921-25 level.

14. De Vries, "Het economisch leven," p. 22.

15. Ibid., p. 22.

16. Ibid., p. 13.

17. E. de Vries shows the ratios of the values of outlying island exports to Java as 39 in 1920, 92 in 1925, 82 in 1930, 106 in 1935, and 121 in 1940. De Vries, "Het economisch leven," p. 13.

18. Polak, *The National Income*, p. 10.

19. De Vries, "Het economisch leven," p. 17; and Polak, pp. 66 and 66A.

20. One estimate of the magnitude of surpluses on merchandise trade account (merchandise exports minus merchandise imports) is given in W. F. Wertheim, *Indonesian Society*, p. 101. Wertheim's data show five-year averages from 1876 to 1930. Export surpluses as a percentage of the export values were as follows: 1901-05, 28 per cent; 1906-10, 38 per cent; 1911-15, 37 per cent; 1916-20, 49 per cent; 1921-25, 35 per cent; 1926-30, 33 per cent.

21. Polak's results for per capita incomes of the various ethnic groups in 1930 were as follows (in guilders): Indonesians, 59; Europeans, 2,500; foreign Asiatics, 310. Polak, Table 15.7, p. 66A.

22. These programs are described in G. H. C. Hart, *Towards Economic Democracy in the Netherlands Indies* (New York, Institute of Pacific Relations, 1942), and in Jan O. M. Broek, *Economic Development of the Netherlands Indies* (New York, Institute of Pacific Relations, 1942), especially Chapter 5.

23. Imports (in thousand tons) were 500 in 1925, 616 in 1930, 377 in 1935, 252 in 1939, and only 31 in 1940. E. de Vries, "Het economisch leven," p. 15.

24. Broek, *Economic Development*, pp. 82-85.

25. Ibid., p. 84.

26. To quote Allen and Donnithorne, "This was not, of course, a symptom of prosperity, but rather of the loss of the advantages of the international division of labor." G. C. Allen and A. G. Donnithorne, *Western Enterprise in Indonesia and Malaya* (New York, Macmillan, 1957), p. 35.

27. De Vries, "Het economisch leven," pp. 18-19.

28. See Wertheim, *Indonesian Society*, pp. 108-17, for reference to a number of scholarly and official reports substantiating this conclusion.

29. De Vries, p. 19.

30. Wertheim, p. 117.

31. Ibid., pp. 117-20.

32. Whereas Java and Madura produced 18 per cent of export value in 1950, they contributed only 13 per cent in 1959: Rp. 1,295.5 million out of a total export value of Rp. 9,944.1 million estimated at the

official exchange rate of Rp. 11.40 to US $1.00. In 1959 the Sumatran share of exports was Rp. 6,786.9 million, or 68 per cent of total export value; Borneo's was Rp. 1,565 million (16 per cent); and the other islands produced Rp. 296.6 million, or 3 per cent. Java's contribution in the 1950-55 period fluctuated between a low of 15 per cent (1952) and a high of 19 per cent (1951 and 1954); since then it declined rather steadily: 17 per cent (1955), 16 per cent (1956), 14 per cent (1957), and 13 per cent (1958 and 1959). See Biro Pusat Statistik, *Statistical Pocketbook of Indonesia 1957* (Djakarta, 1958), p. 105; and ibid. *1960* (Djakarta, 1961), p. 111.

33. Donald J. Blake, "Labour Shortage and Unemployment in North East Sumatra," *Malayan Economic Review*, 7 (1962), 109.

34. Clark E. Cunningham, *The Postwar Migration of Toba-Bataks to East Sumatra* (New Haven, Yale University, Southeast Asia Studies, 1958).

35. For a brief survey of the structure of one part of this bueaucracy, see J. A. C. Mackie, "Indonesia's Government Estates and Their Masters," *Pacific Affairs, 34* (1961-62), 337-60.

36. This conclusion is apparent from Central Bureau of Statistics data. See Biro Pusat Statistik, *Statistical Pocketbook of Indonesia 1960,* p. 171; and Centraal Kantoor voor de Statistiek, *Statistisch jaaroverzicht van Nederlandsch-Indië, 1938* [Statistical Annual of the Netherlands Indies], p. 372.

37. J. J. Polak, *The National Income of the Netherlands Indies, 1921-1939,* pp. 59-60, Table 15.7, pp. 66, 66A. According to Polak's study, 39 per cent of total personal income distributed was earned in the Outer Islands, and 35 per cent of the income earned by ethnic Indonesians. Moreover, Polak's study showed per capita income of all groups substantially higher in the Outer Islands than on Java in both 1930 and 1939.

38. See Mohammad Sadli, "The Relation of Guided Economy to the Development of Socialism in Indonesia," in R. Johnson, M. Sadli, and Subroto, eds., *Readings in Business Administration and Economics* (Djakarta, Faculty of Economics, University of Indonesia, 1961), p. 3.

39. This conclusion emerges from a map showing interregional movement of goods. See *Statistical Pocketbook of Indonesia 1960*, p. 143.

40. See Douglas S. Paauw, *Financing Economic Development: The Indonesian Case* (Glencoe, Free Press and the Center for International Studies, M.I.T., 1960), pp. 188-89.

41. Since August 1960 the effective export rate has been Rupiah 40.5 per U.S. dollar while the average import rate has been about Rupiah 117.5 per U.S. dollar.

42. For an excellent survey of the variations in exchange rate policy, 1950-60, see W. M. Corden and J. A. C. Mackie, "The Development of

the Indonesian Exchange Rate System," *Malayan Economic Review*, 7 (1962), 37-60.

43. The late Professor J. H. Boeke led a school of Dutch thought which interpreted Indonesian society in terms of an economic dualism reflecting differences between "Eastern" and "Western" society. See Boeke, *Economics and Economic Policy of Dual Societies as Exemplified by Indonesia* (New York, Institute of Pacific Relations, 1953).

44. See R. S. Eckaus, "The Factor Proportion Problem in Underdeveloped Areas," *American Economic Review*, 45 (1955), 539-65.

45. Benjamin Higgins, "The 'Dualistic Theory' of Underdeveloped Areas," *Economic Development and Cultural Change*, 4 (1956), 113.

46. J. J. Polak, *The National Income*, p. 74. Polak's figures for calories per head from seven main food crops on Java and Madura are as follows (average for five-year periods): 1921-25, 1,803; 1926-30, 1,722; 1931-35, 1,658; 1935-39, 1,718.

47. Ibid., pp. 69-70.

48. Thus the 1930 per capita income of Indonesians in Java and Madura was 55 guilders, while in the Outer Islands it was 66. Europeans in Java and Madura received an average income of 2,300 guilders in that year, while those on the Outer Islands had a per capita income of 3,200; and Asians who were not ethnic Indonesians earned an average of 310 guilders in Java and Madura and 320 in the outer territories. For the Netherlands Indies as a whole, the average per capita income in 1930 was 59 guilders for ethnic Indonesians, 310 guilders for non-Indonesian Asians, and 2,500 guilders for Europeans. Polak, Table 15.7, p. 66A.

49. Polak's results for 1939, for example, show wages earned in plantation and mining activities contributing about 10 per cent of income by industrial origin for the Outer Islands, compared to about 6 per cent for Java. Polak, Table 15.4, p. 61.

50. An estimate of Indonesian national income for the 1921-39 period was complied during World War II from materials available outside Indonesia. For an estimate of income in 1939, see J. J. Polak, "Het nationale inkomen van Nederlandsch Indië, 1921-1939" [The National Income of the Netherlands Indies, 1921-1939], reprinted from *Statistische en econometrische onderzoekingen*, No. 4 (1957), pp. 2-3.

51. S. Daniel Neumark, "The National Income of Indonesia, 1951-1952," *Ekonomi dan Keuangan Indonesia*, 7 (1954), 345-91.

52. An estimate of the industrial origin of Indonesian net domestic product from 1951 to 1959 may be found in United Nations, *Economic Survey of Asia and the Far East, 1960* (Bangkok, 1961), Table 6, p. 127.

53. Statistical Office of the United Nations, *Yearbook of National Accounts Statistics, 1960* (New York, United Nations, 1961), p. 114.

54. See, for example, Biro Pusat Statistik, *Perusahaan-perusahaan Industri, 1958* [Manufacturing Industries] (Djakarta, 1960), pp. xi-xv.

55. *Perusahaan-perusahaan Industri, 1958*, Table 1B, pp. 4-5.

56. Leon A. Mears, "Indonesia," Chapter 14 in A. Pepelasis, L. A. Mears, and I. Adelman, *Economic Development: Analysis and Case Studies* (New York, Harper and Brothers, 1961), pp. 440-41.

57. P. H. W. Sitzen, *Industrial Development of the Netherlands Indies* (New York, Institute of Pacific Relations, 1943), p. 5.

58. Polak, p. 30, quotes Sitzen's estimate for the total number of factories in 1939 as "over 5,000" even though official statistics registered only 2,809 establishments. The Central Bureau of Statistics, in a tabulation of all establishments with more than ten laborers, reports 9,807 by 1955, a postwar maximum of 10,972 for 1956, and 10,175 for 1958. These data are taken from annual issues of *Statistical Pocketbook of Indonesia.*

59. Mears, "Indonesia," p. 442.

60. Statistical evidence supporting this conclusion has been marshaled by Benjamin H. Higgins in his Introduction to *Entrepreneurship and Labor Skills in Indonesian Economic Development,* Yale University, Southeast Asia Studies, Monograph No. 1 (New Haven, 1961), pp. 22-24. Similar evidence is presented in terms of licensed capacity in the National Planning Bureau's *Report on the Execution of the Five-Year Development Plan, 1956-1960,* Table 40, p. 48, in which fairly steady growth of most consumer goods manufacturing is shown through the end of 1957, but in which 1958 is shown to be a year of advance in some major industries and retrogression in others, particularly spinning.

61. Sumitro Djojohadikusumo, ed., "The Government's Program on Industries," *Ekonomi dan Keuangan Indonesia,* 7 (1954), 702-36; and Wanda Mulia, "The Mechanization of Small-Scale Industries," *Ekonomi dan keuangan Indonesia, 11* (1958), 702-36.

62. S. Daniel Neumark, p. 354.

63. United Nations, *Economic Survey of Asia and the Far East, 1960,* p. 127.

64. *Statistical Pocketbook of Indonesia 1960,* Table 1, p. 86.

65. Ibid.

66. Neumark, p. 354.

67. The ratio of export value to domestic product can be calculated on the basis of Polak's domestic product estimates and his balance of payment data for 1925-39. See Polak, Annex II, pp. 83-84; and Table 15.1, p. 59.

68. The volume of Indonesian exports excluding petroleum was as follows for the 1950-60 period (in thousand tons): 1950, 2,420; 1951, 3,009; 1952, 2,422; 1953, 2,637; 1954, 2,892; 1955, 2,785; 1956, 2,522; 1957, 2,558; 1958, 2,025; 1959, 2,235; 1960, 2,121. See the *Report of the Bank Indonesia* for the 1950-51 period; for subsequent years, see Biro Pusat Statistik, *Monthly Survey* (September-October 1961), p. 34.

69. *Report of the Bank Indonesia, 1959-1960,* p. 181. Output of crude petroleum by the three foreign companies was reported as follows

for 1959: Shell, 4,394,000 tons; Standard-Vacuum, 4,602,000 tons; Caltex, 8,197,000 tons.

70. National Planning Bureau, *Report on the Execution of the Five-Year Development Plan*, p. 102.

71. Paauw, *Financing Economic Development: The Indonesian Case*, Table 22, p. 179.

72. Figures for government expenditures are taken from Biro Pusat Statistik, *Monthly Survey* (September-October 1961), p. 107, and for national product from United Nations, *Yearbook of National Accounts Statistics, 1960*, p. 257. Gross domestic product is measured at factor cost.

73. Sumitro Djojohadikusomo estimated the nonmarket sector at 25 per cent of gross national product for 1952. "The Budget and Its Implications," *Ekonomi dan Keuangan Indonesia, 6* (1953), 15. Subsistence activities may have declined since 1952: during certain periods the supply of money increased somewhat more rapidly than the price level, and some observers interpret this as evidence that a greater part of production was becoming monetized. I am grateful to Professor Bruce Glassburner for this suggestion.

74. Leon A. Mears, "Rice Marketing in the Republic of Indonesia," *Ekonomi dan Keuangan Indonesia, 11* (1958), 54.

75. *Report of the Bank Indonesia, 1959-1960*, p. 138.

76. See Chapter 4 for a further discussion of this point.

77. *Report of the Bank Indonesia, 1959-1960*, p. 139.

78. Mohammad Sadli, "The Public Sector, Private Sector and Economic Growth Experience in Indonesia" (paper mimeographed by the Faculty of Economics, University of Indonesia, January 1962).

79. Ibid., p. 23.

80. In an attempt to narrow wage and salary differentials in the newly nationalized estates, the PPN (government plantation enterprises) undertook a general reduction in salaries in late 1959. It has been argued that this measure produced serious decline in morale, loss of experienced employees, and adverse effects on efficiency and output. See Lim Kim Kim Liat, "The Deli Tobacco Industry: Its History and Outlook," in *Prospects for East Sumatran Plantation Industries: A Symposium* (New Haven, Yale University, Southeast Asia Studies, 1962), pp. 16-17.

81. For a discussion of incentive problems in agriculture, see Chapter 4.

82. In April 1962 an agreement was signed between the United Nations Special Fund and the Indonesian government providing for the establishment of a Statistical Research and Development Center "which will undertake research activities for statistical development, including the preparation of current estimates of the national income. It will also undertake field research activities and train statisticians through in-

service training and at the Academy of Statistics, which will be incorporated in the Center." Assistance is to be provided by the UN Special Fund in the form of experts and equipment over a five-year period. American-Indonesian Chamber of Commerce, Inc., *Information Bulletin*, No. 688 (May 18, 1962), p. 17.

83. To quote the Economic Commission for Asia and the Far East on the problem: "Except for the years 1951-1952, no extensive work has been done on the computation of the national income for the subsequent years. Estimates for these years are arrived at by rough extrapolations and are not supported by extensive surveys and field work as conducted in the past." Economic Commission for Asia and the Far East, *Economic Survey of Asia and the Far East, 1961* (Bangkok, 1962), footnote on p. 110.

84. An Indonesian estimate of national income per capita, in rupiah at 1938 prices, shows the following results: 1938, 39; 1951, 28.3; 1952, 29.4; 1953, 35.9; 1954, 36.4; 1955, 37.6. Muljatno, "Perhitungan Pendapatan Nasional Indonesia untuk 1953 dan 1954" [Estimate of Indonesian National Income for 1953 and 1954], *Ekonomi dan Keuangan Indonesia, 13* (1960), 184. The 1961 census suggests that Muljatno worked with low estimates of population growth and hence overstated postwar per capita income.

85. ECAFE, *Economic Survey of Asia and the Far East, 1961*, p. 109.

86. Ibid., p. 110

87. For the ECAFE estimate of real gross aggregate, per capita product, and real gross investment for 1951 to 1959, see *Economic Survey of Asia and the Far East, 1961*, Table 3-23, p. 109.

88. The ECAFE quotation above indicates a growth rate of 4 per cent for this period. This is inconsistent with the data presented in the same report on p. 109, where the geometric average of the rate of increase in real gross national product (1951-57) used is 5.2.

89. Assuming a ten-year interval between the UN population estimate of 75 million for 1950 and the census results of 1961 (95.9 million)—the census began early in 1961—the geometric average rate of increase would be 2.5 per cent per year.

90. National Planning Bureau, "A Study of the Indonesian Economic Development Scheme," *Ekonomi dan Keuangan Indonesia, 10* (1957), 600-42.

91. Ibid., calculated from Table I, p. 614.

92. Muljatno, "Perhitungan Pendapatan Nasional Indonesia untuk 1953 dan 1954," p. 185.

93. Calculated from National Planning Bureau, *Report on the Execution of the Five-Year Development Plan, 1956-1960, Covering the Years 1956, 1957 and 1958* (English edition, Djakarta, 1960), Table 75, p. 92.

94. United Nations, *Yearbook of National Accounts Statistics, 1960*, p. 114.

95. National Planning Bureau, *Report on the Execution of the Five-Year Development Plan, 1956-1960*, p. 96.

96. See the price series presented in Table 17.

97. This result is suggested by a comparison of calculations of the 1958 value of the agricultural sector's contribution in terms of 1957 and 1958 prices. Working Group of the National Income Committee, *The Contribution to the National Income of Indonesia, 1957 and 1958 by the Agricultural Sector* (Djakarta, 1960), Table C, p. 5.

98. For a discussion of the details of agricultural output behavior, see Chapter 4.

99. Changes in major food crops production between 1957 and 1958 by crop were reported as follows: rice, +4.6 per cent; maize, +42 per cent; cassava, +11 per cent; and sweet potatoes, +17 per cent. Calculated from *Statistical Pocketbook of Indonesia 1960*, p. 53.

100. *Report of the Bank Indonesia, 1957-1958*, p. 145; and *1958-1959*, p. 168.

101. United Nations data show a decline in the value added by the manufacturing sector (including electricity, gas, and water) from 16.1 billion rupiah in 1957 to 9.8 billion rupiah in 1958 (both in 1955 prices) or a loss of 39 per cent; United Nations, *Yearbook of National Accounts Statistics, 1960*, p. 114. The same source reports value added in manufacturing rose in 1959 to 10.4 billion rupiah in 1955 prices, approximately the value of output in 1954, while value added in mining, after having dropped by approximately 40 per cent in 1958, fell by another 5.5 per cent in 1959.

102. *Report on the Execution of the Five-Year Development Plan*, p. 99.

103. See, for example, the *Report of the Bank Indonesia, 1959-1960*, p. 17, where the assertion is made that "according to estimates, the major part of industries operate at a production level 50 per cent below their capacity. For the major part, this has been caused by the shortage in raw materials and auxiliaries, which in turn resulted from factors beyond the control of such undertakings."

104. *Statistical Pocketbook of Indonesia 1959*, pp. 94-95; and ibid. *1960*, pp. 92-93.

105. Ibid. *1960*, p. 99. Textile production in large weaving mills fell from 56.3 million meters in 1957 to 55.7 million in 1958 and to 40.5 million in 1959. Sarong production fell from 2.7 million units in 1957 to 2.3 million in 1958 and 1.8 million in 1959.

106. Economist Intelligence Unit, *Three Monthly Economic Review: Indonesia* (January 1960), p. 6. This review reported textile mills in the Bandung area operating at only 30 per cent of full capacity. The manager of a large, modern, and well-equipped textile plant in North Sumatra

reported to me in December 1959 that the plant was being operated at only 10 per cent of capacity because of shortages of imported raw material supplies. The plant in question had been built with funds provided by the Bank Industri Negara and was completed in 1956. At no time prior to the interview had it been utilized near full capacity.

107. *Report on the Execution of the Five-Year Development Plan,* p. 102.

108. Ibid.

109. *Monthly Survey* (January-February 1961), pp. 94-95.

110. One report suggests that Indonesian shipping companies could handle only 22 per cent of total traffic at the time the KMP shipping line was withdrawn from Indonesian waters; Economist Intelligence Unit, *Three Monthly Economic Review: Indonesia* (June 1961), p. 8.

111. *Report of the Bank Indonesia, 1959-1960,* p. 203.

112. This procedure has been followed in all estimates prepared by the National Planning Bureau and its successor, the Bureau of Finance and Economics. See, for example, National Planning Bureau, "A Study of the Indonesian Economic Development Scheme," *Ekonomi dan Keuangan Indonesia, 10* (1957), 613-19; and Muljatno, p. 185. In both, gross investment is estimated by assuming that the local component rises from 60 per cent of total investment costs (for nonvillage investment) in 1951 to 67 per cent in 1955. The same basic procedure, with different ratios for the local component, was followed by Lance Castles of the University of Indonesia's Institute for Economic and Social Research in an estimate for the years 1951-58. See Lance Castles, "An Approach to the Study of Saving in Indonesia," *Warta Research, 1* (1960), 34-42.

113. A similar problem is discussed above, with reference to the valuation of interregional trade balances.

114. This is confirmed by many recent observations on performance in individual firms or industries. See, for example, J. A. C. Mackic, "Indonesia's Government Estates and Their Masters," p. 347; Lim Kim Liat, "The Deli Tobacco Industry: Its History and Outlook," in *Prospects for East Sumatran Plantation Industries;* pp. 13-14; Sayuti Hasibuan, "The Palm Oil Industry on the East Coast of Sumatra," ibid., pp. 35-38; Dahlan Thalib, "The Estate Rubber Industry of East Sumatra," ibid., pp. 58-59; and *Report of the Bank Indonesia, 1959-1960,* pp. 189-99.

115. Paauw, *Financing Economic Development: The Indonesian Case,* p. 295.

116. J. D. Legge, "The Retreat from Autonomy," Chapter 9 in *Central Authority and Regional Autonomy in Indonesia: A Study in Local Administration, 1950-1960* (Ithaca, Cornell University Press, 1961).

117. The percentage share of investment in government expenditures was as follows for the 1951-58 period: 17 (1951), 13 (1952), 11 (1953), 20 (1954), 17 (1955), 14 (1956), 11 (1957), and 9 (1958); ECAFE,

Economic Survey of Asia and the Far East, 1960, Table 25, p. 72. The share of government investment as percentage of the gross national product was: 2.7 (1951), 2.5 (1952), 1.9 (1953), 3.3 (1954), 2.3 (1955), 2.0 (1956), 1.6 (1957), and 1.7 (1958); ibid., Table 24, p. 71.

118. Paauw, *Financing Economic Development: The Indonesian Case,* pp. 58-61.

119. Polak, *The National Income,* p. 60.

120. Wertheim, *Indonesian Society,* pp. 112-14.

121. See Chapter 4, Tables 5 and 6.

122. *Statistical Pocketbook of Indonesia 1958,* p. 213; ibid. *1960,* p. 213. For Java and Madura, a comparison with the average for the prewar period 1936-40 is possible. The total rice equivalent of all cereals and roots available per capita is shown as 194.3 kilograms in 1936-40, 169 in 1956, and 177.1 in 1959.

123. *Statistical Pocketbook of Indonesia 1960,* p. 112.

124. Benjamin Higgins, Introduction to *Enterpreneurship and Labor Skills in Indonesian Economic Development,* Yale University, Southeast Asia Studies, Monograph No. 1 (New Haven, 1961), pp. 22-24.

125. *Statistical Pocketbook of Indonesia 1960,* p. 115.

126. Ralph Anspach shows a fairly close correlation, with the exceptions noted, in a graph picturing relative changes in money (deflated for real income changes) and changes in the consumer price index. "Monetary Aspects of Indonesia's Economic Reorganization in 1959," *Ekonomi dan Keuangan Indonesia, 13* (1960), Graph II, p. 12.

127. This point is thoroughly examined in Anspach, pp. 7-13.

128. Mohammad Sadli, "The Relation of Guided Economy to the Development of Socialism in Indonesia," in Johnson, Sadli, and Subroto, *Readings in Business Administration and Economics* (Djakarta, 1961), p. 1.

129. Public argument revolved about the central issue described in this paragraph for more than a decade after the Indonesian declaration of independence in 1945. For an excellent summary of much of this debate see John O. Sutter, *Indonesianisasi: Politics in a Changing Economy, 1940-1955* (4 vols. Ithaca, Southeast Asia Program. Cornell University, 1959). For evidence on the reality of the issue in the years immediately after the transfer of sovereignty, see Volume IV, Chapter 25, pp. 1106-83; and Chapter 26, pp. 1184-1229.

130. Even during this period, Sutter notes a shift toward more radical leadership, beginning with the first Ali Sastroamidjojo cabinet in 1953. This shift, however, had little effect in changing the tenor of economic policy. Sutter, p. 1228.

1.31. The meaning of Guided Economy has been expounded as follows: "The political goal of Guided Economy is *to carry out a shift in the balance of economic power,* i.e. *a shift in the balance of ownership (of the forces of production).* The national revolution seeks to shift the balance of ownership from foreign hands (viewed as a vestige of the colonial system) to national control, and the social revolution (toward socialism as the social structure) intends to shift the balance of power (and partially to shift ownership also) from the private side to the side of the state (or society)." Sadli, "The Relation of Guided Economy," p. 2.

132. Ibid., pp. 1-2. Emphasis in the original.

133. Broek, *Economic Development of the Netherlands Indies*, Chapter 5, pp. 52-75; and Allen and Donnithorne, *Western Enterprise in Indonesia and Malaya*, pp. 28-30; 34-37.

134. Allen and Donnithorne, pp. 60-61.

135. In 1961 the Bank Industri Negara was merged with the newly established Bank Pembangunan (Development Bank).

136. A partial listing of the Bank Industri Negara's industrial interests can be found in M. Sadli, "Structural and Operational Aspects of Public (Especially Industrial) Enterprises in Indonesia," *Ekonomi dan Keuangan Indonesia, 13* (1960), 233.

137. Government Ordinance Number 10/1959.

138. Government Ordinance Number 140/1961 gave to cooperatives monopoly distribution rights over all basic materials in areas where cooperatives exist.

139. For a critical view of the effectiveness of these retail outlets, see Economist Intelligence Unit, *Three Monthly Economic Review: Indonesia* (July 1961), p. 4.

140. Herbert Feith believes that sandan-pangan organization has also been involved in black market operations (see Chapter 8).

141. Wanda Mulia, "The Processes of Changes in the Marketing Structure Since the Implementation of Guided Economy," *Ekonomi dan Keuangan Indonesia, 14* (1961), 63.

142. Ibid.

143. M. Sadli, "The Public Sector, Private Sector and Economic Growth Experience in Indonesia" (paper mimeographed by the Faculty of Economics, University of Indonesia, January 1962), p. 8.

144. Central Management Board of the State Trading Enterprises, *A New Era in Indonesian Export* (Djakarta, 1961).

145. Karl Pelzer notes an exception to this in the case of sugar production, however; see Chapter 4.

146. Bruce Glassburner and Kenneth D. Thomas, "The Swing of the Hoe: Retooling Begins in the Indonesian Economy," *Asian Survey, 1* (1961), 7.

147. This implies, as suggested above, that the volume of internal trade has fallen since the Guided Economy program was applied to the trading sector.

148. The argument over interpretation of these phrases is documented in Sutter, *Indonesianisasi, 2,* 275-78.

149. Sutter, pp. 672-73.

150. M. Sadli, "The Public Sector," p. 11.

151. Ibid., p. 23.

152. See Glassburner and Thomas, p. 6.

153. Bruce Glassburner, "Problems of Economic Policy in Indonesia, 1950-1957," *Ekonomi dan Keuangan Indonesia, 13* (1960), 311.

154. Kementerian Perekonomian, *Berita Ekonomi Indonesia* (April 28, 1951).

155. Ministry of People's Industry, *A Review and Progress Report of the Loan Project for the Mechanization of Privately Owned Factories, Covering the Period February 1952 to April 1960* (Djakarta, 1960), *passim*, esp. p. 37.

156. Bruce Glassburner, "Economic Policy-Making in Indonesia, 1950-1957," *Economic Development and Cultural Change, 10* (1962), 125-26.

157. The National Planning Bureau began its work in 1952, under the direction of Dr. Sumitro; later Ir. Djuanda assumed the position of director-general, assisted by Ali Budiardjo as his deputy. In 1956, when the drafting of the First Five-Year Plan had been completed, Ir. Djuanda joined the cabinet as Minister of National Planning, and Ali Budiardjo became Director-General of the National Planning Bureau.

158. *Garis-garis Besar Rentjana Pembanguan Lima Tahun, 1956-1960* [General Outline of the Five-Year Development Plan, 1956-1960] (Djakarta, Biro Perantjang Negara, 1956). Important aspects of the plan are summarized in English in Paauw, *Financing Economic Development: The Indonesian Case,* Appendix A, pp. 363-92. The Indonesian parliament did not approve the five-year plan until November 1958, when it was made retroactive to January 1, 1956.

159. Chapter 1 of the volume presenting the framework of the plan (cited in the footnote above) gave the essentials of the aggregative model taken as its frame of reference. This model was elaborated and revised in some important respects in an article by the National Planning Bureau published in Indonesia's leading economics journal. See National Planning Bureau, "A Study of the Indonesian Economic Development Scheme," *Ekonomi dan Keuangan Indonesia, 10* (1957), 600-42. Widjojo Nitisastro believes that the statistical data employed in building the model were of such poor quality that its practical usefulness was negligible if not negative. See Widjojo Nitisastro, in a review of Benjamin Higgins, *Indonesia's Economic Stablization and Development* in the *Journal of Asian Studies, 17* (1958), 638-41.

160. See, for example, Benjamin Higgins, *Indonesia's Economic Stabilization and Development* (New York, Institute of Pacific Relations, 1957), pp. 40-47.

161. In 1957 Djuanda became prime minister; and after Sukarno assumed the position of prime minister in 1959, Djuanda became first minister, a position he still holds.

516

162. Biro Perantjang Negara *Laporan Pelaksanaan Rentjana Pembangunan Lima Tahun, 1956-1960, Mengenai Tahun-tahun 1956, 1957 dan 1958* (Djakarta, 1959). An unofficial version was translated into English and published by the National Planning Bureau in August 1960, under the title *Report on the Execution of the Five-Year Plan, 1956-1960, Covering the Years 1956, 1957, and 1958.*

163. The decision to emphasize shipping was forced upon the government in any case with the loss of Dutch shipping, which had represented 70 per cent of interisland tonnage, after the ousting of Dutch navigation at the end of 1957.

164. Biro Perantjang Negara, *Report on the Execution of the Five-Year Development Plan, 1956-1960,* p. 109.

165. *Report on the Execution of the Five-Year Development Plan,* pp. 5 and 7.

166. The entire plan is a massive document consisting of 4,675 pages, divided into 8 parts, 17 volumes, and 1,945 paragraphs (8-17-1945, the date of the declaration of independence). The official document and an official summary have been published only in Indonesian. Brief reviews in English may be found in Guy J. Pauker, "Indonesia's Eight-Year Development Plan," *Pacific Affairs,* 34 (1961), 115-30; and Glassburner and Thomas, pp. 8-11. Several extracts from the plan and its summary have been published in English in 1960 and 1961 issues of circulars published by the Commercial Advisory Foundation in Indonesia (*Warta CAFI*).

167. Pauker, pp. 115-30.

168. From the discussion above, it is clear that there is no reliable basis for estimating the rate of investment. It should be noted, however, that the National Planning Bureau's estimate was based on a 1960 figure for national product of Rp. 236 billion and that plan investment of Rp. 30 billion would work out to approximately 13 per cent of this magnitude. With rapid inflation, rising monetary value of national product, and serious doubt about the government's capacity to invest Rp. 30 billion annually, it is apparent that the projected public investment rate is much too high.

169. A translation from the plan reflects the passing nature of the reference to stabilization: "We must endeavor to revive the equilibrium in the monetary fields as soon as possible each time said equilibrium is disturbed." *Warta CAFI,* Circular No. H354 (March 30, 1961), Enclosure II.

170. "There is none amongst us who wishes to aggravate the people's burden, whether directly or indirectly, through monetary channels (contributions or deficits) to obtain the developmental capital." *Warta CAFI,* Circular No. H354 (March 30, 1961), Enclosure III.

171. Guy Pauker writes that "the Indonesian public was told that these Rp. 240 billion were to come not from 'domestic savings' but from

direct foreign investments. Closer inspection shows that this is not quite true; the B projects would yield $2,462.5 million (about Rp. 111 billion)." Pauker, p. 125.

172. The projects by location listed in the announcement are: (1) fertilizer plant, Palembang; (2) rayon plant, Palembang; (3) blast furnace, Lampung (South Sumatra); (4) steel mill, Tjilejon (West Java); (5) window-glass factory, Djakarta; (6) superphosphate plant (fertilizer), Tjilatjap (Central Java); (7) paper mill, Makassar (South Celebes); (8) paper mill, Takengon (Atjeh); (9) cement factory, Makassar; (10) fertilizer plant, Surabaja. This listing differs somewhat from that in the Presidential Decree, suggesting considerable revision at the ministry level.

173. For an excellent review of the history of Indonesia's foreign exchange policies, 1950 to 1960, see W. M. Corden and J. A. C. Mackie, "The Development of the Indonesian Exchange Rate System," *Malayan Economic Review*, 7 (1962), 37-60.

174. It is estimated that in 1952 budgetary changes raised aggregate demand by Rp. 23.4 billion, while balance of payments changes reduced it by Rp. 11.4 billion. Paauw, *Financing Economic Development: The Indonesian Case*, Table 11, p. 113.

175. This paradox is explained by the fact that Indonesia had undertaken a de facto devaluation with different import and export rates in March 1950. Under this system, the exporter sold his foreign exchange to the government for Rp. 3.80 per dollar and was given foreign exchange certificates in equivalent amount, to be sold to importers for an additional Rp. 3.80 per dollar. Thus exporters received a total of Rp. 7.60 for each dollar's worth of foreign exchange; importers were obliged to purchase foreign exchange at Rp. 3.80 per dollar and to supply in addition foreign exchange certificates in 200 per cent of this amount, one-half purchased from exporters and one-half from the government. The effective import rate was Rp. 11.40 per dollar, the effective export rate Rp. 7.60 per dollar, the differential amounting to a tax on exports.

176. Benjamin Higgins, *Indonesia's Economic Stabilization and Development*, p. 3.

177. *Statistical Pocketbook of Indonesia 1958*, p. 112.

178. *Report of the Bank Indonesia, 1956-1957*, Table 89, p. 181.

179. Ralph Anspach, "Monetary Aspects of Indonesia's Economic Reorganization in 1959," *Ekonomi dan Keuangan Indonesia*, 13 (1960), Graph I, 3.

180. Ibid.

181. Ibid. Anspach gives the source for the output decline as the National Planning Bureau, *Report on the Execution of the Five-Year Plan* (Indonesian edition). In fact, the Report showed a decline of 12.6 per cent in real gross national product, a result referred to in the previous section.

182. Hans O. Schmitt, "Some Monetary and Fiscal Consequences of Social Conflict in Indonesia, 1950-1958" (unpublished dissertation, University of California, Berkeley, 1958).

183. Ibid., p. 226.

184. Ibid.

185. Ibid., p. 267. Schmitt writes, "It can be said, therefore, that the political parties favoring inflation supported the interests of importers and of the bureaucracy in Java, whereas the opposition to them represented the indigenous trading interests in the outer regions."

186. These measures were introduced in a series of government regulations promulgated on August 25, 1959. They are reproduced as appendices to the *Report of the Bank Indonesia, 1959-1960*, p. 279 and pp. 285-97. In August 1960 the 20 per cent tax was replaced by a ten per cent duty, raising the effective export rate from Rp. 36 per U.S. dollar to Rp. 40.5.

187. Ralph Anspach, pp. 2-42.

188. Benjamin Higgins, Introduction to *Entrepreneurship and Labor Skills in Indonesian Economic Development: A Symposium*, p. 36.

189. Paauw, *Financing Economic Development: The Indonesian Case*, pp. 105-07, 138-39.

190. Ibid., pp. 149-54.

191. The Chartered Bank, the Oversea Chinese Banking Corporation, the Hong Kong and Shanghai Banking Corporation, and the Bank of China.

192. *Report of the Bank Indonesia, 1958-1959*, pp. 106-07.

193. *Report of the Bank Indonesia, 1959-1960*, p. 76.

194. Ibid., p. 76.

195. Ibid., p. 77.

196. More recent data on credit outstanding from these sources are not available at the time of this writing.

197. *Report of the Bank Indonesia, 1959-1960*, pp. 83-84. Examples of credits extended to "vital" enterprises cited in this report are those to the Central Trading Company to distribute essential commodities and to export copra, to PELNI (Indonesian Navigation Company) for chartering ships, and to PPN-Baru (the new estate management agency).

198. Albert O. Hirschman, *The Strategy of Economic Development* (New Haven, Yale University Press, 1958), pp. 7-11.

199. Ibid., p. 10.

BIBLIOGRAPHY

I. *Basic Statistical Sources*

Central Bureau of Statistics (Biro Pusat Statistik) publishes a number of regular periodicals containing economic information. The interested student should consult a full listing of the Central Bureau's publications. Many are published using both Indonesian and English in the same volume, a few are published in English only, and several in Indonesian only. A comprehensive survey of Central Bureau and other official statistical publications prior to 1954, written by a former director of the Central Bureau, is available in E. A. van de Graaff, *De statistiek in Indonesië* [Statistics in Indonesia] (The Hague and Bandung, W. van Hoeve, 1955), in Dutch.

Statistical Pocketbook of Indonesia (in English) published annually in August by the Central Bureau of Statistics in Djakarta, roughly covering the previous and several prior calendar years. Major areas covered include geography; population; education; health; government organization; agriculture, forestry and fishing; mining; manufacturing; international and interisland trade; transport and communications; public finance and monetary data; consumption; prices and labor.

Monthly Survey (English subtitle of Statistik Konjunktur). Originally published monthly by the Central Bureau of Statistics, but recently appearing on a bimonthly basis, this publication provides English translations of the Indonesian used in the statistical tables and notes. It contains sections on production, labor, foreign trade, prices, transport and communications, finance, consumption, and international conditions.

Report of the Bank Indonesia, published in Indonesian and English editions by the Bank Indonesia in Djakarta, on a fiscal year basis covering the period July 1 to June 30. In recent years it has appeared late; the most recent available (in June 1962) being the report covering the year 1959-60, which appeared late in 1961. This publication is the basic source for financial data, but it also covers many other economic phenomena. The commentary provides a useful review of policies in fiscal and financial fields.

Bank Indonesia Bulletin, regularly published in Indonesian and English editions, although occasionally in Indonesian with English translations of table headings. Previously this bulletin was published quarterly by the Bank Indonesia, but each issue now covers two quarters and appears as much as a year after the end of the period covered. It now contains only statistical tables, covering mainly fiscal, financial, and balance of payments data, whereas previously it included a verbal commentary on current developments.

Data submitted by the Indonesian government to the UN and related agencies are published in several periodicals. The most important outlet for such statistics, published by the Economic Commission for Asia and the Far East (ECAFE), is the *Economic Bulletin for Asia and the Far East,* which appears quarterly in June, September, December, and March of each year. The March issue contains the annual *Economic Survey of Asia and the Far East* (also published separately), which includes a more comprehensive series of statistical data, including many covering Indonesia, than do quarterly issues of the *Economic Bulletin*. Financial data are published in the International Monetary Fund's *International Financial Statistics,* and balance of payment data in the Fund's *Balance of Payments Yearbook.* National income and product data have occasionally appeared in the *Yearbook of National Accounts Statistics,* published annually by the United Nations Statistical Office.

In addition to the citations above, estimates of Indonesia's national income and product have appeared in a number of sources:

ECAFE, *Economic Survey of Asia and the Far East* annually publishes a series on Indonesia's national income, industrial origin of net domestic product, and composition of gross capital formation.

POLAK, J. J., *The National Income of the Netherlands Indies, 1921-1939,* New York, Institute of Pacific Relations, 1942, is the only source covering the prewar period. A summary of this study was published in Dutch as "Het nationale inkomen van Nederlandsch Indië, 1921-1939," in *Statistische en econometrische onderzoekingen,* January 1947.

NEUMARK, S. DANIEL, "The National Income of Indonesia, 1951-1952: Report Prepared at the Request of the National Planning Board," *Ekonomi dan Keuangan Indonesia,* 7 (1954), 348-91. This study continues to be the only postwar estimate of Indonesian national income and product based on a certain amount of empirical research. The methodology and results have been challenged by many later writers. See for example C. Bakker, "Some Remarks about Dr. Neumark's Estimation of the National Income in 1951 and 1952," *Ekonomi dan Keuangan Indonesia,* 7 (1954), 597-602; and William C. Hollinger and A. D. Tan, "The National Income of Indonesia, 1951-1952: A Critical Commentary on the Neumark Estimates," *Ekonomi dan Keuangan Indonesia,* 9 (1956), 785-98.

National Planning Bureau, "A Study of the Indonesian Economic Development Scheme," *Ekonomi dan Keuangan Indonesia,* 10 (1957), 600-42. This article contains an estimate of national income and product aggregates for the period 1951-55, in conjunction with the presentation of models showing the projected growth of domestic product during the Five-Year Plan period. The estimates for 1951 and 1952 are revisions of the Neumark results.

MULJATNO, "Perhitungan Pendapatan Nasional Indonesia untuk Tahun 1953-1954" [Estimate of Indonesian National Income for 1953-1954], *Ekonomi dan Keuangan Indonesia,* 13 (1960), 162-216. This study presents an estimate of national income and product aggregates, 1951-55, based on an independent evaluation of the basic statistical data. It attempts to compare postwar per capita real income with the prewar (1938) level.

II. Books and Articles

ALLEN, G. C. and A. G. DONNITHORNE, *Western Enterprise in Indonesia and Malaya*, New York, Macmillan, 1957. A valuable collection of information, with perceptive generalizations comparing the impact of foreign investment and management in Indonesia and Malaya.

ANSPACH, RALPH, "Monetary Aspects of Indonesia's Economic Reorganization in 1959," *Ekonomi dan Keuangan Indonesia*, 13 (1960), 2-47. A detailed analysis of important monetary and fiscal aspects of the 1959 monetary reform with some suggestive interpretations.

CHARLESWORTH, HAROLD K., *A Banking System in Transition*, Djakarta, New Nusantara Publishing Company, 1959. A descriptive study of the Indonesian banking system as it existed in the late 1950s.

CORDEN, W. M. and J. A. C. MACKIE, "The Development of the Indonesian Exchange Rate System," *Malayan Economic Review*, 7 (1962), 37-60. An excellent descriptive review of the exchange rate and related policies covering the period 1950-60.

GLASSBURNER, BRUCE, "Economic Policy Making in Indonesia, 1950-1957," *Economic Development and Cultural Change, 10* (1962), 113-33. A systematic presentation of economic policy changes against the background of political conflict.

HIGGINS, BENJAMIN, *Indonesia's Economic Stabilization and Development*, New York, Institute of Pacific Relations, 1957. The best general study of Indonesia's struggle for economic stability and development from the transfer of sovereignty (December 1949) through 1956.

JOHNSON, ROSSAL J., MOHAMMAD SADLI, and SUBROTO, eds., *Readings in Business Administration and Economics*, Djakarta, Faculty of Economics, University of Indonesia, 1961. A collection of writings by members of the University of Indonesia's Faculty of Economics. Several contributions are important for their analysis of the impact of Guided Economy measures in various sectors.

MEARS, LEON, "Indonesia" in A. Pepelasis, L. Mears, and I. Adelman, *Economic Development: Analysis and Case Studies* (New York, Harper and Brothers, 1961), 418-67. A brief but useful survey of the Indonesian economy and its prospects for development. A representative bibliography of thirty-three items is included.

MULIA, WANDA, "The Processes of Changes in the Marketing Structure Since the Implementation of Guided Economy," *Ekonomi dan Keuangan Indonesia, 14* (1961), 58-70. The only published account of the major distributional changes that have occurred since 1957.

The author has written several unpublished papers on other aspects of Guided Economy, and has published some brief summaries of current economic research in progress at the Institute for Economic and Social Research of the University of Indonesia in that institute's *Warta Research.*

National Planning Bureau, *Report on the Execution of the Five-Year Development Plan 1956-1960, Covering the Years 1956, 1957 and 1958* [unofficial English translation of Biro Perantjang Negara, *Laporan Pelaksanaan Rentjana Pembangunan Lima Tahun, 1956-1960*], Djakarta, 1960. This report is useful for its compilation of data to evaluate progress in many fields of economic activity during the period covered.

PAUKER, GUY, "Indonesia's Eight-Year Development Plan," *Pacific Affairs, 34* (1961), 115-30. A summary and brief evaluation of the current Indonesian development plan.

SADLI, M., "Structural and Operational Aspects of Public (Especially Industrial) Enterprises in Indonesia," *Ekonomi dan Keuangan Indonesia, 13* (1960), 227-53. An objective evaluation of the structure and problems of public enterprise by a leading Indonesian economist.

Senat Mahasiswa Fakultas Ekonomi, Universitas Indonesia, *Bunga Rampai Ekonomi* [English subtitle: Readings in Economics], Djakarta, 1960. A collection of essays, many explicitly focusing on the Indonesian economy, written by economists associated with the University of Indonesia. Its chief value lies in the application of economics and business analysis to problems of the new Guided Economy policies in Indonesia.

SUTTER, JOHN O., *Indonesianisasi: Politics in a Changing Economy, 1940-1955,* 4 vols. Ithaca, Cornell University, Southeast Asia Program, 1959. This ambitious study contains a wealth of information on the history of Indonesian economic policy and the effects of the Indonesian nationalism on patterns of ownership and enterprise.

United States Department of Commerce, *Investment in Indonesia,* Washington, 1956. A useful collection of data relative to conditions affecting foreign investment in Indonesia and the patterns of foreign investment in various economic fields. Much of the material is now out of date, however.

WERTHEIM, W. F., *Indonesian Society in Transition: A Study of Social Change,* The Hague, W. van Hoeve, 1959. This is the closest approximation to a modern social science view of Indonesia's economic history. Chapters of particular interest to the student of the Indonesian economy are: Chapter 5, "Shifts in the Economic System" (a useful review of the Western impact on the economy and the response); Chapter 7, "Urban Development"; and Chapter 9, "Changing Patterns of Labor Relations."

Notes and Bibliography for *Labor in Transition*

1. Clark Kerr, F. H. Harbison, J. T. Dunlop, and C. A. Myers, *Industrialism and Industrial Man* (Cambridge, Harvard University Press, 1960). A brief summary of these ideas appeared in *International Labour Review, 82*, 1960.

2. These categories are analyzed by Alice W. Shurcliffe in *Limits to Trade Union Possibilities in Independent Underdeveloped Countries* (Washington, 1960).

3. For a further discussion of the transmigration efforts and the problem of Java's overpopulation, see Chapter 1.

4. It should be noted in this context that unions can bring dismissal cases before the government arbitration boards, requiring the employer to show cause; this is, in fact, one of the most important types of labor dispute. Moreover, the employer who wishes to lay off more than ten men must get permission to do so from the authorities.

5. Biro Pusat Statistik, *Sensus Penduduk 1961 [Population Census 1961] Republik Indonesia* (Djakarta, 1962).

6. Departemen Perburuhan R. I., *Report on Labour Force Sample Survey in Java and Madura* (Djakarta, 1961).

7. Ibid., p. 38.

8. Bureau of Economic Research, Gadjah Mada University, *Consumer Finances in the Region of Jogjakarta: A Preliminary Report on Research Conducted in August 1959* (Jogjakarta, 1960).

9. Departemen Perburuhan, *Report on Labour Force*, p. 22.

10. Ibid., pp. 25, 29.

11. Ibid., p. 15.

12. For a description of these restrictions on the economic activities of the Chinese, see Chapter 3.

13. Departemen Perburuhan, *Report on Labour Force*, p. 13.

14. For a discussion of the problem of labor commitment in undeveloped countries, see Wilbert E. Moore and Arnold S. Feldman, eds., *Labor Commitment and Social Change in Developing Areas*, (New York, Social Science Research Council, 1960).

15. A discussion of the implications of these factors for economic development, in particular for the case of North Sumatra, can be found in Chapter 5.

16. The Ministry of Labor compiles data from its 127 employment exchanges scattered throughout the country, but since only 17,000 to 30,000 persons were placed each year from 1954 through 1960 out of 147,000 to 170,000 new applicants, it is not surprising that many of the unemployed did not bother to register. Most of the applicants in the 1950s tended to come from primary schools; in the course of that decade there was a rise in middle-school applicants and a decline in others, including the unskilled. See the *Statistical Pocketbook of*

Indonesia 1961, p. 242; and Ministry of Labor, *Report of the Two Years April 1957-April 1959*, p. 33.

17. Sample studies in Bandung confirm the 7 per cent figure, showing 7.2 per cent unemployed in 1957 plus 4.4 per cent who were not actually working when the survey was made. Direktorat Tenaga Kerdja Kementerian Perburuhan, "Laporan Penjelidikan Angkatan Kerdia Berdasarkan (Labor Force Sample Survey) Daerah Kota Besar Bandung" [Report on the Labor Force Sample Survey of the District of Greater Bandung], *Ekonomi dan Keuangan Indonesia*, 11 (1958), 571-99.

18. Departemen Perburuhan, *Report on Labour Force*, p. 34.

19. For an interesting analysis of how social and economic factors reinforce each other in Javanese rural underemployment, making it a very difficult pattern to break, see C. Geertz, *The Development of the Javanese Economy: A Socio-Cultural Approach* (Cambridge, M.I.T., 1956).

20. This estimate was based on the premise that the 15,740,000 people employed in the peak season in agriculture could have worked for 305 days at 7 hours a day or a total of 33.604 billion manhours, whereas they actually worked only an estimated 22.352 billion, giving an underemployment rate of 33.48 per cent.

21. Departemen Perburuhan, *Report on Labour Force*, p. 27, Tables 12A and 12B.

22. Thus the proportion of Indonesian intermediate and secondary school students in programs outside the liberal arts was about one-third in 1957, while in Pakistan it was under one per cent. See United Nations Educational, Scientific, and Cultural Organization, *Basic Facts and Figures* (Paris, UNESCO, 1960), pp. 40-42.

23. Indonesian sugar workers have generally been organized in unions separate from those of other estates.

24. For a description of the political aspects of Indonesian labor organization in the 1920s, see Ruth T. McVey, *The Comintern and the Rise of Indonesian Communism* (Ithaca, Cornell University Press, in press).

25. For a detailed discussion of the development of Indonesian unions during the revolution and the early 1950s, see H. J. Wijnmaalen, "Aantekeningen betreffende het ontstaan, de ontwikkeling en het optreden van de vakbeweging in Indonesië na de Onafhankelijkheidsverklaring van 17 Augustus 1945" [Notes Concerning the Origin, the Development, and the Activity of the Labor Movement in Indonesia after the Independence Declaration of August 17, 1945], *Indonesië*, 5 (1951-52), 434-61, 539-63.

26. Center for International Studies, M.I.T., *Stanvac in Indonesia* (Washington, National Planning Bureau, 1957).

27. For a further discussion of this point, see Douglas S. Paauw, ed.,

Prospects for East Sumatran Plantation Industries: A Symposium (New Haven, Yale University, Southeast Asia Studies, 1962), pp. 53-54.

28. For an English text of this code, see International Labour Office, *Legislative Series: Indonesia,* 1951-1.

29. This number excludes more than seven million hours lost from a one-day political protest strike over the West Irian question at the end of 1957.

30. For accounts which deal with the problems of management in the seized enterprises, see Paauw, *Prospects for East Sumatran Plantation Industries,* passim; and J. A. M. Mackie, "Indonesia's Government Estates and Their Masters," *Pacific Affairs, 34* (Winter 1961-62), 260-79.

31. The central organization of BUMIL was the Labor Consultative Council, which met daily; each member organization appointed a permanent and an alternative delegate to this body. In addition, BUMIL had regional and local councils.

32. For an account of this meeting, see Department of Labor Affairs, *Conference on Presidential Regulation on the Establishment of the Indonesian Workers' Association Organization, July 14-16, 1960* (Djakarta, 1960).

33. The first three also belong to a separate grouping representing the NASAKOM principle, which acts as an advisory council to the Minister of Labor Affairs. For a discussion of NASOKOM, see Chapter 8.

34. Since the Perkappen units are not organized by private company managers and thus are not true company unions, it would seem better to describe them as "government managerial labor organizations."

35. Donald J. Blake, in his carefully reasoned article "The Role and Functions of Labor Organisations in Socialist Economic Development," concludes: "If, for example, labor organisations are created by government fiat and left without the possibility of meaningful functions, they will remain mere paper organisations, lacking the life-giving impulses of member participation. It is this participation which is the essence of self-fulfillment for the members as social participation is the quintessence of the socialist society." In Johnson, Sadli, and Subroto, eds., *Readings in Business Administration and Economics* (Djakarta, University of Indonesia, 1961), p. 82.

BIBLIOGRAPHY

Biro Pusat Statistik, *Perusahaan-perusahaan Industri Besar* [Large Manufacturing Industries], *Triwulan 1-1961,* Djakarta, 1962. This publication, issued in Indonesian and English by the Central Bureau of Statistics, gives data for 1960 and the first quarter of 1961 on wages, salaries, and number of persons employed, in detailed industrial classifications. The Bureau has also issued several comparable studies covering earlier periods.

————, *Upah Pada Perkebunan, 1959* [Wages Paid on Estates], Djakarta (1960). A series of reports on plantation wages published by the Central Bureau of Statistics. For other statistics on labor, see the annual reports of the Bank Indonesia and the yearly *Statistical Pocketbook of Indonesia.*

BLAKE, DONALD J., "The Role and Functions of Labor Organisations in Socialist Economic Development," in Rossall J. Johnson, Mohammad Sadli, and Subroto, eds., *Readings in Business Administration and Economics,* Djakarta, University of Indonesia, 1961. Although devoted to broad theoretical considerations, this carefully reasoned article has special pertinence to the position of Indonesian labor under Guided Democracy.

Coolie Budget Commission, *Living Conditions of Plantation Workers and Peasants on Java in 1939-1940,* trans. Robert Van Niel, Ithaca, Cornell University, Modern Indonesia Project, 1956. This exhaustive study, instituted by the Netherlands Indies government, provides a real benchmark with which to compare postwar labor conditions on Javanese estates.

Departemen Perburuhan R. I., *Report on Labour Force Sample Survey in Java and Madura,* Djakarta, 1961. This is by all odds the most important labor force survey made since Indonesia achieved independence. Some of the data for rural and urban areas are presented separately because different definitions were used in their collection; the reader should bear this in mind when comparing them. In addition, he should check the figures against the 1961 census statistics when these are published in detail. Other research reports in the labor field have been issued by the Manpower Directorate and the Office of Statistics of the Department (formerly Ministry) of Labor.

Department of Labor Affairs, *Conference on Presidential Regulation on the Establishment of the Indonesian Workers' Association Organization,* Djakarta, 1960. This report on the meeting which attempted to set up OPPI reveals many of the motives behind the positions taken by the Minister of Labor Affairs and the various unions on the question of a single, government-sponsored labor organization.

HAWKINS, EVERETT D., "Indonesia," in Walter Galenson, ed., *Labor in Developing Economies,* Berkeley and Los Angeles, University of California Press, 1962, pp. 71-137. A discussion of the emergence of an Indonesian labor force, the development of labor organizations, problems of management, and the increasing role of the government in labor relations.

International Labour Office, Expanded Programme of Technical Assistance, *Report to the Government of Indonesia on Wage Policy and*

Industrial Relations, Geneva, International Labour Office, 1958. This account, which contains useful data, was drawn up by W. J. Hull, a technical expert provided by the ILO to the Indonesian government at the latter's request. Other valuable reports to the Indonesian government by the ILO cover vocational training, labor statistics, accidents, social security, productivity, etc. In addition, the ILO publishes the texts of important Indonesian labor laws in its *Legislative Series.*

KAT ANGELINO, P. DE, *Batikrapport: Rapport betreffende eene gehouden enquête naar de arbeidstoestanden in de batikkerijen op Java en Madoera* [Batik Report: Report Concerning an Investigation of Working Conditions in the Batik Enterprises in Java and Madura], 3 vols. Weltevreden, Netherlands Indian Labour Bureau, 1930-31. An exhaustive study of wages, working conditions, and output in a traditional Javanese industry.

LASKER, BRUNO, *Human Bondage in Southeast Asia,* Chapel Hill, University of North Carolina Press, 1950. The description of "Bondage through Worker Indebtedness in the Batik Industry of Java," in Appendix C, is of special value.

McVOY, EDGAR, "Some Aspects of Labour and Economic Development in Indonesia," *Ekonomi dan Keuangan Indonesia,* 7 (1954), 800-07. An ILO expert working with the State Planning Bureau suggests the role of labor in Indonesia's economic development. *Ekonomi dan Keuangan Indonesia,* the major Indonesian journal of economics, has published a number of articles in the labor field. See, for example, the issues of December 1955; January, March-April, July, and October 1958; and April 1959.

Persatuan Buruh Kereta Api, *Laporan Kerdja 3-Tahun, Nopember 1955 sampai Achir 1958, untuk Kongres ke-V* [Report on Three Years' Work, from November 1955 to the End of 1958, for the Fifth Congress], Bandung, Persatuan Buruh Kereta Api, 1958. A very full description of the activity of a major non-Communist union, the KBSI-affiliated Railway Workers' Union (PBKA). The report, which is illustrated, contains statistical materials and a discussion of various mutual aid projects sponsored by the union.

RICHARDSON, J. HENRY, "Indonesian Labor Relations in their Political Setting," *Industrial and Labor Relations Review,* 12 (1958), 56-78. An article stressing the political aspects of Indonesian unionism.

SANDRA, *Sedjarah Pergerakan Buruh Indonesia* [A History of the Indonesian Labor Movement], Djakarta, PT Pustaka Rakjat, 1961. A detailed history published by the Ministry of Labor. Part I covers the period up to 1945; Part II deals with developments during and after the revolution, providing details by federation and region. The appendix includes several valuable documents.

SOBSI, International Department, *Indonesian Trade Union News.* A monthly English-language publication by the Communist-oriented labor federation, giving political and economic news of the various SOBSI unions. It appears somewhat irregularly now. The principal Indonesian-language SOBSI journal is *Bendera Buruh* [Workers' Flag]; in addition, SOBSI and its affiliates publish numerous periodicals, pamphlets, and reports of their major meetings in Indonesian.

TEDJASUKMANA, ISKANDAR, *The Political Character of the Indonesian Trade Union Movement*, Ithaca, Cornell University, Modern Indonesia Project, 1959. Written by a former Indonesian Minister of Labor, this monograph discusses the impact of various political ideologies and parties on trade unions in both the colonial and republican periods. The author's doctoral dissertation in the same field (Cornell University, 1962) should also be consulted.

THOMPSON, VIRGINIA, *Labor Problems in Southeast Asia*, New Haven, Yale University Press, 1947. Chapter 4 (pp. 117-66) gives an important account of labor conditions in Indonesia, primarily during the colonial period.

Tindjauan Masa'alah Perburuhan [Survey of the Labor Question], Djakarta, Kementerian Perburuhan, monthly. The official journal of the Ministry of Labor, this is an important source for laws and government regulations, as well as decisions of the Central Disputes Committee, labor statistics, and occasional signed articles. In recent years it has tended to appear irregularly.

United States Department of Labor, Bureau of Labor Statistics, *Summary of Labor Conditions in Indonesia*, Washington, International Cooperation Administration, 1955. A good brief summary in its day, this report is being completely rewritten; the new version should be published in 1963.

WERTHEIM, W. F., *Indonesian Society in Transition*, 2d rev. ed. The Hague and Bandung, W. van Hoeve, 1959. Chapter 9, "The Changing Pattern of Labour Relations," concentrates on the Dutch period, with short sections on the Japanese occupation and postwar years.

WIJNMAALEN, H. J., "Aantekeningen betreffende het ontstaan, de ontwikkeling en het optreden van de vakbeweging in Indonesië na de Onafhankelijkheids-verklaring van 17 augustus 1945" [Notes Concerning the Origin, the Development, and the Activity of the Labor Movement in Indonesia after the Independence Declaration of August 17, 1945], *Indonesië*, 5 (1951-52), 434-61, 539-63. An important account of the relations between labor unions and political groupings in the Indonesian Republic during and immediately after the revolution.

WIT, DANIEL, *Indonesian Labor: A Management Survey*, International Studies, Foreign Labor Practices Series, Washington, Governmental

Affairs Institute, 1961. This report, drafted by E. D. Hawkins as senior professional consultant, provides considerable detailed information on manpower resources, recruitment, employment conditions, personnel management, and labor relations.

NOTES AND BIBLIOGRAPHY FOR *The Course of Indonesian History*

1. This lack of information on early, purely indigenous Indonesian civilization was a major reason why Western scholars tended until recently to portray Indonesia's history in the light of influences from abroad rather than in terms of the country itself. Thus the archipelago's history was usually divided into Hindu (Indian), Islamic, and European periods and considered almost solely in terms of the role of these exogenous elements in the area. The Dutch historian van Leur, writing in the 1930s, presented the major counterargument to this interpretation, maintaining that the foreign elements must be viewed not as determining factors but as influences on an essentially healthy and unique Indonesian society. J. C. van Leur, *Indonesian Trade and Society* (The Hague and Bandung, W. van Hoeve, 1955), pp. 94-95, and *passim*.

2. For a stimulating attempt at a reconstruction of this development by an anthropologist, see C. Geertz, *The Development of the Javanese Economy: A Socio-Cultural Approach* (Cambridge, M.I.T., 1956), pp. 39-43, 79-85.

3. F. D. K. Bosch, "The Problem of the Hindu Colonisation of Indonesia," *Selected Studies in Indonesian Archaeology* (The Hague, M. Nijhoff, 1961), presents most of the theories on the spread of Hindu influence.

4. Whether Sandjaja's realm actually extended beyond Java is open to question; Hall declares that all we can accept with certainty is that he was able to force the various regional rulers of Central Java to render him obedience and tribute. D. G. E. Hall, *A History of South-East Asia* (London, Macmillan, 1955), p. 42.

5. Hall (pp. 46-50) discusses the various theories concerning the Sailendras, whose origin and identity have been subject to much dispute.

6. W. F. Stutterheim, *Het hindoeïsme in de archipel* [Hinduism in the Archipelago] (Djakarta and Groningen, J. B. Wolters, 1952), p. 31.

7. The major theories regarding the reasons for this transfer are reviewed in B. Schrieke, *Indonesian Sociological Studies* (The Hague and Bandung, W. van Hoeve, 1957), Part II, pp. 287-301. Schrieke concludes that the major reason for the shift of the population center to the Brantas River basin was peasant migration to escape heavy military and corvée duties imposed by the Central Javanese rulers.

8. In spite of Sriwidjaja's power and its rulers' evident religious concern, the Sumatran kingdom did not produce great monuments such as those found on Java. The most satisfactory explanation offered thus far appears to be that of Coedès, who has argued that the interests of the Sriwidjaja rulers were devoted less to enhancing their stature in the interior than to establishing their importance on the seas, principally for controlling traffic through the Straits of Malacca. G. Coedès, *Les états hindouisés d'Indochine et d'Indonésie* (Paris, E. de Boccard, 1948), p. 221.

9. C. C. Berg, "Kertanagara de miskende empirebuilder," *Oriëntatie*, No. 34 (July 1950), pp. 3-32; and also his "De geschiedenis van pril Majapahit" [The History of Early Madjapahit], *Indonesië, 4* (1950-51), 481-520; and *5* (1951-52), 190-202.

10. Ibid. Hall, on the other hand, is of the opinion that Gadjah Mada undertook a program of military conquest, breaking with the Kertanagara tradition of a ritually symbolistic empire (Hall, p. 76).

11. Stutterheim, pp. 116-26.

12. For a discussion of the early penetration of Islam into Indonesia, see Schrieke, pp. 230-67, and van Leur, pp. 110-16. A description of the culture of the Pasisir city-states, especially those on the Outer Islands, may be found in Chapter 2.

13. H. J. de Graaf, *Geschiedenis van Indonesië* [History of Indonesia] (The Hague and Bandung, W. van Hoeve, 1949), pp. 87-93.

14. For a discussion of the *santri* and other major Javanese life patterns, see the discussion of Java in Chapter 2.

15. Hall, p. 183. See also M. A. P. Meilink-Roelofsz, *Asian Trade and European Influence in the Indonesian Archipelago between 1500 and About 1630* (The Hague, M. Nijhoff, 1962).

16. de Graaf, p. 92.

17. H. J. de Graaf, *De regering van Sultan Agung, vorst van Mataram 1613-1645 en die van zijn voorganger panembahan Séda-ing-Krapjak, 1601-1613* [The Government of Sultan Agung, Prince of Mataram 1613-1645, and that of his predecessor, Séda-ing-Krapjak, 1601-1613] ('s-Gravenhage, M. Nijhoff, 1958), p. 129.

18. de Graaf, *Geschiedenis*, p. 112.

19. Hall, p. 251. For an extensive discussion of the rise and decline of the Dutch mercantile effort in Asia, see K. Glamann, *Dutch-Asiatic Trade, 1620-1740* (Copenhagen and The Hague, Danish Science Press, M. Nijhoff, 1958).

20. The standard work on Coen and his policies is H. T. Colenbrander, ed., *Jan Pietersz. Coen: Bescheiden omtrent zijn bedrijf in Indië* [Jan Pietersz. Coen: Documents Concerning His Activity in the Indies] (7 vols. The Hague, M. Nijhoff, 1919-52).

21. D. H. Burger, *De ontsluiting van Java's binnenland voor het*

wereldverkeer [The Opening of Java's Interior to World Trade] (Wageningen, H. Veenman, 1939), pp. 3-4.

22. J. Bastin, *Raffles' Ideas on the Land Rent System in Java and the Mackenzie Land Tenure Commission* (The Hague, M. Nijhoff, 1954), especially Chapter I. Raffles' activities in Java were not limited to the governing of the area: he made studies of the local flora and fauna and wrote a splendid history of the island, *History of Java*, which was published in 1817.

23. Detailed information on land holdings was only obtained after 1867 and made available during the course of the next three decades. For a summary of these findings see *Eindresumé van het bij Gouvernements-besluit dd. 10 Juni 1867 No. 2 bevolen onderzoek naar de rechten van den Inlander op den grond op Java en Madoera samengesteld door den Chef der Afdeeling statistiek ter Algemeene Secretarie* [Final Resumé of the Investigation into Native Land Rights on Java and Madura, Compiled by the Head of the Statistical Department of the General Secretariat in Accordance with Government Decision No. 2 of June 10, 1867] (3 vols. Batavia, Ernst, Landsdrukkerij, 1876-96). Cadastral surveys were also undertaken in this period.

24. For discussions of the liberal-conservative conflict in this period, see D. W. van Welderen Rengers, *The Failure of a Liberal Colonial Policy* (The Hague, M. Nijhoff, 1947) and S. J. Ottow, *De oorsprong der conservatieve richting: het kolonisatie rapport Van der Capellen* [The Origin of the Conservative Persuasion: The Colonization Report of Van der Capellen] (Utrecht, A. Oosthoek, 1937).

25. Schrieke, Part I, pp. 192-93.

26. J. S. Furnivall, *Netherlands India: A Study of Plural Economy* (Cambridge, University Press, 1944), p. 192.

27. C. Th. van Deventer, *Overzicht van den economischen toestand der Inlandsche bevolking van Java en Madoera* [Survey of the Economic Position of the Native Population of Java and Madura] (The Hague, M. Nijhoff, 1904), pp. 248-49.

28. Furnivall, pp. 209-12.

29. A more detailed discussion of the educational system in the Netherlands Indies may be found in Chapter 6.

30. A further description of the government's new role in the villages may be found in Furnivall, pp. 381 ff.

31. The Volksraad's membership was partially appointed by the governor-general and partly chosen by a limited electorate. European representatives dominated the council until 1931, when a majority of seats was allotted to the Asian (Indonesian and Foreign Oriental) population groups. For a description of the development of the Volksraad's role, see B. H. M. Vlekke, *Nusantara: A History of Indonesia* (Chicago, Quadrangle, 1960), pp. 361-62, 385.

32. For a more detailed account of the early Indonesian political movements, see J. Th. P. Blumberger, *De nationalistische beweging in Nederlandsch-Indië* [The Nationalist Movement in the Netherlands Indies] (Haarlem, Tjeenk Willink, 1931), and R. Van Niel, *The Emergence of the Modern Indonesian Elite* (Chicago, Quadrangle, 1960).

33. H. J. Benda, *The Crescent and the Rising Sun: Indonesian Islam under the Japanese Occupation, 1942-1945* (The Hague and Bandung, W. van Hoeve, 1958), pp. 39-47.

34. The results of government-sponsored investigations into the causes of these revolts may be found in Schrieke, Part I, pp. 83-166; and H. Benda and R. McVey, eds., *The Communist Uprisings of 1926-1927 in Indonesia: Key Documents* (Ithaca, Cornell University Modern Indonesia Project, 1960).

35. For details on the development of the Indonesian political movements in the 1930s see J. M. Pluvier, *Overzicht van de ontwikkeling der nationalistische beweging in Indonesië in de jaren 1930 tot 1942* [Survey of the Development of the Nationalist Movement in Indonesia from 1930 to 1942] (The Hague and Bandung, W. van Hoeve, 1953).

36. For descriptions of colonial policy and administration in the twentieth century, see A. D. A. de Kat Angelino, *Colonial Policy, 2* (The Hague, M. Nijhoff, 1931); Amry Vandenbosch, *The Dutch East Indies: Its Government, Problems, and Politics* (Berkeley and Los Angeles, University of California Press, 1944); and J. S. Furnivall, *Colonal Policy and Practice: A Comparative Study of Burma and Netherlands India* (Cambridge, University Press, 1948).

37. For a further discussion of this point see Furnivall, *Netherlands India: A Study of Plural Economy*, pp. 446 ff., passim. An economist's analysis of Indonesia's plural society may be found in J. H. Boeke's *Economics and Economic Policy of Dual Economies as Exemplified by Indonesia* (Haarlem, Tjeenk Willink, 1953), and a sociologist's interpretation in W. F. Wertheim's *Indonesian Society in Transition* (The Hague and Bandung, W. van Hoeve, 1956), pp. 148 ff.

38. Hall, p. 640.

39. An account of the development of the nationalist movement during the Japanese occupation may be found in G. McT. Kahin, *Nationalism and Revolution in Indonesia* (Ithaca, Cornell University Press, 1952), pp. 101-33. The evolution of the Islamic movement under the Japanese is described in Benda, *The Crescent*.

40. The story of the proclamation and early years of the Indonesian Republic is best told by Kahin and his account is generally followed here.

41. For a description of the early Indonesian reactions to the federal proposals, see C. Wolf, Jr., *The Indonesian Story* (New York, John Day, 1948), pp. 44-45. A detailed description of the federal structure established in the Dutch occupied areas of the archipelago may be found

in A. A. Schiller, *The Formation of Federal Indonesia* (The Hague and Bandung, W. van Hoeve, 1955).

42. For a history of the Dutch-Indonesian negotiations and the role of the United Nations, see A. M. Taylor, *Indonesian Independence and the United Nations* (Ithaca, Cornell University Press, 1960).

BIBLIOGRAPHY

BAUDET, HENRI and I. J. BRUGMANS, eds., *Balans van beleid: Terugblik op de laatste halve eeuw van Nederlands-Indië* [Balance of Rule: Reflections on the Last Half Century of the Netherlands Indies], Assen, Van Gorcum, 1961. Essays by leading Hollanders, giving their impressions of events in colonial Indonesia during the twentieth century. Some excellent essays on literature and the Eurasian population, and reflections on a life now past.

BENDA, HARRY J., *The Crescent and the Rising Sun: Indonesian Islam under the Japanese Occupation 1942-1945*, The Hague, W. van Hoeve, 1958. An excellent study of Islam in Indonesia—surveyed from earliest times, detailed for the war years.

BLUMBERGER, J. TH. PETRUS, *De nationalistische beweging in Nederlandsch-Indië* [The Nationalist Movement in the Netherlands Indies], Haarlem, Tjeenk Willink, 1931. A detailed record of early Indonesian nationalism, generally unsympathetic to the movement.

BOEKE, J. H., *The Evolution of the Netherlands Indies Economy*, New York, Institute of Pacific Relations, 1946. A study of economic development emphasizing the dualism between the indigenous and Western worlds in Indonesia.

BURGER, D. H., *De ontsluiting van Java's binnenland voor het wereldverkeer* [The Opening of Java's Interior to World Trade], Wageningen, H. Veenman, 1939. A study of the impact of Dutch colonial policies on the society of nineteenth-century Java.

COEDÈS, G., *Les états hindouisés d'Indochine et d'Indonésie*, Paris, E. de Boccard, 1948. A famous work on the Hindu period containing invaluable information, though challenged on some points by later research.

COOLHAAS, W. PH., *A Critical Survey of Studies on Dutch Colonial History*, 's-Gravenhage, M. Nijhoff, 1960. A bibliography of historical works concerned with Dutch policies and impacts in the Indonesian archipelago as well as other parts of the world.

DAM, P. VAN, *Beschrijvinge van de Oostindische Compagnie* [Descriptions of the East India Company], 4 vols. The Hague, Rijksgeschiedkundige publicaties, 1927-32. An early eighteenth-century piece which shows keen insight into the operation and problems of the East India Company.

DAY, CLIVE, *The Policy and Administration of the Dutch in Java*, New York, Macmillan, 1904. A liberal view of Dutch policy which stresses the adverse nature of the Dutch impact upon Indonesia.

DEVENTER, S. VAN, *Bijdragen tot de kennis van het landelijk stelsel op Java* [Contributions to an Understanding of the Agriculture System in Java], 3 vols. Zaltbommel, J. Norman, 1865-66. The major source work on the land rent system and the application of nineteenth-century colonial policy.

ELSBREE, WILLARD H., *Japan's Role in Southeast Asian Nationalist Movements, 1940-1945*, Cambridge Harvard University Press, 1953. A comparative view of Japan's activities during World War II in stimulating nationalist causes.

Encyclopaedie van Nederlandsch-Indië [Encyclopedia of the Netherlands Indies], 4 vols. The Hague, M. Nijhoff, 1917-21; 5 supplements, 1927-40. A storehouse of historical, geographical, and cultural articles—an invaluable reference work.

FURNIVALL, J. S., *Netherlands India: A Study of Plural Economy*, Cambridge, University Press, 1944. An excellent socioeconomic history of East Indian developments under Dutch impact from 1600, and more specifically since 1800.

GEERTZ, CLIFFORD, *The Development of the Javanese Economy: A Socio-Cultural Approach*, Cambridge, Center for International Studies, M.I.T., 1956. A thought provoking socioeconomic analysis of major shifts in Indonesian history.

GLAMANN, KRISTOF, *Dutch-Asiatic Trade, 1620-1740*, Copenhagen, Danish Science Press, 1958. Interesting insights into the nature and development of the Asian trade of the Dutch East India Company.

GRAAF, H. J. DE, *Geschiedenis van Indonesië* [History of Indonesia], The Hague and Bandung, W. van Hoeve, 1949. A competent survey of Indonesian history, especially useful for developments in the fifteenth and sixteenth centuries.

HAAN, F. DE, *Priangan: De Preanger-regentschappen onder het Nederlandsch bestuur tot 1811* [Priangan: The Preanger Regencies under Dutch Rule to 1811], 4 vols. Batavia, G. Kolff, 1910-12. A meticulous account of early Dutch activities in the Preanger district of West Java.

HALL, D. G. E., ed., *Historians of South East Asia*, London, Oxford University Press, 1961. Essays on indigenous and Western historical writings with coverage of all Southeast Asian lands.

————, *A History of South-East Asia*, London, Macmillan, 1955. A masterful survey of historical developments from earliest times, excellent for fitting Indonesia into its larger setting.

HATTA, MOHAMMAD, *Verspreide geschriften* [Collected Writings], Djakarta, Amsterdam, and Surabaja, C. P. J. van der Peet and Penerbitan dan Balai Buku Indonesia, 1952. Essays, mostly on politics and economics, by one of the leaders of Indonesia's nationalist movement, later vice-president of the independent Republic.

JONGE, J. K. J. DE, *De opkomst van het Nederlandsch gezag in Oost-Indië (1595-1811): Verzameling van onuitgegeven stukken uit het oud-koloniaal archief* [The Rise of Dutch Power in the East Indies (1595-1811): A Collection of Unpublished Pieces from the Early Colonial Archives], 13 vols. The Hague, M. Nijhoff, 1862-88.

ROO, L. W. G. DE and G. P. ROUFFAER, *Documenten omtrent Herman Willem Daendels, gouverneur-generaal van Nederlandsch Oost-Indië* [Documents Concerning Herman Willem Daendels, Governor-General of the Netherlands East Indies], 2 vols., supplement to vol. 13 above, The Hague, M. Nijhoff, 1909.

TIELE, P. A. and J. E. HEERES, *Bouwstoffen voor de geschiedenis der Nederlanders in den Maleischen archipel* [Materials for the History of the Dutch in the Malay Archipelago], 3 vols., supplement to the series above, The Hague, M. Nijhoff, 1886-95. This series forms the major collection of documents for the period of the East India Company's activity in the archipelago.

KAHIN, GEORGE MCTURNAN, *Nationalism and Revolution in Indonesia*, Ithaca, Cornell University Press, 1952. The best work for the period of the Indonesian revolution against the Dutch after World War II.

KAT ANGELINO, A. D. A. DE, *Colonial Policy*, 2 vols. The Hague, M. Nijhoff, 1931. An English translation of a masterful work representing the cultural synthesis concepts prevalent in the early twentieth century.

KLERCK, E. S. DE, *History of the Netherlands East Indies*, 2 vols. Rotterdam, W. L. & J. Brusse, 1938. A history of the Dutch in the archipelago with emphasis upon military affairs—a rather dry work.

KOCH, D. M. G., *Om de vrijheid: De nationalistische beweging in Indonesië* [For the Sake of Freedom: The Nationalist Movement in Indonesia], Djakarta, Jajasan Pembangunan, 1950. A short but stimulating history of Indonesian nationalism by one of its most sympathetic Dutch observers.

KROM, N. J., *Hindoe-Javaansche geschiedenis* [Hindu-Javanese History], 2d. rev. ed. The Hague, M. Nijhoff, 1931. Full of information on the "Hindu" period of Indonesian history; it is now outdated on some points of interpretation but still has much valuable material.

LEUR, J. C. VAN, *Indonesian Trade and Society: Essays in Asian Social and Economic History*, The Hague and Bandung, W. van Hoeve, 1955. Based on Weberian concepts, this study has done much to revise opinions with regard to both the focus and the interpretation of Indonesian history.

NATSIR, MOHAMMAD, *Capita selecta*, Bandung and 's-Gravenhage, W. van Hoeve, (1955?). Collected Indonesian essays on politics and religion by an outstanding younger Indonesian Moslem leader.

PIGEAUD, TH. G. TH., *Java in the Fourteenth Century: the Nagara-Kertagama*, 5 vols. The Hague, M. Nijhoff, 1960–. An English translation with commentary of a highly significant Javanese chronicle.

PLUVIER, J. M., *Overzicht van de ontwikkeling der nationalistische beweging in Indonesië in de jaren 1930 tot 1942* [Survey of the Development of the Nationalist Movement in Indonesia from 1930 to 1942], The Hague and Bandung, W. van Hoeve, 1953. The most detailed account of Indonesian political developments during the 1930s.

PRINGGODIGDO, A. K., *Sedjarah Pergerakan Rakjat Indonesia* [History of the Popular Movement in Indonesia], Djakarta, Pustaka Rakjat, 1950. An outstanding account of the nationalist movement by a leading Indonesian statesman and scholar.

RADJAB, MUHAMAD, *Perang Paderi di Sumatera Barat (1803-1838)* [The Padri War in West Sumatra (1803-1838)], Djakarta, Perpustakaan Perguruan Kementerian P. P. dan K., 1954. An account of a conflict which played a major role in Indonesia's social, religious, and political history.

RAFFLES, THOMAS STAMFORD, *A History of Java*, 2 vols. London, Black, Parbury, and Allen, 1817. A brilliant history and survey of Indonesian life, still invaluable for understanding Raffles and his time.

SCHRIEKE, B., *Indonesian Sociological Studies*, 2 vols. The Hague and Bandung, W. van Hoeve, 1955-57. Social historical studies of an exceedingly high caliber, these writings have been instrumental in creating the modern historical view of Indonesia.

SJAHRIR, SOETAN, *Out of Exile*, New York, John Day, 1949. An English translation of a most eloquent statement of Indonesian nationalist aims by an outstanding leader in the independence movement and revolution.

SOEDJATMOKO, *An Approach to Indonesian History: Towards an Open Future*, Modern Indonesia Project, Translation Series, Ithaca, Cornell University, 1960. A brilliantly argued brief against nationalist distortions of history.

STAPEL, F. W., *Geschiedenis van Nederlandsch-Indië* [History of the Netherlands Indies], 5 vols. Amsterdam, Joost van den Vondel, 1938-40. Multiauthor work of uneven quality; the later volumes are an example of Dutch-oriented colonial history.

TAYLOR, ALASTAIR M., *Indonesian Independence and the United Nations*, Ithaca, Cornell University Press, 1960. A balanced account of the

537

role of the United Nations in the creation of Indonesian independence.

VALENTIJN, FRANÇOIS, *Oud en nieuw Oost-Indiën* [The Old and New East Indies], 5 vols. Dordrecht and Amsterdam, J. van Braam and G. onder de Linden, 1724-26. A mass of information on the history and geography of the archipelago, collected by a minister of the Dutch Reformed Church.

VANDENBOSCH, AMRY, *The Dutch East Indies: Its Government, Problems, and Politics*, Berkeley and Los Angeles, University of California Press, 1942. Detailed and accurate account of the Dutch colonial government—especially good for the nineteenth and twentieth centuries.

VLEKKE, BERNARD H. M., *Nusantara: A History of Indonesia*, rev. ed. Chicago, Quadrangle, 1960. A readable general history of the archipelago which provides a good survey.

VOLLENHOVEN, C. VAN, *Het adatrecht van Nederlandsch-Indië* [Adat Law of the Netherlands Indies], 3 vols. Leiden, E. J. Brill, 1918-33. The great work on customary law in the Indonesian archipelago, it has had much influence on historical interpretation.

WERTHEIM, W. F., *Indonesian Society in Transition: A Study of Social Change*, 2d rev. ed. The Hague and Bandung, W. van Hoeve, 1959. Thought provoking sociological analysis premised on Marxian and Weberian concepts of change in Indonesia.

YAMIN, MUHAMMAD, *Proklamasi dan Konstitusi Republik Indonesia* [The Independence Proclamation and Constitution of the Republic of Indonesia], Djakarta, Djambatan, 1951. An interpretation by a leading Indonesian nationalist of the events from 1945 through 1950, as reflected in the major government decrees.

————, *Sedjarah peperangan Dipanegara, Pahlawan Kemerdekaan Indonesia* [History of the War of Diponegoro, Hero of Indonesian Freedom], Djakarta, Jajasan Pembangunan, 1952. A brilliant effort at nationalist historiography, taking as its subject the Java War of 1825-30.

NOTES AND BIBLIOGRAPHY FOR *Dynamics of Guided Democracy*

1. The following section is based almost entirely on Herbert Feith, *The Decline of Constitutional Democracy in Indonesia* (Ithaca, Cornell University Press, 1962).

2. Biro Pusat Statistik, *Statistical Pocketbook of Indonesia 1957* (Djakarta, 1957), pp. 51, 66, 78, 93.

3. The Pantja Sila (Five Principles), enunciated by Sukarno in June 1945, had become Indonesia's official philosophy of state; the principles are: The One Deity, Nationality, Humanity, Democracy, and Social

Justice. See Sukarno, *The Birth of the Pantja Sila* (Djakarta, Ministry of Information, 1952); and Chapter 7.

4. Clifford Geertz, *The Religion of Java* (Glencoe, Free Press, 1960).

5. Herbert Feith, *The Indonesian Elections of 1955* (Ithaca, Cornell Modern Indonesian Project, 1957), p. 58.

6. For a discussion of the exchange rate by one who regards it as of central importance for political alignments, see Hans O. Schmitt, "Foreign Capital and Social Conflict in Indonesia, 1950-1958," *Economic Development and Cultural Change, 10* (1962), 284-93.

7. Donald Hindley, "The Communist Party of Indonesia, 1951-1961: A Decade of the Aidit Leadership" (doctoral dissertation, Australian National University, 1961), pp. 471-72.

8. On the take-overs see J. M. van der Kroef, "Disunited Indonesia," *Far Eastern Survey, 27* (1958), 49-63; Louis Fischer, *The Story of Indonesia* (New York, Harper, 1959), pp. 227-30, 300; and Leslie H. Palmier, *Indonesia and the Dutch* (London, Oxford University Press, 1962), pp. 100-10.

9. Biro Pusat Statistik, *Statistical Pocketbook of Indonesia 1957*, p. 29.

10. As used here the term "political elite" refers to the small group of persons—200 to 500 in the 1949-58 period, fewer since then—who contribute actively to the decision-making which produces political crises or ends them. The term "political public" refers to the much larger group of the politically aware, those who have mentally stepped out of their traditional society and translate the resulting new attitudes and perceptions into political opinions. This group is roughly coterminous with the two million or so Indonesians who are regular newspaper readers. Most of the members are white-collar city dwellers.

11. The term "stable conflict" was suggested to me by Daniel S. Lev, to whom I am indebted for many of the ideas in this section, and indeed in the whole chapter.

12. Brigadier-General G. P. H. Djatikusumo, *Antara News Bulletin* (New York), May 8, 1958.

13. V. Hanssens, "The Campaign against the Nationalist Chinese in Indonesia," in B. H. M. Vlekke, ed., *Indonesia's Struggle 1957-1958* (The Hague, Netherlands Institute of International Affairs, 1959), pp. 56-76.

14. Chief of Staff Nasution declared on December 19, 1958 that a remote possibility of a military coup existed and that he was doing all he could to prevent it. Prime Minister Djuanda stated on the following day that the government and parliament could avoid an army coup only if they proved themselves capable of carrying out a sound policy. *Antara News Bulletin* (Djakarta), December 20 and 21, 1958.

15. Guy J. Pauker, "The Role of the Military in Indonesia," in J. J.

Johnson, ed., *The Military in the Underdeveloped Areas* (Princeton, Princeton University Press, 1962).

16. For a full statement of this point of view by a former head of the army information service, see Rudi Pirngadie, "The Problem of the Government and the Army in Indonesia" (unpublished paper, Harvard University Center for International Affairs, 1960), especially pp. 89-104.

17. On the *pamong pradja* system see Donald R. Fagg, "Authority and Social Structure: A Study in Javanese Bureaucracy" (unpublished doctoral dissertation, Harvard University, 1958). See also J. D. Legge, *Central Authority and Regional Autonomy in Indonesia, 1950-1960* (Ithaca, Cornell University Press, 1961), pp. 171-83. For a discussion of the local context of government in Java and other areas, see Chapter 2.

18. For a discussion of the miltary-labor group, BUMIL, see Chapter 6.

19. Sukarno accused the Front of not being genuinely concerned with the liberation of West Irian. See the President's address of August 17, 1959, in *Toward Freedom and the Dignity of Man* (Djakarta, Department of Foreign Affairs, 1961), p. 66.

20. However, one development which occurred as this chapter was being completed may bring about a partial reversal of this trend. On June 23, 1962, Major-General Achmad Jani, previously commander of West Irian operations, was installed as Chief of Staff of the Army, with General Nasution assuming the new post of Chief of Staff of the Armed Forces, as well as remaining Deputy First Minister for Defense and National Security. This change and other personnel shifts which have followed it are certainly of great importance for the army's role as a political organization, but it is too early to describe their effects with any confidence.

21. Aidit was included in his capacity of third deputy chairman of the Provisional People's Consultative Assembly (MPRS), Lukman as third deputy chairman of Parliament.

22. This part of the argument leans heavily on Hindley, "The Communist Party of Indonesia," pp. 591-648. See also Donald Hindley, "President Sukarno and the Communists: The Politics of Domestication," *American Political Science Review, 56* (1962), pp. 915-26.

23. Hindley, "The Communist Party," pp. 641-43.

24. Guy J. Pauker, "Current Communist Tactics in Indonesia," *Asian Survey, 1* (1961), 28-35.

25. Ir. Sakirman, "Apa Arti Sokongan PKI kepada Undang-undang Dasar 1945 dan Demokrasi Terpimpin" (What Is the Meaning of PKI Support for the Return to the Constitution of 1945 and Guided Democracy?), *Bintang Merah*, May-June 1960, pp. 194-219, and July-August 1960, pp. 320-40, 348; quoted in Hindley, "The Communist Party," pp. 611-12.

26. Donald Hindley, "The Indonesian Communists and the CPSU 22nd Congress," *Asian Survey, 2* (1962), 20-27.

27. Numerous caveats must be entered in relation to this use of "pro-Western groups" as an umbrella term for the Masjumi, PSI, and (ex-) PRRI. It is much more than a cold-war position which marks these groups off from other players on the political stage—for instance, their long-standing hostility to President Sukarno and their links with entrepreneurial groups on the islands outside Java. In addition they are certainly not dependent on Washington, or devoted to many of its ideological formulations. And as for having a general preference for the US-led bloc of states over the Communist bloc, this is something they share with other groups in Indonesian politics. The term's best justification is probably the negative one that it is far less misleading than "rightwing groups" with its suggestion of conservatism and reaction.

28. For an abridged version of this essay, which was subsequently banned in Indonesia, see Mohammad Hatta, "Indonesia's Misguided Democracy," *New Leader, 43* (1960).

29. James Mossman, *Rebels in Paradise: Indonesia's Civil War* (London, Jonathan Cape, 1961), pp. 159-60 and passim.

30. Late in 1961 the army launched a major new drive against the Darul Islam. In the following months it succeeded in surrounding groups of Darul Islam rebels in a number of their mountain hideouts and on June 4, 1962 it captured the rebel leader S. M. Kartosuwirjo. After his capture Kartosuwirjo ordered his followers to lay down their arms, which all or virtually all of them did forthwith, leaving all West Java secure. The ending of this thirteen-year-old West Java rebellion was a signal victory for both the army and the government as a whole. Kartosuwirjo was subsequently convicted and sentenced to death on a charge of masterminding a May 1962 attempt to assassinate the President.

31. For an exposition of this policy in the words of one of its architects see Mohammad Hatta, "Indonesia's Foreign Policy," *Foreign Affairs, 31* (1953), 441-52.

32. For reviews of the history of the West Irian dispute and discussions of the cases of the two parties, see Robert C. Bone, Jr., *The Dynamics of the Western New Guinea (Irian Barat) Problem* (Ithaca, Cornell University Modern Indonesia Project, 1958); and J. M. van der Kroef, *The West New Guinea Dispute* (New York, Institute of Pacific Relations, 1958).

33. Guy J. Pauker, "General Nasution's Mission to Moscow," *Asian Survey, 1* (1961), 13-22.

34. The official figure for membership of the army was "approximately 200,000" between 1951 and 1960. Since 1961 it has been "approximately 300,000." See *Harian Rabjat*, September 14, 1961. The army's size probably grew further in the period of West Irian mobilization in the first half of 1962.

35. *Revolusi, Sosialisme Indonesia, Pimpinan Nasional* [Revolution,

Indonesian Socialism, National Leadership] (Djakarta, Departemen Penerangan, 1961), p. 29.

36. For a description of the 1945 constitution and the events surrounding its introduction, see Chapter 7.

37. Departemen Penerangan, *Kembali kepada Undang-undang Dasar 1945* [The Return to the 1945 Constitution] (Djakarta, Departemen Penerangan, 1959), pp. 5-10. See also J. A. C. Mackie, "Indonesia's Search for a New Constitution," *Australia's Neighbours, 98,* 3rd Series (1959).

38. In later versions the third point of the program was often stated as "Return of West Irian to the Republic."

39. J. D. Legge, *Central Authority and Regional Autonomy in Indonesia,* pp. 209-29.

40. It was decided in mid-1961 that ten parties met all these requirements. They are the PNI, PKI, Partai Katholik (Catholic), PSII (a minor Moslem party), Parkindo (Protestant), Murba, NU, Perti (a small, largely Sumatran, Islamic party), IPKI (minor, with army connections), and Partindo (a group which broke away from the PNI in 1958 with Sukarno's blessing).

41. For a full discussion of the Guided Democracy institutions in their general political context, see J. A. C. Mackie, "Indonesian Politics under Guided Democracy," *Australian Outlook, 15* (1961), 260-79.

42. *Toward Freedom and the Dignity of Man,* pp. 75, 39-76.

43. *Haluan Politik dan Pembangunan Negara* [Political Direction and the Building Up of the State] (Djakarta, Departemen Penerangan, 1961), pp. 27-39.

44. For perceptive analyses of its appeals see Moehammad Slamet, *Kembali Kepribadian Bangsa Indonesia* [More on the Return to Indonesian National Identity], Social Research Centre Occasional Papers (Padjadjaran State University, Bandung, 1960); and Selo Soemardjan, "Some Social and Cultural Implications of Indonesia's Unplanned and Planned Development," *Review of Politics, 25* (1963), 64-90. Compare J. M. van der Kroef, "Javanese Messianic Expectations: Their Origin and Cultural Context," *Comparative Studies in Society and History, 1* (1959), 299-323.

45. J. A. C. Mackie has written, "This confidence that agreement will be reached about the 'national interest' and that all parties will accept it even when their sectional interests are affected is in many ways comparable with the assumptions of early Western democratic theorists that education and public discussion will always prevail." "The Army and the Cabinet in Indonesia," *Nation* (Sydney), December 30, 1958.

46. These statistics have been obtained from the Department of Information, Djakarta. The lower circulation resulted principally from government decisions to reduce imports of newsprint along with other

types of imports. In addition more and more newsprint is being used for the government's own printing.

47. Harold D. Lasswell and Abraham Kaplan, *Power and Society* (New Haven, Yale University Press, 1950), pp. 73 ff.

48. J. M. van der Kroef, "New Religious Sects in Java," *Far Eastern Survey, 30* (1961), 18-25.

49. Among the many Manipol-USDEK jokes current is the story, apparently true, of the Protestant synod which was not content with making the expected declaration that Manipol-USDEK accorded with the teachings of the Bible. Instead it declared that the Bible accorded with Manipol-USDEK!

50. In this respect Indonesian practice accords fully with the tendencies described in S. N. Eisenstadt, "Changes in Patterns of Stratification Attendant on Attainment of Political Independence," *Transactions of the Third World Congress of Sociology* (London, 1956), 3, 32-41.

51. For a fascinating case study see M. A. Jaspan, "Productivity Inhibition among Workers in a Nationalized Industry: A Factory Case Study in Java," *Anthropological Forum, 1* (University of Western Australia, 1962).

52. Harold D. Lasswell and Abraham Kaplan, p. 138.

53. Fred W. Riggs, *The Ecology of Public Administration* (Bombay, Asia Publishing House, 1961), pp. 100-17.

54. Selo Soemardjan, "Land Reform in Indonesia," *Asian Survey, 1* (1962), 23-30.

55. On the social bases of the main political parties in Javanese villages see Clifford Geertz, *The Social Context of Economic Change: An Indonesian Case Study* (Cambridge, M.I.T. Center for International Studies, 1956) pp. 141 ff.; and Geertz, "The Javanese Village," in G. William Skinner, ed., *Local, Ethnic and National Loyalties in Village Indonesia* (New Haven, Yale University, Southeast Asia Studies, 1959), pp. 34-41.

56. For a full theoretical discussion of this phenomenon see Fred W. Riggs, *The Ecology of Public Administration*, pp. 104-11.

57. Discussion of this proposition owes a great deal to the theoretical arguments presented by Riggs in *The Ecology of Public Administration* and his "Prismatic Society and Financial Administration," *Administrative Science Quarterly, 5* (1960), 1-46.

58. Clifford Geertz, "Religious Belief and Economic Behavior in a Central Javanese Town: Some Preliminary Considerations," *Economic Development and Cultural Change, 4* (1956), 134-58.

59. The importance of this trickling down as a factor stabilizing the whole political system has been stressed to me by David P. Mozingo, who sees it as being in sharp contrast to the situation which prevailed in Kuomintang China.

60. The metaphor is Hatta's. See his *Past and Future* (Ithaca, Cornell University Modern Indonesia Project, 1960), p. 15.

61. The above paragraphs are based in part on information I have received from Donald Hindley and Alexander Shakow. See also Alexander Shakow, "Foreign Economic Assistance in Indonesia: 1950-1961" (doctoral dissertation, University of London, 1962).

62. Lasswell and Kaplan, *Power and Society*, pp. 9 ff., 244 ff.

63. Most of the persons to whom I spoke were either civil servants (mostly of the senior and middle ranks), university teachers, or students; but the group also includes significant numbers of men from business firms, government-run or private, officers and soldiers, politicians, lawyers, and religious functionaries.

64. This general view finds public expression in many of the writings of Mohammad Said. See, for instance, "Kesungguhan—Itulah jang Kita Perlukan" [Honesty—That Is What We Need], *Basis, 10* (Jogjakarta, 1960), 1-6.

65. For a possible parallel between this fall in expectations and that which characterized the Indonesian nationalist movement for much of the fifteen-year period after the defeat of the Communist revolts of 1926-27, see Ruth T. McVey, "Indonesian Communism and the Transition to Guided Democracy," in A. Doak Barnett, ed., *Communist Strategies in Asia* (New York, Praeger, in press).

66. For one example of the government's taking arguments out of its critics' mouths, see Sukarno's speech of August 17, 1961, *Revolusi, Sosialisme Indonesia, Pimpinan Nasional,* especially pp. 28-30.

67. Donald Hindley, "The PKI [Partai komunis Indonesia] and the Peasants," *Problems of Communism, 11* (1962), 28-36.

BIBLIOGRAPHY

BONE, ROBERT C., JR., *The Dynamics of the Western New Guinea (Irian Barat) Problem,* Cornell University, Modern Indonesia Project, Interim Reports Series, Ithaca, 1958. A valuable compilation of data based on much research—and a warmly pro-Indonesian heart.

DUYNSTEE, F. J. F. M., *Nieuw Guinea als schakel tussen Nederland en Indonesië* [New Guinea as a Link between the Netherlands and Indonesia], Amsterdam, De Bezige Bij, 1961. Valuable account of the development of the West Irian issue.

FEITH, HERBERT, *The Decline of Constitutional Democracy in Indonesia,* Ithaca, Cornell University Press, 1962. A detailed study of Indonesian politics in the pre-1957 period.

————, "Indonesia," in George McT. Kahin, ed., *Governments and Politics of Southeast Asia,* Ithaca, Cornell University Press, 1959. A general introduction to the subject; the forthcoming second edition of this volume contains a revised and updated version.

FISCHER, LOUIS, *The Story of Indonesia*, London, Hamish Hamilton, 1959. The impressionistic and readable report of a visit in 1958, and of numerous conversations with President Sukarno.

Haluan politik dan pembangunan negara [Political Direction and the Building Up of the State], Djakarta, Departemen Penerangan, 1961. A collection of major documents elaborating the ideology of the state.

HANNA, WILLARD A., *Bung Karno's Indonesia*, New York, American Universities Field Staff, 1960. A racily written book by a sensitive and well-informed but deeply disillusioned author-journalist.

HATTA, MOHAMMAD, *Demokrasi kita* [Our Democracy], Djakarta, Pandji Masjarakat, 1960. An attack on the current trend of political developments.

HINDLEY, DONALD, "The Communist Party of Indonesia, 1951-1961: A Decade of the Aidit Leadership" (doctoral dissertation, Australian National University, Canberra, 1961). An important analysis based on considerable field work.

KAHIN, GEORGE McT., "Indonesia," in George Kahin, ed., *Major Governments in Asia*, Ithaca, Cornell University Press, 1958. An excellent comprehensive survey of government and politics up to 1958. A revised edition is in press.

————, *Nationalism and Revolution in Indonesia*, Ithaca, Cornell University Press, 1952. The standard work on the Indonesian revolution, this sensitively written book is essential reading for students of contemporary politics.

KROEF, J. M. VAN DER, *Indonesia in the Modern World, 1*, Bandung, Masa Baru, 1954; *2*, Bandung, Masa Baru, 1956. Sociological essays on a wide range of subjects. Stimulating but occasionally inaccurate.

————, *The West New Guinea Dispute*, New York, Institute of Pacific Relations, 1958. A compact summary of the rival claims along with a survey of the issue's history.

LEGGE, JOHN D., *Central Authority and Regional Autonomy in Indonesia: A Study in Local Administration, 1950-60*, Ithaca, Cornell University Press, 1961. Illuminating on many aspects of regional government and regional feeling.

MACKIE, J. A. C., "Indonesia's Government Estates and Their Masters," *Pacific Affairs*, 34 (1961-62), 337-60. A valuable case study of the economic and political effects of nationalization of Dutch firms.

————, "Indonesian Politics under Guided Democracy," *Australian Outlook*, 15 (1961), 260-79. Good coverage for the 1959-61 period.

MARYANOV, GERALD S., *Decentralization in Indonesia as a Political Problem*, Cornell University, Modern Indonesia Project, Interim

Reports Series, Ithaca, 1958. A rigorously executed examination of the symbols used in the regional conflict.

MOSSMAN, JAMES, *Rebels in Paradise: Indonesia's Civil War*, London, Jonathan Cape, 1961. A British journalist's account of the regionalist rebellion of 1958.

NATSIR, MOHAMMAD, *Some Observations Concerning the Role of Islam in National and International Affairs*, Cornell University, Southeast Asia Program, Data Paper No. 16, Ithaca, 1954. A good introduction to the thinking of a major representative of Indonesian Islam.

NOTOSOETARDJO, *Kembali kepada Djiwa Proklamasi 1945* [Return to the Spirit of the Proclamation of 1945], Djakarta, Harian Pemuda, 1959. A collection of documents on the return to the 1945 constitution.

PALMIER, LESLIE H., *Indonesia and the Dutch*, London, Oxford University Press, 1962. A provocative essay which interprets Indonesia's hostility to Holland in terms of conflict between the Javanese and non-Javanese.

PAUKER, GUY J., "Indonesian Images of Their National Self," *Public Opinion Quarterly*, 22 (Fall 1958), 305-25. An illuminating study of political values, based on analysis of entries submitted in a press-conducted essay competition.

————, "The Role of the Military in Indonesia," in J. J. Johnson, ed., *The Military in the Underdeveloped Areas*, Princeton, Princeton University Press, 1962. Includes valuable historical material as well as a discussion of the most important current issues.

ROESLAN ABDULGANI, *Pendjelasan Manipol dan USDEK* [An Explanation of the Political Manifesto and the Principles of USDEK], Djakarta, Departemen Penerangan, 1960. An authoritative exposition.

SKINNER, G. WILLIAM, ed., *Local, Ethnic and National Loyalties in Village Indonesia*, Yale University, Southeast Asia Studies, Cultural Reports Series, New Haven, 1959. A collection of excellent papers in which several anthropologists—Edward M. Bruner, Clifford and Hildred Geertz, Peter R. Goethals, Andrea Wilcox Palmer, and G. William Skinner—speak on issues of political importance.

SLAMET, MOEHAMMAD, *Kembali Kepribadian Bangsa Indonesia* [The Return to Indonesian National Identity], Social Research Centre, Occasional Papers, Bandung, Padjadjaran State University, 1960. Perceptive psychological analysis.

SOEKARNO, *Toward Freedom and the Dignity of Man*, Djakarta, Department of Foreign Affairs, 1961. A valuable collection of the President's speeches, it includes the famous "Birth of Pantja Sila" speech of 1945 as well as four speeches delivered in the 1956-60 period.

SOEMARDI, SOELAEMAN, "Some Aspects of the Social Origins of the Indonesian Political Decision-Makers," in *Transactions of the Third World Congress of Sociology*, London, International Sociological

Association, 1956. Important conclusions from research on the biography of cabinet ministers, parliamentarians, and senior civil servants.

SOEMARDJAN, SELO, "Some Social and Cultural Implications of Indonesia's Unplanned and Planned Development," *Review of Politics*, 25 (1963), 64-90. A penetrating sociological essay on "Returning to Our National Personality."

————, *Social Changes in Jogjakarta*, Ithaca, Cornell University Press, 1962. Covers many aspects of the life in this town-village complex, and includes an important study of its sultanate.

SUTTER, JOHN O., *Indonesianisasi: Politics in a Changing Economy, 1940-1955*, Cornell University, Southeast Asia Program, Data Paper No. 36, 4 vols. Ithaca, 1959. Brings together an immense volume of data on efforts to Indonesianize the economy. An indispensable work of reference.

WERTHEIM, W. F., *Indonesian Society in Transition*, 2d ed. The Hague and Bandung, W. van Hoeve, 1959. A major work of neo-Marxist social analysis, historical as well as contemporary.

WILLMOTT, DONALD E., *The National Status of the Chinese in Indonesia, 1950-1958*, Cornell University, Modern Indonesia Project, Monograph Series, Ithaca, 1961. Comprehensive treatment of political issues related to the role of the Chinese.

NOTES AND BIBLIOGRAPHY FOR *Genesis of a Modern Literature*

1. For a general introduction to the early history of Malay and Javanese literature, see A. Teeuw "The History of the Malay Language," *Bijdragen tot de taal-, land- en volkenkunde, 115* (1959), 138-56; R. O. Winstedt, "A History of Classical Malay Literature" in *Journal of the Royal Asiatic Society, Malayan Branch, 31* (1958); J. G. de Casparis, *Prasasti Indonesia* [Indonesian Inscriptions] (2 vols. Bandung, 1950 and 1955); Poerbatjaraka, *Kepustakaan Djawa* [Javanese Literature] (Djakarta, Djambatan, 1952).

2. J. Noorduyn, "Some Aspects of Macassar-Buginese Historiography" in *Historical Writing on the Peoples of Asia, 2* (London, Oxford University Press, 1961), 29-36.

3. See the list of manuscript catalogues referred to in Winstedt, pp. 250-51.

4. A. H. Johns, *Rantjak di Labueh: A Minangkabau Kaba* (Ithaca, Cornell University, Southeast Asia Program, Data Paper No. 32, 1958).

5. A. H. Hill, *The Hikayat Abdullah*, an annotated translation in *Journal of the Royal Asiatic Society, Malayan Branch, 28* (1955).

6. G. H. Bousquet, *A French View of the Netherlands East Indies* London, Oxford University Press, 1940), p. 79.

7. All of these works were published by Balai Pustaka. *Sitti Nurbaja* has gone through eight reprints (most recent 1957), *Salah Asuhan* six (most recent 1956), *Karena Mentua* two (most recent 1958), and *Kalau tak Untung* five (most recent 1956).

8. Teeuw notes that Balai Pustaka refused to accept *Salah Asuhan* in its original form. It is interesting to speculate what parts the editors found too forthright. A. Teeuw, *Pokok dan Tokoh dalam Kesusasteraan Indonesia Baru* [Themes and Personalities in Modern Indonesian Literature], *1* (Djakarta, Pembangunan, 1958), 156.

9. The work was first published in *Pudjangga Baru* in 1940; it has gone through four reprints put out by Pustaka Rakjat, the most recent being 1957.

10. This is a collection of Armijn Pané's short stories written between 1932 and 1952; it was published by Balai Pustaka in 1953. A few of the tales are sketches and experiments for *Belenggu*.

11. There are probably sociological reasons too, which I have touched on briefly elsewhere. A. H. Johns, "The Novel as a Guide to Indonesian Social History," *Bijdragen tot de taal-, land- en volkenkunde, 115* (1959), 232-48.

12. Of the few Indonesians who chose to write in Dutch, the most important were Noto Suroto and Suwarsih Djojopuspito. It is interesting to note that Suwarsih, whose novel *Buiten het Gareel* [Out of Harness] was published in Holland in 1940, had previously submitted it in Sundanese to Balai Pustaka, which had rejected it.

13. Teeuw, *Pokok dan Tokoh, 1,* 71.

14. Ibid., p. 77.

15. Armijn Pané, "Sifatnja Kesusasteraan Baru" [The Characteristics of the New Literature], *Pudjangga Baru, 1* (1933), reprinted in *Indonesia, 3* (1952), 18-23.

16. Quoted by R. B. Slametmuljono in *Sari Pustaka Indonesia* [Themes in Indonesian Literature] (Djakarta, Wolters, 1952), p. 152. The *Pudjangga Baru* reference is not given.

17. Armijn Pané, *Kort Overzicht van de Moderne Indonesische Literatuur* [Brief Survey of Modern Indonesian Literature] (Djakarta, Balai Pustaka, 1949), pp. 9-10.

18. Achdiat Karta Mihardja, ed., *Polemik Kebudajaan* [Debates on Culture] (Djakarta, Balai Pustaka, 1954); and A. H. Johns, "Indonesian Tensions: The Literary Record," *Quadrant* (Sydney, 1961), pp. 51-60.

19. A. H. Johns, "Amir Hamzah: Malay Prince, Indonesian Poet," in *Essays in Honour of Sir Richard Winstedt* (London, Oxford University Press, 1963).

20. H. B. Jassin, *Kesusasteraan Indonesia Dimasa Djepang* [Indo-

nesian Literature during the Japanese Occupation] (Djakarta, Balai Pustaka, 1954), pp. 6-27.

21. His most characteristic works are to be found in the collection: *Dari Ave Maria ke Djalan Lain ke Roma* [From Ave Maria to Another Road to Rome] (Djakarta, Balai Pustaka, 1948). A couple of his stories have appeared in English: "Och, och, och" in "Perspective of Indonesia," *Atlantic Monthly* (1956), supplement, and his novelette *Aki* (Djakarta, Balai Pustaka, 1949) in John M. Echols, ed., *Indonesian Writing in Translation* (Ithaca, Cornell Modern Indonesia Project, 1956).

22. Quoted by H. B. Jassin in *Chairil Anwar, Pelopor Angkatan '45* (Djakarta, Gunung Agung, 1956), p. 118.

23. W. A. Braasem, *Moderne Indonesische Literatuur* [Modern Indonesian Literature] (Amsterdam, Van der Peet, 1954), pp. 61-66.

24. *Pudjangga Baru,* Nomor Peringatan Sepuluh Tahun [Ten Year Commemorative Number] (1949), pp. 1-3.

25. Teeuw, *Pokok dan Tokoh, 2,* 130-31.

26. Rosihan Anwar introduced the term in an article appearing in the January 9, 1949 issue of *Siasat.* For an example of an early objection to the use of the label, see Achdiat Karta Mihardja's open letter to "Mr. X," published in *Pudjangga Baru* (Nomor Peringatan), 1949, p. 17.

27. For an example of the Lekra argument, see A. S. Dharta's comment in "Kepada Seniman 'Universil'" [To the "Universal" Artist], in Aoh K. Hadimadja, ed., *Beberapa Paham Angkatan '45* [Views of the Generation of '45] (Djakarta, Tintamas, 1952), pp. 82-91.

28. For example, see the periodical *Budaya* (Nomor Puisi) [Culture: Poetry Number], *6* (1957), which includes 76 poems by 35 poets. Teeuw notes (*Pokok dan Tokoh, 2,* 47) that it is increasingly difficult to form even a provisional judgment about recent poems, for the majority are characterized by a sameness of form as well as content.

29. The exact meaning of the title is difficult to determine. *Kuak* can mean (1) bellow at (2) open out, sweep aside, penetrate. Lexically *takdir* means fate, but when the book first appeared in 1949, the title was widely understood as "Three Bellow at Takdir [Alisjahbana]," the leader of the old generation. From the content of the book, however, the idea expressed by the title as I have translated it must have been uppermost in the minds of the authors.

30. Teeuw, *Pokok dan Tokoh, 2,* 77.

31. J. U. Nasution, "Sitor Situmorang sebagai Penjair dan Pengarang Tjerita Pendek" [Sitor Situmorang as a Poet and Short Story Writer], *9,* 345-67, 405-24.

32. *Kisah, 4* (1956), 27.

33. Jassin has recently published a substantial essay on his work, in *Kesusasteraan Indonesia Modern dalam Kritik dan Esei* [Modern Indonesian Literature in Criticism and Essay], 2 (Djakarta, Gunung Agung, 1962), 47-66.

34. *Keluarga Gerilja* (Djakarta, Pembangunan, 1950), p. 38.

35. "Lahirnja sebuah Tjerita Pendek" [The Birth of a Short Story], *Kisah*, 4 (1956), 21-24.

36. This has appeared in translation in L. Wigmore, ed., *Span* (Melbourne, 1958).

37. "Hamid" has appared in *Span* and the *Atlantic Monthly* (1956) supplement and "Sensation at Top of Coconut Palm" in the Australian quarterly, *Meanjin* (1960), Part 4.

38. The best account of the Indonesian short story will be found in Ajip Rossidi, *Tjerita Pendek Indonesia* [The Indonesian Short Story] (Djakarta, Djambatan, 1959), in which Rossidi discusses published collections of short stories by 21 authors.

39. See Pramudya Ananta Tur, "Mentjari Sebab-sebab Kemunduran Kesusasteraan Indonesia Modern Dewasa Ini" [Seeking the Causes of the Present Decline in Modern Indonesian Literature], *Indonesia*, 4 (1953), 330-33.

40. *Konfrontasi* (first issue July-August 1954) was intended to fill the gap left by the demise of *Pudjangga Baru*, which had been revived in 1948 and discontinued in 1954, and to inaugurate a new approach to the cultural and economic problems facing Indonesia. The editorial board included Takdir Alisjahbana and Achdiat Karta Mihardja.

41. "Mengapa *Konfrontasi*" [Why *Encounter*?], *Konfrontasi*, 1 (1954), 3-4.

42. Jassin, *Kesusasteraan*, 2, 11.

43. "Sastra Muda, Bumi Muda" [A Young Literature, A Young Country], *Kisah*, 4 (1956), 18.

44. H. B. Jassin, "Satu Tahun *Sastra*" [One Year of *Sastra*], *Sastra*, 2 (1962), 4.

45. *Kepribadian Nasional*, the K of USDEK. For a further discussion, see the chapter on government and politics.

46. This was not the first time the government had taken a hand in cultural affairs, though it was the first serious attempt to dictate artistic policy. The government had subsidized the Badan Musjawarah Kebudajaan Nasional (Consultative Body of National Culture), a federation of cultural groups founded in 1952. Although Lekra belonged to it, the association tended to lean toward the universal humanist side—a fact which Lekra, leaping on the National Personality bandwagon with understandable alacrity, lost no time in pointing out. See *Zaman Baru* (September 15, 1960), pp. 1-2.

47. *Kisah*, which began in 1953, was a monthly periodical devoted

principally to the short story; it expired in 1957. *Sastra*, in effect a resurrection of *Kisah*, began publication in 1961.

48. It is most difficult to form any accurate estimate of the serious reading public in Indonesia. One would expect it to include university students—at least those following the liberal arts curricula—school teachers, high school students, and aspirant writers. A serious interest in Indonesian literature on the part of Indonesians remains low, however. *Atheis* sells about five thousand copies in three years. The literary monthly *Sastra* has an impression of two thousand copies for nationwide distribution.

49. Teeuw, *Pokok dan Tokoh*, 2, 42-43.

50. E. Muir, *Essays on Literature and Society* (London, Hogarth Press, 1949), p. 144.

51. Ibid., p. 142.

BIBLIOGRAPHY

Critical Works and Anthologies

ALI, AHMED, *The Flaming Earth: Poems from Indonesia*, Karachi, Friends of the Indonesian People Society, 1949. A selection of some of the best Indonesian poetry to appear between 1945 and 1949, including renderings of works by Chairil Anwar and Rivai Apin. As far as literary impact is concerned, this is the most successful anthology of Indonesian poetry in English yet to appear.

ALISJAHBANA, SUTAN TAKDIR, *Dari Perdjuangan dan Pertumbuhan Bahasa Indonesia* [From the Pioneering and Development of Bahasa Indonesia], Djakarta, Pustaka Rakjat, 1957. A selection of Alisjahbana's essays and papers on Indonesian language and literature written between 1932 and 1952. This volume is thus of special interest and importance.

————, "Le développement de la langue et de la littérature indonésienne," *Cahiers d'Histoire Mondiale*, 2, No. 3, 1955. A brief account of the genesis and early development of the Indonesian national language and its literature by one of its major pioneers.

BRAASEM, W. A., *Moderne Indonesische Literatuur* [Modern Indonesian Literature], Amsterdam, Van der Peet, 1954. A general survey of the development of Indonesian literature between 1930 and 1950. It is particularly useful because the author, in large measure, allows the protagonists to speak for themselves (through Dutch translations). It includes a biobibliography of Indonesian authors. Another useful biobibliography can be found in *Cultureel Nieuws: Indonesië*, Nos. 28-29 (Amsterdam, 1953), 748-69.

DREWES, G. W. J., *Maleise Bloemlezing uit Hedendaagse Schrijvers* [A Modern Malay Reader], 2d ed. The Hague, Servire, 1949. A well-chosen anthology of selections from works appearing between 1920 and 1940.

ECHOLS, JOHN M., ed., *Indonesian Writing in Translation*, Cornell Modern Indonesia Project, Translation Series, Ithaca, 1956. Unfortunately many of the renderings lack stylistic merit, and in some cases accuracy of comprehension; thus the literary dimension of the original is largely lost. This is particularly true of the poetry. It is a unique compendium, none the less.

GONDA, J., *Letterkunde van de Indische Archipel* [Literature of the Indies Archipelago], Amsterdam, Elsevier, 1947. An anthology of traditional literature selected from the various cultural areas of the archipelago in Dutch translation, with a useful introduction.

HOLMES, JAMES S, "Angkatan Muda: A Checklist of Writings in Western Language Translations," *Indonesië*, 5. A comprehensive list of translations of recent Indonesian works into West European languages. An expanded version of this article exists in Dutch: "Angkatan Muda: Proeve van een bibliographie van vertalingen uit de naoorlogse Indonesische letteren," *Cultureel Nieuws: Indonesië*, No. 28-29, 1953.

————, "Modern Indonesian Prose: A Total Revolution," *Pacific Spectator*, 7, 1953. Another version of this article appeared in Dutch as "Modern Indonesisch proza: Een Totale Revolutie," in *Indonesië*, 7, 1954. A survey of modern Indonesian literature, emphasizing the radical break between the new literature and the older style of writing.

HOOYKAAS, C., *Literatuur in Maleis en Indonesisch* [Literature in Malay and Indonesian], Groningen and Djakarta, J. B. Wolters, 1952. Also from the same publisher a version of this work in Bahasa Indonesia: *Perintis Sastra* [An Introduction to Literature], 2d ed. 1953. The book gives a good survey of the whole field of Malay-Indonesian literature from 1400 to 1947 illustrated by a varied and well-chosen selection of extracts. A new more up-to-date edition in Malay (Oxford University Press, Kuala Lampur) will appear in 1963 or 1964.

————, *Over Maleise Literatuur* [On Malay Literature], 2d ed. Leiden, Brill, 1947. A lucid and well-documented account of the various genres of traditional Malay literature and their history.

JASSIN, H. B., *Analisa* [Analysis], Djakarta, Gunung Agung, 1961. A selection, by Jassin, of stories appearing in the periodical *Kisah*, together with his analysis of each one at the time of its appearance.

————, *Gema Tanah Air* [An Echo of the Fatherland], 4th ed. Djakarta, Balai Pustaka, 1959. The most substantial and representative anthology extant of Indonesian writing from 1942 onward.

————, *Kesusasteraan Indonesia Dimasa Djepang* [Indonesian Literature during the Japanese Occupation], Djakarta, Balai Pustaka,

1948. An anthology of the early works of the new group of writers who were to rise to prominence after the Proclamation of Independence, with a valuable introductory essay on the predicaments of writers under Japanese rule.

——————, *Kesusasteraan Indonesia Modern dalam Kritik dan Esei* [Modern Indonesian Literature in Critiques and Essays], 2 vols. Djakarta, Gunung Agung, 1962. This compilation of essays and reviews since 1946 from the pen of the most well-known and meticulous Indonesian chronicler of his country's literary development is a rich and indispensable source book for any study of Indonesian literature.

JOHNS, A. H., "The Novel as a Guide to Indonesian Social History," *Bijdragen tot de taal-, land- en volkenkunde, 115* (1959), pt. 3. "Indonesian Tensions: The Literary Record," *Quadrant*, No. 4, Sydney, 1961; "Amir Hamzah: Malay Prince, Indonesian Poet," in *Essays in Honour of Sir Richard Winstedt*, London, Oxford University Press, 1963; "The Writer as Outsider: An Indonesian Example," (the work of Pramudya Ananta Tur), *Meanjin Quarterly*, Pt. 2, Melbourne, 1963. The first two of these essays attempt to understand and interpret Indonesian literature in its sociocultural setting. The latter discuss in some detail the work and attitudes of two outstanding Indonesian writers.

KARTAHADIMADJA, A., ed., *Beberapa Paham Angkatan '45* [Some Views on the Generation of '45], Djakarta, Tintamas, 1952. A valuable compilation of essays written from various standpoints discussing the significance and validity of the expression "Generation of '45.' "

PANÉ, ARMIJN, *Kort Overzicht van de Moderne Indonesische Literatuur* [Brief Survey of Modern Indonesian Literature], Djakarta, Balai Pustaka, 1949. This short book by one of the founders of the periodical *Pudjangga Baru* is of particular value for its highly intelligent and sophisticated assessment of Indonesian literary developments in the 30s.

"Perspective of Indonesia," supplement to the *Atlantic Monthly*, 1956. Includes translations of short stories by Pramudya Ananta Tur, Armijn Pané, Mochtar Lubis, Asrul Sani, Idrus, and Achdiat Karta Mihardja, as well as poems by Chairil Anwar, Amir Hamzah, Takdir Alisjahbana, and Rivai Apin.

ROSSIDI, AJIP, *Tjerita Pendek Indonesia* [The Indonesian Short Story], Djakarta, Djambatan, 1959, A discussion of 21 collections of short stories by Indonesian writers that is both perceptive and balanced.

TEEUW, A., "The History of the Malay Language," *Bijdragen tot de taal-, land- en volkenkunde, 115*, Pt. 2 (1959). A brilliant and succinct delineation of the history of Malay and the richness of its dialectical development.

——————, "Iets over de jongste Indonesische Letterkunde: Het Werk van Sitor Situmorang" [A Note on More Recent Indonesian Literature: The Work of Sitor Situmorang], *Bijdragen tot de taal-, land- en volkenkunde, 112*, pt. 1. A valuable essay on the poetry and personality of Sitor Situmorang.

————, *Pokok dan Tokoh dalam Kesusasteraan Indonesia Baru* [Themes and Personalities in Recent Indonesian Literature], 4th ed. 2 vols. Djakarta, Pembangunan, 1958. The only full-scale work on modern Indonesian literature that has attempted to keep pace with literary developments in its successive editions.

WIGMORE, L., ed., *Span: An Adventure in Asian and Australian Writing*, Melbourne, F. W. Cheshire, 1958. Contains works by ten Indonesian authors, including Sitor Situmorang and Pramudya Ananta Tur.

WINSTEDT, RICHARD O., "A History of Classical Malay Literature," *Journal of the Royal Asiatic Society, Malayan Branch, 31*, 1958. The only work on traditional Malay literature in English comparable in scope to Hooykaas' *Over Maleise Literatuur*. Although difficult to read and pre-emptory in some of its judgments, it is detailed and well documented.

Important Literary Periodicals

Bahasa dan Budaya [Language and Culture]. A literary and cultural monthly founded in 1952 and published by the Lembaga Bahasa dan Budaja (Linguistic and Cultural Institute), University of Indonesia, Djakarta.

Budaya [Culture]. A literary and cultural monthly founded in 1951 and published by the Cultural Office of the Ministry of Education (Bagian Kesenian P. P. dan K.) in Jogjakarta. Deserving special note is *Nomor Puisi* (March-April 1957), an anthology of seventy-six poems by thirty-two new poets.

Buku Kita [Our Books]. A literary and cultural quarterly founded in 1955 and published in Djakarta by Gunung Agung, listing new publications and featuring valuable essays and reviews.

Indonesia [Indonesia]. A literary and cultural monthly founded in 1949 and published by the Consultative Body of National Culture (Badan Musjawarah Kebudajaan Nasional) in Djakarta.

Kisah [Short Story]. A monthly published by Djakarta Press, Djakarta, 1952-58. Devoted principally to the short story, but also including critical essays and poems. Succeded by *Sastra*.

Konfrontasi [Encounter]. A literary and cultural monthly founded in 1954 to replace the postwar revival of *Pudjangga Baru*. Published by Pustaka Rakjat, Djakarta. At present suspended.

Pembimbing Pembatja [The Reader's Guide]. A quarterly bulletin founded in 1947 and published by Balai Pustaka in Djakarta, listing reprints and new publications in Bahasa Indonesia and the regional languages issued by Balai Pustaka itself and other publishers.

Pudjangga Baru [The New Poet]. A revival, in 1948, of the prewar periodical of the same name, published by Pustaka Rakjat in Djakarta. Discontinued in 1954.

Sastra [Literature]. A literary monthly devoted principally to the short story and founded in 1961. Published by Interpress, Djakarta.

Siasat [Scrutiny]. One of the oldest postwar political weeklies (founded 1946, Djakarta), it included the valuable literary and cultural supplement *Gelanggang* [Forum] later entitled *Cahier Seni Sastra* [Cultural Notebook].

NOTES AND BIBLIOGRAPHY FOR *The Enduring Tradition: Music and Theater in Java and Bali*

1. For a discussion of the ancient coexistence of Indian and autochthonous musical styles on Java, see Mantle Hood, "The Effect of Medieval Technology on Musical Style in the Orient," *Papers Read and Proceedings of a Symposium on Music and History in Africa and Asia* (Royal Anthropological Institute of Great Britain and Ireland, in press, 1962).

2. Mantle Hood, "The Reliability of Oral Tradition," *Journal of the American Musicological Society, 12* (1959), 201-09.

3. For discussions of aspects of Indonesian art and handicrafts not dealt with in this chapter, see Frits A. Wagner, *The Art of Indonesia* (New York, Crown, 1959), passim. Other suggested sources on the arts of Indonesia are: C. K. Coomaraswamy, *A History of Indian and Indonesian Art* (London, 1927), with extensive bibliography; M. Covarrubias, *Balinese Art,* 37 (Asia, 1937); J. H. Jager Gerlings, *Sprekende weefsels* [Woven Cloths That Speak] (Amsterdam, 1952), with extensive bibliography; J. E. Jasper and Mas Pirngadie, *De Inlandsche kunstnijverheid in Nederlandsch Indië* [The Native Applied Arts in the Netherlands Indies] (5 vols.) The Hague, Mouton, 1912-30); "Indonesië," in *Oosthoek's encyclopaedie* (Utrecht, 1950), with extensive bibliography; W. F. Stutterheim, *Cultuurgeschiedenis van Indonesië* [Cultural History of Indonesia] (3 vols. Groningen and Djakarta, Wolters, 1951); as well as the works recommended in the bibliography.

4. R. L. Mellema, *Wajang Puppets* (Amsterdam, Koninklijk instituut voor de tropen, 1954), pp. 10-44.

5. Ibid., p. 5.

6. Poerbatjaraka, "De geheime leer van Soenan Bonang" [The Secret Teachings of Sunan Bonang], *Djawa, 18* (1938), 178-80.

7. See further on the discussion of the Balinese kayon.

8. Mellema, *Wajang Puppets,* p. 8.

9. Ibid.

10. Jaap Kunst, *Music in Java* (2d ed. The Hague, Martinus Nijhoff, 1949), pp. 137-39.

11. Occasionally at the radio station in Djakarta in the course of a wajang kulit performance gamelan sléndro may yield briefly to gamelan pélog, at which point the players move to the appropriate pélog instruments.

12. Colin McPhee, "The Balinese Wajang Koelit and Its Music," *Djawa, 16* (1936), 6.

13. Wagner, *The Art of Indonesia,* pp. 119-20, 126-27.

14. Ibid., p. 117; and Mellema, *Wajang Puppets,* p. 9.

15. Mellema, p. 9.

16. Wagner, p. 131.

17. This is an English translation of Jaap Kunst quoting the Dutch writer Leonhard Huizinga. Kunst also gives the following two observations, the first from the piano virtuoso, Leopold Godowsky: "The sonority of the gamelan is so weird, fantastic and bewitching, the native music so elusive, vague, shimmering and singular, that on listening to this new world of sound, I lost my sense of reality, imagining myself in a realm of enchantment." The second is from the art historian Otto Fischer: "Wie ich aus der Beglückung dieser Nacht nach Hause fand—ich weiss es nicht mehr. Aber eine solche Vollendung himmlischer Klänge werde ich wohl nie mehr vernehmen." These remarks were published in: Jaap Kunst, *De waardering van exotische muziek in den loop der eeuwen* [The Evaluation of Exotic Music through the Centuries] (The Hague, Martinus Nijhoff, 1942), pp. 35-36. Kunst also reported that before World War II there were more than seventeen thousand gamelan in Java.

18. Hood, "The Effect of Medieval Technology."

19. The term *buron wana,* mentioned above, is a classification denoting animals other than monkeys. *Keték* is the designation for monkeys, separating them from other animals probably in deference to their important role in the Ramayana and Mahabarata. Hanuman, General of the Monkey Army, is one of Shiva's sons, according to the Javanese.

20. M. Soeriadiradja and I. Adiwidjaja, trans. R. Ibrahim Singadilago, "De Soendaneesche dans" [The Sundanese Dance], *Djawa, 10* (1930), 115-21.

21. For many of the particulars in connection with Balinese dance I am particularly indebted to: Beryl de Zoete and Walter Spies,

Dance and Drama in Bali (London, Faber and Faber, 1938; reprinted by Bradford and Dickens. 1952).
22. Jane Belo, *Trance in Bali* (New York, Columbia University Press, 1960), passim.
23. De Zoete and Spies, p. 134.

BIBLIOGRAPHY

BERNET KEMPERS, A. J., *Ancient Indonesian Art*, Amsterdam, C. P. J. van der Peet, 1959. A well-illustrated, scholarly survey of Java's ancient plastic arts, from an archaeological point of view.

BRANDTS BUYS, J. S. and A. BRANDTS BUYS-VAN ZIJP, "De toonkunst bij de Madoereezen" [The Music of the Madurese], *Djawa*, 8, 1928. This sizable monograph devoted to the music of the island of Madura is the only work of its kind on the subject. It affords a basis of comparison with Javanese music.

DEWANTARA, KI HADJAR, *Serat Sariswara, 1*, The Hague and Weltevreden, J. B. Wolters, 1930. A valuable book in the Javanese language which discusses the theory and practice of singing. It includes some examples of children's songs, e.g. *Matjapat, Sekar Gending*, and *Lagon*, in the sléndro tuning system.

EMPU SEDAH and EMPU PANULUH, *Bharata Yuda Kakawin*, with an introduction by J. G. H. Gunning, The Hague, M. Nijhoff, 1903. The original version of the Javanese Bharata Yuda Kakawin is given here in the Javanese language. It offers an interesting comparison with actual performances today.

HARDJAWIROGO, ed., *Sedjarah Wajang Purwa* [History of the Wajang Purwa], Djakarta, Perpustakaan Perguruan Kementerian P. P. dan K., 1955. A valuable book giving the chief attributes and descriptions of 165 wajang characters, including their principal participation in the stories of wajang.

HOLT, CLAIRE, *Dance Quest in Celebes*, Paris, Les Archives Internationales de la Dance, 1939. A vivid description of some dances of the Buginese, Makassarese, and Toradja groups in South Celebes.

————, *Théâtre et danses aux Indes Neerlandaises, Java, Bali, Celebes, Nias: Catalogue et commentaires*, Paris, Gustave–Paul Maisonnieve, 1939. Fifty illustrations of the dances of Java, Bali, Celebes, Sumatra, and Nias, with brief commentary.

HOOD, MANTLE, "The Challenge of 'Bi-musicality,'" *Ethnomusicology*, 1960. This is a presentation of some of the problems which face the Westerner in learning to perform on non-Western musical instruments, especially those of Java and Bali.

————, "Changing Patterns in the Arts of Java," *Bulletin* of the Institute of Traditional Cultures, Madras, 1959. Emphasizing the music and dance of Java, this article discusses the significant impact of Western technology on the arts.

————, "Indonésie," "Pélog," and "Sléndro," in the *Encyclopedie van de Muziek,* Amsterdam, Elseviers, 1958. Three concise articles, the first treating separately the music of Java, Bali, and the Outer Islands, and the other two giving a brief explanation of the two major tuning systems of Java and Bali.

————, *The Nuclear Theme as a Determinant of Patet in Javanese Music,* J. B. Wolters, 1954. After an introductory summary, this book is an analytical study of Javanese modal practice.

————, "The Reliability of Oral Tradition," *Journal of the American Musicological Society, 12,* 1960. The persistence of Sundanese, Javanese, and Balinese music through centuries of contact with foreign cultures is discussed in terms of the strength and weakness of oral tradition.

KATS, J., *Het Javaansche tooneel,* Deel I, *Wajang poerwa* [The Javanese Theater, Part I, Wajang Purwa], Weltevreden, Volkslectuur, 1923. This is probably the best-known reference on the Javanese wajang kulit, although it is rather disappointing in its lack of specific details. It presents thirty-seven principal characters in the wajang with some description of clothing ornaments, physical types, and coloring. The discussion of story content is very general.

KUNST, JAAP, "Hindoe-Javaansche muziek-instrumenten, speciaal die van Oost Java" [Hindu-Javanese Music Instruments, Especially Those of East Java], in collaboration with R. Goris, in *Studiën over Javaansche en andere Indonesische muziek, Deel II* [Studies on Javanese and Other Indonesian Music, Part II], Weltevreden, Koninklijk Bataviaasch Genootschap, 1927. Excellent presentation of musical instruments found in the Hindu-Javanese period. A second edition in English will appear sometime in 1963.

————, *Music in Flores,* trans., Emile van Loo, Leiden, E. J. Brill, 1942. This is the only study of any size devoted to the music of Flores; it contains music examples as well as explanatory notes.

————, *Music in Java,* trans., Emile van Loo, 2d rev. ed. 2 vols. The Hague, M. Nijhoff, 1949. These two volumes are the most important standard reference in Javanese music. It is extremely valuable for its descriptive treatment of history, theory, and techniques. It is richly illustrated, well-documented and contains a large bibliography.

————, "Music in Nias," *Internationalarchiv für Ethnographie, 38,* 1939. This is the only substantial work devoted to the music of Nias and contains musical illustrations as well as explanations of musical style.

————, *Muziek en dans in de buitengewesten* [Music and Dance in the

Outer Islands], Leiden, Indisch Instituut, 1946. A good but brief exposition of some types of music and dance in the Outer Islands.

LELYVELD, TH. B. VAN, *De Javaansche danskunst* [The Javanese Dance], Amsterdam, Van Holkema en Warendorf, 1931. This is the only book published to date on the subject of Javanese dance. For this reason it is valuable, though it is often lacking in important details.

MANGKUNEGARA VII of Surakarta, K. G. P. A. A., *On the Wajang Kulit (Purwa) and Its Symbolic and Mystical Elements*, Claire Holt, trans., Cornell University, Southeast Asia Program, Ithaca, 1957. This is an excellent translation of a paper read by His Highness Mangkunegara VII before members of a "cultural-philosophical study circle" in Java. It is a particularly sensitive examination of the mystical and philosophical implications of the wajang kulit.

MCPHEE, COLIN, "Angkloeng Gamelans in Bali," *Djawa*, 17 (1937), 322-66. An excellent discussion of gamelan angklung, its temporary disappearance and revival.

————, "The Balinese *Wajang Koelit* and Its Music," *Djawa*, 16, 1936. The only thorough treatment of this subject in the literature, including important music examples and explanations.

————, "The Five-Tone Gamelan Music of Bali," *Musical Quarterly*, 35, 1949. One of the best discussions in the literature of the manner in which the Balinese gamelan performs.

————, *A House in Bali*, New York, John Day, 1946. An excellent book for its power of provoking the genuine atmosphere of Bali, as seen through the eyes of a composer sensitive to the arts of the island.

————, *Music of Bali*, Yale Press, 1963. This book will become the equivalent in Balinese studies of Kunst's *Music in Java*. It is an excellent descriptive presentation of all forms of Balinese music, including ample musical illustrations.

PIGEAUD, TH., *Javaanse volksvertoningen* [Javanese Folk-Plays], Batavia, Volkslectuur, 1938. This is the definitive work on various types of Javanese folk-plays. It is both extensive and intensive in treatment, containing examples which today no longer survive.

SISWOHARSOJO, KI, *Pakem Makutarama*, Ngajogjakarta, Pesat, 1954. This very valuable book on wajang gives monologues, dialogues, and texts to such songs as the *suluk, ada-ada, sendon*, including music in cypher notation.

SNELLEMAN, JOH. F., "Muziek en muziekinstrumenten" [Music and Music Instruments], in the *Encyclopaedie van Nederlandsch Oost-Indië*, 2, 2d ed. 1918. The best comprehensive article available on the subject, based on information known up to 1918. Especially valuable for the Outer Islands.

WAGNER, FRITS A., *The Art of Indonesia*, New York, Crown, 1959. This is an excellently produced volume, devoted to a discussion of the arts including their historical background from an ethnographic point of view. It includes a useful chronological table, a bibliography, a glossary of technical terms, and an index.

ZOETE, BERYL DE, and WALTER SPIES, *Dance and Drama in Bali*, with a preface by Arthur Waley, New York, Harper and Bros., 1939. This is the finest and most complete introduction to the many forms of dance and drama found in Bali. Accurate description is complemented by a sensitivity to mood and imagery fitting the subject.

Phonograph Records

Columbia Masterworks Series. An LP recording of Balinese gamelan and another of Javanese gamelan performed by UCLA students will be released in 1963 and 1964 respectively. Both illustrate a variety of representative traditional music.

Dancers of Bali, Columbia. The most successful of all commercial recordings of Indonesian music released to date.

Music of Indonesia, Folkways Record. This album contains selections from Celebes, Ambon, Bali, Java, and Sumatra. Although the background material in the descriptive brochure is not reliable, there are some good recordings in this album. The Javanese (as opposed to Sundanese) selection is not representative of gamelan but is an accompaniment for the folk dance, Djatilan.

Music of the Orient, Decca, 1951. An LP repress of this old album of 78 recordings has made available some good material on the music of Java and Bali as well as an example from Sunda (West Java).

World Library of Folk and Primitive Music, Vol. VII, "Music of Indonesia," Columbia, 1954. A small sampling of some of the music of the Outer Islands, with a concentration of the music of Bali as well as an illustration of Javanese music; edited by Jaap Kunst.

List of Tables

List of Tables

563

TABLES FOR *From Colonial to Guided Economy*

TABLES FOR *Labor in Transition*

TABLE FOR *Dynamics of Guided Democracy*

Index

Index

Iraq, 356
Irian. *See* New Guinea; West New Guinea
Iron ore, deposits of, 9
Irrigation, 5, 6, 17, 19, 45, 54f., 78, 120, 134, 136, 145, 162, 173, 221, 274, 291; Irrigation Service, 125, 501. *See also* Land, *sawah;* Rice, wet-rice
Iskandar Nur, Sutan, 415
Islam, 24, 31, 49, 58, 66f., 67f., 69f., 78, 93, 112, 316f., 349, 359, 360f., 368, 411, 427, 437, 448, 450, 464; cultural influence of, 30f., 69f., 80, 84, 85, 413, 416, 425, 447, 468f., 483; during colonial period, 284, 286, 290, 295, 298; in early history, 276-9; in Java, 42f., 48, 295; role in education, 61, 66f., 68, 69, 295. *See also* Moslems; Pasisir peoples; Political parties, Sarekat Islam; *santri*
Islamic Trading Union. *See* Sarekat Dagang Islam
Islamic Union. *See* Political parties; Sarekat Islam
Italy, 230, 401, 429
Iwa Kusumasumantri, 370f., 378

Jakarta. *See* Djakarta
Jani, Achmad, 540
Japan, 11, 30, 90, 231, 301, 355, 401; occupation by, 90, 109, 114, 163, 203, 258, 298ff., 302, 303, 309, 328, 331, 414, 422-6
Jassin, H. B., 430, 435
Java, 1, 2, 4, 11, 31, 41-9, 83, 85, 93, 150f., 152, 153, 204, 210, 294, 297, 301, 303, 304, 305, 320, 328, 346f., 378, 382, 421, 450, 476, 498, 502, 505, 506, 514, 519; agriculture in, 79, 119, 120, 121, 122, 124f., 126, 130f., 131f., 136ff., 141, 160, 164, 173, 174f, 282, 284f., 499, 508f.; Chinese in, 97, 98f., 99f., 101, 103, 104ff., 107, 110, 112, 293, 301, 492; cities, 30, 33, 38f., 41, 42f., 300; during colonial

period, 280-7, 289, 292, 306, 532; in early history, 42, 60, 272-9, 384, 410, 438, 482, 530, 531; geography of, 3, 5f., 7, 25; government center, 317, 318, 324; industry and trade, 156, 157, 158-67, 168ff., 171, 179, 181, 216, 238, 239, 507, 508; labor force in, 250-4, 255f., 257, 258, 262, 525; land resources, 6, 7, 16f., 18, 19, 41, 46, 120f., 124f., 128, 130, 146, 147, 151, 158f., 160f., 164, 173, 174, 499; migration from, 20, 21f., 23, 291; mineral resources, 9, 10, 174f.; population, 5f., 8, 13, 14, 16f., 18, 19f., 21f., 23, 30, 41, 46, 59, 128, 158f., 160f., 164, 165, 173f., 249, 291, 480. *See also* Central Java; East Java; Javanese; West Java
Java Sea, 25, 49
Java War, of *1825-1830*, 283f., 424
Javanese, 39, 58, 60, 61, 90, 308, 319, 407, 419, 432; aristocracy, 37, 42f., 284ff., 323, 368; art forms, 30, 42, 50, 59, 438-48, 449, 450-5, 458-65, 470f.; attitudes, 42, 49, 158f., 249, 294, 323, 328; occupations, 157f., 165, 255; religion, 42ff., 45, 46, 47f., 439; role in politics, 48f., 292-7, 300, 368; social structure, 30, 45-9, 54, 57, 59, 91, 285f., 301, 482; values, 25, 42, 43ff., 48, 96, 368, 399, 427, 442, 444f., 470f., 480, 483. *See also* Java; Peasants; Villages
Javanese language, 26, 28, 441, 479; literature, 410f., 413, 419, 421, 447; puppet theater, 441, 443, 447. *See also* Madurese; Sundanese
Jogjakarta, Special Territory of, 14f., 17, 18, 42, 251, 253, 284, 444, 480
Jogjakarta, city, 19, 33, 38, 42, 273, 274, 279, 307, 444, 451, 459, 461, 492
Jogjakarta, Sultan of, 42, 321, 404-7
Johore, state, 282
Journalists, 369, 377, 378
Judicial system, 373. *See also* Law, Islamic; Legal system
Junk trade, 97